WOMEN WRITING IN INDIA

Regional Language Editors

WOMEN WRITING IN INDIA

600 B.C. TO THE PRESENT

Volume I: 600 B.C. to the Early Twentieth Century

EDITED BY SUSIE THARU
AND K. LALITA

THE FEMINIST PRESS
at The City University of New York
New York

Published 1991 by The Feminist Press at The City University of New York,
311 East 94 Street, New York, N.Y. 10128
Distributed by The Talman Company, Inc., 150 Fifth Avenue, New York,
N.Y. 10011

Library of Congress Cataloging-in-Publication Data

Women writing in India : 600 B.C. to the present / edited by Susie Tharu
and K. Lalita.
   p. cm.
  Includes bibliographical references (p.) and index.
  Contents: v. 1. 600 B.C. to the early twentieth century.
  ISBN 1-55861-026-X (cloth : v. 1 : alk. paper) : $59.95. — ISBN
1-55861-027-8 (pbk. : v. 1 : alk. paper) : $29.95
  1. Indic literature—Women authors—Translations into English. 2. English
literature—Translations from Indic languages. 3. Indic literature (English)—
Women authors. 4. Indic literature—Women authors—History and criticism.
5. Indic literature (English)—Women authors—History and criticism. I.
Tharu, Susie J. II. Lalita, K.
PK2978.E5W57 1990
891'.1—dc20   90-3788
                                           CIP

Permissions acknowledgments begin on page 530.

This publication is made possible, in part, by public funds from the New
York State Council on the Arts. Funds have also been provided by the Ford
Foundation and the L. J. Skaggs and Mary C. Skaggs Foundation. The
Feminist Press is also grateful to Ellen Bass, Sallie Bingham, Judith Birsh,
Alida Brill, Johnnetta Cole, Creative Graphics, Inc., Allan Ecker, Marilyn
French, Carolyn Heilbrun, Florence Howe, Deborah Light, McNaughton &
Gunn, Inc., Joanne Markell, Nancy Porter, Margaret Schink, Barbara
Sicherman, Domna Stanton, Gloria Steinem, and Alice Walker for their
generosity.

Text design: Paula Martinac

Cover design: Lucinda Geist

Cover art: Detail from an eighteenth-century painting from *Nal Daman,*
manuscript collection of the Victoria Memorial Museum, Calcutta,
reproduced by permission of Hiren Chakrabarti, Secretary and Curator

Typeset by Creative Graphics, Inc.

Printed in the United States of America on acid-free paper by McNaughton
& Gunn, Inc.

*For all the writers
we have not been able to include,
for the many we do not yet know about*

CONTENTS

PREFACE

We began work on these volumes with the premise that critical assumptions, historical circumstance, and ideologies generally have been hostile to women's literary production and have crippled our ability to read and appreciate their work. In the two volumes of *Women Writing in India* we have attempted to make available for English-language readers in India and around the world a group of works that together will illuminate the conditions in which women wrote; bring more significant women's writing to light; help us reevaluate writers who were reasonably well known but had been misunderstood or dismissed; give us a sense of the themes and literary modes women drew on and made use of; and help us capture what is at stake in the practices of self or agency and of narrative that emerge at the contested margins of patriarchy, empire, and nation.

When we began work we were repeatedly warned, often by reputed scholars, that we would find few significant women writers in Marathi or Kannada or Urdu literature. One of the editors had been teaching courses in Indian writing in English for several years, little suspecting that the nineteenth or early twentieth centuries would hold such gems as Cornelia Sorabji's autobiography, Pandita Ramabai's letters or memoirs, Krupa Sattianadhan's novels, Rokeya Sakhawat Hossain's utopian fiction, the many pieces that first appeared in the influential

Indian Ladies Magazine over the first two decades of the twentieth century, or the memoirs of such independent political thinkers as Muthulakshmi Reddi. Even the celebrated Indo-Anglian poet Toru Dutt, whose work invariably found place in syllabuses, was usually presented as a brilliant, but protected, upper-class child-poet, who died early of consumption. Rarely did students learn that, like her uncle Romesh Chunder Dutt, she was a nationalist and a passionate republican; that she was widely read in the history and literature of the French Revolution; or that she had translated speeches made in the French Chamber of Deputies around the time of the Revolution for Indian nationalist journals. Hardly ever is it mentioned, in the context of the literature classroom, that Sarojini Naidu was called the Nightingale of India as much for the rhythm and modulation of the speeches she made during the Independence movement as for her delicate verse.

We began, therefore, somewhat tentatively—hopeful, but uncertain. We read against the grain of literary histories, taking special note of writers who were criticized or spoken about dismissively, and controversies that involved women. Social histories, biographies, and autobiographies, we found, often provided information that literary histories had censored. From these we learned about debates in which women had intervened; about wives, companions, and mothers who "also" wrote; about the prostitutes of Benares who had written a *Shraddanjali* (a collection of elegies) when a famous Hindi writer died; about a women's *kavi sammelan* (poets' meet) organized by Mahadevi Varma; about Vai Mu Kodainayakiammal, who in the early 1920s bought a publishing house, which then published her 115 novels and many works by other women writers, as well as the journal *Jaganmohini,* which she edited. To our surprise we found that the early twentieth century, commonly considered a period when the women's movement was at a low ebb, had been a high point of women's journalism. In almost every region women edited journals for women (though clearly men also read them) and many hundreds of women wrote in them. Our list soon included the testimonies of Buddhist nuns from the sixth century B.C., rebel medieval poets, sixteenth-century court historians, and many unknown women poets, novelists, and polemical writers of the nineteenth and twentieth centuries, and several published memoirs.

Confident that there was a great deal more to be discovered, we began to travel through different parts of the country meeting scholars, women writers, and feminist activists—and it was only as we talked to these people that the project actually took concrete form. We found ourselves slipping past the disciplinary gatekeepers we had first come up against, and searching out, or being directed to, a whole range of other people: historians, sociologists, activists, as well as writers and critics outside the mainstream, who shared information about little-known writers, told us about major works, and discussed what they considered dimensions of cultural history that helped us understand both the cultural economy in which women write and the politics of canon building as it affected women. In most languages, the literary canons had been established in the early 1950s, shortly after Independence. They were therefore charged with constructing an imagined community and sculpting the new citizen. But, as the section introductions also point out, the relation between articulations of the women's question and the discourses of an emerging nationalism was a very troubled one. Critics whose major concern had been to establish the universal dimensions of a literature that was at the same time also authentically "Indian" seemed to have had little interest in probing such unsettling configurations, or asking what these tensions implied for the woman writer or for literary form. They did not ask why, for instance, the central fictional relationship had changed between the 1880s and the 1920s from that of husband and wife to that of mother and son. Or what were the urgencies that were condensed onto the recurring figure of the Hindu widow in the nineteenth-century texts. Neither could they ask, therefore, how this figure had been transformed in the twentieth century by women writers such as Nirupama Devi, Subhadra Kumari Chauhan, Indira Sahasrabuddhe, or Bahinabai Chaudhari, and why. Critics did not seem interested in how the question of the education of women into citizenship and identity, as fascinatingly broached in Chandu Menon's *Indulekha,* 1889, and in Rabindranath Tagore's *Ghare Bhaire* (The Home and the World), 1916, had been recast by Indira Sahasrabuddhe or Rokeya Sakhawat Hossain. No one asked what it meant for a writer to live in times and in situations where she was doubly "Other"—as woman and as colonized person—even in her own vision. Yet these are complexities in the cultural fabric that must be recognized if we are to approach the elusive nature of an identity that emerges at the margin, or understand the peculiar tension between public and private realities that underwrites women's writing.

The more than 140 authors included in the two volumes of this project were selected from an initial list, itself selective, of over 600 writers. The detailed research into the literature of each of the eleven languages represented here—Bengali, Gujarati, English, Hindi, Kannada, Malayalam, Marathi, Oriya, Tamil, Telugu, and Urdu—was done by different scholars, each working in one of these regional languages. The scholars searched through archives and spoke with writers and critics before they made the initial selections. They also did the substantial original research for the biographical headnotes. Many of our most exciting discoveries were made at this stage. Each of us has different anecdotes about tracking down books and information, about surprise finds, and about unlikely people who helped us out with crucial details. Once we had searched out the information about the writers, we ran into the problem of actually locating the texts. Libraries had often not acquired the books, and even when they had, the copies were badly preserved. The pages were moth-eaten, the paper faded and brittle, reproduction sometimes impossible. S. S. Kalpana had to copy out entire texts by hand. Susie Tharu found one archive had just sold some nineteenth-century titles she had been looking for as junk. All Jharna Dhar could locate of Mokshodayani Mukhopadhyay's satiric poem was a long extract, quoted by an indignant literary historian. At other times we were luckier. Many of us found copies of early texts with individuals—women and men—who had carefully preserved them. K. Lalita discovered to her delight that the Saraswata Niketanam, an old library in the small, out-of-the-way town of Vetapalem, had a rare collection of early twentieth-century books and journals. Afeefa Banu located a fifty-year-old private library in Hyderabad that had maintained a special interest in women writers. Once Vidyut Bhagwat had convinced the historian G. B. Sardar that her project might be worthwhile, he made several priceless suggestions. Then she met Geeta Sane, who had just turned eighty and was overjoyed to find a new generation searching out her books. It wasn't long before Vidyut learned about a whole group of women writers unheard of in the corridors of the Marathi literary establishment. K. Lalita had almost given up in despair when she located handwritten copies of Tarigonda Venkamamba's poem's in her aunt's prayer room. Though Venkamamba's work had found no place in public systems of distribution, it had been kept alive in an alternative mode, as it was handed across from woman to woman. The translator of Mary John Thottam's "Lokame Yatra" (Farewell to the World), who knew the poem by heart, told us he had never seen a printed copy before, but his mother had had a handwritten copy, which she kept in her Bible. Jancy James discovered that the "ghost" that appears in Lalithambika Antherjanam's story was the ghost of a real woman, and tracked down the early twentieth-century newspaper reports of her trial. Shirin Kudchedkar unearthed clearly feminist stories and poems by writers who were not commonly regarded as feminist. Vijaya Dabbe came up with extraordinary selections from Kannada *bhakti* poetry.

Gathering information for the biographical headnotes was an equally challenging and adventure-filled task. We located and interviewed contemporary writers, but finding out about little-known authors who had died in the forties or earlier was unexpectedly problematic. There were few biographies we could drawn on, little formal documentation, and almost no criticism. Occasionally we came across memoirs or could piece together letters kept by a relative or a friend. Sometimes we learned about writers' lives from published interviews, preserved by writers themselves or their friends, but dates and bibliographical information began to seem something of a miracle. Small presses often didn't record a date of publication and on occasion even children could not tell us when their mothers had been born or their major works published. Sometimes the writers themselves were depressed or reduced to penury and didn't have the space or inclination to keep copies of their own books. Ashapurna Debi could not remember when she had written the story she wanted us to translate for this collection. What a contrast it was to learn about box after box of Cornelia Sorabji's papers neatly labeled and filed in the India Office Library in London!

The physical problems we ran into were compounded, at more levels than we had imagined, by conceptual ones. Conventions of representing a life vary—historically across periods, but also spatially across a culture. The carefully preserved biographies of Buddhist nuns with which these volumes open, for instance, provide information about their previous lives and record the occasion on which each nun attained enlightenment and subsequent release from the cycle of birth and death, but tell us nothing about the rest of their lives or their other compositions. In keeping with the conventions of eighteenth-century Telugu court literature, Muddupalani traces her poetic lineage, naming as her mentors her grandmother and her aunt and telling us about her literary achievements. About her other experiences we know almost nothing. Much of the information we were able to glean about the important nineteenth-century novelist Krupa Sattianadan was from speeches made at a memorial meeting held shortly after she died. Colonial administrators cited her life as testifying that education or intellectual achievement did not destroy the modesty or sensitivity natural to women. The Indians who spoke at the meeting considered her novels important because they demonstrated that education had in no way alienated Krupa from her roots in Hindu society. Most of the head-notes therefore carry this double mark, some more interestingly than others, of the "standard" forms of our present-day investigation and the biographical imagination our sources represented.

A few observations about translation. Formulations that set up the problem of translation as one of judging how faithful a translation has been to the original, or how well it reads in the target language, divert attention from the fact that translation takes place where two, invariably unequal, worlds collide, and that there are always relationships of power involved when one world is represented for another in translation. We have been very aware that in India, when we translate a regional language—Tamil or Oriya, for instance—into English, we are representing a regional culture for a more powerful national or "Indian" one, and when this translation is made available to a readership outside India, we are also representing a national culture for a still more powerful international culture—which is today, in effect, a Western one. We have tried, therefore, in the translations (not always successfully) to strain against the reductive and often stereotypical homogenization involved in this process. We preferred translations that did not domesticate the work either into a pan-Indian or into a "universalist" mode, but demanded of the reader too a translation of herself into another sociohistorical ethos. We have taken pains, therefore, to preserve the regional grain of the work, and to create a historical context that might open the text up for a materialist and feminist reading.

On the whole we have required that a reader use the context a story or poem provides, which the other pieces and the introductions fill out and complicate, to make her way into the writer's times and the writer's world; we are asking that a reader—in India or abroad—learn slowly, as she relates to the objects, the concerns, the logic of the worlds women have inhabited over the years, to *live* a mode of life, and not just read about it. We have therefore kept the glosses to a minimum, presenting them only when we felt the information was difficult to locate and crucial to an informed reading of the text.

Unfortunately we have had to leave some important selections out because the translations "failed." For volume 2, we wanted to include the work of Krishna Sobti, one of the leading contemporary Hindi writers, but she writes in a dialect translators felt would be difficult to render into standard English and uses an earthy, lewd diction. Standard forms of English, sanitized as they have been over the last two hundred years, just did not stretch into anything that resembled the scope of

Sobti's idiom. Very reluctantly we had to abandon the effort to translate Balamani Amma, a major Malayalam poet of the 1940s and 1950s, because her grand, public verse about motherhood presupposes an ethos we found difficult to recreate in the context of a few poems and a short biography. We are also sorry we were not able to include a story by Qurratulain Hyder, a leading Urdu writer, because of disagreements over the translation.

Considerable discussion went into deciding how Indian-language words would be transliterated into roman script in the body of the book. We began by developing a system of transliteration that was subtle enough to capture regional differences without becoming so elaborate that it would alienate an ordinary reader. Since each Indian language has sounds that others do not have, and we wanted the translation to retain the mark of the original regional language, this was no easy task. Vasanta Duggirala, who helped us with this task, had to go over each headnote and each piece with someone who spoke the standard form (not always easy to identify) of Gujarati, Malayalam, and so on. When we had finished, the page looked like one in an Orientalist or anthropological text. Since anthropology and Orientalism were colonial disciplinary contexts into which our book might so easily be assimilated, we had deliberately and consistently strained against those currents when we made the selections, did the translations, and wrote the headnotes and introductions. We were, to say the least, unhappy about that effect. So were the editors at the Feminist Press. We then talked the problem over with several people in India including publishers and editors. Most people in the trade seemed to think that the kind of elaborate transliterations Indological studies had established as a norm were not really necessary or useful. As far as we know, few readers vocalize words when they read. New words are "recognized," visually, but not necessarily formulated aurally, even as a sort of mental image.

We also found that there were many words, in fact a great many more than we had originally envisaged, that appeared in common English and American dictionaries and therefore had conventional spellings. A great many other commonly used words were in the process of acquiring such standardized spellings, *akam, dalit, kisan,* and *hartal,* for example. We finally decided that we would keep the use of Indian-language words that did not appear in the *Webster's New Collegiate Dictionary* to a minimum, and spell other words as they would normally be spelled in newspapers and journals published in India—without diacritical marks or combinations of letters that seem strange in English (such as -*chch*-). In one sense we might be regarded as taking the initiative in standardizing the spelling of these words. The same idea underlay the decision to italicize an Indian-language word the first time a reader meets it, but not later. What we had gained as a result of all this was a "reader-friendly" page that did not look like an Orientalist text. What we had lost—and we are sad about it—was the variety of the regional languages.

We have provided, for a reader who wants to pronounce the writers' names and the titles of works correctly and is willing to take trouble over it, an appendix in which the names and titles have been systematically transliterated.

It must by now be clear that when we made the selections we were not just looking for uncontroversially "well-formed" works or indeed simply for an individual writer's "achievement" that would appeal immediately across time and space. We looked more specifically for pieces that illuminated women's responses to historical developments and ones that gave insight into the dimensions of self-fashioning and the politics of everyday life as they affected women. We paid special attention to writers we thought had been underestimated or whose work ought to be far better known.

Not all the texts or authors, therefore, were chosen for the same reasons. We might have included one piece because it was moving, another because the writer was already very well known, another precisely because she ought to be better known, or represented a class or other group whose creative activity is rarely taken into consideration in traditional literary histories and the canons they construct. Yet another might be raising an important issue, dramatizing a typical conflict, or representing a formal development.

It goes without saying that the collection is *not* exhaustive. Very regretfully we had to exclude Assamese literature, which has a long and distinguished tradition of women writers, and were not able to work on women's writing in Punjabi, Rajasthani, Kashmiri, or Sindhi. We would have liked to include in volume 2 an extract from the Telugu writer Raganayakamma's (b. 1939) *Janaki Vimukti* (Janaki's Liberation), 1977, but could not obtain permission to do so. Since the work of those who wrote in English would be more easily available to the reader, we included only rare pieces from the nineteenth and early twentieth centuries in English. This means we have not presented major contemporary figures such as Attia Hossain (b. 1912), Anita Desai (b. 1937), Shashi Deshpande (b. 1938), or Meena Alexander (b. 1951). We would have liked, had space permitted, to introduce, in oral autobiographies, the voices of peasant women and women workers. We have too little material by dalit writers and nothing that represents the tribal traditions of resistance and celebration. We hope *Women Writing in India* will inspire future volumes that can make available more of this rich literature.

ACKNOWLEDGMENTS

No book of such scope could have been written without the support and cooperation of the many people who helped us in more ways than we had thought would be possible. We would like to thank all those who argued with us, introduced us to writers, unearthed biographical information, helped us locate rare books, put us up, fed us, and—most of all—shared our excitement. For any omissions we might inadvertently have made, we sincerely apologize.

Nirmalya Aharya
Hari Adiseshuvu
Wajid Aktar
Sukirat Anand
Madhavi Apte
Sumati Ayyar
Mohammad Abdul Aziz
B. N. Sumitra Bai
Kamakshi Balasubramanian
Samik Bandopadhyay
Shukla Banerjee
Jilani Banu

Ram Bapat
Shakira Begum
Leelavati Bhagwat
Sukumari Bhattacharji
Ashutosh Bhattacharyay
Salma Bilgrami
Brojendra Nath Bondopadhyay
Chittaranjan Bondyopadhyay
Sondeep Bondyopadhyay
Vaddera Chandidas
Narayan Chandran
Priya Chandrasekhar

Enakshi Chatterjee
Ratnabali Chattopadhyay
Girish Chandra Chaudhary
Abburi Chayadevi
Raghu Cidambi
Susan Daniel
Kalpana Dasgupta
Usha Datar
G. P. Deshpande
K. Sita Devi
Deepa Dhanraj
Tilottama Dhar
Susannah Driver
Narain Singh Dubey
Vasanta Duggirala
Arup Dutta
Lalitha Eapen
Nissim Ezekiel
Shailaja Ganguly
B. Gayathri
Mamani R. Goswami
Yogendra Nath Gupta
Dibyendu Hota
Hridayakumari
Akhtar Hussain
Qurratulain Hyder
Susan Jacob
Gigy Joseph
Svati Joshi
Yusuf Kamal
Y. Kameswari
Kalpana Kannabiran
Lakshmi Kannan
Anuradha Kapoor
Geeta Kapur
Abid Ali Khan
Deepti Khandelwal
Komali
Kondapalli Koteswaramma
Rambhatla Krishnamurthy
Durgadas Lahiri

K. Vijaya Lakshmi
T.S.S. Lakshmi
Utukuri Lakshmikantamma
Marjorie Lightman
Yasmeen Lukmani
Runu Mahapatra
Uma Maheswari
Swapan Majumdar
A. A. Manavalan
Celine Mathew
Bina Mazumdar
Jaya Mehta
Vijaya Mehta
Rama Melkote
Taki Ali Mirza
Aditi Mukherjee
Sujit Mukherjee
Romoni Mohan Mullick
Banda Muralikrishna Murthy
S.R.J. Muthukrishnan
Shama Narang
Vadrevu Narayanamurthy
Anupama Niranjana
Tejaswini Niranjana
Evashisha Nongrang
Joanne O'Hare
Mrinal Pande
Ayyappa Pannikar
P. Parvathy
B. D. Phadke
D. D. Punde
Ashraf Rafi
Chudamani Raghavan
N. Raghavendrarao
Polapragada Rajyalakshmi
Nita Ramaiya
V. Ramakrishna
Chekuri Ramarao
Vakati Panduranga Rao
Abburi Varada Rajeswara Rao
R. V. Seshagiri Rao

Shanta Rameshwar Rao
Roopkamal Rastogi
M. Ravinder
N. G. Krishna Reddy
K. Sajaya
Tarun Sannyal
Saomi Saran
G. B. Sardar
Sannidhanan Narasimha Sarma
Nabaneeta Dev Sen
Jyoti Seshan
Syed Ali Shafee
Tanuja Shammohan
D. P. Sharma
Veena Shatrugna
Nilima Sheikh
Gulam Mohammed Sheikh
Syed Sirajuddin
Krishna Sobti

Souda
Rajendra Kumar Srivastava
R. Srivatsan
K. Subramanyam
R. S. Sudarshanam
S. Sivapatha Sundaram
Vivan Sundaram
Suvarchala
Rajsekhar Thakur
Thomas Tharu
J. P. Vasandani
Vattikonda Visalakshi
Uma Viswakumar
Volga
Rajendra Vora
Rajendra Yadav
Robert J. Zydenbos

Anveshi Research Centre for Women's Studies, Hyderabad, for housing this project and for providing a context for discussion and exchange.

Central Institute of English and Foreign Languages, Hyderabad, for granting Susie Tharu leave during which the initial work on these volumes was done.

And special thanks

to Maithraiyee Mukhopadhyay, Vasantha Kannabiran, Meenakshi Mukherjee, and Jashodhara Bagchi, colleagues and friends, who never failed to respond to the many demands we made on them, and treated this work as if it were their own.

to Florence Howe, who has been so much more than a publisher, and who made the process of editing an instructive and genuinely stimulating one.

to Shoshanna, Shamuel, Diya, Vithal, and Jim, who not only put up with our enthusiasms, our anxieties, and our despair through the years in which the book became a permanent guest in our homes, but also made it feel welcome.

WOMEN WRITING IN INDIA

INTRODUCTION

What was the point, we were sometimes asked when we began work on the two volumes of *Women Writing in India,* of putting together an anthology such as this? Why did we think women's writing was different or that it called for special attention? Weren't women writers as much victims to social ideologies about the subordinate status of women as men? If we were arguing that women writers had been marginalized and their work misrepresented or misjudged, how did we suggest they should be read? Our answers to these questions have changed over the years we have been working on these collections, often because we learned a great deal, not only from the erudite and generous writers and critics we met in unexpected places, but also from our most skeptical interlocutors.

I

In 1910, when Bangalore Nagaratnamma reprinted the classic *Radhika Santwanam* (Appeasing Radhika), she was quite certain why she wanted to present the work of the eighteenth-century Telugu poet Muddupalani to the reading public again. "However often I read this book," she wrote, "I feel like reading it all over again."[1] And as if that were

---

[1]Bangalore Nagaratnamma, "Afterword," in Muddupalani, *Radhika Santwanam,* ed. Bangalore Nagaratnamma (Madras: Vavilla Ramaswami Sastrulu and Sons, 1910), p. 80.

1

not reason enough, "since this poem, brimming with *rasa,* was not only written by a woman, but by one who was born into our community, I felt it necessary to publish it in its proper form."[2] The word *rasa* literally means "juice" or "essence." According to classical aesthetic theory, in a well-formed work of art all the nine rasas, or basic emotions such as joy, anger, or sexual pleasure, are evoked in fit measure to the subject at hand. In Nagaratnamma's judgment, *Radhika Santwanam* had achieved that rare balance: it was filled—to the brim—but not spilling over. Even Muddupalani's harshest critic, Kandukuri Veereshalingam (1848–1919), was forced to admit that "there is no doubt that this woman's poetry is soft and melodious, and that she is a scholar, well versed in the literature of Sanskrit and of Telugu."[3]

Nagaratnamma had first found mention of Muddupalani's name in an early commentary on the Tanjavur period of Telugu literature. The authors had spoken about Muddupalani as a great poet and had quoted some extracts from *Radhika Santwanam.* She tried to get hold of the original and finally managed with difficulty to locate a copy. It was poorly printed and difficult to read. Friends who learned about her interest sent her another edition, with a *vyakhyanam,* or commentary, appended, but it was only when she came by the manuscript that she realized what a perfect creation it was: "as adorable," she writes, "as the young Lord Krishna."[4]

The pleasure of the text was clearly the principal impetus for the new edition, but Nagaratnamma was also dissatisfied with the editing and the printing of a version of Muddupalani's poem put out in 1887 by Venkatanarasu, who was a classicist and associate of the Orientalist lexicographer C. P. Brown. Venkatanarasu had not included the prologue in which, as was conventional in classical verse, Muddupalani proudly traced her literary lineage through her grandmother and her aunt, and gave an account of herself and her not inconsiderable standing as a poet in the court of Pratapasimha, who reigned between 1739 and 1763. He had also omitted the *charanam,* or concluding couplets of several poems, and left other couplets out completely. Besides, the printing was poor and there were many orthographic mistakes. "I have compared the manuscript with the published edition," she wrote, and

---

[2]Ibid., p. iv.
[3]Kandukuri Veereshalingam, *Andhra Kavula Charitramu* (History of Andhra Poets), Vol. III: *Adhunika Kavulu* (Modern Poets) (Rajamundry: Hitakarini Samajam, 1950; 1st ed. 1887), p. 142.
[4]Nagaratnamma, p. ii.

"have prepared a new version."[5] If we were to look today for a precursor for these volumes of women's writing, we would locate one in the *Therigatha,* an anthology of lyrics composed by the Buddhist *theris,* or nuns, in the sixth century B.C. But for a figure who anticipates our critical initiative, we must surely turn to Bangalore Nagaratnamma.

Nagaratnamma was a patron of the arts, a learned woman, a musician, and a distinguished courtesan, and she approached her editorial task with confident professionalism and admirable feminist partisanship. But neither she nor her publishers, Vavilla Ramaswami Sastrulu and Sons, who Krishnaswami Aiyangar, professor of Indian history and archaeology at the University of Madras, spoke of as "one of the oldest and most reputable publishers in Madras . . . doing very useful work by issuing correct editions of Telugu and Sanskrit classics," could have been quite prepared for the furor that followed the publication.[6]

Muddupalani's poem had already aroused some controversy. Kandukuri Veereshalingam, father of the social reform movement in Andhra and a novelist himself, had, in his definitive history of Telugu poets, scornfully dismissed the poet as "one who claims to be an expert in music, classical poetry and dance," and denounced her work in no uncertain terms. "This Muddupalani is an adultress," he wrote. "Many parts of the book are such that they should never be heard by a woman, let alone emerge from a woman's mouth. Using *sringara rasa* as an excuse, she shamelessly fills her poems with crude descriptions of sex." That is not surprising, in his view, because "she is born into a community of prostitutes and does not have the modesty natural to women."[7] The poem, he concluded, was pernicious.

Nagaratnamma retorted equally sharply. Perhaps, she wrote, Veereshalingam considered modesty natural only to women. "He can denounce a poet because she is a 'prostitute' and he claims that she shamelessly fills her poems with crude descriptions of sex. But if that is so, it should be just as wrong for men who are considered respectable to write in that manner. But, [as everyone knows] several great men have written even more 'crudely' about sex."[8] Her spirited de-

<hr />

[5]Ibid., p. iv.

[6]Krishnaswami Aiyangar, Note appended to Government Order No. 355, Home, Public, Confidential, dated 22.4.27. "Petition of V. Venkateshwara Sastrulu and Sons, Sanskrit and Telugu Publishers, established 1856." Hereafter cited as Petition, 22.4.27.

[7]Veereshalingam, p. 143.

[8]Nagaratnamma, p. iii.

fense was of little avail, however. The government translator Goteti Kanakaraju Pantulu also declared that parts of the book were objectionable. Once he had translated the sections he considered improper into English, the British government was convinced that the book would endanger the moral health of their Indian subjects. In 1911, Police Commissioner Cunningham seized all the copies, and the government charged Nagaratnamma's publishers with having produced an obscene book.

The order met with considerable resistance. The publishers sent up a petition denying the charge, which was also directed against eight other classics they had published, though *Radhika Santwanam* was clearly the most "objectionable" one. It was "unduly straining the language of Section 292 of the Indian Penal Code," they argued, "to suggest that ancient classics that have been extant for centuries, could be brought within the meaning of the section." The petitioners respectfully submitted "that classics in all languages and in all lands contain passages similar to those that are now complained of and would come equally under the purview of this section, if construed in this manner."[9] Other pressures were also brought to bear on the government. A conference of pandits and scholars was held under the auspices of the Telugu Academy of Letters, and its members submitted a resolution to the government claiming that "such proceedings were inexpedient and undesirable and highly detrimental to the preservation and progress of Telugu culture."[10] Several distinguished scholars added the weight of their standing to the appeal. Peri Narayana Murthy, a well-known lawyer, who, like Vavilla Venkateshwara Sastrulu, was also involved in nationalist politics, argued for the publishers.

Despite these efforts, the petitions were dismissed, as was the plea that the case should be heard by a judge who knew Telugu. The British government banned the books. The publishers were allowed to bring out totally expurgated editions of some works; others could be reprinted with the offensive sections deleted; but all copies of *Radhika Santwanam* were to be unconditionally destroyed. The tree of Telugu literature, Nagaratnamma's publisher wrote, had received an ax-blow.

Much to the chagrin of the government, the books clearly continued to circulate. On March 3, 1927, the Vavilla Press in Tondiarpet as well as its shop in Esplanade was raided again. The police also raided a

---

[9]Cited in Petition, 22.4.27.
[10]Petition, 22.4.27.

bookshop in Rajamundry and even tracked down two readers in Sri-kakulam who had ordered copies by post. In an indignant letter of protest, written shortly afterward, Venkateshwara Sastrulu agreed that copies were being circulated. But he had taken care, he said, to sell the unexpurgated editions only to scholars. The versions that were being commercially circulated had been modified as required by the government. Each of these works, he argued, had been written centuries ago and occupied an important place in Telugu literature. It would be a travesty of justice if they were regarded as coming under the purview of Section 292 of the Penal Code. Prof. Krishnaswami Aiyangar endorsed these claims. "It is possible that the extreme purist may take exception to a verse here and a verse there," he commented, "but having regard to the genius of these languages, such a complete expurgation would be impossible without sacrificing the substance of the work. . . . It is hardly necessary to do so, however, as these passages hardly jar upon Indian feeling or sentiment."[11] All the same, the colonial government banned the books again. It is interesting that in the petition they filed in response, the publishers make no mention of *Radhika Santwanam,* although they contest the seizure of the other books.

Only with the support of a nationalist leader and spokesman for Andhra Pradesh as influential as Tanguturi Prakasam (1872–1957), who had just become chief minister, were the ban orders withdrawn in 1947. It had been a battle, Prakasam said, for pearls of great beauty to be replaced in the necklace of Telugu literature. Permission was also granted for Nagaratnamma's edition of *Radhika Santwanam* to be re-published, and the Vavilla Press brought out a new edition in 1952. When in the late 1980s, our curiosities aroused by the harsh dismissals of Muddupalani's work in almost every contemporary literary history, we searched for a copy of her poem, it was difficult to find one. Critic after critic assured us that her work was obscene and simply not worth reading, though many of them had never seen the text.[12] Students of Telugu literature, even ones sympathetic to women, echoed their judg-

---

[11]Petition, 22.4.27.

[12]Yandamuri Satyanarayanarao's comment is an exception: "These epic poems are well-formed works, complete with all the nine *rasas.* If we look at them with our present view of women, they might appear low and unrefined. That is the inadequacy of our culture, and not that of the epic or the poet." (*Saradadhwajam Thanjavur Rajulakalamloni Telugu Sahitya Charitra* [The Flag of Scholarship: The History of Telugu Literature in the Thanjavur Era] [Hyderabad: Sahitya Academy, n.d.], p. 231.)

ment. The book was no longer banned, but *Radhika Santwanam* had been decreed out of existence ideologically.

There is no evidence to suggest that Muddupalani's work was attacked or dismissed in her own times. The autobiographical prologue conventional in such works indicates that she was a respected poet and also accomplished in music and classical dance. It was not customary for male artists to dedicate their writing to a woman mentor, but Muddupalani records with pride that several works had been dedicated to her. She speaks of her beauty and of her learning with the directness and self-confidence of one who has never been required to be apologetic or coy, and records instances when she herself expressed her appreciation of other poets with gifts and money. If the honors and rewards bestowed on her by Pratapasimha, her royal patron, can be taken as the response of a contemporary reader, there can be no doubt that her work was truly appreciated in her own times.

The Thanjavur court, which provided the context, and the audience for Muddupalani's compositions, was famous for its patronage of the arts. The period is spoken of as the golden age of Telugu literature. Music, dance, and literature flourished, as did painting and sculpture. Many of the kings in this powerful southern dynasty were also scholars and poets, and the evidence we have suggests that there were several eminent literary women at the court. Ramabhadramba and Madhuravani, for instance, both composed poetry in three languages and were experts in *ashtavadhanam* (the capacity to attend to eight different intellectual activities at the same time). Ramabhadramba was also a historian and left behind accounts of the political and military events in Raghunadhanayaka's reign. She documents the presence of several women composers in the court. Muddupalani herself traces her literary heritage through her grandmother and her aunt, who were both poets. Unlike a family woman in her time, as a courtesan Muddupalani would have had access to learning and the leisure to write and practice the arts. She would have owned property and expected and enjoyed a functional equality with men. Obviously, the esteem in which Muddupalani was held and the acclaim her work received can be attributed as much to the contexts, literary and social, she drew upon as to her own talent.

Developments in literary form suggest a changing society. Even Muddupalani's harshest critics comment on her scholarship and on the diction of her poetry, which subtly shifted the rhythms of classical Telugu verse closer to those of the spoken form. Other writers of her period were extending established courtly forms to criticize rapacious landlords and describe the everyday lives of craftspeople. Secular prose narratives had also begun to make an appearance. *Radhika Santwanam* was a *sringarapra-bandham,* a genre associated in the history of Telugu literature with the Thanjavur era. Epic poems in this genre usually retold, with significant transformations of plot, atmosphere, theme, and worldview, the story of the divine lovers Radha and Krishna. The principal rasa evoked was srin-gara, or erotic pleasure. Muddupalani's composition, which captures moods and tones of voice with a rare humor and subtlety, is one of the formally and linguistically more sophisticated works in the genre. But what must have drawn Nagaratnamma to her work and what strikes us today is Muddupalani's remarkable subversions of the received form. Traditionally in such literature, the man is the lover, the woman the loved one; Krishna woos and makes love to Radha. Though Radha is invariably portrayed as longing for him, the narrative has as its focus his pleasure. Not so in *Radhika Santwanam,* where the woman's sensuality is central. She takes the initiative, and it is her satisfaction or pleasure that provides the poetic resolution. With a warmth unmatched in later poetry, Mud-dupalani celebrates a young girl's coming of age and describes her first experience of sex. In another section, Radha, who is represented as a woman in her prime, instructs her niece, Iladevi, in the art and joy of love. Radha encourages her to express her desire and to recognize and value her pleasure.

Some of the most startling and unusual verses in the epic, however, come from the section that gives the poem its title. Though Radha encourages the liaison between Iladevi and Krishna, she is herself in love with Krishna and cannot bear the separation. She calls him names, accuses him of ignoring her, and demands that he keep up his rela-tionship with her. Krishna responds warmly and appeases her with sweet talk and loving embraces. What makes the work so radical to-day, if not in its own time, is the easy confidence with which it con-tests the asymmetries of sexual satisfaction commonly accepted even today, and asserts women's claim to pleasure. In fact Muddupalani transgresses today as much in her attitude as in her themes and her person.

When Nagaratnamma reprinted the poem a little over a century after it had first been written, Victoria was queen of England and empress of India, and major political and ideological shifts, which affected women's literary production and consumption, had taken place. As the British established their commercial and military authority over India during the second half of the eighteenth century, the old rulers were overthrown or marginalized, and the earlier centers of trade and ad-ministration lost their importance to the new port cities. By 1799, all revenues from the Thanjavur kingdom went to the British. Those driven to destitution as a result of these changes were principally artisans and craftspeople, but poets, musicians, architects, scientists, indeed scholars and artists of all kinds who depended on the patronage of the courts were deprived of a means of sustenance. Large numbers of women artists, mainly folk singers and dancers, who depended on wealthy households for patronage, but also court artists like Muddupalani were driven into penury and prostitution.

Important ideological changes, which also served to discredit such women artists as Muddupalani, were taking place at the same time. Increasingly over the nineteenth century the respectability of women from the emerging middle classes was being defined in counterpoint to the "crude and licentious" behavior of lower-class women. Decent (middle-class) women were warned against unseemly interaction with lower-class women and against the corrupting influence of the wandering women singers and dancers whose performances were laced with bawdy and a healthy disrespect for authority.[13] As we shall see, the sculpting of the new respectability was one of the major tasks taken on by the social reform movement, which set out to transform a traditional society into a modern one. Artists, such as Muddupalani, who had been acceptable figures in royal courts came to be regarded as debauched and their art as corrupting.

A similar process of class differentiation, on the basis of (among other things) redefined sexual mores for women, had taken place in Europe during the late eighteenth and early nineteenth centuries as the new bourgeoisie inscribed its identity on the bodies and souls of women and the proper lady was born.[14] Indian women's sexual propriety, however, was also to be vindicated under the glare of the harsh spotlight focused right through the nineteenth century on what was

---

[13]Among the other books banned at the same time as *Radhika Santwanam,* for instance, was a sixteenth-century text, Ayyalaraju Narayanamatya's *Hamsavimsathi* (The Twenty Swan Stories), a colorful and somewhat bawdy work, which represents the culture of the artisan classes, and which the publishers described as comparable to Boccaccio's *Decameron.* The collection of twenty stories, they point out, presents "twenty different handicrafts and professions, and [is] intended to give the readers a picture of the life and manners of the sixteenth century." The text contained several technical terms now lost to the language. Petition, 22.4.27.

[14]See Cora Kaplan, *Sea Changes: Culture and Feminism* (London: Verso, 1986), pp. 31–50.

described as the moral degeneration of Indian society. Bureaucrats, missionaries, journalists, and Western commentators of various kinds filed sensational reports about Indian culture, and made authoritative analyses of Indian character, which was invariably presented as irrational, deceitful, and sexually perverse. The thrust of these descriptions was usually quite clear: the situation in India was so appalling that it called for intervention by an ethical and rational power. The British quickly persuaded themselves (and the huge profits remitted to imperial coffers no doubt hastened the process) that India was the white man's burden and their government essential to its salvation.

Equally important to our understanding of what made a work that was so well regarded in the mid-eighteenth century unacceptable by the early twentieth century is an appreciation of the new curricular and ideological services literature itself was being pressed into. British colonial administrators and political thinkers, Thomas Macaulay, John Stuart Mill, and Charles Trevelyan among them, were agreed on the need to shape an Indian subject who would be able to not only understand their laws but also appreciate their efforts. The "greatest difficulty the Government suffers in its endeavours to govern well springs from the immorality and ignorance of the mass of the people . . . particularly their ignorance of the spirit, principles and system of the British Government," one administrator reported.[15] "The natives must either be kept down by a sense of our power or they must willingly submit from a conviction that we are more wise, more just, more humane and more anxious to improve their condition than any other rulers they could have," another observed.[16] Indian literatures, they were convinced, contained neither the literary nor the scientific information required for the moral or mental cultivation so essential if good government was to be desired and appreciated. Only suitably selected and carefully taught English literary works, thought of as embodying a "secular Christianity," could be entrusted with the fine-grained transformations of thought, emotion, and ethical sensibility necessary if the moral and political authority of the British was to be recognized,

---

[15]W. Frazer, Letter to the Chief Secretary, Fort William (now Madras), 25.9.1828. H. Sharp, *Selections from Educational Records,* Vol. I (Calcutta: Superintendent, Govt. Printing, India, 1923), p. 13.

[16]Minute of J. Farish, 28.8.1938. Quoted in B. K. Boman-Behram, *Educational Controversies of India: The Cultural Conquest of India under British Imperialism* (Bombay: Taraporevala Sons and Co, 1942), p. 239.

and a sense of public responsibility and honor to develop.[17] Imperial interests clearly underlay the fashioning of the literary curriculum—a fact that becomes all the more significant when we realize that English literature was taught in Indian universities several years before it was in Britain. Readers critically trained to "appreciate" such carefully selected "canons" of English literature would probably have found not only *Radhika Santwanam* but the culture and the society that sustained the writer to be reprehensible, even dangerous. Gradually, as the new powers staked their claims over the land and over the minds of the people, not only individual works but whole literary traditions were delegitimated and marginalized.

Colonial restructurings of gender and the curricular institutionalization of literature both worked to undermine the authority of Indian literatures and undercut the societies that gave rise to them. On the face of it, Orientalist scholarship, which "retrieved" and put into circulation many classical Sanskrit and Persian texts, would appear to have reauthorized Indian literature and reaffirmed the significance of an Indian tradition. But, as we argue later, it was a highly restructured version of the past that emerged in the Orientalist framework. Scholars like Max Müller popularized the idea of an idyllic Aryan community, which was a learned, highly disciplined and ascetic one, governed by a sacred (and priestly) order. After this golden vedic age, they argued, Hindu civilization had declined. Historians have pointed out that the Indian past, reconstructed and reempowered by such scholarship, was not only the idealized paradise untouched by the disturbing changes taking place in European society that the Romantics longed for, but also a brahminic one in which the Indian society and its history was reduced to what could be found in the ancient sacred texts. One of the consequences of reaffirming the high brahminical image in the context of a history that was ostensibly in decline was the marginalization of the more recent literatures as well as the literatures that emerged from historically changing and secular contexts. Since these literatures often treated divine figures such as Radha or Krishna with familiarity or irreverence and undermined traditional hierarchies of caste and gender, Orientalist scholarship paid little heed to them, or, as Venkatanarasu and Brown did when they reprinted *Radhika Santwanam* in 1887, these works were trimmed and recast. It is interesting that they excised not

---

[17]Gauri Viswanathan, "The Beginnings of English Literary Study in India," *Oxford Literary Review* 9, 1987, pp. 2–26. The author quotes the evidence of Thomas Macaulay and Charles Trevelyan, *Parliamentary Papers,* Vol. 32 (Great Britain 1852–53).

only the verses they considered sexually explicit or obscene but also the *peetika,* or colophon, in which the woman writer traced her female lineage and spoke with confidence, unusual for later times, about her achievement as an artist.

There are other angles to the story. The cultural history of nineteenth-century India is commonly presented as a battle between the social reformers, who are considered modernizers charged with the interests of women, and the traditionalists, who are considered opposed to the movements for reform and in favor of the preservation of a traditional society. Figures such as Nagaratnamma and the cultural forces she represents, who are neither "modern" nor "traditional" in the sense that the modernizers represented tradition, are obscured by these categories, which also reduce the complex and heterogenous forces at work to a simple dichotomy between the progressive and the reactionary.

A reader might still want to ask why, if the ban was lifted in 1947 and the book reprinted in 1952, copies could not be found in the late 1980s.[18] Why, she might want to inquire, is the book still condemned by most literary critics? The lifting of a ban imposed by the British was clearly a nationalist act. But the interests of empire and of nation are not always in contradiction. As we will repeatedly find, the institutions of literature and the issues of gender and class that the book and its history raise remained illegitimate.

The story of Muddupalani's life, her writing, and the misadventures of *Radhika Santwanam* could well be read as an allegory of the enterprise of women's writing and the scope of feminist criticism in India, for it raises, in an uncanny way, many of the critical questions that frame women's writing. These include questions about the *contexts,* structured and restructured by changing ideologies of class, gender, empire, in which women wrote, and the conditions in which they were read; questions about the *politics,* sexual and critical, that determined the reception and impact of their work; questions about the *resistances,* the subversions, the strategic appropriations that characterized the subtlest and most radical women's writing. In Nagaratnamma's efforts to reprint Muddupalani's poem, we encounter not only an episode in the unwritten history of feminist criticism in India but also the hitherto invisible questions of the woman reader and her requirements for the

---

[18]We have, after combing through libraries in Hyderabad, Rajamundry, Vetapalem, Madras, and Thanjavur, located a copy of each of the 1887, 1911, and 1952 editions. The palm-leaf manuscript is not available even in the famous Saraswati Mahal Library in Thanjavur.

literary text. That the narrative should take in the historical span of the two volumes of *Women Writing in India* is a bonus. Patriarchies, reconstituted in the interests of Orientalism, imperialism, the Enlightenment, nationalism, among other forces, provide the horizon within which the text articulates its feminist challenge. We move from the precolonial times in which Muddupalani wrote through, in Veereshalingam's and Prakasam's responses, the social reform period and the period of high nationalism into this moment, when we read both the original text and the controversy that surrounds it anew, engaged as we are in the unusual text we are preparing.

II

Given the dominance of English as a world language, and the political economies not only of publication but also of the circulation of knowledge, the principal feminist critical traditions we have access to in India are the American and British ones. The work of the French theorist Julia Kristeva has been available in translation for some time now, but the writings of other French thinkers such as Helene Cixous or Luce Irigaray have become available in English only recently. Their work, however, is still not widely circulated, and has not been influential. (Our knowledge of Kenyan, Latin American, or Soviet feminist criticism is sadly limited.) Though the early work of the Marxist Feminist Literature Collective and of the critic Cora Kaplan are exceptions, British feminist criticism, which is, broadly speaking, more Marxist and more theoretical in inclination than its American counterpart, has steered clear of engagement with women's writing, possibly because it was difficult to reconcile the privileging of women's "voices," which underwrote the early initiatives, with the idea, which several British theorists have explored, of female subjectivity or selfhood as also ideologically constructed. British feminist critics have chosen instead to focus on questions of representation and genealogy.[19] Strictly speaking, of course, neither Cixous's concept of *ecriture feminine* (feminine writ-

---

[19]See, for instance, Rosalind Coward and John Ellis, *Language and Materialism* (London: Routledge and Kegan Paul, 1977); Rosalind Coward, *Patriarchal Precedents: Sexuality and Social Relations* (London: Routledge and Kegan Paul, 1983), as well as the important work done in feminist film theory by Laura Mulvey, Claire Johnston, and Annette Kuhn. In America Catherine Gallagher and Gayatri Spivak in cultural history and Teresa de Lauretis and others in film theory have taken up related issues.

ing)[20] nor Kristeva's notion of femininity as marginality[21] is concerned with *women's* writing.[22]

Solitary figures such as Virginia Woolf or Rebecca West apart, the involvement with *women's writing* or the idea of retrieving a lost tradition of women's literature has actually developed only over the last twenty years and *has been largely an American one.* Since this is the work that is also most easily available and most easily assimilable into existing critical paradigms, it has seemed very attractive to many feminist scholars and to sections of the literary establishment in India. We have therefore chosen to focus our attention on it.[23]

The interest in women's literature in American feminist criticism grew out of an earlier polemical moment, best represented perhaps by Kate Millet's *Sexual Politics,* 1969, in which attention had been focused on the images of women in mainstream literature. Disturbed by the sudden realization that women had invariably been represented in stereotypical ways by a literary heritage that claimed universality, feminist critics turned to women authors for alternative images of women.

---

[20]"Most women are like this: they do someone else's—man's—writing, and in their innocence sustain it and give it voice, and end up producing writing that's in effect masculine. . . . The fact that a piece of writing is signed by a man's name does not in itself exclude femininity." Helene Cixous, "Le Sexe ou la tête" (Castration or Decapitation?), trans. Annette Kuhn, *Signs* 7:1, 1981, pp. 41–55.

[21]"What can 'identity,' even 'sexual identity,' mean in a new theoretical and scientific space where the very notion of identity is challenged?" Julia Kristeva, "Women's Time," trans. Alice Jardine and Harry Blake, *Signs* 7:1, 1981, pp. 13–35.

[22]For a useful assessment of these theories, see Gayatri Spivak, "French Feminism in an International Frame," in *In Other Worlds* (London: Methuen, 1987), pp. 134–153.

[23]Our discussion of American criticism would have been greatly enriched had we learned earlier about Hazel Carby's path-breaking work on black women writers: *Reconstructing Womanhood* (New York: Oxford University Press, 1989). Carby's analysis of black women novelists proceeds from a theoretical position closely related to the one we have developed in this essay. Her argument traces "ideologies of womanhood as they were adopted, adapted, transformed to effectively represent the conditions of black women and it explores how black women intellectuals reconstructed the sexual ideologies of the nineteenth century to produce an alternative discourse of black womanhood" (p. 6). Though the rhetoric of sisterhood obscures this contradiction, ideologies of white womanhood too, Carby points out, were "sites of racial and class struggle which enabled white women to negotiate their subordinate role in relation to patriarchy and at the same time to ally their class interests with men and against establishing an alliance to black women" (p. 18). We are extremely grateful to Florence Howe for having drawn our attention to this important book.

Women reared on the idea that great literature embodied, in some quasi-mystical, transcendent sense, a universally and perhaps eternally valid ethic were understandably agitated by what they now experienced as the masculine biases of the classics. Some critics spoke in terms of correcting a deficiency in the record, enshrined in the canon, of the culture's finest literary achievements. Others, especially those who wrote as teachers, were more concerned with the cumulative effect such literature would have on the reader-student's understanding and response to life, and emphasized the similarity between the images of women found in popular literature, in advertisements, or in children's literature, and those in the canonical texts.

Literary texts, Mary Anne Ferguson's widely circulated anthology demonstrated, commonly cast women in sexually defined roles.[24] Women were mothers, good submissive wives or bad dominating ones, seductresses, betrayers, prim single women, or the inspiration for male artists. In Ferguson's scheme of things, these were clearly regarded as *false* images of women, which she counterposed in the concluding section, "Woman Becoming," with fictional accounts, by women writers, of women's working lives, their relationships with each other, their struggles, and their aspirations. She assumed, in keeping with the empiricist basis of her criticism, that women's writing would reflect women's *real* worlds and their real experiences, and much of the most persuasive feminist criticism of the early 1970s worked from the same principle. Although it is difficult for us to share her assumptions, we must acknowledge with admiration that her collection, and other efforts that followed, did locate several women writers whose portrayal of women was clearly more complex and less stereotypical than that of the canonized fathers.

It is to this critical moment, and the initiatives it led to in publishing and curricular reform, that we owe the "rediscovery," not only of formerly undervalued works such as Charlotte Perkins Gilman's *The Yellow Wallpaper* and Susan Glaspell's *Trifles,* but such classics of women's working-class literature as Agnes Smedley's *Daughter of Earth,* Rebecca Harding Davis's *Life in the Iron Mills,* and Tillie Olsen's *Tell Me a Riddle,* as well as the extraordinary work of the black novelist and folklorist Zora Neale Hurston.[25]

---

[24]Mary Anne Ferguson, *Images of Women in Literature* (Boston: Houghton Mifflin, 4th ed., 1986; 1st ed., 1973).

[25]Charlotte Perkins Gilman, *The Yellow Wallpaper* (New York: The Feminist Press, 1973); Susan Glaspell, *Trifles and A Jury of Her Peers* (New York: The Feminist

An equally powerful propelling force for the turn toward women's writing was the growing realization that critical estimates of women's literature were invariably prejudiced. The tendency in Western culture, Mary Ellmann argued in an important early book, was "to comprehend all phenomena, however shifting, in terms of original and simple sexual differences; and . . . classify almost all experience by means of sexual analogy."[26] What she called "phallic criticism," or the criticism practiced by male academics and reviewers, extended this mode of thought by sexual analogy to criticism when it was faced with a woman writer.

> With a kind of inverted fidelity, the analysis of women's books by men will arrive punctually at the point of preoccupation, which is the fact of femininity. Books by women are treated as though they themselves were women, and criticism embarks, at its happiest, upon an intellectual measuring of busts and hips.[27]

Ellmann's witty exposé of "phallic criticism," elaborated a decade later with equally devastating aplomb by Joanna Russ,[28] demonstrated, with example after hilarious and infuriating example, that the critical establishment had been unjustly hostile to women writers. Writers who were widely read and critically acclaimed in their own times had, over the years, been so discredited as to be forgotten or even damned. Others, such as Virginia Woolf, had found a place in the canon but only after the radical, political edge of their work had been blunted. Clearly feminist works such as *A Room of One's Own,* 1929, and *Three Guineas,* 1938, rarely feature in critical discussions, though her experiments with the stream of consciousness technique are well known. Yet others, and Emily Dickinson is a commonly cited example, never received the serious attention they so richly deserved. Feminist critics soon pointed

---

Press, forthcoming); Agnes Smedley, *Daughter of Earth* (New York: The Feminist Press, 1973, 3d. ed. 1987); Rebecca Harding Davis, *Life in the Iron Mills and Other Stories,* ed. Tillie Olsen (New York: The Feminist Press, 1985); Tillie Olsen, *Tell Me a Riddle* (New York: Dell, 1976); the excellent collection of work by Zora Neale Hurston, *I Love Myself When I Am Laughing . . . And Then Again When I Am Looking Mean and Impressive,* ed. Alice Walker (New York: The Feminist Press, 1979); Zora Neale Hurston, *Their Eyes Were Watching God* (Urbana: University of Illinois Press, 1978).
[26]Mary Ellmann, *Thinking about Women* (New York: Harcourt, 1968), p. 6.
[27]Ibid., p. 29.
[28]Joanna Russ, *How to Suppress Women's Writing* (London: The Women's Press, 1984).

out that the problem was much larger in its scope than the prejudice of male critics. Subsuming the female into the category of human was a political act. With its universalist assumptions, literary criticism systematically obscured questions relating to women as writers, women as readers, and the representation of women in literary texts. Besides, questions relating to the social, historical, and ideological contexts in which literary production and consumption took place, which were crucial to an understanding of women's literature, had no legitimacy in such criticism. Feminist critics also pointed out that the "ideal reader," privileged by critical modes that stressed the universal, was white, upper-class, and clearly male and that the reader addressed by the canonical texts bore the same social imprint. In fact, the focus of disciplinary interest had become so restricted that what were regarded as classics could be read, to purloin a phrase from the American critic Nina Baym, as "melodramas of beset manhood."

By the late 1970s, three major book-length studies that set up women's writing as a new disciplinary field had appeared. Serious work on the tasks of writing feminist literary histories and evolving critical paradigms sensitive to the issues at stake in the study of women's writing had begun. In the earliest of these books, *Literary Women,* Ellen Moers admitted to an initial reluctance to separate writers on the basis of gender, but cited three reasons why she began to think otherwise. First, the astonishing results such separation does produce. Second, the realization that "we already practise a segregation of major women writers unknowingly," and third, a better understanding of women's history.[29] Implicit in the second reason is the recognition of the covert politics of subsuming women into the category of human, but restricting at the same time their importance within it. But more important, we feel, is the realization that existing critical practices had a hidden political agenda and that a politics could only be challenged and undermined politically, however much the critical decorum might discourage such unseemly behavior. It might have been difficult to construct theoretically tenable reasons for dealing separately with women writers. But the political value of such a move was undeniable.

Moers argued that women's writing was actually a rapid and powerful undercurrent distinct from, but hardly subordinate to, the mainstream. Women writers, she demonstrated in her chapter on literary

---

[29]Ellen Moers, *Literary Women: The Great Writers* (New York: Doubleday, 1976), p. xv.

history with impressive lists compiled from their letters and other private papers, read each other's books and even kept up an international correspondence. Their writing therefore drew upon women's experiences but also on a literary subculture of women writers that the mainstream was hardly aware of. In fact, Moers's book touched on almost every theme that was to be elaborated and refined in the subsequent discussion on women's writing in America: the exclusion of women writers (who had been misread and misjudged by the literary establishment), the need to find new strategies to open up canonical texts for feminist readings, the idea that a knowledge of feminist history was crucial for an understanding of women's writing, and the suggestion that women writers had shared a subculture that they often secretly kept alive. It had all the components of a rousing argument: evidence of gross injustice countered with a tradition of secret solidarity and resistance.

Elaine Showalter's meticulously researched *A Literature of Their Own,* which came out a year later, covered much the same conceptual ground. But Showalter took issue with Moers's characterization of women's writing as an ongoing international movement and emphasized the transience of female literary fame. Though the "lost continent of the female literary tradition [had] risen like Atlantis from the sea of English literature," each generation of women writers had found itself, she claimed,

> in a sense, without a history, forced to rediscover the past anew, forging again and again the consciousness of their sex. Given this perpetual disruption and also the self-hatred that has alienated women writers from a sense of collective identity, it does not seem possible to speak of a "movement."[30]

Showalter set out to trace "the female literary tradition" in English fiction from about the 1840s to the present day, working not so much on the continuity of that tradition as on the identity it found in resistance. Any minority group, she argued, finds its self-expression relative to a dominant society.[31] She posited three major phases that she claimed were common to all literary subcultures. First, a phase of imitation; second, one of protest; and third, "a phase of *self-discovery,* a turning inward, freed from some of the dependency of opposition, a

---

[30]Elaine Showalter, *A Literature of Their Own: British Women Novelists from Brontë to Lessing* (Princeton: Princeton University Press, 1977), pp. 11–12.
[31]Ibid., p. 11.

search for identity."[32] Showalter's own political biases probably make it difficult for her to acknowledge the theorist and revolutionary Frantz Fanon as the best-known source for this thesis about emerging subcultures. What is also obscured as a result is her transformation of Fanon's theory, domesticating an idea of revolutionary action to a liberal-conservative one of self-discovery and individual fulfillment as the goal of literary endeavor. Phases one and two in Fanon's argument about the emergence of a national culture from colonialism broadly coincide with those Showalter posits, but in Fanon's third phase, which is a "fighting phase," the artist "composes the sentence which expresses the heart of the people and becomes the mouthpiece of a new reality in action."[33]

A Literature of Their Own is, all the same, an important book, for Showalter provided women's writing with the kind of careful scholarly attention it had probably never received in the academy. She repopulated the period whose literary history she felt was marred by a residual "Great Traditionism" with many little-known writers, and deftly reopened the case for writers who were widely read and well regarded in their time but had been subsequently forgotten. We find it quite astonishing, however, that although the period covered by Showalter's book coincides with the age of high imperialism, neither Britain's colonial "possessions" nor the complicity of Englishwomen, writers not excluded, in the ideologies of class and of empire are seriously dealt with. In part, as we shall see, Showalter's own schemes replicate an imperialist design.

In two articles published a few years later, both reprinted in a widely circulated 1985 collection of feminist criticism, Showalter developed a theory of women's writing. Feminist criticism, she argued, could be regarded as functioning in two distinct modes: "feminist critique" and "gynocritics." The former is concerned with the woman "as the consumer of male-produced literature, and the way in which the hypothesis of the female reader changes our apprehension of a given text." She coined the term "gynocritics" for "scholarship concerned with woman as the producer of textual meaning, with the history, themes, genres and structures of literature by women."[34] Feminist critique is

---

[32]Ibid., p. 13.

[33]Frantz Fanon, *The Wretched of the Earth,* trans. Constance Farrington (Harmondsworth: Penguin, 1967; 1st ed. 1961), p. 179.

[34]Elaine Showalter, "Towards a Feminist Poetics," in *The New Feminist Criticism,* ed. Elaine Showalter (London: Virago, 1986), p. 128.

essentially political and polemical, with affiliations to Marxist sociology and aesthetics, whereas "gynocritics is more self-contained and experimental."[35] Showalter's own separatist inclinations become clearer as she extends her argument. "If we study stereotypes of women, the sexism of male critics and the limited roles women play in literary history, we are not learning what women have felt and experienced," she writes, "but only what men have thought women should be."[36] She is herself interested, like the historians and anthropologists she quotes, with the newly visible world of "feminist culture," which she argues will provide a setting and the rationale adequate to recovery of a tradition of women's writing. The problem is understood as analogous to that faced, say, by American literature as it sought to consolidate its independence from British literature and establish itself as the cultural arm of a new and sovereign nation. The idea is developed in a later essay, "Feminist Criticism in the Wilderness," where she reaffirms her distance from the Jeremiahs of feminist critique, who protest too loudly and whose concerns, according to her, do not remain strictly feminist.[37]

In their influential analysis of the major Anglo-American women writers of the nineteenth century, *The Madwoman in the Attic,* which came out in 1979, Sandra Gilbert and Susan Gubar set out to explore anew a "distinctively female literary tradition" and develop a theory of "female literary response to male literary assertion and coercion."[38] The focus of their attention was "female literary creativity," conceived of in their argument as a kind of essence, struggling to find its way out of the strictures that contain it. The study charts "the difficult paths by which nineteenth century women overcame their anxiety of authorship, repudiated debilitating patriarchal prescriptions, and recovered or remembered the lost foremothers who could help them find their distinctive female power."[39]

Patriarchal ideology in the nineteenth century, Gilbert and Gubar argue, thought of the writer as one who in the image of the Divine Creator *fathers* his work; the pen, they demonstrate, is invariably im-

[35]Showalter, "Towards a Feminist Poetics," p. 129.
[36]Ibid., p. 130.
[37]Showalter, *The New Feminist Criticism,* pp. 243–270.
[38]Sandra Gilbert and Susan Gubar, *The Madwoman in the Attic: The Woman Writer and the Nineteenth-century Literary Imagination* (New Haven: Yale University Press, 1979), p. xii.
[39]Ibid., p. 59.

aged as phallic. Women could not, therefore, both write and remain feminine without transgressing the norms set up by patriarchal authority. Thus, the woman writer is faced with a double burden. She has to confront these myths of creativity, but she also has to work past the ideal of the "eternal feminine" that was set up as inspiration and complement to the male. This ideal was a combination of angelic beauty and sweetness: passive, docile, selfless. But, the authors point out, "to be selfless is not only to be noble, it is to be dead. A life that has no story like the life of Göethe's Markarie is really a life of death, a death-in-life."[40] Behind this frozen angel lurks the monster woman who has a story to tell, and she is one of the terrible sorceress-goddesses such as "the Sphinx, Medusa . . . Kali . . . all of whom possess duplicitous arts that allow them both to seduce and steal male generative energy."[41] If such a proudly masculine cosmic author is the sole legitimate model for all early authors, and women are by virtue of their sex defined as angels or monsters and denied the autonomy to formulate alternatives to the authority that has imprisoned them and kept them "from attempting the pen," what are the options open to the woman writer?[42] Gilbert and Gubar provide an answer, which they develop through the seven-hundred-odd pages of the book.

> Women from Jane Austen and Mary Shelley to Emily Brontë and Emily Dickinson produced literary works that are in some sense palimpsestic, works whose surface designs conceal and obscure deeper, less accessible (and less socially acceptable) levels of meaning.[43]

The woman writer projects her uneasiness about literary creativity onto the emblematic figure of the madwoman, who, like Bertha Mason in Charlotte Brontë's *Jane Eyre,* is "usually in some sense the *author's* double, an image of her own anxiety and rage."[44] It is principally through these dark doubles that female authors both identify with and revise the definitions of femininity and female authorship that their culture proffers. But the woman writer is also engaged at another level with "assaulting and revising, deconstructing and reconstructing those

---

[40]Ibid., p. 25.
[41]Ibid., p. 34.
[42]Ibid., p. 13.
[43]Ibid., p. 73.
[44]Ibid., p. 78.

images of women inherited from male literature, especially the paradigmatic polarities of angel and monsters."[45]

The theoretical perspective, which we have summarized here, is really the weakest and most whimsical part of this energetic book. Their sparkling style, apparently never at a loss for a meaningful turn of phrase or a surprising metaphor, is a constant pleasure. Not least among the achievements of this widely circulated work is that it uncovers in women's writing formal strategies of such complexity and depth that they live up to the academy's most stringent New Critical demands. In this sense *The Madwoman in the Attic* has probably done more than any other single work to provide feminist criticism and women writers with a "respectable" berth in the academy, not only in the United States but in any other country in which English (or American) literature is studied.

Yet, as they naturalize a "female literary creativity," Gilbert and Gubar fix—and universalize—women and literary creativity in the image of the high subjectivist aesthetics of nineteenth-century Europe. History or geography can only touch their schemes tangentially as incident or as locale. Patriarchal ideology seems to bear no relation to class, race, or empire, and once it enters the literary text it has a life entirely independent of its counterpart in the world.

III

Over the last decade and a half, American feminist criticism would seem to have arrived at a framework for the study of women's writing. Tasks have been assigned, themes located, areas of debate defined, and women's writing authoritatively established as an object for disciplined investigation. The confidence of having drawn up no less than a world picture of the history of women's literature rings through the introduction of Elaine Showalter's 1985 collection of essays. "Since 1979," when *The Madwoman in the Attic* was published, she writes,

> insights have been tested, supplemented, extended, so that we have a coherent, if still incomplete, narrative of female literary history, which describes the evolutionary stages of women's writing during the last 250 years from imitation through protest to self-definition and defines and traces the connections, throughout history and across national

---

[45]Ibid., p. 176.

boundaries of the recurring images, themes, and plots that emerge from women's social, psychological and aesthetic experience in male-dominated cultures.[46]

The claims are awesome; the tone, one that colonized peoples have heard on many earlier occasions. An anthology of women's writing compiled, as this one was, in the late 1980s inherits a space—conceptual and political—opened up by these critical initiatives but also shaped by their assumptions. The metaphors we have used state the case too weakly, too neutrally. Feminist criticism has not merely developed a methodology to study a phenomenon that already exists: women's writing. Feminist criticism has actually shaped a new discipline and in the process created, as the object of its study, a new field: women's writing. There's no denying that women have written, or, to put it more accurately in the context of this anthology, that women have created literature in the past. But as those artifacts are studied as *women's writing,* which is charted as an area of study and sculpted into a tradition, they take on a significance that is a contemporary invention. As a discipline, "gynocritics" has designated its archives, forged its tools, asserted its authority, and made its political alignments.

There are several reasons why artifacts from "other" cultures might find hospitality in the space created by this new discipline: its self-proclaimed international scope, the increasing self-consciousness among Western liberals about the ethnocentrism of their white middle classes, the wild celebration of pluralism that postmodernism decrees, and the growing multinationalist scope of industry and commerce ensure a ready welcome, at several levels, for other cultures. Yet the assumptions of this criticism as well as the mode in which it extends a welcome to other literatures make it difficult and compromising terrain for an anthology such as this to enter or negotiate, and we feel the imperative to frame this critical moment and examine in some detail the disciplinary politics of gynocritics as it affects a project such as ours. It is a disturbing step, this, for we are as aware of our solidarities and the need to consolidate them as of our differences. But we hope as we engage critically with the bias of its feminism, and the political agenda hidden in its aesthetic, that we will also open up questions for Western feminism itself and make new, more self-conscious, more risky, and more radical, solidarities possible.

There are several dimensions along which a critique of the discipline

---

[46]Showalter, *The New Feminist Criticism,* p. 6.

as it has established itself might be developed. We have chosen, however, to pick out four major strands in its conceptual weave and tease out the implications of bringing them to bear on the study or reading of women's literature in India. We investigate, first, the idea of loss, which underwrites so much of the "recovery" of women's writing; second, the notion of release or escape, which tropes itself into a feminist poetics in works such as *The Madwoman in the Attic;* third, the problem that arises as the concept of experience, which in feminist practice has a critical, deconstructive charge, is uncritically conflated with an empiricist privileging of experience as the authentic source of truth and meaning; and finally, the hidden politics of what some strands of Western feminism have set up as women's real experiences, or female nature itself.

Notions of "loss" and "exclusion," for instance—lost women writers, lost classics, exclusion from the canon—are always underwritten by a dream of wholeness or completeness. A lost or excluded object can be recognized when it is found, and restored to the place from which it was missed. When it frames the problem as one of loss or exclusion, therefore, contemporary feminism sets up its present and the aspirations that stem from that as a covert norm against which the past is measured. Indeed, what gynocritics actually locates as it raids the past or picks its way through other cultural wares (and even the histories of other peoples) are the scattered fragments of its own dream. As it enumerates the themes and sets up the agenda for women's writing the world over, therefore, the present-day concerns of Western feminists are writ large to encompass the world, and the world collapses into the West. When women's literary history, for instance, culminates in what Showalter categorizes as the "female phase" turned in on itself, seeking its identity, history becomes a plot that finds its resolution in the current aspirations of Showalter's form of feminism.

If we ask the questions—apparently illegitimate, because the criticism seems to take for granted that the answer is such common knowledge that it does not even need to be stated—who has lost these writers, or rather, to what cause have they been lost, several answers suggest themselves. At one level they are obviously lost to feminists today, lost to a tradition of women's writing, lost to literary studies, lost to the reader's experience. But more significantly they are missing from another, more deeply embedded cultural institution that has over the last century or so provided literary studies with its legitimacy. It is this institution feminist scholars must invoke when they voice their grievances. In so doing, of course, they reaffirm its authority and align their concerns with it. These writers, the unstated argument is, are lost to the select company of great (male) writers whose works were charged with the task of providing post-Enlightenment Western society in general, and the nation in particular, with its ethical capital. In other words, even as the feminist act of recovery establishes a historical legitimacy for women's writing, it consolidates the hold of a (liberal) humanism and with it the political imperatives that underwrote the setting up of literary studies as a major agent of that ideology. In a recently published study, Gauri Viswanathan, for instance, argues that "humanistic functions traditionally associated with the study of literature—for example, the shaping of character, or the development of an aesthetic sense or the disciplines of ethical thinking—are also essential to the process of sociopolitical control." Drawing on evidence from parliamentary debates and educational policy, she demonstrates that "literary study gained enormous cultural strength through its development in a period of territorial expansion and conquest."[47] Other commentators have explored the process through which the discipline was institutionalized and its imbrication in the shaping of gender and class. The story of its establishment as a humanistic discipline in the "mother

---

[47]Gauri Viswanathan, "The Beginnings of English Literary Study in British India," *Oxford Literary Review* 9, 1987, pp. 2–26. Viswanathan argues that the growth of English as a discipline in England took place somewhat later in the nineteenth century, and had as its basis "a shape and an ideological content developed in the colonial context." A reader might enjoy the following extract from a toast proposed in 1846 in Edinburgh by Thomas Macaulay (1800–1859), the British statesman and historian who was the principal architect of English education in India and the important spokesman for literary studies in Britain: "To the literature of Britain, to that literature, the brightest, the purest, the most durable of all the glories of our country, to that literature, so rich in precious truth and precious fiction, to that literature which boasts of the prince of all poets and the prince of all philosophers; to that literature which has exercised an influence wider than that of our commerce and mightier than that of our arms; to that literature which has taught France the principles of liberty and has furnished Germany with models of art; to that literature which forms a tie closer than the tie of consanguinity between us and the commonwealths of the valley of the Mississippi; to that literature before the light of which impious and cruel superstitions are fast taking flight on the banks of the Ganges; to that literature which will in future ages, instruct and delight the unborn millions who will have turned the Australasian and Catfrarian deserts into cities and gardens. To the literature of Britain, then! And wherever the literature of Britain spreads may it be attended by British virtue and British freedom!" Thomas Macaulay, *Miscellaneous Writings,* vol. 3 (London: Longman's Green and Co., 1880), pp. 398–399.

country" and that of its more nakedly dominative functions in the colonies are closely meshed.[48]

Gynocritics forces open the doors of a literary sanctum where only male writers—and that too, only some male writers—seemed to have rights of entry, in order to let a few women in. The unwritten rules that once debarred them are cleverly exposed. But the deeper political commitments that govern the teaching of literature are not subjected to serious theoretical scrutiny. Neither the legitimacy nor the function of the sacred monument itself can be radically questioned by those who wish to restore its fullness and thereby endorse its authority.

Structurally, the idea of "release" is not dissimilar to that of "loss." When it asserts the presence of a repressed female creativity struggling over the last two hundred years or more for release, which is recognized at last by the feminist critic and restored through her reading to a female literary tradition, *The Madwoman in the Attic,* for instance, extends the reach of the authors' present-day feminist consciousness to a point where it is naturalized and enshrined as female nature itself. The scope of what they conceive of as women's bondage or imprisonment, however, is clearly laid out. The "release" is to be principally from "male houses and male texts." A further qualification sharpens the focus: and "escape" through ingenuity and indirection may turn for its metaphors to the other paraphernalia of middle-class "women's place."

> Ladylike veils and costumes, mirrors, paintings, statues, locked cabinets, drawers, trunks, strong boxes and other domestic furnishings appear and reappear . . . to signify the woman writer's sense that, as Emily Dickinson put it, her life has been "shaven and fitted to a frame," a confinement she can only tolerate by believing that "the soul has moments of escape / when bursting all the doors / she dances like a bomb abroad."[49]

In the process, all women's writing, or at least women's writing that merits serious literary attention, becomes feminist in the precise mode

---

[48]See Chris Baldick, *The Social Mission of English Criticism 1848–1932* (Oxford: Clarendon Press, 1983). Francis Mulhern in *The Moment of 'Scrutiny'* documents the deep complicity of the Leavisite tradition, often thought of as humanist in contrast to the formalism of American New Criticism, in the ideologies of the Tory middle classes in Britain (London: Verso, 1981).
[49]Gilbert and Gubar, *Madwoman,* p. 85.

and to the precise extent that the authors themselves understand and experience feminism. Their reading gestures toward history. The subtitle itself indicates the focus as a specific period, the nineteenth century, and the text makes mention of earlier periods. But the past is a collection of intense, more or less univocal moments in which the authors identify the themes and concerns of contemporary American feminism. The paraphernalia of a European middle-class woman's place is regarded as an adequate metaphor for all women's worlds. Other times and other places are only a feature of dispersal, not transformation or change. Gender subordination imaged in these domestic, middle-class terms defines the entire scope of the woman writer's world, in which, as Gilbert and Gubar image it, there appears to be only the fundamental antagonism repeatedly played out in its primal tune: that of a monolithic, unchanging patriarchy, which would seem to have no connections with other hegemonies, say, of class or race, and an equally fixed and resilient female self: "The striking coherence we noticed in literature by women could be explained by a common female impulse to struggle free from social and literary confinement through strategic redefinitions of the self, art, and society."[50]

The idea of a natural being straining for release echoes the Rousseauist formulations of the Enlightenment. But in Gilbert and Gubar's argument, there is a significant reversal of the priorities set up at that time for the emerging bourgeois male. It is a reversal disturbingly reminiscent of the radically different and unequal programs the Enlightenment itself so confidently proposed for men and for women. The man was to direct his revolt outward against the Church and the king. *His* natural being, once it was released to enjoy the earth, which was his inheritance, would be governed by reason, which was also part of male nature. Woman, however, and it is important to remember that even the feminist philosopher Mary Wollestonecraft agreed on this, had to turn her energies onto her self. She had to refashion her nature to emerge as fit complement to the new man. The agenda for the colonies was structurally similar. In its most enlightened mode, imperialism regarded the colonized peoples as requiring a remolding, not of course to be fit complement to bourgeois males, but to be fit subjects for its rule. We will have occasion to return to this configuration from the point of view of the middle-class woman in India, and for the woman writer—the stresses it set up and the opportunities it

---

[50]Ibid., p. xi–xii.

opened up. But for the present it is enough to point out that, in Gilbert and Gubar's scheme, as the woman writer struggles for release, she redefines her self and with it the symbolic world of the literary text. As for society, that ghostly appendage does not seem solid enough to throw even a shadow on the imaginative world of the book.

The "last parable" through which this particular gospel of redemption explicates itself is that of the

> the woman artist [who] enters the cavern of her own mind and finds there the scattered leaves not only of her own power but of the tradition that might have generated that power. The body of her precursor's art, and thus the body of her own art, lies in pieces around her, dismembered, dis-remembered, disintegrated. How can she remember it, and become a member of it, join it and rejoin it, integrate it and in doing so achieve her own integrity, her own selfhood?[51]

Like the messages on the sibylline leaves of Mary Shelley's story on which this "parable" is based, these fragments are written in several languages. Some of the scripts are faded, others unfamiliar. But they are inscribed on the elements of the natural world, bark and leaf, and on the secret inner lining of the female body, as Gilbert and Gubar quote Shelley: "a white filmy substance resembling the inner part of the green hood which shelters the grain of unripe Indian corn."[52] With effort, they can be deciphered. In Gilbert and Gubar's reading of Shelley, these misunderstood, and therefore scattered, pieces of the woman writer's literary heritage rise now like a "lost Atlantis ... whose wholeness once encompassed and explained all those figures on the horizon who seemed 'odd,' fragmentary, incomplete. . . ." Here memory declares itself as an hermeneutic act, for as lost or forgotten works are "remembered . . . by the community of which they are and were members, such figures gain their full authority."[53] The cultural context for women's writing is a sort of female enclave untouched by masculinist assumptions and the woman writer is imaged as free from ideology. The mystic energy that attends the vision is invoked with a confidence that does not doubt its power to absorb the whole world into its project.

It is not surprising, therefore, to find that their equally monumental *The Norton Anthology of Literature by Women,* 1986, which is in many

---

[51]Ibid., p. 98.
[52]Ibid., p. 95.
[53]Ibid., p. 99.

other ways a superb collection, places women from all over the world (who write in English) quite unself-consciously against the backdrop of Euro-American social history.[54] Even the idea that a sizable proportion of British or American society itself does not consider the history or culture of Western Europe as *its* past, that the history and culture of Africa—and not just of the slave trade—may be an important prehistory of the United States, for example, and that of India or the Caribbean of Britain, is simply suppressed. British imperialism is referred to—in one sentence—but it does not appear to have touched any of the women writers in a serious way. As the editors project it, the immediate contexts for women's writing are only the images of women in mainstream literature. But nowhere in the book do we find even an awareness that there are many "mainstream" literatures; or that women who write in English cannot so casually be gathered into the same fold; or that it is not the same essential female nature that is struggling, the world over, to free itself from male bondage.

Like Showalter, Gilbert and Gubar speak as if feminist "poetics" has finally arrived at its destination. Women writers, they indicate, can now set aside their palimpsestic plots and engage directly with their experience, as male writers whose full authority was never repressed have always been able to do.

Underlying both Showalter's empiricist literary history and Gilbert and Gubar's symbolic recreation of the woman writer's consciousness and her female literary inheritance is an assumption as deeply embedded in the practices of popular reading in the twentieth century (in India as much as in the West) as in literary criticism. Literary texts, the assumption is, express the author's experience and reveal the truth about his or her world, and as they do so, they provide us with access to the universal dimensions of human nature. As an aesthetic theory, expressive realism emerged in the second half of the nineteenth century, more or less in conjunction with the realist novel. It has been subjected to extensive critique in recent times, and its function, in shaping a reader, "cut to the measure" of the white bourgeois world, analyzed at several levels. The notion is, however, reaffirmed and given new life today by feminist critics who counterpose women's writing, which they choose to read as a transparent expression of women's authentic experience, to the stereotypes of mainstream literature, often

---

[54]Sandra Gilbert and Susan Gubar, *The Norton Anthology of Literature by Women: The Tradition in English* (New York: W. W. Norton, 1985).

spoken of as "male" literature, which is regarded simply as distorting the reality of women's lives.

Within feminist criticism, the idea that women's experience is a critical resource also draws its strength from the consciousness-raising groups that were so crucial to the development of feminist theory and feminist politics in the United States in the late sixties and early seventies. Several commentators have pointed to the similarities between the politics of consciousness-raising and those of the "speaking bitterness" campaigns of the Chinese Cultural Revolution.[55] The parallel helps us focus on dimensions of consciousness-raising that are often blurred over as the immediacy, intimacy, and spontaneity of these groups are highlighted. In fact, consciousness-raising was as carefully structured a political exercise as the "speaking bitterness" campaigns. It worked by challenging and recasting a dominant ideology's characterizations of women and interrogating authoritative interpretations of every dimension of social and personal experience. The focus was not, as it tended to become in literary criticism, on distorting stereotypes but on the wide-ranging strategies, social, economic, and psychic, through which mastery was exercised and subordination maintained. From the supportive contexts of the consciousness-raising groups, feminists confronted the institutions and practices of everyday life, and extended their micropolitical analysis into the domain of the family and even of desire. Women's experiences were used as a resource for critical discussion, making it possible for women to share dimensions of their lives they had earlier kept secret or felt too insecure to confront or even recognize. Groups encouraged women to focus on and articulate anger and dissatisfaction, and evolved through discussion new interpretations of their experience that questioned and rejected earlier modes of processing and making sense of what they had observed or felt. But these sessions were less a spontaneous outburst and more a reading against the grain, which was often so risky— socially and psychically—for the individual that they needed the

---

[55]According to Florence Howe (in "Women and the Power to Change," written in 1973), Juliet Mitchell first noted the analogy in *Women's Estate* (New York: Pantheon, 1971, p. 62). Howe adds that there were also "several elements in the United States culture that allowed for the spread of such groups: the coffee klatch, for example, the quilting bee, and other forms of female social or work groups." Further, "in the southern civil rights movement, discussion groups, especially on the subject of racism, also provided a precedent." *Myths of Coeducation* (Bloomington: Indiana University Press, 1987), p. 172.

combined resources of a group to make the "reading" possible. The new "feminist" significations that emerged were provided legitimacy through group consent and were consolidated and put into circulation through active and considered political or personal programs.

Not least among the achievements of consciousness-raising was the solidarity it generated among women who were closely involved in it, as well as the new self-confidence and sense of power it produced. Many women felt their lives had been completely transformed and that they had finally been "released" from the constrictions of patriarchal ideology. But consciousness-raising was also an extremely significant development in political practice. Though the politics of ideology and of representation had been discussed for well nigh a century, it was in the women's movement that a critique of culture first emerged as a viable political program. Consistently extended, this attention to the minute, everyday practices of subordination and expropriation has implications for the politics of class, caste, colonialism, ethnicity, and a whole range of other structures of domination that determine the lives of women—and men. But unfortunately the critical use of experience and the sense of release consciousness-raising generated were quickly annexed in several ways: most blatantly by a consumerism that addressed and orchestrated women's "freedom" in its own interests; but also by a powerful strand of feminist scholarship within several disciplines that naturalized and privileged the new "feminist" significations as they conflated the freedom they experienced, and their sense of having inherited the earth anew, with an essential—and visionary—femaleness. When the new validity women's experience acquired as a resource that could be drawn on for critical discussion was conflated with the empiricist idea that experience was the source of true knowledge, experience lost the critical edge it had acquired as a political tool. And to the extent that feminism accepted or promoted this conflation and the consequent valorization of female nature, it acquiesced to and even collaborated in the annexation of one of the most powerful political movements of our age into a dominant bourgeois humanist scheme of things. In ways that soon obscured the critical functions of consciousness-raising, many liberal feminists simply endorsed the authenticity of what were increasingly referred to in universalist and naturalistic terms as *women's* experiences. Liberal feminists invented a *female* tradition that was imaged as a lost city, submerged but intact, unaffected by history, waiting to be recovered, and they spoke of an essential difference between male and female. They argued for a privileged affinity between women and peace or women and nature, the body or the unconscious. When this popular strand of feminism set up its significations, won no doubt at considerable cost and in the thick of struggle, as a kind of covert norm, or began to think of these significations as "natural," or as constituting some sort of female essence struggling in the work of the woman writer to express itself, it effectively brought the critical politics feminist practice had so brilliantly designed and set going in the consciousness-raising groups to a grinding halt.

We believe that there are powerful alliances feminists of all classes the world over can make, and equally powerful alliances feminists can make with other oppressed groups if we accept the challenges held out to us. But since the kind of feminist criticism that naturalizes the experiences and issues of Western feminism in this way is so easily co-opted by the academy and so widely circulated among third-world scholars (while the more historically aware work done by feminist scholars is marginalized), we must explain in more detail why we find the subsuming of a critical method into a celebration of female nature so disturbing. We must also explore why it is that if we simply apply the theories of women's writing that have been developed over the last decade or so to women's writing in India, we will not merely reproduce its confusions, but compound them.

It might be useful, as a starting point, to unpack the concept of "reality" as it emerges in the work of the critics we have discussed, whether it is in the idea of "women's real experiences," which are transparently available in women's writing, especially in realist fiction and in lyric poetry, or in the related idea of a real or authentic female voice that can, if only we pay the right kind of attention, be heard in a woman writer's work.

In gynocritics the real is clearly invested with an oppositional force and with the sense of a knowledge preserved in the face of opposition, and is contrasted with "unreal" or "untrue" portrayals of women in the work of most male writers. The idea of the "real," therefore, carries the impress of a *truth* that emerges as the shackles of prejudice—or false consciousness—are thrown off. As one might have expected, the major contradictions middle-class feminists in the West experienced in the initial stages of the movement were those between the promises of freedom and equality that liberalism held out to them and the social and psychic determinations that limited women's access to these rights. Though the movement drew on many existing resources—theoretical and political—to develop a powerful and original critique of patriarchy, when the dominant strand in Western feminism articulated its own solutions to those problems, it did so in a way that only addressed the contradictions principally as women from such social formations experienced them. Other contradictions, which had their source, say, in patriarchy as it was historically constituted by class, by colonialism, or by caste, which would have shaped the subordination of a working-class woman in India—Bangalore Nagaratnamma, for instance—and determined her selfhood or subjectivity, were simply not addressed. Besides, even the contours of what might be more strictly defined as gender subordination were so normatively invoked that they could not accommodate other histories that shaped the contours of desire or of power. As a result, the shifting reciprocal relationships that determine women's worlds and female subjectivities are obscured. Further, the complicity of white women or middle-class women in the structures of domination are never subjected to informed or serious scrutiny. The myriad conflicts women came up against in their everyday lives were invariably woven into a fictional world or a "real" world in which an adequate "resolution" to problems was achieved as middle-class women uncovered the processes, material and ideological, that had "excluded" them from full citizenship in their society, and developed strategies to ensure their "inclusion."[56] Oppressions of class, of imperialism, of race, which for many women—white middle-class women not excluded—compound and reciprocally constitute those of patriarchy, were glossed over in a narrative logic that focused its attention exclusively on what it defined as *women's* concerns. Both the author and the reader such narratives assumed—and therefore produced and consolidated—as "woman" belonged to a social configuration the narratives took as norm. Of course, this was precisely how the narrative of the realist novel had a century earlier set up the world as home for its bourgeois hero. That world fell into place and acquired the aura of the real from the viewpoint of the white bourgeois male. Its objects were delineated from his perspective, in his image, and the world was ordered in his interests. Realism was an effect of his gaze. Only from his location could memory, actuality, and language achieve that perfect confluence which produced the "reality

---

[56]Betty Friedan's *The Second Stage* (New York: Summit Books, 1981) represents the anxiety to close the movement off once these initial demands have been met in its most intense and explicit form. Other closures are more subtle and more covert. See Susie Tharu, "The Second Stage from the Third World," *Indian Journal of American Studies* 13:2, 1983, pp. 179–184.

effect." But feminists who accepted a place in these frameworks and these narratives—whether in the passive sense of allowing them to take over and avoiding more risky initiatives, or in the active sense of choosing their allies—shortchanged feminism too.

We are not, of course, suggesting (what even a decade ago we might have easily been interpreted as doing) that feminism is only a white middle-class, or Indian middle-class, women's issue. What we are saying is that in the process of posing, elaborating, analyzing, and resolving questions of gender and projecting their resolutions as female reality, Western feminists from the liberal mainstream drew on a whole range of significations and inferential logics attached to them already in circulation, which constituted the common sense of their society. As they did so, they underwrote afresh their society's consensus about the "real" or the plausible. They questioned the ideological processes that endorsed their subordination as women, but they acquiesced broadly in the consensus on the significations of other cultural and conceptual objects, disciplinary commitments, feelings, tastes, everyday practices, and, indeed, narrative fragments of various kinds that were operative in their society and underwrote the politics of class, race, or imperialism, without subjecting them to the same vigorous critique they had extended to the social construction of middle-class femininity. Feminism drew attention in quite spectacular ways to the subtle strategies of power written into the shaping and differentiation of the feminine in the everyday practices of the family, of education, of the workplace, of the law, and of medicine and psychology. But feminisms that projected the results of this initial deconstructive move as *true* or *natural,* as essentially female, projected not only present-day middle-class subjectivities as normatively female but also the problem as they construed it, as the limits of feminism, and their present-day concerns as the great female themes. Such feminism inevitably aligned itself with the many splendored apparatus of power that liberal capitalism, which was also inalienably imperialist, developed over the not inconsequential history through which it established its "natural" dominions.[57]

---

[57]For analysis of a replay of the liberal feminist problematic in the "new realism" of the late 1970s and early 1980s, see Susie Tharu, "Third World Women's Cinema: Notes on Narrative, Reflections on Opacity," *Economic and Political Weekly* 21:20, 1986, pp. 864–867.

IV

At one level the two volumes of *Women Writing in India* are a joyous retrieval of artifacts that signify women's achievement. At another, they represent a difficult and inventive moment in the theory and practice of feminist criticism. We have reread established writers and are introducing several comparatively little-known ones. There will be surprises—even for, say, Telugu readers in our collection of Telugu literature. In English translation, what we have is a stupendous body of new work. Judged by conventional standards, many of the pieces collected here are classics. Some have stood the test of time—biased and hostile though that test might have been. Others will not require unusually persuasive advocates to argue for their rehabilitation in the canons of Marathi, Kannada, or Urdu literature, or for that matter in an international canon of women's literature. Our collection might well provide an impetus for such a venture, but the refurbishment of canons was not the primary task we ourselves addressed. Had the recovery of literature, lost or damned in the conduit of male criticism, been our major interest, we might have translated different authors, made somewhat different selections, and used different working norms for the translations. We may not have felt the need to attend, as we did, separately to each of the regional literatures or work carefully through their archives and their histories. We would probably not have spent so much time dredging out information about the writers' lives, or attempted to reconstruct the changing ideological configurations in which women wrote and were read.

We have not, then, simply tried to make good the loss for literary studies. The interests of that monumental institution as it stands are ones we wish to transform, not entrench. Neither do we claim that these texts, simply because they are authored by women, express women's *real* experiences or portray *real* women, or indeed that they therefore speak to women in other times, other places, or other social positions with an immediacy that affirms the universality of patriarchal oppression and the common experience of women. Women writers—critics and editors of anthologies no less—are clearly as imbricated in the ideologies of their times as men are; patriarchies take shape and are transformed in specific historical circumstances. Not all literature written by women is feminist, or even about women. Neither is the scope of women's writing restricted to allegories of gender oppression. Besides, even when the writing is specifically feminist, as most of the pieces selected for translation here are, opposition to the dominant ideologies of gender can be discomfitingly class or caste bound and draw on assumptions about race or religious persuasion that reinforce the hold of those ideologies and collaborate in extending their authority. Middle-class women, white women, upper-caste Hindu women might find that their claims to "equality" or to the "full authority" of liberal individualism are at the expense of the working classes, the nonwhite races, dalits, or Muslims. For, as we shall see, given the specific practices and discourses through which individualism took historical shape in India, these groups had to be defined as Other in order that the Self might gain identity.

Women writers may not be exempt from the ideologies that shape their worlds, but it does not follow, as some critics have argued, that there is no sense in which women's writing can be regarded as different or as warranting separate attention. Women articulate and respond to ideologies from complexly constituted and decentered positions within them. Familial ideologies, for instance, clearly constitute male and female subjectivities in different ways, as do ideologies of nation or of empire. Further, ideologies are not experienced—or contested—in the same way from different subject positions. What may appear just and rational from a male or upper-class point of view may seem exploitive and contradictory from a working-class woman's point of view. If we restrain ourselves from enthusiastically recovering women's writing to perform the same services to society and to nation that mainstream literature over the last hundred years has been called upon to do, we might learn to read compositions that emerge from these eccentric locations in a new way; we might indeed learn to read them not for the moments in which they collude with or reinforce dominant ideologies of gender, class, nation, or empire, but for the gestures of defiance or subversion implicit in them.

Readers trained in the appreciation of artifacts that assume and reinforce the power of the center, readers bred on the standard narratives of resolution, victory, or liberation and on an aesthetic designed to smooth over contradictions and celebrate authority (in both senses of the term), readers searching through other times and other cultures for mirrors that reflect their current concerns may initially feel insecure and disoriented as they find their way into texts that take shape at the margins. There will be few gratifications here to replace those domestic fires burning in polished hearths, few testimonies of liberation, or bugle calls that herald the nation or the revolution.

Women Writing in India represents a critical moment that requires us to strain against many earlier formations, but also one, we hope, that makes significant initial moves in developing an aesthetic that does not lessen discontinuity, dispossession, or marginality but dramatizes and clarifies it. It is an aesthetic that must undo the strict distinctions between the literary and the social text, abdicate the imperious functions it has been charged with over the last century and a half, and redesign itself to orchestrate contradictions and cherish the agonistic forms of insurgency and resistance. The promise it holds out is that of a critical practice that is by no means restricted to literature—or to the academy—but, in Gayatri Spivak's phrasing, fills the "literary form with its connections to what is being read: history, political economy— the world."[58] It is also an aesthetic that holds the promise of the many worlds that will appear as the old universalism fades and begins to look dull and simplistic; its self-confident posturing melodramatic; the tastes and feelings it nourished somehow decadent and sentimental.

What we have tried to do, therefore, principally in the section introductions, but also in the biographical headnotes, is to create a context in which women's writings can be read, not as new *monuments* to existing institutions or cultures (classics are, by definition, monuments), but as *documents* that display what is at stake in the embattled practices of self and agency, and in the making of a habitable world, at the margins of patriarchies reconstituted by the emerging bourgeoisies of empire and nation. Our stress is on what forms the grain of these women's struggles. How were their worlds shaped? we ask. How have they turned figures, plots, narratives, lyrical and fictional projects set up for different purposes to their use? With what cunning did they press into service objects coded into cultural significations indifferent or hostile to them? How did they tread their oblique paths across competing ideological grids, or obdurately hang on to illegitimate pleasure? What forms did their dreams of integrity or selfhood take? Most important, and this has been the major principle for our selections: what modes of resistance did they fashion? How did they avoid, question, play off, rewrite, transform, or even undermine the projects set out for them?

In other words, we are interested in how the efforts of these women shaped the worlds we inherited, and what, therefore, is the history, not of authority, but of contest and engagement we can claim today. But

---

[58]Gayatri Spivak, *In Other Worlds* (London: Methuen, 1987), p. 95.

we also ask, what was the price they paid in these transactions, what did they concede, and how do those costs and those concessions affect our inheritance? Through these texts, therefore, we look back to a feminist inheritance more powerful and complex, but at the same time more troubling, than narratives of suppression and release might allow us to suspect.

LITERATURE OF THE ANCIENT AND MEDIEVAL PERIODS

LITERATURE OF THE ANCIENT AND MEDIEVAL PERIODS: READING AGAINST THE ORIENTALIST GRAIN

The broad sweep of twenty-four centuries between the religious poetry of the early Buddhist period and the court literature of the seventeenth and eighteenth centuries allows us only to highlight the major movements and major figures. Although some of these artists are known today only to a few specialist scholars, the songs of others have been kept alive over several centuries through the oral traditions of their regions. These figures come to us, therefore, firmly set in the scenarios of classical scholarship, or shaped by the popular imagination. As anyone who has struggled with the problems of writing feminist, or indeed any alternate, history will quickly appreciate, it is impossible to ask new questions about the past without confronting and making one's way through such earlier formations. As we read lightly against the grain of these earlier determinations, several interesting questions emerge.

Euro-American feminist theory has tended to concentrate its efforts principally on exposing the *patriarchal* urgencies that underwrite representations of women and shape the conceptual and methodological apparatus of a discipline. Though they admit the need to take race and class, and occasionally even imperialism, into account, these theories usually treat patriarchy as an isolatable system responsible for the subordination of women, to which, in the interests of a more complete analysis of the workings of power in a particular society, oppressions of race and class might be "added." Even as an initial, consciousness-raising gesture, such an approach seems curiously inadequate. Patriarchies are clearly formed through historical processes and structured by other dominant ideologies—of colonialism, of class, and of caste, which they in turn structure. Right through the nineteenth century and well into the twentieth, for instance, tradition and the past—ancient India and, indeed, women in ancient India—were major issues of debate, not only for historians and students of literature but also for artists, novelists, jurists, political philosophers, social reformers, imperial administrators and policy makers, and nationalist thinkers of all kinds. Though their characterizations of it were sometimes totally opposed, colonizers and colonized alike from all schools of thought regarded "ancient India" as holding the key to the understanding of the subsequent history of the subcontinent and to its contemporary condition. "So great an influence," wrote Friedrich Max Müller (1823–1900), the Anglo-German scholar whose works popularized the idea, "has the Vedic age . . . exercised upon all succeeding periods of Indian history . . . so deeply have the religious and moral ideas of that primitive era taken root in the mind of the Indian nation, so minutely has almost every private and public act of Indian life been regulated by old traditionary precepts, that it is impossible to find the right point of view for judging Indian religion, morals and literature without a knowledge of the literary remains of the Vedic age."[1] These controversies are particularly important for us because it was through them that the question of women, which was umbilically tied by all parties in the debate to that of ancient India, took on some of the contours it did in the nineteenth century—contours that continue, in many respects, to determine its scope today.

This section of the anthology, therefore, has a double function. On the one hand it provides a glimpse of an astonishing and varied body of women's literature in the precolonial period on which hardly any serious feminist research has been done. On the other, as it considers precolonial literature from a feminist perspective, it questions powerful

---

[1]Max Müller, *A History of Ancient Sanskrit Literature,* 1859, quoted in Nirad C. Chaudhuri, *Scholar Extraordinary: The Life of Professor the Rt. Hon. Friedrich Max Muller P.C.* (Delhi: Oxford University Press, 1974), p. 135.

representations of the past. These representations have shaped the debate on women (their status in Indian society, their role in the family and in the nation, their education, their freedom, their sexuality) and, consequently, the debate over women's subjecthood and women's writing in the nineteenth and twentieth centuries.

From our point of view, the most significant of the initial frameworks set up for the study of Indian history was that of Orientalist scholarship. Since the term *Orientalism* has taken on much broader connotations in the wake of Edward Said's well-known argument, we have chosen to refer to Indian Orientalists as Indologists. Both the Indologists and the Utilitarians (who were their fiercest opponents in India) were Orientalists if we think of Orientalism in Said's sense of the term, as "a way of coming to terms with the Orient that is based on the Orient's special place in European western experience," as its "cultural contestant" or Other, and the persistent schemes and tropes by which the Orient is *"contained and represented* by dominating [Occidental] frameworks."[2] The beginnings of Indological studies are associated with William Jones (1746–1794), who was an official of the British East India Company, and others. The studies arose in response to the demands made by the company, as it extended its early commercial interests into political ones, for a knowledge of the history, the legal practices, and the customs of the people who were to be governed. It is not surprising, therefore, that these interests structured the knowledge that was acquired.[3] The expanding requirements of the imperial enterprise, and the unexpectedly large numbers of texts Jones and his colleagues "discovered," took the project beyond its original mandate into the study of Sanskrit literature and philosophy and the Hindu religion. As we shall see, however, the designs of power it embodied remained unchanged.

The Indologists developed the thesis of a common Indo-European heritage, based on the similarities between Sanskrit, the language associated with the Aryans who had invaded the subcontinent around

[2]Edward Said, *Orientalism* (New York: Pantheon, 1978), p. 40.
[3]See Ranajit Guha, *An Indian Historiography of India: A Nineteenth-century Agenda and Its Implications* (Calcutta: Centre for Studies in Social Sciences, 1988), for a penetrating analysis of how imperialist interests shaped nineteenth-century historiography. Also James Mill, whose three-volume *The History of British India,* published in 1817, was regarded as the authoritative work in the area for almost a century. Mill quite explicitly states that he is attempting in his history to provide the knowledge required for the enlightened government of Britain's new overseas dominions.

1700 B.C., and the classical European languages, Latin and Greek. They set up a distinction between the languages (in Europe as well as in India) derived from this lineage, increasingly referred to as Aryan, and the non-Aryan, Dravidian, or Semitic languages.[4] Their writings spoke of the ancient India preserved resplendent in the thirty-five-hundred-year-old text of the *Rig Veda* as the lost heritage of Europe. The idyllic, unchanging village communities of the vedic period, they argued, sustained the natural human qualities of gentleness, truthfulness, and otherworldliness, and ancient India thus became a sort of utopia for the Romantic imagination. The study of Oriental cultures, Jones himself believed, would help invigorate European culture.[5] It was in the Orient, the poet August Schlegel (1767–1845) proclaimed, that "Europe should search for the highest Romanticism.[6] And through his much reprinted book, *India: What It Can Teach Us,* 1892, Max Müller propagated the idea of ancient India as the answer to the ills of contemporary Europe. Unlike Europe, which had become materialist and self-indulgent, the governing principles of vedic society, he wrote, were not the active, combative, and acquisitive, but the passive, meditative, and reflective. In other words, ancient Indian civilization had the qualities Europe required for a richer, more total humanity. Müller himself seems to have had little to say about women, but the omission is compensated for, Uma Chakravarti shows, in other Indological writings such as that of Clarisse Bader (1845–?).[7] Bader argues that Western women had much to learn from the ancient Aryan civilizations, in which women were characterized by spiritual and ascetic tenderness, complete abnegation of self-interest, and unlimited devotion to the

---

[4]In Sanskrit the word *arya* means "noble" or "freeborn"; otherwise it designates a member of the three higher castes (brahmin, kshatriya, and vaisya) and excludes the fourth caste (sudra). *Aryan* as it is used in modern discussions of ancient India did not have such currency until the late eighteenth century; the term acquired an entirely different meaning when it was used by the National Socialists in Germany.
[5]John Drew, *India and the Romantic Imagination* (Delhi: Oxford University Press, 1987), pp. 45–82.
[6]"Im Orient mussen wir das hochste Romantische suchen," quoted in Romila Thapar, *Ancient Indian Social History: Some Interpretations* (Delhi: Orient Longmans, 1979), p. 23.
[7]Clarisse Bader, *Women in Ancient India* (London: Longmans Green, 1925), cited in Uma Chakravarti, "Whatever Happened to the Vedic Dasi? Orientalism, Nationalism and a Script for the Past," in *Recasting Women: Essays in Colonial History,* ed. Kumkum Sangari and Sudesh Vaid (Delhi: Kali for Women, 1989), pp. 44–45. Uma Chakravarti discusses related questions at some length.

family. Their awe-inspiring spiritual courage, she and others seemed to think, was still evident in the women who mounted the funeral pyres of their husbands to commit sati. Bader traced contemporary degradation of Indian women to later accretions on vedic beliefs and practices, and to the growth of the sensuous Vaishnava cults. According to her, the decline of vedic society also held a lesson for Europe: it showed to what depths of "physical and moral degradation the most gifted of people could fall, once it exchanged the yoke of duty for that of passion."

The transformative intent of the Indologist mission, however, was not restricted to Europe. The ethos and practices of the ancient civilization they had discovered were to be returned to a present-day India, which, they felt, had in the intervening years lost touch with the primitive roots of its own culture. Embedded in the Indologist thesis was a teleology that sought to erase history. Their argument was that as vedic culture absorbed elements from other indigenous nonvedic, non-Aryan practices (among which were the traditions spoken of as Vaishnava), it gradually degenerated. The process culminated in the precipitous fall that marked the medieval period—and Muslim rule. The only way to excise the parasitic growths of the last three thousand years, Max Müller, for instance, declared, was to show present-day India the real vedic roots of its religion.

The tendency to essentialize vedic culture and exaggerate its virtues, Romila Thapar writes, was in part a result of the Romantic search for a distant Edenic world, a utopia, "to escape from the bewildering changes taking place in nineteenth century Europe and in part to counteract the highly critical attitudes current among Utilitarian thinkers in Britain from whose ranks came the more influential writing on India."[8] However kindly the intentions, the effects were hardly benign, but we shall return to those questions after a brief discussion of the direction taken by Utilitarian historiography, notably by James Mill's *History of British India.*

Writing in 1817, Mill maintained that Indian society had remained substantially unchanged over three or four millennia, from its beginnings in the Aryan invasions to the period when the British arrived in India. But unlike Müller and the Romantics, with their more mystic predilections, who were attracted to that ancient civilization, Mill considered Indian culture as primitive, immoral, and "rude," and funda-

<hr />

[8]Romila Thapar, *Ancient Indian Social History,* p. 3.

mentally lacking, therefore, in the qualities that "preside over the progress" of civil society, especially, in his view, reason and good government. A series of despotic rulers had, he believed, stunted the growth of the people. Their imagination—and Mill based his observations on the entire scope of Indian mythology—therefore, was still "wild and ungoverned," their fictions "audacious," "unnatural," and "monstrous."[9]

It is to Mill's view of the world that we owe the pride of place that the question of women acquired in this debate. The most telling index of the level of civilization a society had arrived at, he claimed, was the status it accorded its women. "Among rude people, the women are generally degraded; among civilized people they are exalted."[10] If one were to go by that rule, his argument would seem to need no further endorsement: "Nothing can exceed the habitual contempt which Hindus entertain for their women," he wrote. "Hardly are they ever mentioned in their laws, or other books, but as wretches of the most base and vicious inclinations on whose nature no virtuous or useful qualities can be engrafted."[11] What seemed to offend him most was "that remarkable proof of barbarity, in the wife held unworthy to eat with her husband [a custom] prevalent in Hindustan."[12] Though so much had been written about the mildness, the refinement, and the beauty of Indian women, the women themselves, Mill was horrified to note, lacked even the natural delicacy one would find in an Englishwoman. He cites the difficulties faced by the Indologist Mr. Wilkins, who translated "the popular and moral work, entitled *Hitopadesa.*" He quotes Wilkins, who wrote, "The translator has carefully refined a great many indelicate expressions, which a Hindu lady, from grosser habits, might hear without a blush; and even omitted whole passages when that could not be effected but by a total change of the author's meaning."[13]

Mill's observations were echoed and elaborated on in the writings and attitudes of many British politicians, but also by administrators in India, and in the British fiction, journalism, and travel writing in the nineteenth century, which increasingly became dossiers of moral lapses

---

[9]James Mill, *The History of British India* (Delhi: Associated Publishing House, 1972; 1st ed. 1817), p. 32. All other quotations in this paragraph are taken from pp. 24–32, in which he lays out his basic thesis on ancient India.
[10]Ibid., p. 279.
[11]Ibid., p. 281.
[12]Ibid., p. 287.
[13]Ibid.

or accounts of sensational practices. The widow burning on her husband's funeral pyre or the child-bride became equated with India in the Western imagination. One cannot help wondering today in what ways the popularity of these texts meshed with the history of sexuality in the West. Katherine Mayo's *Mother India,* 1927, for instance, which provided a detailed and indignant account of the sexual excesses of Indian men and the terrible sufferings of their child wives, became a best-seller. In the 1930s C. F. Andrews writes that he found *"Mother India* being sold all over the world in a cheap edition, even on railway bookstalls, and having an honoured place in the libraries of private persons. Furthermore I found it had been published in different translations . . . numerous editions . . . to be retailed at popular prices."[14] Other accounts speak of public libraries in England and America restricting the borrowing to a few hours, since the demand for the book was so heavy. Moral indignation and pornographic titillation were obviously closely aligned in this phenomenon, which was clearly structured more to fit the requirements of the Western imagination than to aid Indian women. *Mother India,* we must not forget, came out at a time when the nationalist movement was growing stronger, and was enthusiastically supported by the British government. As one reviewer put it, Mayo's book "makes the claim for *Swaraj* (self-government) seem nonsense and the will to grant it, almost a crime."[15]

The ideas Mill drew on can also be found in another powerful British group involved in the work of empire: the Evangelicals, who broadly agreed with Mill about the dismal state of affairs in contemporary India, and were quite willing to accept that matters had not changed in any substantial way for three thousand years. Nevertheless, they felt that Mill and the other progressives had been carried away by their ideals. India's disease was endemic. Neither legislation nor good government could provide a solution without a rational religion—Christianity—to replace the superstitious religions of India and transform the Indian character.

Despite these controversies, Mill's representation of India gained enormous authority. Considering that he simply dismissed the Indian past as barbaric and raided the ancient texts for example after example

---

[14]C. F. Andrews, *The True India: A Plea for Understanding* (London: George Allen and Unwin, 1939), pp. 17–18.

[15]*The New Statesman and Nation* (London, 1927), quoted in Joanna Liddle and Rama Joshi, *Daughters of Independence: Gender, Caste and Class in India* (Delhi: Kali for Women, 1986), p. 31.

to confirm his thesis, it might seem surprising that his history acquired such a powerful hold even over the study of ancient India. We have, however, only to probe a little further to understand how and why it happened. As Mill painstakingly interrogated the history, the laws, the manners, and the art of India to tell his three-volume story of the civilization, he drew quite unself-consciously and in great detail on the assumptions and the logic of the (upper-class, British) common sense of his times. Mill invoked this common sense—which, we must remember, also grounded liberal Utilitarian notions of human nature and civilized behavior—in a tone that indicated that he regarded its soundness as obvious and its authority as rational and indisputable. And as he did so he translated the alien world he encountered into one in which he and his (English) readers could feel at home. The process was consolidated as he wove his observations and his judgment into a coherent narrative. The India that appeared through the fine mesh of his narrative logic was a strange, irrational, and even grotesque one, but it held no secrets and posed no threat, for the logic itself was familiar and assigned these disturbing forms to their "proper" places. In fact, it was a logic that reaffirmed the primacy of the world Mill shared with his readers and underwrote afresh their sense of reality. We might observe in passing that Indian novelists of later generations had to contend with the fantastic forms into which Western common sense, and the reality effects achieved by its narratives, had translated colonial worlds, as they devised strategies to rewrite those worlds and render them plausible for readers in India. The task that confronted them was not just the taking-up of a point of view, but the remaking of a world. But of that more later.

For now it is enough for us to also note that as Mill elaborated his political program through his history, he was working with a capillary substratum of the Western imagination, "a detailed logic, governed, not simply by empirical reality, but by a battery of desires, investments, projections."[16] His arguments, therefore, had the moral urgency of truths that *had* to be faced and interventions that *had* to be made. By the middle of the nineteenth century, such views were so firmly established that Max Müller and Clarisse Bader had little choice but to structure their defense of ancient India as detailed replies to Mill's indictments. They claimed (and later nationalist writers, as we shall see, would echo these sentiments) that few of the "evils" Mill and others

---

[16]Said, *Orientalism,* p. 8.

called attention to had existed in the vedic period. In those times women assisted men in performing the most important tasks of religious life; they chose their own husbands, had access to education, and even composed poetry; there was no polygamy or child marriage, and the caste system did not exist. Clearly, the Utilitarian critique as well as the bedrock of assumptions it drew on—which of course the Indologists shared—had completely infiltrated Indological scholarship.

Early nationalist studies forced open the question of historiographical biases and exposed the imperialist interests that underwrote such versions of Indian history or culture. But their battles were fought, as all initial battles perhaps are, on ideological ground laid out by the very powers they opposed. It is true that as nationalist thinkers politically appropriated the terms of Orientalism, they undermined its functions, for their efforts were not to consolidate but to confront and displace British rule. But it is also true that the women's question remained fixed into remarkably similar schemes as one patriarchy confronted the other. The novelist and historian R. C. Dutt (1848–1908), for instance, drew on the Indologists to attack the edifice Mill and others had developed when they had elaborated the Utilitarian thesis into a call for Britain's permanent presence in India. In Dutt's *History of Civilisation in Ancient India,* too, the vedic woman becomes the highest symbol of Hindu womanhood. There was evidence to show, Dutt argued, that "women were honoured in ancient India, more perhaps than among any other ancient nation on the face of the globe. They were considered the intellectual companions of their husband . . . affectionate helpers in the journey of life, and . . . inseparable partners in their religious duties."[17] As late as 1938, A. S. Altekar, in *Position of Women in Hindu Civilization,* claimed once more that the status of women is one of the best gauges of the "spirit of a civilization," its "excellencies and its limitations," and went on to argue that the vedic age was one in which women enjoyed singular freedoms.[18] Like the Indologists, Altekar traces a steady decline from this golden age to the shadowy valleys of the period before the Muslim invasion.

Clearly a whole network of concerns shapes the representations of India and of Indian women that emerge in these writings. If the German Romantics read Indian history as an allegory of Western man's

---

[17]Romesh Chunder Dutt, *History of Civilisation in Ancient India* (Delhi: Vishal, 1972; 1st ed. 1888), p. 67.

[18]A. S. Altekar, *Position of Women in Hindu Civilization* (Delhi: Motilal Banarsidass, 1962; 1st ed. 1938), pp. 1, 13.

soul, the British Utilitarians found in imperial policy and imperial administration a cause in which their historical thesis about mankind and the universe could be writ large, and earned considerable profit. As they defined and structured the past, Orientalist perspectives *translated* ancient, and by implication contemporary, India into something that was accessible, familiar, and above all structured for intervention and control. In other words, they not only described it as something that was in need of good government, but *restructured* it as something that was governable.[19]

In the process, we must not forget that they also "translated" vedic patriarchies into contemporary Western ones. Further, and feminists in the West will find this interesting, by setting itself off against Oriental patriarchy, Western patriarchy reaffirmed its identity and gained authority. The cross-hatchings through which this took place, and continues to do so, is one of the many themes that can be traced right through *Women Writing in India*. In addition, these representations *contained* the past. The many histories and many practices of a changing heterogeneous society were contained in a narrative that obscured or subordinated other narratives and other schemes of which, as even this small collection shows, there was no dearth. Third, they *produced* vedic India—produced it in the sense that they set up the scenarios, invented the principal characters, the major events, the significant themes, the points at issue—to extend their aspirations. Even now, to conceive of such structurings as "fictions" that feminists might set aside as we go back to the *real* past is to grossly misjudge their significance and their extended, capillary hold, and also to underestimate the power systems that underwrote and continue to underwrite them.

The subject bristles with problems and we will discuss several of immediate importance to our understanding of women's writing in India in the precolonial period. We will have reason to return to other questions as we introduce the writing of the later periods.

Of considerable importance is the epochal deployment of time that was brought into play in Indologist or Utilitarian readings of Indian history. The Indologists regarded the three thousand years that followed the vedic golden age as a continuous process of degeneration.

---

[19]See Talal Asad, "The Concept of Cultural Translation," in *Writing Culture: The Poetics and Politics of Ethnogaphy,* ed. James Clifford and George Marcus (Berkeley: University of California Press, 1986), pp. 141–164. See also Tejaswini Niranjana, "Representation, History and the Case of Translation," *Journal of Arts and Ideas* 17–18, 1988, pp. 109–116.

But since the spiritual power of ancient India was also prescribed as the cure for contemporary ills—in a gesture that connected the present directly to this past—the entire span of Indian history from the vedic period until the nineteenth century froze into a single still. Mill's history is as sweeping and imperious in its stand. Mill considered Indian society as not having changed in any significant way—in other words, as being without history—since despotic rulers had never allowed the society to develop, as the European nations had, into the mainstream of world history. (Mill's influence, it is useful to remember, extended to the German philosopher G. W. Hegel, and through him to Karl Marx.) As they denied Indian history and absorbed India into their narratives these schemes ensured their hold over it. But in the process they also obscured and delegitimized the enormously important demographic, economic, political, and cultural changes taking place and the literatures that accompanied these shifts.

The freeze was so total and uncompromising that only in the last decades of the nineteenth century, principally in the work of M. G. Ranade (1842–1901), did even the medieval *bhakti* movements, from which we have such an impressive collection of women's compositions, come up for discussion. Ranade and others somewhat hesitantly compared the bhakti cults to "protestant" and humanist developments in the West, but it was some time before their ideas were paid heed to. We have still not proceeded much further in our understanding or assessment of that movement. Further, as the focus remained so firmly fixed on an Aryan Hinduism, secular writing, including the court literature, was suppressed and even today is often known only in the dismissive and prudishly Victorian readings of the nineteenth century.

Just as significant as the denial of history is the setting up, in the discussions hung on the vedic texts and on ancient India, of the Aryan man as the centerpiece of Indian civilization. It was in his (newly minted) archaic, upper-caste image that the entire scope of Indian history and Indian culture was reconstructed. Indian history became the history of Aryan man; the Indo-Gangetic plain, which was the major focus of his initial wanderings, defined the extent of India, and time, even if essentially static, measured his fortunes. The Aryan woman, perfect adjunct to the Aryan man, shadow of that shadow character, haunted almost all writing on women in precolonial India, which had in effect become vedic India. Nearly all the discussions of women's writing were centered on the two hymns of the *Rig Veda* attributed to Ghosha, and on the verses that might have been composed by eight other female seers. These were held up as evidence that women were educated and regarded as capable of the highest spiritual and literary achievements. In the long years of decline that followed, the implication was that nothing of import had taken place. Women's literature from the later periods was not, however, ignored. It was discussed, but discussed in a way that totally absorbed it into the polemic about the Aryan woman. Accounts stressed the erudition (not the rebellion) of the bhakti saints, and somehow found in each major figure qualities (often moral) that would do the Aryan woman proud. As we will find, the Mirabai now standardized and strategically placed as the cornerstone of the ideology of conjugal sacrifice and domestic composure stands in total contrast with the Mirabai held dear in the Gujarati and Rajasthani folk traditions.[20]

Women's Writing in the Ancient Period

If we look even at the small collection of women's writing from the precolonial period in this anthology, it is clear that nearly all of it is either from pre-Aryan or non-Aryan sources. Further, we see that women often found opportunities for involvement in literary creation in the context of powerful historical movements that questioned Aryan or brahminic dominance and represented the claims of rival political groups or emerging social classes. Scholars point out that there are no references to Aryan mythology in the Tamil Sangam poetry of the first to third century A.D., suggesting that the valley civilizations that gave rise to this stupendous body of work were pre-Aryan, agricultural societies.[21] Both the Buddhist and the bhakti poetry came from movements that opposed caste discrimination and the ritualized Hinduism dominated by the brahmin priests. Much of the secular literature of the later period can be traced to the patronage of the courts, especially the Mughal courts, which by all accounts seem to have had space for artists of various kinds in their entourages. The women's folk songs in nearly every region are sung mainly to celebrate the cycles of the agricultural year, and have their sources in local non-Aryan cultures.

Scholars today seem agreed that the remarkable corpus of sacred texts and secular literature that developed over the two millennia after

---

[20]See Parita Mukta, "Mirabai in Rajasthan," and Madhu Kishwar and Ruth Vanita, "Modern Versions of Mira," in *Manushi* 50, 51, 52, 1989, pp. 94–101.

[21]George L. Hart III, "Ancient Tamil Literature: Its Scholarly Past and Future," in *Essays on South India,* ed. Burton Stein (New Delhi: Vikas, 1975), pp. 41–63.

the first Aryan invasions, around 1700 B.C., emerged in the ongoing interplay between the Aryan and the indigenous, or nonvedic, cultures. The spectacular discovery in 1925 of the immense urban ruins of Harappa and Mohenjodaro dating back to around 3000 B.C. (of which there was no mention in the vedic corpus) suggests that the agricultural civilizations the Aryans found when they came through the Himalayan passes were flourishing ones, with well-developed civic organization, a regular coinage, and trade links with other parts of the known world. Their art forms were visual, in contrast to the oral narratives of the pastoral Aryans and in keeping with the more sedentary life of agricultural societies. The Aryans overran these civilizations and gradually, over the next two thousand years, established their dominance over large parts of the Indian subcontinent. What seems to have taken place culturally—and politically—was a sort of loose assimilation: the practice of the indigenous nonvedic societies, their rituals, and their deities were absorbed into an expanding vedic repertoire. In the process, vedic culture itself underwent major transformations. As the later Vedas, the Puranas, and the epics took shape, D. D. Kosambi writes, indigenous deities were "equated to standard brahmin gods" or "new brahmin scriptures" were created to give unassimilable gods vedic legitimacy.

> The worship of these newly absorbed primitive deities was part of the mechanism of acculturation, a clear give-and-take. First, the former worshippers, say of the Cobra, could adore him while bowing to Siva, but the followers of Siva simultaneously paid respect to the Cobra in their own ritual services; many would then observe the Cobra's special cult-day every year, when the earth may not be dug up and food is put out for the snakes. Matriarchal elements had been won over by identifying the mother goddess with the "wife" of some male god, e.g. Durga-Parvati (who might herself bear many local names such as Tukai or Kalubai) was wife to Siva, Lakshmi for Vishnu. The complex divine household carried on the process of syncretism: Skanda and Ganesa became sons of Siva.[22]

Later formations such as Vaishnavism, which is centered on the worship of Vishnu and his incarnations, notably, the dark Krishna, are attributed to this syncretic assimilation of indigenous mythologies and

---

[22]D. D. Kosambi, *The Culture and Civilization of India in Historical Outline* (Delhi: Vikas Publishing House, 1987; 1st ed. 1965), p. 170. See also Romila Thapar, "The Image of the Barbarian in Early India," in *Ancient Indian Social History,* pp. 152–192.

cultural practices. (The Indologists, we remember, found this process contaminating.)

Feminist cultural historians will find Debiprasad Chattopadhyay's extension of this thesis of particular interest. Working from "a few fragmentary survivals . . . but all these as preserved in the writings of its opponents, i.e. of those who wanted to refute or ridicule it," he reconstructs what is spoken of in the ancient texts as the Lokayata. Etymologically, *Lokayata* means "that which is prevalent among the people" and "that which is essentially this-worldly."[23] As the pastoral Aryans, who were also patriarchal and philosophically idealist or "otherworldly," subordinated the existing agricultural societies, which were materialist and in which *prakriti,* or the female principle, was viewed as fundamental, Lokayata worldviews were displaced and overlaid. Further, the social supremacy the female enjoyed in these societies was undermined by the male-dominated vedic traditions of the Aryans.

Reading against the grain of the classical texts, to find evidence of the societies and the worldviews that were subsumed into the vedic mainstream, Chattopadhyay concludes that these materialist orientations form the substratum of late vedic idealism. He also argues that vedic idealism itself was shaped by the struggle against matriarchal, materialist cultures and still carries the marks of the engagement. The gods mentioned in the early *Rig Veda,* he points out, are male, yet the Hindu pantheon soon included important female deities drawn principally from the nonvedic traditions of Sankhya and Tantra, which venerate the female principle.[24] The "Devi Mahatmya" sections of the *Markandeya Purana* (ca. A.D. 250), which relate the exploits of the warlike female deity Canda and celebrate her powers, are nonvedic in origin, but as they were absorbed into the Sanskrit text in the sixth century A.D., they were "translated" into the broad scope of vedic idealism.[25] Again compared to the *Rig Veda,* the later vedic texts, especially the practices probably codified around the first century A.D. in the *Manusmriti,* are fiercely misogynist. Critics have pointed out that the cosmology of those agricultural societies was not based on transcendental notions. Even today in parts of India, in the rituals associated with sowing and harvest the male deity is assigned female

[23]Debiprasad Chattopadhyay, *Lokayata: A Study in Ancient Indian Materialism* (Delhi: People's Publishing House, 1959; 4th ed. 1978), p. xv.
[24]Ibid., p. xvii.
[25]See Thomas B. Coburn, *Devi Mahatmya: The Crystallization of the Goddess Tradition* (Delhi: Motilal Banarsidass, 1985).

attributes or sometimes, after the initial ceremonies, the male icon is replaced by female symbols. It is important to remember that the female principle Chattopadhyay writes about is, in these agricultural societies, a vigorous, aggressive, and dangerous force with several attributes that would commonly be considered masculine today.

In the folk traditions, moreover, which have, if anything, only been superficially overlaid by Sanskrit forms we also find the contemporary strength of these early worldviews. A recent study of a famous *adivasi,* or tribal, revolt in Gujarat in the early 1920s (which formed the basis for the Bardoli Satyagraha) shows that their protest against the Parsi owners of the liquor shops was shaped and legitimated in the idioms of Goddess worship.[26] A careful reader will sense the power women have in these traditions, not only in the folk songs collected in this anthology but in the bhakti literature, in the poetry of Bahinabai Chaudhari (ca. 1880–1950), and in the awesome presence of tribal or adivasi peoples, which is the theme of several stories, especially those of Mahasweta Devi and Meherunissa Parvez (in volume two).

Though, as we saw, two hymns and a few verses in the *Rig Veda* are attributed to women, very little that has actually been *written* by women has survived from vedic Sanskrit or from the later classical Sanskrit literature. This explains the long gap in this collection between the early years of the first millennium A.D., when the Sangam poetry was written, and the twelfth century, which brings the early bhakti poetry. What little we have access to are extracts included in anthologies or stanzas cited by scholars. Some commentators compare the genius of Vijjaka or Vidya (ca. 650), a poet from what is present-day Karnataka, with that of the great fourth-century poet and dramatist Kalidasa, but we know almost nothing about Vidya's life, though a few pieces of her work have survived in later anthologies such as that of the Buddhist scholar Vidyakara, compiled around A.D. 100. One of her stanzas, often quoted by commentators, begins, it was "without knowing about me, Vijjakka, dark, like the petal of the blue lotus, / That the poet Dandin [vainly] said that the Goddess of learning was all-white."

The commonly cited explanation for the paucity of women's writing in classical Sanskrit is that it was the language of religion and of courtly art, and was used only by upper-caste men. Women and men from the lower castes spoke the local Prakrits. Accounts of Rajasekhara, the

---

[26]David Hardiman, *The Coming of the Devi: Adivasi Assertion in Western India* (Delhi: Oxford University Press, 1987).

ninth-century scholar and dramatist, best remembered for his pioneering work in Prakrit, sometimes mention his learned wife Avantisundari. Even from the scanty evidence we have, Avantisundari, who herself wrote poetry in Prakrit, seems to have been much more than a wife who supported her brilliant husband's projects. Rajashekhara quotes her views in his aesthetics, and his Prakrit play, *Karpuramanjari,* is said to have been written and staged "at her request." At one point in the *Kavya-Mimamsa,* his treatise on aesthetics, he writes, "Women also can be poets. Sensibility and sophistication know no difference of sex. We have heard and can see princesses, daughters of minsters, courtesans and wives of court-jesters [who were scholars] who are possessed of extensive knowledge of the sacred texts, of the sciences and of poetry."[27] We cannot help wondering as we read these words today what role Avantisundari actually played in making the "low" language of the people a respectable one for literary composition. It is clear that her poetry was well known and widely read, for Hemachandra uses quotations from it in the twelfth century for his dictionary *Deshinamamala* to illustrate the meanings of certain Prakrit expressions. Some scholars believe that it was also at her initiative or "for her benefit" that Dhanapala compiled the Prakrit dictionary (ca. 972). Today, only the fragments of her poetry quoted in the *Deshinamamala* remain. As for the many women who possessed "singular poetic talent," we have no record of their work.

Women's Writing in the Medieval Period

With the eighth-century Tamil poet Karraikal Ammaiyar, to whom the very first lyrics of the Nayanar movement are popularly attributed, begins a long line of women poet-saints in the medieval bhakti movements. The word *bhakti* means "devotion," and these powerful religious upheavals, which mocked pedantry, rejected ascetic withdrawal, and emphasized the intense, mystic experience of personal devotion, emerged, century after century, first in different regions of southern India: the Alvars and the Nayanars in Tamilnadu as early as the eighth century; the Virasaivas in Karnataka in the twelfth century; and the Varkaris and Manubhavs in Maharashtra in recurring phases from the twelfth to the seventeenth centuries. Later, in the fifteenth and six-

---

[27]Rajashekhara, *Kavya-Mimamsa,* ed. Ganga Sagar Rai (Varanasi: Chowkhamba Vidya Bhavan, 1977), p. 138.

teenth centuries, the movement spread north through Rajasthan, Gujarat, Kashmir, Punjab, to the Vaishnava groups in Bengal and Assam, fusing the songs of Kabir and Lal Ded with Sufi traditions. Of the poets translated here, Akkamahadevi, Sule Sankavva, Janabai, Rami, Gangasati, Ratanbai, Mirabai, Molla, Bahinabai, and Tarigonda Venkamamba may be regarded as bhakti poets.

The movements arose in different parts of the country apparently independently, and developed various idioms, but they also had several things in common. In each place these artisan groups led what has been called a people's revolt against the domination of the upper castes and the lifeless ritual of vedic Hinduism practiced by the brahmin priests. Washerpeople, leather workers, oil pressers, stonecutters, potters, weavers, silversmiths, artisans, and small tradespeople of all kinds swelled the movements' ranks. And, what is perhaps most significant from our point of view, the path of devotion set up no barriers of caste or sex. The women poets of the bhakti movements did not have to seek the institutionalized spaces religion provided to express themselves, and women's poetry moved from the court and the temple to the open spaces of the field, the workplace, and the common woman's hearth.

The bhakti poets composed in the regional languages, deliberately breaking the literary and religious hold of Sanskrit. They addressed their popular lyrics to the people in the languages the people spoke and could understand. "Sanskrit is the stagnant water of the Lord's private well," Kabir sang, whereas "the spoken language is the rippling water of the running stream." Most of the regional literatures locate their beginnings in the poetry of the bhakti saints. For many years after Lal Ded lived and died, the *vakhya* form she shaped continued to dominate the literary tradition in Kashmir, which traces its roots to that colorful rebel poet and mystic.[28]

The devotees, or *bhaktas,* set their poetry in familiar contexts and found their imagery in the everyday lives of working people. As a result, scholars have also argued, they drew their symbolism primarily from nonvedic sources. Their verses cultivate a rough-hewn directness. The devotee cajoles, chides, woos, rages against God, who is a personally chosen husband/lover to the bhakta imaged as wife/lover, and

---

[28]Madhu Kishwar and Ruth Vanita, "I Drank the Wine of My Own Verse: The Life and Work of Lal Ded, Kashmiri Poet and Mystic," *Manushi* 32, 1986, pp. 17–22. The article is derived from Jayalal Kaul, *Lal Ded* (Delhi: Sahitya Academy, 1973).

the mystic union is often imagined in sexual terms. In fact status, masculinity, scholarship are seen as *obstacles* to bhakti. Though their poetry often circulated for one or two centuries before it was recorded, the lyrics are easily attributed to individual poets because embedded in the text is the composer's *ankita,* or signature, which is usually the form in which she addresses her lord. Akkamahadevi, for instance, uses the ankita Chennamallikarjuna, which literally means Mallika's beautiful Arjuna, but is rendered in the best-known translations of her poetry as "Lord white as jasmine."[29]

A surprising number of the bhakti poets were women. Many of them were people who chafed at the strictures of the household and the family. Lal Ded's songs describe her mother-in-law's taunts and the numbing triviality of domestic chores. The young Bahinabai, hemmed in and cornered by marriage, sees visions of Tukaram, who calls her to another life. Mirabai chafes at the restricted life in her husband's home. The movement held for them the promise of other things. Biographies of the bhakti saints usually begin with the break—from the family and community—and chart the wanderings of the poet-saints. Yet there is evidence that women had to struggle to find acceptance even within these movements. Women saints are often put to the test in a major debate with the male leaders. Akkamahadevi, for instance, left her husband and her family and wandered through large tracts of Karnataka and Andhra before she joined the Virasaiva poets Allama and Basavva at their monastery in Kalyana. In a brilliant encounter with Allama, documented for us in a set of finely chiseled lyrics, she proves herself his equal—or better—as a philosopher and poet, and insists on spiritual equality with the men. Mirabai faces a similar trial.

Scholars continue to speculate about the origin, the nature, and the importance of these movements. The most commonly proffered theory, and the one the feminist historian Neera Desai also proposes, is that the bhakti movement was a response from medieval Hindu society to the threat posed by the growing political power as well as the monotheistic and egalitarian ideas of the Muslim invaders.[30] Hindu society, which had gradually become more and more rigid, was forced to respond, these historians argue, to demands of equality from the lower

---

[29]A. K. Ramanujan, *Speaking of Siva* (Harmondsworth: Penguin, 1973).
[30]Neera Desai, "Women in the Bhakti Movement," *Samya Shakti* 1:2, 1983, pp. 92–100.

castes, who might otherwise have converted to Islam. I. H. Qureshi, on the other hand, regards the movement as a characteristically subtle attempt by Hindu society to lure Muslims into its field.[31] The more conciliatory Tarachand argues that the movement represents a creative synthesis of the great religious traditions.[32]

The difficulty with these theories is that each of them plucks these varied, complex, and energetic movements out of their social contexts, and recasts them as an episode in another drama—one that stages the struggle of two monolithically imaged, dominant religions. The problem is not only that the idea of Hinduism or Islam conceived of in this way, as an all-India religion, is of fairly recent origin, but also that such formulations tell us little about the social and political ground on which the movement took root or indeed about its significance for the people who took part in it. They provide no leads, therefore, for one interested in finding out how the movement affected ordinary women's lives, why it produced so many women poets and thinkers, and what it might mean for us, as women today.

More sociologically oriented analysts, when they have not simply dismissed the movement as misguided, provide more useful observations. Irfan Habib argues that, with the new crafts introduced and with the technological development of the twelfth and thirteenth centuries, artisan production increased dramatically.[33] The more stable, centralized administration made for more trade, and thus the period saw an increasingly affluent artisan population who aspired to a better social status. Since women's labor is always an integral part of home-based artisan production, it seems possible that in the initial stages of the movement at least, women shared the same aspirations. This would also help us understand the bhakti emphasis on the life of the householder, and the importance given to domestic responsibilities as well as the rich detail in which the everyday lives of these men and women appear in the poetry.

Most commentators seem agreed that the bhakti movements did not have any explicit political focus. But G. B. Sardar, taking issue with

---

[31]I. H. Qureshi, *The Muslim Community of the Indo-Pakistan Subcontinent 610–1947: A Brief Historical Analysis* (The Hague: Mouton & Co., 1962), pp. 104–124.

[32]Tarachand, *The Influence of Islam on Indian Culture* (Allahabad: Indian Press, 1963).

[33]Irfan Habib, "The Historical Background of the Popular Monotheistic Movement of the 15th–17th Centuries," cited in *History and Society*, ed. Debiprasad Chattopadhyaya (Calcutta: K. P. Bagchi, 1976), p. 451.

some Marxist scholars who regard the movement as one without social or political importance, argues that though the Varkaris in Maharashtra did not call for a social revolution or question feudal power, the Varkari movement was nonetheless significant, for it "destroyed the stupor that prevailed in the hearts of women and sudras and brought into their lives an activating faith. . . . [It] . . . infused into the soulless existence of lakhs of people in Maharashtra a knowledge of the spirit."[34] The bhaktas, Neera Desai also argues, "were not social emancipators," but, as she points out, they were individuals, trying to lead a liberated life. It is their individualism, she writes, that continues to inspire us.

Given the impressive body of women's writing that has come down from the bhakti movements, it is tempting to think of the period as one in which patriarchal control was radically questioned and the lives of ordinary women changed. But there is little evidence that this might have been so. It is possible that the new prosperity of these classes, the new sense of self-worth, the new dignity even domestic chores were endowed with did give women a new self-confidence. For those who left their homes to become bhaktas, it also gave access to a wider world, but the options were still very limited.

Other interesting observations can be made about the movements and the openings they provided for women. It appears that in terms of both the number of women who took part and the depth of their rejection of patriarchy, the earlier phases of the movements were more hospitable to women. Thus the Tamil Alvar and Nayanar movements, the predominantly Kannada Virasaiva movement, and the Varkari sects of Maharashtra seem to have provided support for more radical women poets and thinkers than the later movements associated with Tulsidas and Nanak, which developed in the north. By the early seventeenth century, and considerably earlier in many southern regions, the movements had been pushed into cults structured around vedic gods. The movements lost their critical edge and were reabsorbed into the very hierarchical and temple-ritual-centered system they had initially opposed. That some of the most magnificent temple architecture in India dates back to this period supports the hypothesis. These temples, which were endowed by the king or ruler, legitimized the authority of the brahmin priests, but were built with the skills of the artisans.

Similar co-optations may be traced in the way some of the major

---

[34]G. B. Sardar, *The Saint Poets of Maharashtra,* trans. Kumud Metha (Delhi: Orient Longmans, 1969), p. 20.

figures in the movements have been recast in the popular imagination. In her times, the sixteenth-century poet Mirabai, for instance, was attacked and persecuted for leaving her husband and taking up a religious life, but her life and poetry have been accommodated into schemes about which patriarchies in her time, or in ours, would seem to have little to complain. Though she is a rebel, once she chooses the divine Krishna for a lover, her spiritual idiom becomes that of a chaste and dutiful wife who observes, in every minute detail, her household tasks. She makes no mention of the suffering of other women or of the injustices that prevail in society at large. A feudal order is her support, not her enemy, and her concern is to find fulfillment through an ever more intense involvement in a spiritual recreation of the good wife's temporal role.[35] Similarly Bahinabai, who was a contemporary of the seventeenth-century bhakti poet Tukaram, does not seem to have the options open to an Akkamahadevi, who centuries earlier broke with the family and took to the road, declaring the joy of her calling in song. Bahinabai struggles at home with a husband who is jealous of her importance, and her extraordinary account of her soul's journey ends with a paean of glory to the wife.

Detailed feminist scholarship on the primary materials will one day tell us a great deal more about the lives of ordinary women of this period and will offer new interpretations of what the movement meant for women. It is possible also that, in the process, new figures will emerge from such research to be set alongside or to replace the women poets whom an earlier tradition has chosen to honor.

Though the Mughals left a rich store of documents and several histories, the centuries that history books refer to as the era of Muslim rules was, until recently, one of the least carefully researched periods in Indian history. The thesis developed by Western Orientalist scholarship in the nineteenth century was largely taken over by historians with a nationalist perspective, who also argued that, after the period in which Hindu society was consolidated (roughly the first to fourth centuries), religion ossified, literary and philosophical texts became more ornate and abstract, and political authority fragmented. The Muslims were therefore easily able, in a series of invasions between the seventh and twelfth centuries, despite valiant resistance by the Rajputs in the west and from Shivaji and the

---

[35]See Kumkum Sangari, "Mirabai and Gandhi: Reformulating Patriarchies," Paper read at the Third National Women's Studies Conference, Chandigarh, India, October 1986.

Marathas and the Vijayanagar Empire in the south, to overrun India. What followed was regarded as an age of courtly decadence, despotic rule, and social stasis. For women especially it was seen as one of the most oppressive periods in the history of India.

Scholars have subsequently questioned this view. They have unearthed evidence about not only the agrarian economy and artisan production but also systems of education, science and technology, and the arts and political thought, which shows that India in the seventeenth and early eighteenth centuries was a well-developed and industrialized country. Statistics collected in the nineteenth century by British officials suggest that there were more girls in school in the eighteenth than in the early twentieth century. Women must have shared the prosperity of what was, by all accounts, a thriving economy when the British first came to India as traders in the seventeenth century.

Mughal histories and the accounts written by European travelers in the sixteenth and seventeenth centuries paint a picture of well-planned cities, a prosperous and sophisticated urban life, a developed export economy, and a general sense of plenty. Architecture, painting, music, and poetry, which were the arts of the court, also flourished. So too did the sciences and philosophy in general. A well-designed system of canals and tanks, maintained by the state, irrigated fields. Roads and caravanserais, or resting places, allowed merchants and others to travel in reasonable comfort. "Even in the smallest villages rice, flour, butter, milk, beans and other vegetables, sugar and other sweatmeats dry and liquid can be procured in abundance," Tavernier, a seventeenth-century visitor from France, observed.[36] Manouchi, the Venetian doctor in Aurangzeb's court, was even more enthusiastic. Indian textiles, especially silks, brocades, and muslins, were famous all over the world; the quality of iron and steel produced in foundries, unmatched. But equally well known were the other metalwork and the artisan crafts in general. In a series of brilliantly documented studies, the early twentieth-century art historian Ananda Coomaraswamy demonstrates how over centuries of development artisan products had achieved a balance of form and function. These products spoke of a worldview, he argues, quite at odds with that of the Occident.[37]

Tavernier's account of the villages might, just possibly, reflect what

---

[36]William Crooke, ed., Jean-Baptiste Tavernier, *Travels in India,* trans. Valentine Ball (1889) (Oxford: Oxford University Press, 1925 [1676]), p. 238.

[37]Ananda Coomaraswamy, *The Dance of Shiva* (Delhi: Munshiram Manoharlal, 1970; 1st ed. 1947), esp. pp. 21–38, 39–51, 115–139.

was set out for an important visitor and not the everyday repast of a peasant woman, but there is evidence to suggest that she had enough to eat and that her right to cultivate the land was secure. Her part in the family's labor—in the field or at the loom or at a hundred other crafts—was not at issue. Besides, she might find in the egalitarian philosophies popularized by the bhakti cults, which often cut across the divisions of Hindu and Muslim, an added sense of self-worth.

As we contrast life in this period with the terrible hardships that were to come in the nineteenth century, we might be tempted to think of the ordinary peasant's or artisan's life as secure and comfortable. Without going into the controversy that rages today over the term "Oriental despotism," we can still heed the warning against thinking of these village communities as idyllic. Peasants may have had security of tenure, but it was almost impossible to leave a tenancy even if one wanted to. Further, as Chandrabati's narrative poem "Sundari Malua," included here, also tells us, taxes were not fixed and unscrupulous officials could extract arbitrary amounts from helpless villagers. Punishments were harsh and in some areas the city cultures flourished entirely at the cost of the countryside.

Patriarchal social norms and practices, however, were taken for granted. Though it was rare in the villages and among the lower classes, upper-class women practiced purdah. Nevertheless, no one who has read Gul-Badan Begum's history of her brother Humayun's reign, excerpted here, or looked at the records of the life and work of Zebunissa, can think of the women in the zenana as repressed. Women of the Mughal royal families obviously had access to learning and commanded respect. They knew Persian and could read the religious texts. Many were well versed in the arts. Paintings show women from the royal families in serious discussion with jogins (women lay ascetics).[38]

The story of Nur Jehan is well known, but bears repetition. She married the emperor Jehangir in 1611 at the age of thirty-four, some years after her first husband, Sher Afgan Khan, died, and soon rose to be one of the most powerful people in the empire. She is remembered today for her courage, her diplomacy, and her skill in archery. In addition, scholars attribute new designs for jewelry and dress as well as innovations in cuisine to her. For eleven years she practically ruled what was the greatest

---

[38]See Rekha Misra, *Women in Mughal India* (Delhi: Munshiram Manoharlal, 1967), for a carefully documented study of women in this period.

empire in the world. *Farmans,* or edicts, were issued under her seal, and her name was struck on coins, which bore the legend "By the command of Emperor Jehangir, gold has acquired a hundredfold beauty with the name on it of Nur Jehan, the Emperor's royal consort."

From this period also come the compositions of the great *tawaifs.* The word *tawaif* has sometimes been translated as "courtesan," but such a rendering, into a language in which the concept has no associations or history, hardly captures the regard and the affection in which these learned and accomplished women were often held. Nor does the translation give us a sense of the wide circle of other artists and connoisseurs of culture to which some of them belonged. One of the first Urdu novels, Mirza Ruswa's *Umrao Jan Ada,* is a transcription of the story the famous Umrao Jan told of her life.[39] Mahlaqa Bai from Hyderabad was not only a much sought-after composer and singer but also a powerful patron of the arts. She endowed caravanserais for travelers and built monuments. Other records indicate that women owned estates and large public gardens.

Women artists found patronage in other courts too. We recounted the fortunes of Muddupalani's *Radhika Santwanam* in the opening pages of the Introduction. Muddupalani belonged to the Thanjavur court and lived during the reign of Pratapasimha (1739–63). Also from the south all the records of the powerful Maratha queens, especially Tarabai (1675–1761) and Ahalyabai Holkar (1735–1795), who had the eighth-century Buddhist caves at Ellora repaired, adding stucco reliefs to them.

These noblewomen and courtesans were not the only women artists of this period. The coals of the bhakti movement continued to smolder and inspire such women as the legendary late eighteenth-century religious poet Tarigonda Venkamamba. We can decipher a great deal of what was happening in the folk literature of the period from both the songs and stories that have been collected. The most accurate measure of the power of the bhakti movements, however, can be found in the massive effort to break the hold of the Vaishnava artists, and the culture they represented, in early nineteenth-century Bengal. Of that we will have more to say as we introduce the later literature.

---

[39]Extracts from the account would have given us a glimpse of one of the major artists and social figures in the Lucknow of her time, which, if we are to go by the accounts of Western travelers, was one of the greatest cities in the world. There has been so much controversy about Umrao Jan's authorship of this work, however, that we decided against excerpting it for this anthology.

THERIGATHA

(Songs of the Nuns, 6th Century B.C.)   *Pali*

The earliest known anthology of women's literature—in India certainly,
but possibly anywhere in the world—took shape when the songs composed by the Buddhist *theris,* or senior nuns, which date back to the sixth
century B.C., were collected into the *Therigatha.* The poets were evidently
contemporaries of the Buddha, though the 522 stanzas of the collection
that has come down to us were committed to writing only around 80 B.C.
Each lyric in this collection as well as in the companion volume of songs
composed by the monks is a testimony, for it bears witness to a life transformed by the Buddha's teachings and celebrates a release, sometimes from
the toil and hardship of everyday life, but more often from a "hidden
shaft" lodged in the heart, or from a consuming anxiety. For Mutta, the
release is from "pestle and mortar," and from her "twisted lord." Vasitthi
wanders light-headed, crazed with grief, "naked, unheeding, streaming
hair unkempt," until she meets the "banisher of pain" and her errant mind
comes back to her.

Accompanying the anthology is a commentary, the *Paramatta Dipani,*
which provides us with notes on the songs and information about the
theris' lives. The biographies are accounts of the soul's journey and describe the poets' previous births as well as the circumstances in which they
attained enlightenment and subsequent release from the cycle of death and
rebirth. Scholars consider it probable that these compositions, which were
used by the itinerant theris as they wandered around preaching their message of release, were reworked over the five centuries in which they were
circulated orally. In the process the sound values, the images, the color
and detail in which feeling and situation were evoked would have been
recast as the preachers responded to the requirements of the women they
addressed. Obviously the biographical accounts would have gone through
a similar dialogical process of refinement before they were collected and
committed to writing in the fifth century A.D.

Buddhism arose in the egalitarian ethos of the republican territories in
the north of present-day Bihar. There is some disagreement about whether
these republics were democratic or not, but commentators seem broadly
agreed that in contrast to the neighboring monarchial states, in these areas
power was vested with a group and not with an individual. The people
were primarily agricultural, though there is evidence that they also kept
cattle. Accounts of trade and city life suggest that the economy was flour-

ishing, that the lives of peasants and artisans were changing, and that there was enough agricultural surplus to allow urban growth. Many heterodox sects, principal among which were the Jains and Buddhists, emerged in the ensuing period of doubt, turmoil, and experimentation. Different groups of wandering ascetics and itinerant almspeople questioned orthodoxy and preached revolutionary ideas. The Buddha's own followers came from all walks of life and included married as well as unmarried women. Among them were several city women, including the powerful courtesan Ambapalli, famed for her beauty, who finally became a theri herself.

As an ideology Buddhism is marked by its antagonism to the sacrificial rituals prescribed by the Vedas, and its rejection of the authority, religious or social, of the brahmins. It stressed the importance of experience as a basis of knowledge and ethics as the guiding principle of spiritual practice. Truth, the Buddha preached, must not be sought in the law or accepted out of reverence for the teacher, but tried out, as gold is tried by fire. The lyrics rest, therefore, on experiences that might otherwise have been considered trivial or merely personal, and the poets allow feelings to sculpt experience into a critique in a way that would not have been legitimate in the metaphysical traditions of vedic Hinduism. The songs provide us with rare glimpses into the personal lives of the wide range of women who joined the ascetic communities. Among them were poor peasants, small artisans, wealthy wives and daughters of businessmen, noblewomen, and courtesans. Many poems describe what we would today think of as oppressions of class or gender. Others provide a critique of a religion that has no space for the pain or the longing of individuals. Everyone, regardless of status, caste, or gender, the Buddha preached, was united in Buddhism, "as are the rivers in the sea." The three jewels commonly referred to in the poems are the three authorities of Buddhism: the Buddha himself; the *Dhamma,* or the rules of Buddhist life; and the *Sangha,* or the ascetic community.

But though Buddhism accepts that both men and women might attain *nirvana* and though both monks and nuns were provided the same rigorous meditative training and philosophical education, and entrusted with preaching the doctrine, the general tone of Buddhism, the feminist historian Uma Chakravarti points out, was antagonistic to women. Detailed accounts of the exchanges that took place before women were finally allowed to renounce the life of the household and join the community of the "houseless" in the Sangha have survived, and are worth recounting for the insight they give us into patriarchal ideologies and women's status in the early Buddhist period.

Mahapajapati Gotami, the Buddha's royal foster mother, who wanted to join the Sangha, the story goes, walked long distances through dust and heat to find the Buddha and make her request, but he would not hear of it. She appealed again and again but nothing would persuade him. Finally, one of his younger disciples, Ananda, intervened. There could be no reason, given the tenets of their belief, Ananda argued, why women should not be allowed into the Sangha. The Buddha was forced to agree, but he laid down "eight weighty laws," which any woman who entered the order would have to obey. We cite a few: no theri was ever to rebuke a thera, or monk, but all theris, however senior, could be subjected to reproof by a thera; after the two-year novitiate, a theri was to seek confirmation from both congregations, but the monk needed only to present himself to the male Sangha. Gotami willingly accepted all the conditions, but the Buddha was still unhappy. If women had not joined the Sangha, he is reported to have said, the doctrine would have endured a thousand years; now it would die out after a mere five hundred. That is why, "just as a man of property builds a dyke so that the water may not transgress its bonds, in the same way [I have] laid down eight weighty laws, to safeguard the doctrine." (It is not without some pleasure, therefore, that we provide Buddhism with yet another incarnation in these volumes.) Despite these restrictions, women did join the Sangha in considerable numbers, and from their songs it is clear they found the possibilities the new life opened up preferable to the confinement of a domestic life.

The focus of each lyric in the *Therigatha* is an epiphanic experience in which the painful constrictions of secular life fall away and the torment of feelings subsides as the peace and freedom of nirvana are attained. Nesting within and shaping the moment is an autobiographical fragment, for as the poets testify to the transformative power of Buddhism and exult in their new life, they contrast it to the painful worlds they leave behind. The rhetoric of testimony trims each experience into a similar form and assigns it the value of that-from-which-the-message-of-the-Buddha-will-provide-relief. The rhetoric continuously urges us to go beyond the fact or the statement to its significance. But even though the structural focus is on the message of the Buddha, that message itself depends for its texture and quality on the actual lives it transforms, and acquires fresh currency in each lyric. If one reads the songs of the theris only for the resolutions they offer—as one would if one read them in the context provided by the Buddhist canon—the structural design of testimony dominates the experience. If on the other hand our interest is in the historical detail of women's lives, their sufferings and aspirations, and on Buddhism as it articulated a world that included women, then we must strain against that resolution. We can focus instead on the way women used the spaces Buddhism opened up, individually and collectively, to contest the powers that determined their lives. We can ask how women inflected the concerns of Buddhism, extending its scope and infusing its schemes with their aspirations. But we must also ask how and why these gestures were contained as they were annexed into its architecture.

About the lives of the poets translated here we have some shards of information. The commentary on the *Therigatha* tells us that Mutta, "heaping up good under former Buddhas was in this dispensation, born in the land of Kosala as the daughter of a poor brahmin. . . . Come of proper age she was given to a hunchbacked brahmin, but she told him she could not continue in the life of the house, and induced him to consent to her leaving the world. Though she exercised herself in insight, her thoughts still ran on external objects. So she practiced self-control, and repeating her verse, strove after insight until she won [it]." Then, exulting, she spoke the lines attributed to her.

Sumangalamata, or Sumangala's mother, was daughter and wife to workers in the rushes. Her son, Sumangala, was a thera and from him we have a lyric strikingly similar in form to that of Mutta, suggesting that the oppression of gender and class found equal expression in the contexts Buddhism provided: "Well rid, well rid, O excellently rid / Am I from three crooked tasks and tools. / Rid of my reaping with your sickles, rid, / Of trudging after ploughs and rid's my back / Of bending over these wretched little spades," he sings. Mettika also "heaped up merit under former Buddhas." In an earlier birth she was the daughter of a wealthy merchant family and offered a jeweled girdle at a shrine. In this birth she was the child of an eminent brahmin at Rajagaha. Of Ubbiri, we know only what the poem tells us, but the translators point out the interesting fact that only women sing of bereavement or think of the Sangha as a refuge for those who have suffered such loss.

◆

MUTTA
[So free am I, so gloriously free]

So free am I, so gloriously free,
Free from three petty things—
From mortar, from pestle and from my twisted lord,
Freed from rebirth and death I am,
And all that has held me down
Is hurled away.

Translated by Uma Chakravarti and Kumkum Roy.

UBBIRI
["O Ubbiri, who wails in the wood"]

"O Ubbiri, who wails in the wood
'O Jiva! Dear daughter!'

Return to your senses. In this charnel field
Innumerable daughters, once as full of life as Jiva,
Are burnt. Which of them do you mourn?"
The hidden arrow in my heart plucked out,
The dart lodged there, removed.
The anguish of my loss,
The grief that left me faint all gone,
The yearning stilled,
To the Buddha, the Dhamma, and the Sangha
I turn, my heart now healed.

Translated by Uma Chakravarti and Kumkum Roy.

SUMANGALAMATA
[A woman well set free! How free I am]

A woman well set free! How free I am,
How wonderfully free, from kitchen drudgery.
Free from the harsh grip of hunger,
And from empty cooking pots,
Free too of that unscrupulous man,
The weaver of sunshades.
Calm now, and serene I am,
All lust and hatred purged.
To the shade of the spreading trees I go
And contemplate my happiness.

Translated by Uma Chakravarti and Kumkum Roy.

METTIKA
[Though I am weak and tired now]

Though I am weak and tired now,
And my youthful step long gone,
Leaning on this staff,
I climb the mountain peak.
My cloak cast off, my bowl overturned,
I sit here on this rock.
And over my spirit blows
The breath
Of liberty

I've won, I've won the triple gems.
The Buddha's way is mine.

Translated by Uma Chakravarti and Kumkum Roy.

THE SANGAM POETS ──────────────

(ca. 100 B.C.–A.D. 250)   *Tamil*

The ten anthologies and eight long poems of the Sangam age are the oldest
and most distinguished body of secular poetry extant in India. The relative
absence of Sanskrit words and mythology suggests they were composed
in a period before an Aryan culture took hold in that area. A total of 154
of the 2,381 poems carry women's signatures, and it is possible that some
of the 102 poems that have not yet been attributed to specific composers
were also written by women. Anonymous, we know from other cultures,
was often a woman.

Working from the evidence in the poetry and from the aesthetic schemes
that classified all compositions, by theme, into two complementary categories—*akam* (inner/romantic) and *puram* (outer/martial), each supported by an extended symbology of seasons, places, plants, and animals—
scholars have reconstructed the world that housed these distinguished
poets. The fertile river valleys in the north of what is Tamilnadu today
were occupied by several small kingdoms. The symbolic repertoire celebrates a thriving agricultural economy: the mountain slopes where the
coarser and hardier millet was grown, the forests, the pastures, the low,
well-watered valleys where rice was the main crop. Other poems pay
homage to the king's power and extol the bravery of warriors who protected the valleys against invaders. Cattle seem to have been the main
index of wealth, and the wars in which kingdoms were extended and
power consolidated were also cattle raids. Sangam poets write of cities and
attractive markets, of busy streets and tall buildings. Ships from abroad
(coins in the area indicate trade with the Roman Empire) stand in the
harbor. The poems, one commentator writes, "express the delight of a
fairly new civilization with its material culture."

It was a culture that took poetry seriously, for kings extended their
patronage to poets who, in turn, sang of the ruler's glory, though not
always without irony. When a defeated king "faced north" to starve ritually to death, the poets in his court joined him. But poetry and song were
also part of daily life. The commentaries that accompany these poems
mention songs women used to sing while transplanting seedlings, drawing

water, and husking paddy. Women apparently sang as they kept vigil on the ripening grain—to keep the birds away—but also to charm the spirit of the growing plant and coax it along as it reached fruition; they sang to soothe the pain of men who had been mauled by animals or were injured in wars. But the collections that have survived contain only the court poetry.

The elaborate aesthetic divides the poems into two genres, akam and puram, and codifies the connections among landscape, flower, season, and mood. Akam poems are usually love poems and deal with an inner space, whereas puram poems take everything else into their scope: the yard, the court, the battlefield, public life. The love poetry sets up a fictive situation in which the characters are ideal types: the heroine, the hero, the heroine's mother, her foster mother, her woman friend, the courtesan, the courtesan's woman friend, the hero's friend, passersby who witness the event. These are the *dramatis personae* of the akam poems. Puram poems, on the other hand, deal with historical figures and real events. The wild jasmine in bloom and the dark clouds of monsoon rain represent and evoke the grief of lovers who are separated; the *kurinci,* a wild mountain flower, alludes to a first, and often illicit, sexual experience, and so on. It is enough to mention one element in a cluster to evoke the others.

The distinguished translator of these poems, A. K. Ramanujan, points out that an interesting convention usually restricts the imagery for different speakers within the poems. "The heroine's images are confined to what surrounds her house or to general notions and hearsay. Her girlfriend or foster mother has more ranging images: they are of a lower class, their experience is wider. The man's imagery has great range. Apparently there are no limits to his experience and therefore to his imagery." Divisions of gender are also evident in the way the love poems deal with the body. The woman's body is sensuously evoked: her skin like young mango leaf, her dark hair musk with the scent of jasmine, her eyes shot with red, her loins glistening with ornaments. Of the man we hear only of his hairy chest, his actions, his horses, and his spears. The woman in the akam poems is young and made for love; the man a warrior in his prime or one who (foolishly) leaves a woman and goes "in search of riches." In the puram poems the woman is older, a mother of grown sons, a poet in the court, a widow forced to shave her hair and eat only "white seeds," a courtesan. Chastity and fidelity were clearly much at stake.

What we can recover of the philosophy of the Sangam age suggests that it is what we might today call animist. The idea is one of a spirit immanent in things and not of a transcendent or divine being who has to be worshiped. The home or the woman (akam) and the king (puram) were the two spheres of the sacred. As in agricultural societies all over the world, women were the symbols of fertility and were regarded as infused with sacred powers. They were considered especially dangerous at certain times: while they were menstruating, after they had given birth, and after the death of a husband. Under control, female power was auspicious, but if it broke loose, it could wreak havoc. We might be tempted, as we read the few poems reproduced here, to conflate the stress on chastity with modern notions of virtue, and the control of women's bodies at crucial points in their life cycle with contemporary sexual politics. Yet the remarkable sense of equality, of freedom to move around, to make relationships, and take on responsibilities that women obviously had would suggest that this society's concept of women as sacred, and therefore both powerful and dangerous, cannot simply be translated into forms familiar to us today.

Similarly, though the archaic language makes access to the original poems difficult, the direct, dramatic cast of the verse and the startling, compact imagery form a remarkably modern aesthetic. As lovers meet at night, in secret, on the hill slopes or long for each other, "The north wind / mocks my loneliness / Tell what she, / her eyes cold flowers, / said for me," we are tempted to blur Orient and Occident, Aryan and Dravidian, then and now into a timeless humanity, to which it would seem access is immediate and perennial.

> Her bright ornaments of fresh gold gently radiant,
> she climbed the *marutam* tree on the bank
> and plunged into the water,
> and her cool, fragrant hair
> was as splendid as a peacock descending from the sky.

> *(Orampokiyar, trans. George L. Hart III)*

But other poems force us to acknowledge that the urgencies and the passions of the Sangam poets belong to a world very different from our own. In exquisitely crafted poem after poem, mothers sing of rearing their sons for war and of their pride, only richer when touched by grief, in a son killed on the battlefield. In one celebrated poem a mother, beside herself with anxiety that her son might have deserted, searches the battlefield. Her unrestrained joy at finding her son's body there, mangled but recognizable, legitimates her maternal virtue as much as it celebrates his heroic action and glorifies the war as well as the king who fought it.

> Many said,
> "That old woman, the one whose veins show
> on her weak dry arms where the flesh is hanging,
> whose stomach is flat as a lotus leaf,
> has a son who lost his nerve in battle and fled."
> At that, she grew enraged and she said,
> "If he has run away in the thick of battle,
> I will cut off these breasts from which he sucked,"
> and, sword in hand, she turned over fallen corpses,
> groping her way on the red field.

Then she saw her son lying there in pieces
and she rejoiced more than the day she bore him.

(*Kakkaipatiniyar Naccellaiyar, trans. George L. Hart III*)

It is difficult to say whether the poem gives us a glimpse of what it meant to be a mother of a son in times when wars and cattle raids established not only the extent and prosperity of a kingdom but also the poet's livelihood and the security of a people, or whether the woman poet is simply drawing on a woman's life for an image that will evoke all the more intensely what the people (or so she tells him) are willing to sacrifice for the patron of her art, the king.

If we are to go by the poems that have survived, the most active, or perhaps the most powerful, of the women poets was Auvaiyar. Fifty-nine lyrics by her have come down to us, thirty-three of the puram mode and twenty-six of the akam. Auvaiyar wrote of kings and of war and of politics as much as she did of love. About the other women poets we know only what we can glean from the poems. The poems translated here are selected from the akam anthology *Kuruntokai* (Anthology of Short Poems) and the puram anthologies *Purananuru* (Four Hundred Puram Poems) and *Patirruppattu* (Ten Tens of Songs).

◆

VENMANIPPUTI
KURUNTOKAI 299
[What she said to her girlfriend]

What she said to her girlfriend:

On beaches washed by seas
older than the earth,
in the groves filled with bird-cries,
on the banks shaded by a *punnai*
clustered with flowers,
                    when we made love
my eyes saw him
and my ears heard him;

my arms grow beautiful
in the coupling
and grow lean
as they come away.
                    What shall I make of this?

Translated by A. K. Ramanujan.

VELLI VITIYAR
KURUNTOKAI 130
[He will not dig up the earth and enter it]

He will not dig up the earth and enter it,
he will not climb into the sky,
he will not walk across the dark sea.
If we search every country,
every city,
every village,
can your lover escape us?

[The friend speaks to the heroine about her lover,
who has left on a journey and not returned.]

Translated by George L. Hart III.

VELLI VITIYAR
KURUNTOKAI 58
[You tell me I am wrong, my friend]

You tell me I am wrong, my friend,
that I should stop seeing her.
Yes, I know it would be good
if I could do what you say,
but my pain
is like butter melting
on a ledge scorched in the sun
while a man who has no hands or tongue
tries to save it.
It spreads through me
no matter what I do.

Translated by George L. Hart III.

AUVAIYAR
KURUNTOKAI 28
What She Said

Shall I attack these people, shall I strike them?
I do not know.
Or shall I find some reason and cry out
to this city that sleeps
not knowing my suffering
while the moving wind swirls
and pulls me to and fro.

Translated by George L. Hart III.

AUVAIYAR
PURANURU 92
[You cannot compare them with a lute]

You cannot compare them with a lute.
The tenses are wrong, the meanings unclear,
and yet the words of a little son
fill a father with love.
The words of my mouth are like that also,
O Netuman Anci
who have taken many enemy forts with guarded walls,
for they make you show your love.

Translated by George L. Hart III.

KAVAR PENTU
PURANURU 86
[You stand and hold the post of my small
    house]

You stand and hold the post of my small house,
and you ask, "Where is your son?"
Wherever my son is, I do not know.
This is the womb that carried him,
like a stone cave

lived in by a tiger and now abandoned.
It is on the battlefield that you will find him.

Translated by George L. Hart III.

KAKKAIPATINIYAR NACCELLAIYAR
PATIRUPPATTU 60
[His armies love massacre]

His armies love massacre,
he loves war,
yet gifts
flow from him ceaselessly.

Come, dear singers,
let's go and see him in Naravu

    where, on trees
    no ax can fell,
    fruits ripen, unharmed
    by swarms of bees,
    egg-shaped, ready
    for the weary traveler
    in fields of steady, unfailing harvests;

    where warriors with bows
    that never tire of arrows
    shiver
    but stand austere
    in the sea winds
    mixed with the lit cloud
    and the spray of seafoam.

      There he is,
      in the town of Naravu,
      tender among tender women.

Translated by A. K. Ramanujan.

OKKUR MACATTIYAR
PURANURU 279
[Her purpose is frightening, her spirit cruel]

Her purpose is frightening, her spirit cruel.
That she comes from an ancient house is fitting, surely.
In the battle the day before yesterday,
her father attacked an elephant and died there on the field.
In the battle yesterday,
her husband faced a row of troops and fell.
And today,
she hears the battle drum,
and, eager beyond reason, gives him a spear in his hand,
wraps a white garment around him,
smears his dry tuft with oil,
and, having nothing but her one son,
"Go!" she says sending him to battle.

Translated by George L. Hart III.

AKKAMAHADEVI ————————————

(12th century)   *Kannada*

It was like a stream
   running into the dry bed
   of a lake,
            like rain
   pouring on plants
   parched to sticks.

It was like this world's pleasure
   and the way to the other,
                        both
   walking towards me.

Seeing the feet of the master,
O lord white as jasmine,
   I was made
   worthwhile.

                (trans. A. K. Ramanujan)

Embodied in this terse and deceptively simple poem is the philosophy of the brilliant medieval Kannada poet, rebel, and mystic Akkamahadevi. A reader familiar with the themes and conventions of Virasaiva (see the Introduction) poetry will find the analogies quite clear: as the waters of the monsoon regenerate the land, parched by the long days of summer heat, a mystic union with the Lord will regenerate a religion of dry, lifeless ritual or orthodox belief. The second stanza introduces another recurrent theme. Her god is not to be found, as the vedic traditions suggested, through ascetic withdrawal, but is to be embraced in the fullness of life's pleasures, indeed, is found only through them. It is in the third stanza, however, that Akkamahadevi arrives at the radical humanism that marks all bhakti poetry. In the intimacy of union with her personal deity, her Self is given a new legitimacy.

Akkamahadevi was born in Udutadi, a village near Shimoga in present-day Karnataka, and initiated into Virasaivism when still a young girl. Apparently, the ankita (see the Introduction) she chose, Chennamallikarjuna, which appears in each of her poems and helps us identify them as hers, is the form in which Shiva was worshiped in the temple at Udutadi. A. K. Ramanujan translates it as "lord white as jasmine," though literally rendered it would read "Mallika's beautiful Arjuna." The most popular legends about Akka claim that Kausika, the king of that land, chanced upon her one day and desired to have her as his wife. Kausika was a Jain, and it is important to remember that in Karnataka the Virasaiva movement was focused as much against this dominant commercial community as it was against the religious orthodoxy of the brahmins. It is possible that Akka might have married him, but the claims of Shiva were stronger. A couple of her powerful poems, or *vacanas,* dramatize the tension. Each time she rejects the human lover, who would turn her body into an object of his desire, in favor of her Chennamallikarjuna, who gives form to her Self. Another touching lyric tells us how she severed her links with her mother and her birthplace and set out in search of her Lord Chennamallikarjuna, to whom she betrothes herself.

She wandered, some legends say, naked, across most of what is now Karnataka in search of her divine lover. Defiant and furious with the men who molest her and misunderstand her quest, she arrives at Kalyana where Allama and Basavva, the two principal male saints of the Virasaiva movement, lived. Basavva is often spoken of today as Karnataka's first socialist, for he spoke out against the caste system and united the artisan groups into the *lingavantas,* or those who worshiped Shiva. About herself Akka sang: "she has lain down / with the lord white as jasmine / and has lost caste." Allama's vacanas are more philosophical and stress the importance of personal salvation. Both strands join in Akkamahadevi's poetry, though the mystic complexity of her verse and the power of her many-hued images that shift and glow into life are often lost in translation. From Kalyana, Akka traveled further north to Kadali in Srisailam, where she spent her last days.

Of the 350 vacanas that bear her ankita, many of the most complex and stunning ones are attributed to the extensive dialogue she had with Allama before joining the community at Kalyana. Akka's poetry uses the metaphor of illicit love for her intense, all-encompassing relationship with Shiva, whom she addresses as Chennamallikarjuna. It is a relationship *she* seeks out, one she is intoxicated by and willingly abandons herself to, with a directness of address surprising even today. The three conventional poetic themes of love forbidden, love fulfilled, and the longing of separated lovers are often compressed into the same vacana, and sometimes into one dominant image. The growth of carnal love becomes a symbol of mystic progression. Akka's poems are moving, haunting, unforgettable. For women, her work embodies a radical illegitimacy as she struggles in her poetry to go beyond much of Virasaiva poetry to include the struggles of her body, struggles against the pettiness of roles she is forced into as a woman, struggles against a man who is also a prince and a Jain, and against the social expectations that restrain her.

◆

[Don't despise me]

Don't despise me as
   She who has no one
I'm not one to be afraid,
   Whatever you do.
I exist chewing dry leaves,
   My life resting on a knife edge
If you must torment me,
   Chennamallikarjuna,
My life, my body
   I'll offer you, and be cleansed.

Translated by Susan Daniel.

[Brother, you've come]

Brother, you've come
   drawn by the beauty
   of these billowing breasts,
   this brimming youth.

I'm no woman, brother, no whore.

Everytime you've looked at me,
  Who have you taken me for?
All men other than Chennamallikarjuna
  Are faces to be shunned, see, brother.

Translated by Susan Daniel.

[Not one, not two, not three or four]

Not one, not two, not three or four,
but through eighty-four hundred thousand vaginas
have I come.
            I have come
through unlikely worlds,
                  guzzled on
pleasure and pain.
            Whatever be
all previous lives,
            show me mercy
this one day,
      O lord
      white as jasmine.

Translated by A. K. Ramanujan.

[Would a circling surface vulture]

Would a circling surface vulture
  know such depths of sky
  as the moon would know?

would a weed on the riverbank
  know such depths of water
  as the lotus would know?

would a fly darting nearby
  know the smell of flowers
  as the bee would know?

O lord white as jasmine
  only you would know
  the way of your devotees:
  how would these,

these
  mosquitoes
  on the buffalo's hide?

Translated by A. K. Ramanujan.

SULE SANKAVVA ─────────────

(12th century)   *Kannada*

The only poem by Sankavva that has survived is the one translated here. Sankavva uses the ankita Nirlajjeshwara, literally, "God/Shiva who is without shame," translated in the poem as "libertine Shiva." To a contemporary sensibility the easy juxtaposition of sacred and profane in this poem is startling. While at one level it simply presents a dramatic moment in the everyday life of a prostitute, at another the encounter is a symbolic one in which she reaffirms her personal allegiance to Shiva. There is a suggestion in the original, which does not come through clearly in translation, that the second man is not a Virasaivite.

Of course we chose this poem as much for the author as for the poem itself. Although many of the poet-saints of the bhakti movement were artisans and people who plied small trades, it is unusual to find one who was a prostitute.

◆

[In my harlot's trade]

In my harlot's trade
having taken one man's money
I daren't accept a second man's, sir.
And if I do,
    they'll stand me naked and
       kill me, sir.

And if I cohabit
    with the polluted,
My hands nose ears
    they'll cut off
    with a red-hot knife, sir.

Ah, never, no,
    Knowing you I will not.

My word on it,
    libertine Shiva.

Translated by Susan Daniel.

JANABAI ———————————————————

(ca. 1298–1350)   *Marathi*

Let me not be sad because I am born a woman
In this world; many saints suffer in this way.

So wrote Janabai, who is perhaps one of the best known and best loved
of Maharashtra's Varkari saint-poets. The Varkaris are the most influential bhakti sect among the Marathi-speaking peoples. Like many of these
saint-poets, Janabai was born into a low-caste sudra family. Her parents,
who were also Varkaris, lived in a village on the banks of the Godavari.
It was not unusual at the time for children from poor families to be sent
to live in a household where they would work as domestic servants, and
when Janabai was hardly seven, her parents handed her over to the family
of Dama Shetty, father of the revered Varkari poet Namdev. Janabai spent
the rest of her life in that household. Tradition would have required that
she be well looked after, and this would have been all the more so in this
particular household, steeped as it was in the egalitarian Varkari ethos, yet
Janabai often speaks of the restrictions, even with regard to worship, that
her status as servant, or *dasi,* imposed on her and of the heavy, never-
ending household tasks that fell to her lot. The hardships of being a woman
and the burden of domestic labor are ever present in her writing.

   In Janabai's poetry we find a response that gives a sense of how women
translated the concerns of a dominant ethos as they pressed it into service.
The result is an incipient feminism that is also truly Varkari in spirit and
in act (see the Introduction). Vithoba, the deity at Pandharpur, who is of
special significance to the Varkari sect, Janabai proclaims, is a friend, a
support, a constant helpmate in her arduous domestic work. He is there
to help her carry and heat the bathwater, to sweep the leaves from the
courtyard, to scour the vessels until they gleam, to scratch her scalp when
the lice bite her. Her sensitive poetry, which is popular even today, illuminates the everyday life of ordinary women and addresses its joys and
its strains. The poems also embody the dream of the *jodi,* or the hope of a
perfect companionship to comfort her in her loneliness. It is in the love
she has for God that Janabai can imagine and reach out toward a freedom
and a power her life could hardly have provided for her.

Of the two poems translated here, one is representative of several in which she images Vithoba as an everyday helpmate and companion. The other is a more suggestive and radical one in which Janabai speaks of herself as a wandering singer. Such women were also considered of easy virtue, but Janabai portrays them as free and rebellious, not restricted by the rules of decorum (such as that of keeping the breasts covered with the *pallav* of the sari), which "virtuous" family women are bound by. Though this nuance has not been captured in the translation, the original suggests that she might be speaking not only of selling her body but also of setting up trade as an independent artist, in her song.

◆

[Cast off all shame]

Cast off all shame,
and sell yourself
in the marketplace;
then alone
can you hope
to reach the Lord.

Cymbals in hand,
a *veena* upon my shoulder,
I go about;
who dares to stop me?

The pallav of my sari
falls away (A scandal!);
yet will I enter
the crowded marketplace
without a thought.

Jani says, My Lord,
I have become a slut
to reach Your home.

Translated by Vilas Sarang.

[Jani sweeps the floor]

Jani sweeps the floor,
The Lord collects the dirt,
Carries it upon His head,
And casts it away.

Won over by devotion,
The Lord does lowly chores!
Says Jani to Vithoba,
How shall I pay your debt?

Translated by Vilas Sarang.

RAMI

(ca. 1440)   *Bengali*

About two hundred years ago scholars came across a sheaf of poems, in manuscript, written after the death of the famous fifteenth-century Vaishnava poet Chandidas. When these poems were attributed to his distinguished contemporary and companion Rami, a love story that had already given rise to countless Bengali folk plays and folk songs sprang to life and Bengali literature found its first major woman poet.

Ramoni, or Rami, was born of low-caste washerfolk. The poems tell us how she wandered, destitute, from place to place until she reached Nanur, a village in what is now the district of Bankura. There Rami found work cleaning the Bashuli Devi temple where the well-known Bengali bhakti poet Chandidas also lived. She worked hard and through her devotion won the respect of the entire village. Soon Rami began composing verses in praise of the deity. These are the earliest extant verses by a Bengali woman.

It was not long before the friendship between Rami and Chandidas grew into an intimacy that was noticed and disapproved of by the village. Overtly the complaint was that Chandidas was a brahmin and she of low caste. A relationship between them was improper. But the evidence of the poems suggests that it was more the warmth of their companionship and the intensity of their involvement that broke the sanctions at a far deeper level. Chandidas was exiled from the village and boycotted by his community. Rami lost her job at the temple.

In one of his verses, Chandidas expresses the desire to touch her feet. Coming from a man, and a brahmin at that, this image, which embodies a total inversion of the social hierarchy, was truly revolutionary. Needless to say, later Vaishnavite scholars have domesticated the image by interpreting it as a spiritual metaphor of mystic abandonment. On the whole, however, what we find in Chandidas's verses is a sanitized, spiritual representation of their love, whereas Rami's poems are passionate and brutally frank.

The first of the two poems we have chosen is taken from Rami's early poetry and the second from a sequence of powerful poems, which scholars regard as her most outstanding work, written after the death of Chandidas. They refer to another episode in Rami's life. The Nawab of Gaur, an important nobleman, invited Chandidas to sing at his palace. His wife, the Begum, was so charmed by Chandidas's poetry that she fell in love with him. Worse still, she made no secret of her feelings. Chandidas, Rami's poems bitterly admit, was attracted to her. Rami was clearly hurt. Pain and anger ring through her verse as she speaks of the betrayal. The Nawab was infuriated. He ordered that Chandidas be tortured and put to death even as the Begum watched. Chandidas was tied to the back of an elephant and beaten to death. All through his extended torture, Chandidas kept his gaze fixed on Rami, who was there too. The Begum was so distraught that she killed herself. A moving lyric tells us how Rami, her anger and resentment now set aside, wept at her feet.

Rami's verses are unlike other Vaishnava lyrics of the time, which were often abstract and philosophical. These poems express directly the yearnings of a woman in love. There is no attempt to be discreet or to hide her passion. She curses and rages and laments. And as she does so, the poems bring to life a flesh-and-blood woman, angry, proud, and in love. In the poems written after the death of Chandidas, though she is overcome by grief at his suffering, she does not allow him to forget that he betrayed their love and the pledge he had made to her in the temple. Never once does she whine or plead; she demands from life a right that should be hers because of her great love.

◆

[Where have you gone?]

Where have you gone,
    my Chandidas, my friend,
Birds thirst without water,
    despair without rain.
What have you done,
    O heartless lord of Gaur?
Not knowing what it means to love,
    you slay my cherished one.
Lord of my heart, my Chandidas,
    why did you break
The vows you made
    and sing in court?
Now evil men and beasts come swarming round;
    heavens turn to hell.

Betrayed by you, I stand in shame;
     you've crushed my honor in your hands.
Once, heedless, untouched by Vasuli's threat,
     you told the court with pride
You'd leave a brahmin home, you said,
     to love a washergirl.
Now, lashed to an elephant's back,
     you reach me with your eyes.
Why should the jealous king heed
     a washerwoman's cries?
Soul of my soul, how cruelly on your fainting limbs
     the heavy whip strikes and falls,
Cleave through my heart, and let me die
     with Chandidas, my love.

And then the queen fell on her knees,
     "Please stop, my lord," she cried.
"His singing pierced me to the heart.
     No more of this, I plead.
Why must you thus destroy
     limbs made for love alone?
Free him, I beg of you, my lord,
     don't make love your toy.
O godless king, how could you know
     what love can mean?"
So spoke the queen, and then, her heart
     still fixed on Chandidas, she died.
Rami trembled, hearing her,
     and hastened to the place.
She threw herself at those queenly feet
     and wept the tears of death.

Translated by Malini Bhattacharya.

[What can I say, friend?]

    What can I say, friend?
    I don't have enough words!
Even as I weep when I tell you this story
    My accursed face breaks into laughter!
Can you imagine the cheek of the sinister men?

They have stopped worshipping the Devi
And have started tarnishing my reputation.

Let the thunderbolt crash on the ehads of those
Who from their housetops shout abuses at good people
    I won't stay any longer in this land of injustice,
I'll go to a place where there are no hellhounds.

Translated by Sumanta Banerjee.

GANGASATI ———————————————————

(12th–14th century)   *Gujarati*

Though today Mirabai is the best known of the Gujarati saint-poets, several other women belonged to the medieval devotional tradition and composed their lyrics in Gujarati. Gangasati is one of several women poets we know of, others being Radhabai, Krishnabai, Gauribai, and two poets named Ratanbai. Gangasati's compositions have all been handed down through the oral tradition and what has been recorded of her life was written down so long after her time that we do not know even roughly the period in which she lived. It is said, however, that she was married to Kahlubha in the village of Samdhiala in Saurashtra. She was already deeply religious when she married and prevailed upon her husband to adopt her way of life. Their home became a center for religious discourses and meditations and a meeting place for holy men. Her son was brought up in this atmosphere. Her husband's rejection of the world was so absolute that he decided to put an end to his earthly existence by entering into *samadhi,* which is a state of trancelike stillness achieved through intense concentration in meditation. The contemplator is absorbed in the object (usually the divine) contemplated and the self negated. But when Gangasati resolved to follow the same course of action, he persuaded her to defer it till she had perfected her daughter-in-law, Panabai, in the path of bhakti.

Gangasati's compositions consist of around forty *bhajans* or hymns addressed to Panabai, instructing her in the ways of truth. It is noteworthy that when Gangasati speaks of God, she is not involving any one of the deities in the Hindu pantheon, but the ultimate Brahma, pure spirit without attributes or form *(nirguna),* with whom the human soul could attain union only through arduous discipline and self-surrender. She stresses the importance of submission to the true Guru. The qualities of the true Guru are those the disciple must also seek to cultivate: the conquest of desire and passion, the casting aside of the ego, single-minded devotion to God. Her bhajans mark the stages by which the devotee advances in religious experience, stages by which she seeks to lead Panabai. Gangasati has no use for ritual or for the doctrines of various sects, but she relies quite considerably on yogic exercises for the attainment of transcendental experience. The poem translated here is typical of her oeuvre and exhorts Panabai to be resolute in her commitment.

Whereas accounts of the lives of other women devotional poets tend to show them as abandoning the family and attaching themselves to a guru, Gangasati is presented as striving to make worship and religious or intellectual search the fundamentals of her family tradition and a woman, the daughter-in-law, the bearer of that tradition. The mountain referred to in the poem is Meru, a legendary mountain of gold, which supports the earth and round which the planets revolve. We have made no attempt to translate the word *harijan,* which means "a person of God," since it suggests not only that the person worships God wholeheartedly but that God regards that person as one of His own. Six centuries later Gandhi used this term for the lower castes, saying that they were not untouchables but those whom God regarded as His own. Gangasati, however, uses the term in its earlier sense.

◆

[Oh, the Meru mountain may be swayed]

Oh, the Meru mountain may be swayed, but not the mind of the
    Harijan,
Let the whole universe be shattered into fragments.
But the mind uncorroded by misfortune—
That's the true measure of the Harijan,
        The Meru mountain may be swayed, but not the mind of the
            Harijan.
O brother, this is one unaffected by joy and sorrow,
Whose head is willingly offered in sacrifice,
Who shows courage in adhering to the true Guru's teachings,
Who surrenders the ego in full submission—
        The Meru mountain may be swayed, but not the mind of the
            Harijan.
O brother, this is one who lives in the company of the enlightened,
Who rejoices all hours of the day,
Who does not waver between resolution and counterresolution,
Who has broken all the bonds of worldly life—
        The Meru mountain may be swayed, but not the mind of the
            Harijan.

Devote yourself to God, O Panabai!
Be faithful to your words;
Here's a word of advice from Gangasati,
Submit yourself wholly to the true Guru—
>   The Meru mountain may be swayed, but not the mind of the
>   Harijan.

Translated by Nita Ramaiya.

RATANBAI ————————————————

(12th–14th century)   *Gujarati*

We were able to find out very little about this bhakti poet, who composed
her songs in Gujarati. She is usually mentioned in literary histories as one
of the women poets who was well known in her time. Unlike Mirabai
(the next poet in our collection), who came from a royal family, Ratanbai
made her living at the spinning wheel. Since the bhakti movement was
primarily a movement of artisans and small tradespeople, it would not
have been unusual for a spinner to compose poetry.

◆

[My spinning wheel is dear to me, my sister]

My spinning wheel is dear to me, my sister;
My household depends on it.
My husband married me and departed;
He went abroad to earn a living.

After twelve years he returned,
With a copper coin and a half;
He went to bathe in the Ganga,
Dropped the copper coin and a half.

Mother, father, father-in-law, mother-in-law,
One and all rejected us;
The spinning wheel was our savior,
To it we clung.

I paid off all my husband's debts
And over and above

Tying coin after coin in the corner of my sari
I earned a whole rupee.

Translated by Nita Ramaiya.

MIRABAI

(ca. 1498–1565) *Gujarati and Hindi*

Mirabai is a relative latecomer in the bhakti movement, which began in
the south around the eighth century and moved north in wave after wave,
through what is now Karnataka and Maharashtra into Mira's own Gujarat
and Rajasthan. The legends that surround the life of Mira in the popular
imagination today are as significant a source of information about this
much-loved poet as the oldest extended biographical account: Priyadas's
commentary in Nabhadas's *Sri Bhaktammal,* 1712, itself no doubt a mixture
of fact and legend.

Mirabai belonged to a leading Rajput clan and was married into another
powerful royal family. In one poem she speaks about a childhood vision
of Krishna, which made such an impact on her that she declared herself
his bride and dedicated her life wholly to him. Though she consented to
marriage with the crown prince of Mewar, it was a marriage in name only.
In her heart she was wedded to Giridhar Naagar (Giridhar Gopal in the
Hindi-speaking regions) and acknowledged no other husband. When the
marriage festivities were over and it was time to leave with her husband,
Mirabai had no desire to take with her any of the magnificent gifts of
clothes and jewels she had been given; she insisted instead on carrying her
personal image of Krishna with her.

Central to the accounts of Mirabai's life are the struggles with her husband and his family. Her sisters-in-law, for instance, try to stop her from
seeking the company, so improper for a highborn woman, of wandering
saints and mendicants. In the most popular legends concerning her, her
husband, the Rana, makes two attempts to kill her, but she is miraculously
saved both times. Once a poisonous snake is concealed in a basket, but
when she opens it, the snake turns into a garland of flowers. On another
occasion a deadly poison is mixed into her drink, but she swallows it,
fully aware of what it is, and emerges unscathed, glowing with even
greater radiance and health. It would appear that Mira spent most of her
adult life in worship and devotion and in the company of holy men. She
soon left Mewar and traveled east to places of pilgrimage associated with

the life of Krishna, such as Vraj, near Mathura, and later back west to Dwarka in Saurashtra. The date and manner of her death are uncertain.

In Mirabai's poetry it is not the devotee who pursues God, but Krishna who pursues the devotee as he pursued the milkmaids. The relationship is intense and erotic, their love a source of joy to both. She suffers deeply in periods of separation. In several lyrics Mira speaks of herself as "mad," and the religious experience is one of ecstasy and abandon. All Mira's poems are intended to be sung, and she may have herself composed or selected the melodies. Although the musical quality of her poems is marked even when they are read aloud, they gain immensely when sung. Fourteen hundred short compositions have been attributed to her, of which four hundred are in Gujarati. Since Mirabai's poetry cannot be traced back to any reliable manuscript, it is difficult today to say how many of these are her own compositions and how many were subsequently attributed to her.

The language spoken in the area where she originally lived was western Rajasthani, though her poems are also in Vraj *bhasha,* which is the dialect of Hindi in which much devotional poetry was composed, as well as in Gujarati. The critic Niranjan Bhagat argues that she composed her poems in the language of the area she was in at the time. Alternatively, he argues also that all her poems may have been originally composed in western Rajasthani and then altered over the years as they were sung all over northern India. Her gift for the exact word and her fine sense of rhythm make Mira one of the best loved poets of the bhakti movement. The Mira story has been made into at least ten films, which go back to the earliest days of Indian cinema, and the revered classical singer M. S. Subbalaxmi's rendering of Mira's songs is perhaps one of the most influential recordings of religious music produced in India.

Feminist scholars like Neera Desai have pointed to the contradiction between Mira's rebellious life and her poetry, which seems to affirm a woman's traditional place in the family. Her religious imagery, Desai argues, is drawn from the household and all the duties of a wife are celebrated, down to their minutest detail. As lover, Mira images herself as the dasi (or slave) of Giridhar. Unlike other bhaktas, or devotees, she never seems to question the authority of the brahmin, the hierarchies of caste, or the degeneracy of ritual. Parita Mukta, who has worked on the figure kept alive in the oral traditions of places associated with the Mira legend, argues, however, that for the peasants in the areas where she lived she is a symbol of resistance, both to the rule of the Rana and to the authority of a husband. She retains an identity as a historical figure through whom their hopes and grievances are expressed.

Even within the mainstream popular tradition, the intensity of Mira's devotion and her courage in resisting every pressure to deviate from her chosen way of life can be a source of strength to women who regard her as an intimate and personal support in their suffering and pain.

The two poems chosen for translation are taken from Niranjan Bhagat's collection of Mira's Gujarati songs. The term rendered in the poem as "bundle of suffering" literally refers to the burden of forced labor demanded of a vassal. The names Ranchodrai Sheth, Shamalsha Sheth, and Giridhar Naagar all refer to Lord Krishna. Ranchodrai is the Krishna who saves human beings from the desertlike aridity of life. There is a legend that Krishna came to the house of his devotee, Narsinh Mehta, in the guise of Shamalsha Sheth, a wealthy businessman, to help him financially. Giridhar, Mira's chosen form of Krishna, is the "lifter of the mountain," and a youthful, heroic, protective aspect of the deity. Giridhar lifted a mountain on the tip of his finger to protect the cowherds from a storm that Indra, the god of rain, had raised in jealous anger.

◆

[I am pale with longing for my beloved]

I am pale with longing for my beloved;
    People believe I am ill.
Seizing on every possible pretext,
    I try to meet him "by accident."

They have sent for a country doctor;
    He grabs my arm and prods it;
How can he diagnose my pain?
    It's in my heart that I am afflicted.

Go home, country doctor,
    Don't address me by my name;
It's the name of God that has wounded me,
    Don't force your medicines on me.

The sweetness of his lips is a pot of nectar,
    That's the only curd for which I crave;
Mira's Lord is Giridhar Naagar.
    He will feed me nectar again and again.

Translated from the Gujarati by Nita Ramaiya.

[Having taken up this bundle of suffering]

Having taken up this bundle of suffering, this body,
How can I throw it away?

It belongs to Ranchodrai Sheth,
It belongs to Shamalsha Sheth,
How can I throw it away?

The hot sand burns my feet,
The scorching wind of summer blows,
How can I throw it away?

Mira's Lord is Giridhar Naagar;
I am longing to reach the ultimate,
How can I throw it away?

Translated from the Gujarati by Nita Ramaiya.

[I am true to my Lord.]

I am true to my Lord.
O my companions, there is nothing to be ashamed of now
Since I have been seen dancing openly.

In the day I have no hunger
At night I am restless and cannot sleep.
Leaving these troubles behind, I go to the other side;
A hidden knowledge has taken hold of me.

My relations surround me like bees.
But Mira is the servant of her beloved Giridhar,
And she cares nothing that people mock her.

Translated from the Hindi by F. E. Keay.

[The Bhil woman tasted them, plum after plum]

The Bhil woman tasted them, plum after plum,
  and finally found one she could offer him.
What kind of genteel breeding was this?
  And hers was no ravishing beauty,
Her family was poor, her caste quite low,
  her clothes a matter of rags,
Yet Ram took that fruit—that touched, spoiled fruit—
  for he knew that it stood for her love.
This was a woman who loved the taste of love,
  and Ram knows no high, no low.
What sort of Veda could she ever have learned?
  But quick as a flash she mounted a chariot
And sped to heaven to swing on a swing,

tied by love to God.
You are the Lord who cares for the fallen;
  rescue whoever loves as she did:
Let Mira, your servant, safely cross over,
  a cowherding Gokul girl.

Translated from the Hindi by J. S. Hawley and M. Jeurgensmeyer.

ATUKURI MOLLA

(early 16th century)   *Telugu*

In Molla's times if a brahmin were to read through the *Ramayana* once, it would be an event to be celebrated with joy and feasting. One can imagine what an extraordinary achievement it must have been for a woman from the lowly potter caste to write a new version of the epic. Atukuri Molla did so, legend has it, in five days. In place of the customary introductory flourish, with which poets of her time presented their work—establishing their ancestry, their literary heritage, and the distinctiveness of their own poetry—Molla plays a simple tribute to her artisan father:

> I am god's gift to him
> they call me Molla.

She describes her own attempt with a gesture of self-depreciation that barely masks her self-confidence:

> I am no scholar,
> distinguishing the loanwords
> from the native stock.

> I know no rules of combination
> no large vocabulary

> I am no expert
> in composition and illocution,
> semantics and style.

She writes, she adds, only by the grace of the famous Lord Kantha Mallesa. Although it was the convention for poets in her time to claim divine inspiration, given Molla's own circumstances as a low-caste woman, it was perhaps mandatory that she do so, if her work was to be acknowledged or read.

Molla and her father were both Virasaivas (see the Introduction). The movement had emerged in the Telugu-speaking areas, now in Andhra Pradesh, around the twelfth century, about the same time as it did in the

Kannada-speaking areas further south, and remained strong well into the sixteenth century. In Andhra too, the Virasaivas condemned ritual and animal sacrifice, opposed caste discrimination, and tried to raise the status of women. Molla and her father were persecuted for their unorthodox beliefs.

The *Molla Ramayanam* is such an astonishing achievement that many legends grew up to explain how she came to write this Telugu epic. One story has it that during the reign of Krishnadevaraya, the court poet Tenali Ramakrishna threw a challenge at a senior poet from another village, in the process insulting the whole village. To restore the honor of her village, Molla accepted the challenge and swore she would compose the *Ramayanam* itself in five days. Tenali Ramakrishna heaped scorn on the idea. How could a woman, especially one so low born, boast like this! But to his dismay and the amazement of the world, the story goes, she sat in the temple, hard at work, and finished her version of the epic in the promised five days.

Molla was the first woman to write in Telugu whose work has been preserved. But as with most women writers, even those who lived much later, there is no source that tells us more than these legends do about the life or work of this remarkable poet. Literary histories place her in the early sixteenth century. For many years scholars assumed that Molla was a brahmin, or at least that she was a brahmin foundling adopted and brought up by the potter Kesava. Since knowledge and scholarship were, in those times, the exclusive prerogative of the brahmins, it is not surprising that scholars came to these conclusions. The fact that Kesava was himself a poet did not seem to affect such speculations. Other critics dismissed her as one of Krishnadevaraya's concubines.

Sources in the oral tradition, however, make it clear that Molla was a rebel. She lost her mother quite early, we are told, and was reared by her father, whom she loved greatly. So she grew unwomanly and bold in her ways. Since she used her parental family name—Atukuri—it is probable that she did not marry. Though it was the custom for poets to dedicate their poems to kings or other powerful persons, seeking in the process their patronage and favor, Molla ignored that tradition and chose to dedicate her work directly to Rama. Molla also seems to have been consciously arguing for a new poetic diction that would appeal to the immediacy of the senses as much as to the learning of scholars.

The *Molla Ramayanam* consists of 138 *slokas,* or verses, sung in praise of a deity, in six *kandas,* or sections. Critics point out that the language of her composition was revolutionary as it was much closer to the spoken forms of Telugu than was conventional in her time. In her *Ramayanam* Molla dwells on Sita's childhood and celebrates her vitality, her strength, and her joyousness. There are explicit descriptions of Sita coming of age and of the time spent in Ashokavanam, a beautiful forest of *ashoka* trees in Ravana's kingdom. We have chosen to translate the introductory autobiographical slokas in which Molla traces her lineage and comments on her idea of poetry. The other slokas are from the main body of the work, and give us a sense of the sensuous imagery and vigorous diction typical of her composition. The last extract, celebrating Sita's beauty, is from the Swayamvara section of the poem, in which Sita chooses her husband from among several princely suitors.

◆

From MOLLA RAMAYANAM
[My father Kesava]

My father Kesava
was pious, friendly,
devoted to his guru,
and God, in all His manifestations,
fixed and mobile.

Shiva's devotee
he was a guru in his own right.

I am God's gift to him;
they call me Molla.

Translated by B. V. L. Narayanarow.

From MOLLA RAMAYANAM
[I am no scholar]

I am no scholar
distinguishing the loanwords
from the native stock.

I know no rules of combination
no large vocabulary.

I am no expert
in composition and illocution,
semantics and style.

Nor do I know
phonetics, case relations,
roots of verbs and figures of speech,
meter and prosody, either.

Untrained though,
in composing poems and epics
in mastering lexicons and rules
I do write poems
by the grace of the famous Lord
Sri Kantha Mallesa.

Translated by B. V. L. Narayanarow.

From MOLLA RAMAYANAM
[As honey sweetens]

As honey sweetens
the mouth readily
a poem should make sense
right away.

Obscure sounds and sense
are no better than
the dumb and the deaf conversing.

Translated by B. V. L. Narayanarow.

From MOLLA RAMAYANAM
[Telugu writing]

Telugu writing
embellished with idioms and proverbs
make it right, delicious,
and a feast for the ears
of the scholars.

Translated by B. V. L. Narayanarow.

From MOLLA RAMAYANAM
[The sun moved in the sky]

The sun moved in the sky
from the East to the other end.

Fatigued, and perspiring, he dived
into the western ocean
for a bath.

Translated by B. V. L. Narayanarow.

From MOLLA RAMAYANAM
[Are they lotuses]

Are they lotuses
or the arrows of Cupid?
    Difficult to say
    of her eyes.

Are they sweet chirpings of birds
or of celestial women?
    Difficult to say
    of her words.

Is it the moon
or the looking glass?
    Difficult to say
    of her face.

Are they golden pots
or a pair of *chakravaka* birds?
    Difficult to say
    of her breasts.

Is it a flow of sapphires
or a flock of bees?
    Difficult to say
    of her hair.

Is it a sand dune
or a dais for Love God's wedding?
    Difficult to say
    of her thighs.

People got confused
as they watched
elegant her.

Translated by B. V. L. Narayanarow.

GUL-BADAN BEGUM ─────────

(1523–1603)   *Persian*

The learning and the sophistication of women in the Mughal royal families
are common knowledge. It was not unusual to find among them scholars,
poets, stateswomen, and even architects. Yet as we look back at their
achievements, Gul-Badan's history of her brother Humayun's reign, the
Humayun Nama, completed around 1587, stands out as exceptional. Such
histories commonly gave accounts of the major public events that had
taken place, political crises that threatened the state, battles that had been
fought, and grants or honors that had been given. Not so Gul-Badan
Begum's. The focus of her unusual account is the everyday life of the royal
family. She speaks of anxieties and pressures as the womenfolk experience
them. Even the emperor's travels are charted through the minds of the
women in his household. We watch with them from the ramparts as the
men ride away to war and anxiously scan the horizon for them to return.
Gul-Badan Begum's history is one of life in that large household and of
warm enduring friendships.

Gul-Badan's history, Annette Beveridge, her distinguished translator,
wrote in 1898, "lights up a woman's world." Her father, Babur, his wife
Masuma, her brothers Humayun and Askari, and Humayun's wife Hamida come alive as they might in a modern psychological novel, as warm,
rounded characters. When Babur goes into battle, or Humayun returns,
it is no less the much loved head of the family as the powerful king.
Particularly vivid is her account of the battle of Khanua in which Babur,
ignoring the warning of his astrologer, fought against the Rajput princes—
and won. The book also gives us a rare account of a pilgrimage to Mecca
the women undertook.

Scholars down the centuries have remarked on the unconventional,
spontaneous quality of Gul-Badan's original Persian prose, enlivened with
words and phrases from the Turki she would have spoken every day. The
book was written in response to a royal command from Akbar, son of
Humayun. Gul-Badan pleaded lack of scholarship, but the emperor insisted. The history was finally completed several years after his untimely
death in 1556. Gul-Badan herself lived to be eighty. The last years of her
life were spent in acts of charity and devotion. When she died, Hamida
was with her. Akbar himself helped carry her bier.

Annette Beveridge recounts how she began work on Gul-Badan's
manuscript, annotating and translating it, thinking it to be only a minor

document. But she soon decided it was a "most valuable contemporary record of the period." Like her, we are enthralled by Gul-Badan's forthright tone and the unexpected detail of her description, and like her we are left wishing this unusual woman had given us more.

We have chosen to excerpt for this book Gul-Badan's amusing account of how the independent young Hamida first refused the emperor's hand in marriage, though later she was persuaded to accept. The story as it is told here portrays Hamida as a warm, impulsive girl, an individual with her own ideas, reluctant to become a queen, and perhaps also reluctant to marry a man so much older than she, who was also, to quote Beveridge, "an opium eater and already much married." Early twentieth-century commentators, embarrassed perhaps by this show of spirit on Hamida's part, have suggested that she refused to appear before the emperor because she did not want to break the rules of purdah. Annette Beveridge's translation, done in the best conventions of Orientalist scholarship, also gives us a sense of what a feminist intervention in that tradition amounted to. So we have chosen to excerpt from her translation, completed in 1899 and published in London by the Royal Asiatic Society in 1902, rather than provide a new one.

◆

From HUMAYUN NAMA
(The History of Humayun)

As at this time Mirza Muhammad Hindal crossed the river, some said he might be going to Qandahar.[1] On hearing this his Majesty sent several people after him to make inquiry and to say: "It is reported that you plan going to Qandahar." When questioned, the mirza said: "People have given a wrong impression." On this the Emperor came[2] to see her Highness my mother.

The mirza's *haram* and all his people paid their respects to his Majesty at this meeting. Concerning Hamida-banu Begam, his Majesty asked:

---

[1] He encamped at Pat (text, Patr), about twenty miles west of the Indus and about forty miles north of Sehwan. Pat is in the *sarkar* of Siwistan, a little to the east of the highroad to Hyderabad, and not far north of Meani, the scene of Napier's victory of 1843. I am indebted to Major-General Malcolm R. Haig for the information that "Pat is now a ruin, having been destroyed in the latter part of the eighteenth century when two Kalhora chiefs of Sind called in the Afghans to quell domestic troubles."

[2] Leaving his troops to prosecute the siege of Bhakkar, and passing through Darbila where was his cousin, Yadgar-nasir. From the wording it might be supposed that Gul-Badan was with her mother in Pat, but I believe she was in Kabul at this time.

"Who is this?" They said: "The daughter of Mir Baba Dost." Khwaja Muazzam was standing opposite his Majesty, who said: "This boy will be one of my kinsmen (too?)." Of Hamida-banu he said: "She, too, is related to me."[3]

In those days Hamida-banu Begam was often in the mirza's residence *(mahall)*. Another day when his Majesty came to see her Highness my mother, he remarked: "Mir Baba Dost is related to us. It is fitting that you should give me his daughter in marriage." Mirza Hindal kept on making objections, and said: "I look on this girl as a sister and child of my own. Your Majesty is a king. Heaven forbid there should not be a proper alimony, and that so a cause of annoyance should arise."[4]

His Majesty got angry, and rose and went away. Then my mother wrote and sent a letter, saying: "The girl's mother has even before this been using persuasion.[5] It is astonishing that you should go away in anger over a few words." He wrote in reply: "Your story is very welcome to me. Whatever persuasion you may use, by my head and eyes, I will agree to it. As for what they have written about alimony, please Heaven, what they ask will be done. My waiting eye is on the road." My mother fetched his Majesty, and on that day she gave a party. When it was over, he went to his own quarters. On another day he came to my mother, and said: "Send someone to call Hamida-banu Begam here." When she sent, the begam did not come, but said: "If it is to pay my respects, I was exalted by paying my respects the other day. Why should I come again?" Another time his Majesty sent Subhan Quli, and said: "Go to Mirza Hindal, and tell him to send the begam." The mirza said: "Whatever I may

---

[3](?) interrogative, but the preceding verb is *guftand,* and not *pursidand.*

[4]This looks like a side-glance at the wasted fortunes of royalty. No kingdom! No revenues! Whence then the dowry? It is clear from the sequel that the important point was being pressed.

Jauhar says that Hamida had been already asked in marriage, but not betrothed or perhaps promised. Her objections to marry Humayun seem personal, and may indicate preference for another and dislike for him. She is said to have been fourteen years old and Humayun was thirty-three, an opium-eater, and much married already. Her objections, whatever their true basis, must have been strong or they could hardly have survived, for Gul-Badan to record, through the many years of prosperity and proud motherhood which her husband's renewed sovereignty in India and her son's distinction secured to her.

Behind Gul-Badan's story of the wooing of Hamida there were doubtless many talks over "old times" when the royal authoress was freshening her memory for her literary task, begun (it seems probable) when she was about sixty-five and Hamida some few years younger.

[5]*Madar-i-dukhtar az in ham, peshtar naz mikanad.* Perhaps, "caressed the idea."

say, she will not go. Go yourself and tell her." When Subhan Quli
went and spoke, the begam replied: "To see kings once is lawful; a second
time it is forbidden. I shall not come." On this Subhan Quli went and
represented what she had said. His Majesty remarked: "If she is not a
consort *(na mahram)*, we will make her a consort *(mahram).*"

To cut the story short: For forty days the begam resisted and discussed
and disagreed. At last her highness my mother, Dil-dar Begam, advised
her, saying: "After all you will marry someone. Better than a king, who
is there?" The begam said: "Oh yes, I shall marry someone; but he shall
be a man whose collar my hand can touch, and not one whose skirt it
does not reach." Then my mother again gave her much advice.

At last, after forty days (discussion), at mid-day on Monday (fault)
Mumi du-l-awwal *(sic)* 948H (September, 1541), and in Patr *(sic)*, his
Majesty took the astrolabe into his own blessed hand and, having chosen a propitious hour, summoned Mir Abul-baqa and ordered him to
make fast the marriage bond. He gave the mir two lakhs of ready
money for the dower *(nikahana)*, and having stayed three days after the
wedding in Patr, he set out and went by boat to Bhakkar.

Translated by Annette Beveridge (1899).

CHANDRABATI ─────────────────

(ca. 1550–1600)   *Bengali*

The relationship between art and spiritual experience or religious reform
was clearly established in the bhakti tradition that continued well into the
seventeenth century. In Chandrabati, however, we have one of the earliest
artists whose compositions were more explicitly political. Her long poem
Sundari Malua was directed against unjust laws and focused on the problems they created for women.

Chandrabati's father, Bansidas, came from Paturi, a village now in
Bangladesh, scenically situated on the banks of the river Phuleswari. Bansidas earned his living as a poet-singer, composing and performing the
popular ballads of the time. Some of his compositions have come down
to us, and his *Maanasa Bhajan* is well known even today. Scholars have
suggested that Chandrabati might have helped in its composition. Besides,
she herself wrote a short *Ramayana, Dasyu Kenaram* (Kenaram the Dacoit),
and the important text, *Sundari Malua,* which we have excerpted from
here. Chandrabati composed this long poem in the *pala gan* form, which

the dictionary defines as a narrative opera, in ballad meter. It usually deals with mythological themes and is sung. Chandrabati's *Sundari Malua* has 1,247 verses and is divided into 28 parts.

Poetic convention in her time required that a writer preface the work with a biography in verse. In the prologue to her *Ramayana,* Chandrabati describes the extreme poverty, verging on destitution, in which her family lived. They were wholly dependent on Bansidas's meager earnings as a poet. Her father educated her, however, and also taught her the rules of poetic composition. Legend has it that she, like the heroine, Malua, of her poem, was very beautiful and attracted many suitors. But she was in love with Joychandra, a childhood sweetheart, and rejected all other offers of marriage. Joychandra and Chandrabati had studied together, played together, and, as adolescents, even composed verses together. It seemed inevitable that they would marry each other. But Joychandra fell in love with someone else. He even took on her religion to marry her. Chandrabati, we are told, never recovered from the shock.

Seeking to rebuild her life, she asked of her father two things: that he build a temple for her and that he allow her to remain unmarried. Chandrabati dedicated her life to worship. She continued to compose her verses and worked on a version of the *Ramayana.* Meanwhile Joychandra seems to have tired of his wife and returned in search of Chandrabati. But for him the doors of the temple were barred. Chandrabati would not meet him. In anguish he left verses addressed to her on the door of the temple, written with the sap of a poisonous plant before he drowned himself in the Phuleswari. Chandrabati, the legend has it, stopped writing after this. Archaeologists have recently found the remains of the temple at which Chandrabati worshiped.

Some critics of Bengali literature dispute the authorship of *Sundari Malua,* but the biographical details in the prefatory dedication are Chandrabati's, and the ballad singers of Mymensingh attribute it to her. The pain and anxiety of a woman in love are movingly evoked, and the descriptions of household activities, the accounts of how food is prepared, and the recipes discussed in such detail indicate that the author must have been a woman.

The story is set in the reign of the Mughul emperor Akbar (1556–1606). Akbar had the reputation of being one of the most enlightened, just, and benevolent of emperors, but Chandrabati's poem was directed against two laws that caused a great deal of hardship for the people. These laws were enacted in the thirteenth century, during Allauddin Khilji's rule, but continued to be enforced. Both laws required the payment of taxes, but since there were no amounts specified, people were at the mercy of local landlords or officials, who could set extortionist rates. Property could be seized and the womenfolk in the family kept in custody or sent to the *hauli,* which was a prison for women. *Sundari Malua* depicts the sufferings of women under these unjust laws.

Chandrabati's women characters, the critic Jharna Dhar comments, are nearly always more liberal and magnanimous, stronger and more determined, than her men. The relationships between women, too, are refreshingly unstereotypical. Indian literature of all kinds is full of the enmity between daughter-in-law and mother-in-law. But in this story, when Malua is released from the hauli, her mother-in-law stands up for her and argues, in a remarkable passage, against the elders of the village, who want to exile her. Chandrabati also depicts the village women as joining together to argue Malua's case.

A brief outline of the elaborate plot will help the reader place the extracts translated here. Binod, the son of a poor widow, and Malua fall in love. Malua is extraordinarily beautiful. Though her father, Hiradhar, has received several offers for her hand, none of them meets with his approval. He likes Binod, but hesitates because the boy is poor. Irked by Hiradhar's attitude, Binod sets out to earn enough money to ask for Malua in marriage. The first extract translated here describes the wedding night. The first night after a wedding is passed in revelry. Young people, friends, and relatives of the bride and groom play traditional games and make merry. The bride and groom are not allowed to sleep. On the second night, the *kaal raat,* or Black Night, the bride sleeps beside her mother-in-law. The third night is the Bright Night, or night of consummation. A bed of flowers is prepared for the young people and they are alone for the first time. A description like this is often a set piece in such narratives, but the freshness of Chandrabati's imagery and the dramatic presentation are remarkable.

The main sections of the narrative poem deal with two episodes in which the family is harassed and attacked by priests and administrators, who use the black laws, which are Chandrabati's principal concern in the poem, to further their personal ends. Malua, her husband, and her mother-in-law, the story goes, live together happily for a while, but problems arise when the local *qazi* (magistrate), attracted by Malua's beauty, propositions her. Angered by her rejection, he imposes a fine of five hundred silver coins. Because the family is impoverished, Malua and Binod have to sell their property to pay the fine and again to find money to support themselves. Malua struggles to keep herself and her mother-in-law alive. Binod returns and is able to redeem his land, but they are soon in trouble once more. Encouraged by the qazi, the diwan (a powerful local administrator), demands that Malua be sent to live with him as his mistress. Unless his wishes are complied with, he decrees, Binod will be buried alive. Malua is determined to save him. She goes to the hauli and tells the diwan that she is bound by a vow to sleep with no man for a period of time. The diwan agrees to wait. Meanwhile, Malua's brothers come to the rescue. In a surprise attack they kill the diwan's guards, though he himself escapes. Malua, Binod, and Binod's mother decide to go back to Malua's parental village and set up house there.

The second extract translated here is taken from section 27 and refers to a subsequent episode. Since Malua has lived in the hauli, she cannot, the elders declare, be allowed back into the village. So Malua sets up house on its outskirts. Her mother-in-law goes with her, but Binod stays behind. Once, while out hunting, Binod is bitten by a snake and almost dies. Malua finds him and nurses him back to health. This time the village women rally round Malua and demand that she be allowed back into the village. It is the power of her virtue that has brought Malua's husband back to life, they claim. But the elders will have none of it. Binod, his mother, and the other women comfort Malua, but disappointed, unwilling to burden the family further, she drowns herself in the river.

◆

From SUNDARI MALUA
Section 15 [After the Black Night comes the
Bright Night]

After the Black Night comes the Bright Night
And the bed of flowers awaits bride and groom
With a lamp, like the evening star, lighting the room.
While Malua stands by the door, the night
Deepening, her eyes heavy with sleep, as Binod
Gently raises the veil from her face that
Glows like new gold, like the full moon.
Passionate, Binod lifts Malua's heavy hair,
Which hangs down to her feet, and spreads it wide.

"Friend of my heart," breathes Malua, "What
Are you doing? Wait, the time's not ripe. Do bees
Come to a flower before it fills with honey? Do we
Pluck buds before they blossom? Don't we
Leave the hot rice to cool before we eat? Let
The night grow chill. Your brothers' wives are yet
Awake, watching through chinks in the wattled
Wall, listening to our clothes rustle, to
My jewelry tinkle, waiting to tease us, to make
Their jokes in the morning, so no more tonight, I beg."

Now the lamp is out, the room quiet, auspicious
The night, auspicious the hour. At dawn
They rise and wash with water drawn
The day before: Binod, on a low stool, washes
His hands and feet.

Section 27 [Back to life she'd brought her husband]

Back to life she'd brought her husband
The faithful wife, the virtuous wife.
In crowds women thronged to see her
Greeting her with triumphant cries
Singing her praises everyone.

. . . .

   "How can you welcome her with flowers?"
Asked the elders, "How offer her pan?
Is she so virtuous? So faithful? Why should she
Resort to sorcery then?"

. . . .

   The brother of Binod's mother, Halwal Sardar,
A village elder, decreed: "Taking this woman back
Will cost us rank and caste. For three long months
She lived between Muslim walls. The shame of it
Would shatter a tiger! Who can save a doe
Caught in the wild beast's claws? We can do
Nothing once chastity and caste are gone.
Have we not turned away other weeping
Women who came back in shame from the Hauli?"

Then the brother-in-law of Binod's father spoke
After careful thought: "No. We cannot
Take such a woman into our house. I warned
Binod's mother at the wedding, but she thought
She knew better. Is it easy, in times like these,
To protect a beautiful woman? Even
The wives of kings are not safe. Muslims
Veil their women. Only peasants' wives
Go about openly, taunted at market and riverside,
Deaf to news of the times. Binod should not
Have married such a beauty!
Now she's lost both caste and standing. Beauty
Invites disaster. We've supervised her conduct,
Chastised her, wasted money to protect her—
And all for what? Don't let her into the house!
What more shall I live to see!"

"She's my heart's gold," Binod's mother said.
"My son's wife. No matter what you decree,
I shall never renounce her. She stood by me
In times of trouble, toiled long days
To keep us alive. She brought Binod back
From the clasp of death; no truer Sati
Can you find. She's the light of our
Sorrow-dark house, the roof of a hut
That had none. How can I live without her?
You think she's a sorceress. You want
To turn her away. She sleeps out of doors,
Lives like a fieldhand. I'll make my bed
With her, she'll sleep in my arms, we'll weep
The whole night through. I know I won't
Live long. Banish her, if you must,
But not before I die."

Translated by Madhuchhanda Karlekar.

BAHINABAI ⎯⎯⎯⎯⎯⎯⎯⎯⎯⎯

(1628–1700) *Marathi*

The Vedas cry aloud, the Puranas shout,
"No good may come to woman."

I was born with a woman's body
How am I to attain Truth?

"They are foolish, seductive, deceptive—
Any connection with a woman is disastrous."

Bahina says, "If a woman's body is so harmful,
How in this world will I reach Truth?"

Though these verses have invariably been read as Bahinabai's lament over the fate of being born a woman, to the contemporary reader what comes through in the bold, dramatic cast of this abanga is her skepticism, her rebelliousness, and her insistent refusal to abandon her aspiration for the truth. The abanga is an elaborated, regularized form of the popular Marathi *ovi* meter, which is used in the songs women sing as they grind flour or husk grain. An abanga has rhymed lines and expresses religious sentiment. The form is associated with the Varkari sect, especially with the saint-poet Tukaram, and flourished between the end of the thirteenth century and the seventeenth century.

Autobiographical writings are rarely found outside the tradition of individualism and the sense of personal worth it inculcates. Yet, of the 473 abangas of this seventeenth-century poet and philosopher that are available today, the first 78 are an *atmanivedana,* an autobiographical account of her soul's journey through twelve previous lives as well as through her present one. In the first section of these 78, Bahinabai traces her life from the childhood spent in the village of Devgar in what is today northern Maharashtra. Her parents, Aaudev and Janaki, were both brahmins. Bahinabai was the first child in the family. Since her birth had been foretold by a holy man, and shortly after she was born her father found a gold mohur wrapped in an auspicious yellow cloth by the wayside, she was regarded as a child who would bring good fortune to the family. Clearly Bahinabai was a cherished child and accounts of her childhood are happy ones, but she preferred reciting the "names of God" to playing with other children.

When she was three, her parents arranged for her to be married to a relative in a nearby village. He was thirty and had been married before, but, writes Bahinabai, he was a scholar and "an excellent jewel of a man." After she was married she continued, as custom required, to live with her parents until she attained puberty. But as a result of a family quarrel, Bahinabai, her parents, and her husband left Devgar. They journeyed along the banks of the Godavari, and a month later they arrived at the Mahadeva forest where they joined other pilgrims in worship: "seeing Sankara we were comforted, and through our bhakti we asked that his hand of assurance might rest upon us," she says. The family begged, as wandering holy people customarily do, for grain, which they cooked. "It tasted to me like nectar, for in the eating of it one's sins seemed burnt away. I was nine years of age and I have revealed my heart's emotions."

By the time she was eleven the family had moved to Kolhapur, where Bahinabai had the unusual experiences with the calf that are reported in the sections of her atmanivedana excerpted here. According to Shivaji Narahar Bhave, the author of a dictionary of terms used in Varkari literature, the calf must have been a *yogabhrasta,* a person who had reached a high state of yogic concentration in a previous life, but had, for some failing, been reborn as a calf; all the same, the calf was destined to have a human companion like Bahinabai and to be part of a religious community.

Some years later Bahinabai began to experience the visions of Vithoba and his famous seventeenth-century low-caste (sudra) poet-devotee, Tukaram, that were to change the direction and scope of her life. In these visions, Tukaram appeared to her, fed her nectar, and taught her a mantra. The poems of the last sections are the moving, reflective writings of one who has "seen her death" and found "it is a good omen." Many of Bahinabai's unusual abangas explore the tensions in her marriage and their resolution. Despite attempts by early twentieth-century commentators such as Justin E. Abbot to see it otherwise, the emphasis in her poems is clearly more on the conflict between husband and wife than on its resolution. Nevertheless, it is remarkable that she nearly always portrays her husband's feelings with empathy even when they are hostile or destructive toward her.

Unlike many of the women saints in the bhakti period, Bahinabai does not present herself as one who breaks free of the constraints of marriage and wanders abroad in search of God who is imaged as a lover. Her bhakti is not the ecstatic release of a Mirabai or an Akkamahadevi. Perhaps out of sagacity, perhaps out of timidity, she reconciled her duties to her husband with her devotion to God and His saints. Because the archaic Marathi and the elaborate patterning of the original make this a particularly difficult text to translate, we have retained an early prose rendering. The intratextual numbering indicates the verses, or the units of rhymed lines, in the original.

The following translation is reprinted from *Bahinabai: A Translation of Her Autobiography and Verses* by Justin E. Abbot (Poona: Scottish Mission Industries, 1929).

◆

From ATMANIVEDANA

Abanga 14

(1) Now it happened on a certain occasion, when I was in my eleventh year, that there was a great festal event on a Monday. (2) During this festival a cow was given to Bahirambhat, the donor having found a cow about to calve. (3) This one-coloured cow was wholly black. He made a *pradakshina,* waved the tail over himself, and gave the cow away. (4) Her horns were gilded with gold leaf, her hoofs were silvered, and she was covered with a yellow robe. (5) The cow was given with all the proper ceremonies, and everybody came to see her. (6) A calf was born to the cow, and Bahirambhat took her to his house. The calf drank the milk that was milked from the cow. (7) Ten days passed, and on the eleventh day a Brahmin appeared to Bahirambhat in a dream and said: (8) "Offer this one-coloured cow to the Brahmin who is occupying your veranda." (9) Bahirambhat made the dream come true, and gave the cow with sincere good wishes to my husband. (10) The hearts of us all rejoiced in this gift, and the care of the cow fell to us.

(11) My father and mother went every day to get grass. She was cared for carefully, and it was done with joy.

(12) The calf of the cow was also of one colour, and it had a great affection for me. (13) Only if I unfastened it, would it go to get its milk, and as I milked the cow it was with me. (14) I was the only one to give it water, and the only one to feed it with grass. Without me it was unhappy. When I went out to draw water, the calf would bawl aloud, and with tail erect, would follow me. (16) The people watched us and thought all this a strange thing while the calf and the cow looked casually at us. (17) When the calf was loosened, it would not even go to the cow. (18) Only when I gave it grass, would it eat. Only when I gave it water, would it drink. (19) At night it slept on my bedding. As it listened to the reading of the Purana it would sob with emotion.

(20) When I went to a *kirtan,* it would come along with me and stand quietly listening. (21) The cow would be in her stall at home, but the calf would be at the *kirtan.* When I went to my bath the calf would follow me. (22) People would remark to me in various terms, "The calf acts most extraordinarily with you." (23) Some remarked, "The calf must be a *yogabhrashta.*" Some said of me, "Its habits are bad." (24) Others said, "The calf is her debtor and only when the debt is paid will she be rid of it." (25) The calf, however, would not leave me, and I loved to be with it. (26) If the calf was not in sight, I was troubled; I felt like a fish out of water. (27) Whether I was grinding, or pounding grain or carrying water, I was unhappy, though with others, without the calf. (28) My husband was of a fiery temper, and he did not like this, but finally his heart yielded to pity. (29) Said he, "Let it be. You have no child, and this calf is a plaything for your heart. (30) You enjoy listening to the puranic stories and *kirtans,* and the calf costs you nothing."

(31) It was at this time that Jayaram Gosavi happened to come there. (32) He conducted *kirtans* from house to house where the Brahmins worshipped, and he began to feed them. (33) He conducted his *kirtans* both at night and during the day. My father and mother attended them with much pleasure. (34) I also went with them to these *kirtans,* and the calf used to go with me also. (35) Where my mother sat, there I sat also, and the calf would rush in and stand beside me. (36) Inoffensive in its actions, it stood listening to the *kirtan* and the loud acclaim of God's names. (37) After the verses of praise, when all bowed to the ground, the calf also placed its head on the floor.

(38) Everybody laughed when they saw this, but they were kindly and happy over it. (39) They said, "It is a *yogabhrashta,* a worshipper

of Hari in a former birth. In the form of a calf see how it acts as one indifferent to the things of this world."

(40) It now happened on a certain day that Moropan invited the *bhaktas* to the performance of a *kirtan*. (41) The day was the eleventh of the month, and at noon with great rejoicing the *Hari-kirtan* was begun. (42) Jayaram Gosavi, with his multitude of disciples, sat in the assembly on special seats. (43) There was singing accompanied with cymbals and drums. A large crowd had gathered there. (44) Among them were myself, my parents and my brother, and we listened with exceeding joy to the recitation of the *Puranic* stories. (45) The calf seated itself by me, but some people dragged it away to the door. (46) They said, "There is no sufficient seating space for the people. Is a beast a proper creature to be a listener?" (47) I began to weep for my calf, and the Gosavi heard me. (48) And as the calf cried, I fell to weeping. Someone explained the matter to the Gosavi. (49) They said, "This is a little girl living at the house of Bahirambhat. She has come to this *Shri Hari-kirtan*. (50) She has a calf with her, which she has always following her. (51) The calf has been taken outside, because of the seating difficulties. For this reason the girl is sulking and crying. (52) The calf is outside crying out, and she is crying here inside, hence this commotion." (53) Jayaram Swami was a discerner of the soul. He recognised the soul of the calf. (54) "Bring the calf here," he said. "Can Hari, the knower of the soul, not be in the soul of a calf? (55) It is overcome with desire to listen to the *kirtan*. One should not call it a beast." (56) So he had the calf brought in, and had it stand by him.

As Jayaram looked at the calf, he had a feeling of joy. (57) On account of my *prarabdha,* because of good deeds done in a former birth, the kindly man called me to him. (58) Looking intently at us, he caressed us both though this was unacceptable to the people. (59) The *katha* (Puranic recitation) continued with very loud refrains, for the hearts of the Vaishnavas were full of joy. (60) Jayaram Gosavi thought that both parties were true hearted and of good deeds. (61) He said, "The calf stands during the *katha,* in its actions showing intense attention. (62) This is a little girl, of tender age. It is very strange that she so loves to listen to these stories. (63) Is there anyone here at the *katha* belonging to her?" (64) One replied, "Yes, her father and mother. She has a husband, a very worthy man. But her *vairagya* seems very great. (65) She comes to these readings of the *Puranas* with her father and mother and brings the calf along with her." (66) At this point I acted for myself. I prostrated myself at his feet. (67) The calf also fell at his feet as I did. To all the people it was extraordinary. (68) At his left and right there were two persons. They raised us up, the calf and myself. (69) When the *katha* was ended, the people went away, remarking to themselves on the event, such as had never occurred before. (70) Bahirambhat and many others also said, "Who knows what this is a sign of." (71) Says Bahini, "This is what happened at Kolhapur, and now I will tell you what happened thereafter."

Abanga 15

(1) With my father, mother, and brother and accompanied by the calf, we then returned to our lodgings. (2) At that time only two *ghatikas* of the night remained. The calf was fed, and the cow was milked. (3) Bahirambhat performed his bath in the spirit of fire-worship, and the *kartik* lamps twinkled in the sky. (4) I swept and cleaned the floors, performed my bath, and caressed the cow and calf. (5) My husband also performed his bath. Kolhapur is the Gaya of the South country.

(6) It happened that at that time there was a certain woman named Nirabai. (7) She began relating what had happened at the *katha*. (8) She let fall on my husband's ears a recital of all the events at the *katha,* as being most extraordinary, the actions of the calf, and my crying. His ears were filled with her recital. (9) She added how Jayaram Gosavi, while in an ecstatic state, had placed his hand upon her head. (10) Great was her good fortune that he should speak to her, and give her his gracious blessing. (11) My husband was a religious mendicant by profession, but a man of very angry disposition. He rushed up to the house. (12) He seized me by the braids of my hair, and beat me to his heart's content. Bahirambhat was greatly distressed at this, (13) but could not restrain him from beating me. The cow mourned aloud, and the calf also was in great distress. (14) All this happened to me when in my eleventh year. In what duty to my husband had I failed? (15) My mother, father, and brother kept quiet, until my husband gradually restrained his rage. (16) When he became quiet, they asked him why he was so troubling his wife? (17) He replied, "In last night's *katha* what special greatness or devotion did she notice in Jayaram! (18) Who cares for the *Purana!* Who cares for the *Hari-katha!* I'll give her a beating and nothing else." (19) Thus talking, my husband again could not control his rage, just like a fire out of control. (20) Says Bahini, "My body accepted it, who can ward off the force of Fate?"

Abanga 16

(1) When it came to his mind to do so he beat me violently. He tied me (hand and foot) into a bundle and threw me aside. (2) Bahirambhat cried to him, "Get out of here! He seems like a murderous wretch!" (3) My father and mother pleaded with Bahirambhat and soon quieted him. (4) "Have mercy on us this day," they said, "tomorrow morning we will seek for another place." (5) In the meantime the cow and the calf would eat no grass, nor drink water. (6) And my husband, seeing this refusal of the cow and calf, untied me and set me free. (7) And as I came close to the cow and the calf, they lowed, just as a mother coos over her son. (8) When I saw the calf and the cow, I said to myself, it is better that I should die. (9) Says Bahini, "It was their great affection for me that made them refuse the grass and water given to them."

Abanga 17

(1) They would eat no grass and drink no water. I also refused all food. (2) They would not arise from the place on which they were lying. Everybody came to see what was happening. (3) Someone told Jayaram Svami of what was going on, and he also came to see, at this time of my extremity. (4) My husband made him a *namaskar,* with a mind sincerely devoted to him. (5) He gave Jayaram Svami a special seat, and Bahirambhat worshipped him. (6) People gathered to see with their own eyes what was taking place. The Svami also at that time experienced a sense of joy. (7) He said, "O Brahmin, you are her husband. I am going to tell you the truth; listen with attention. (8) Your wife is a *Yogabhrashta,* and the manner of life she must adopt is of a very austere kind. Now do not distress her any more. (9) By her special wifely duties she will do you service; and you will save your soul. (10) You must possess some good deed done in a former birth. By means of it you have become associated with her. (11) The cow and the calf are her companions and one with her in her religious life. (12) The calf is her guru; the calf is her means of salvation, for it destroys the cord that binds it, (13) and all who live in association with her, will joyfully drink the sweet juice of *bhakti.* (14) If you listen to me, it will be well for you. But what authority have I here?" (15) Says Bahini, "As Jayaram thus advised, he saw that all signs were favourable."

Abanga 32

(1) My husband now began to say, "We are Brahmins. We should spend our time in the study of the Vedas. (2) What is all this! The *shudra* Tuka! Seeing him in a dream! My wife is ruined by all this! What am I to do? (3) Who cares for Jayaram, and who for Pandurang. My home has been destroyed! (4) What care I for singing the names and praises of Hari? Even in my dreams I know not *bhakti*. (5) Who cares for saints and *sadhus!* Who cares for the feelings of *bhakti!* Let us always be found in the order of the religious mendicants." (6) Says Bahini, "Thus did my husband think and discuss the matter in his own mind."

Abanga 33

(1) This is how my husband considered the subject in his own mind: "I will abandon her, and go into a forest, (2) for people are going to bow down to her, while she regards me as worth but a straw. (3) They will discuss with this woman the meaning of the *kathas,* but she herself will consider me a low fellow. (4) The people make regardful enquiries about her while I, who am a Brahmin, have become a fool! (5) They are all calling her a Gosavin. Who will show me respect in her presence?" (6) Says Bahini, "Thus my husband discussed the matter in his own mind, and gave his own mind advice."

Abanga 34

(1) He said to himself, "This is my wife's condition. Do not remain here any longer. (2) Let me rather go to some sacred river, for asceticism is now my lot." (3) He made his *namaskar* to his mother-in-law and father-in-law saying, "My wife is advanced three months in pregnancy. (4) I am going on a pilgrimage to sacred places; my wife has become mad after God; look after her. (5) I do not wish to see her face any longer. Who is to make up to us our loss in reputation? (6) Who is going to stay here and suffer humiliation at her hands? Who cares to keep such a wife as she is!" (7) Says Bahini, "Thus did my husband talk, and I then began to think to myself."

Abanga 35

(1) What am I to do with my Fate? I must bear whatever comes to my lot. (2) I am not one who is possessed. My body is not subject to demoniac possession. (3) Therefore, holding to my own special duties, I will give my mind to listening to the Scriptures, and the winning of

God. (4) My duty is to serve my husband, for he is God to me. My husband himself is the Supreme Brahma. (5) The water in which my husband's feet are washed has the value of all the sacred waters put together. Without that holy water, (all I do is) valueless. (6) If I transgress my husband's commands, all the sins of the world will be on my head. (7) The Vedas in fact say that it is the husband who has the authority in the matter of religious duties, earthly possessions, desires, and salvation. (8) This is then the determination, and the desire of my heart. I want my thought concentrated on my husband.

Translated by Justin E. Abbot.

SANCIYA HONNAMMA ————————

(late 17th century)   *Kannada*

"The stories I tell are of wives who understood their husband's moods and desires and served them well," wrote this well-known Kannada poet whose *Hadibadeya Dharma* (Duties of a Devoted Wife) is still so popular that verses from it are recited in ordinary homes even today. For a woman like Honnamma, who was only a servant in the king's palace, to have written a book at a time when only noblewomen or bhaktas composed poetry was an exceptional achievement. It is also remarkable that the book continues to be read today and that Honnamma has not been forgotten.

Honnamma worked in the palace of the Mysore king Chikadevaraya (1672–1704). The appellative Sanciya suggests she had the task of preparing and rolling the betel leaves, or pan, for members of the royal household to chew. *(Sanci* means bag, and probably refers to the bag that she must have carried to hold the paraphernalia for rolling pan). Legend has it that Honnamma was a great favorite of the queen, Devajammanni, and that the court poet Singaracharya recognized her talent for words, taught her how to read and write, and trained her in the rules of poetic composition. He was so pleased with his pupil that he called her *sarasasahityada varadevata,* literally, a "goddess of exquisite poetry." Honnamma is a traditional thinker and writes about socially accepted mores. She was loyal to the king and upheld the values of her times, but her poems are sensitive to the pain in women's lives and are unusually sympathetic for such normative writings. The verses chosen for translation are from *Garathiya Haadu* (Song of a Married Woman).

◆

From GARATHIYA HAADU
(Song of a Married Woman)
[Wasn't it woman who bore them]

Wasn't it woman who bore them,
Wasn't it woman who raised them,
Then why do they always blame woman,
These boors, these blind ones.

In the womb they're the same
When they're growing they're the same
Later the girl will take, with love, what's given
The boy will take his share by force.

For money's sake, for trust
And friendship's sake
Don't give a girl to a walking corpse
Bereft of virtue, youth, and looks.

Don't say, "We're poor people, where
Can we get jewels from?"
Instead of spending on yourself
Provide your daughters with clothes and ornaments.

Translated by Tejaswini Niranjana.

MUDDUPALANI ——————————————

(ca. 1730–1790)   *Telugu*

Which other woman of my kind has
felicitated scholars with gifts and money?
To which other woman of my kind have
epics been dedicated?
Which other woman of my kind has
won such acclaim in each of the arts?
You are incomparable,
Muddupalani, among your kind.

These are the verses in which Muddupalani introduces herself in the autobiographical overture to her erotic epic *Radhika Santwanam* (Appeasing
Radhika), which was to become so controversial in the early twentieth

century. Significantly, she traces her literary lineage through her mother, her grandmother, and her paternal aunt, each of whom she describes in some detail. Of herself, Muddupalani has more to say:

A face that glows like the full moon,
skills of conversation, matching the countenance.
Eyes filled with compassion,
matching the speech.
A great spirit of generosity,
matching the glance.
These are the ornaments
that adorn Palani,
when she is praised by kings.

Muddupalani was a courtesan attached to the retinue of Pratapasimha (1739–1763), one of the Nayaka kings of Tanjavur. These rulers were scholars and poets, well versed in Telugu, Tamil, Marathi, and Sanskrit. They were lovers of music and literature and great patrons of the arts. There were other distinguished women poets and scholars in their courts. One of them, Ramabhadramba, writes in her *Raghunadhaabhyudayam* about women in the Thanjavur courts who composed poetry in eight languages. Traditionally the only women who had access to scholarship and the arts of dancing, music, and literature were courtesans. They also enjoyed an unabridged right to hold and inherit property and therefore retained control of their wealth. They had the status of freewomen, whose place in the public sphere was undisputed, and many of them commanded respect for their learning and their accomplishments. Their right to choose their lovers and friends was seldom questioned. About Muddupalani herself, we know little more than her poem tells us.

Radhika Santwanam consists of five hundred and eighty-four poems, divided into four sections. It tells the tale of Radha, Krishna's aunt, a woman in her prime who brings up Ila Devi from childhood and then gives her in marriage to Krishna. The poem describes in detail Ila Devi's puberty and the consummation of her marriage to Krishna. Radha advises the young bride on how she should respond to Krishna's lovemaking, and Krishna on handling his young bride tenderly. But the poem also captures at the same time the pain of a woman in her prime who must give up her own desire and yearning. At one point, unable to bear the grief of her own separation from Krishna, whom she desires herself, Radha breaks down and rages against Krishna for having abandoned her. Krishna gently appeases her and she is comforted by his loving embrace. It is from this section that the poem takes its title.

In an unusual third section, Krishna complains that Radha insists on making love even though he does not want to. No other Telugu poet—man or woman—has written about a woman taking the initiative in a sexual relationship. In another section, Muddupalani speaks of men as inconsistent, impatient, and unreliable. The impression a reader carries away from the poem is of a poet who drew on her own everyday experience to rewrite the classical story of Radha and Krishna. Muddupalani also wrote several seven-lined songs, or *saptapadalu,* which are not available today. The genre in which Muddupalani wrote *Radhika Santwanam,* the *sringara- prabandham,* was a popular one in her times, but she is the only woman to have written an erotic epic and it is possible that the work became so controversial a century later principally because it was written by a woman.

The epic poem was first published in 1887 and a second edition, with a commentary, was brought out in 1907 by Venkatanarasu, a linguist work- ing with the lexicographer C. P. Brown. Neither of these editions, how- ever, satisfied Bangalore Nagaratnamma, a courtesan herself, who "compared the published versions with the manuscript," and brought out what she considered the "proper work" in 1911. "I find the work im- mensely beautiful," she wrote in the preface, "and as it has been com- posed, not only by a woman, but a woman of our community, I felt it was necessary to publish the proper work."

Nagaratnamma's edition was banned and a long controversy followed. For a discussion of that, the reader must turn back to the Introduction.

◆

From RADHIKA SANTWANAM
(Appeasing Radhika)
[Move on her lips]

Move on her lips
the tip of your tongue;
    do not scare her
    by biting hard.
Place on her cheeks
a gentle kiss;
    do not scratch her
    with your sharp nails.
Hold her nipple
with your fingertips;
    do not scare her
    by squeezing it tight.
Make love
gradually;
    do not scare her
    by being aggressive.
      I am a fool

to tell you all these.
When you meet her
and wage your war of love
would you care to recall
my "do's and dont's," Honey?

Translated by B. V. L. Narayanarow.

From RADHIKA SANTWANAM
(Appeasing Radhika)
[Honey, / why do you think / I stamped on Kali?]

Honey,
Why do you think
I stamped on Kali?
    The snake seemed to rival
    your lovely plait.
Why do you think
I broke the bow of Kamsa?
    It seemed to rival
    your shapely brows.
Why do you think
I uprooted the Govardhan?
    The mountain seemed to rival
    your firm breasts.
Why do you think
I hurt Kuvalayaapeeda?
    The elephant seemed to rival
    your comely gait.
Please, therefore,
ask yourself
if it is fair for you
to treat me shabbily.

Translated by B. V. L. Narayanarow.

From RADHIKA SANTWANAM
(Appeasing Radhika)
[If I ask her not to kiss me]

If I ask her not to kiss me,
    stroking on my cheeks
    she presses my lips hard against hers.

If I ask her not to touch me,
    stabbing me with her firm breasts
    she hugs me.

If I ask her not to get too close
for it is not decorous,
    she swears at me loudly.

If I tell her of my vow not
to have a woman in my bed,
    she hops on
    and begins the game of love.

Appreciative,
she lets me drink from her lips,
fondles me, talks on,
making love again and again.
    How could I stay away
    from her company?

Translated by B. V. L. Narayanarow.

MAHLAQA BAI CHANDA ————————

(1767–1824)   *Urdu*

The end of the eighteenth century, the period in which Mahlaqa Bai
Chanda grew up and received the elaborate education that was expected
for her as a *tawaif*, was in some ways as turbulent a period in the history
of the Asaf Jahi Sultanate as it was in the Mughal Empire. Mahlaqa was
born in Aurangabad, which was the center of Asaf Jahi culture at that
time. In 1776, when Nizam Ali Khan shifted the capital to Hyderabad,
she moved along with the court. Though we do not find much evidence

of it in her writing, as a well-known and powerful courtesan, she would have witnessed many of these public events at close quarters.

Etymologically, *tawaif* is the plural of the Arabic word *taifa*, meaning "group"; but the word *tawaif* as a singular in Urdu is the term for a prostitute. The common and less respectable word for a prostitute in Urdu is *randi*. There were various types of tawaifs, those who lived permanently with a man on payment and eventually might have married him, those who led an itinerant life moving from city to city, and those who kept permanent house in a city. In some cities, especially in Lucknow, the tawaif had a more or less respectable place in society and was admired for her sophistication and culture. The elite of the town sent their sons to her for education in manners and letters.

As a young girl Mahlaqa was influenced by the work of Siraj Allahabadi, a famous court poet of that time. She was a singer of high caliber, and, as was customary, composed her own songs. She is also remembered for her dynamism, her sense of humor, and her beauty. Sameena Shaukat, her biographer, argues that Mahlaqa reached the peak of her career as a poet and singer in Hyderabad and that among her many admirers were powerful noblemen and members of the royal family. A patron of the arts, she gave large sums of money away and endowed several shrines, some of which still stand. When she died, her enormous wealth comprising gold, silver, and jewelry was distributed among homeless women.

It was not uncommon for women of her profession to write and to acquire learning or indeed to cultivate a sophisticated wit, yet very little of their work has been recorded or preserved. Fortunately, Mahlaqa's poems were compiled and published after her death as *Gulzar-e-Mahlaqa* (Mahlaqa's Garden of Flowers).

Most of her poems are composed in a popular poetic form known as the *ghazal*. The ghazal originally developed in Iran and consists of couplets, varying in number, each complete in itself. The couplets may or may not relate to one another thematically, for the integrity of the poem lies in the rhyme scheme, the quality of which is particularly difficult to capture in translation. The first two lines, forming the verse called the *matla*, have end rhymes. The rhyme is repeated in the second line of each verse. The poet's *nom de plume* appears in the last two lines, or the *maqta*. Ghazals are usually recited or sung, and draw on a whole set of conventional images and symbols. Since they are repeatedly used, they develop layers of meaning and nuance for a cultivated audience. For instance, in the ghazal translated here, Mahlaqa's use of *bulbul*, a Persian songbird, which is a symbol of the male lover and of devotion, and the *gul*, or rosebud, which is the symbol for beauty and the sweetheart, is conventional, but her images echo and build on the bulbul and the gul in other poems, classical and contemporary. *Saqi* is one who served wine in a drinking house in Iran, hence symbolically a source of inspiration.

The critic Sameena Shaukat considers Mahlaqa the first woman to compose poetry in Urdu. Thirty-nine of her ghazals, each comprising five couplets, have been preserved. Though Urdu was commonly spoken, especially in areas where there were communities of Muslims, it was not the language of the court or of learning in the north. In the southern Dakkhani regions of Golconda (present-day Hyderabad) and Bijapur, however, poetry was composed in Urdu as early as the sixteenth and seventeenth centuries. Most commentators think north Indian writing in Urdu emerged under the influence of the Dakkhani form.

◆

[Hoping to blossom (one day) into a flower]

Hoping to blossom (one day) into a flower,
Every bud sits, holding its soul in its fist.

Between the fear of the fowler and (approaching) autumn
The bulbul's life hangs by a thread.

Thy sly glance is more murderous than arrow or sword;
It has shed the blood of many a lover.

How can I liken a candle to thy (glowing) cheek?
The candle is blind with the fat in its eyes.

How can Chanda be dry lipped, O saqi of the heavenly wine!
She has drained the cup of thy love.

Translated by Syed Sirajuddin.

TARIGONDA VENKAMAMBA ⸻

(ca. 1800–1866)   *Telugu*

The anxiety that her devotion, her talent, her scholarship, and her beauty were excessive for a woman whose rightful place was in the home dominates almost every anecdote about this poet-saint's childhood. As her reputation grew, and stories about her piety spread "like the fragrance of a flower," the initial concern about her unruly obsessions gradually turned into admiration for this "rebel in the highest cause." Right through her lifetime, however, Venkamamba continued to be criticized and persecuted for her unorthodox behavior.

Venkamamba was born in the village Tarigonda in the southeast of Andhra Pradesh, the only child of her parents, Krishnamacharya and Mangamamba. Rather than play with others of her own age, young Venkamamba would sit apart, engrossed in worship. Even as a child she could compose and sing devotional songs extempore. Even such extraordinary natural ability, her father realized, could profit from formal training. So he sent her to work under the guru Subramanya Desika, who was quick to recognize her talent and intelligence, and taught her "everything he knew." Venkamamba's fame spread rapidly. Unnerved, her father put a stop to her education and began efforts to find her a husband. The story goes that when she was asked to help her mother with domestic tasks, Venkamamba, in what was in her society an unthinkable act, refused, declaring she would "work only for God." Each prospective bridegroom who came to see her rejected her, saying she was either too beautiful or too intelligent to be a wife. Finally Venkatachalappa, who had fallen in love with her beauty, agreed to marry her. Her father ordered her to be a submissive wife and take good care of her husband's household. Venkatachalappa decided he would get rid of her religious fervor and tame her, but Venkamamba would not allow him near her.

Not long after, he died. Now began another ordeal. Brahminical tradition insisted that widows shave their heads, and her relatives tried to compel Venkamamba to do so. "What right do you have to make me shave my head and sit in a corner," she retorted. "I am married to God, and no one can make me a widow." In defiance she continued to adorn her hair with flowers and wear her jewelry. She also immersed herself in writing poetry and was so engrossed in it that she was often unaware of what happened around her and forgot to eat or drink. As might be expected, she incurred the wrath of the society she had so summarily rejected. She was called a prostitute, and people criticized her pride in her beauty and her youth, and her arrogance in wearing flowers and ornaments even after her husband had died. They called her mad, and demanded that she be excommunicated.

According to the legend, a complaint against her reached as far as the Sringeri Shankaracharya. She was summoned, but when she arrived, she refused to offer obeisance to him. While the brahmins insisted, she asked the Shankaracharya to rise from his seat and then bowed before it. It burst into flames. Awed by her superhuman powers, the Shankaracharya ordered that she be taken back into the community.

Venkamamba wrote songs and composed for Yakshagana, a folk theater popular in Andhra Pradesh and Karnataka. Her work was apparently well known in her time, although it is scarcely read even in scholarly circles today and is difficult to locate in library collections. We found only scattered references. The linguist C. P. Brown, for example, comments in his Telugu–English lexicon (1852) that "the *Dwipada Bhagawatam* (Life of Lord

Krishna in Couplet Form) was (also) written by a poetess who was living in the year 1840," which we presume is a reference to Venkamamba. We were able to locate references to fourteen other works by Venkamamba; notable among them are *Siva Natakam* (The Dance of Siva), *Parijatapaharanam* (Stealing the Celestial Parijata Flower), *Narasimha Satakam* (A Hundred Poems on Narasimha), *Venkateswara Mahatyamu* (On the Greatness of Venkateswara), and *Chenchu Natakam* (A Play about Chenchu).

In a critical essay written in 1887, the social reformer Veereshalingam, who had so disparaged Muddupalani's poetry, spoke well of Venkamamba. Probably because of its religious themes, he considered her poetry "delightful" but hastened to qualify his praise by adding that it was "marred by some minor faults." Although some of her religious lyrics have survived, her Yakshaganas, which were obviously popular, are lost. S. V. Joga Rao, in *Andhra Yakshagana Vangmaya Charitra* (History of Andhra Yakshagana Literature), 1961, comments, "There were no women, what is more, even men, who wrote so many Yakshaganas and with such skill." Her songs, composed for different occasions (lullabies, bathing songs, bride-dressing songs, and so on), were popular and continue to be sung. Women today enjoy their strong, simple forms and evocative language. Venkamamba wrote many songs imagining Vishnu in his incarnation as the dark deity, Lord Venkateswara, to be her husband, and said in the *Venkateswara Mahatyamu* that when there was need to describe lovers or write erotic verse, she invoked the help of Lord Krishna, since she had had no direct experience.

Despite all her achievements, Venkamamba is, like Molla, often apologetic about her poetry and writes deprecatingly about herself. "No teacher ever taught me / How can I compose verse?" she asks in the beginning of the *Dwipada Bhagawatam,* and she apologizes again, a few stanzas later, for her ignorance of prosody. We have chosen an extract from her poem "Vishnuparijatamu," which is based on a legend about Lord Krishna giving the celestial *parijata* flower to his first wife, Rukmini. His other wife, Satyabhama, known for her proud and quick temper, is enraged. She turns away from Krishna and insults him. To placate her, Krishna brings her the whole parijata tree from paradise. The parijata is one of the five trees produced at the primal churning of the oceans; its flower is of intoxicating fragrance. Venkamamba's poem, which is still popular with women, is richly sensuous and imbues the traditional legend with a new romance.

◆

From VISHNUPARIJATAMU
(The Divine Flower of Vishnu)
[Gently he lifts me up]

Gently he lifts me up
Wipes the stream of tears from my eyes
Trails his fingers softly through my twisted hair
Braids my tresses and decks them with flowers
Gently requests I change my crumpled clothes
Into a flowered raiment of his choice
And adorns me with trinkets of gold and silver.
On my forehead he places the
Vermilion mark of fidelity and artfully
Darkens my reddened eyes with *kajal*
And on my breasts with his own hands
Playfully rubs a sandal salve to
Cool my burning flesh:
Slowly guides me to his chamber
And cajoles me with
Loving appeals to "let me know"
The secret reason for my sulk
(As if he didn't know)
And I, like a fool, tell him
About the flower that he
Gave Rukmini, the other one.
Whereupon he laughs lightly,
"Oh that," he says sweetly,
"To poor Rukmini I have given
A single petal of the Parijat.
To you I'll present the whole
Tree if you wish.
And now come into my arms
I cannot tarry much longer."
And so again, fool that I am,
I believe the charming rogue
And suffocate him with my kisses.
And as I lie in love-drugged sleep,
He leaves me, as is his wont,
For another bed.
Tell me, my dear, where Tarigonda's Lord is now.

Find him, my dear, the beloved libertine,
And bring him back into my arms.

Translated by Srinivas Rayaprolu.

FOLK SONGS ————————————————————————————

The folk songs translated here represent the oldest, richest, and liveliest traditions of poetry in India and introduce to the modern urban reader the hundreds of non-literate women poets (and storytellers) of the country.

We found the folk songs to be among the most difficult pieces to select and translate. Each of the states from which are drawn the ten regional literary traditions represented in this anthology also nurtures separate oral traditions in each of its many dialects—and sometimes, as with adivasi songs, in different languages altogether. We had no difficulty finding these songs—they are still sung all over the country and several collections are now available. But the variety and the range stunned us. The songs were vivid, witty, moving—and radical.

Most folk literature belongs to the indigenous traditions of the different regions. As is common in agricultural societies, women are the principal makers and users of these songs, which accompany sowing, transplanting, weeding, reaping, and threshing in the fields, as well as the husking, pounding, and grinding of grain by hand. The rhythm of the handmill, or the rhythm of pounding, forms the basis of the meter in most of the verse. But lullabies and songs women sing while they are swinging have different rhythms and different meters. In many regions women sing while attending childbirth and announce the event in song. Marriages are celebrated with different songs for each stage in the ceremonies. Every tradition has the tearful lyrics sung when the daughter leaves home after marriage, and women's keening marks the passing of life.

The songs of yearning for the beloved, associated with the sudden darkening of the skies as the clouds gather and the monsoon breaks after the long hot summer, are sung by both men and women. Other songs entertain, or let the imagination run wild; yet others pass on the knowledge of the land and seed and of the weather as well as of illness and its treatment. In some parts of the country, there are still professional troupes of women singers and entertainers such as the *mirasanis,* who are an inalienable part of the culture of Urdu, the *brahminis* in Kerala, and, of course, the Vaishnava singers all over northwestern India.

Some of the songs we have chosen celebrate the bonds between women.

Others speak of childlessness, of the hardship of a woman's lot, and of the pain of separation from daughters. Yet others ridicule men and poke fun at the husband's family, or create situations in which the victim, usually the daughter-in-law, finally wins in a battle of wits with the father or mother-in-law. But there are also songs of love and nearly all the songs reflect philosophically upon life.

The compositions are sometimes completely spontaneous, but more often they add to or ring changes on existing ones. Pounding songs, for instance, are often sung in a duet, with the two women who are working together composing verses in counterpoint. The results can be moving, cuttingly satirical, or hilarious—depending on the occasion or the mood of the singers. Each song, therefore, has many versions, and songs change as the experiences of the people change. The traditional motif of the longing of Radha for the absent Krishna is more recently infused, in some of the songs we have translated, with the new suggestion that the man might have had to leave the family and the village to seek a living in the town.

◆

[The ladies are giving the groom a bath]

The ladies are giving the groom a bath,
They've given him a golden-wood seat.
He's sitting embarrassed like a thief who's harassed
By the police.
        Let's go take a look, girls, it's a treat!

What a creep, he won't touch mustard oil!
But he uses *Jabakusum*.★ That's neat!
        Let's go take a look, girls, it's a treat!

Turmeric on handloom towels,
But he won't rub his body with those.
His thick beard is flowing with the froth of soap,
Oh what an incredible feat!
        Let's go take a look, girls, it's a treat!

He hates river water, he does,
Only tapwater for him, he says,
Even to wash his feet, he says.

★*Jabakusum* is a brand name for a scented oil. The term helps us date this version to the early twentieth century.

Let's go take a look, girls,
      The groom on the golden-wood seat.

Bengali. Collected by Tilottama Dhar from Comilla. Translated by Chandreyee Neogy.

[In the backyard seedlings I sowed]

In the backyard seedlings I sowed
And a charming father-in-law I gained

Like black basil is my mother-in-law
Fair and slim is my sister-in-law
In my sister-in-law I found a friend
Oh, but how jealous is my husband!

A measure of rice he gave me
I pounded it and cleaned it
But it became so much less
I cooked it and served it
But it did not fill even a bowl
How long will I stoop and serve?
The laughter of enemies hurts
How much more can I tolerate?

I shall bear this
I shall bear this
And in the well across the yard
This life of mine I shall end.
You will end your life, O Beautiful,
But I will pull you out.

You will pull me out, O Handsome,
And I'll become the grass near the well
You will become this grass near the well, O Beautiful,
I will let the black cow graze.

You will graze the black cow, O Handsome,
I will become dust on the road.
You will become dust on the road, O Beautiful,
I will make a hundred people walk.

You will make a hundred people walk, O Handsome,
I will become the *sahada* tree by the road.

You will become the tree by the road, O Beautiful,
I will brush my teeth with a twig of yours.

You will brush your teeth with my twig, O Handsome,
I will be the roadside blackberry tree.
You will become the roadside blackberry tree, O Beautiful,
I will pluck and relish your berries day after day.

You will pluck and eat the berries every day, O Handsome,
And I will become the star near the moon.
You will become the star near the moon, O Beautiful,
And I will look on straining my neck.

You will look on straining your neck, O Handsome,
And I will hide in the dark clouds. . . .*

Oriya. Translated by Jyotsna Mahapatra.

[I am being robbed of my colorfully striped sari]

I am being robbed of my colorfully striped sari,
    Oh my sister-in-law claims my sari, my friend!

The sari that my grandfather gave me, my friend,
With the edging sewn on by my mother,
    Oh my sister-in-law claims my sari, my friend!

Four boxes of jewelry in the four corners of the room,
O sister-in-law, choose the best of them.
    Oh my sister-in-law claims my sari, my friend.

O woman, what shall I do with your boxes of jewelry,
I have been longing for a colorfully striped sari.
    Oh my sister-in-law claims my sari, my friend.

Four pitchers in the four corners of the room,
O sister-in-law, take the best of them.
    Oh my sister-in-law claims my sari, my friend.

O woman, what shall I do with your pitchers?
I have been longing for a colorfully striped sari.
    Oh my sister-in-law claims my sari, my friend.

---

*In such songs, verses usually composed extempore can be added until the singers
run out of ideas or finish their task.

Four horses stand in the opposite stall,
O sister-in-law, pick the best of them.
    Oh my sister-in-law claims my sari, my friend.

O woman, what shall I do with your horses?
I have been longing for a colorfully striped sari.
    Oh my sister-in-law claims my sari, my friend.

There hangs my sari, on the rail on the opposite wall,
O sister-in-law, take it and disappear.
    Oh my sister-in-law claims my sari, my friend.

Gujarati. Translated by Nita Ramaiya.

[Daughter-in-law, dear]

Daughter-in-law, dear,
wife of my dear son, O Mother!

Where is the cream
on the fresh milk? Aha! Aha!

And where is the butter
on the boiled milk? Aha! Aha!

Mother-in-law, dear,
great fault-finder, O Mother!

How does one get
cream off fresh milk? Aha! Aha!

How does one get
butter off the boiled milk? Aha! Aha!

*

Daughter-in-law, dear,
whatever happened to the sweets
stored in the sling
hanging from the ceiling? Aha! Aha!

Whatever happened
to those goodies of ours? Aha! Aha!
Who else but
our tomcat, boss of all.

Who else can get
the goodies to eat? O Mother!

"Get lost!
Drop dead:
I will teach you a lesson,"

so saying the mother-in-law
came to the threshold
fire-brand in hand, O Mother!

The scorpion lying in wait
stung her again and again
forcing her to retreat.

Ouch, ouch, oh my,
Ouch, ouch!

Telugu. Translated by B. V. L. Narayanarow.

[Kamakshi, married / into a prosperous family]

1

Kamakshi, married
into a prosperous family,
was washing the peas in a pot.

There arrived then
her elder brother.

She gave him water
and stood there silent
with tears in her eyes.

2

Why, what is the problem, dear,
wipe your tears, comb your hair
Just tell your in-laws
and go with me.

3

Mother-in-law
seated on the high seat!

My brother is here
to take me home.

Will you let me go with him, please?

I know nothing, she said,
ask your father-in-law.

4

Father-in-law, sir,
reclining on your bed!

My brother is here
to take me home.

Will you let me go with him, please?

I know nothing, he said,
ask the senior daughter-in-law.

5

Madam Sister,
engrossed in the kitchen!

My brother is here
to take me home.

Will you let me go with him, please?

I know nothing, she said,
ask your brother-in-law.

6

Brother-in-law, sir,
studying the *Mahabharata!*

My brother has come
to take me home.

Will you let me go with him, please?

Oh dear, he said,
ask your husband.

7

Oh Royal Enjoyer,
seated in the veranda!

My brother is here
to take me home.

Will you let me go with him, please?

Of course, go get dressed
wear your jewels
pick up our child
and get into the carriage.

Have a nice time
at your parental home.

Telugu. Translated by B. V. L. Narayanarow.

[Brother-in-law, my dearest friend]

Brother-in-law, my dearest friend,
Take me home to the land of my father and brother.

Father and brother, they are wicked men;
They sold me to a drunkard in a faraway land.
He drinks
And I serve him all night long.

Father and brother, they are wicked men;
They sold me to a pot smoker in a faraway land.
He smokes
And I light his pipe all night long.
The smoke of his pipe has darkened my face.

Now the wild *kash* flowers have made the river
                             festive all the way,
But who will take me home across the river?
The one who will take me home,
I'll lay down my necklace and my youth at his feet.
Take all my jewels, brother,
And bid me farewell with a smile.
Oh how can I go across the river?

Bengali. Collected by Nihar Barua from Gauripur. Translated by Chandreyee Neogy.

[O Boatman, brother from the upstream country]

O Boatman, brother from the upstream country,
When you meet my father tell him about me. Tell him

My husband's sister treats me like poison and to his mother
I am no better than a pikestaff. A witch's luck is
Not worse than mine! I pass my days in mourning.
O boatman, brother from the upstream country.

When you meet my father tell him about me. I watch
The boats come and go. So many of them!

If my brother doesn't hasten to take me home,
Tell him he should bring a bamboo bier to carry me to the grave.
Tell my mother, O brother boatman, about me,
I throw myself at your feet.

Bengali. Collected from Kishoregunj by Ranen Roy Choudhury. Translated by Lila Ray.

[Ten months and ten days]

Ten months and ten days
The mother dreams on ever,
I'll have a son I'll see him grow,
Now she's a daughter's mother.

The cruel Fates have sent her
At last a little daughter;
To an alien home she soon must go,
So weeps the daughter's mother.

It was the mother's dearest wish
To keep the daughter near her,
Wed her to the boy next door,
But weeps the daughter's mother.

Your seven sons with seven wives
Can be with you forever;
But a daughter stays as long as a dream,
So grieves the daughter's mother.

Mother weeps and father weeps,
So does the bride's brother;
For she goes away this very day
And breaks the heart of her mother.

Bengali. Collected by Tilottama Dhar from Comilla. Translated by Chandreyee Neogy.

[You nurtured me to be a carefree bird, O Mother]

You nurtured me to be a carefree bird, O Mother
You counted the days to make me fly, O Mother
Now the cage is bare without a bird, O Mother
Without me your home is empty, O Mother
Who shall coax me to eat, O my Mother
Who shall wake me from sleep, O Mother
Who will feel the yearning of my heart, O Mother
For they shall only exaggerate my words, O Mother
And they shall make fun of them, O Mother
Oh their harsh words I cannot bear, O Mother
They shall flay my skin to the bone, O Mother
Oh how I was afraid of the dark, O Mother
But now I have freed you from my care, O Mother
And when the first hibiscus blooms, O Mother
Darkness shall reign on your hearth, O Mother
The camel drinks with its long neck, O Mother
But you have none to caress, O Mother.

Oriya. Translated by Jyotsna Mahapatra.

[Come to my arms, Uma, come]

Come to my arms, Uma, come,
Let me take you onto my lap.
Lay your neck against mine.
Dear little daughter, Tarini,
You are this sad woman's life!

Now go to our son-in-law's, dear,
Your mother's room will be empty.
When I have bidden you good-bye
I shall be a sorrowing parent.

Listen to your husband! Become
His lifelong beloved and devote
Yourself to his care!

Bengali. Collected from Kishoregunj by Ranen Roy Choudhury. Translated by Lila Ray.

[Father sat in the inner room, O Mother]

Father sat in the inner room, O Mother
The money came in the afternoon, O Mother

Just as life flows through me in earnest, O Mother
All this money shall soon turn to coal, O Mother

Under the pounder the paddy lies husked, O Mother
There at the *mandap* sits the bald old man, O Mother

As he walked bedecked with flowers, O Mother
How he stumbled and fell on his knees, O Mother

My father sits at the embellished mandap, O Mother
With magic words he whispers in his ears, O Mother

Mouth toothless, his gums all bared, O Mother
How he sat and stared at the mandap, O Mother

The fruit ripens even on the mountaintop, O Mother
But where is your honor,
How can you place a flower on an old man's head, O Mother

Not a bit of shame has that old man, O Mother
He sits there at the mandap
To be wedded, O my Mother
Look at the bullocks he has tied to the door, O Mother.

Oriya. Translated by Jyotsna Mahapatra.

[If you keep away from your husband's elder brother]

If you keep away from your husband's elder brother
and are pleasant to your father-in-law lightly
we will be able to say you are the worthy daughter
of a noble landowner.

A stranger takes the girl child from her mother.

If you are the first to take your bath, the last
to eat, we shall be able to say you are
truly the daughter of a deserving father.

A stranger takes the girl child from her mother.

If you serve milk and rice to everyone
and content yourself with plain rice alone
we shall be able to say you are the proper
daughter of a wise father.

A stranger takes the girl child from her mother.

Bengali. Collected from Kishoregunj by Beena Majumdar. Translated by Lila Ray.

[Don't go away]

Don't. Don't go away.
Don't take a job somewhere
Far from home! My friend!
You yourself are my treasure,
The chain of gold around my neck.
How can I live alone if you go?
How many build great houses?
I am a woman, weak, strengthless!
Stay at home with me, my friend.
What need have we for ready cash?
I shall oil and comb your hair and
Make piles of the stakes that fall!

Bengali. Collected from Kishoregunj. Translated Lila Ray.

[Elder sister, elder sister]

Elder sister, elder sister,
to have a talk
heart to heart,
let's push open
the attic door
then untie our hearts.

Have a talk
heart to heart
with the sacred *tulsi* plant
swaying in the courtyard.
The moon has gone
behind the attic;
sweet is the talk
between mother and daughter.

Put a double wick
into the lamp;
elder sister, elder sister,
let's talk all night.

For such give and take
a mountain is not enough!
I live on the courage
your words give me,
elder sister, elder sister.

Marathi. Translated by Vilas Sarang.

[Tell me, Bird, if you see my friend!]

Tell me, Bird, if you see my friend!
If he returns to this unlucky woman,
Bird, you shall perch on a high branch
And survey all the wide earth. Do you
Know the whereabouts of my friend, Bird?
Take this note I've written to him then.
Give my writing to my heart's friend!
If my beloved comes home
Show him my home, dear bird.
My home is under the *kadam* on the river bank.
My home is the grave, dear bird.

Bengali. Collected from Kishoregunj by Ranen Roy Choudhury. Translated by Lila Ray.

[Jee Jee Ho Re Ho Re]

Jee Jee Ho Re Ho Re
I say Ho, I sing Ho,
I sing my little one to sleep in his cradle
I say Ho, I sing Ho,
I am all yours!★
I would die for you, my beautiful child.

★The expression "I am all yours" has been used to translate an expression used
repeatedly in the poem, *re marun,* which literally means, "Oh, I die." It appears
to be used on joyful occasions or as a greeting with the meaning, "I would die
for you."

May everything good come to you,
I am all yours!
May your life be free of all illness, my child.
I pray to God,
I urge him to shower blessings on you.
I am all yours!
May you grow fast! May you live a long life.
I am all yours!
May my little one stand out among all his playmates.
May you receive the blessings of Meher Ijad.*
May Sharori Ijad protect you!
A pair of toy parrots hangs on the rod of your cradle,
I am all yours!
Crowds of children run through our house to play with you.
The children of aunts and uncles have all gathered together,
I am all yours!
Go and play together under the fragrant flowering plants.
I will pick the fragrant flowers of the *kerado* and *mogaro,*
I am all yours!
I will cover my little one with a coverlet of roses.
You are my very life,
I am all yours!
I light a lamp of ghee and offer sugar and flowers to God.
I light the lamp with a thick lump of ghee.
I am all yours!
You are the source of joy and comfort to your mother, your
    aunts, your grandmothers.

*Gujarati. Either composed or collected by Dhanbai Bamanji Wadia (1929).
Translated by Nita Ramaiya.*

[My courtyard has been cleaned and plastered]

My courtyard has been cleaned and plastered
Give me a child who will print it with his footsteps, O Rannade!**
Mother, the taunts of childlessness are hard to bear.

---

*Meher Ijad and Sharori Ijad are names of angelic beings in the Zoroastrian tra-
   dition.
**The idol of Rannade, the sun queen, is installed in the house when a woman is
   expecting her first child. This song was located in a collection of lullabies, from

I stand here after grinding the grain,
Give me a child who will scatter the heap of flour, O Rannade!
Mother, the taunts of childlessness are hard to bear.

I stand here after fetching water from the river,
Give me a child who will hang on to the corner of my sari, O
    Rannade!
Mother, the taunts of childlessness are hard to bear.

I stand here after churning the curds,
Give me a child who will demand butter, O Rannade!
Mother, the taunts of childlessness are hard to bear.

I stand here after cooking the chapatis,
Give me a child who will ask for a tiny one, O Rannade!
Mother, the taunts of childlessness are hard to bear.

I am wearing a clean white sari,
Give me a child who will spring up and down in my lap, O
    Rannade!
Mother, the taunts of childlessness are hard to bear.

Gujarati. Translated by Nita Ramaiya.

[With a piece of broken earthenware rubbing herself bright]

With a piece of broken earthenware rubbing herself bright,
The trader's wife of Morvi goes for water to the Machhu River's
    bank.

> Ahead goes the king's courtier,
> Behind, the king of Morvi,
>   Taking their horses to the water.

O trader's wife, will you tell me your pitcher's price?
    Let me go, king's courtier,
    Let me go, king of Morvi,
    I don't want to name the price,
In my pitcher your two elephants will vanish in a trice.

---

which it must be assumed that the woman in the poem is confident of bearing a
child and has not, as might appear, undergone a prolonged period of childlessness.

O trader's wife, tell me the price of the embroidered
            ring on which your pitcher rests?
    Let me go, king's courtier,
    Let me go, king of Morvi,
    I don't want to name its price;
In my ring your two horses will vanish in a trice.

O trader's wife, of your pitcher's lid, how do you rate the price?
    Let me go, king's courtier,
    Let me go, king of Morvi,
    I don't want to name the price;
In my pitcher's lid your kingdom will vanish in a trice.

O trader's wife, tell me the price of the arches of your feet?
    Let me go, king's courtier,
    Let me go, king of Morvi,
    I don't want to name the price;
In my arches your two queens will vanish in a trice.

O trader's wife, tell me the price of your beautiful knot of hair?
    Let me go, king's courtier,
    Let me go, king of Morvi,
    I don't want to name the price;
In my knot of hair your own head will vanish in a trice.

Gujarati. Translated by Nita Ramaiya.

[In the forest Seethamma gives birth]

In the forest Seethamma gives birth
No water to wash her thighs, and Hanumanta
Builds a bridge over the ocean

To the mother who loves me
I'll be a good daughter,
To my enemy who rejects me
I'll be a naked sword flashing

A daughter's born and the house falls to pieces
A son's birth sets rejoicing even the latch
On the door, the pictures on the wall

What a match for a girl soft as jasmine
It was like setting the grass afire
Like pouring water over hard rock

Lives of women without children:
Like oxen hired out
Like a plantain leaf discarded after the meal

Those who couldn't say enough about the couple
Turn their faces now from the widow
Her life's become a stinking drain

A fig tree in the barren woman's yard
On every branch a parrot sits
Saying, "Your labor's only for others."

Kannada. Translated by Tejaswini Niranjana.

[I'm at the grindingstone, the child on my lap]

I'm at the grindingstone, the child on my lap!
Do not argue with me, sister-in-law,
I'll finish your work within the hour.

Cry if you're tired, cry if you're bored
But not if I die, my mother!
I'll have done my woman's term.

The meal will be late in your mother-in-law's house;
The child will be hungry, dear daughter,
Take some sugar in your clothes.

Kannada. Translated by K. V. Tirumalesh.

LITERATURE OF THE REFORM AND NATIONALIST MOVEMENTS

LITERATURE OF THE REFORM AND NATIONALIST MOVEMENTS

Background

Gradually, from about the middle of the seventeenth century onward, British presence, mercantile, military, and political, established itself. The East India Company was initially restricted to the trading centers at Surat, Calcutta, Bombay, and Fort St. George (Madras), but by the late eighteenth century it had established its military and administrative authority over large parts of the country. Indian historians and their British counterparts broadly agree that what followed was a period of wholesale plunder. Enormous revenues—principally from land taxes and unequal trade exchanges—were remitted back to England. Company shareholders and officials amassed huge personal fortunes. In 1764 and 1765, the last year of Indian administration in Bengal, the land revenue totaled £817,000. Company administration realized £1,470,000 from 1765 to 1766; the Permanent Settlement was fixed in 1793 at £3,400,000. In many Bengal provinces one-third of the inhabitants died in the terrible famine of 1770. With surplus siphoned off so systematically, the peasant cultivators had no reserves to fall back on when the crops failed. Nevertheless, in 1771 the Company was pleased to report to its shareholders that revenue collection had actually increased.

Economic historians have argued that the Industrial Revolution in Britain could not have occurred without the capital that became available from the plunder of India. The sudden acceleration of the revolution in Britain, R. P. Dutt points out, coincides with the establishment of British rule in India. He writes, "In 1757 came the battle of Plassey and the wealth of India began to flood the country in an ever growing stream. . . . In 1764 came the spinning jenny of Hargreaves; in 1765 came Watt's steam engine, patented in 1769; in 1769 came the waterframe of Arkwright followed by his patents in 1775 for carding, drawing and spinning machines; in 1779 the mule of Crompton and 1785 the powerloom of Cartwright; and in 1788 the steam engine was applied to blast furnaces."[1] These inventions, Dutt argues, did not result from some "special and unaccountable burst of inventive genius," but from the accumulation of enough capital to make possible the large-scale outlay needed to turn the inventions into functional fortunes.

Contemporary accounts attest to the devastation that followed in India. "This fine country," one of the East India Company's own residents reported, "which flourished under the most despotic and arbitrary government is verging towards ruin."[2] Francis Buchanan, who surveyed the country in the early 1800s, wrote: "The natives allege that, although they were often squeezed by the Mogul officers, and on all occasions were treated with utmost contempt, they preferred suffering these evils to the mode that has been adopted of selling their lands when they fall in arrears, which is a practice they cannot endure. Besides, bribery went a great way on most occasions, and they allege that, bribes included, they did not actually pay one half of what they do now."[3]

Both agricultural self–sufficiency and what by many accounts was a growing industrial economy were broken down. For the peasant, insecurity, impoverishment, and indebtedness followed. The shadow of famine stalked the next century.[4] The new system of land taxes introduced with the Permanent Settlement of 1793 turned the zamindars, who were originally tax collectors, into landowners with new rights to evict the peasants who cultivated the lands for not paying the revenues. In earlier years taxes varied—with drought, or flood, or un-

---

[1]Rajani Palme Dutt, *India Today* (Calcutta: Manisha, 1947; 1st ed. 1940), p. 109.
[2]Becher, Company Resident at Mushirabad, 1769, quoted in Dutt, p. 107.
[3]Francis Buchanan, "Statistical Survey," Fifth Report of the Select Committee of the House of Commons, 1872, quoted in Dutt, p. 224.
[4]In the first half of the nineteenth century there were seven famines, in the second half, twenty-four, with an estimated total, according to official estimates, of twenty million deaths.

foreseen expense, but the new tax structure called for the same amount to be transferred to British coffers come whatever calamity. Half the rapidly increasing number of landless and impoverished peasants, pushed further and further into indebtedness by the burden of the new taxes, and evicted when they were unable to pay, were women.

Many thousands of people were also affected by the deindustrialization, most so, perhaps, by the collapse of the textile industry, but also of iron, glass, paper, pottery, and jewelry.[5] For centuries India had been exporting fine cloth—silks and muslins—to the whole world. In 1813, under pressure from the Lancashire textile industry, the British government imposed a high tariff on the import of Indian textiles. British goods, on the other hand, had virtually free entry into India. The shattering results are well known: between 1814 and 1835 British cotton goods exported to India rose from one million yards to thirty-one million yards; the value of Indian cotton goods exported in the same seventeen years fell to one-thirteenth its original size. The thriving textile towns— Dacca, Mushirabad, Surat, Madurai—were laid waste.

The weavers in the cities had generally specialized in creating the fine muslins and brocades in demand among the aristocracy in India and famous the world over. But equally badly hit by the new tariff structure were the weavers in the countryside. During months when there was little to do in the fields, and in years when the rains failed and the harvests were poor, women and men working in their homes spun and wove the coarser cotton cloth into the colors and designs of the saris and dhotis worn in the areas they lived in. The new tariffs and the shifts in textile production left the peasants, now solely dependent on agriculture, even more vulnerable. In Europe the peasants and the handloom weavers who had been displaced found jobs in the new industries, which employed many women. In India even the men had few such alternatives. For the women there were almost no openings.

Both women and men who were forced off the land left to find work in the new plantations. But many more men were able to do so than women. Women stayed back caring for the household, dependent on what little of the men's earnings they were able to send back, and what little they were able to earn. They were always insecure, always

---

[5]For a stimulating discussion of this phenomenon, see A. K. Bagchi, "Deindustrialization in India in the Nineteenth Century: Some Theoretical Implications," *Journal of Development Studies* 12, 1975–1976, pp. 135–164.

anxious. One could reconstruct a parallel narrative for the women who went with their husbands and children to work on the new indigo, rubber, jute, and tea plantations that the British had set up; another for the women who moved to the already overcrowded cities in search of work; and yet another for the women who sometimes with their men, but surprisingly often alone, were taken as "indentured labour" to plantations in other British colonies as far abroad as South Africa and the West Indies.[6]

The pauperization of the peasantry and the decline in artisan production would certainly have affected men and women in different ways. In times of hardship and want, the most marginal are the worst hit. "The bones of the cotton weavers are bleaching the plains of India," the governor general himself wrote in 1834.[7] We can hardly read that chilling statement today without wondering how many of them were women, and what happened to them before that great leveler struck. New evidence indicates the sale of girls by distressed families to pay new taxes. But women were also affected in other less spectacular ways. Women's traditional role in the economy—in the processing of grain, as part of artisan production, and in the service sector—Nirmala Banerjee shows, "slowly became redundant, while their gains in the modern sector remained negligible."[8]

The peasants and artisans were not the only ones hit by the violent changes that were taking place. As the flourishing textile cities of Dacca, Murshidabad, Surat, and Madurai declined in importance and the old urban aristocracy lost power, a whole community of women court artists, poets, singers, musicians, and dancers was displaced.

There were also other, less visible ways in which women were marginalized culturally. In many parts of India, sowing and transplanting are primarily the work of women. Women sort, select, treat, and preserve seeds. They are the genetic bankers of traditional agriculture. In parts of India and Nepal, 60 to 80 percent of the work done in the

---

[6]See Rhoda Reddock, "Freedom Denied: Indian Women and Indentureship in Trinidad and Tobago, 1845–1917," *Economic and Political Weekly* 20:43, Oct. 1985, pp. WS-79–87. Also Brij V. Lal, "Kunti's Cry: Indentured Women on Fiji Plantations," in *Women in Colonial India: Essays on Survival, Work and the State,* ed. J. Krishnamurthy, (Delhi: Oxford University Press, 1989), pp. 163–179.
[7]William Bentinck quoted in Dutt, *India Today,* p. 82.
[8]Nirmala Banerjee, "Working Women in Colonial Bengal: Modernization and Marginalization," in *Recasting Women: Essays in Colonial History,* ed. Kumkum Sangari and Sudesh Vaid, (Delhi: Kali for Women, 1989), pp. 269–301.

selection and storage of seed is by women. The science they practice is one empirically refined, through many generations, by observation and practice.[9] It is well known that as a result of the new tax pressures and the growth of the market economy, many of the smaller farmers were forced to shift from growing food to cultivating cash crops, which would provide the raw material for British industry. This meant there was less for the village to eat and less of reserves for times when the crop failed. But it also meant that the agricultural knowledge preserved and practiced by women, now illegitimate and vestigial, shriveled up from disuse, as did knowledge in other areas: medicine, forest conservation, and, as we shall see, song and storytelling.

A series of peasant and adivasi, or tribal, rebellions spread right through the country, and dogged the British Raj as it marched imperiously through the century.[10] Recent attempts to document these conflicts and understand their implications acknowledge the involvement of women in the struggles.[11] Many of Mahasweta Devi's extraordinary stories and novels deal with these movements. Her highly acclaimed *Aranyer Adikar* (The Rights of the Forest), 1979, is a closely researched novel on the Munda Insurrection of 1899 to 1900 in which Mahasweta "begins putting together a prose that is a collage of literary Bengali, street Bengali, bureaucratic Bengali, tribal Bengali and the language of the tribals," as she recreates the forces at play in those struggles.[12]

It seems surprising, therefore, that right through the nineteenth century the issues that came center stage in public life and became the focus of fierce controversy were those of the social reform movements. A weighty historical guarantee accompanied these efforts, which announced their intent in no uncertain terms: a traditional, religious, and hierarchical society was to be transformed and set on the road to modernity, secularism, and progress. And women, it would seem, were

---

[9] See Vandana Shiva, *Staying Alive: Women, Ecology and Survival in India* (Delhi: Kali for Women, 1988), p. 121, also pp. 61–67.

[10] Kathleen Gough documents seventy-seven such uprisings during colonial rule. "Indian Peasant Uprisings," in *Peasant Struggles in India,* ed. A. R. Desai (Delhi: Oxford University Press, 1979).

[11] Gayatri Spivak commends the efforts of the subaltern studies group on this count, in her "Subaltern Studies: Deconstructing Historiography," *In Other Worlds* (London: Methuen, 1987), p. 215, but adds that a feminist historian of the subaltern must frame the issue with greater theoretical rigor, and "raise the question of woman as a structural rather than marginal issue" (p. 219). And we are still a long way from doing that for the struggles of this period.

[12] Ibid., p. 180.

both the focus and the principal beneficiaries of these changes. "Social reform as commonly understood in India," one of the activists and best-known chroniclers of the movement writes, "is largely related to changes affecting the structure of Indian society and family and was [only] slightly concerned [with] changes affecting relations between economic classes, which in the West go by the name of social reform."[13]

The 1820s, for instance, are associated with Rammohan Roy's (1772–1833) efforts to abolish sati (often spelt "suttee" in early texts). Rammohan used as his principal argument the lack of vedic precedent for this barbarous practice. Legislation making sati illegal came in 1829, though the controversies that ensued continued well into the 1830s and 1840s. The 1850s are marked by the work of Ishwarchandra Vidyasagar (1820–1891) in Bengal and Vishnusastri Pandit (1827–1876) in Maharashtra. They focused on the plight of the large number of widows (often young brahmin girls), who were socially restricted to a life of hardship and self-denial and not allowed to remarry. These reformers also cited the scriptures as support, and the 1856 act, which made remarriage legal, was largely a result of their work. Efforts to make the idea of remarriage socially acceptable, however, continued right through the second half of the century, receiving fresh momentum in the work of Kandukuri Veereshalingam (1848–1900) in coastal Andhra.

By the 1860s women's education had staked its claims as a major issue. In Maharashtra and Tamilnadu, and most spectacularly in Bengal, there were heated discussions over a suitable curriculum for women, schools for women were set up, and efforts to bring women out of purdah renewed. The need to discourage child marriage was of major interest in the 1880s and 1890s.[14]

Sociologists and political scientists have pointed out that many of these problems affected only a small proportion of upper-caste women.

---

[13]S. Natarajan, *Century of Social Reform in India* (Bombay: Asia Publishing House, 1959), p. 5.

[14]See Vina Mazumdar, "The Social Reform Movement in India from Ranade to Nehru," in *Indian Women: from Purdah to Modernity,* ed. B. R. Nanda (Delhi: Vikas, 1962), pp. 41–66, for more detailed feminist analysis of these movements, Gulam Murshid, *The Reluctant Debutante* (Rajashahi: Rajashahi University Sahitya Samsad, 1983), for a discussion of the movement in Bengal, supported by important archival research, and V. Ramakrishna, *Social Reform in Andhra (1848–1919)* (Delhi: Vikas, 1983).

Sati, for instance was a Rajput practice taken over, especially in Bengal, by the brahmins. It is difficult to imagine the restrictions on diet and the practices of self-abnegation that haunted the life of the brahmin widow finding place among the lower-caste women, who worked in the fields or at a trade for a living. Among other groups—the Jats in Punjab, or the Muslims—widows commonly remarried. Purdah was practiced only in upper-class families. Child marriage was more widespread, though norms about when a girl would move to her marital household varied a great deal. When the question of women's education was raised, it was the education of these women from the upper strata that was at issue. It is essential, we would argue, to grapple with these apparent contradictions if we are to appreciate the scope and genius of women's writing in this period.

A Critique of Historiography

Histories have commonly dealt with the changes that took place after the British arrived in India in two mutually exclusive schemes. Political and economic histories study the transformations that took place in the agrarian structure, the changes in the market economy, and the laws that formalized the idea of private ownership of property, especially of land. Social histories, on the other hand, deal with the social reform movements—many of which concerned women—that arose, decade after decade, from the 1820s onward. Despite the attention it pays to the "woman question," such scholarship obscures more than it reveals about gender. Political history occasionally stops to record events in which women were involved, but it rarely asks whether women and men were affected in different ways by the changes they describe and seems incapable of capturing the structural importance of gender in colonial politics. Social histories cite the liberal democratic ideals of the Enlightenment as the inspiration for the nineteenth-century reform movements in India, but portray the reform movements as engaged in the moral transformation of a perverse society. The revolutionary demands of liberty and equality are not considered as arising, in India, from the politics of oppression or exploitation, but from an ethical concern for regeneration.

Further, since scholarship based on such a dichotomy between the political and the social confined the scope of women's history to the ideological issues taken up in the reform movement, it did not investigate how patriarchy itself might have been reconstituted as a result, say, of the old zamindars being reempowered within a colonial economy or by the changing market, or by the new rule of property itself.[15] Besides, the focus on the explicit concerns of the social reform movements and their proclaimed intent did not help explain why these issues, which seemed to concern only a small upper-caste stratum, roused such passionate debate and absorbed so much energy.

If we shift our attention from the issues overtly addressed by the reformers—sati, widowhood, or child marriage (and the women's literature of this period seems to demand that we do so)—to a more general economy of the transformations that were taking place, the hidden agendas of the social reform movement emerge in more telling form. Embedded in the explicit programs of the reform movement were massive ideological reconstructions of patriarchy and gender that underwrote the consolidation of imperial power. These reconstructions often took place at the interface of patriarchy with class and caste. Not surprisingly, it is these hidden agendas, whose effects were by no means restricted to upper-caste or middle-class women, that were being played out in the agitated discussions of the time. And it is these agendas, their strategic intentions and the interests underlying them, that the more radical and subversive women's literature of the period addresses.

We are not claiming, as some powerful contemporary voices seem to be, that the problems the reform movement addressed itself to did not exist, or even that they were false.[16] We are not saying that widows did not lead a hard life or that sati is not a terrible practice, or that women had no need of schooling. We are saying that it is not useful to consider social reform as the framework from which to write a cultural history of gender in nineteenth-century India and that such a framework does not aid an appreciation of the literature. We are also saying that by doing so we might have altogether missed other, more covert and far-reaching processes, for, finally, this recasting of women into the new molds of the time was not merely social but political.

Many, though not all, for we have tried to strain against this powerful determination, of the writers translated in these volumes are middle-class and upper-caste women (and in this respect writers and

---

[15]See Kumkum Sangari and Sudesh Vaid, "Introduction," in *Recasting Women,* pp. 1–25, for a related discussion of feminist historiography.

[16]For example, Veena Das, "Strange Response," *The Illustrated Weekly of India,* 28 February 1989, pp. 30–32; Ashish Nandy, "The Human Factor," *The Illustrated Weekly of India,* 17 January 1989, pp. 20–23.

readers of literature in India are no exception to the general rule). As the writings reveal in poignant detail, their lives too changed as imperial rule established itself. They were faced with new demands to fulfill—from husbands and fathers, who had new hopes for them, but also from the changing times—and new worlds to negotiate. But they also had new aspirations themselves. Some of the issues commonly associated with the reform movement—the evils of purdah, the ideal of companionate marriage, the hardships of widowhood, an utopian vedic community—are clearly recognizable in their writings, as are the questions raised later by an emerging nationalism. But these issues are rarely thematic. The narrative and figural schemes of these writings call our attention to the fine-grained drama of the many and often conflicting ideological transformations that were taking place in those momentous times. The writings display the complex dimensions in which woman's subjectivity was being sculpted, and the way particular women negotiated, redeployed, or subverted these blueprints.

Except in the two texts (Anonymous, 1881 and 1889) in which the widows themselves testify to the horror of their lives and, as the narrative makes amply clear, the barbarity of a society that treats them so brutally—and these are pieces we deliberately included to set off the other voices—none of the concerns of the reform movement appears in the familiar forms in the women's writings translated here. What we find instead are unexpected changes (and sometimes reversals) in the function of these discourses, subtle shifts in emphasis or point of view, redeployments of the projects, the concepts, the enunciative modalities or the rhetorical strategies, of the period. Other texts introduce voices that the loud conventional coverage of the period had totally drowned.

As we read these texts we find all the grand abstractions of the times—Empire, Human Nature, Ethical Responsibility, Tradition, Nationalism, Indianness, Masculinity, each with important stakes in the woman question—imaged in the unfamiliar mirror of these changing subjectivities. For gender, as we shall see, was far from being marginal to the new world. It had a major role to play in the structuring of a whole range of social institutions and practices. Neither the authorial selves, nor the readers they address, can, therefore, be thought of in an ahistoric mode or as primordially female. Their selfhood or subjectivity cannot be separated from the specific historical and political conjunctures that constituted their worlds.

It is crucial, therefore, that we restrain ourselves (and this is all the more true for readers outside India and especially in the West) from reading these texts simply for confirmation of our present-day experience, or, in the more historically self-conscious version of the same gesture, from reading them as earlier, "less advanced" realizations of contemporary (feminist/liberal/nationalist/Marxist) sensibilities. For to do that is simply to lose out on the rich drama that is staged in these texts, not only in their overt themes, but also in the fine detail of their form. These writers contested the structures that were shaping their worlds: they tactically redeployed dominant discourses, held onto older strains and recharged them with new meanings and even introduced new issues, new emphases, new orientations. And in so doing, they left their marks on the worlds we inherit. What emerges from the writings, then, it a subtle and closely textured sense of the struggles and counterstruggles through which women's subjectivities took shape as new worlds were formed around them.

Only in the last decade or less have we had access to the kind of research that allows us to reread these writings not as shadows of a greater (male, Western) reality, or even of a Western feminist reality, but as texts that display the oblique and subtle dramas of these off-off-center subjectivities. The gestures here do not have the "self-evident" logic or the transparency that accompanies an uncontested centrality. Nonetheless they are (and this is easy to forget) the hidden underbelly of that centrality. Indeed, the issues, of self and of agency as well as of worlds recast by empire or nation, at stake in these writings make the traumas of mainstream Western literature seem simple, even melodramatic.

Colonial Rearticulations of Gender

We might, for a start, explore the way gender was being rearticulated in relation to class as both institutions were re-formed. Among the many women artists delegitimated and marginalized as the new "respectable" middle-class woman was being shaped were the Vaishnava poets and singers. In a fascinating recent study, Sumanta Banerjee traces the fortunes of this popular cultural mode in the second half of the nineteenth century. Traditionally, Vaishnavism, with which the bhakti movements in the north and the east are associated, provided a legitimate space for those rejected by society. Vaishnavas, the Census of India, Bengal 1872, reported, "open their arms to those who are rejected by all others—the outcasts, the crippled, the diseased and the unfortunate."[17] Lurking somewhere under the umbrella of that last category were also widows and other women, married and single, who had been driven out of or had left their families. "Contemporary records," Banerjee writes, "abound with references to women in villages—widows, married as well as unmarried women—deserting their homes to join some Vaishnavite *akbara* or monastery. Here religious norms allowed them a freedom of movement, an access to all corners of society, both high and low, and a certain liberty in their relations with men—privileges which were out of reach for rich and middle class Bengali women of this time. Many of these Vaishnavite women went around singing and begging from door to door."[18] Some who had learned to read and write in their homes taught the girls and boys in upper-class homes their first lessons. In the Tagore household, for instance, all the children were taught to read and write by an elderly Vaishnava woman whom Tagore's sister, Swarnakumari Devi, describes in an autobiographical fragment as a warm and learned person. In nineteenth-century Bengal, these popular artists also had a wide female audience ranging from the lower-caste and lower-class self-employed women of the marketplace to the sheltered wives and daughters of wealthier, "respectable" families. Their well-known compositions were often frankly realistic, tough, sensuous, even bawdy, and used the familiar, domestic terms and forms of address associated with women's dialects.

One of the tasks the social reform movement set itself, Banerjee demonstrates, was to break this unregimented and indecorous intercourse between women of all classes and create the respectable middle-class housewife, the *bhadramahila*. The purity and domestic virtue of this newly created being was defined by setting it up as the antithesis of the "unbridled movement" and the "licentiousness" of the Vaishnava poets.[19] For women it was a double-edged process, for as this

---

[17]Cited in Sumanta Banerjee, "Marginalization of Women's Popular Culture in Nineteenth Century Bengal," in *Recasting Women,* ed. Sangari and Vaid, p. 134.

[18]Ibid., p. 134.

[19]The new middle-class woman's virtue, as the early twentieth-century fortunes of Muddupalani's *Radhika Santwanam* clearly indicate, was also aligned to that of the "proper lady" in the West. Mary Poovey explores the hold of this ideological configuration on the early nineteenth-century British women writers in her excellent study, *The Proper Lady and the Woman Writer: Ideology as Style in the Works of Mary Wollstonecraft, Mary Shelley and Jane Austen* (Chicago: University of Chicago Press, 1984). Unfortunately, Poovey does not touch in this book on im-

popular culture was discredited and the artists reduced to penury and often forced into prostitution, the new respectable upper-caste woman was shaped, her sexuality elaborated, and in the process also contained.

The figures speak best. The 1891 Bengal Census lists 17,023 actresses, singers, and dancers. In 1901, there were only 3,527. Some of the displaced women must have found jobs in the new mills being set up. Others tried to become teachers in the new schools being established, which, the reformers never tired of announcing, were desperately in need of women teachers, but the women were turned away. On the other hand, prostitution was spreading like the plague in Calcutta.[20]

It is with some pride, therefore, that this volume features the work of the folksingers Jogeswari and Bhabani, and an extract from the autobiography of the actress Binodini Dasi. These pieces testify to a line of women artists and a great tradition of women's art that was turned into an illegitimate Other and eliminated, not without violence, as the new middle-class writing took shape. Its shadow must stand over the achievements that follow.

The forces at work in the demarcation of women as citizens under the law, and consequently as the "free individuals" of a liberal society, involved much more than class differentiations. Brought into play in the new conjugations of gender were the powerful ideological counters of tradition, caste, religion, and a culture's "authentic essence": an Indianness, which was to be preserved. It goes without saying that as they were drawn into the new configurations and put to new use, tradition, caste, religion, and so on were also rearticulated and reendorsed. The legal system introduced with the Permanent Settlement,

perialism as a formative force in that ideology. Even Mary Wollstonecraft, whose work she analyzes at length, holds Western civilization up in contrast to the barbarous "Mohametan" or Chinese cultures, and argues that it is therefore required to treat its women as equals. This argument, as we saw earlier when we discussed Mill's history, was a common one, and is one of the rocks on which white middle-class femaleness was built in the nineteenth century. See her *Vindication of the Rights of Women* (Harmondsworth: Penguin, 1985; 1st ed. 1792), pp. 100, 128. See also Catherine Hall, "Gender Divisions and Class Formation in the Birmingham Middle Class, 1780–1850," in *People's History and Socialist Theory,* ed. Raphael Samuel (London: Routledge and Kegan Paul, 1981), pp. 164–175.

[20]A. K. Dutt, "Kalikatar Bartaman Durbastha" (The Present Degeneration of Calcutta), *Tattvabodhini Patrika* 13, July 1846, pp. 96–104, quoted in David Kopf, *The Brahmo Samaj and the Shaping of the Modern Indian Mind* (Princeton: Princeton University Press, 1979), p. 92.

for example, had distinctively different implications for women and men. The new law defined (and protected through a judiciary set up at the same time) the rights of the new Indian subject, principal among which was the right to property. The political philosophy that underlay the initiative, Ranajit Guha argues, was drawn from Whig political ideas and European physiocratic economic theory, and it was claimed that it would transform Indian society by creating a modern possessive individualism.[21] Private or personal law, however, was based on principles sharply opposed to those that determined the public sphere, and reflected a totally different vision of the future. Whereas the public law was designed to encourage and safeguard the freedom of the individual in the marketplace, and was established by statute, personal law was intended to *limit* the extent of this freedom by prescribing the social and ethical obligations to which the individual was traditionally subject. Further, whereas public law evoked the social contract, personal law reaffirmed ascriptive status, which, as we shall see, was freshly recast, as the basis of individual rights and assigned a new political function.

What is more important from our point of view, though, is the fact that personal law was to be formulated and standardized through the "discovery" of existing customary and religious norms. Courts were to look to the vedic texts, redesignated by the evangelical temper as "scriptures," and endowed with prescriptive status, for information about these "laws." Since tradition was equated in this procedure with the sacred *texts,* and the courts used brahmin pandits (spelled "pundit" in the earlier literature) to interpret these texts, some historians have argued that consolidated in the process was a *brahminical* view of society, one that regarded its "structure in terms of immutable religious principles," and applied "a theological definition to the concept of family and to the proper basis of relations within it."[22]

Lata Mani's analysis of the actual processes—the court hearings, the

---

[21]Ranajit Guha, *A Rule of Property for Bengal: An Essay on the Idea of Permanent Settlement* (Delhi: Orient Longman, 1982; 1st ed. 1963).

[22]D. A. Washbrook, "Law, State and Agrarian Society in Colonial India," *Modern Asian Studies* 15:3, 1981, pp. 649–721. Washbrook's conclusion represents the broad consensus among Western South Asianists. See also S. Rudolf and L. Rudolf, *The Modernity of Tradition* (Chicago: University of Chicago Press, 1967). It is surprising that the connections with the powerful theological definition of the family in Western society, and the connection between those redefinitions and what was happening in this period to gender in Europe, so completely escapes Washbrook's notice.

administrative exchanges, the debates through which the legal codes on sati were established—however, suggests that the dynamic at work involved much more than a brahmin view of society. Brahmin authority was recreated, elaborated, and endorsed by the colonial administration in its interests. The exchanges between the pandits and the judges, she argues, demonstrate "how the very formulation of the official questions shapes the responses of the pandits and how the answers of the pandits are interpreted in specific ways by the officials."[23] It was the framework in which these officials operated, Lata Mani shows, that became the filter through which the vedic or brahminical tradition was meticulously "recovered" (or invented) to suit contemporary ends. In other words, the official discourse of imperial government and its interests structured the recovery of "tradition." Further, this "tradition" acquired significance only as an element in that structure. A newly standardized rigid "brahminical" version of Hindu law, reempowered by Orientalist scholarship and by colonial authority, extended its hold over other castes and other areas that possessed their own more localized, nonscriptural laws and legal procedures. In the process, a changing and heterogenous society, with conventions, laws, legal institutions, and ideological formations that embodied the different historical experiences of its people, was reconstituted and confined not only by the law but also by the whole range of social practices that took their cue from legal procedure, into a stunted upper-caste image.[24] A similar reversion to "tradition" took place with Muslim personal law, for which the *Al Hidayah* (of which the Orientalist scholar Charles Hamilton had made a highly selective and dubious translation) was to be the principal normative text. As a result, women's "individuality," their "citizenship," their "freedom" were defined and contained in the domain of the personal not only by the law but also in the agitated debates on other issues that accompanied the setting-up of the law. But as many of the texts that follow show, the personal domain, newly constituted in exclusively religious terms, had complex and problematic connections with caste, tradition, Victorian norms of feminine propriety, and imperialist ambitions. A

---

[23]Lata Mani, "Contentious Traditions: The Debate on Sati in Colonial India," *Cultural Critique,* Fall 1987, pp. 119–156. Reprinted in *Recasting Women,* ed. Sangari and Vaid, pp. 88–126.

[24]See Prem Chowdhry, "Customs in a Peasant Economy: Women in Colonial Haryana," in *Recasting Women,* ed. Sangari and Vaid, pp. 302–336.

more detailed analysis should explore each of these formations in depth; we offer instead the women's texts that stage the drama.

There is evidence, in our collection as well as in historical studies, that other processes bringing about changes in family structure and in women's autonomy were actually set in reverse as colonial rule established itself. The young Hamida's sixteenth-century reluctance to marry the emperor Jehangir (reported with such evident approval by Gul-Badan Begum) was interpreted by the Begum of Bhopal in 1910 as an index of her modesty and her reluctance to appear unveiled before the emperor. There seems to be no way in which, isolated as she was in a small village, the unapologetic sense of self-worth that characterizes Rassundari Devi's narrative can be thought of as a product of liberal individualism. In Kerala, despite their loud avowals that there would be no interference in personal law, the imperial state intervened quite blatantly to recast the matrilineal Nair *taravads* (households) into what they spoke of as a "natural" patriarchal mold.[25] The taravad consisted of siblings, women and men, and the women's children. Taravad land was subject to matrilineal inheritance, but was held by all in common and administered by the eldest brother. Women were free to cohabit with other (usually Namboodiri brahmin) men, but no rights or duties were attached to these *sambandhams.* In a series of Nair Regulation Laws, starting in 1868 and continuing well into the 1930s, this form of family organization, which gave a woman economic power and sexual freedom or, in the phrasing of the Marriage Commission, the right to terminate a union "at any time, from wantonness or caprice," was brought to heel.[26] The ideological pressures probably had even more powerful effects on actual practices. The sociologist Irawati Karve reports after a survey conducted in the early 1960s that the younger men were ashamed of their parents' relationship and thought of their fathers as male concubines to their mothers.[27]

---

[25]See *Report of the Malabar Marriage Commission with Enclosures and Appendixes* (Madras: Government Printers, 1891). Also, Maria Mies, *Indian Women and Patriarchy* (Delhi: Concept, 1980), pp. 84–90.

[26]Malabar Marriage Commission, Section 47.

[27]Irawati Karve, *Kinship Organisation in India* (Bombay: Asia Publishing House, 1953), pp. 297–299.

One cannot fail to be struck by the extraordinary number of autobiographies (many of them published) that were written in the second half of the nineteenth and the early twentieth centuries, especially in Marathi and Bengali but also in other languages. Many of these texts are a personal testimony of the new sense of worth these women experienced as "individuals," whose specific lives were of interest and importance. But nearly all of them also focus in one way or another on the tension and contradictions built into the promises liberalism held out to colonized peoples and especially to colonized women. These life stories are therefore fascinating historical documents of how women worked out these conundrums. As a genre, autobiography, especially modern autobiography, exhibits a certain ambivalence. The accent is on the personal. The existential contours of a life and the preoccupation with intimate, even confessional, detail often obscure the fact that autobiography always draws on the repertoire of life scripts that cultures provide at particular junctures in their history. Recurrent themes in many nineteenth-century memoirs are the woman's joy in the love and support of a progressive husband and her education and the new possibilities that opened out to her. But even in relatively conventional accounts we come across passages that give us a glimpse of the many-faceted struggles involved: the pain of being constantly watched and corrected; the feeling that they were not good enough; the exhausting demands of the new housework; the uncertainty and anxiety involved in raising children in the new mode, outside the reassuring circle of the traditional family; the longing for the support of a world they had lost, and so on.

Other autobiographies reveal more dramatic tensions. "I have with great effort freed myself from the yoke of the Indian priestly tribe," Pandita Ramabai writes in reply to a letter from her Christian mentor, criticizing her independence of mind, "so I am not at present willing to place myself under another similar yoke."[28] The assumption, which rings through Cornelia Sorabji's unusual memoir, that she was the equal of a white man, set her in such conflict with the world that her last years were spent in an asylum for the mentally deranged in England. The self-deprecating humor of Lakshmibai Tilak's autobiog-

---

[28] *The Letters and Correspondence of Pandita Ramabai,* ed. A. B. Shah (Bombay: State Board for Literature and Culture, 1977), p. xxx.

raphy develops into a fine-honed tool that cuts in many surprising ways.

Literary historians often emphasize Rassundari Devi's pious conclusions to promote her autobiography as that of a God-fearing Bengali housewife. In the process they blur over other, less "exemplary" aspects of her unusual self, which actually form the body of her work: the strength of her bond with her mother, the shadowy presence of her husband (who seems a totally unimportant figure in her life), and the brief mention she makes even of her children.

Both Lakshmibai Tilak's and Ramabai Ranade's memoirs are rare records of the little-explored but politically significant struggle of women caught between the bold public gestures of the new Westernized men they were married to, the public promises of freedom held out to them, and personal lives that were bound anew into private spheres. Their stories capture the oblique paths they trod across these grids.

If these autobiographies of marriage provide us with one picture of what the new individualism held in store for middle-class women, the extracts from the life stories of the actresses Binodini Dasi and Hamsa Wadkar (1923–1972; see volume 2), though separated by almost half a century, represent its hidden obverse. Binodini and Hamsa, gifted artists with colorful personalities, were among the leading figures of their times. Yet their struggles to make a living and survive humanely in the male worlds of theater and cinema were met with surprising resistance, and they were pushed back, time and again. Even the qualified promises of progress and freedom held out to middle-class women were obviously not meant for them.

If we consider the questions more closely, we will find that what emerged as the idea of the past was elaborated and reaffirmed—in the legal procedures, or in the arguments in which the social reformers proclaimed that none of the evils besetting contemporary society had plagued a vedic one—was a powerful double-jointed alliance, endorsed by the authority of millennia, between imperial interests and the dominance of brahminic culture. The newly homogenized Indian "tradition," indeed the new Hinduism, took on an unprecedented upper-caste color. And women, set up in the discussion as emblematic of it, were drawn willy-nilly into its schemes.[29] The direction taken in

---

[29]For a fascinating discussion on the invention of tradition, see Romila Thapar,

Maharashtra by the writing and the activism of the Satyashodhak Mandal, set up in 1873 by Jotiba and Savithribai Phule, challenges this dominant configuration. The Satyashodhak Mandal called for a broad alliance of sudras, ati-sudras, and women in the fight against brahmin domination. Jotiba's reinterpretation of history ascribed the success of the seventeenth-century Maratha hero Shivaji, in resisting the Mughals, to his sudra and ati-sudra armies and not to his influential brahmin ministers, the Peshwas.[30] Conflict between the brahmins and the lower castes, he argued, had always been a central feature of Marathi culture. The schools Jotiba and Savithribai Phule started in Pune were meant especially for lower-caste girls. Their colleague, Fatima Sheikh, was a Muslim woman. In the letters Savithribai wrote to her brother, which we have reprinted here, we get an inkling, from the many levels at which they were attacked, of the many interests they were undermining.

From the context of the Satyashodhak Mandal we have also taken the essay in which Muktabai, a student at one of their schools, scornfully rejects the tendency to go back to the Vedas for the answer to all contemporary problems, and rages against the present-day brutality of the brahmins. The gesture, in which she takes up her pen and marks the paper, has been centuries in the making, centuries during which neither book nor pen came within reach of the lower castes—or of upper-caste family women—for learning had been the preserve mainly of brahmin men. In another time and another social space, that gesture itself would have been cause for celebration. But this fourteen-year-old has no time to wait, for it is not enough that she must write, she must write for a people who have many stories to tell, but have not been heard. With a directness that still electrifies us, she takes on the Peshwas themselves and tells a story that gives us a totally different understanding of the heroes of Maharashtrian history.

Muktabai's anger against the Peshwas, whose cruelty toward the sudras matches the callousness with which they treated women, is one expression of this powerful movement. But it is in the extraordinary

---

"Traditions versus Misconceptions," Interview with Madhu Kishwar and Ruth Vanita, *Manushi*, 42–43, 1987, pp. 2–14. Also, Romila Thapar, "Imagined Religious Communities? Ancient History and the Modern Search for a Hindu Identity," *Modern Asian Studies*, 23:2, 1989, pp. 209–231.

[30]See Gail Omvedt, *Cultural Revolt in Colonial India: The Non-Brahmin Movement in Western India 1873–1930* (Bombay: Scientific Socialist Education Trust, 1976), for an excellent discussion of this movement.

piece by the feminist Tarabai Shinde, who was inspired by the context of the Satyashodhak Mandal, that we find the most meticulously worked-out critique of the men who had sold the nation for a few comforts and were content to ape their rulers. These men, Tarabai writes, toyed with their new-found pleasures, but were blind to the sufferings of the artisans who were starving to death and the grinding poverty in which the women and children existed. It was a scathing indictment, for "in the face of male misadventure, treachery, duplicity and faithlessness," she had no option, she says, but to be blunt. In a deliberate rejection of the literary language of the time, which she regarded as decadent, she adopted a roughshod colloquial style. Her critique of the popular adventure-romances of that period is not merely a call for a more realistic portrayal of women, though some recent critics have read it as such, but a demand for a literature more sensitive to the problems of the time. What inspires us today is the broad scope of her feminism. As she (a Maratha) takes up the cause of Vijayalakshmi, a Gujarati brahmin widow, and connects it to the plight of the artisans and the ordinary people under imperialist rule, she gives voice to a nationalist force unmatched elsewhere in India, although one, we must sadly admit, that was soon to be driven underground.

The whole question of women's education was similarly riddled with contradictions. On one level education promised freedom and equality and was projected as a program that would shape the child for responsible citizenship. Yet underlying much of the discussion in the nineteenth century was the need felt as urgently by missionaries and such women as Mary Carpenter and Annette Beveridge as by the new Indian men to break into the zenana, or the private spheres of household and family, and make women into more fitting homemakers, mothers, and companions for the emerging urban middle-class men. Clearly freedom and equality meant different things for women and for men. All over the country the beginnings of women's education were plagued by disagreements about what might constitute a suitable curriculum for women. The more conservative supporters of their cause argued that women really needed to acquire only the skills that would make them better wives and better mothers. They proposed a little writing, a smattering of history and arithmetic, but wanted the emphasis to be on hygiene, moral education, and needlework. Music and sport were controversial because so much activity—of spirit or of body—might excite the passions. And as for English, there was no useful purpose served by teaching women *that* language, since it was spoken only outside the household. Fortunately the opposition was also strong. But even those who argued for a common curriculum seemed agreed that the ultimate purpose of female education was to make women more efficient homemakers and more enlightened mothers.

Many of the women writing in the late nineteenth and early twentieth centuries echo the same sentiments, and there seems to be little that distinguishes their work from the male writing of the time. The writers translated here, however, speak of the norm by refuting it. Rassundari Devi's autobiography is so astonishing because she grew up, reared her children, and struggled in secret to learn how to read, in a village, a long distance away from the metropolis of Calcutta where debating societies were arguing about women's education, and long before the new schools for women had been set up in the city. Perhaps it is a desire to escape that moves her, perhaps the love of words, or the longing for her parental home, where she watched her brother learn to write as a child. But it is also a powerful sense of self-worth as well as the need to extend the spiritual dimensions of her life that drives her. Her awe-inspiring efforts to read are illegitimate in more than one sense. We know that a Hindu wife laid hands on a book or a pen at the risk of losing her husband. But as Rassundari Devi scratches her letters, like a prisoner in solitary confinement, onto the blackened kitchen wall, she also subverts the reform movement's educational project into a totally different, personal one. Her desire for literacy, as we pointed out earlier, has a composition quite different from that postulated by the new individualism. There is absolutely no place in her hunger to read for domesticity or motherhood, or indeed for any of the other much-flaunted ends of female education.

Women's education is one of the many controversies Rokeya Hossain addresses in the jocular inversion of the familiar world she creates in "Sultana's Dream." The tasks education has to equip a woman for, the story makes amply clear, are the tasks of rebuilding the entire world. Women need the knowledge of modern science and a training in the fearless use of reason. As for domesticity, Rokeya is willing to acknowledge the pleasure of cooking or the arts of embroidery, not as fit tasks for the virtuous housewife, but as dimensions of the art of living well.

The nineteenth century also spawned an enormous body of normative literature, which functioned as a kind of supplementary education for women. The more popular among these authoritatively written conduct books ran into several editions and some continue to be reprinted today. The traditionalists, as well as those who argued for modernity and progress, put out rival versions of what they regarded as fit behavior for women. Every detail of the middle-class woman's life was commented on. As we read them today, we are struck more by what they seemed agreed on than by their disagreements. The "conservative" Maulana Thanawi belonged to the theological seminary at Deoband, which fiercely opposed the modernization associated with Syed Ahmed in Aligarh. But his *Bihishti Zevar* (Jewels of Paradise), 1905, and the progressive Nazir Ahmed's *Miratul Uroos* (A Mirror for the Bride), 1869, are both agreed on the need for the bourgeois virtues of thrift, sacrifice, forbearance, and meticulous attention to housekeeping and child rearing, as is the Hindu traditionalist Bhudhev Mukhopadhyay's *Paribarik Prabandam* (Essays on the Family), 1883.[31] While all three explicitly address the need for sexual decorum and restraint, and the need to pay careful attention to rearing children to be proper citizens, also important is the idea that a woman should be a companion to her husband, a person he might turn to when he needed to unburden himself, one who would share his troubles and his joys.

For the novelists with their new "realist" ambitions, however, the problem of sculpting a new woman took on added dimensions. As Meenakshi Mukherjee argues in her subtly conceived book *Realism and Reality,* fiction had to negotiate the uneasy fit between the myriad microscopic assumptions that went into creating the "reality-effect" of the nineteenth-century European novel and the everyday worlds—in Rajahmundry, Calcutta, or Pune—that was mediated by a thousand other forms (institutions/discourses/symbologies) that the novelists and their readers lived in.[32] For these writers it was not enough that the woman should be an efficient homemaker and supportive companion. They needed a new woman molded into such proportions that the hero could plausibly fall in love with her. One of the major projects of the nineteenth-century novel is the making of this woman.

It is difficult to imagine what it might have meant for a woman in that period to be the object of a transformative mission of such penetrating reach. In women's writing we get a glimpse of how women wrestled with these projects, infusing them with totally illegitimate extensions and indecorous deviations. Swarnakumari Devi's *Kahake,* for example, subverts the question of finding a fit domestic companion

---

[31]See Barbara Metcalf, "Islamic Reform and Islamic Women: Maulana Thanawi's Jewelry of Paradise," in *Moral Conduct and Moral Authority in South Asian Islam* (Berkeley: University of California Press, 1984), pp. 184–195.

[32]Meenakshi Mukherjee, *Realism and Reality: The Novel and Society in India* (Delhi: Oxford University Press, 1985).

for the new man, and turns it into the story of a woman's search for a soul mate. The narrative is structured so as to pose the problem, and chapters in which the plot is developed are interspersed with ones in which the heroine discusses the events and the characters with her sister. As she engages the conventional wisdoms of her time and defines herself in opposition to them, the protagonist gradually discovers what she is looking for in a life partner. The functionalist schemes in which the reform movement announced its program of personal transformation are displaced as the novel's imaginative field shifts the woman from the periphery, where she is an object to be molded according to male and, in turn, societal requirements, into the center, where her aspirations shape the plot.

Many writers, Mokshodayani Mukhopadhyay, Tarabai Shinde, and Rokeya Hossain among them, engaged in a different kind of oppositional logic. Historical accounts are often full of the hostility and persecution male reformers had to face, but the corrosive everyday hostility from *both* the modernizers and the traditionalists that women themselves lived with is very rarely acknowledged. The impatience the social reformers themselves felt toward the women they were trying to help, but who rarely seemed worthy of the effort that was taken on their behalf, is so typical of such missions of charity that it does not surprise us. But what is often glossed over is that the woman herself is imaged in reform literature as inefficient, ignorant, superstitious, prone to waste time gossiping and listening to street singers, in short, as incapable of initiative. Education, it was argued, would broaden her mind and school her into becoming more prudent and rational. On the other hand, from those who felt the sanctity of a traditional society was being invaded by these newfangled and dangerous "Western" notions about women, there was scathing indictment and outright attack. Women must have dealt with the ridicule, the insult, and the corrosive dismissal in a thousand ways that have never found a place in the records that have come down to us. But the fragments that remain in Mokshodayani Mukhopadhyay's satirical poem "Bangalir Babu" (Bengali Babu), but more so in Tarabai Shinde's *Stri Purush Tulana* (A Comparison of Men and Women), are documents that stand witness to the ways women turned the censure directed against them onto the men.

Mokshodayani's poem, composed as a reply to a satirical piece written by one of the leading poets of the time, matches his derisive attack on feminine vanity, malice, and superstition in apt polemical counterpoint, with a damaging description of the gentlemen reformers. Tarabai recasts the common charges made against women and demonstrates in her prose that the men themselves are invariably far more guilty of everything they accuse women of. She rounds off the earliest full-length polemical piece in the history of feminist writing in India with a scathing analysis of the female characters in the stories and plays popular in her time, showing them up as fictions of fertile male imaginations, and as having little to do with real women.

The mode acquires a whole new range of possibilities in Rokeya Sakhawat Hossain's *Sultana's Dream*. The story cheekily turns the tables on men, inventing, in a carnivalesque inversion of the *zenana,* the female quarters to which women of the aristocracy and upper classes were traditionally restricted, a culture where the men are confined in a *murdana*. But the genius of this unusual story lies in its bold transformation of an issue—purdah—the reformers had taken up with such zeal, and the witty treatment of the theme. Purdah in Rokeya's story is not merely a curtain behind which a woman must live or only the veil she must wear. Purdah is a whole range of patriarchal practices and ideas that shut out the possibility of another world, a world, the writer suggests, that could easily be realized if women were allowed to exercise the wisdom and skills they already have.

Women's Periodicals

Historians often remark on the sudden disappearance of women's issues from the agenda of public debate in the last decades of the nineteenth century. The women's question, they argue, bowed out as nationalism swept in and replaced the social concerns of the reform movement with political ones. There is certainly a sense in which this *is* true, and we shall have cause to discuss it later. But what is rarely recognized is that between the 1880s and the 1920s, as its limelight faded, the movement was enthusiastically carried forward, expanded, and transformed by women. All over the country women had hardly begun to read and write before they were editing and publishing in journals that had surprisingly long runs. Important among these were *Bharati* (Bengali), edited by Swarnakumari Devi, Hiranmayi Devi, and Sarala Kumari Devi between 1884 and 1912; the *Indian Ladies Magazine* (English), edited by Kamala Sattianadan between 1901 and 1938; *Savithri* (Telugu), by Pulugurti Lakshminarasamamba in the early years of the century; *Stree Darpan* (Hindi), by Rameshwari Nehru, started in 1909; *Karnataka Nandini* (Kannada), edited by Nanjanagudu Thirumalamba between 1917 and 1922. In such others as *Bamabodini Patrika*

(Bengali), *Sundari Subodh* (Gujarati), *Hindu Sundari* (Telugu), *Zenana* (Telugu), *Stree Bodh* (Gujarati), *Khatoon* (Urdu), *Tehzib Niswan* (Urdu), and *Ismat* (Urdu) women were the sole or major contributors. These journals were circulated widely, but there were dozens of others, and it is obvious from the articles that they were intended for women readers.[33]

The issues that roused the concern of earlier reformers—the hardships of widows, the evils of purdah, the need for education—are discernible here, too, but they acquire complex new dimensions that come, on the one hand, from the flexibility the movement itself acquired as it shifted away from the center of public debate to the less-visible and less-policed peripheries, and, on the other, from the fact that women had taken the causes over and, in the process, had transformed them. The widow remarriage agitations, for instance, had envisaged the reabsorption of young widows into the institution of the family. The stress in reformist arguments was as much on the barbarity of a society that treated women so badly and on the danger of their "unharnessed" sexuality, as on the hardships the widows themselves had to face. In the journal literature produced by women, the emphases clearly shift to education for widows and the possibility of their leading independent and self-reliant lives. Rarely, we found, did women themselves campaign for remarriage or support men's efforts in that direction. Sometimes, as Pulugurti Lakshminarasamamba did with Veereshalingam, they actually confronted the male reformers and accused them of bad faith. In the women's journals, Vir Bahadur Talwar shows, purdah was seen more as an obstacle to education, and as part of a larger oppressive system, than as a blot on a nation's self-respect. He quotes Saubhagyavati, writing in 1918 in *Stree Darpan,* as saying, with "neither power nor real knowledge, nor education, nor freedom . . . what point will the mere removal of purdah serve?"[34] Nazar Sajjad Hyder, whose piece has been translated here, also regards purdah thus, as obstacle, not as "social evil."

Quite a few of the writers from this period were frequent and popular contributors to the women's journals and we have taken pains to include their writing. They received little attention from mainstream critics or readers and have over the years been totally forgotten. The

---

[33]For a discussion on Urdu journals see Gail Minault, "Urdu Women's Magazines in the Twentieth Century," *Manushi* 48, 1988, pp. 2–9.
[34]Vir Bahadur Talwar, in *Recasting Women,* ed. Sangari and Vaid.

Kannada writers Tirumalamba and Kalyanamma, for instance, were major literary figures in their time, but are not known today outside a small circle of feminist scholars.[35] Darisi Annapurnamma's satires of superstitious men and fake ascetics, which appeared initially in the journals, are among the best works in that genre, but are also forgotten.

One could add to this list of those who not only kept alive but transformed the concerns of the reform movement Sughra Humayun Mirza, Tallapragada Viswasundaramma, Nazar Sajjad Hyder, Shyamala Devi, Homvati Devi, Saraswati Bai Rajwade, and the early work of Lalithambika Antherjanam. Considered individually, some, though certainly not all, of these writers may be "minor" in that their total output is not large, but as a group they provide us with a clear sense of what women were thinking and writing about and from far-flung areas of the country. And as for the myth that the women's question died out after its spectacular flowering in the second half of the nineteenth century, these writers offer evidence that women hung on to ideas of freedom and justice, and infused them with their aspirations, even as they responded to the call of the nation.

Women's Literature in the Nationalist Movement

It would seem useful, by way of a chronicle that might provide a backdrop to the literature, to record some of the events in what was to grow into an anti-imperialist struggle that inspired colonized and other oppressed peoples the world over. It is impossible to say exactly what precipitated it. By the end of the nineteenth century India was one of the poorest countries in the world. Famine and plague had added their toll to that of exploitation. But what forcibly hit the middle-class intelligentsia, who gave the movement a leadership, was the uncompromising racism of the British. As the British defined themselves as the efficient, ethical, hardworking, courageous, and masculine rulers of India (and of the world), they came to characterize Indians increasingly as slothful, deceitful, and immoral.[36] Indians were

---

[35]See C. N. Mangala, "Nanjanagudu Tirumalamba (1887–1982)," *Aniketana* 1:1, 1988, pp. 128–133.

[36]Francis G. Hutchins, *Illusion of Permanence: British Imperialism in India* (Princeton: Princeton University Press, 1967), esp. pp. 29–78, for an analysis of the process in which this took place. Several other studies and some fiction document the phenomenon.

allowed little say in the government of the country and were debarred from important posts in the administration or judiciary. The ethnocentrism that underlay James Mill's arrogant readings of Indian culture and Indian history was writ large into an elaborate cultural apparatus designed to keep the empire going. As one viceroy admitted in a letter, "We could only govern by maintaining the fact that we are the dominant race."[37] In 1883, during the famous controversy over the Ilbert Bill, which made it possible for Indian judges to hear cases in which white people were the accused and to pass judgments, the "English women of India" addressed a petition to the queen, expressing the "grave alarm" with which they contemplated the proposed change. "No native of India, however highly educated," they wrote, "can possess the knowledge or sympathy essential to a correct appreciation of the feelings and conduct of European women."[38] But as Sumit Sarkar points out, "For the less fortunate racism took the cruder forms of kicks and blows and shooting 'accidents' as the *sahib* disciplined his *punkha* coolie or bagged a native by mistake when out on *shikar."* No less than eighty-one "accidents" were recorded in the years between 1880 and 1900.[39] White courts awarded ridiculously light penalties. Some of the pieces translated here touch on these issues. Krupa Sattianadan's autobiographical novel *Saguna* has several episodes in which the young Saguna exposes the arrogance and stupidity of white racism; few things disrupt the even-keeled composure of Lakshmibai Tilak's narrative or her ability to laugh as much as the missionaries she and her husband had to interact with; and Pandita Ramabai's correspondence with Sister Geraldine holds up a mirror to a little-explored aspect of white racism, the violent desire to crush independent thought of any kind.

Though the Sepoy Rebellion of 1857, later renamed the First Indian War of Independence, is sometimes cited as the beginning of active nationalist politics, most historians trace the beginning to the outcry against the 1905 partition of Bengal into a predominantly Muslim Eastern Bengal (now Bangladesh), with its capital in Dacca, and Bengal proper, which was to include more Oriya and Hindi speaking peoples than Bengalis. The British claimed administrative convenience, but In-

---

[37]Lord Elgin, Letter to Roseberry, July 1895, quoted in Sumit Sarkar, *Modern India* (Delhi: Macmillan, 1983), p. 23.
[38]From Richard Cody, "British Attitudes: A Selection of Documents," Ph.D. dissertation, Columbia University, 1970, pp. 191–195.
[39]Sarkar, 1983, p. 22.

dians were convinced that the partition was designed to break up the increasingly powerful pressure group among the middle-class intelligentsia of Bengal.

The widespread agitations that followed, known as the Swadeshi (of one's own country) movement of 1905 to 1908, seemed finally to turn the tide against reform in the public eye. This movement was perhaps even more important than the later struggles in bringing about transformations in cultural practices. Swadeshi activists roundly rejected the "mendicant" politics of petition and appeal, and called for a boycott initially of foreign goods, especially textiles, which soon expanded to include government schools and colleges, courts, titles, government services, and Western education as such. Women refused to use foreign goods, including utensils and bangles, and, like Swarnakumari Devi's daughter, Sarala Devi Choudhurani, organized *samitis* to propagate the Swadeshi message through speeches, discussions, songs, and magic lantern lectures. Sarala Devi herself toured all over northern India lecturing and setting up branches of the Bharat Stree Mahamandal, which she declared were to preserve the memory of the past, study history and science, master the regional languages, and strive for women's rights.[40] At the height of the movement, she was in Lahore, where she was full-time manager of the *Hindustan Press.* She set aside three of the machines for job work and three for the regular printing of the paper, making sure in the process that if a confiscatory order was passed, the subversive work could be carried on with the other three.[41] The movement expanded rapidly. In Maharashtra, under the leadership of Lokmanya Tilak (1856–1923), the Savarkar brothers, and several others, the boycott grew into a major force. Its reverberations were felt all over northern India and in the Punjab as well as in Madras and parts of what is now Andhra.

Culturally, it was an extremely fertile period. Popular festivals were revived and given a new nationalist slant, as were folk theater forms. The songs composed in this period were sung in the ensuing decades. Painters broke with Western realism and looked to Rajput, Mughal, and Kangra paintings and to the art of Ajanta and Ellora for inspiration. The beginnings of Indian film are self-consciously Swadeshi. Describing his inspiration—a film on the life of Christ—

[40]Sarala Devi Choudhurani, "A Women's Movement," *Modern Review,* Oct. 1911, pp. 344–350.
[41]Home Political Confidential Files: 63–70, November 1908, cited in Manmohan Kaur, *Women in India's Freedom Struggle* (Delhi: Sterling, 1985), p. 98.

Dadasaheb Phalke writes, "While the life of Christ was rolling fast before my eyes, I was mentally visualizing the gods Sri Krishna, Sri Ramachandra, their Gokul and Ayodhya. Could we, the sons of India, ever be able to see Indian images on the screen?"[42] Major new theories of Indian art and Indian philosophy emerged.[43] Among those who turned to the literature of the people and began collecting folk songs and stories were several women, including Shovana Devi, a younger member of the distinguished Tagore family.

The boycott of government noneducational establishments was accompanied by a Swadeshi national education program on "national lines and under national control," which included physical and moral training and instruction in Indian history and culture, but also relevant technical and scientific education.[44] Perhaps most important for women's writing was the emphasis on *atmashakti* (self-reliance), which implied self-help and constructive village work but also the building of character and the reassertion of national dignity, honor, and confidence. Patriotism demanded a supreme sacrifice, and though men and women were both required to make it, it was the women who were to provide the lead. Tanika Sarkar quotes a collection of proscribed articles by nationalist leaders that make it quite clear that unless the vital principle of *shakti* (power), which the women hold, is released, the great act of sacrifice will not be complete.[45] A couplet from a later poem captures the contrast, seen from the nationalist point of view, between the prospects offered women by the reform movement and by nationalism. "A wife used to be the goddess Shakti to us / Now she is just a 'dear.' "[46]

A powerful new female figure emerged in the nationalist imagination and can be encountered in text after text of the period. She was, in keeping with the now-naturalized Victorian ideals of domestic virtue, patient and long suffering. But the new woman was also self-confident

---

[42]Dadasaheb Phalke, quoted in Ashish Rajadhyaksha, "The Phalke Era: Conflict of Traditional Form and Modern Technology," *Journal of Arts and Ideas* 14–15, 1987, pp. 47–78.

[43]See Ratnabali Chattopadhyay, "Nationalism and Form in Indian Painting," *Journal of Arts and Ideas* 14–15, 1987, pp. 5–46.

[44]The quoted phrase is from Bipan Chandra et al., *India's Struggle for Independence* (Delhi: Viking, 1988), p. 130.

[45]Tanika Sarkar, "Politics and Women in Bengal—The Conditions and Meaning of Participation," in *Women in Colonial India,* ed. J. Krishnamurthy, p. 236.

[46]"Shiksha Bipad," *Bangabani,* 10 April 1933, quoted in Tanika Sarkar, p. 241.

and autonomous, conscious of her power and of the strength she could find in tradition: a gentle but stern custodian of the nation's moral life. And this was a figure that dominated the literary imagination for several decades to come.

In reality pedestals are extremely precarious places, but in an imaginative world they have a certain power. The reform movement's image of women as uneducated, ill-bred victims of atrocity and burdens on a nation's self-respect shifted, and women became part of the struggle, indeed the real guardians of the nation's spiritual essence. It is not at all difficult to appreciate why this self-affirming image had such popular appeal, or why women felt empowered by it and by the significant positions it provided them in the tasks that faced the nation. The heroines of Nirupama Devi's immensely popular novels, for instance, are traditional and quietly resolute, yet have tremendous strength. Nirupama herself was a widow who scrupulously followed the prescriptions laid down for a Hindu widow's life. Her characters too draw their energy from a vital connection with tradition, and the resulting strength is one that every other element in the world of the novel is forced to acknowledge in the course of the narrative. Similar schemes emerge in the poetry and the memoirs of Mahadevi Varma, Subhadra Kumari Chauhan, and many other writers in the early twentieth century.

Cultural historians commonly cite the popular historical novels of Bankimchandra Chatterjee (1838–1894) and R. C. Dutt (1848–1909) as the beginnings of nationalist thought in literature. More interesting from our point of view than Bankimchandra's *Anandamath,* 1882, which has definite nationalist themes, is *Devi Chaudhurani,* 1884, in which the protagonist, Prafulla, thrown out of her husband's family, becomes Devi Chaudhurani, a robber queen with an almost demonic power. It is a curious allegorical work, nationalist, and, despite the ending in which the protagonist goes back to the family as a good daughter-in-law, feminist. The thugs in her band are the keepers of the nation's soul and their battles finally ethical. In Bankimchandra's social and historical novels, Jashodhara Bagchi writes, womanhood "becomes both symbol of a ravaged order and of the resistance to such ravages." Bankimchandra successfully appropriates the mythology of power as a feminine force, as Shakti. "In the late novels the stereotype is given a distinctive turn . . . Preoccupied with the heroic obligations of preserving a Hindu order, he threw up, one after another these images of women who have defied the normal canons of femininity in order to join the resistance against the crisis in the order."[47] Rabindranath Tagore's (1861–1941) brilliant novel, *Ghare Bhaire* (The Home and the World), 1916, mirrors the tensions of this creative period in the life of Bimala, who is torn between the quiet liberal humanism of a husband devoted to her growth and the compelling attraction she feels for the Swadeshi leader Sandeep and what he and his cause demand of her.[48]

Much of the tractlike normative literature and the polemical narratives commonly associated with the nineteenth-century social reform movement tended to feature a limited set of characters in a predictable scenario: child widows, victims of sati, wives in purdah, women embattled against tradition and superstition. The narrative trimmed and shaped the problem in such a way that the self-evident solution in the early years of the century was Christianity, whereas in the later decades it was Progress with due respect for Tradition. To put it this way may caricature these efforts somewhat, but the intent is not to belittle the pain of a widow's hard existence or the terrible restrictions of purdah. Instead, we mean to give a sense of the harsh, flat light that focused on the women's question in the mainstream literature of that period and created figures of women out of morality plays to act out its dramas. Women's literature of the late nineteenth century and the early decades of the twentieth century breaks totally out of these programmatic molds. Landscapes and figures neither imagined nor missed in the earlier years move onto the page. Stories have new shapes and are told from new points of view. The shift is gradual, initially uncertain and tentative, but clearly discernible all the same. What emerged was a many-faceted and often contradictory phenomenon not easily held down in a single formulation or an inert sense of period. Obviously the spread of women's education had a great deal to do with it. In 1863 there were 95 girls' schools in Bengal with a registration of 2,500. By 1890, the number had shot up to 2,238 schools with an

---

[47]Jashodhara Bagchi, *Economic and Political Weekly* 20:43, Oct. 1985, pp. WS-58–62.

[48]Mihir Bhattacharya explores Tagore's critique of the female figure set up by militant nationalism. "It is part of Tagore's design in *Chaturanga* to negate a version of subjective liberation in which the whole world is dipped in the font of erotic, theological femininity," he writes. "Rabindranath Tagore and the Oriental Woman: A Reading of *Chaturanga*," unpublished paper read at a seminar entitled "Literature, Society and Ideology in the Victorian Era," Jadavpur University, March 1987.

attendance of over 80,000. Figures from other regions reflected similar trends. But equally important was the new nationalist mood and the self-confidence it inspired. In fact it is only as we place literary production in the next three or four decades in the context of these changes that we can appreciate what was at stake in the moves women made through their writing.

In some ways the mood is prefigured in the late nineteenth century in Tarabai Shinde's critique, but also in Mokshodayani's impatience with the reformers who make speeches and give themselves airs even as they cringe before the white sahibs. More subtle in its understanding is a fine short story by Swarnakumari Devi, "Biroda" (Mutiny/Revolt). The story records the thoughts of an Indian woman as she listens to white women speak about sati and about the mutiny of 1857 with the easy authority of those whose worldview has never been contested. The heroine privately transforms each statement the others make to give it the meaning it would have for an Indian, but is unable to break into their conversation or make her point.

The novels Kashibai Kanitkar and Hari Narayan Apte wrote after they met each other in 1884 reveal a similar interweaving of nationalist sentiment with a feminism more subtle and creative than that which emerged with the social reform movement. Kashibai's brilliantly constructed utopian novel, *Palkicha Gonda* (The Silk Tassel in the Palanquin), was published in 1928, but it reflects her concerns at the turn of the century. The state that has the *palkicha gonda* as a symbol is ruled by a wise woman. The heroine, Tai, is an educated woman, forced through her mother's ambitions into marriage with a prince, who turns out to be insane. Supported by her mother-in-law, Tai takes over the administration of his state. Both men and women are happy and fulfilled in her new regime. The prologue, in which Kashibai explains how she "came across" the story, is important. Her curiosity roused by a woman she meets on a journey, Kashibai goes to Palkicha Gonda, and stays at the village high school. Many of the students there, she found, were married women, some driven away from their homes by husbands who were drunkards, others deserted or abandoned. She learned that women in this country did not face destitution outside marriage. They practiced their hereditary occupations, and fulfilled important social functions. She learns about Tai and finds a manuscript written by Tai's younger sister, which tells the story of this wise administration. The novel, Kashibai writes, is based on that manuscript. A certain nostalgia for a lost village community and its organic order is evident here, but so is a sense of women as a vital part of that regenerated world, and not merely helpmates, as in the vedic utopias, in sacrificial rituals.

An important group of almost forgotten women writers in Maharashtra, among whom were Indira Sahasrabuddhe, Geeta Sane, and Vibhavari Shirurkar, for instance, specifically directed their attention to the terrible contradictions in the promises of freedom and equality that were held out by the liberal reformers; implicitly demanding that the questions be addressed more honestly by the nationalists. Needless to say, they met with little success. Indira Sahasrabuddhe casts the controversial novel *Balutai Dada Ghe* (Learn a Lesson, Balutai), which was also the last one she wrote, as an autobiographical narrative in which the protagonist's aspirations are crushed by her "progressive" father even as she is deserted by her "progressive" lover. "Progressive" commitments, in the message offered to the younger girl, are double-edged and hollow, and a woman who takes them seriously will suffer. Vibhavari Shirurkar raises the question of what a woman wants from marriage and of women's sexuality outside it. She brings a new image of woman—the single independent working woman—into Marathi fiction. Her controversial *Virlele Swapna* (The Dream That Disintegrated) investigates the question of "love" in marriage. The wife, Rohini, is a strong-willed and independent person and her views on her own status in the relationship, as well as on what constitutes sexual morality and social ethics, emerge in sharp focus. These ideas are more than the husband's much paler, more simplistic world can cope with. In a series of unusual and grossly underestimated political novels, Geeta Sane connects the ongoing, hidden discriminations against women with questions of class and nation.

But the journal literature was also forging new bonds with nationalism. As we noticed earlier, from the 1880s well into the early decades of the twentieth century, journals edited by women or meant for a female readership had provided a supportive base for women's writing and had kept alive and developed the issues raised in the reform movements. These writings broadened the scope of the women's question as it had been posed in the reform movement, infused it with new feminist strains, and even subverted its original commitments. It is difficult to pick out one figure or one work as representative of the widespread nationalist movement because it was a broad-based, popular development, somewhat at odds with the form of this anthology, which is designed around major figures and major works. Nevertheless, we have attempted to capture a little of this significant movement through the work of our first feminist historian, Bandaru Acchamamba, who was also a distinguished nationalist; the Kannada writer and activist Shyamala Devi; and the Hindi writers Homvati Devi and Kamla Chaudhry. The unusual piece of historical fiction by Kalyan-amma represents an angle some women writers added to the militant Hinduism of Tilak, Rajwade, and the Savarkar brothers.

Though its influence on nationalist thought and culture was far-reaching, by 1908 the Swadeshi movement had been broken politically. Political action, however, was revived during the First World War in the Home Rule agitations, with which the name of Annie Besant (1847–1933), the Irish suffragist, is associated. The nationalist movement picked up momentum after 1917, when important demonstrations were organized in different parts of the country. In a series of *satyagrahas* (literally, "to persist in the truth"), organized to use the Gandhian strategy of nonviolent, passive resistance, specific issues were taken up, including the plight of the workers in the indigo plantations and textile mills, and the distress of peasants who, despite drought and crop failure, had not been given remission of land taxes. The most famous of these was organized in 1919 on a nationwide scale to protest against the Rowlatt bills, which were designed to curtail the civil liberties of Indians. One of the responses to the series of meetings and protests all over the country was the Jallianwala Bagh massacre, in which British troops fired continuously for ten minutes at an unarmed crowd of women, children, and men, leaving (these were British government estimates) 329 dead and several injured.

In 1930, the Congress launched a civil disobedience movement prior to which Gandhi addressed a letter to the British viceroy. British rule, he said, "has impoverished the dumb millions by a system of progressive exploitation. . . . It has reduced us politically to serfdom. It has degraded us spiritually. . . . On the 11th day of this month, I shall proceed with such co-workers of the Ashram as I can take, to disregard the provisions of the salt laws. . . . It is, I know, open to you to frustrate my design by arresting me. I hope that there will be tens of thousands ready, in a disciplined manner, to take up the work after me, and, in the act of disobeying the Salt Act to lay themselves open to the penalties of a law that should never have disfigured the statute-book."[49] What followed was the famous Salt Satyagraha, which many writers in this collection make reference to. Together with seventy-

---

[49]M. K. Gandhi, *Collected Works,* Vol. 43 (Delhi: Ministry of Information and Broadcasting, 1971), pp. 3–7.

eight other members of his ashram at Sabarmati, Gandhi walked the 240 miles to the coast at Dandi, where they were to break the law and collect salt from the beach. They stopped in the villages on the way to speak to the people and explain their action.

The event made world headlines, but more important, it riveted the attention of the nation. Huge crowds met the marchers: the route was festooned with banners and leaves. Men and women sat outside their homes spinning on the *charka* as the marchers passed. By the time the marchers reached Dandi, they had become a crowd of two thousand people, who approached the waiting police cordons, with Gandhi, Sarojini Naidu (who could not be dissuaded from joining), and a few others in the front ranks. As they came closer, the police rushed forward with their steel-tipped *lathis* (sticks) and set upon the nonresisting protesters. Row upon row of the injured were carried away on makeshift stretchers as others took their places. "Not an arm was raised in defence, and by 11:00 A.M. When the temperature in the shade was 116 degrees farenheit, the toll was already 320 injured and two dead."[50] The American journalist Webb Miller wrote that never before in his long experience of reporting such events had he "seen unresisting people being methodically bashed into a bloody pulp."[51]

In 1942 came the Quit India call. It was, from then on, to be a head-on, though nonviolent, confrontation "on the widest possible scale." In a surprise move, the British government arrested all the main leaders of the Congress party and jailed them in different parts of the country. The reaction from the people was massive, and it came from the workers and the middle classes in the towns as well as from the peasants in the villages. By the end of 1943, 91,836 people had been arrested; 208 police outposts, 332 railway stations, and 945 post offices had been destroyed or severely damaged.[52] The brutality of the reprisals was unmatched by anything that had gone before. The British were out, they clearly proclaimed, to break the movement.

But after the Second World War, with the Labour party in power in Britain, popular elections were declared in India. Though there had been several rounds of discussion, the final decision, arrived at not without pressure from the All India Women's Conference, which resisted *all* proposals for partial enfranchisement whether on the basis of

---

[50]Chandra et al., *India's Struggle for Independence,* p. 275.
[51]Quoted in Sumit Sarkar, *Modern India,* p. 290.
[52]Sumit Sarkar, p. 395.

property ownership or gender, was "universal franchise." The Congress party won the 1946 elections with a clear majority. The year that followed was a period of extended negotiation: among the Congress, the Muslim League, and the British. Clashes between Hindus and Muslims increased, and with political independence in 1947 also came the partition of India and Pakistan and the terrible riots that followed.

By all accounts women's participation in the Congress-led freedom movement was impressive. In the early stages, Congress women picketed shops selling foreign goods and made huge bonfires in which foreign cloth was burned.[53] What the enemy is forced to concede is always more telling. Sumit Sarkar quotes a white police official from Uttar Pradesh, who wrote in 1930, "The Indian woman is struggling for domestic and national liberty at the same time, and like a woman she is utterly unreasonable and illogical in her demands and in her methods, but like a woman she has enormous influence over the stronger sex. . . . Many local officials including police officers have . . . suffered more from taunts and abuse from their female relatives than from any other source."[54] Peasant women took more risky initiatives. At Indas in Bankura, for instance, hundreds of women lay down on the road and successfully barred the exit of distrained goods from the village for three whole days.[55] In several villages, when the men were arrested or had to go underground, women moved into positions of leadership and continued the fight. Women were also part of more militant action. In 1931 two teenaged girls assassinated the district magistrate at Comilla. Shortly afterward Preetilata Waddadar, Kalpana Joshi, and a group of others attacked the Chittagong European Club.[56] Bina Das fired at Governor Anderson at a Calcutta University convocation. In the peasant movements of Telangana and Tebhaga, women were involved in large numbers and as key figures. Recently compiled oral histories of the women who took part in the Telangana movement

---

[53]See Usha Bala, *Indian Women Freedom Fighters* (Delhi: Manohar, 1986), for brief portraits of major figures; Manmohan Kaur, *Women in India's Freedom Struggle,* for a narrative account based on detailed archival work; and Kamaladevi Chattopadhyay, *Indian Women's Battle for Freedom* (Delhi: Abhinav Publications, 1983), for a fascinating personal account by one who was the secretary of the All India Women's Conference during the 1930s and 1940s.

[54]Quoted in Sumit Sarkar, *Modern India,* p. 290.

[55]Tanika Sarkar, in *Women in Colonial India,* ed. J. Krishnamurthy, p. 237.

[56]See Kalpana Joshi, "Remembering Preetilata Waddadar," *Manushi* 3:1, 1982, pp. 39–40.

suggest that the peasant struggles for land, and against the repressive state, opened up life possibilities they would earlier not even have dreamed of.[57]

Tanika Sarkar points out that even socially conservative, upper-caste families applauded women's participation in the nonviolent Gandhian movement. "There can be no denying,"she writes, that this step must have been "preceded by an acute, even revolutionary, struggle with their own sensibilities and inhibitions, but even that must have been facilitated by sure knowledge of social approval."[58] Several commentators, Vina Mazumdar (1976), Madhu Kishwar (1985), and Devaki Jain (1986), consider the Gandhian movement in some ways a feminist one. Gandhi, Mazumdar argues, respected women's "personal dignity" and "without belittling their roles as mothers and wives . . . [gave them] . . . equal tasks to perform in the achievement of freedom."[59] He repeatedly emphasized, she points out, that they were not to be regarded as sexual playthings and that they were the real foundations on which Indian society was built. Devaki Jain centers her analysis on the early notion of self-reliance, which the Gandhian movement also emphasized. It involved, she writes, simplicity and identification with the poor, but also self-confidence and the desire for peace. Gandhi, she points out, insisted that women should not be treated as sex objects. Further, the bonds with tradition and "the rules of the ashrams made it possible for women to 'come out' of the narrow worlds of their homes to participate in a wider community."[60] Madhu Kishwar, who provides us with the most detailed analysis, both of Gandhi's writings and his actual relationships with women, argues that Gandhi's success was less ideological than strategic: he drew on traditional symbols of female power, emphasized women's strength, and appealed directly to them, addressing them as "self-conscious arbiters of their own destiny."[61] She acknowledges that Gandhi sought personal and ethical transformations for women and not material ones, but regards the

---

[57]Stree Shakti Sanghatana, *"We Were Making History . . .": Life Stories of Women in the Telangana People's Struggle* (Delhi: Kali for Women, 1989; 1st ed., in Telugu, 1986).

[58]Tanika Sarkar, in *Women in Colonial India,* ed. J. Krishnamurthy, p. 237.

[59]Vina Mazumdar, in *Indian Women,* ed. B. R. Nanda, p. 58.

[60]Devaki Jain, "Gandhian Contributions Towards a Theory of 'Feminist Ethic,' " in *Speaking of Faith: Cross-Cultural Perspectives in Women, Religion and Social Change,* ed. Devaki Jain and Diana Eck, (Delhi: Kali for Women, 1986), pp. 255–270.

[61]Madhu Kishwar, "Women in Gandhi," *Economic and Political Weekly* 20:40, 41, 1985, pp. 1691–1702; 1753–1758.

movement as having empowered women all the same. Sujata Patel qualifies these claims. Even though Gandhi did emphasize women's power, she argues, Gandhian ideology also restricted the scope of their political involvement and growth. The spinning wheel became a symbol of women's participation in the regeneration of the country without having to leave their homes. In the later stages of the movement, 1932 to 1948, a new ideal took over. Women were seen as the ones whose strength lay in their weakness. And that strength, Gandhi proclaimed, was one toward which *all* satyagraha must strain, and, in the process, draw on a nonviolent feminine strength against the brute masculinity of British power.[62]

It comes as no surprise, therefore, that women's militancy was always sharply censured. The popular novelist Saratchandra, who is famous for his sympathetic portraits of suffering upper-caste women (he was also a support and inspiration for the novelist Nirupama Devi), for instance, ridiculed educated, Westernized women who sought roles outside their homes and especially in politics in his influential novel *Pather Dabi* (Bid for the Pathway), 1926. Perhaps the harshest rejection came from Rabindranath Tagore, who in *Char Adhyaya* (Four Chapters), 1934, made his revulsion for militant women clear. When the revolutionary Ela breaks down and admits her mistake, the protagonist Atin is triumphant: "At last I see the real girl . . . you reign in the home with a fan in your hand and preside over the serving of milk, rice and fish. When you appear with wild hair and angry eyes on the arena where politics has the whiphand, you are not your normal self but unbalanced, unnatural."[63]

We were ourselves initially surprised to discover that these momentous happenings in public life were hardly reflected in women's writing. We have extracted a section from Sudha Chauhan's account of her mother's life in jail, and could have included similar accounts from biographies and autobiographies written in the 1950s and 1960s. Tallapragada Viswasundaramma's poem "Jailu Gadiyaramu" (Jailhouse Clock) is the only piece we found that was actually written at the time and speaks of a woman's experience in the freedom struggle. We were puzzled about this and searched again, more carefully, to find writers

---

[62]Sujata Patel, "The Construction and Reconstruction of Women in Gandhi," *Economic and Political Weekly* 23:8, 1988, pp. 377–387.
[63]Rabindranath Tagore, *Char Adhyaya* (Four Chapters), 1934, quoted by Tanika Sarkar, in *Women in Colonial India,* ed. J. Krishnamurthy, p. 240.

and texts we might have overlooked, but we did not meet with much success. Sarojini Naidu, one of the country's best known poets and a popular speaker on Congress platforms, wrote very little after the early 1920s when she became involved in politics.[64] Mahadevi Varma, who gave her life to women's education in the Swadeshi mode, wrote only memoirs and lyric poetry in which the public events of those times are barely discernible. Kuntala Kumari Sabat, who was also actively involved in the nationalist movement, writes poetry that dwells mostly on personal experiences. From other regions too the evidence was disappointing: a story by Dhirubhen Patel in which the backdrop was the freedom movement but the plot itself centered on an apparently unrelated personal trauma; and a much translated story by Lalithambika Antherjanam, "Koddunkattilpetta Orila" (A Leaf Caught in the Whirlwind), written in 1950, about a young girl caught in the riots at the time of Partition.

The most significant of these works is perhaps Lalithambika's award-winning novel *Agnisakshi* (Witness by Fire), which traces what she regards as the fortunes of the women's movement itself in the life of the protagonist. Thetikutty courageously breaks with the deadening oppression of a Namboodiri household, and joins a Gandhian ashram, but leaves, disillusioned. Her last years are spent as a religious mendicant on the banks of the Ganges. The husband she has left behind has gradually moved further and further into a life of austerity and prayer. They have taken different paths, this strange couple marked out for each other by the stars: he accepts the stern demands of his Namboodiri tradition; she rebels, but her restless soul arrives, of its own free will, after its arduous journey, at a very similar resolution. It is a disturbing prognosis—the author herself admits as much in the preface—which seems to suggest that whatever the passing rebellion, one is drawn irresistibly back to a waiting destiny. Yet it is a conclusion that several women writing in the context of the nationalist movement arrive at. Lalithambika's story, however, is told in flashback by a younger sister-in-law, now settled in domestic life, who was always compellingly drawn to this rebel figure, after a chance meeting that unnerves them both. The narrative is inflected by the attraction between these two women, one powerful enough, the novel seems to

---

[64] For a sensitive discussion of Sarojini Naidu's poetry that reflects also on this question, see Meena Alexander, "Sarojini Naidu: Romanticism and Resistance," *Economic and Political Weekly* 20:43, 1985, pp. WS–68–71.

suggest, to undermine the painstakingly constructed equipoise of both their lives.

Nationalist Rearticulations of Gender

Cultural historians have recently turned their attention to what is termed the sudden disappearance of the women's question from the forums of public debate as nationalism began to establish a hold over the minds of the middle-class intelligentsia. Why did it happen? they ask. Some (and there are many), like the Bangladeshi historian Gulam Murshid, regard the mid-nineteenth-century efforts to lift the status of women as part of the modernization process. They relate the social reform movements to the new ideals of equality, rational inquiry, and individual worth that emerged as a result of the contact with liberal *Western* ideas.[65] Whereas the modernizers demanded a critique of tradition, Murshid argues, the cultural politics of nationalism glorified the past and tended to demand that everything traditional or Indian be defended. Any questioning of traditional practices began to be regarded as "Western" and antinational, and was, when it was not actively attacked, simply dismissed. In his view, as far as women were concerned, nationalism was clearly retrogressive. This tension is clearly visible in a figure like Muthulakshmi Reddi (1891–1968), who took an active part in the work of the women's India Association right from its inception in 1917, and who supported the nonbrahmin movement in Tamilnadu all her life, but was reluctant to support the Congress until it made its commitments on the women's question clear.

Joanna Liddle and Rama Joshi bring imperialism more directly into their analysis of this conflict. One of the limitations in the way the women's question was taken up in the nineteenth century, they argue, was that it was caught between the political agendas of British colonialists and Indian nationalists. Thus, women could not, under the circumstances, envisage an independent program. Women were inhibited in this manner, since they "not only had to fit their understanding of women's oppression within the conceptual framework of the national movement, they were also limited in how far they could confront male dominance as a major cause of women's subordination because of the way this would be used by the foreign rulers against the whole na-

---

[65]Murshid, *The Reluctant Debutante*.

tion."[66] Like Murshid, Liddle and Joshi seem to have few questions about what constitutes women's interests, or even about "progress," but they are willing to acknowledge necessary constraints on women's quest for freedom.

Scholars who have questioned such a linear or progressive understanding of history claim that the liberal ideals of reformers could not have been realized under the economic and political conditions of colonial rule, and warn against applying such simple, linear narratives of progress to the study of nineteenth-century India. What appears as retrogressive in nationalism was not a conservative backlash, but the logical limits of reformist programs in a colonial situation that would never, as Sumit Sarkar writes, allow more than a "weak and distorted" caricature of "full blooded" bourgeois modernity, either for women or for men.[67]

Partha Chatterjee agrees with Sumit Sarkar. The question of women illuminates the contradiction between "progress" and nationalism with a spectacular flourish, he argues, suggesting that nationalism is "retrogressive" only from the point of view of Enlightenment liberalism. As he sees it, the women's question was not repressed; it "disappeared" with nationalism only because, as far as nationalist ideology was concerned, the problem had been resolved. His thesis is provocative, and he draws on popular novels, plays, songs, and advice books, mostly written by men, to argue his case. Nationalist self-identity, he argues, was predicated on a division between material life, in which it was acceptable to take the lead from the West, and spiritual life, in which the East was clearly superior. It was necessary, therefore, if an Indian identity was to be consolidated, that the spiritual essence of the national culture be preserved and strengthened. This distinction between the material and the spiritual, he claims, was condensed into "an analogous, but ideologically far more powerful dichotomy between the inner and the outer. The home and the world." Although the "outer," which was associated with male domains, could change, the sanctity of the "inner," which was to be preserved by women, could not be touched. The constant anxiety, for instance, that education or reform of any kind would result in the Westernization of women—and the subsequent collapse of an essentially Indian identity—can be traced

---

[66]Joanna Liddle and Rama Joshi, *Daughters of Independence: Gender, Caste and Class in India* (Delhi: Kali for Women, 1986), p. 40.

[67]Sumit Sarkar, *A Critique of Colonial India* (Calcutta: Papyrus, 1985), esp. pp. 1–17 and 71–76.

back, he believes, to this ideological scheme. "To ridicule the idea of a Bengali woman trying to imitate the ways of a memsahib . . . was a sure recipe calculated to evoke raucous laughter and moral condemnation in both male and female audiences."[68] Moreover, the burden on women to maintain the spirituality of the national character was all the more heavy because men were being forced to change in response to the pressures of the material world. "Each of these capitulations had now to be compensated by an assertion of spiritual purity on the part of the women."[69] This did not mean that women had to be confined to the home. So long as their spirituality was adequately and self-evidently protected and its purity demonstrated, they could take part in public life.

The emphasis on the nationalist *resolution* of the women's question completely obscures what is at stake in the narrative that precedes and leads up to that conclusion, but the evidence from women's writing seems broadly to support Chatterjee's conclusion. If we look at the work of the major writers of the 1920s to the 1940s—Nirupama Devi, Subhadhra Kumari Chauhan, Mahadevi Varma, Lalithambika Antherjanam, Dhirubhen Patel, Balamani Amma, Nanjanagudu Tirumalamba, or M. K. Indira—the most compelling imaginative task they address seems to be the creation of this new resilient self, one that is not easily understood or explained, but is, all the same, a power to be reckoned with. The backdrop is often, though, as Lalithambika's extraordinary novel *Agnisakshi* shows, not always, domestic. Further research into the cultural formations of this period would help us appreciate more richly the work of reclamation and reorientation that is taking place in these writings. As we saw earlier, other trends, such as those found in the women's journals and in the critiques of the reform movement, made by writers who did not use the images and the idiom of national movement, run parallel, but the concerns of the writers influenced by mainstream nationalism are quite distinct.

Compared to the positions of Tarabai Shinde, Bandaru Acchamamba, or Rokeya Hossain, in earlier decades, these works seem conservative, restrained, confined to spaces that have always been

---

[68]Partha Chatterjee, "The Nationalist Resolution of the Women's Question," Occasional Paper No. 94, Centre for Studies in Social Sciences, Calcutta, 1987, p. 9.
[69]Ibid., p. 19.

sanctioned to women, cautious to a fault. The pattern of everyday life is rarely broken by the spectacular or the grotesque. History, politics, antagonisms of gender or class do not intrude in immediately recognizable forms. Yet this fiction seems to chart women's slow but unmistakable and moving struggles for dignity and personhood outside the double-edged promises of the Enlightenment and the social reform movement. It is a lonely struggle, but if we are to go by the popularity of some of these writers, it is a struggle other women recognize and regard as realist—as against that of popular romances, which they accept as escapist. In contrast to the earlier writing that focused on the landed aristocracy or the intelligentsia in big cities, or sometimes the peasantry, these stories are set in small towns and are about middle-class lives. Consider Dhirubhen Patel's *Vishrambkatha* (Revelation), for instance.[70] A son, typically insensitive to the mother he has "dutifully" accompanied on a pilgrimage, waits impatiently—his meal will be late—as his mother stops to talk to a childhood friend she runs into. The two have not met for several years. They are married, their children grown. The mother introduces her son. The friend looks puzzled. He doesn't resemble Vinayak at all, she remarks. The mother smiles. I never married him, she explains. That brief phrase shatters the son's image of his mother—and cracks open his world. He had never imagined that the mother he had so casually taken for granted as "traditional" could have had a male friend or that she was once young. The reader too is overwhelmed by the new awareness of the hidden reserves this "ordinary," "conservative" housewife and mother holds. Dhirubhen captures the moment in a few deft strokes, remarkable for their understatement. The mother is not a rebel. Far from it. But in the story a revolution of sorts has indeed been achieved. The Bengali writer Ashapurna Debi's best stories have similar shock waves waiting just below the surface.

---

[70]Translated by Bina Bhakta in *Manushi* 23, 1984, p. 43 and reprinted in *Longman Anthology of World Literature by Women, 1875–1975,* ed. Miriam Arkin and Barbara Schollar (New York: Longman, 1988), pp. 771–773.

JOGESWARI ──────────────────

(early 19th century)   *Bengali*

Contemporary records tell us that between the 1820s and 1830s, around
the time when the well-known *kabiyals* Bhola Moira and Nilu Thakur
were at the height of their fame, a woman named Jogeswari formed her
own group and toured the districts. *Kabigan* is a form of poetic duel or
repartee, invariably spontaneously composed, which flourished between
the middle of the eighteenth and the middle of the nineteenth centuries.
Two teams of artists (kabiyals) compete in a performance, which was often
sponsored by a rich patron. Folksingers generally moved freely among
different strata, but this roving band of women artists must have been an
outstanding exception to the norms even of those times, since they were
widely known in many parts of Bengal. Yet the profiles of kabiyals that
Ishwarchandra Gupta featured in his journal *Sambad Pravarkar,* right
through 1854, do not include one on Jogeswari.

In their compositions, women kabiyals make no secret of the various
forms of harassment they were subjected to by male kabiyals and the high
price they had to pay to pursue their art. The well-known historian of
folk literature, Prafulla Chandra Pal, records an episode in which Bhola
Moira insults Jogeswari in a retort to one of her songs:

Why have you appeared before this gathering?
Why do you bellow here like a cow in labor?
Your time must be near.
Shameless women with no sense of decorum
Bellow in gatherings of respectable men.

Jogeswari's compositions, only a few of which have been recorded, depict the situation of women in her time. Women's grief over separation
from their husbands and lovers, their desertion by men, and the charges
women made against their debauched husbands are the themes of her
songs. The song translated here is a *jhumur,* sometimes described by literary critics as a tribal song and dance performance. Many jhumurs present
variations on the themes and episodes of the Radha-Krishna story (lovers
separated, lovers united, sensuous lovemaking) but obviously also refer to
the experiences of the contemporary listener and touch on contemporary
issues in public life. The bawdy, satirical humor and the explicit sensuality
of such folk songs came in for much criticism from the nineteenth-century
reformers, who felt they were not suitable for proper middle-class women.

◆

[If fortune has brought you my way at last]

If fortune has brought you my way at last,
Sit a while, my lord, I implore you
And allow me to lay bare my heart.

You brought me to this cloister of love
And now I can see you no more,
You have deserted my chapel forever.

I am a faithful wife,
I do not care for any but my lord.
But it's not for you to turn and look at me
For you possess me heart and soul.
You have thrown the jewel away that was your home
And now you go around playing with tinsel.

Neither spring nor monsoon brings you back.
You have trampled on the hopes
Of an honest woman's heart
And showered your attention on the whore.
This empire of yours shall fall, my lord,
You know not how to love.

Translated by Chandreyee Neogy.

BHABANI ————————————————

(early 19th century)   *Bengali*

Two of the most important folk forms in Bengal are the *tarja* and the
jhumur. These compositions, which are sung extempore, reflect the life and
problems of the poor and use a racy, colloquial language. Tarja is a form
of repartee, and jhumur a song and dance turn. A bawdy humor counter-
points themes of melancholy and loneliness. Questions that preoccupied
the upper strata of Bengali society in the nineteenth century such as sati
or female education rarely find place in these compositions. But laws and
administrative strictures enacted by the British government that had direct
bearing on the lives of the poor are often the themes of these songs.

Durgadas Lahiri records in his *Bengalir Gaan* (Bengali Songs), 1906, that around 1850, in the Ghatal area of Midnapore district, there lived a tarja and jhumur artist called Bhabani. She came from a goldsmith's family and was also known as Bhaba Rani. She led two troupes that gave tarja and jhumur performances and was one of the most eminent exponents of these forms at the time. Many of Bhabani's songs parody the themes and conventions of religious songs and are hilariously subversive. In her time she was as well known as her male contemporary Bhola Moira and her compositions continue to be sung today. Troupes such as these, however, came under attack as the urban middle-class culture established its dominance. The songs were considered improper, and the artists, women of easy virtue. Sometimes the police were called in to disband gatherings and there was a sharp decline in the number of tarja and jhumur troupes. Bhabani died in Calcutta sometime in the 1860s.

◆

[Knock knock knock]

Knock knock knock
    What a shock!
There's someone at the door
In the middle of the night,
    What a fright!

Hark!
It's desire that calls me
Out into the dark.
I shan't look around,
Nor care if there's sound,
To call me a sinner would be trite.
There's someone at the door
In the middle of the night,
    What a fright!

Ram's real sweet,
Shyam's the same;
It's only my husband who's sour,
Too boring to suffer for an hour
Except when we're having a fight.
There's someone at the door
In the middle of the night,
    What a fright!

Shyam's uncle's father-in-law
    Is one hell of a man

Jadu's cousin's brother-in-law
    Now he's my latest fan.
Ma Mitter's got hysterical
    Oh what an awful sight!
There's someone at the door
In the middle of the night,
    What a fright!

Translated by Chandreyee Neogy.

RASSUNDARI DEVI ⎯⎯⎯⎯⎯⎯⎯⎯

(1810–?)   *Bengali*

Rassundari Devi's autobiography *Amar Jiban* (My Life), 1876, is an astonishing achievement. It was the first autobiography to be written in the Bengali language and it was more than two decades before the next one, by the eminent Bengali litterateur Debendranath Tagore, was published, in 1898. Rassundari Devi was an ordinary housewife who had taught herself to read and write in secret by scratching the letters of the alphabet onto a corner of the blackened kitchen wall. Yet her Bengali prose is so crisp and readable that it could be mistaken for modern text. Rabindranath Tagore's elder brother, Jyotirindranath, a popular dramatist of his time, somewhat patronizingly conceded: "this writing is by a woman, an elderly, mature woman of 88 [sic]. I therefore read this piece with great curiosity. I was interested in marking those sections which I found well written and significant. However as I read I found I would have to underscore every line were I to do this." Though her work is rarely spoken of in those terms today, its publication was a major event for modern Bengali prose, which was still in an incipient stage.

Rassundari Devi was born in the small village of Potajia in Bengal. Because she lost her father very early in her life, she grew up thinking of herself as her mother's child. In her autobiography she described how upsetting it was for her to be introduced as her father's daughter. A persistent, almost tenacious sense of her individual identity, one that she struggles to hold onto in the most adverse of circumstances, is a striking feature of her narrative. Rassundari gives us few details about her childhood, but she does tell us that she was a timid child and her mother taught her how to pray when she was frightened. She was very close to her mother and deeply resented that she had not been allowed to go to her, or care for her, when she lay dying. Had she been a man, Rassundari writes, surely she would not have been denied the right to fulfill this basic human duty.

As was the custom in her time, she was married young and left her mother's home when she was twelve to live in what she describes as "bondage and imprisonment." Fortunately for young Rassundari, her mother-in-law was kind to her. She did not have to bear the insults and the taunts or do the heavy domestic work that fell to the lot of most newly wedded girls. But, when her mother-in-law was bedridden after a serious illness, Rassundari had to step in and run the large household single-handed. Her autobiography is an amazingly detailed account of the exhausting drudgery of this household work, which, especially after the children came along, was never over, day or night. Some critics have held her narrative up as a celebration of the patient and long-suffering Bengali housewife. It is not surprising, considering the ideology of her times, that this note is apparent in some of the chapters. What is surprising, indeed astonishing, are the impatience and discontent, however mellow and understated, that come through as clear protests against the trapped lives of Bengali women and as laments over their helplessness. Some of the most moving parts of her account describe her struggle to escape the grind of petty domesticity and teach herself how to read and write. "Is this my fate because I am a woman?" she asks. "Just because I am a woman does it necessarily mean that trying to educate myself is a crime?"

Unusual too is the frank and detailed description of her experience of pregnancy and childbirth. At eighteen she is overcome by wonder at the child growing within her, but when she has had many children, she regrets that her identity is limited to being their mother. Her husband is only a shadowy figure in her account. There are passing references to him including a brief description (rare for her time) of his physical appearance, in the fifteenth composition. When he died in February 1869, her head was shaved in keeping with the humiliating customs of the times, which, for Rassundari, were "more painful than death." As always for her, her personal experience was a means of thinking also about others. She writes, "Toward the end of my life I have been widowed. I feel ashamed and hurt by the realization that even if a woman has lived her life fully, has brought up her children and leaves behind her sons and daughters to carry on, her widowhood is still considered a misfortune."

Amar Jiban is written in two parts. The first, consisting of sixteen compositions, which tells the story of her life, was published in 1876. The second part, consisting of fifteen compositions, was published in 1906. Each composition is preceded by a dedicatory poem, and the compositions in the first part are relatively longer. We have excerpted for translation a section from the first part of *Amar Jiban* that provides an account of Rassundari's everyday life and an account of how she learned to read. Both episodes are factual. The tone, typical of Rassundari's writing, is one of understatement and restraint, but what emerges is a clear indictment of the way Bengali society in her time treated women like her.

◆

From: AMAR JIBAN
(My Life)
The Third Composition

. . . The news made me very happy indeed. I would be married. There would be music, I would hear the women ululating. How exciting that would be! Yet I felt scared at the same time. I cannot express the apprehensions that came to my mind. Meanwhile the various things necessary for the ceremony began to arrive. Relatives and guests began pouring in. I was scared to death by all this. I did not talk to anyone and spent most of the time weeping. Everybody did their best to reassure me. They embraced me, but the unspoken agony in my mind did not lift.

Later on I was cheered up by the ornaments, the red wedding sari, and the wedding music. I forgot my earlier worries and went about laughing and watching the elaborate preparations. My happiness knew no bounds. When everything was over the next day, I heard people asking my mother, "Are they leaving today?" I thought they were referring to the guests. Then the music started. There was an air of festivity. The guests must be leaving now, I thought. It made me happy and I went about following my mother. Presently everybody assembled inside the house. Some looked happy, but others were in tears. That made me feel really frightened. Then my brother, aunts, uncles, and my mother all took me in their arms by turn as they burst into tears. Their tears made me so sad that I began to cry too. I knew mother was going to hand me over to the other family. I tightened my hold on her and pleaded, "Don't give me over to them, Mother!" That made everybody present even more upset. They broke down and tried to say nice words to console me. My mother took me in her arms and said, "You are a good girl, you understand everything, don't you? God is with us, you needn't be afraid. You are going to come back to us in a few days' time. Every girl has to go to her in-laws' house. Nobody else cries like this. There is no reason to be so upset. Please calm down and talk to me." But I was trembling all over with fear. I was quite unable to speak. Somehow I managed to say through my tears: "Are you sure that God will go with me?" Mother promptly reassured me that he most certainly would. "He will be with you all the time, so stop crying now." But in spite of her soothing words my apprehensions kept growing and I could not check my tears.

With great effort they took me away from my mother. I still feel sad when I think of the state of mind I was in and the agony I was going through. As a matter of fact it is indeed a sad thing to leave one's parents, settle in some other place, and live under other people. A place where your parents are no longer your own. But such is the will of God, so it is praiseworthy.

I clung to whomever came to pick me up and went on weeping incessantly. Everyone, old and young, was moved to tears. Eventually they managed to put me into a palanquin, which was not the one intended for me. No sooner was I seated inside than the bearers started marching off. With none of my near ones close by I sank into a deep depression. Since there was no way out, I started praying through my tears: "Please be with me, God." If I am asked to describe my state of mind, I would say that it was very much like the sacrificial goat being dragged to the altar, the same hopeless situation, the same agonized screams. I could see none of my relatives near me. I was miserable, and in tears I kept calling for my mother. I also prayed with all my heart as Mother had told me to. If you ever feel afraid, think of God, she had said.

All these thoughts went through my mind as I sat weeping. Very soon I felt too parched to cry.

The Fourth Composition

Unable to cry any more I fell into deep sleep. I had no idea what happened after that and where I was taken.

When I woke up the next morning I found myself on a boat with none of my relations near me. All the people who came and talked were strangers. I thought of my mother and other members of the family, the affectionate neighbors, my playmates. Where were they now and where was I? So I started to weep once again. My heart felt as if it would break. All the people in the boat tried to console me. But that increased my misery because their kind words reminded me of the affection of my own people. Tears streamed down endlessly—I just couldn't stop them. I cried till I was out of breath. Besides the boat ride was a new experience and it made me feel sick. All I could do in my desperation was to think of God, and I did that, though the predominant emotion I felt was fear. But Mother had said, speak the name of God if you are afraid. So I just kept on repeating my prayers.

Only God will understand the predicament I was in—nobody else can have any idea. Even now I remember those days. The caged bird, the fish caught in the net.

Since it was the will of God, however, it was no use feeling sorry for myself. I am only writing about what I felt at the time. I do not know how other girls feel. Perhaps they do not feel as miserable as I did. Actually there are no obvious reasons for my sadness but the tears came constantly because I had to leave my own people.

People put birds in cages for their own amusement. Well, I was like a caged bird. And I would have to remain in this cage for life. I would never be freed. We spent a few more days on the boat. Then I heard people say that we were about to reach home. For one moment I thought they meant my home. It gave rise to mixed emotions and also to fear. God only knows what went through my mind. All I could do was cry—I spent all my days and nights crying. Strange are the ways of God! Your laws are so wonderful! You have taken me from my dear mother and from others I love so much and have brought me to this distant place. That night we landed. We arrived at their house and saw different people taking part in all sorts of merrymaking. But none of them was from my part of the country. I did not know a single one of them. I began to weep again. I was so upset that the stream of tears did not cease. Everybody tried to assure me that this was my home— that all these people and everything that I saw was mine—and that I had no reason to cry. From now on I would have to live here and look after the house. There was no reason to be upset. But even as they spoke, my longing increased because I knew I wouldn't be able to see my family. Sorrow engulfed me like a raging forest fire. Those who have had such experiences perhaps know how useless words seem in times of sorrow. If somebody loses her son, is it wise to rebuke her? Or ask her not to lament, saying he must have been an enemy in an earlier birth: "He was not your son really. He wouldn't have left you if he had been so. He was a plunderer—don't ever utter his name. . . ."

The Fifth Composition

My day used to begin very early—and there was no respite from housework till long past midnight. I could not rest, even for a moment. But thanks to the grace of God I did everything in a spirit of duty. No work seemed too tiring. Because God wished it, I managed to gradually finish all the household tasks. I was only fourteen then. Around this time, the idea that I should learn how to read books entered my mind. But unfortunately girls were not supposed to read in those days. "What is the world coming to?" they used to say. "To think that women will be doing the work of men! Never heard of it before. In this new age even this has come to be true! These days women are becoming famous and men seem good for nothing. Such strange things never happened before. There was even a woman ruler on the throne. Who knows what other changes are in store for us! The way things are going, a decent man will very soon lose his caste. Pretty soon the womenfolk will get together and study books."

When I overheard these conversations I used to feel really scared. I had never dared to tell anyone about my desires—but now I became afraid that they might come to know what was on my mind. I dared not look at a page with written letters on it, in case they attributed it to my desire for learning. But I prayed constantly to God. I said, "Please, God, help me learn, so that I can read religious books. Dear God, friend of the poor, I invoke your name only for this." I used to say, "God, you have brought me so far from my village Potajia—a journey of three days and three nights to Ramdia. You have made me leave my friends and my relations and have brought me to this faraway place. And now, this village of Ramdia has become my home. How strange that is! When I did not know how to do any housework, even the slightest attempt would please my mother. She used to praise me before the others. Look at me now. I am no longer free. I have learned to work for others. And there is so much I should do. These people have become very dear to me. . . ." All these thoughts raced through my mind and I would shed tears, hiding my face in the sari that was drawn over my head. Nobody knew of my sorrow. How could they know, for my face lay hidden. "Only you knew because you are my father, my God, the heart of my heart, the life of my life, the very cream of kindness. I float in your kindness all the time. You have been with me through good days and bad days. You know all that I have experienced; I cannot keep anything back from you."

I left my village at the age of twelve. Ever since then I have lived in Ramdia. But I must admit the people here are very good. They are fond of me. Whenever I was physically ill they were so concerned that I forgot all the discomfort. Even the neighbors and the servants were kind. It was as though God had asked them to be particularly nice to me. I was confident that they loved me more than they loved people from their own family. In fact none of them was ever rude to me or showed displeasure in any way. Everyone was extremely kind. And I include my immediate family also, who are good beyond comparison.

Everybody loved me sincerely. No one ever spoke a harsh word. Even now they are nice, but I do not know how long this will continue. I do not know how much longer I'll have to be here. Only God knows what will happen to me in my last days—whether people will still be as kind as they were.

Dear Master, all-pervading Father of the Universe! Your glory is without end. Who can fathom your actions! Only you know their reason. It is a mistake for mortals even to try to think about such things. I came to the village of Ramdia at the age of twelve. For the next six years I was treated like a new bride. My mind too was playful, like that of a child. That was how I spent the first eighteen years of my life. But it was a very happy time for me. I had little to worry about. My only effort was to please people through the work I did in the house. My only regret was that I was not able to read and write because I was a girl. Women of today are so lucky. Many parents educate their daughters. I think this is a good practice.

Now I am going to describe the children who were born to me. I had a son, Bipinbehari, when I was eighteen. At twenty-one, I had another son, Pulinbehari. At twenty-three, I had a daughter. She was named Ramsundari. Another son was born when I was twenty-five. He was called Pearylal. The next son, Radhanath, was born when I was twenty-eight. At thirty, I had another son, Dwarakanath. When I was thirty-two, I had another son, who was called Chandranath. When I was thirty-four I had another son, Kishorilal. Then another child, a son, lived in my womb for six months, but then he died. After this, when I was thirty-seven, I had one more son, who is called Pratap Chandra. Then at the age of thirty-nine I had a daughter, Shyamsundari. When I was forty-one I had my youngest—a son named Mukundalal. My first child was born when I was eighteen and the last when I was forty-one. God only knows what I had to go through during those twenty-three years. Nobody else had any idea either.

There were eight maidservants in the house, but all of them lived outside the household. There was nobody to do the household chores in the inner quarters. I was the only one. As was the custom, I had to do all the work and look after the children as well. I had to work right through the day and the night, without a moment's rest. Suffice it to say that I had no time to think about my own health. So much so that I often did not eat either of the two meals. There were days when the pressure of work did not let me even have one meal during the course of the day. I should not dwell on those things, however. I feel ashamed even to mention them. Yet I think I should speak briefly of one or two incidents. I used to get up before the children woke up in order to do all the work around the house. I even started cooking before they were up. After feeding the children I finished whatever else was left to be done. Then I had to make my offerings to the family deity and get ready to prepare the meals for the rest of the family. I had to cook quite a lot—about twelve *seers* of rice for each meal. The master of the house had to eat his meal of rice just after he had bathed in the morning. He would not eat anything else. So I had to cook specially for him first. In the next round I cooked for the entire family. So it used to be about four in the afternoon before the cooking was done.

One afternoon I was just about to sit down to eat, having cooked and served the family, when a guest arrived. He was of a low caste and he refused to cook for himself. He said, "I would like to have some rice if I may." He refused to eat anything else. There was no time to cook again. So there was no other way. I had to offer him the food I had served for myself. I thought I'd cook something in the evening and went back to do the household chores. I put the children to bed and went into the kitchen. I was feeling extremely hungry. There was nobody else at home and I could easily have helped myself to some of the food that was there. There was nobody to stop me. Besides, the other members of the family would only have been happy to see me eating. But the problem was I never served myself anything except rice, which automatically ruled out many other foodstuffs. If others came to know that I had not eaten, they'd have made a lot of fuss—that was what I told myself. Besides, the children always bother the mother if they find her eating. What was the point of creating all that fuss? I went into the kitchen and began to cook. I finished the cooking. It grew late but my husband was still in his office in the outer house. There was no sign of him, so I served all the others and waited up for my husband. It was so late that pretty soon the children would be up, I kept thinking. That meant going without food again. Then my worst fears came true. As soon as my husband came in, one of the children woke up and started whining. I served my husband and picked up the child hoping to put him to sleep by the time my husband had finished. I could manage to eat with the sleeping child on my lap. But presently another one was up and joined the chorus. "Never mind," I said, "I'll hold both of them and manage to eat." So I picked up the other child from his bed. Suddenly, when I began to eat, a storm started blowing. The lamp went out. This scared the children and they began to cry again. I was so hungry that I would have eaten in the dark if I did not have to hold the children. There were maidservants but they were outside. How could I send the children outdoors in the darkness. My husband was sure to ask why the children were crying. It was better that I did not eat. So I had to leave my plate there and go into the adjoining room. Later on the storm blew over. The children were asleep. But I felt too tired to eat. I had been forced to fast the whole day. Next day I went through the routine and hurried to the kitchen. Nobody knew that I had not eaten the previous day. After everybody ate, I thought I'd finally have the time to have something myself. But that was not to be. I had to serve the servant who was holding the baby. Then the baby needed milk too. I attended to both of them and sat down with a plate of rice, the baby in my lap. No sooner had I done so than the baby decided to have a motion and urinated in such a way that all the rice was washed away.

This was an act of God and it made me laugh. I did not tell anyone that I had been without food for the last two days. It was an embarrassing subject and I did not want others to discuss it. So I preferred to keep quiet about it. Thus on many occasions I was forced to go without food. By the grace of God I had excellent health. It would have been difficult to bring the children up if I had been sickly. Dear God! Who can fathom your glory? I feel overwhelmed to think of your kindness to your daughter. I am ignorant of your greatness. I call on you only because my mother asked me to do so. Blessed is my life, my birth. I am grateful for everything.

Merciful God! I am only an unfortunate girl. I hardly know you. I don't know what I would have done without you. If I had had a sickly body I couldn't possibly have raised my children. I would have been most miserable with a sick body. I thank you a hundred times. Friend of the poor! It is only through your good grace that I have come to know what it takes to bring up a child, what agony the mother has to go through. I never knew that a mother has to suffer so much for the sake of her children. People never realize these things unless they go through similar pressures. Now I know perfectly well the tortures a mother has to undergo because of her children. Every human being should know this. Most people do not have any knowledge about the matter.

I regret to say that I have not taken good care of my own mother, who was so affectionate. A mother is a very precious thing—it is my misfortune that I did not understand it. She suffered so much for my sake. But I was not of any use to her. She did not derive any benefit from me. She used to cry for me and wanted to have me over. But I am a virtual prisoner here. They never sent me to her because the household work here would suffer. I was allowed to go back to attend some family festival but had to return in a couple of days like a slave. About fifteen people accompanied me on the boat along with two senior men and two maidservants. I was allowed to visit my people only under certain conditions. I was allowed to go only on special occasions, not otherwise. When my mother lay on her deathbed she wanted very badly to see me. I have caused her sorrow, hateful sinner that I am. I tried my utmost, but could not go. It is my misfortune. It is a matter of no ordinary regret. Alas my God, why did you let me be born as a human being? It is indeed a very rare fortune to be born a human being. Birds and beasts are inferior beings. And to think of the sin I have committed even after being fortunate enough to be born a human. Why was I ever born a woman? Shame on my life! A mother is the most affectionate person in the world, the representative of God on earth—and I could not even be of any use to her. My grief knew no bounds. If I were a son I would have flown directly to my mother's bedside. But I am helpless. I am a caged bird.

The Sixth Composition

I was so immersed in the sea of housework that I was not conscious of what I was going through day and night. After some time the desire to learn how to read properly grew very strong in me. I was angry with myself for wanting to read books. Girls did not read. How could I? What a peculiar situation I had placed myself in. What was I to do? This was one of the bad aspects of the old system. The other aspects were not so bad. People used to despise women of learning. How unfortunate those women were, they said. They were no better than animals. But it is no use blaming others. Our fate is our own. In fact older women used to show a great deal of displeasure if they saw a piece of paper in the hands of a woman. So that ruled out my chances of getting any education. But somehow I could not accept this. I was very keen to learn the alphabet. When I was a child I used to sit in the schoolroom and listen to the chanting of the students. Could I remember any of that? By and by I recalled the thirty letters with all their vowel combinations. I could recognize the letters, but was still not able to write them. What was I to do? Actually one cannot learn without a teacher. Besides, I was a woman, and a married one at that, and was not supposed to talk to anyone. If anyone spoke a harsh word to me I would die of shame. That was the fear that kept me from talking to anyone. My only hope was God and my constant prayer was, "Dear

God, I can only learn to read and write if you teach me. Who else is there to be my teacher?" Days passed in this manner.

One day I dreamt that I was reading the *Chaitanya Bhagavata*. When I woke up I felt enthralled. I closed my eyes to go over the scene. It seemed that I was already in possession of something precious. My body and my mind swelled with satisfaction. It was so strange! I had never seen the book yet I had been reading it in my dream. For an illiterate person like me, it would have been absolutely impossible to read such a difficult book. Anyhow I was pleased that I was able to perform this impossible feat at least in a dream. My life was blessed! God had at last listened to my constant appeals and had given me the ability to read in my dream. Thank you, dear God. You have made me so happy. He had given me what I had wanted so much, and I was happy.

Our home contained several books. Perhaps the *Chaitanya Bhagavata* is one of them, I thought to myself. But what did it matter to me after all? An illiterate woman like me wouldn't even recognize the book. So I prayed to God again, saying, "You are the friend of the poor; allow me to recognize the book. You must let me have that book. You are the only one whom I can approach." That was how I prayed to God silently.

How strange are the ways of God and the effects of his kindness! He heard my prayers and set out to grant me my wish. My eldest son was then eight. I was working in the kitchen one day when my husband came in and said to him, "Bipin, I am leaving my *Chaitanya Bhagavata* here. Please bring it over when I ask you to." Saying that he put the book down there and went back to the outer house.

I listened from the kitchen. No words can express the delight I felt when I heard his words. I was filled with happiness and rushed to the spot to find the book there. Pleased with myself, I said to God, "You have granted my wish," and I picked the book up. In those days books were made differently. There were illustrated wooden frames to hold the sheets. Since I did not know how to read, I tried to remember the illustrations.

When the book was brought into the room I detached one sheet and hid it. But I was afraid lest it were found. That would be a disgrace. I might even be rebuked. It was not easy to face criticism or rebuke. I was very sensitive about those things. Those days were not like present ones. We were completely under the control of men. And I was particularly nervous. I was at a loss with that sheet. Where should I keep it so that nobody would find it? But if they did, what would they say?

Finally I decided to put it in some place where I would be present most of the time and nobody else was likely to go. The *khori*★ in the kitchen was the only hiding place I could think of. Housework kept me busy the whole day. There was no time even to look at it. In the evening the cooking continued until it was very late. By the time I was free, the children had awakened. Some demanded to be taken to the toilet, some were hungry, some wanted to be picked up, some started crying, so I had to attend to their demands. Then I felt sleepy myself—so where was the time for my education? I did not see any way out. No one could learn without the help of a teacher. There were some letters that I could recognize but I wasn't able to write them. How can one be literate without being able to write? So how was I to read that sheet? I thought and thought about it but could not find a way out. Besides, the danger of being seen was very much there.

Gradually I began to lose hope, but I prayed to God constantly, "Please, God, teach me how to read. If you don't, who else will?" That was my constant prayer. Sometimes I used to think that I would never succeed. Even if I tried hard and somebody was willing to teach me, where was the time? It was useless. I'd never learn. The very next moment I thought, Of course I will. God has given me hope. He can never disappoint me. Encouraged, I kept that sheet to myself. But I had no time to look at it. I kept the sheet in my left hand while I did the cooking and glanced at it through the sari, which was drawn over my face. But a mere glance was not enough, because I could not identify the letters.

I decided to steal one of the palm leaves on which my eldest son used to practice his handwriting. One look at the leaf, another at the sheet, a comparison with the letters I already knew, and, finally, a verification with the speech of others—that was the process I adopted for some time. Furtively I would take out the sheet and put it back promptly before anybody could see it.

Wasn't it a matter to be regretted, that I had to go through all this humiliation just because I was a woman? Shut up like a thief, even trying to learn was considered an offense. It is such a pleasure to see the women today enjoying so much freedom. These days parents of a single girl child take so much care to educate her. But we had to strug-

---

★The *khori* is an elevated bamboo platform, used as a storage space in East Bengali (now Bangladeshi) village kitchens.

gle so much just for that. The little that I have learned is only because God did me the favor.

Actually the man who was my master happened to be a likable person. But it is difficult to ignore or reject accepted customs and practices. That was why I had to undergo all that misery. Anyway it is no use crying over spilled milk. In those days people considered the education of women to be wrong. Even now we come across some who are enemies of education. The very word excites their displeasure. Actually they were not really to blame; it was a time that was very precious. If you compare that period with the present you find many changes—beyond count. If the people of the earlier generation were here to witness all these changes, they would have died of disgust and shame. But whatever God directs seems to be for the good. The heavy dress of the women in those days, the heavy jewelry, the conch-shell bangles, and large vermilion dots used to look very nice. Of course not all clothes were like that.

But I have no reason to complain. God has looked after me well and I spent my time with a happy heart. Suffice it to say that whatever he does is for the best. As a child I used to sit with the other children in the primary school. This proved to be useful when I compared the letters of the palm leaf and sheet of the book with the memory of the alphabet I had. All through the day I went on doing this in my mind. After a great deal of time and with great effort I somehow managed to stumble through the *Chaitanya Bhagavata*. Books were not printed in those days. The handwriting was difficult to decipher. Oh, the trouble I had to take to read. In spite of all that, I did not learn to write. One needs a lot of things if one is to write: paper, pen, ink, ink pot, and so on. You have to set everything before you. And I was a woman, the daughter-in-law of the family. I was not supposed to read or write. It was generally accepted as a grave offense. And if they saw me with all the writing paraphernalia, what would they say? I was always afraid of criticism. So I gave up the idea of writing and concentrated on reading. I never thought I would be able to read. It seemed an impossible task in my situation. The little that I have learned was possible because God guided me. I was deeply engrossed in whatever I could read and the idea of writing did not cross my mind.

Translated by Enakshi Chatterjee.

HANNAH CATHERINE MULLENS ——————

(1826–1861)   *Bengali*

Phulmani O Karunar Bibaran (The Story of Phulmani and Karuna), 1852, is
the first work of prose fiction written in Bengali. Three thousand copies
were printed when the book was first brought out, and it has gone through
several subsequent editions. In Hannah Mullens's obituary written ten
years later, *The Friend of India,* a missionary paper, reported that her book
had "been translated from its exquisite Bengali into every vernacular of
India, and has become to the native Church what Bunyan's *Pilgrim's Progress* has been to the masses in England."

There still exists some controversy as to whether Hannah Mullens was a
Bengali. Literary historians hold widely different views on the subject. In
A Descriptive Catalogue of Bengali Works, 1885, Long and Murdoch mention
Mullens as a Bengali writer. Some scholars claim that she was born at
Chakraberia to a Bengali brahmin and that she changed her name after
she married a Christian and was converted to Christianity. More recently
researchers have disputed this and declared that she was an Englishwoman
by birth. Evidence from her book would seem to support the latter claim.
But despite these controversies, certain recorded facts about her life are
undisputed. Hannah Catherine Mullens was born in Calcutta on 1 July
1826. She was educated at home. At the age of twelve, she taught one
class a day at the newly founded Bhawanipore Mission School for girls.
Her biography, Meenakshi Mukerjee comments, "reads like a page out of
a Victorian novel: the devoted daughter and dutiful wife whose endless
task of childbearing and social obligation in a hostile climate is punctuated
by the secret pleasures of reading and writing—secret because her stern
father thought writing was an indulgence and because she herself thought
she derived too much pleasure from these activities." Yet she was a meticulous and disciplined writer. It was apparently at her initiative that the
first zenana schools, aimed at educating the cloistered women of upper-
class Bengali families, were founded in 1855. In 1858, Mullens traveled
to England with her husband, who was a missionary. On her return to
Calcutta in 1861, she began work on another novel, which she wanted to
publish by that year's end. Her ambition remained unfulfilled, however.
On 20 November 1861, after having worked all day, she developed an
acute abdominal pain. On the following day, at 7:00 P.M., she died. She
was thirty-five. Her last book remained incomplete and is untraceable.

Women are the main characters in *Phulmani O Karunar,* which depicts the everyday life of ordinary village folk, their superstitions, religious traditions, and customs. The plot is centered on their experiences, more specifically on Karuna's change, from a rather shrewish, quarrelsome character who loves to gossip to a charitable Christian woman. "I have endeavored," the author writes in the preface, "to show the practical influence of Christianity on the various details of domestic life [which are] worked into the little story, fictitious on the whole, but founded on facts, for many of the incidents related in it have come under my own notice." Critic Jharna Dhar points out that, with its carefully evoked rural setting and lower-caste characters, this was in a sense a realist novel. Written at a time when literary circles in Calcutta were preoccupied with reformist polemic, and written on themes that would have been considered unromantic and not worthy of literary attention, *Phulmani O Karunar* is a path-breaking work. For the first time in Bengali literature, children are portrayed as human beings (though later Rabindranath Tagore would develop the tradition), and women are shown as capable of developing a responsible individuality. Although the book was written to propagate her faith, Mullens takes care that this preoccupation does not interfere unduly with her fictional mode. The characters are rounded and the changes in their lives are gradual and plausible.

The story is told by a district magistrate's wife, who makes friends with both Phulmani and Karuna and is gradually drawn into their families, and it is this friendship among the women that structures the plot. One of the episodes is particularly interesting for it shows Sundari, Phulmani's daughter, being drawn to Christianity, but unwilling to follow the dictates of the priest and marry a man of his choice. Against the wishes of the religious leader, she chooses the man she will marry and the author clearly supports her decision. Another interesting feature of the book is that Mullens writes about women who leave home to earn their living. In doing so she discusses, nearly a century and a half ago, the problems of working women.

Why then, one might ask, is this book largely forgotten? One explanation offered for its neglect centers on the conflict that arose between the Hindus and the Christian missionaries in the wake of a number of conversions to Christianity, in 1845, of college-going Hindu boys. Since *Phulmani O Karunar* was published by a Christian publishing house, it was likely to have been ignored by educated Hindu readers. This is not a sufficient explanation, however, for its absolute neglect for over a century after those controversies have been dead and buried. A more plausible explanation may be that researchers were unwilling to grant the honor of having produced the first Bengali novel to a woman writer and a "foreigner" at that.

Hannah Catherine Mullens's other works include *Voyages and Travels of a Bible,* 1851; *The Missionary on the Ganges: or, What Is Christianity,* 1856;

and *Prasanna and Kamini,* 1885. Her *Faith and Victory: A Story of the Progress of Christianity in Bengal,* also left unfinished at her death, was completed by other members of her family and published in 1865.

The two chapters translated here deal with issues that women like Hannah Mullens would have been working on: women's health, especially in childbirth, and their right to choose their own life partners. Mullens obviously regarded the practices of Bengali midwives as unscientific and unchristian. In her mind there seems to have been little distinction between the two. The novel contrasts the characters of Phulmani and Karuna. Phulmani is an ideal Christian woman, friendly and charitable; her family, too, is an ideal Christian family. Karuna on the other hand tells lies and is lazy and quarrelsome. The reader sees Karuna gradually changing as she faces life's adversities. Toward the end, this irresponsible and shrewish woman also becomes an ideal Christian woman. Such novels were being written in many parts of India in the middle decades of the nineteenth century, but Mullens's novel stands out because it portrays the life of ordinary village people in great detail and presents the change in Karuna in a way that does not seem contrived. Phulmani's daughter Sundari is the central character in the second extract. In the first extract we witness the birth of her school-friend Rana's first child.

◆

From PHULMANI O KARUNAR BIBARAN
(The Story of Phulmani and Karuna)
Chapter 4

Two days after Madhu's burial I visited his mother's house again as I had promised. This time, by God's blessings, I was happy to be able to give a little help to those unfortunate people. Specially since I noticed on arrival that Rani was in labor and suffering greatly. Her mother-in-law told me that she had been in acute pain for a whole night and day, but still there was no sign of delivery.

The tumult and confusion that the women had created when Rani's husband died was being repeated over again; some dozen of them were standing around encircling Rani. If one of them says one thing, another says quite the opposite: "Sit up," instructs one, "No, no, walk around," says another. A third brings a potion from some ignorant woman and feeds it to her. All these useless processes seemed to delay the birth rather than speed it along and that increased Rani's suffering even further.

There was something else that distressed me, and that was how, Christian though they were all of them, they seemed to indulge in groundless beliefs. Superstitions such as if someone sneezes when you are about to do some work, that work should not be undertaken; if you hear a lizard call when you are about to go on a journey, don't go out that day; a monkey's face shouldn't be the first thing you see in the morning; nothing should be cut during a lunar eclipse; if you're ill you should wear a magic amulet round your neck; and so on. It is not just in Madhu's family that I saw these senseless observations; many Christian families I know do the same. Dear Lord, may You will that these ignorant people should open their eyes and see sense, may they reject these illogical and ridiculous beliefs as the work of Satan himself.

Rani had said to her mother-in-law a couple of months ago that an owl or some night bird had flown over her head squawking the night before. The old woman remembers this now and keeps saying that the childbirth would not take place until the bird returned. All the other women agreed except one old one who says, "No, I don't think owls have any evil influence, because once four or five of us were sitting out in the courtyard when an owl flew over our heads; my young niece was nearly nine months gone at that time, so we were naturally very worried. But no harm came to her. She delivered a son a month later, and that too after just one hour of labor."

At that, another woman says, "I will never believe this. Everyone knows that no delivery is possible until that bird returns; perhaps the bird has come back but you people haven't noticed it."

The first speaker replies, "No, dear, no! It hasn't come back; don't we all have eyes? And the child was born at two o'clock in the afternoon. Do owls fly then? But I can tell you very well what has happened to Rani. She ran away sometime ago and stayed with an old woman in Kalipur. That woman worked some spell on her to put her to sleep, and then stole all her jewelry. If she hadn't worked a spell, Rani would have surely awakened. So I think that that woman was a witch, and she must have jinxed Rani to stop her from having a baby." Since this new theory is even more astonishing than the previous one, all the women nod in agreement and say, "Yes, yes, that must be it." Madhu's mother has been moaning incessantly, "Oh when shall I take my son's child in my lap?" But she is not in the least bit worried over what might happen to the daughter-in-law. Now she is convinced by the neighbors' talk that unless something is done about the daughter-in-law, the baby too might be lost. So she says on hearing about the witch, "I will send someone to Kalipur to plead at the old woman's feet to break the spell on my son's wife."

On hearing this, Rani turns to me in desperation, "Oh Memsahib, don't you know of any medicine for my condition? Kalipur is two days' journey from here; by the time someone gets back from there, I will be dead. Oh, Memsahib, I beg you, tell these people not to give me any more of their wretched potions. I throw up every time I take them." One woman hears this and says, "No, we won't give you any more of that stuff, since it's not working anyway."

So I tell them, "Does that useless stuff ever work? Why don't you give her some food instead? That might help." To which the mother-in-law says, "That's all very good! We will think of feeding her later; let her deliver the baby first."

I get really angry when I hear this. I tell her straight, "You are a wicked and ignorant woman. Just look at her face, she's about to faint. How will you get your grandson then?"

Next I turn to the neighbors. "Could any of you bring over some fish soup? That would help." A young woman responds to this and rushes off home. But the old ones shake their heads and say, "That sort of thing is fine for English wives, but for us Bengalis our own systems of medicine work much better. You feed soup to an expectant mother and it's sure death."

By now the young woman has returned with the soup. So I take the bowl and offer it to Rani. She drinks it eagerly and says, "I feel much stronger now. Now if they would let me lie down for a little, I might bear the pain much better."

Those stupid women have kept her sitting on her knees for three hours. That itself has made her exhausted and weak, so I tell the midwife, "What harm would there be if you let her lie down for a while? Women in England always give birth like that." The woman looks displeased to hear that and says, "There's plenty of difference between English and Bengali women; if you've come here with the birthing methods of the English, then do as you please; I don't know anything about the good or bad of such methods."

"So leave her to me then," I say. "I know exactly what needs to be done in such cases; I've been well trained. So with God's blessing, she won't come to any harm."

Saying this, I made Rani lie down on her left side, and I made her sip hot milk three or four times within the next hour. I noticed later that the midwife had tied a piece of cloth firmly around her stomach. I promptly took it off. The women kept saying that now the baby would move up again. But Rani said, "No, no, the memsahib knows much better about these things; let her do what she wants."

HANNAH CATHERINE MULLENS ◆ 207

Some more time passed, and now they all realized that the time for the delivery was close. At this point the midwife, wanting to get some credit for herself, said, "If you permit me, Memsahib, I can deliver her this minute." But I said, "No, no, you've helped thrice already, and only increased her pain. Let her be now; God will deliver her in His own time." No sooner had I said this than Rani gave birth to a live baby girl. I was quite surprised at this, because the way those women had been treating her, I strongly suspected that the child would be stillborn. I have seen myself how very often Bengali women lose their babies in the womb because of the ignorance of these midwives. Be that as it may, in this instance, the Lord smiled on Rani and gave her a living baby girl.

Chapter 10

After that first meeting with Sundari, we saw each other quite regularly. Sometimes I would go to her home, or she would come over to mine and teach my *ayah* to knit stockings. On these occasions we would talk a great deal, and I was really impressed by her knowledge and understanding of religion. So when it was time for her to go back to Calcutta, I was extremely sorry. I would have paid her double the salary she received from the doctor's wife to keep her back with me; but I couldn't be so unfair to her old employer. Probably Sundari would not have left her either, because there was no trace of ingratitude in her mind. Sundari's mistress was a very wise and religious woman, and since there were no other English friends I had in town, I would visit the padre's house frequently to converse with her.

On one such occasion when I called on them, the padre informed me, "Your friends in 'Sukhshala' (that is, Phulmani's house) are in a bit of a dither; their daughter Sundari is creating great difficulties."

But I saw a smile on his face as he said that, so I knew that it could not be any major mishap. But I was still surprised and said, "Impossible! Sundari can never cause her parents any worry."

The padre replied, "Oh, it's all to do with her marriage. Just as our own young girls feel sometimes that they know better about marriage than their parents, Sundari too thinks the same way, so she refuses to marry the young man Premchand and Phulmani have chosen for her. But you won't understand unless you hear it all from the beginning, so listen. Last Wednesday, a handsome young man came here from Calcutta in search of a bride. He had brought a letter of recommendation from his padre, which said this young man had been a brahmin but had been converted to Christianity three years earlier and had shown excellent conduct ever since. He was the headmaster of an English school, and earned twenty-five rupees a month. When I read this letter, I turned to my sister and said, "O Lucy! This man would be an ideal match for Sundari; would you agree to let her go?" She said, "I would agree to whatever is best for Sundari." So I called Premchand and Phulmani over and explained the contents of the letter to them. Later they talked to the young man for a long time, particularly about religion, and found him to be a true follower of the Lord. Then Premchand asked me to read once more what the letter had said about his religion. I read out a portion that said, "I firmly believe that this young man is one of Christ's chosen people; one clear proof of this is his constant efforts to help others in distress." Premchand and Phulmani were delighted to hear this, for they had been searching long for such a religious young man who would in every way be a suitable match for Sundari. Later, by my advice, they invited him over to their home for dinner, so that he could see Sundari. So last evening he dressed up very nicely and went off to Premchand's house. Before he left, I told him all about Sundari and how deeply religious she was. Phulmani had not told her daughter why he had been invited. She had simply said, "We have asked that young gentleman from Calcutta who is staying at the padre's house over for dinner." The minute he saw Sundari, he was so struck by her beauty he told Phulmani, "Ask your daughter after I leave. If she does agree to marry me, I will be only too happy." But this morning when her parents told her, Sundari refused even to consider it. And she gave no other reason except that she didn't know him, and he did not know her either, so there was no certainty the marriage would turn out happy. Phulmani could see no sense in such talk. She said, "I didn't know Sundari's father before we got married; how am I so happy then? If you find someone we all know to be religious, there's no need for you to know him personally."

So I said to the padre, "I think our friend Phulmani has not acted too wisely this time; what do you feel?"

The padre replied, "It is true, madam, that among the English, we do look for a lot of qualities in a husband or wife other than religiousness. If a man and a woman have similar tastes, natures, habits, and ambitions, their marriage is far happier than others, so we should look for these common qualities when arranging a match. But consider this too: Bengali girls get no opportunity to meet a man before marriage, like the English. And if they don't meet, how do they come to know each other's tastes? So I say that as long as Bengali girls are not able to select their own husbands, let their parents and the council of elders guide them in these matters."

I said, "Yes sir, that may be true, but I would still say that I will be really happy when the girls of this country begin to show some degree of independence in selecting their life partners. But, coming back to this issue, has anything been decided yet?"

The padre said, "Madam, Phulmani is coming here this evening with her daughter; we might come to some decision then. Phulmani wants me to speak to Sundari, and convince her somehow; but I will not do that. Because it is extremely difficult to intervene in such matters. Anyway, I will ask Sundari why she is unwilling to marry this young gentleman. I think she probably has some special reason."

Eager to know the outcome, I stayed on at the padre's house, waiting for Phulmani to arrive.

After nearly an hour she arrived with Sundari. We talked of this and that for a while, and then the padre asked Sundari straight out, "You have refused to marry this gentleman, Sundari, because, as you've told your mother, you don't know him. Good, so meet and talk to him for a few days, and then give your answer. But if you do not wish to do that, then you must tell me truthfully why you do not wish to marry him."

Sundari had no desire to meet the gentleman. She hung her head and said, "Sir, if you ask me so directly, I must speak out. There is a special reason why I do not wish to marry this gentleman, but if I reveal it, my own countrymen will consider it to be very shameful, although I know surely that I have done no wrong."

When she heard this Phulmani said, "Sundari, you can speak your mind without fear. If you have not done anything that is contrary to God's laws, then your parents will never blame you. Never mind what other people might say."

I said, "Truly, Sundari, you must not keep anything secret from your parents; so tell us frankly why you do not wish to marry the gentleman."

Sundari half-raised her eyes and said, "Because I love someone else. My mistress knows him; he is her old gardener's son."

Translated by Madhuchhanda Karlekar.

SAVITHRIBAI PHULE ——————

(1831–1897)   *Marathi*

Few people today think of Savithribai Phule as a poet or a scholar or
indeed as an activist in her own right. If she is remembered at all, it is as
the wife of Jotiba Phule (1827–1890), who, in 1873, formed the Satyashodhak Mandal, one of the earliest and most significant movements of the
lower castes against the oppressive power of the high-caste brahmins.
Though Jotiba and Savithribai themselves never used the phrase, and always referred to these castes as *mang-mahar,* mangs and mahars were traditionally "untouchables". The anthropologist Irawati Karve points out
that the mahars, who are possibly the largest caste in Maharashtra, were
important village servants: they carried messages, guided strangers, and
assisted the headman. They also guarded the boundaries of the village and
kept it clean. Besides, they often settled land disputes, for they were living
reference books of village and family history and contemporary social
relations. As village economies broke down, their importance declined.
The mangs were rope makers, basket weavers, and musicians. Both castes
lived outside the village and were allowed to draw water only from separate wells.

Savithribai was the first woman teacher in modern Maharashtra. Together, she and her husband started the first school for women, in 1848.
Though there was a period in which Jotiba Phule's work was also trivial-
ized and dismissed, today he is remembered as the father of the nonbrahmin movement in Maharashtra. But it is only after the work of scholars
such as G. B. Sardar and M. G. Mali, whose biography of Savithribai was
published in 1980, and who brought out her collected works in 1988, that
we have begun to appreciate her important role in that movement.

Savithribai was married to Jotiba in 1840, when she was nine. With his
support she was able to study. In 1848, when Savithribai was only seventeen, they opened five schools in and around Pune, and in 1851, one
meant especially for the girls from the mang and mahar castes. Savithribai
and Jotiba, together with another colleague, Fatima Sheik, taught in them
until 1856 when Savithribai fell seriously ill and went back to her parental
home in Naigaon (Khandala taluk, Satara district), where she was nursed
back to health by her elder brother, "Bhau." The letter translated here was
written at that time. Both Savithribai and Jotiba Phule were maligned,
socially ostracized, and attacked by the orthodoxy whose authority and
power they had questioned. Yet Savithribai had special burdens to carry.

Women are traditionally charged with the responsibility of preserving societal "purity" and maintaining its norms. When they rebel, they are policed and punished in a thousand ways that rarely touch the men. Like the wives and co-workers of so many of the enthusiastic male reformers of that period, Savithribai bore the brunt of the attack against the Phules and the Satyashodhak Mandal even as she strained to shield her husband. Another letter, written in 1868, also from Naigaon, gives us a glimpse of a different aspect of Savithribai's life. It tells the story of a mahar girl and a brahmin boy who fell in love. The girl got pregnant and the infuriated villagers wanted them both killed. Savithribai rescued them and sent them to Jotiba in Pune. A third letter, written in 1877, describes the work of the Satyashodhak Mandal during the fierce drought and famine of 1876. All three extant letters have recently been published in M. G. Mali's edition of her collected works.

Savithribai and Jotiba were not alone in their crusade. They were part of a group whose impact, as Gail Omvedt has shown, was strong and widespread, and from whose work grew a remarkable body of writing. The independence of thought and the sharpness of argument that mark the work of Muktabai, for example, who studied at the Phules' school in Pune, or of Tarabai Shinde, whose vigorous polemical style has been associated with Jotiba's, were not matched for many years to come.

Savithribai was not only a teacher and an activist but also a writer. Her first collection of forty-one poems, *Kavyaphule* (Poetry's Blossoms), was published in 1854. Many of the poems are nature poems; others speak in the main of the wealth that comes with education, give advice to children, and decry the caste system. Her second book, *Bavankashi Subodharatnakar* (The Ocean of Pure Gems), 1892, a more ambitious book, is a biography, in verse, of Jotiba Phule. Jotiba had developed a critique of the brahmin interpretation of Maratha history in the ancient and medieval periods. He presented the Peshwa rulers, who were overthrown by the British, as decadent and oppressive, and Savithribai reiterates these themes in her biography. In addition to these two books, Savithribai edited for publication four of Jotiba's speeches on Indian history.

A few of her own speeches were published in 1892. Because Savithribai's correspondence is so unique, and especially because of the insights it provides into her life and into women's experiences in one of the most important social movements of the times, we have chosen to include a letter rather than poetry.

◆

Letter to Jotiba Phule

10 October 1856

To My Lord Jotiba, Who Is the Image of Truth,
Many humble greetings from Savithri.

After a great many vicissitudes, my health has ultimately been perfectly restored. Bhau nursed me indefatigably throughout the illness. That shows how loving he really is! I'll come to Pune as soon as I have completely recovered. Please don't be worried about me. This must be causing a lot of trouble to Fatima. But I am sure she will understand and won't grumble.

While we were talking one day, Bhau said, "You and your husband have rightly been excommunicated. You help the lowly castes like the mangs and mahars and that, undoubtedly, is committing sin. You have dragged our family name in the mud. Therefore, I want to tell you that you must behave according to the customs of our caste and follow the dictates of the brahmins." Mother became livid when she heard these wild and irresponsible remarks. Bhau is otherwise kindhearted, but he is extremely narrow-minded and he did not hesitate to criticize us and blame us squarely. Mother was distressed. She did not scold him but tried instead to reason with him. She said, "God has given you the ability to speak sweetly. It doesn't become you to misuse it so." When he heard her, Bhau was so ashamed that he didn't say a word. To refute his argument, I said, "Bhau, your point of view is extremely narrow and, moreover, your reason has been weakened by the teachings of the brahmins. You fondle even animals like the cow and the goat. You catch poisonous snakes on the day of Nagpanchami and feed them milk. But you consider the mangs and mahars, who are as human as you, untouchables. Can you give me any reason for this? When the brahmins are in their 'holy' clothes, they consider you also untouchable and they are afraid that your touch will defile them. They treat you just like a mahar then." When he heard this, he turned red in the face and asked me, "Why do you teach those mangs and mahars? I can't bear it when people criticize and curse you and create trouble for you for doing that." I told him what the English had been doing for the mangs and mahars and said, "The lack of learning is nothing but gross bestiality. It was the possession of knowledge that gave the brahmins their superior status. Learning has a great value. One who masters it loses his lowly status and achieves the higher one. My master is a godlike man. No one can ever equal him in this world. My swami,

Jotiba, confronts the dastardly brahmins, fights with them and teaches the mahars and mangs because he believes that they are human beings and must be able to live as such. So they must learn. That is why I also teach them. What is so improper about it? Yes, we both teach the girls, the women, and the mangs and mahars. The brahmins believe that this will create problems for them and therefore they chant the mantra "Abrahmanyam" (Unholy!) and go on reviling us and poisoning the minds of people like you.

"You surely remember that the English government had organized a ceremony to felicitate my husband in honor of his great work and had put these vile people to shame. Let me assure you that my husband does not merely chant God's name and do pilgrimages like you. He is doing God's own work. And I help him in that. It's such a pleasant task that I feel immeasurably happy. Besides, it also demonstrates the horizons to which a human being can reach out." Mother and Bhau were listening to me intently. Bhau repented what he had said and begged me to forgive him. Mother said, "Savithri, the Goddess Saraswati herself must be speaking through your mouth. I feel so intensely satisfied to listen to your wisdom." I was overwhelmed to hear both of them say so. From this you may realize that there are several idiots here, as in Pune, who try to poison people against you. But why should we give up the work we have undertaken from fear of such people? It would be better to be involved with the work instead! And then success will be ours in future.

What more could I add to this?

With most humble regards,

Yours,
Savithri

Translated by Maya Pandit.

MUKTABAI ————————————————

(1841–?)   *Marathi*

We have little biographical information about Muktabai. We know only that she studied at the school in Pune founded by Savithribai and Jotiba Phule and when she wrote this essay in 1855 she was fourteen. Of what happened to her later, or indeed of any of her other writings, we have no record. Yet through her vivid and acerbic polemic we get an unmistakable impression of intelligence and self-confidence. For an untouchable, and a woman at that, to write "O learned pandits, wind up the selfish prattle of your hollow wisdom and listen to what I have to say," would be surprising even today. In Muktabai's time it was awe-inspiring.

This piece was originally published in 1855 in *Dnyanodaya,* an Ahmednagar journal that was designed to disseminate information about such new scientific disciplines as physics and astronomy and also discussed religion and morality. The essay was reprinted in the *Dnyanodaya Centenary Volumes,* edited by B. P. Hivale, in 1942. It is probably the earliest surviving piece of writing by a mang woman, an "untouchable."

◆

MANG MAHARACHYA DUKHAVISAYI
(About the Griefs of the Mangs and Mahars)

If one attempts to refute, on the basis of the Vedas, the argument of these brahmins, the great gluttons, who consider themselves to be superior to us and hate us, they counter that the Vedas are their own property. Now obviously, if the Vedas are only for the brahmins, they are absolutely not for us. Teach us, O Lord, thy true religion so that we all can lead our lives according to it. Let that religion, where only one person is privileged and the rest are deprived, perish from the earth and let it never enter our minds to be proud of such a religion.

These people drove us, the poor mangs and mahars, away from our own lands, which they occupied to build large mansions. And that was not all. They regularly used to make the mangs and mahars drink oil mixed with red lead and then buried them in the foundations of their mansions, thus wiping out generation after generation of these poor people. Under Bajirao's rule, if any mang or mahar happened to pass in front of the gymnasium, they cut off his head and used it to play "bat ball," with their swords as bats and his head as a ball, on the grounds. If the victim managed to save his life and Bajirao came to know of it, he used to say, "How dare they save their lives? Do these untouchables expect the brahmins to hand over their duties as revenue officers to them and to start roaming with their shaving kits, all over the town, shaving the heads of widows?" With such remarks he used to punish them.

Second, were these brahmins satisfied with prohibiting the knowledge of writing to us? No. Not them. Bajirao went to Kashi and died a dusty death there. But the mahars here, no less untouchable than the mangs, have absorbed some of his qualities through their contact with him, and consider themselves to be superior to the mangs, so much so that they do not allow even the shadow of a mang to fall over them. Do the merciless hearts of these brahmins, who strut around in their so-called holy clothes, ever feel even a grain of pity for us when we suffer so much grief on account of being branded as untouchables? Nobody employs us because we are untouchables. We have to endure miseries because we do not have any money. O learned pandits, wind up the selfish prattle of your hollow wisdom and listen to what I have to say.

When our women give birth to babies, they do not have even a roof over their houses. How they suffer in the rain and the cold! Try to think about it from your own experience. Suppose the women suffered from some puerperal disease, from where could they have found money for the doctor or medicines? Was there ever any doctor among you who was human enough to treat people free of charge?

The mang and mahar children never dare lodge a complaint even if the brahmin children throw stones at them and injure them seriously. They suffer mutely because they say they have to go to the brahmins' houses to beg for the leftover morsels of food.

Alas! O God! What agony this! I will burst into tears if I write more about this injustice. . . .

Translated by Maya Pandit.

MOKSHODAYANI MUKHOPADHYAY ——
(ca. 1848–?)   *Bengali*

Even though her writing caused quite a stir in the literary world in her time, very little is known about Mokshodayani's life. Her year of birth can be given approximately as 1848, but nothing is known of the circumstances or date of her death. The dearth of biographical detail is all the more significant when we consider that the author came from a well-known family. She was the sister of W. C. Bonnerjee, the first president of the Indian National Congress, and her father was the renowned lawyer Girish Chandra Bannerjee. The family was famous for its scholarship and Mokshodayani grew up in an atmosphere of learning.

What little we were able to learn of Mokshodayani's writing came from *Kalyan Pradip,* 1928, the biography of her nephew, Captain Kalyankumar, a doctor in the army who was killed in Turkey. In April 1870, Mokshodayani brought out the first issue of *Banga Mahila* (Woman of Bengal). There are no extant copies of the journal, but the June 1880 issue of *Tattvabodhini Patrika,* the influential women's journal brought out by the Brahmo Samaj, announced that it was "the first effort at publishing by a Hindu lady." *Banga Mahila* was intended as a newsletter, designed to support the exchange of information among women. It stood for women's rights and pledged it would fight for women's causes. One article, probably an editorial written by Mokshodayani, from the first issue, "Swadinata" (Freedom), was reprinted by Brajendranath Bandhopadhyay in 1950 in a collection of pieces from women's journals. The writer makes a distinction there between real freedom for women and the aping of Western manners and thoughts that often passed for freedom but was actually only wantonness. Western women, she argues, were not "free." They had merely lost their dignity. She did not agree with those who claimed that Bengali women were suppressed, or not free. What Bengali women needed, she insisted, was not "freedom" but access to higher education and a new style of dressing that would make it easier for them to move about in public.

Mokshodayani's first collection of poems, *Bana Prasun* (A Bunch of Wild Flowers), was published in 1882 and helped her secure a prominent though controversial position in the literary circles of the times. The book was critically acclaimed, but one of the poems in the collection roused exceptional protest. It was entitled "Bangalir Babu" (The Bengali Babu) and was a fitting and witty riposte to a well-known satirical poem written in the 1870s, "Bangalir Meye" (The Bengali Woman), by Hemchandra Bandhopadhyay (1830–1903), the leading poet of the time. Mokshodayani matches Hemchandra's attack on feminine vanity, malice, and superstition with an equally damaging list of male attributes. The supposedly educated and emancipated babu in her poem is vain, pompous, slavish, and degenerate. The poet says she replies as a representative of all the women who were insulted and angered by Hemchandra's attack.

The nineteenth-century social reform movements are commonly thought of as representing male efforts to improve society and especially the status of women. Most accounts discuss the issues that the movement raised—sati, widow remarriage, purdah—"objectively" as social questions, and portray the women who were touched by the activism as passive beneficiaries. Mokshodayani's witty attack on men, similar in some ways to that of her contemporary in Maharashtra, Tarabai Shinde, whose work is also collected in this volume, is an extremely important piece because it is a woman's impatient response to the widespread nineteenth-century concern, especially in Bengal, with the "improvement" of women and her own "rewriting" of the issues. It is the men, not the women, in Mokshodayani's view, who need improvement! Like Tarabai Shinde and Rokeya Hossain, she stresses education (rather than remarriage) and the need to provide opportunities for women to be independent, and is skeptical about the integrity or seriousness of male reformers.

All the leading journals of the time, including the most important literary journal, Bankim Chandra Chatterjee's *Bangadarshan,* reviewed her first book of poems. The *Bangadarshan* comment, a masterpiece of evasion, is worth quoting at length.

> The title of the collection, *Bana Prasun,* will indicate to the reader that this is a book of poems. . . . A reading of the poems will reveal that the lady is a powerful writer. I am always afraid to praise poems written by women, since it might instigate other women to desert their household duties and take up the pen. And what would be the hapless condition of the men in this circumstance! I hope that Mokshodadevi will forgive me if I am not overgenerous in praising her work. Of course if the writer had been a man, I would not have asked for forgiveness, since men are unused to praise. But women have got so used to being extolled for what they are—their beauty, their culinary abilities, their beautiful needlework—that it may not be worth their while to receive praise from unknown men. Therefore, leaving aside all the other things that she is good at, I will write only about Mokshodadevi's poetry.
>
> We are all aware that Hemchandra Bandopadhyay is a famous poet whose contribution to Bengali literature is unequaled. His famous poem "Bangalir Meye" has irked the sensibilities of many women and continues to do so. It is obvious that it is as a fitting rejoinder to this poem that Mokshodadevi has taken up her pen in "Bangalir Babu." It is an interesting poem, and ought to be read with care. We have published most of it, with some deletions. I hope that the author will forgive us. On reading the poem I have two questions to ask the readers:
>
> Will men be able to cope with the injury to their pride?
> Does Hemchandra think this is sweet revenge?

In spite of the furor, *Bana Prasun* is not available anywhere today and the extracts that follow were retrieved from an early history of Bengali literature. Mokshodayani also wrote a novel, *Safal Swapna,* 1884, which was later translated into English by Nalini Blair as *Dreams Unfulfilled.*

◆

From BANGALIR BABU
(The Bengali Babu)

Who's that rushing through his breakfast and bath?
The Bengali babu! He's terribly pressed:
The sahib will scold him, should he be late
So he's got to get ready, and bustles about.
There he comes, decked in trousers and jacket!
On his head a pith helmet, tied round with a scarf,

Just like a basket! He can't bear to wait
For anything. Loses his temper and shouts.
Furious, he'll slap or snap at his boy
If the child should happen to call out, "Father!"
Everything's a rush, but he takes his own time
Over his hookah, and puffs it at ease.
Should his heart soften, as he dreams in the smoke,
A half-chewed betel leaf will console the child.
The carriage costs five annas, but it hurts him to walk.
Alas, there goes our Bengali babu!

Alas, there goes our Bengali babu!
He slaves away from ten till four,
Carrying his servitude like a pedlar's wares.
A lawyer or magistrate, or perhaps a schoolmaster,
A subjudge, clerk, or overseer:
The bigger the job, the greater his pride;
The babu thinks he's walking on air.
Red in the face from the day's hard labor,
He downs pegs of whiskey to relax when he's home.
He's transported with pride at the thought of his rank—
But faced with a sahib, he trembles in fear!
Then he's obsequious, he mouths English phrases,
His own tongue disgusts him, he heaps it with curses.
The babu's learned English, he swells with conceit
And goes off in haste to deliver a speech.
He flounders while speaking, and stumbles and stutters,
But he's speaking in *English:* you must come and hear.

Alas, there goes our Bengali babu!
The lackey's livery is shed when he's home.
Bare-chested in slippers, he's a sight to be seen;

Clad in plain cloth, pleated by his servant,
He relaxes in slippers, or in native sandals.*
He enjoys his tobacco, lolls about on cushions;
Hookah at his mouth, he thinks he's in heaven.
The sitting room's resplendent, and echoes with laughter,
The spittoon's in front of them, but they spit on the mat.

Alas, there goes our Bengali babu!
Cane in hand, wearing shoes, smoking a cheroot;
Some, sahib-fashion, are hatted and coated.
Not a thought of religion, they lie about and sing,
Crying out on occasion "Bring the tobacco and pan!"

The oil lamp burns brightly, they can't wait to impress.
Their valor's displayed to any fool who passes.
With his cronies the babu plays cards or chess.
Alas, there he sits, the Bengali babu!

He longs to be fair, scrubs vigorously with soap;
Rubs with a towel till his skin peels off;
Parts his hair in front in the style of Prince Albert,
Scents himself liberally, and reeks like a civet.

. . . .

He has fashionable tastes. He loves watching plays;
His mouth stuffed with betel, he smiles with a twist.
He roars like a bull, "Excellent! Encore!"
And by the grace of the shopkeeper, he gets a lungful of smoke.
Head over heels in debt, but he won't leave his pleasures,
Alas, there goes our Bengali babu!
Here's one who doesn't drink, swells with pride at the thought—
The country's deliverance lies in his hand!

He writes himself down as a Brahmo and turns religious,
Tradesmen and pedlars are amazed at his sermons—
One becomes Brahmo to emancipate women,
Drags out of seclusion the ladies of his clan;
Another, a drunkard, is liberated by drink,
And launches a struggle to deliver the country.

---

*Not really sandals, but a kind of slipper, worn and popularized by Iswarchandra
  Vidyasagar.

The babu speaks a patter of Bengali and English
But he berates the English with all his heart.
These sports are but nocturnal; wiping his mouth, in the morning
The babu is respectful and sober* again.

Translated by Supriya Chaudhury.

TARABAI SHINDE ⸺⸺⸺⸺

(ca. 1850–ca. 1910)   *Marathi*

Though Jotirao Phule mentions *Stri Purush Tulana* (A Comparison of Men
and Women), 1882, in the second issue of *Satsar,* the journal of the Satyashodhak Mandal, which he started in 1885, this extraordinary work by
a courageous and original feminist thinker and critic remained virtually
unknown until 1975 when it was found and republished by S. G. Malshe.

We know very little about Tarabai Shinde's life. Malshe draws on oral
evidence to suggest that she was born into a high-caste, well-to-do Maratha family and that she was an only child. She studied Marathi, Sanskrit,
and English and was obviously well read in classical and modern literature.
She married very young and seems to have soon lost regard for her husband. She had no children. There are stories, perhaps apocryphal, that
speak of her as a fiercely independent and self-confident person who rode
a horse and wielded a sword as well as most soldiers could. Of the rich-
ness, the variety, and the clarity of her intellect, as of the vitality of her
personality, we have no dearth of evidence in the only work this philosopher, social analyst, and literary critic left behind.

Stri Purush Tulana, an essay of about forty pages published in book form,
was initially written in response to an article that appeared in the
Pune Vaibhav, a weekly known for its extremely orthodox and antireform-
ist politics, following an incident over which there was charged discussion
in the city. It is difficult to tell from the reports of that time whether the
accused, Vijayalakshmi, had had an abortion or whether she had committed infanticide, but the court sentenced her to death. The *Pune Vaibhav*
came out with a virulent article attacking her, and women in general, for
their "new" loose morals. Tarabai Shinde's response shows, first, how
men are invariably guilty of the very vices they accuse women of, and,
next, that men are often responsible even for the few vices women do

---

*The Bengali word is *bhadra,* an untranslatable term of social reference, implying
a variety of attributes such as decent, gentlemanly, respectable.

have. It is an impressive riposte. She writes, she says, out of pride for her sisters and to clearly establish that women are braver than men.

> Though every day we see new and more terrible examples of men's violence, audacity, and cunning, yet no one pays any attention to these; instead people continue to heap the burden of all wrongs onto the women themselves.

Parts of the essay suggest she is speaking of her own experience—of being married to a man who did not come up to her expectations or hold her interest—and other parts obviously refer to Vijayalakshmi's situation. It is possible that contemporary readers would have associated many other sections of this long essay with specific incidents and specific people.

Tarabai speaks of herself as a "powerless dull woman, prisoner within a Maratha household." Even so, she says, in the face of male treachery, duplicity, and faithlessness, she is forced to adopt a crude and blunt manner: "I cannot restrain myself from writing in such fiery language." But in any case she prefers her direct rough-hewn language and style to the sophisticated diction, manufactured by male conspiracy, of "standard" language. She makes no plea to the men that they pay attention to her work. In fact, she does not count on their goodwill or chivalry. If they are true to the images of rationality and objectivity they project, she says, they will be forced to accept her arguments. But if they respond from self-interest or merely retort out of wounded pride, she warns, she will continue her battle against male injustice and sow the seeds of universal sisterhood. In that battle, reason will be her sword and her shield.

Tarabai is as irreverent as she is incisive. She subjects both God and man to the same devastating logic and the same scathing wit. The critic Maya Pandit describes her writing as "racy and absolutely full of fire. She uses many idiomatic expressions and phrases that occur particularly in the language of women. The syntactic structure is conditioned by the balance of ideas." Other scholars claim that the style of her argument and the rhetorical diction link her work to that of the reformer Jotiba Phule. In fact, in the second issue of *Satsar,* Jotiba criticizes men who attacked Tarabai without even reading what she had to say carefully.

Stri Purush Tulana is probably the first full-fledged and extant feminist argument after the poetry of the bhakti period. But Tarabai's work is also significant because, at a time when intellectuals and activists alike were primarily concerned with the hardships of a Hindu widow's life and other easily identifiable atrocities perpetrated on women, Tarabai Shinde, apparently working in isolation, was able to broaden the scope of the analysis to include the ideological fabric of patriarchal society. Women everywhere, she implies, are similarly oppressed.

Most of the second half of her essay is translated here. It moves on from a response to the accusations against Vijayalakshmi and Tarabai's own introductory observations to a more general critique of patriarchal culture in her time. She begins by taking up for consideration two verses that she felt epitomized the misogyny of the culture and refuting them, point by point. The first verse comes from the *Ramvijaya* (The Victory of Ram), a sixteenth-century Marathi text written by Shridhar, the prolific pandit of Pandharpur. The second is taken from the Sanskrit *Sataka Trayam* (Three Centuries of Verses), compiled by the poet Bhartrhari.

Tarabai also has the distinction of being the first Indian feminist literary critic. Her "exposure of male stereotypes and images of women," Vidyut Bhagwat points out, "appeared almost a century before Simone de Beauvoir's *The Second Sex*. Besides, Tarabai's forthright polemical style stands in sharp contrast to de Beauvoir's."

◆

STRI PURUSH TULANA
(A Comparison of Men and Women)

Let me ask you something, Gods! You are supposed to be omnipotent and freely accessible to all. You are said to be completely impartial. What does that mean? That you have never been known to be partial. But wasn't it you who created both men and women? Then why did you grant happiness only to men and brand women with nothing but agony? Your will was done! But the poor women have had to suffer for it down the ages.

One comes across several charges against women both in the written literature and in everyday discourse. But do men not suffer from the same flaws that women are supposed to have? Do men not cheat as women do? Theft, incest, murder, robbery, deception, fraud, swindling of government funds, taking bribes, changing truth to falsehood and falsehood to truth—do men not do any of these? . . .

First, if, as you claim, a woman has more power than a device for witchcraft or black magic, let me ask you, you who are endowed with an intellect far more powerful than hers, what have you not achieved with your intellect? You who have made possible what was believed to be impossible, of what worth can a woman's power be before your valiant deeds? Of none.

Second, it may be true that women are a whirlpool of suspicion. But that is because they are uneducated and all kinds of doubts inhabit their minds. But even then, it must be borne in mind that their suspicions are usually and necessarily about their own relationships. But if one casts just a fleeting glance at the webs of doubt in your minds, one's eyes will surely be dazed. Your minds are full of all kinds of treacherous plans. "Let's bluff this moneylender and pocket a thousand rupees from him." Or, "Let's tell that *jagirdar* such and such a thing and swindle him out of some five hundred rupees." Or, "Let's lie to that officer about that particular case and change his judgment in X's favor." Or, "Let's register those false documents instead of the true ones." Or, "That woman Y, what a coquette she really is! What airs she gives herself! Must corner her one of these days, and see whether some affair with her can be managed. My current affair has begun to bore me. This is the chance to end it once and for all and begin a new one." Such disgusting thoughts never enter a woman's mind. This is, of course, not to say that all the women in the world are as luminous as the sun and as pure as the waters of the Holy Ganges. But even if one takes into account the entire female community in the world, it would be difficult to come across more than 10 percent of them who, like you, are caught in the whirlwind of such insidious perfidies, though not a single one of you is free of them.

Third, women are called the acme of impudence. But does your own species lack this quality in any measure? A judicious comparison would reveal the balance weighted far heavier on your side in this respect. Fourth, women are considered a megapolis of inadvertent acts. But what about you, the dastardly, perfidious, treacherous people that you are? You, who would not hesitate even for a moment in cutting somebody's throat immediately after winning his confidence. Do you never commit such insidious acts? You speak as if you are Holy Temples of Reason! Bravo! Bravo, indeed! You consider yourselves erudite and judicious, don't you? Yet can you find a match, anywhere, at any time, for the perfidious acts that you commit every day? On top of all this, you have the audacity to call yourselves judicious! What can anyone say?

Granted, women are as stupid as buffaloes in the cow pen! They are ignorant and do not know how to read or to write. But does that mean God did not grant them even an iota of intelligence? Thoughtless and rash they may sometimes be, but even then they are far preferable to you. Yes! To you who are the bastions of erudition and wisdom! Why, one has only to visit a prison to get a proof of this! The prisons are packed to capacity with such people. One can't even find a place to stand there, they are so packed! As for the "wisdom," the "knowledge" that they have, it's a little too much, if you really ask me! Everyone there has a "wise" head on his shoulders, and a "wise" deed to his credit! Some come there because they have printed false notes, some have taken bribes,* some for having eloped with someone else's wife, some for having been in a rebellion, some for poisoning people, some for treason, some for perjury, some for impersonating kings and deceiving the public, some for murders. . . . Or would it be more correct to say that the government has most reverently offered you an honorable place in this prison, I mean, this palace, of merriment for committing such great, why, such superbly valiant deeds? Now tell me, what woman ever commits such atrocious deeds? Can you show me any prisons that claim to hold only women prisoners in their fold? I am sure the number of such women will not be more than a hundred at the most for every two thousand men.

Furthermore, we need to ask, what is the greatest crime that women commit? Adultery. That is the highest peak of their criminal ventures. They behave recklessly only because of such inclinations. But then, who takes the first step of sowing the seed of such designs in their minds? Who else but you? However shameless a woman may be, she will never throw herself into the arms of a strange man. That is an eternal truth. Do you know what a woman's idea of happiness is? First, a husband of her choice. One whom she can love. Once their hearts are united, she will not worry about poverty. She will endure any

---

*Look, the government employs you for various jobs. It pays you salaries ranging from ten rupees to a couple of thousand, according to your qualifications, puts its complete trust in you, and agrees to whatever terms and conditions you make! Why? For merely putting your signatures across some papers here and there! Now, is it any of the government's fault that you pocket the pay and insist upon taking bribes as well? You never hesitate in accepting anything—just anything—as bribe. From hard cash to horses, cows, cloth, gold, and even pots and pans! And in the absence of any of these, even shoes! No one can escape from your clutches. You have no scruples whatsoever in extracting bribes from both the rich and the poor. Now doesn't this prove beyond any doubt that you are treacherous? That you commit treason? Further, if you fail to get any of these things, you are willing to accept as bribes any other thing, like provisions for a day, guavas, a couple of sticks of sugarcane, or even wood, jaggery, or even the husk of grain! But you will make people cough up something and grab it. Do you ever let anybody escape without paying up? Never! By hook or crook, grab you will—anything that you can lay your hands on! Do you know what you are? Slimy beggars! Yes, that's what you are! All the paper in the world wouldn't be enough to write a panegyric on these most noble, excellent and commendable merits of yours! Why, there won't be any place in the world large enough to stock all those papers! The entire world would overflow with them. And the oceans won't be sufficient to make ink to write that eulogy! And armies of carpenters will have to be employed to carve pens to write it with!

calamity for him. She will suffer hunger or thirst and put up with any kind of harassment for the sake of the man she loves. She will be happy even in the worst circumstances possible. But she will never, in her remotest dreams, think on her own of committing that crime. But let me tell you something. Can adultery really be considered an act of the most heinous nature? Our shastras* certainly do not seem to think so! There is no need to think that such things did not happen in the past. In fact, those very shastras that you so very glibly quote are full of the most supreme confusion regarding this problem. For example, the shastras most freely sanctioned such practices in several circumstances. Suppose a king died, leaving behind him a queen who did not have a son, she could select any rishi** of her choice and beget sons from him in order to augment the family. And she could keep him till she had as many children as she wanted. What was this if not adultery? But wasn't it sanctioned by the shastras? Now, instead of sanctioning such things, had they sanctioned widow remarriages, that would have made even the kingdom of the deceased king stronger. As you know, many of our states, *jahagirs, inams,* and other hereditary revenue rights were dissolved by the government for want of legal heirs. Now that could easily have been avoided and even the country need not have become a slave [had widows been allowed to remarry]. The estates and properties of many were seized by the government and added to the treasury, for lack of legal heirs. Besides, many times it so happened that when a king died, he left behind him a bunch of widows and there was no one to protect that crowd. What happened then? You men swooped down on them like a swarm of locusts and caused downright ruin. Those royal women, whose feet were never soiled with earth, were as beautiful as goddesses; but your insatiable lust reduced them to nothing but beggars in exile.

Another charge against women is that they are extremely mean minded and shallow. But they are never obsessed by such thoughts as "How will I get promoted to a higher office? How will I get more money? When will I rise to dizzy heights in public esteem? When will people address me as 'Sir' or 'Sahib' and speak humbly and meekly to me?" Women never waste their lives as you do, trying to achieve such impossible things. Then why do you pretend all these things are ab-

---

*The term *shastra* here refers to ancient books of law, guidelines for moral, social, and political action; compilations belonging to the postvedic period.—Ed.
**Rishi* is a sage, seer.—Ed.

solutely unknown to you and charge women with being the sole pro-
prietors of "reckless vanity"?

The fifth charge against women is that they are the treasure houses
of transgressions. But in fact, it is you who fit that description best.
It's you who cause women to transgress. Let me substantiate this. Many
fathers give away their beautiful and very young daughters, who are
hardly ten or eleven years old, to men who are eighty or ninety in
exchange for a purse of gold. They do it with an eye only on his
wealth. Their reasoning is, "Even if the husband dies, there's no need
to worry. She will be rolling in money. She will be able to get the best
of things to eat, and be able to wear nice clothes—at least for a few
days. She will have nothing to worry about. So what if she doesn't
have a husband?" That is what they think. So without any scruples,
they give their daughters away to such old men as lambs to a tiger.
But once he who is her love, her real happiness, passes away, what
meaning does life hold for her? The only man to delight in her new
clothes, admire her, and consider her more precious than his life is her
husband. Without him her life is like a desert. Then why would she
hanker after those dry festivities? It might seem far better in the past
when women used to burn themselves on their husbands' funeral pyres.*
At least when one was reduced to a heap of ashes along with the
husband, there was nothing left to worry about. In this world who is
there who would love a woman as much as the husband does, apart
from her mother, of course? That is a fact. But what about her who
loses both? Who can she depend on when the red-hot fire of youth is

---

*What a great service the Sarvajanik Sabha in Pune has rendered to women! In
their journal, or whatever it is that they publish annually or biannually, they very
pompously declared, "It would be better if the government allowed women to
burn themselves on the funeral pyres of their husbands." But tell me, if you want
women to do that, why don't you propose the same plan for yourselves? Why
do you want to survive your wives? To knead cow dung and pat it into cakes
for your own cremation? Why shouldn't you burn yourselves on the pyres of
your wives? Better you than her. Because her passing away proves to be far more
detrimental than yours. Do you want to know how? Well, she is always survived
by her young children. Who would look after them for her?

There is a proverb, "Let a prosperous father die but even a pauper of a mother
should never die." If the father dies, the mother will endure any amount of grief and
sorrow but maintain her children. But what do you do in such circumstances? If
your wife dies today, you rush to bring another the very next day and render your
children homeless. Don't you? Admit it now! Already there is a great outcry about
this! In fact it's you who should be thrown into that pyre before your wives.

burning in the pallav of her sari? This, then, is the fate of the women who are married off to old husbands. . . .

Many rich men get their favorite daughter married to a boy of rather humble origin and keep the couple in their house because they love their daughter. Everything goes well while the boy and the girl are both young and immature. But once she comes of age, this daughter of the rich man, clever, pampered, and used to wealth right from her birth, starts realizing the difference between herself and her husband. Now, that boy is a wretched creature of a lowly origin and is ignorant of the real comforts in life. As a result of the marriage, he is able to experience them for the first time. It is probably solely because of the good deeds he had done in a previous birth that he married into such a family. But his behavior is far from becoming to his newly acquired prosperity. The wretched creature is used only to the coarsest things in life! Even if a donkey is fed twice a day and decorated with silken threads, a saddle, a plume of feathers, and silver knobs, will it ever equal a noble horse though it be lean and on the brink of death? Naturally she doesn't like him, since he is a rough patch on a delicate shawl—and then the inevitable happens. I don't have to write about that extensively. All those ridiculous and despicable things that result from such a state of affairs are public knowledge. Now of what use is the father's pampering to the daughter? Had he found a suitable husband for her in the first place it would have been better. He would have the joy of seeing her happily settled in her married life.

You would not like a bad, ugly, cruel, uneducated wife, full of vices; why then should a wife like such a husband? Just as you desire a good wife, she also longs for a good husband. Let me remind you of something. When you are young and your parents are very poor, they are greatly worried about your marriage. At that time, they borrow heavily and somehow manage to marry you off. In such circumstances you can hardly expect to get a beautiful girl for a wife. At that time, even a wife who is as ugly as an owl seems like a Venus to you. But later on, when you are blessed by the goddess Saraswati, and have become "learned" and educated, when you get promoted in your job, you are ashamed of this first wife. Because you are wealthy now, you consider her to be worthless. She is nothing more to you than a servant or a cook whom you can hire to keep house for you for a few small coins. For you, she is just a slave you have bought for a thousand rupees. Perhaps you love even your dog or your horse more than your wife. A wife is nothing but a dark corner or a heap of rubbish in the house. Who cares for her? But why would a rich man care for his wife? For him wives come a dime a dozen. The rich are ready to be bridegrooms any day—indeed every day. It is only because Yama, the God of Death, doesn't have time to carry off their wives so fast. Otherwise they wouldn't mind tying the knot thrice a day. Such men find it very difficult to call an ugly wife their own. When they were poor, in the past, nobody took any notice of them. But now that they have acquired wealth and prestigious jobs, they have risen in public esteem. So they want a wife who will match that pomp with her beauty. Just watch all those silly pranks they get up to at the time of their second or third marriages. Now tell me, do women ever behave in this fashion? Whether in prosperity or in poverty, they always behave obediently, according to your commands. Have you ever heard of a woman running off with another man just because her husband is ugly or poor? Now who deserves to be blamed? Women or men?

The sixth argument against women is that a woman is enveloped in a hundred guises of fraud and deceit. My friends, as far as these particular merits are concerned, the honor of the first rank undoubtedly goes to you. How can I describe your deceit? One comes across it virtually at every step. Oh, what guises you don! Those yellow-black stripes that you draw on your body—like a tiger! You are a Gosavi, a fakir, a Haridas, a brahmachari, a sadhu, a dudhahari, a Giripuri, a bharati, a Nanak, a kanfate, a yogi* . . . what a fanfare you create. You smear your body with the so-called holy ash, grow your hair long into a mass of matted locks, proclaim that you have renounced the world, and roam all over cheating and deceiving people with your beguiling tricks. "Who's this?" "Ramgirkarbuwa." "Who's that?" "Shastribuwa." "And this?" "The great sage, Ganpatbuwa Phaltankar, a mahasadhu!" "That one there?" "A follower of Nanaka." Somebody just has to say "Look at his virtues! They defy any description! He's wonderful. Besides, he is free from all worldly desires. He has great magical powers," and so on. That is enough of an introduction for a credulous public! Then the fake sadhu goes on prolonging his stay, putting on grander and grander pretensions. He gorges himself with rich, sweet food like a fat tomcat, and then begins his "worship." That is, reposing in a corner, he closely eyes all the women who come for an audience with him, and selects a few beautiful ones whose names he reiterates on his rosary. That's the end! All gods are forgotten promptly and forever. And these "goddesses," in the form of beautiful women, oc-

---

*These titles for holy men are Tarabai's satirical inventions.—Ed.

cupy that place. In his eyes, their lovely, smiling faces and in his heart a burning desire for money. Torn between these two cravings, the sadhu hovers between the worlds of sanity and madness. . . .

A tulsi necklace around the neck, God's name on your lips . . . with this paraphernalia you roam around in the guise of a Haridas, but what are you really? Nothing but beggars! Respectable-looking beggars! You go to Kashi, don't you? But just because you have shaved off your mustache and your beard, do you think you are absolved of all sin? . . .

Once you become sannyasis, you shouldn't hanker after any worldly ambitions. With your holy saffron clothes, your staffs and pails of holy water in your hands, you declare that all the creatures in this world are the manifestations of God. You sit on the *ghats* after bathing in the river, smearing yourselves with sackfuls of ash, pretending to be lost in meditation. But at the first sound of tinkling anklets, don't your eyes race up all the fifty steps of the ghat? The *buwa* is so utterly flustered that he drops the pail of holy water from his hand. . . . With what words can I describe your guile? You will assure somebody that he is like a brother to you, but at the same time wish for his ruin in your heart. You call another your father, but with your eye on his purse. And when you are friends with someone, you eye everything, from his dog to his wife, with malicious desire. There are very few among the male sex who are pure. One should hear your gossip with your friends. "Why, that Mr. X shows off so much these days! What fun if he is ruined! How that Mr. Y has risen! What a marvel it is! There were times when that son of a donkey didn't have enough food to eat! But now the son of a bitch goes around in a two-horse carriage!" This is your favorite hobby, isn't it? The moral of the story is, with evil in your mind, like a crow, you roam around looking for the weaknesses of people to wreck them. Do women ever behave like that? Tell me. Did any woman ever disguise herself as a sadhu and carry any man off? Give me just one example. . . .

The next argument against women is this: A woman is temptation incarnate. All right. A woman is full of charm from top to toe. Everything about her—her limbs, her voice, her gait, her speech—fascinates and attracts men like a magnet, like a honeycomb attracts a honeybee. But is that any of her fault?

If a great brahmachari sadhu is asked to choose between a pot of gold coins and a beautiful woman, he will undoubtedly forsake the pot of gold for the golden complexion. . . .

In these days, because of the spread of education and because of the printing press, many works of fiction have been published. For example, *Manjughosha, Muktamala,* the play *Manorama,* and so on. Now it is true that no story becomes really interesting without a sprinkling of romance, humor, and pathos. But the composers of these stories should at least check whether such stories are plausible, or whether they have any historical validity, before starting the composition.

Let's take a look at *Manjughosha* first. Manjughosha is the favorite daughter of an emperor. Is it possible that she could deceive her old father and impudently run away with Vasantamadhava in his airplane? Wouldn't she have any sympathy for her old father, who treated her with so much love and affection? She was known as virtue incarnate; then how could she desert her jeweled palace and forsake its pleasures for a strange prince whose name and origin she did not know? Didn't the image of her old father rise before her eyes when she left? Didn't she feel guilty in any way? Dear readers, you can judge for yourselves the truth of such a story. It's thousands of years since the Dwaparyuga ended and the Kaliyuga began.* Even the English rule in this country is two hundred and fifty years old. The writer of this book, I'm sure, was born in this century itself. But I'm sure that all our ancestors put together couldn't ten generations ago visualize anything like Vasantamadhava's airplane.

The English people have invented many machines: trains, airplanes, and so on. But even they haven't got the trick of using an airplane for anything they want to. You can decide for yourselves how incredible it is to imagine that Vasantamadhava mastered its entire intricate mechanism for the sole purpose of carrying off Manjughosha.

Another book in the same tradition is *Muktamala.* Muktamala was the daughter of a famous knight. Her husband had been thrown into prison as a result of the king's wrath. In her attempts to meet him, she got into the clutches of the despotic officer Bhadraksha. He tortured her and kept her prisoner in a thick forest. But she never surrendered her virtue, which is a woman's true religion. It is probably the intention of the writer to demonstrate this. Now what I want to debate is this. A woman is as frail as an ant compared to the towering strength of a man; why, all the strength in the whole of her body would be less than the strength contained in the arm of a man. If such a lustful tiger chased a poor helpless cow in a lonely and unprotected place, would he refrain from killing her as well?

---

*Dwaparyuga is the third of the world's four ages; Kaliyuga is the present age.—Ed.

Why, even your gods are treacherous. No wonder you are the same. Indra impersonated Gautama to seduce a virtuous wife like Ahalya. Didn't His Holiness, Lord Krishna, go and ruin the virtue of a great wife like Chandrawal, who loved her husband so much? No, if you start wrecking houses treacherously, what can a woman's *pativratadharma** do? How can a woman protect her true religion, her loyalty to her husband?

Krishna at least is a God. He holds in even balance sins and moral achievements. He is omnipotent and knows the truth. A woman could save herself from your hands only if God himself takes pity on her and cuts you into tiny pieces at such times. Otherwise she can't even dream of being rescued. Such stories are true only in books. The preacher tells us from his pulpit that eating aubergines is forbidden in the Puranas and one shouldn't eat them. But the moment he is back from his preaching, all that he has said is promptly forgotten and he stuffs himself with a hearty meal of those very vegetables. Obviously what he preaches is only for other people to follow. What use is such knowledge? And who follows such dicta? Who cares about the sufferings of a woman? She can escape a tyrant only by smashing her head at his feet. Otherwise escape is impossible. So what is the intention behind writing such books? They are based on such obviously childish logic. One who knows the ways of the world can easily see how false the whole thing is.

Let us now turn to the play *Manorama.* The playwright has delineated four types of situations here. In the first, the couple Manorama and Ganapatrao are shown to have come to a good end because they are both cultured and educated. The couple Godubai and Ramrao Phadnis, on the other hand, are most ill matched. This is apparently to show how young wives ignore their old husbands and how contemptuously they treat them. Later on the writer presents elaborate descriptions of Godubai reveling in her native vileness after Ramrao's death, her becoming a laughingstock in the court of law, the police inspector's style of working, and the testimony of Saraswatibai and Tuka the barber. In the third situation, we have the couple Gangu and poor Vinayakrao. Gangu doesn't love her husband because of his poverty, and through the machinations of Saraswatibai, she becomes friendly with loafers

---

Pativratadharma refers to a wife's religion. This is a concept somewhat like that of "virtue" with many dimensions and many implications. A wife's religion is the worship of a husband, whom she must consider a god.—Ed.

and runs off to Karachi to openly become a whore. There, once again we find descriptions of the false affections of whores, their false words, their hollow promises, and so on.

The fourth section consists of the account of Rambhatji's daughter-in-law Thaku, who is a widow. Later she becomes pregnant and after going through every kind of suffering imaginable, she dies in extreme distress of some horrible disease in Bottlebhoy's hospital in Bombay.

All these different types of stories have been cooked up by the dramatist, but the question is, To what end? In fact, by writing such a play the writer has exposed himself in public and made himself a butt of ridicule. It's true that a clenched hand contains a million, every house has skeletons in its cupboards, and every house has some darkness and some light. Every house, however, also has a widow—either a sister, or mother, or daughter-in-law, or daughter. A stigma to one is a stigma to all. What a grand achievement it is that this author has managed to malign all widows by one stroke of his pen! Who can claim that all parents will learn their lesson from this play and get their daughters married only to good and virtuous husbands; and that Lady Luck will smile upon all women as she did on Manorama!

Similarly, old dogs like Ramrao will never learn a lesson from the play just because they see how Ramrao married a young adventuress only to have his prestige auctioned off in the crowded court of law. That will never stop them from marrying young girls in their old age. There shouldn't be any doubt that those who marry when they are so old will be disgraced and subjected to ridicule both in private and in public. But it is impossible to believe that all women will run away from husbands who are inferior to them.

Now it is hardly surprising that Thaku died in the hospital. After all, she was going to die anyway. Either at home or in the hospital. Dear authors, please don't imagine, even in your wildest dreams, that you will be able to strike terror into the hearts of people and persuade them never to do such things again simply by writing such stories.

In short, it is you who are vice incarnate. Why blame women? Women like Anadibai, the aunt of the Peshwas who was notorious for her murderous deeds, are far less in number than similar men. There will not be more than ten women like Vijayalakshmi in a hundred, either.

And even if a woman is guilty of any monstrous deeds, she is, nonetheless, superior to man. Once you win her over with your various tricks, and become the king of her heart, she trusts you implicitly and loves you with every fiber of her being. Then you become the most precious thing for her, next to her virtue, of course. She offers you nothing less than her life. How can she see through your treacherous game? Because at such times you behave like a slave to her. You win her favors with such an obtrusive and officious manner that you are ready to even lick her shoes. Yes, your love knows no bounds, but for how long? Until your lust is satiated. Once your desire is fulfilled, and she becomes pregnant, you leave all the worrying and suffering to her and hide your face like a scorpion, behind a stone. When that mortified woman, innocent as a deer, crushed to death by that burden on her soul, begs the wicked man, that beast in disguise, to help her, he answers her with such indifference as if it were none of his concern. "What can I do about it? You have sinned and now you must suffer for it." Ah, what an answer! What must she feel when she hears such words from the same mouth that had uttered words dripping with love, which she regarded with utmost love, for which she was prepared to throw away her life and soul? They are not words, they are poisoned arrows. Think of her condition when she hears such words. But what can the poor woman do? Utterly destitute, she had no courage left but to abandon the child, her own flesh and blood, to save the honor for which she has to undergo so severe a punishment.

Here under the British rule, not a leaf can be moved without a witness! But in such delicate affairs, witnesses are conspicuously absent. The government also deserves to be blamed for this. They have passed a law that the punishment given to him who offers a bribe will be double that given to him who accepts it. Similarly, I would suggest that they should pass a law in such cases as well by which the man should get twice as much punishment as woman gets. Why shouldn't it be so? Even in ancient civilizations like Rome and Greece such crimes used to be punished most severely. I have one suggestion to offer in this regard. The government should brand the stupid prattling mouths of these men with red-hot irons. This will strike terror in their hearts and such crimes will never be committed! Think of that miserable woman who later on spends her life in some godforsaken corner, or in the jail, mourning her fate, weeping her heart out, trying to wash the stains off her character. All her honor is torn to rags by such public disgrace. Many commit suicide, many abandon their relatives, give up their wealth, and go into exile. Even a cobra is preferable to you. At least it kills immediately. But the poison that you inject into her afflicts her with intolerable agony and causes her to die a slow, slow death. Thus, you are more treacherous than even a poisonous snake. You can judge who has a more generous mind. Will you ever suffer as much as she does for you?

Never, never will you be so kind! Never can you be so generous! No sooner have you ruined one than you are ready to go after another. Then you won't remember the first one even in a dream. But a woman's love is as deep as an ocean. She will value the man she loves even more than her own life. He may torture her, but she will always be on his side. Thus her heart is always full of tender love for him, but look how she's rewarded.

I'm sure there are very few men who are ruined by women. But it would be difficult even to guess at the number of women ruined by men. You are far too clever for women. You are, in fact, nothing but scoundrels of the first order! You are so cunning that you will pass through a sugarcane field without letting those sharp leaves touch you, let alone scratch you. You organize big meetings every day, deliver impressive speeches, offer unwanted advice to all and sundry, and do a hundred other such stupid things. You are nothing but learned asses! Yes, that's what you are really. It is said that it's always dark just under a lamp! You are no exception to that rule! If only you realized how much evil you contain, it would break your heart! . . .

Translated by Maya Pandit.

SWARNAKUMARI DEVI ———————————

(1856–1932)   *Bengali*

The history of modern Bengali literature and culture is inextricably intertwined with the history of the Tagore family of Jorasanko, which was to Bengali society what the Medici family was to Europe during the Renaissance. The most illustrious member of the family was undoubtedly Swarnakumari Devi's younger brother, the poet and novelist Rabindranath Tagore (1861–1941), but Swarnakumari herself, novelist, poet, playwright, songwriter, and journalist, was one of the most distinguished literary figures of the time, and a torchbearer in the tradition of women's writing in Bengal. As Anurupa Devi (1882–1942), also a famous name in Bengali literature, put it, "The advent of Swarnakumari on the literary scene of Bengal heralded a new era for women. Many women had written poems and stories before her, but these were looked upon patronizingly. She was the first writer to show up the strengths of women's writing and raise women's creations to a position of respect."

During her lifetime Swarnakumari's novels were as popular as those of the great novelist Bankim Chandra Chatterjee. Yet today it is difficult to lay one's hands on the writings of this versatile artist. A whole publishing house was set up to preserve and reprint the works of her brother, Rabindranath. But whereas these prestigious publishers have brought out two children's books written by another woman of the Tagore family, Jnanadanandini Devi, as writer and critic Bani Roy points out, the more serious, more distinguished work of Swarnakumari Devi is in danger of being lost to history.

Swarnakumari, the tenth child of Debendranath Tagore, was born just before the Sepoy Rebellion of 1857, which she later described in her short story *Mutiny*. The major reform movements—advocating education for women and the remarriage of widows—which spanned the second half of the nineteenth century, form the backdrop to some of her books. The Tagore girls did not go to school, but great attention was paid to their education. Private tutors were hired to teach them Sanskrit and English, and obviously the more important education was the discussions—on literature, painting, music, science, religion, politics, and education—that were constantly going on in the sprawling Calcutta mansion of this large family. Both the men and the women designed costumes and experimented with gardening, cooking, interior decor on such a scale that the phrase *Thakur-bari* (of the Tagore household) is, even today, synonymous with a particular elegant style of living. Swarnakumari Devi was already writing when, at thirteen, she married Janakiram Ghosal, who was then a deputy magistrate.

In 1870 a novel with the title *Dipnirban* (The Snuffing Out of the Light) hit the literary scene in Calcutta. It was widely acclaimed. Since the name of the author had initially been withheld, though, to quote the notice in the *Hindu Patriot,* "it became known in course of time that the accomplished writer was a young Hindu lady," there was much speculation about who she might be. The *Calcutta Review's* praise was unstinting: "We have no hesitation in pronouncing this book to be by far the best that has yet been written by a Bengali lady, and we should no more hesitate to call it one of the ablest in the whole literature of Bengal." Her brother Satyendranath, who was in England when the novel appeared, was a little more hesitant. He found it difficult to believe that a woman had written the book. All the same, he wrote, "I have received a novel of unprecedented merit for review. I have heard that it is the work of a woman of a learned and cultured family. I feel greatly excited to find that a Bengali woman is capable of writing a novel of such artistic merit. The erudition, style, and sincerity are hard to find in Bengali literature; in fact they would be difficult to find in other cultures also."

That was only a beginning. Important among the several other works in her varied oeuvre are *Chinna Mukul* (A Picked Flower), 1879, which explores the friendship of sisters, *Virodha* (Revolt), 1890, a historical novel about tribal revolts against the Rajputs, *Snehalata ba Palita* (Snehalata and Palita), a novel in two volumes, 1892 and 1893, respectively, as well as what is perhaps her best work, *Kahake* (To Whom?), 1898 (translated by her as *The Unfinished Song*). In it she captures for the first time in Bengali fiction the ethos of the new urban middle class that was her milieu. Her two farces *Koney Badal* (Evening Dust Clouds/Time for Seeing the Bride), 1906, and *Pakchakra* (Wheel of Fortune), 1911, were immensely popular, as were her expertly crafted short stories.

Among her major achievements is the journal *Bharati*, founded in 1878, which she edited for more than thirty years. The first editorial board had Rabindranath and Jyotirindranath on it, but from 1885 to 1905 and again from 1909 to 1915, Swarnakumari Devi was the sole editor. Her second daughter, Sarla Devi, was also involved in this venture. Though *Bharati* was primarily a literary magazine, there was no aspect of Bengali life or culture that did not feature in it. Leading thinkers and activists of the time, including such women writers as Girindramohini, Sarat Kumari Chaudhurani, and Anurupa Devi wrote for it. Swarnakumari made it a matter of editorial policy to give priority to popular articles on science so that women who couldn't speak English would have access to new scientific ideas and new information. She herself wrote seven articles on geology, having first made a careful study of several important works in the subject. She was among the first people to coin Bengali names for the new scientific concepts.

In 1879 Swarnakumari published what must have been the first opera written in Bengali—*Basanta Utsav* (Spring Festival). Bani Roy points out that Tagore's more popular *Balmiki Protiba* (Balmiki's Genius) was only composed later, and that Swarnakumari often used forms that her more famous younger brother later picked up. Many of Swarnakumari's short stories were written before her younger brother had mastered the form. She also wrote the long philosophical poems known as *gatha* long before Rabindranath did. In fact she dedicates her first book of these poems to him with the lines:

> To my younger brother.
> Let me present these poems: carefully
> 	gleaned and strung
> To the most deserving person.
> But you are so playful. I hope you will not
> Snap and scatter these flowers for fun.

The affection is unmistakable, but so is the hurt. Though scholars have rarely mentioned it, the "early Rabindranath," Bani Roy feels, "shows remarkable affinity with the style, techniques, and even the titles of his elder sister," who was probably a model and a support. Rabindranath, however, was not so generous or encouraging. In February 1914, soon after Swarnakumari's *Kahake* had been published in translation, he wrote to William Rothenstein, "She is one of those unfortunate beings who has more ambition than ability. But just enough talent to keep her alive for a short period. Her weakness has been taken advantage of by some unscrupulous literary agents in London and she has had stories translated and published. I have given her no encouragement but have not been successful in making her see things in the proper light." The book, however, was well received in England, and a second edition was published within a year. This novel unfolds an analysis of what love is for a woman. It raises many issues (including whether George Eliot is as great as Shakespeare), but perhaps the fact that it highlighted a woman's independence—and her difference—is its major achievement. Swarnakumari Devi clearly resented being patronized as the famous writer's sister and struggled hard to establish her own reputation as a writer. But it was difficult. In the poem "Likhitechi Dinrat" (Writing, Day and Night) she expresses these resentments and her frustration.

Of her involvement in social reform and nationalist politics there is much to report. In 1887 she helped form the Sakhi Samiti, an organization to help widows and destitute women, and in 1889 and again in 1890, along with Pandita Ramabai, Ramabai Ranade, and Kadambini Gangopadhyay, she participated in the annual sessions of the Indian National Congress. She also started the Ladies' Theosophical Society in Calcutta.

One cannot today claim that Swarnakumari Devi's writing is comparable to that of her brother Rabindranath, whose mature work places him among the most distinguished of twentieth-century writers in India. But one can ask, Had she received the support and encouragement she deserved, what might she not have achieved?

We have chosen to translate the first and eighth chapters of Swarnakumari's novel *Kahake,* which depicts a young woman's growth into selfhood and independence through an understanding of what it means to love. The heroine, Moni, meets and falls in love (a radical act for a middleclass woman at that time) with Ramanath, a lawyer who has just come back to Calcutta from London. She soon finds out that in England Ramanath had been engaged to marry an English girl and that he had deserted her. "It was only a brief flirtation," he tells Moni. Disturbed, and finding that her feelings toward him have changed, Moni breaks off the engagement after a period of traumatic indecision. She finds herself growing closer to another family friend, a doctor, who turns out to be a childhood playmate. She finally marries him.

The novel is structured in crisp alternating chapters: one carries the story forward while the other explores, often in conversation with a sister who cannot understand why Moni is making such a big issue out of what to her is a simple matter, Moni's changing self and her changing understanding of love.

◆

From KAHAKE
(To Whom?)
Chapter 1

> Man's love is of man's life a thing apart
> 'Tis woman's whole existence.

The person who wrote these lines was a man. It is a wonder that a man could so capture the essential nature of a woman. When I consider my own life I feel this to be literally true. However far I look back into the past, ever since knowledge dawned on me, it would seem, I find all I have done is to love. Love and life are synonymous for me. If I detach love from myself, life becomes empty and without substance—I lose my own selfhood.

How old was I then? I cannot exactly tell you the year or the date. Neither my sister nor I have a birth almanac with which we could have settled the matter. I had once noted the date down at the back of a music book, but sure enough, when I went looking for it in the pile of papers, everything turned up, including the useless scraps on which I practiced my first alphabets—everything except that one crucial book, which was missing. Men will probably find all this unconvincing, and will not trust my innocence, but women should appreciate how difficult it is to pin down the exact date or year. It is far easier to recall festive seasons or days, but if you try and ascertain the exact astronomical date, it will doom the occasion to complete oblivion. For instance, when I try to remember my sister's wedding, I see quite vividly the gorgeous, festive full-moon night in spring. But the exact year is not fragrant with the vernal blossoms in Falgun* shining radiantly in the full-moon light. Reliving the atmosphere and color of the occasion does not help one to distinguish one year from the next. And to calculate it by counting back ten years from now is more like contemplating a shapeless and formless Reality. The problem, however, lies in the fact that one cannot determine the exact date of one's own birth by the common means of falling back on the evocative power of one's memory—the Lord has made that impossible. I cannot understand this unique mystery of creation. When human beings are born on earth, the stars immediately enter into close relationship with them, weaving their destiny, but at this stage they have nothing to do with that most

---

*Falgun is a month in the Bengali calendar.

intimate of companions, memory. The main problem now is to try to remember a precise date as an exact mathematical symbol. I constantly forget whether it is 1282 or 1283.* But come to think of it, who stands to lose from such a mistake? Neither the reader nor ourselves. Though, of course, a loss of three hundred and sixty-five days or twelve long months from the puny life span of a man is no light matter. Fortunately or unfortunately, time will not leave me alone, however much it slips out of my mind—my age will remain fixed—down to the last pice.** As for my reader, it makes little difference whether I am twenty instead of nineteen, or twenty-one instead of twenty. As far as I can understand, she or he is only interested in the final denouement. What does it matter if I remember my age correctly or not? Anyway, let us assume that I was then eighteen or nineteen. . . . I am still unmarried. Does this surprise anyone? What is there to be surprised at? Nowadays there are many who remain unmarried even longer—so let me be what I am. But if this is considered surprising, then a greater surprise is to follow—I am in love even before I am married. Besides, I did not fall in love with the person with the idea of getting married. Not only that, this is neither my first, nor last, love. When I did not love this person I loved another, neither was my heart vacant before I had loved the other person. I do not remember my mother. I lost her in childhood, but I doubt if any child could love his or her mother as intensely as I loved my father when I was a child. There is a popular notion that it is inappropriate to compare one's love for one's parents to conjugal love—the two being poles apart. I do not know if you will agree with me, but according to my experience there is very little difference between filial love in childhood and conjugal love in youth. As in the case of one's beloved in one's youth, our parents are our only objects of dependence, worship, and love in childhood. Both the loves have the same symptoms—a constant craving to be near the loved one, wanting to keep them within sight throughout the day, the desire to monopolize the other person, a sense of frustration when it cannot be done, being happy in the other person's happiness, a sense of fulfillment at being able to sacrifice oneself for the sake of the other— all these are common to both.

---

*The dates in the Bengali calendar correspond roughly to 1875–1876.
**A pice was the smallest denomination of currency at that time.

Chapter 8

My sister was having a siesta after the late night dinner party and I was trying to read a novel sitting on an easy chair by the drawing room window—but I could not concentrate. Only a few days back, when I read through some novels, taking time off from the texts prescribed for the examinations, I used to think that the ultimate bliss was to be steeped in novels for the rest of my life—nothing more could be desired. Not even a year has passed since then—how quickly one changes one's conception of happiness!

The book lay open before the eyes. I kept on reading silently, reciting the letters mechanically. I realized very soon that not a single letter had registered in my mind. Was I really reading or musing? But there was no direction even in my musing. Indistinct, unrestrained, indisciplined thoughts, rebellious desires, revulsion against those present and attraction for those absent, not bothering to formulate their exact shape or location. Occasionally my eyes fell on the eastern sky—my empty heart would merge in its expansive, silent beauty like a dream. . . . I would suddenly wake up with a start and turn my gaze to the book. It struck four—I saw a lovely red cloud in the sky and I remembered the sea. This calm, streaked sky suddenly brought to my mind the menacing, storm-tossed look of the sea on the way to Cuttack—who knows how this scene was related to that? It also brought to my mind a few lines from a novel I had read a long time ago: "In certain places and certain periods the aspect of the sea is dangerous—fatal; as at times is the glance of a woman." I had liked the analogy when I had read it; hence it probably lay dormant, tucked away in one corner of my memory. I could remember neither the name of the book nor what I had made of it. It occurred to me that the look that was compared to the sea is bound to be an angry one. Are women's angry looks so frightening to men? I am not a man, so I couldn't identify myself with the sentiments; I only chuckled inwardly at the thought of man's cowardice. I on my part cannot imagine that such an angry look or angry sentiment in a man could throw me off gear, quaking with fright! People think of me as softhearted. In fact, my eyes moisten at even slight provocation; I cannot stand other people's suffering. I give up otherwise uncontrollable desires when it comes to love—but could anger have subjugated me? If my words had made him angry the other day and if he had rudely cursed me and threatened vengeance, would I have felt this pain or become so anxious to alleviate it? More likely it would have roused my contempt for him. The anxiety of love alone is the real anxiety. Is there anything that hurts one more than to hurt someone who loves and who is loved in turn? It is not the angry look but the sad, loving look that is truly "fatally dangerous." I remembered his sad, parting look. I had no more doubt that the author of the book had used the analogy in the latter sense. Such a look quietly inundates the heart just as floods come and wash away trusting people standing on the dry shore—one cannot simply turn back, though one is fully aware of the danger. Most of the time people know the danger yet cannot turn back. Often they do not wish to turn back, but drown voluntarily. That is the most frightening aspect of it.

My reverie was broken by the rustling noise of shoes. I started, turned round, and found *him*. He did not smile but entered in a melancholic grave mood and stretched his hand out. After shaking hands in silence, he sat himself down on the divan nearby. His mood depressed me. I realized that he was disappointed not to have received a letter. It became impossible to explain myself easily—which I might have done if I had found him more cheerful. Despite a thousand wishes to the contrary, how was it possible for me to speak out in such an awkward situation?

After a little while he said, "I hope you received my letter."* I noticed the changed mode of address. My heart froze with his distant manner and his cold, hard language; I too spoke in an unnaturally subdued and grave tone. "I did, but did not answer because you were coming soon."

"May I expect an answer now?"

Of course you may; I am ready to speak. All these days I had mentally rehearsed, ad nauseam, how I was going to explain myself to him in full. Now when I tried to express myself, I realized how different it is to actually *say* it. I could not remember what to say, where one might begin. Words encircled my brain with a haphazard randomness. I blurted out, my head swimming with suppressed emotion, "I, I, what shall I say—your fault!"

He said, "Still the same answer—it is my fault."

I had not intended to say that—I had wanted to say that it was *not* his fault but mine, etc. But he mistook my words before I finished and framed a reply to them.

He said, after what I mentioned above, "All right, perhaps it was my fault, but can you not marry me despite my faults? I am not being

----

*In Bengali this sentence contains the formal second person pronoun.—Trans.

merely selfish. Please consider your own loss if this marriage is broken off. Please do not make your decision only because I love you and will suffer if this marriage does not take place. Please make your decision after considering your own welfare."

These words originated in altruism, but my entire nature rebelled against them. Where were the reasons for which I could have forgiven all his faults? Where was the madness of love in these well-calculated, neatly constructed words? Was the rumor that was circulating true? Had his love been bought by a few thousand silver coins? My pride rose. I said distinctly, without hesitation, "I do not count my losses— you do not need to do that either—I do not wish to marry for convenience. Since your happiness does not depend on it, I beg to be released."

His voice rasped in his dry throat, "Let it be so."

Translated by Jashodhara Bagchi.

PANDITA RAMABAI SARASWATI ————

(1858–1922)   *English*

She was, in the words of a well-known scholar and humanist, "the greatest woman produced by modern India and one of the greatest Indians in all history . . . the one to lay the foundations for a movement for women's liberation in India." Few people would regard A. B. Shah as given to overstatement, yet for one who has been spoken of thus, in superlatives, Pandita Ramabai is a surprisingly hazy presence in contemporary consciousness—if indeed she is a presence at all.

There is no dearth of documentary evidence about this unusual woman, who was a legend in her own lifetime. Her autobiography, *My Testimony,* 1907, has been the main source for the half a dozen or so biographies; notable among these are D. G. Vaidya's *Pandita Ramabai,* in Marathi, and Nicol Macnicol's book with the same title in English. Right through the 1880s and the 1890s, newspapers all over the country reported her movements, celebrated her achievements, and wrote editorials on the controversies that were generated around her work at Sharda Sadan, a widows' home in Pune. Ramabai was one of the few nineteenth-century women who were able to support themselves with their writing. (She also founded and supported a series of homes for widows.) The sales of *Stree Dharma Neeti* (Morals for Women), 1882, paid for her passage to England. The first edition of ten thousand copies of *High Caste Hindu Woman,* 1888, was sold out before she left for the United States in 1889. *My Testimony,* is now in its ninth edition. Unfortunately, perhaps because it is so strongly promoted as a Christian tract, this vivid, moving autobiography has rarely found a place among the literary masterpieces of this period.

Ramabai's childhood, though obviously one of hardship, has a story-book quality to it. Perhaps it was because she grew up a wanderer, never tied down by the conventional demands of a social group, that she was able later in life to achieve more than other women in her time. After a brief initial period when her father, Anant Shastri Dongre, had the patronage of the Mysore royal court, the small family wandered through different parts of India as readers of the Puranas in temples and other places. (The Puranas are collections of tales of ancient times. They became the medium, in the postvedic age, for conveying vedic teaching to the unlettered—all women and lower-caste men.) Dongre, a renowned scholar and teacher himself, believed in women's education and took many risks to teach his wife Lakshmibai to read. There was no sanction, he said, in the scriptures against women reading anything—except the Vedas and the Upanishads. Lakshmibai, in turn, took care with the education of her two daughters. "My pilgrim life began when I was a little baby," Ramabai writes in her autobiography. "When I was about eight years old my mother began to teach me and continued to do so until I was about fifteen years of age. During these years she succeeded in training my mind so that I might be able to carry on my education with very little aid from others." If we are to judge by the incisive grasp Ramabai had of ideas and situations, or by her refusal to sacrifice her freedom of thought or expression at any price, this mother-teacher's achievement was no mean one. Ramabai's sketches of this period portray a close, supportive, almost idyllic family unit. Learning and ideas were at the center of their life, and strength and nobility of character taken for granted. These memories, it is clear, were to sustain her throughout her life.

Among the models her mother held up to her was that of Mirabai, the sixteenth-century saint-poet whose adoration of Krishna is legendary. Ramabai's feminism is evident in her description of Mirabai, whom she sees as "a woman rejecting the worship of the husband and the enslavement it implies, choosing instead a higher symbol of the divine in which her passionate heart can find something more satisfying and enlarging."

Ramabai lost her parents and her elder sister during the terrible famines of 1874–1877. She traveled with her brother to Calcutta, where she caused a sensation by giving lectures in Sanskrit and arguing with the *shastris,* or theologians. She was publicly honored with the title *pandita,* which means eminent scholar and teacher, and spoken of as a modern-day incarnation of Saraswati, the goddess of learning. It was in Calcutta that she met Keshub Chunder Sen, the Brahmo Samaj reformer, who convinced her that women could read the Vedas, and she soon began to study the Vedas and the Upanishads.

Ramabai had become a celebrity, but her personal life was marked by one disaster after another. Soon after her brother died in 1880, she married his friend Bipin Behari Das. Their daughter, Manorama, was born in 1881, but Das died of cholera early in 1882. Ramabai decided to devote her life to the uplifting of women and returned to her homeland, Maharashtra. She was welcomed by the social reformers, who organized several meetings at which she spoke of the need for women's education and their right to freedom and a life of dignity. But as she was to point out bitterly later on, she was disappointed by the "talking-much-but-do-nothingness of these educated orators."

The next twenty years of Ramabai's life were crammed with events and controversy. Her plans to start a widows' home in Pune met with little support. Much to everyone's surprise, and amid speculation in the press, she left for England in 1883, with the intention of studying medicine. Later that year she became a Christian. Though she had, for many years, been critical of Hindu orthodoxy and especially of its treatment of high-caste women, Ramabai's conversion created a sensation. Many of those who had earlier supported her regarded it as a betrayal. The missionaries, on the other hand, were delighted to have this learned, "high-caste" woman as a convert. There was no room amid all this noise for Ramabai herself to be heard—and she seemed little inclined to speak. Only now do we have, in A. B. Shah's thoughtful and scholarly introduction to Ramabai's letters, a sense of what it must have involved for Ramabai herself. She had many differences with her Christian mentors, who, it would appear, were hardly able to follow her theological arguments but insistently criticized her ideas. On one occasion she was moved to write: "I am, it is true, a member of the Church of Christ but I am not bound to accept every word that falls from the lips of priests or bishops. . . . Obedience . . . to the Word of God is quite different from perfect obedience to priests only. I have just, with great effort, freed myself from the yoke of the Indian priestly tribe, so I am not at present willing to place myself under another similar yoke."

From England, Ramabai went on to the United States. She was present at the convocation where her cousin Anandibai Joshi received her degree in medicine in 1886, to become the first Indian woman physician. Until 1889, Ramabai traveled all over the United States, raising money for the home she planned to start. Her visit was widely covered in the American press.

Accounts of Ramabai's return to India later in 1889, her founding of Sharda Sadan, a home for widows, and her work for women's education are more easily available, as are reports of the nationalist leader B. G. Tilak's notorious attacks on the home. Tilak declared that Ramabai was preaching Christianity and converting the residents. The Sharda Sadan, he said in a series of hard–hitting editorials in the *Kesari* in 1891, was "worse than a government or missionary school." Accounts suggest that Ramabai comported herself with dignity and a clear sense of her commitment to the cause of women, though they were very difficult times when even friends like M. G. Ranade and Ramabai Ranade withdrew their support. Ramabai herself was caught, as she put it, between the "missionaries [who] as a rule do not like the idea of my school being wholly secular; and the orthodox Hindu [who] finds it repulsive to have me, a Christian outcast, for his daughter's teacher."

We report by way of conclusion a little-known exchange between Ramabai and Lord Sandhurst, the governor of Bombay, that throws an interesting light both on Ramabai's spirit and on the nature of the commitment the British government really had to the cause of Indian women. Early in 1897 Pune had been hit by plague. In May that year Ramabai wrote a long letter to the editor of the *Bombay Guardian* criticizing the treatment given to people suspected of plague at the segregation camp set up by the government. The letter caused quite a stir and had to be read out in the British Parliament in response to a member's question. She had written:

> The shameful way in which women were made to submit to treatment by male doctors goes to prove that English authorities in general do not believe that Indian women are modest and need special consideration. . . . How would an English woman, poor though she may be, like to be exposed to the public gaze and roughly handled by male doctors? Is not the Indian woman quite as modest as the English woman? Does she not as a woman deserve better treatment at the hands of the Governor and the Plague Committee?

The governor, Lord Sandhurst, simply waved Ramabai's complaints aside as "grossly inaccurate and misleading." Ramabai wrote another letter to the *Bombay Guardian*. This time she minced no words.

> So the Governor of Bombay has declared my statement about the shameful treatment of one of my girls and the bad management of the Poona hospitals as "grossly inaccurate and misleading." Some believe that only Orientals make assertions without giving any proof of their truth. But I see that the Occident also can boast of some people including our worthy Governor who make assertions without giving any proof of their truth. . . . In the name of truth and justice, I ask the conscientious Christian public to say if Lord Sandhurst did right to declare my statements as "grossly inaccurate" when he has never so much as asked me to prove them.

If Sister Geraldine's response is an indication, the "conscientious Christian public" thought Sandhurst quite justified, and Ramabai irresponsible. Sister Geraldine accused Ramabai of adding "fuel to the fire by a childish, sensational and seditious Letter to the Editor." She continued, "Sedition quickly spreads and hardly a month had elapsed after Ramabai's letter when . . . Lt. Ayerst and Mr. Rand were murdered in cold blood."*

We have included an extract from her best known book, *The High Caste Hindu Woman,* and a relatively unknown letter to a friend, Dorothea Beale, who was head of the Ladies' College at Cheltenham and Ramabai's spiritual mentor after her conversion, which reveals little-discussed aspects of Ramabai's life and thought.

◆

From THE HIGH CASTE HINDU WOMAN

Chapter 3. Married Life

It is not easy to determine when the childhood of a Hindu girl ends and the married life begins. The early marriage system, although not the oldest custom of my country, is at least five hundred years older than the Christian era. According to Manu, eight years is the minimum, and twelve years of age the maximum marriageable age for a high-caste girl.** The earlier the act of giving the daughter in marriage, the greater is the merit, for thereby the parents are entitled to rich rewards in heaven. There have always been exceptions to this rule, however. Among the eight kinds of marriages described in the law, there is one form that is only an agreement between the lovers to be loyal to each other; in this form of marriage there is no religious ceremony, nor even a third party to witness and confirm the agreement and relationship, and yet by the law this is regarded as completely lawful a marriage as any other. It is quite plain from this fact that all girls were not betrothed between the age of eight and twelve years, and also that marriage was not considered a religious institution by the Hindus in olden times. All castes and classes could marry in this form if they chose to do so. One of the most noticeable facts connected with this form is this: women as well as men were quite free to choose their own future spouses. In Europe and America women do choose their husbands, but it is considered a shame for a woman to be the first to

---

*When plague broke out, Tilak and Ramabai both stayed on in Pune and helped the government organize relief. Public resentment against the house-to-house searches and the severe and often arbitrary segregation ran high, and both Tilak and Ramabai criticized the government. In June, Rand, the chairman of the Plague Committee, and Lieutenant Ayerst were assassinated by the Chapnekar brothers.

**A man aged thirty years shall marry a maiden of twelve who pleases him, or a man of twenty-four a girl of eight years of age" (*Manu* ix. 94).

request marriage, and both men and women will be shocked equally at such an occurrence; but in India, women had equal freedom with men, in this case at least. A woman might, without being put to shame, and without shocking the other party, come forward and select her own husband. The Svayamvara (selecting a husband) was quite common until as late as the eleventh century A.D., and even now, although very rarely, this custom is practiced by a few people. . . . A great many girls are given in marriage at the present day literally while they are still in their cradles; from five to eleven years is the usual period for their marriage among the brahmins all over India. As it is absurd to assume that girls should be allowed to choose their future husbands in their infancy, this is done for them by their parents and guardians. In the northern part of the country the family barber is generally employed to select boys and girls to be married, it being considered too humiliating and mean an act on the part of parents and guardians to go out to seek their future daughters- and sons-in-law. . . .

Although the ancient lawgivers thought it desirable to marry girls when quite young, and consequently ignored their right to choose their own husbands, yet they were not altogether void of humane feelings. They have positively forbidden parents and guardians to give away girls in marriage unless good suitors were offered them.

> "To a distinguished, handsome suitor of equal caste should a father give his daughter in accordance with the prescribed rule, though she has not attained the proper age."—*Manu* ix. 88.

> "But the maiden, though marriageable, should rather stop in the father's house until death, than that he should ever give her to a man destitute of good qualities."—*Manu* ix. 89.

But, alas, here too the law is defied by cruel custom. It allows some men to remain unmarried, but woe to the maiden and to her family if she is so unfortunate as to remain single after the marriageable age. Although no law has ever said so, the popular belief is that a woman can have no salvation unless she be formally married. It is not, then, a matter of wonder that parents become extremely anxious when their daughters are over eight or nine and are unsought in marriage. Very few suitors offer to marry the daughters of poor parents, though they may be of high-caste families. Wealth has its own pride and merit in India, as everywhere else in the world, but even this powerful wealth is as nothing before caste rule. A high-caste man will never condescend to marry his daughter to a low-caste man though he be a millionaire.

But wealth in one's own caste surpasses the merits of learning, beauty, and honor; parents generally seek boys of well-to-do families for their sons-in-law. As the boys are too young to pass as possessing "good qualities," i.e., learning, common sense, ability to support and take care of a family, and respectable character, the parents wish to see their daughter safe in a family where she will, at least, have plenty to eat and to wear; they, of course, wish her to be happy with her husband, but in their judgment that is not the one thing needful. So long as *they* have fulfilled the custom, and thereby secured a good name in this world and heavenly reward in the next, their minds are not much troubled concerning the girl's fate. If the boy be of rich or middle-class people, a handsome sum of money must be given to him and his family in order to secure the marriage; beside this, the girl's family must walk very humbly with this little god, for he is believed to be indwelt by the god Vishnu. Poor parents cannot have the advantage of marrying their daughters to boys of prosperous families, and as they *must* marry them to someone, it very frequently happens that girls of eight or nine are given to men of sixty and seventy, or to men utterly unworthy of the young maidens.

Parents who have the means to secure good-looking, prosperous men for their sons-in-law, take great care to consult the horoscopes of both parties in order to know the future of their daughters; in such cases, they are anxious to ascertain, over and above all things, that the girl shall not become a widow. If the daughter's horoscope reveals that her future husband is to survive her, the match is considered very satisfactory; but if it reveals the reverse, then a boy having a horoscope equally bad is sought for, because it is sincerely believed that in that case the guardian planets will wrestle with each other, and, as almost always happens, that the stronger, i.e., the husband's planet, will be victorious, or else both parties will fall in the conflict, and the husband and wife die together. A friend of mine informed me that three hundred horoscopes were rejected before one was found that agreed satisfactorily with her sister's guardian planet. Undoubtedly many suitors, who might make good husbands for these little girls, are for this reason rejected, and unworthy men fall to their lot; thus, the horoscope becomes a source of misery instead of a blessing.

It not unfrequently happens that fathers give away their daughters in marriage to strangers without exercising care in making inquiry concerning the suitor's character and social position. It is enough to learn from the man's own statement, his caste and clan, and the locality of his home. I know of a most extraordinary marriage that took place in the following manner: the father was on a religious pilgrimage with his family, which consisted of his wife and two daughters, one nine and the other seven years of age, and they had stopped in a town to take rest for a day or two. One morning the father was bathing in the sacred river Godavari, near the town, when he saw a fine-looking man coming to bathe there also. After the ablution and the morning prayers were over, the father inquired of the stranger who he was and whence he came; on learning his caste, and clan, and dwelling place, also that he was a widower, the father offered him his little daughter of nine, in marriage. All things were settled in an hour or so; next day the marriage was concluded, and the little girl placed in the possession of the stranger, who took her nearly nine hundred miles away from her home. The father left the place the day after the marriage without the daughter, and pursued his pilgrimage with a light heart; fortunately the little girl had fallen in good hands, and was well and tenderly cared for beyond all expectation, but the conduct of her father, who cared so little to ascertain his daughter's fate, is nonetheless censurable.

When the time to conclude the marriage ceremony draws near, the Hindu mother's affection for the girl frequently knows no bounds; she indulges her in endless ways, knowing that in a few days her darling will be torn away from her loving embrace. When she goes to pay the customary visit to her child's future mother-in-law many are the tearful entreaties and soul-stirring solicitations that she will be as kind and forbearing toward the little stranger as though she were her own daughter. The boy's mother is moved at this time, for she has a woman's heart, and she promises to be a mother to the little bride. On the day fixed for the marriage, parents formally give their daughter away to the boy; afterward the young people are united by priests who utter the sacred texts and pronounce them man and wife in the presence of the sacred fire and of relatives and friends. The marriage being thus concluded, it is henceforth indissoluble.

> "Neither by sale nor by repudiation is a wife released from her husband; such we know the law to be which the Lord of creatures made of old."—*Manu* ix. 46.

. . . .

Childhood is, indeed, the heyday of a Hindu woman's life. Free to go in and out where she pleases, never bothered by caste or other social restrictions, never worried by lesson learning, sewing, mending, or knitting, loved, petted, and spoiled by parents, brothers and sisters, uncles and aunts, she is little different from a young colt whose days are spent in complete liberty. Then lo, all at once the ban[ns] of marriage [are] pronounced and the yoke put on her neck forever!

Immediately after the marriage ceremony is concluded the boy takes his girl bride home and delivers her over to his own mother, who becomes from that time until the girl grows old enough to be given to her husband, her sole mistress, and who wields over the daughter-in-law undisputed authority!

It must be borne in mind that both in northern and southern India, the term *marriage* does not mean anything more than an irrevocable betrothal. The ceremony gone through at that time establishes *religiously* the conjugal relationship of both parties; there is a second ceremony that confirms the relationship both religiously and socially, which does not take place until the children attain the age of puberty. In Bengal the rule is somewhat different, and proves in many cases greatly injurious to the human system. In some very rare cases the girls are allowed to remain with their own parents for a time at least. In the north of India the little bride's lot is a happier one to begin with, she not being forced to go to her husband's home until she is about thirteen or fourteen years of age.

The joint family system, which is one of the peculiarities of Eastern countries, is very deeply rooted in the soil of India. There may not unfrequently be found four generations living under one roof. The house is divided into two distinct parts, namely, the outer and the inner court. The houses, as a rule, have but few windows, and they are usually dark; the men's court is comparatively light and good. Houses in country places are better than those in the crowded cities. Men and women have almost nothing in common.

The women's court is situated at the back of the house, where darkness reigns perpetually. There the child-bride is brought to be forever confined. She does not enter her husband's house to be the head of a new home, but rather enters the house of the father-in-law to become the lowest of its members, and to occupy the humblest position in the family. Breaking the young bride's spirits is an essential part of the discipline of this new abode. She must never talk or laugh loudly, must never speak before or to the father and elder brother-in-law, or any other distant male relatives of her husband, unless commanded to do so. In northern India, where all women wear veils, the young bride or woman covers her face with it, or runs into another room to show respect to them, when these persons enter an apartment where she happens to be. In southern India, where women, as a rule, do not wear veils, they need not cover their faces; they rise to show respect to elders and to their husbands, and remain standing as long as they are obliged to be in their presence.

The mothers-in-law employ their daughters in all kinds of household work, in order to give them a thorough knowledge of domestic duties. These children of nine or ten years of age find it irksome to work hard all day long without the hope of hearing a word of praise from the mother-in-law. As a rule, the little girl is scolded for every mistake she commits; if the work be well done, it is silently accepted, words of encouragement and praise from the elders being regarded as spoiling children and demoralizing them; the faults of the little ones are often mistaken for intentional offenses, and then the artillery of abusive speech is opened upon them; thus, mortified and distressed, they seek to console themselves by shedding bitter tears in silence. In such sorrowful hours they miss the dear mother and her loving sympathy.

I must, however, do justice to the mothers-in-law. Many of them treat the young brides of their sons as their own children; many are kind and affectionate, but ignorant; they easily lose their temper and seem to be hard when they do not mean to be so. Others, again, having themselves been the victims of merciless treatment in their childhood, become hardhearted; such a one will do all she can to torment the child by using abusive language, by beating her and slandering her before the neighbours. Often she is not satisfied by doing this herself, but induces and encourages the son to join her. I have several times seen young wives shamefully beaten by beastly young husbands who cherished no natural love for them.

As we have seen, the marriage is concluded without the consent of either party, and after it the bride is not allowed to speak or be acquainted with the husband until after the second ceremony, and even then the young couple must never betray any sign of their mutual attachment before a third party. Under such circumstances they seldom meet and talk; it may therefore be easily understood that being cut off from the chief means of forming attachment, the young couple are almost strangers, and in many cases do not like their relationship; and if in the midst of all this, the mother-in-law begins to encourage the young man to torment his wife in various ways, it is not strange that a feeling akin to hatred takes root between them. A child of thirteen was cruelly beaten by her husband in my presence for telling the simple truth, that she did not like so well to be in his house as at her own home.

In spite, however, of all these drawbacks, there is in India many a happy and loving couple that would be an honour to any nation. Where the conjugal relation is brightened by mutual love, the happy wife has nothing to complain of except the absence of freedom of thought and action; but since wives have never known from the beginning what freedom is, they are generally well content to remain in bondage; there is, however, no such thing as the family having pleasant times together.

LETTER TO MISS DOROTHEA BEALE, CHELTENHAM

St. Mary's Home, Wantage
1st September 1885

My dear Miss Beale,

I was very much delighted to get your letter this morning and have been trying to enter into your thoughts. Although I cannot yet fully enter into them, I must try to tell you one particular thing which I am perhaps wrong taking in that light in which I see it. I was reading your letter over again, when it occurred to me that if "the entering into limitations does not," according to your conception, "affect the essence," why should the stream of Light which flows from the Father through His Word into all human beings—the little channels—not be as pure as that which is in Christ? I am sure in your simile you do not mean the stream of Light and Life is ever defiled or made impure because it flows into some sinful beings. No, if that were so, you would be teaching the same Hindoo religion which teaches that God's essence is so much degraded when it comes into human nature that there does not exist much difference between those two. What do you mean then by the Stream's remaining pure in Christ? To my understanding, it seems impossible that the boundless and most pure essence of our Heavenly Father should ever be limited or mixed with the impurities of the lower human nature, though it is everywhere and in every limited thing it is boundless and pure. Is not the same God who dwells in Christ dwelling in you and me, yet can we ever say that our lower nature can touch Him? No, the Upanishadas—the revelation of God to the Hindoos, if I may call them so—teach that the Great Brahma which is in a manifest atom, yet is in His nature unbounded, and most pure, dwelling in everything, yet untouched by the lower nature, just as the lotus leaf, though it grows in water, yet is not wetted by the water. If we do not agree with this teaching, we must either say that

God is not omnipresent or that His essence can be defiled by or mixed with the lower nature of creatures, which is against Bible teaching.

What are we to understand then when we read the sayings of Christ: "I and my Father are one," and "No one knoweth the Father save the Son," is the question to be answered. It is manifest from some other sayings of Christ that being one with the Father, and knowing the Father, are no proofs of being the Deity itself, for He desires His disciples to be one with the Father, and He tells us that it is possible for any man to know the Father whomsoever the Son will reveal Him. Please do not think that I am answering the question to you; but I am telling you what I at present understand by the two sentences above quoted.

Christ was one with the Father—one in will and design—because He *knew* the Father. We are not and cannot be one with the Father, as long as our sinful nature is alive in us. This is the difference which I see between other men and Christ. If we knew the Father, we should not differ from Him. This thought is I think most beautifully and plainly put into the mouth of the Psalmist in the 95th Psalm, which we sing at morning prayer. "It is a people that do err in their hearts, for they have not known my ways." Whenever we depart from God and cease to know Him or His ways, we err, and the eyes of our mind become blind and do not see Him. The mystery of man's two selves of which you were speaking seems to me to be nothing but man's being conscious of the awful and holy presence of God which makes him shun unrighteous works. This, I think, is like a mirror put before man in which he sees himself exactly as he is, and is then able to find what is wrong in him, and the grace of God is the power by which he judges himself and tries to put things right. When we see ourselves in a looking glass, we fancy we are seeing another person exactly like us, or a second self; but as we know very well it is our own shadow and not a second person, so we should know that the self which judges the self of man seen in the mirror of conscience is nothing but itself reflected in the consciousness of God's presence. Don't you think it is so? When we sin and depart from God, that state of miserable darkness is called the hardening of the heart in the biblical language. It is true, and I know it by my own experience. At the very remembrance of that dreadful time my soul begins to faint. I have several times felt as if there were no light or life in my heart, all was dark and hard and my self could not be reflected into it. I was as it were dead to myself without any consciousness of the Holy Presence of God before which I dare not even think of an unrighteous act. When, through my own sinful intention, the glass of conscience is dimmed and the darkness prevails I go astray, not being able to see the right path. But sometimes God is most gracious to let His light shine in the thick darkness; then the mirror of conscience is cleared a little and my self is reflected where I can see all its impurities and I am sorry. Don't you think this is the mysterious second self which sees itself reflected? I cannot think of anything else. Our Saviour, being a sinless man, never ceased to be conscious of God's presence in Him, which made Him so utterly one with God in will that His human will almost disappeared in the Divine, and His soul was absorbed as it were in the Divine Spirit.

This is how I understand Christ being one with the Father, and so far I agree with you. But I shrink from calling Christ the Supreme God, and from worshiping Him as God. To give the title and worship which belongs only to the God of gods to a man, and a created being is, to my understanding, nothing but idolatry. Christ's not being Almighty and Omniscient is not to me a proof of God's coming into the limitation of creaturely existence, but it is a proof of His [Christ's] perfect and limited human nature. And Christ's goodness is the manifestation of the Divine Light which dwelt in Him, for which I thank and glorify God, because He has given such hope to men. I believe that as God's dwelling in me and you does not limit His power or holiness, so His dwelling in Christ did not bring Him into limitation. But the difference is in being conscious of His Presence only.

I am not quite sure, but I take it for granted that St. John's Gospel is authentic and so is the whole Bible; all that I want you to do is to prove the deity of Christ by reasonably explained words of the Bible, and then I shall be able to believe in it—if it be so—with the help of your philosophical explanation. But until then I cannot accept philosophy as my sole teacher. The definition of Christ's deity as it is taught by the two Creeds and clergy is the chief object which I want to find in the Bible if I am to believe in it; explained and written as clearly in the Word of God as in the word of the third and the fourth and the nineteenth century.

It is too late in the night and I must go to sleep. With much love and honor,

I remain,
Your humble pupil,
Mary Rama

KASHIBAI KANITKAR ─────────

(1861–1948)   *Marathi*

The subordinate position of women was so universally accepted in her time, Kashibai writes in her autobiography, that women simply considered themselves unfortunate beings. Though both her mother and her stepmother were literate, they believed that education only made women harsh and ambitious. As a result Kashibai was given no formal education. When she was nine she was married to sixteen-year-old Govindrao, who had an English education and came from a rich family. He taught Kashibai how to read, but his family made her feel apologetic about her ordinary looks and her lack of education. The well-known critic Sarojini Vaidya considers the tremendous effort Kashibai put into learning how to read and write Marathi and English as primarily a strategy for survival in a very hostile situation.

Kashibai began to attend the weekly meetings for women organized by the reformist Prarthana Samaj when she was still in her teens, and presented her first essay, "Women Past and Present," at one of its meetings. In 1881 the piece was published in an important contemporary journal, *Subodh Patrika*. The most significant event in Kashibai's literary career, however, took place in 1884 when she was writing her first novel, *Rangarao*. She met Hari Narayan Apte (1864–1919), the doyen of Marathi novelists of this period. The friendship between Apte and Kashibai lasted his lifetime and was a major influence on both of them. Their correspondence, which has been preserved, and which Vaidya has drawn on for her biography of Kashibai Kanitkar, speaks of a rich intellectual companionship. He encouraged her to write and obviously discussed his work with her. The friendship also gave her the acccss, so rarely available to women especially in this period, to a community of other writers. They read and discussed Shakespeare, Mill, Spenser, and Gibbon as well as Dnyaneshwar, Tukaram, and Shivaji. It was with Apte that she ventured to read Kalidasa's *Shakuntalam* in the original Sanskrit.

Literary historians invariably point to a dramatic change in the scope of Apte's writing in the mid-1890s. "His social sympathies widened and his artistic insights and abilities also developed," writes M. D. Hatkanaglekar. Apte's reputation had been made on his historical novels in which the heroes were figures like Shivaji, the great Maratha leader who fought against the British in the eighteenth century, and Chandragupta, the powerful fourth-century emperor. His 1887 novel, *Ganpatrao,* is the first of his books that has a social setting. In it, he portrays an intelligent, flesh-and-blood character, Godavari, who is constantly harassed by her mother-in-law. Of Apte's masterpiece, *Pan Lakshyant Kon Gheto* (But Who Takes Notice), 1890, the critic Meenakshi Mukherjee wrote, "If the word 'feminism' had been current in the last decade of the nineteenth century, *Pan Lakshyant* might have been called a feminist novel. At first docile and limited like all other women of her social class, Yamuna [the heroine] gradually grows into a new awareness and begins to ask the kind of radical questions that none of Bankim's heroines are permitted to ask." Could Kashibai, one asks, have had anything to do with this? In fact, while Apte's influence on Kashibai is repeatedly commented on, her contribution to the much-acclaimed realism and feminism of this nineteenth-century Marathi writer has not been documented or adequately explored.

Among Kashibai's writings are two novels, *Rangarao*, 1903, and *Palkicha Gonda* (The Silk Tassel in the Palanquin), 1928, several short stories, and many essays and reviews. *Palkicha Gonda* had first appeared serially in *Navayug*, a widely read popular journal, in 1913. In 1889, shortly after it came out, she reviewed Pandita Ramabai's *High Caste Hindu Woman* for *Manoranjan*, the literary monthly Apte had started. In the same year she edited Anandibai Joshi's letters for publication. In 1911 she reviewed the progress of women's education under imperialism in *Vividhadynvisthar*, a monthly journal of considerable standing in its time, and in a June 1916 article in *Navayug*, she asks, "Are contemporary plays giving good shape to society?" Her autobiography was written in several parts between 1921 and 1947.

Kashibai describes, in her preface to the novel, an event that led her to write *Palkicha Gonda*, which argues that, given a chance, a woman can rule and administer as wisely and well as, or even better than, a man. On one of her travels she met a woman who took her to a village that had been called Palkicha Gonda by the previous queen of the region. Kashibai noticed that many of the girls in the village went to school and that the women also worked at hereditary occupations and generally married late. When she asked about it, Kashibai was told the story of Tai, a woman who had been an able and respected administrator of the state, by her younger sister, Manu. As a young girl, Tai had been married into the royal family by parents who always dreamt of giving their daughters to families of such status that they were carried around in palanquins. Unfortunately they only find out after the marriage that Tai's husband, the prince, is insane. Her parents die of the shock, but encouraged and supported by her mother-in-law, who is conscious of the injustice done to her beautiful young daughter-in-law and who recognizes her ability, Tai takes over the running of the state, and she ensures that the women are educated and economically independent. Tai renames her state Palkicha Gonda not only because she herself had been a victim of that symbol but also because she had triumphed over it. Later the two sisters, and a brother who had always been very supportive, decide to open an institution for women like Dwarki, a childhood friend, who is the subject of the extract translated here.

Though Kashibai Kanitkar clearly advocates love as the basis for marriage, and supports education and economic independence for women, Vidyut Bhagwat feels the worldview in the novels is sometimes ambivalent toward this "progress." Whereas the previous generation emerges as poised and well integrated, Kashibai portrays the new generation as lost and fragmented, broken by their struggle, the modern woman a suffering tragic figure.

◆

From PALKICHA GONDA
(The Silk Tassel in the Palanquin)
Chapter 30

At Sambalpur, our studies were in full swing. At night, after the routine chores were over, we used to sit either at our place or upstairs in Tai's mansion to discuss our plans. Baisaheb sat in her room upstairs, along with her friends, singing *bhajans*. Nanasaheb used to sit with her at that time. In fact, it was the only time when he used to visit his mother. Otherwise, he went with Tai everywhere.

We had decided, by consensus, that our institution would work only for those hundreds of girls like Dwarki who were totally desolate and ruined. We had decided to write to Dwarki and so I had sent a letter to her, inviting her to come and stay with us. Dwarki had studied up to the fifth standard, so she didn't have a problem writing back. Besides, she was now at her mother's house. So it was easy for her to spare a couple of hours to write a letter at her leisure. No tension of any kind like "Will anyone see me writing? Will anyone scold me for it?" I cite below the entire text of her letter, without changing it in any way.

Chiranjeeva Kumari Manu, lots of blessings.

I received your letter. Was very very happy to read it. How can I ever thank you enough for writing to me? You are so learned, so rich! But even then you remembered to write a few affectionate lines to a woman like me who is forsaken by the whole world, forsaken even by the man who had accepted her with all the sacred rituals. These days I feel so grateful if anybody speaks just one or two kind words to me.

And you wrote me an entire letter! How can I express what I felt when I received that letter? Manutai, there isn't one soul in the whole world who will say even one kind word to me. No, not even my mother! Custom forbids her to talk to her own flesh and blood! I know, her heart is full of love for me but the fear of what people will say won't let her show it. That's how it is! Now let me write to you the story of my misfortunes. I am not yet allowed to come to you. But believe me, I'll come to you the moment they allow me. Till then let us talk to each other through letters.

It all began with a theater company that visited our town. Every night "he" used to visit it. Gradually, my parents-in-law came to know of this and that led to minor bickerings in the house. One day "he" demanded the gold ornaments I was wearing. I refused to part with them. I told "him" that mother-in-law would get very angry with me if she knew of it. "He" tortured me throughout the night. Finally "he" hit me on my head with a large club of wood lying in the corner. It gashed my head open. The next day, I had a burning fever and I lay down raving in delirium. Around eight in the morning my mother-in-law and my sister-in-law noticed that I wasn't around. So they came upstairs and saw the terrible condition I was in. When they touched me, they found that I had a burning fever; my eyes were bloodshot and the pillow and mattress were soaked in blood. So they felt about my head and found the gash. They were quite alarmed to find all my ornaments gone. They were convinced that some terrible thing had happened to me. They tried to ask me about it, but it was useless because I was rambling away incoherently and they could not understand a thing I said. So my mother-in-law asked my sister-in-law to sit near me and went down to fetch a doctor to examine me. She told my father-in-law everything.

Now, my husband usually came home in the afternoon but that day "he" didn't. The evening passed and so did the night. Then my brother-in-law was sent into the town to search for "him" at all the haunts that "he" frequented. He looked for "him" everywhere but there was no trace of "him." It was, by now, eight days since the theater company had left the town. So everybody came to the logical conclusion that "he" must have followed them. I was bedridden for about one month because of the deep wound and fever. I came to know about these things through my sister-in-law. They had also inquired in the town where the theater company had come from, but in vain. My father-in-law put notices in the newspapers and offered rewards to anyone who gave any information, but nothing was heard anymore. Now it's almost seven years since then. When I somehow recovered from my illness, I told the people in the house about what had happened. " 'He' demanded the ornaments," I said, "but when I refused to give them, 'he' hit my head with the wooden club and I fell down unconscious." Well, such then is the sad tale of my past *karma*. But that's not all. I have to tell you something more. But Manutai, won't you be unnecessarily distressed by this tale of my misfortunes? I am afraid it might be a heavy blow to your tender heart. One mind says, "Don't you tell her about it." But the other says, "You poor Dwarki, who else would care to listen to you with love? Open up your heart to your friend."

Manutai, although I was recovering physically, mentally I was sinking fast. "His" disappearance had affected the people in our house greatly. Especially me and my mother-in-law! Her womb had been deserted and the only thread of hope of my life had snapped. Now the world has no more pleasure for me. I won't say I was very happy in that house, but at least I was hopeful that "his" behavior might change with age, and that hope was all I had. But now even that I have lost forever. People say to me, "There are girls with a fate worse than yours!" I agree with them fully and say, "Yes, indeed! But our fates are different." Suppose I come to stay with you and begin to learn and then "he" returns home! "He" might stay for a couple of days and go off wandering again! And then I would be neither here nor there.

This is the difference between me and the other girls. Many say to me, "You are more fortunate than the others. You are at least free to mix with the other women with *kumkum* on your forehead." But tell me, Manutai, what freedom is this really? If I go anywhere, people frown at me. I am counted neither among the married women nor among the widows. I am not allowed to take part in any ceremony and I can't even touch anything when they are cooking. I am cast away from both worlds. How can I describe the horrors of this suspended state of mine? When I was at my in-laws' place, it wasn't so bad because it was their problem too. But as the days went by, I became a burden for them. The whole family is happy except me. It's my misfortune that I met such people. And they say, "It's her ill luck! That's why all this happened. We didn't check her horoscope properly. There must be something evil in her." My father-in-law was absolutely convinced of the evil in me. And I had to suffer like hell because of this. I was treated as an unwanted beast of burden. Oh how they tortured me! Finally, they just drove me out of their house. Where could I go in that condition? A girl has either her own home or her father's! My father's home was the only refuge left for me. And that's how I have come to stay with my mother. She is quite old and I serve her in all respects. My brothers tolerate my existence here only for the sake of my mother. God alone will take care of me after her.

This, then, is the story of my life. You have written to me about the arrangements that could be made for me. I will ask my mother about it, and then I'll let you know whatever we decide. For the time being,

that's all that I can write. Please tell Shrimati Sou Tai that I have enquired after her with the greatest of love and regard. My best and most
humble regards to both you and Brother Nanasahib. May God help the
affection between us grow.

Yours, most deserted,
Dwarki.

We read this letter together and then decided to write to her again
and ask her to come away to stay with us. We decided to send money
along with the letter, too, for expenses.

Dwarki was the only daughter of her mother. She had two step-
brothers, who were married and had their own families. She had only
her mother to call her own. Dwarki's mother was a second wife. She
gave birth to only this child—Dwarki. Her father had always intended
to find a good house for her, since she was his only daughter from his
second wife. And eventually, he did manage to marry her off to the
son of a rich moneylender. But in a few days, the real "qualities" of
the son-in-law came to light. He got into bad company and started
stealing from the house. Though his father tried to keep control over
him, he managed to run away with Dwarki's ornaments one day. So
then the family decided not to let Dwarki wear many ornaments. But
ultimately her bangles and necklace also disappeared, as has been already told. After the husband ran away, Dwarki's father lived for another two years but he deliberately didn't bring Dwarki back to his
house because he suspected that once he brought her home, she would
never see the in-laws' house again.

Quite a few years—it must be around six—passed away after that.
Her in-laws had, by now, given up all hope of their son ever returning
home and so drove Dwarki out of their house. The way they did it
was horrible. Generally businessmen deal in various types of things.
Dwarki's father-in-law dealt in opium. One day, her brother-in-law
raised a great hue and cry that the opium in the shop had disappeared,
and started searching for it in the house. While searching, they found
a handful of it in Dwarki's bag. When they asked her about it, she said
that she had no idea how it got there. Then the mother-in-law and the
brother-in-law started to beat her up. They wanted her to confess. But
she kept on saying, "How can I confess to something I absolutely
don't know about? You may kill me but I will never say that I did it."
Finally, after a lot of beating, they kicked her out of the house at night.
It was raining very hard outside and the night was pitch black. But

the mother-in-law just drove the poor thing out of the house, merci-
lessly, into the darkness, with only her clothes on her.

Finally some neighbors took pity on her and gave her shelter. They
gave her a few cast-offs to wear. And then one of the neighbors, a
kind old woman, at her own cost, took Dwarki to her mother's house.

Translated by Maya Pandit.

SARAT KUMARI CHAUDHURANI ——————
(1861–1920)   *Bengali*

Although she is relatively unknown today, Sarat Kumari was an important
writer of her time and a great favorite of Rabindranath Tagore. Born into
an eminent family in Calcutta, she spent much of her childhood in Lahore
where her father, Shashibhushan Basu, was working. She was married at
the age of ten to Akashary Chandra Chowdhary, a poet who had close
links with the Tagore family. Sarat Kumari, too, developed a taste for
literature and, with her husband's encouragement, began writing.

Throughout her literary career, Sarat Kumari was encouraged and supported by Tagore. On one occasion he suggested she write a story on
dowry and discussed the plot with her. In five days, the account goes, she
finished writing it. The story we have translated for inclusion, "Adorer
na Anadorer" (Beloved, or Unloved?), her best work, was first published
in 1891 in a contemporary journal, *Sadhana.* For its time, it is a remarkable
analysis of the neglect and abuse girls are subject to in a society that considers only the male as human. There are no male characters in the story
and the main tension arises between the older women, who are the principal agents of traditional society, and the younger ones, whose hopes and
aspirations are already beginning to challenge the old order.

Only one of Sarat Kumari's works, a novella called *Shuva Bibaha* (Marriage), 1906, was published as a book. Apparently Tagore wanted the
story to be published in *Bangadarshan,* the journal edited by Bankim Chandra Chatterjee, but Sarat Kumari objected. When it was published as a
book, which, like Swarnakumari's *Dipnirban,* did not carry the author's
name, Tagore himself reviewed it in *Bangadarshan.* Sarat Kumari also published a number of thought-provoking essays on the women's question in
Bharati, the journal Swarnakumari Devi edited.

◆

ADORER NA ANADORER?
(Beloved, or Unloved?)

I woke to the solemn ringing of the prayer bells and found myself bathed in the lovely autumn moonlight. Beside me lay my delicate young daughter, my very own, in untroubled slumber. I did not kiss her lest she should wake, even though I longed to. While a soft breeze blew in from outside, I gazed, still drowsy, at Mother Earth as she lay asleep in the serene moonlight, her offspring close to her bosom. They lay there, enveloped in their mother's love, their cares all forgotten. There was no discrimination here: their mother held all equally dear. The enchanting moonlight was a loving smile on the face of Mother Nature: I looked on, spellbound. Memories of days long past came back to me, one by one: I saw myself once again surrounded by my dear ones, as I had been on countless such moonlit nights. The memory of those silvery nights seemed to endow the moonlight outside with an unsurpassed loveliness. A few lines came back to me:

> Who knew whom, then?
> Who knew oneself?
> Who knew of the world's wild ways?

All of a sudden I was startled out of my reverie by a strident voice outside. A conversation had begun at the edge of the pond in front of my window.

"Who's that? Oh, it's you, Keshtodasi. So you've come to the ghat before dawn today, for a change! I heard a conch shell being blown in your part of the village last night. Has your brother's wife had a son this time, then?"

"Ah, no, don't ask me about it—you think we'd be that lucky? My sister-in-law will never have a son in this lifetime of hers! It's a daughter, as usual."

"Does that make three daughters now?"

"Yes, indeed, that makes three."

"Then it's going to be a foursome—perhaps the next'll be a son."

"Looks like it. When my brother heard it was a girl, he said to me, 'Keshto, I can't get up. I feel drained of all my strength.' The midwife went first to take leave of our mother, and then to him; he did not get up from bed, nor did he speak to her. His wife wouldn't pick the baby up; she took it in her arms only after a lot of coaxing, and even then said she'd throttle it. If I hadn't been there the poor little girl would probably have died lying there on the floor. Sorrow hangs over the whole house."

"It would, I'm sure: three girls, no less, to be married off to *kayastha* families—a tough job it's going to be. It's hard on the wretched woman too—giving birth to a lump of earth, having carried it in her womb for ten months!"

"My sister-in-law has grown thin with worry over having a girl again next time. She has lost her appetite completely. She couldn't even swallow water. What good is there? The eldest daughter is just four years old, yet when she heard about her baby sister she said, 'Why don't you give her away to someone else?' "

"She's only a little child after all; she says what she's been hearing said around her. You will have the eighth-day ritual, won't you?"

"I don't know . . . nominally perhaps. Maybe we'll just invite eight boys and have the ceremony of beating the winnowing tray. Mother had hoped for a son so much this time. She had planned for so many things: she'd send out filled-up pots to the neighbors on the eighth day and hand out oil and dry milk sweets on the day of the Shashthi festival [when the baby is given its name]—everything's spoiled now."

"Well, why doesn't your mother get Naresh married again? This wife of his doesn't have a baby for a long time, and now she produces only girls. Naresh is the only son: who'll keep the family name going if he has just daughters?"

"What can my brother do, Auntie? He belongs to the new generation: they're all afraid of quarrels in the family. My brother wouldn't marry even when my sister-in-law couldn't have babies for a long time and our mother grew tired of it. At least now that his wife has started having girls, we can hope for a son eventually. But Mother wants everything to happen quickly: it's because she's got only one son, you see. My sister-in-law didn't have her first child very late, either; she was about eighteen when the eldest girl was born. Even so, Mother became so impatient that she gave the bride medicines and herbal concoctions, made her wear talismans, and visited so many temples and saints—and after all this the eldest girl was born. She thought, now that this girl has been born it'll be a grandson next time—and, oh dear, it's three times running now! How much longer can you bear it? So Mother says she'll get her son to marry again if this one gives birth to another daughter. It's only that my brother won't agree to it. Mother has already inspected a girl and has her in mind for him. And of course Mother has always been a little impatient. So we say, why worry so much and mope about like that? She's had daughters; she'll have a son too—and now we've got nothing to say."

The sun had not risen yet; there was only a faint glimmer of dawn. A waning moon still shone in the western sky. The gentle early morning breeze carried in the fragrance of *ketaki* flowers from far off. The din of people's voices had not yet begun when people all around me started waking up at the loud voice of our familiar acquaintance, a middle-aged matriarch. I, too, rose and sat by the window. It was a rather small pond, sunk in what was called a garden, a tiny space enclosed by a flimsy bamboo fence on one side and by houses on three sides. Now, in the rainy season, the pond was full to the brim. The water near the edge was, however, green with moss of various kinds: only some of the water in the middle was left clear. On one side, at the edge, were a few fruit trees, mango and *jamun* among them; the undergrowth had never been cleared. On another side were five or six banana trees, of which one or the other was often to be seen bent over the pond by the weight of its fruit. On yet another side were a few half-dead marigolds and dilapidated rose bushes, none of which ever bore flowers. Rarely one or two buds came out, but these would wither before they were even half-blown. An uncared-for *aparajita* creeper had climbed over the fence and enshrouded part of the skeleton of the fence. Sometimes it would bear a few flowers, which would then be plucked for worship of the Deity. The creeper had been tended and guarded carefully when it had first been planted, but no one bothered even to look at it now. Yet it still carried on its work, slowly but steadily, on its own.

"Oh dear, it's nearly dawn—I've spent all my time talking, and now I can't go for a dip in the Jahnavi anymore today. Anyway, I'll go and touch a bit of Jahnavi water—better have a bath here straightaway before I go home. Hey, you young woman, come and give me some oil to massage myself with." It was a lucky day for the ghat: the gathering there never livened up unless this matronly housewife was there.

"That's what I say, Keshtodasi, about these children nowadays. Do they ever listen to what their parents tell them? My father-in-law got fed up when my husband's elder wife wouldn't have a baby, and so he got his son married to me. Well, child, the Great Lord was good to me: hardly two years after my marriage my Radhanath was born. Alas, where did he get carried off to, the poor dear boy—only I have stayed on, wretched woman that I am. Thank goodness his two little boys are there; I've remained here for their sake, else I would have gone mad and left for heaven knows where. Would you believe it, dear child, barely a year after his birth the elder wife got her Haralal. When I got married she was still young enough to have children. Her father married her off when she was very young, I believe, and she was about two years younger than our husband—their heights had to be compared by measuring with a thread before they could be married, they were so nearly as tall as one another. I was rather well grown when I was married. I don't look as if I'm my husband's second wife—you can see that—so with age it was I who became more like his wedded 'family.' In those times the master of the house didn't care much for calculations, anyway. He just said to my husband, 'Marry once again.' These men, too, couldn't disobey their parents the way lads of nowadays do. My father-in-law would say, 'If either of you daughters of wretches starts a quarrel, she'll be sent off to live in her father's house: there'll be no room for her in my house.' What power they had over us, those elders. When the master came into the inner quarters we young girls and brides would go numb with fear, and even the mistress would be scared stiff. The way these modern girls meet their husbands at all times of the day—do you know, Keshto, we couldn't even dream of it. Only after everything became still at night would someone accompany me to his room—only then could I go in. Sometimes I fell asleep on the balcony or on the porch and spent the whole night there unless someone called me up and led me to his room. My mother-in-law allowed Radhanath to sleep inside only after he was six months old, and from that day onward each of us would go and sleep in the room according to her turn. We were not allowed to meet our husband till six months after a son was born; however, if it was something essential our husband would come and speak to us secretly in the store-room or in the kitchen. Well, my dear, we wouldn't talk to him in the daytime: we thought it best not to speak when our mother-in-law might get to know of it and rebuke us. And my stomach turns when I see how drastically different the ways of today are."

Her lecture continued without pause while her hands smeared oil all over her body. Gradually, with the sunrise, a number of pretty faces began to be seen at the edge of the pond. Everyone's attention was riveted on our matriarch, their baths forgotten. Some never finished cleaning their teeth, while some never ceased sponging themselves. The crux of the matter was that all of them were condoling the birth of the Mitras' baby girl and regretting that it wasn't a son. One of them tried to smooth things over a little, saying, "All the same, so many people have a son only after seven daughters. My cousin once removed had a baby son only the other day, after four daughters—the boy has just turned a year old."

Within this group of women there were a few young veiled brides and girls bathing. One of them, a girl of fourteen, could restrain herself no longer. Addressing Krishnadasi as mother, she said, "Look, you may not be able to hold your sorrow back at Auntie's having a daughter, and so we're hearing all about it again here at the ghat. Whatever objection you might have, I still like Auntie's daughters far better than that plain, dark little boy of the Ghoshes: seven pretty girls are better than a plain boy like that. You keep on saying the same thing—well, aren't girls of any help to you? You've come here in the month of Asharh, and has Uncle ever taken care of Granny the way you've been doing for the past two or three months? Granny herself speaks of it." "My son never cares for me in times of need in the way my daughter does," she says. "When that happens you need a daughter desperately, don't you? And yet it's a disaster for you whenever you hear of a girl being born. Take our youngest grandma of that house over there, now—Uncle never manages to bring in the tiniest bit of money for her. Thank goodness Auntie Khema was there; she provides for all expenses, and even Uncle lives on that. Yet I've heard that she was named Khema [mercy, forgiveness] because there were two more sisters before her."

Everyone at the ghat was astounded at the rebellious talk. Even the crows seemed to stop cawing and the leaves on the trees were still. Then the matronly housewife laughed. "Now look here, Perbha," she said, "stop jabbering. You'll understand better when you grow up: how would you know now, chit of a girl that you are? Hold your tongue. Such boldness doesn't suit youngsters like you."

"Well, let me tell you, Grandma, our youngest auntie over here, too, says she won't be sorry to have a daughter. Auntie there, too, loves her daughters so much; only she's scared about having a daughter because of Granny's harsh words. Now that she's got daughters she'd like to have a son as well—but she can't even hold her daughters to her or cuddle them properly out of fear of Granny. Even Uncle didn't dare to give them nice clothes for the festival, although he longs to give good things to his daughters. I don't understand what you think— aren't you women, too?"

"Now listen, my dear madam, we are women too—and have you any idea how beloved I was in *my* family? I was my mother's first child and the darling of both my maternal *and* my paternal grandmothers. My grandmother on my father's side used to say, 'She isn't just my granddaughter, she's the equivalent of seven sons; all the same, it's a misfortune for a family to have a dozen daughters.' "

A few more girls of about Perbha's age came and joined the group at the ghat. Haridasi said, "Hullo, Grandma, you seem to have roused the whole ghat today. What's up?"

"Hey, Haridasi, so you've come? As I say, the ghat doesn't look good without you, does it? We're old people after all; we're no longer capable of livening up the ghat; we've only been exchanging a few confidences, no more. It's for people of *your* age to rouse people. So I was saying, I say, Haridasi hasn't come here yet. Was it our grandson-in-law who came last night?"

"How am I to know that, Grandma; it's *you* who would know! We dropped in at Uncle Harakali's house on the way while coming to the ghat. We saw the baby boy they've just had, which is why we're a bit late today."

"Oh, really? Do you see what luck they're in: times are good for them nowadays, so they're getting good things from all sides; the brides of the family have been having sons one after the other. And they celebrate them so grandly, too—what with filling up pots to be handed out on the eighth day, handing out oil and sweets for the Shashthi worship, celebrating the child's Annaprāsana, its first meal of rice, with a lot of pomp and feasting. They do everything on earth. Look at the hard luck Keshto's mother has: only one daughter-in-law, who's having daughters one after another."

Haridasi: "Even if it's so, are girls only fit to be thrown away?"

"Goodness gracious! You're all the same nowadays, the lot of you, I see. Perbha answered sharply too when I was talking about this! What use can girls ever be, eh?"

"Well, what use can't they be, now? Whether it's parents, husband, or children who may be sick, have you ever seen any man take care of them as much as a woman does? Does a son ever look after a mother or try to understand her sorrows as much as a daughter does? Look, a woman is an asset to the family: however wealthy it is, you can see for yourself how mismanaged and neglected a household looks without a woman to look after it, and how uncared for the children look when they have no mother. You people jump up as soon as you hear a girl's been born, and say, 'Now we'll have to marry her off!' Well, don't you have to spend a lot of money on a boy, too? We've all seen the way the girls of the Sen household are given the leftovers to eat from plates the boys have already used. The boys wear shoes and shirts and spotless garments and the girls go around in cheap grimy wraps.

The boys are each given snacks worth two pice and the girls are given three or four plain chapatis each, made from a pice's worth of whole-meal flour. The boys sleep on soft beds with mattresses and the girls sleep on rush mats and a tattered quilt spread out on the floor. Even the older boys are allowed to sleep in their parents' room, whereas the two younger sisters sleep beside the cook. Poor things, have they ever had the slightest bit of care taken of them? The other day the second auntie's daughter out there had come home from her maternal grand-parents and had asked for rice in the morning, and simply because nobody else had eaten yet Granny turned round and said, 'Whoever heard of a girl eating rice with the first lot—to come and ask for rice when nobody has eaten yet! Let your father and your uncles eat first: you can sit and eat off their plates after that.' Poor dear, she's just a little girl of six or seven—how could she know? She started crying for rice, poor thing. Auntie was disgusted with her mother-in-law's atti-tude and sent the child back to her own parents right away. She grieved over it so much before us afterward, saying, 'My poor darling came home for just one day and went away crying for rice—how can I bear it as her mother?' Who knows, then, whether a girl is beloved, or unloved?"

"My goodness, just listen to the way these girls speak nowadays, as if a hurricane's passing by! Get off with you now. Don't dawdle in the water anymore, or you'll fall sick!"

In any case the younger girls did not carry the conversation any further, but finished bathing and went home. Everyone came and went, hearing a part of the conversation in between. The lady of the pond, however, went on rubbing oil, unperturbed. All of a sudden Harakali's mother came onto the scene in a great hurry. What was it? She was very busy. It was in her house that the conch shell had been blown last night: her daughter-in-law had given birth to a son.

"What's this, Thakur-jhi, didn't you go to bathe in the Ganges to-day? I thought it was only I who hadn't been there today. Well, Sister, what could I do? My second daughter-in-law had this baby son last night. How could I leave it, now? You know what ninnies these girls have turned out to be—won't take hot compresses, won't eat anything hot, won't do anything! I'm not a woman of that sort, and that's pre-cisely why I never send them to their parents for delivery. The third one's father is a doctor too. He won't allow her to be given hot com-presses or pepper; he even wants her to be laid on a mattress! Do you know, Thakur-jhi, the doctor tells us to give up the whole lot of rules that we observe, but I'm no woman to do so. I've just come from giving her burning hot compresses all this while, and I'm going to make her eat pepper after I've had my bath here. He may be a doctor—and let him be—but am I to break rules simply because I've brought his daughter into this family? That time her baby daughter died in the confinement shed, the doctor came to see her and said she had become ill from lying in such damp surroundings. He wanted to shift the confinement bed elsewhere, but I'd never let him do that."

"I never heard that the girl had caught any illness. I thought the father's evil eye had fallen on her."

"That's what I'm talking about, dear. They think they understand everything. Dozens of bottles of medicine were brought in, and they wanted to make her swallow those—who'd take them, though? They didn't realize it was Father who held her mouth tightly shut. It was such an illness that even the sorcerer whom we brought in for treatment could do nothing. And what could he do, anyway? The sorcerer said, 'The newly delivered must have walked under a *champak* tree while pregnant and thus drawn the evil eye toward herself.' She's a Westernized heretic's daughter after all; the girl must have walked under some tree or other; she never bothers about such rules. This time I never let her go home once. The girl nearly died that time; no harm was done, however. But this time a boy's been born. It's necessary to give her hot compresses carefully, isn't it? One can have expectations of having a boy only if the expectant mother keeps well: don't you agree, dear?"

"Why, of course! A bride's of value only to keep the lineage alive: for what else does one take on the burden of bringing in an unwanted girl from another family? Anyway, now you've had a boy you must fill up the pots and hand them around on the eighth day. I hope you'll have the postnatal rituals performed?"

"Of course we will—only we can't get the dust off the feet of a hundred thousand brahmins, so it'll have to be just twelve brahmins. The rest of the rituals will, of course, all be observed. The eighth day will be observed for him in the same way we've done it for the sons of the other daughters-in-law: a pot full of dry rice snacks, a four-anna coin each, and four sweets each—these we'll send out to the houses. And for people who come to visit us, we'll give two annas to each of the boys and four pice to each of the girls. And if the child lives and stays well, we'll have to arrange the rice-eating feast, too. We must spend appropriately, now that our darling son has been born. Only yesterday the midwife had to be given a rupee and a metal water jar, and she's coming again for her final fees. When it's a girl she has to be paid just a fixed sum for the cutting of the cord, that's all."

"Since the Great Lord has favored you with good times, it's only proper that you should spend a great deal on celebrations, isn't it? Two of my daughters are staying with me here, so please send three pots of snacks over to my house. Oh! My stepson and his wife have set up house separately, too."

"Yes, dear, it's just as well you told me. I'll have to go home and make a list for the pots right now. There'll be a band of musicians coming too, and then the dancers—they'll have to be paid a great deal of money after they've performed—"

"Have you heard the news? The Mitras have had a baby girl again!"

"Here, what do you mean, *another* girl? Who told you?"

"That Keshto came here before dawn—she had touched the confinement bed, you see—and she grieved and lamented so much, poor girl. I missed my dip in the Jahnavi through talking to her. I had come here at dawn to wash clothes, and then Keshto came too."

"Thakur-jhi, which of your in-laws is called Ganga, now?"

"The name of the wife of my husband's youngest paternal uncle is Phangamani, which is why we say Jahnavi. We're forbidden to pronounce the names of almost all our elder in-laws. Our family's a large one, you see, and so we have to be careful about all names. We aren't like modern women, who'd be careful only about the names of their parents-in-law."

"Indeed, Thakur-jhi, how accursed the Mitras' bride is. I suppose that makes four or five daughters now. Well, my eldest daughter-in-law has been blessed with these two, and two others got spoiled; so my second daughter-in-law has two sons, too, in spite of all our foes' curses, and a daughter. The daughter lives with her maternal grandparents; she's the darling of her grandmother. My second daughter-in-law is an only child, you see. Anyway, that first daughter is being brought up by her grandmother, so we are being spared from worrying about her. Her grandmother spoils her no end. She dresses her up like a boy; her name is Hemantakumari, and they call her Hembabu! A fine spoiled piece of goods she is, that girl. My third son's wife, now, had two daughters, one of whom died while still in the confinement shed, and now she's had this baby son."

"Well, bless him, we'll all attend the feasts in his honor, and we'll eat, and we'll bring back gifts. It's a question of one's family, after all. The girls are there just in vain: no postnatal worship, doesn't matter if you observe the eighth-day ceremony, and as for the baby's rice-eating feast, if you really are that keen you can invite a few people and feed them. Just a bit of sacred food to be tasted: no rites, no ceremony, and not a drop of water goes to the forefathers. The only time a girl's ancestors are given water is when she gets married—that's all."

"I must go, I must be home now: my third daughter-in-law's father may have come already and started kicking up a fuss. My boys are young after all; they can't speak up that much. God knows what would have happened if I hadn't been so assertive! The boys think the same way too, being all modern young men. Anyway, they don't speak up against me much. Whenever they do, I tell them, 'You've grown up now, so you've decided not to listen to me anymore, haven't you? I brought you four boys up all by myself after I was widowed, I suffered so much, and now I've become a stranger to you. Your fathers-in-law are dearest to you now.' So they can't say anything more after that. Only the youngest one—he's a bit outspoken, and he's my little one, you see, so I indulge him a bit—I can't scold him that much, although he messes everything up, handling the confinement bedclothes and all. As soon as confinement is over I make my daughters-in-law wash all the bedclothes, quilt, pillows, and all."

"Ah, my dear, you don't have to mention it. We've all but lost our castes and our births and everything. These modern young men, they're all alike. My youngest son-in-law is like that. When Bidhu came here that time to have her baby, my son-in-law used to come and see her every day; he would sit on her bed itself and chat for a while and then he'd leave. The first day he came I had gone to have a bath. I came back and stopped there, holding my beads in my hand, and all at once he came out of the confinement shed and touched the dust of my feet. What could I do? I just said, 'My son, ought you to have touched me after having touched the confinement bed? And with my beads in my hand, too.' He looked embarrassed and said, 'I had forgotten.' What else could I do? The beads were desecrated, and I had to go and bathe again in the pond. Well, but I had to observe the rules according to my son-in-law's wishes in caring for my daughter. I gave her a bit of ground pepper in secret—these girls are a match for us too—she accepted it willingly enough and ate some of it, leaving the rest, and then she says, 'I feel thirstier than ever, if I have to eat pepper, Mother, and you won't allow me to drink any water. I won't feel thirsty and so I won't need to drink water if I eat only boiled sago all the while.' I don't understand what they say, dear. They don't feel any thirst in confinement, but we used to be so thirsty that we'd secretly drink a bowlful of even the most unclean water. In our days we were given just so much water to rinse our mouths with after we had eaten pepper. Can one ever survive on that?"

"Of course, what else? I've had these four little ones, and for each of them I've bribed the woman and coaxed her into stealing some water for me to drink in confinement. Those scorching hot compresses on the one hand and the platefuls of pepper on the other—it's because of those that you have the terrible thirst and the burning sensation in your body, but it's only because of those that one's body revives. Oh my, the musical band's arrived. I'm leaving now." Saying this, she flung the end of her wet sari over her shoulder with a flourish and, still wringing the water out of her thin towel, made her exit.

Matriarch: "Did you see, Goyla-bou, how conceited Harakali's mother is! Her feet don't seem to touch the ground out of vanity; she must remind everybody all the time that she's got four sons. Well, the Lord of Death hasn't made her suffer any pain yet, hence all this vanity. She doesn't realize that begetting sons isn't everything. They have to survive, and that's what counts. If it hadn't been for the curse of the Lord of Death I, too, would have been the mother of a king."

Dairyman's wife: "Right you are, Ma-thakrun, such pain the Lord of Death can inflict: I lost two sons and two daughters, and am now surviving somehow with two daughters and a son. The eldest has gone to her in-laws and, Ma-thakrun, I've been crying for her ever since. We're poor people, Mother, but my little ones are such darlings, you know; they understand I'm penniless without my telling them. Even though there are so many nice things to buy around where we live, they never ask to eat or buy any of those, lest I can't afford it."

Matriarch: "Hasn't your daughter married into an affluent family?"

Dairyman's wife: "Yes, Mother, thanks to your blessings they *are* pretty affluent, and they take very good care of my Nayantara too. But can a mother's heart ever be set at rest just by that? I feel as if my heart would break when I see that I can't feed my three children even a pice's worth of puffed rice."

Matriarch: "So what can you do? Don't cry, stop now. Going into another's house is the only thing a woman's life is meant for. Which is why I say, Goyla-bou, girls are just in vain: they'll be going into another's house in two days' time anyway. Only it's impossible telling these young girls that it's so."

Dairyman's wife: "But, Mother, it's because they'll be going to live with in-laws two days later that I feel so sorrowful. It's because of this, Mother, that I can't stay without seeing my two daughters. Boys, Mother, will bring in and get their own choice of people and things;

they'll get wives, they'll be cared for all their lives—and my heart will be at rest. Who'll look after the girls, now, if not their mother? No mother-in-law or sister-in-law will ever do as much, and two days later the girls will become mothers themselves and be busy looking after their own children. If I don't care for them today, Mother, who else will care for them later?"

Matriarch: "Oh, indeed! You've lost so many, which is why you're so attached to your girls; otherwise girls are less wanted than boys the whole world over. One swells with pride to say a boy's been born— it sounds so good, and it's celebrated with such pomp too. And no one ever gets tired of having even seven sons. If the first one born is a girl, people say, 'Never mind. Next time it'll be a boy.' Whatever's been born first should survive; the going'll be good only if the first one survives. Only then can one expect a son."

Dairyman's wife: "Yes, Mother, now I must go. It's broad day-light."

Little by little the ghat became deserted. I had come with dream-laden, enchanted eyes, and now returned with the harshness of truth in my heart. Mother Nature no longer had that sweet, loving look of hers: now duty reigned in all its might around me, and everyone was fully taken up with their duties. My eyes had no spell cast over them anymore: everything was clearly and starkly visible in the light of the sun. My heart kept asking, Beloved, or unloved? Even in affection there was discrimination—and not only in affection. It was there in motherly love: even a mother loved and cared more for a son than for a daughter. Deep in thought, I came back to the bedside and saw that my little flower had not opened yet, since the sunlight of my kisses had not yet touched her. As if written on that calm, undisturbed face, I read:

Have mercy, that this be done:
Do not have mercy on this one.

I kissed her. She smiled, opened her eyes, and looked into my face. I drew her to my bosom and asked her, "Little daughter of mine, are you my beloved, or are you my unloved one?"

"I am your beloved!"

Translated by Tista Bagchi.

KRUPA SATTIANADAN ──────────

(1862–1894)   *English*

Krupa Sattianadan was the thirteenth of the fourteen children of Haripant and Radhabai, the first converts to Christianity in the Bombay Presidency (an administrative unit of the colonial government). Her father died shortly after she was born and she was brought up by her mother and by an elder brother, Bhasker, who was an important influence on her life. Very early, Krupa showed signs of unusual intelligence. In spite of protests from her other brothers, who, she writes, loved her but felt her place was in the kitchen, she persuaded the family to let her join the brothers, at least partially, in their studies. But the loss of her elder brother, Bhasker, who sympathized with her and vowed with her to devote his life to high and noble aims, was a serious setback. Her health was affected and she was sent to a zenana mission school in Bombay in the hope that the new surroundings might help her recover. The extract reproduced here, taken from her autobiographical first novel, *Saguna,* relates her experience of this phase in her life.

In 1878, Krupa joined the Madras Medical College, which was the first in India to open its doors to women. She was received by the distinguished theologian and educator Rev. W. T. Sattianadan, the father of her future husband. To their credit, when this young girl, the first to join a medical college in India, entered the class, the other students rose and cheered. By the end of the year she had stood first in every subject except chemistry and won many prizes. Her teachers spoke of her as a conscientious and untiring student, but her physical strength gave way. After the first-year examinations she was not able to resume her medical studies.

In 1881 she met and married Samuel Sattianadan, the son of her friends and hosts in Madras, who had just taken a degree from the University of Cambridge in England. He became the principal of the Breeks Memorial School at Ootacamund. Krupa went with him and devoted herself to teaching in the schools set up for the poorer girls in the area. She also started a school for Muslim girls, which soon grew into an important institution. Though she wanted to establish a home for Hindu widows, her failing health and early death prevented it.

In Ootacamund she began writing articles for the *National Indian Journal* and other magazines. In 1884 her husband was transferred to Rajahmundry. She accompanied him there, but became ill and remained unwell for the rest of the year they spent there. In 1885 they moved to Kumbakonam, the educational center of Thanjavur district. Her health improved and she wrote a great deal, mostly about the people around her. "No one was too poor or too humble to interest her," writes Krupa's friend, Mrs. Grieg, in the preface to her second novel, *Kamala,* subtitled *A Story of Hindu Life.*

In 1886, Samuel Sattianadan was appointed assistant to the director of public instruction and later to the chair of logic and philosophy in Presidency College in Madras. In Madras she took up a more ambitious literary venture—an account of her parents' conversion to Christianity and her own early life. The result, an autobiographical novel, *Saguna: A Story of Native Christian Life,* was published serially in the *Madras Christian College Magazine* in 1887 and 1888.

Her first child was born even as the last chapters appeared, but died a few months later, leaving Krupa very depressed. Her husband took her to Bombay, hoping that the sight of her own home and people would cheer her, but the journey proved too exhausting. On her return to Madras she was hospitalized for several weeks. It was here that she was told that the illness from which she suffered was a fatal one. The year that followed was difficult. She was deeply pained by the death of her husband's mother and father, who had been friends to her, and her own health deteriorated.

In 1893, she had been taken to Kunoor, a hill town in the Western Ghats, in the hope that the air would help her build up strength. While she was there, she worked continuously on her next novel, *Kamala,* some chapters of which she had thought out while still in hospital in Madras. Krupa was afraid she might not live to complete it, but she did, though she had to dictate the last chapters to her husband when her temperature stood at 104° F and she was too ill to hold a pen. The book appeared in 1894, serially, in the same journal that had carried her first major attempt. She died on the eighth of August 1894, at the age of thirty-two.

Several speakers at a memorial service held in Madras in January 1895 spoke warmly of Krupa Sattianadan's exemplary life and supported a move to establish a memorial medical scholarship for women in her name. During the next year, her two novels were translated into Tamil. They were widely read at the time, both in English and in Tamil, though today her work is virtually unknown.

The extract from *Saguna,* included here, is interesting because it is one of the earliest extant accounts of the everyday interactions between the races in nineteenth-century India. The fine eye for detail, significant in the politics of such exchanges, and the satiric voice, no less devastating because of its understatement, are typical of Krupa's writing. Here she tells the story of her encounter with the women missionaries at the zenana mission school she was sent to after her brother Bhasker's death.

◆

From SAGUNA

My sister paid a visit to the city, not long after Bhasker's death. She noticed my retired ways and my peculiar moods and took me to her home. One day as I was sitting in the hall, puzzling my head over some books that I found in the study, two ladies were announced, and before I had time to run away, they were in the hall. The first grasped my sister's hand in hers and gave her a hearty kiss. Her appearance at once attracted my notice. She seemed fresh coloured, tall, as she looked with a good-humoured smile at me over sister's shoulder. There was a twinkle in her eye, as if she wished every one to be a partaker of her high spirits. She was certainly strikingly different from other ladies, I thought, and I listened with great attention to what she had to say. She spoke of her success in her visits in high-flown words, and asked for some more introductions to my sister's zenanas. Then she turned round toward me, and, catching hold of both of my hands, put question after question to me in such a way that I could not but answer. She had large light brown eyes, a fine, full long face, a nose rather blunt, and a broad, high forehead. I liked her. Presently she turned toward my sister and talked aside for a few minutes while her companion smiled to me and drew me toward her. But before we could talk much the other turned toward me, and said, "So that's settled; you are to come next month and stay with me. You will learn to your heart's content there, but mind you are to be very free with me and tell me everything. I mean to quarrel with you very often. Ah! you critical thing. Don't I know what you are thinking?" and with a warm, but rather rough hug and a brushing kiss she left me. My sister said I must go and stay with the two ladies for some time. I liked the idea and made up my mind to go. The first thing that I was told on going to Miss Roberts'—for that was the name of the lady who took charge of me—was that I was a little girl; that in England girls of fourteen and fifteen were considered mere chits, and that I was to lay aside all solemnity of manner and behave as a girl. When it came to the lessons I was asked what I was learning.

I said: "History, geography, &c."

"What in history?"

"I have finished *Landmarks of the History of Greece,* and am reading—"

"Greece! Greece! What have you to do with Greece?"

I had loved this little book. It was like a storybook, and I thought that she would have been pleased, but she only murmured, "Well! I will see. I must get something more suited to you. What about English? Can you read fluently?"

Longfellow's poems were put into my hand. The volume opened at "Pleasant it was when woods were green." I read this fast enough.

"Too fast."

"Oh I know it by heart," I exclaimed, anxious to show my cleverness. I shut the book and repeated the whole thing to her. I had once learnt it in a fit of study, and it had given me much pleasure.

"Well! I tell you what," she said, shutting the book, "you know a little too much. When a horse goes too fast, what does his master do?"

I did not know what he did, but I thought the comparison was not a good one, and I exclaimed abruptly, "I am not a horse."

"Well! Well!" she said laughing, "we won't discuss that point. I think you want occupation. You must teach in my little school this afternoon. Now we have done with our lessons for one day."

To my great surprise she shut up the books and put them by. When dinner time came I saw the other lady for the first time. She gave me a smile and pointed to my place by her side, but Miss Roberts never left me alone. She began by saying to her neighbour, "Girls in England never sit at the table with their elders, but of course we shall allow this one." In my sister's house I had learned to some extent how to use spoon and fork, but when I found the lady's eyes fixed on me my fingers trembled, and I thought I was sure to make all kinds of mistakes to her amusement. Already her eyes were twinkling with fun and laughter. I refused many a tempting thing that was offered, while she kept on remarking: "That's right, don't eat if you don't care. Girls in England don't eat these things." At last came curry and rice, of which I took a little, and enjoyed it.

The other lady had been long resident in India. She shook her head and said that I was a growing girl and must eat. "Oh, give her some gruel," said Miss Roberts. After this I had always some gruel or congee made in various ways both morning and evening. The butler had orders to place mine next to my plate on the breakfast table, and in the evening to serve it in my room, but the utmost I could do was to swallow a few spoonfuls. My brothers, however, used to come often, and they generally brought something from Mother.

My stay with the ladies raised me much in the estimation of my brothers. They paid visits to me regularly, and my little brother, the youngest of the family, became much endeared to me. He told me he missed me at home, and brought little trifles for me, leaving them in my room without my knowledge. The ladies encouraged him to stay a long time, for they were fond of the shy little fellow, and called him the little gentleman of the house. During the day, the school was my delight. This Miss Roberts managed. She instructed me in the art of teaching, in which I found a great delight. I was astonished at the explanations which I was able to give, and the way in which a knowledge of things seemed to spring into existence when it was required. I was in a whirl of delight with the blackboards, the large maps and the pictures, and the new dignity that all these conferred on me. Miss Roberts smiled at my eagerness, and forgot to say that I was only a child. I loved to think myself grown up and important. Miss Roberts used to quarrel with me as impetuously and passionately as if she had been of my own age, and then make it up by giving me a hearty hug and a kiss. She had very peculiar views, and we often had little fights with each other. I can hardly help thinking that she sometimes gave expression to her views for the sole purpose of teasing me. "Oh, Miss D., what made you receive the Bible woman in the drawing room?" she said one day, alluding to a very respectable person, a great friend of our family. "In England we receive them in the kitchen. She is no better than a servant, I assure you."

"In the kitchen?" I said, in amazement and indignation. I was angry, and thought of many grievances that I had heard spoken of. I had also heard that we were the real aristocrats of our country, and that the English ladies who came to India only belonged to the middle class, and I resolved to tell her that, so I boldly added: "What do you think of us? We are real aristocrats of this place." Unfortunately I pronounced the big word wrongly, and she burst out laughing and repeated it again and again, as I had done. "I don't care. Anyhow, you are middle-class people. She is a brahmin, and only takes money from the Mission because she is poor. She is no servant. In your country you are no brahmins. You are sudras." Tears fell from my eyes, and I felt as if I should choke.

"Miss D.," exclaimed the angry lady, now quite beside herself, "do girls ever talk at table like this? I protest against this. I can't have it. I tell you I can't,"—this with so much emphasis that I was quite frightened. Miss D. looked at me and shook her head. The tears that were rolling from my eyes I hastily wiped. "What can I do?" I said, while a shower of words, such as "rude," "bad," "naughty," "disrespectful," &c., fell on my head. Tiffin over, Miss Roberts went with a bounce to her room and I went to mine and began to cry. "Natives," I said to myself, "we are natives. Tomorrow she will say that my mother was a Bible woman too. Oh! I will go away from her," and I began to cry more. About five minutes afterward the door behind me opened, and Miss Roberts rushed in, took hold of me, and kissed me profusely. "Now it is all right," she said, smiling and wonderfully changed. "We won't talk about it."

"And you won't send Bible women to the kitchen?" I said.

She shook her head and rushed away from me laughing.

In the evenings we generally sat together in the lobby. It was our free time, and I was told to say anything I liked. I used to sit far back on the deep seat with my hands on my lap, although there was a table in front. I liked to draw my own pictures, with the stars and shadows outside, and often my thoughts were with Bhasker; but I was always disturbed and told to talk. Generally the ladies had some fancy work in their hands; but I never brought any. One day Miss Roberts rebuked me and said: "Why did you not bring some work?"

I felt guilty, but still as I rose I said somehow, "I thought we were expected to be free at this time."

"Yes, but we must not appear so. I hate laziness."

Something in this remark caught my attention. I stood near the table and looked out. All my pictures vanished. I looked into her face and said, "It is only for appearance, is it? What is the good of that? Won't it be acting falsely?"

She flew into a passion, and when I tried to escape to my room, she forced me down. "Falsely! Sit and be lazy," she said, "and let everyone of us put you to shame."

The second lady, however, calmed her, saying, "Really I don't do anything. I had better sit quietly too."

"Sit, sit," said Miss Roberts, who had by this time nearly spent her wrath and was in a little pet.

The other lady had on various occasions whispered to me, "She is Irish and means nothing," and now she looked and smiled at me.

My greatest trials always came through my tongue. I had got into the habit of thinking loudly. Bhasker had encouraged it, and the discussions carried on by my other brothers, in which I often took part, had made me quite an adept in defending my views. I had had to stand up for my rights from my childhood. I had not then learnt the beauty of silence. One day I was sitting in the lobby in my usual half-sleepy, half-dreamy state, when I heard a visitor announced. As soon as Miss Roberts heard the name, she broke out abruptly, "Oh, how disgusting! What a bore she is! and she wants me, that is true enough." So saying she walked out, and an elderly lady met her near the lobby.

"Oh! I am so glad to see you. How do you do?" Miss Roberts said in a hearty tone as she brought in the visitor. Surely this is somebody else, and I am glad that it is a surprise for Miss Roberts, I said to myself. The talk evidently was cheerful and genial, but as soon as it was over, I was rather taken aback to hear Miss Roberts say, "Oh, what a bore to be sure! How glad I am she is gone! We must really not have visitors at this time."

"She! she!" I said, "was not she a surprise to you?"

"What do you mean?" said Miss Roberts, turning abruptly round on me.

"No! I thought the lady was a surprise to you. You said you were so glad to see her."

"Oh! Oh!" she said, lifting her voice and her hands.

"Miss D., I tell you I can't have this imper—"

"You said free speech was allowed here," I answered, interrupting her.

"Free speech, but not to your superiors, not to me," this with a thump on the table. "You naughty girl."

But it was a little overdone, and there was a burst from the other lady in which Miss Roberts found herself heartily joining.

Later on I came to know that they did not mean anything. It was only the custom, and they used the few set phrases that etiquette compelled them to use. But my readers will understand from this what a boor I was. I loved these two ladies and stayed with them for months, and in spite of little quarrels now and then, I lived very happily with them. Not long after I was attacked with fever, and my sister was compelled to take me away.

RAMABAI RANADE _____

(1862–1924)   *Marathi*

As a writer, Ramabai Ranade is chiefly remembered for her autobiography *Amachya Ayushyatil Kahi Athawani* (Memoirs of Our Life Together), 1910. Ramabai was born in a village in the south of Maharashtra. Her mother went through twenty pregnancies but only seven of her children survived. Though she does speak a little of her childhood and especially of her mother, who, she writes, was a friend to her children, a large portion of her autobiography, as the title indicates, deals with the life that began at the age of eleven, after she was married to the well-known scholar and jurist Mahadev Govind Ranade. Ranade was thirty-two and a widower.

After he lost his first wife, Ranade wanted, in keeping with his commitments to the ideals of the social reform movement, to marry a widow. His father, however, would hear nothing of it and arranged his marriage to Ramabai. Probably in protest—that must have hurt his bewildered young wife more than it angered his father—Ranade, who was a subjudge, did not even take a day off from court on his wedding day. That very night, he began to teach his wife to read and write. If he was a demanding teacher, she was an apt and intelligent pupil. She learned English and Marathi, read the classics, and by 1893, when he became a justice of the Bombay High Court, she was writing letters on his behalf, scanning newspapers and books for ideas that might be of interest to him, and managing many of his affairs. It was she who, after his death in 1901, edited and published his speeches and writings.

She also found time, however, to take part in several women's organizations. From 1918 to 1923 she worked actively for equal political rights for women. She was a popular speaker who drew, to everyone's delight, freely on her wide reading in English and Marathi. In 1904 she was elected president of the Rashtriya Parishad (National Conference), where women from all castes and different religions came together.

Initially both Ramabai and M. G. Ranade were associates of Pandita Ramabai (the distinguished scholar and social reformer whose work is also included in this volume). They helped her to run Sharda Sadan, the widows' home she had founded. But when Pandita Ramabai came into conflict with the fiery and courageous Swadeshi journalist Lokmanya Tilak, and when her work at Sharda Sadan became the center of controversy, the Ranades withdrew their support. M. G. Ranade himself was a "moderate" and never openly came out in favor of the nationalists, but after his death, Ramabai began to express her sympathy for Tilak's uncompromising stands against British rule and on the freedom of the press. She took active part in the movement to boycott British cloth that Tilak organized in Maharashtra. In 1918, Ramabai made a bold public speech supporting Tilak's "extremist" politics and attacking British rule.

We have chosen extracts from the early part of Ramabai Ranade's autobiography that present a vivid and poignant picture of the experiences of women like her who were married to "progressive," Western-educated husbands, many of them in no way less stern or harshly authoritarian than "traditional" husbands. These wives had to respond to many new demands made on them. They also had to find their way through the complex changes in their relationships with other women in the family and with their husbands that marked their times. Ramabai, who was then only twenty-one, deals adroitly and sensitively with the people around her. But what makes her account so rare for its time, and important for us, is that she was able to write critically about her husband, a gesture all the more difficult because she was married to a man widely known and respected for his scholarship and his progressive ideas.

◆

From AMACHYA AYUSHYATIL KAHI
    ATHAWANI
(Memoirs of Our Life Together)
Part III, Chapter 2. Maza Shikshanas Prarambha
    (My Studies Begin)

Now I have to mention one thing here. The men in our house were very much in favor of teaching women to read and write. My father-in-law had taught his wife and daughter to read, write, and keep accounts. And the women too felt proud of this achievement. My mother-in-law and my sister-in-law both knew perfectly well that the men in the house were in favor of women's education. Indeed, they did not just "know" this, they themselves had firsthand experience of it. Yet they were never sympathetic to my learning. On the contrary, they hated it and used to get very angry with me. As if they were just like Taisasubai*—orthodox and illiterate! There were some nine women in our house at that time, including close and distant relations, but no one of my age. So they all formed themselves into one group. Every night my reading would begin as soon as I went upstairs. Since I had just been assigned the task of reading the Marathi books of the Dakshina Prize Committee, prose books were no problem to me. But reading poetry was a problem. Not because I couldn't read it well. The problem was that I had to chant the poems loudly according to the specific tunes of the different meters like the *arya, sloka,* and so on that were used in the poems. If I chanted them in a soft, low voice, "he" would get angry; and if I read them loudly, some woman or other in the house was bound to be eavesdropping, standing either on the staircase or at the door. They used to memorize the tunes and stanzas I had sung at night and mimic my singing the next day. They used to make faces at me, tease me, mock me, and put me to shame in front of the other women in the house. But I never retaliated. Never answered anybody back whatever they did, or said. I just listened to everything

---

*An older widowed sister of her father-in-law. Ramabai speaks of her as the seniormost widow in the household. She was very strict and orthodox.

they said—whether true or false—and kept quiet. Sometimes, they approached me with seemingly benevolent looks on their faces and a pompously mature concern for me and said, "Why do you unnecessarily invite the wrath of these older women by reading books? We too feel very sorry for you, you know. But what can we do? If the menfolk really insist on your reading books, well, read them, but only occasionally. Don't you understand that your reading is an insult to the elder people? What do men understand of these problems? It is we who have to spend most of our time in the company of these women. Tell me, how much time do we really spend in the company of men? They may ask you a hundred times to read, but you can very well choose to ignore it. And that would solve the whole problem! Ultimately, they are bound to get tired of asking you and then they will give up on you. Isn't it in your own hands really?" Whenever they found time, they used to preach to me like this. I knew they had the secret support of the elders. But neither did I agree with them nor did I argue back. I just quietly did what I wanted to.

Part III, Chapter 7. Ingrejis Suruvant (I Begin on English)

After a few months passed like this, my study of Marathi was over, and "he" started teaching me English. Now the time I had at night or at dawn wasn't really sufficient for me to finish my studies. I had to find extra time, at least an hour and a half, to learn the words by heart. Since there was no place downstairs where I could sit and study, I had to go upstairs to work. This infuriated the elder women, and they warned me in no uncertain terms, "Do whatever you want to do upstairs, but we will never tolerate it if you insult us."

Every day my heart literally froze with fear when it was time to go downstairs in the morning. But he used to encourage me. "Try to endure it. Just don't say anything to them, that's all. Your mother-in-law doesn't scold you, does she? Why should you be so upset if somebody else scolds you?" Encouraged thus, I was able to face the day peacefully.

I had to undergo a great deal of harassment to be able to study. But I never gave it up. I was able to survive the torture only because of my two brothers-in-law. It was their kind and affectionate behavior that saw me through those trying times. They used to assure me, saying, "Don't be afraid of these women even if they scold you." And they used to argue with them for me. But it was he, above all, with his loving, calm, and solemn advice, who was a pillar of strength in those trying times. Otherwise a young, immature girl like me would never have been able to endure such harassment and torment. And the peace and harmony in the house would not have lasted for so long. But the ordeal left me constantly depressed. Nobody, it is said, can read your mind so well and so easily, by any means, as your loved ones can. It is very true! Because of the agony that I had to endure, "he" also suffered. "His" peace of mind had disappeared and "he" used to be very disturbed and tense. Had it continued this way any longer, I believe his control over his mind would have just snapped, and that would have created all sorts of problems in the house. But fortunately our luck held, and without any further problems and complications, we were transferred to Nasik. I was not aware at all of what he or his friends in Pune thought when they heard this news. I was too busy making plans for our happy future in Nasik to worry about the joy or grief of our friends. For two weeks, I went around absolutely exalted! Soon afterward, both of us, together with Abadhawji,* went to Nasik. We had deliberately not taken any of the elder women with us. Once again my studies began, according to "his" plans. "He" was very enthusiastic about teaching me and the smooth, happy rhythm of our life was restored once again. But let me give a further account of Pune before our departure for Nasik.

The government had kept a close watch on people from the city since some particularly significant incidents had occurred in Pune in the year 1874–1875 during the movement of public unrest. To make matters worse, when the case of the poisoning of Malharrao Gaikwad** had come up, these people had sent a wire to Baroda, saying, "Though the government hasn't allowed this case to be heard, Pune is ready to spend up to one hundred thousand rupees to assist you. So Your Highness should not give it up." At this time, Sir Richard Temple was in charge of affairs. Intensive investigations were being carried out by the government to find out who was at the root of the movement. No concrete evidence could be discovered against anyone in particular, but the government nevertheless began to regard some people with a sus-

---

*A brother-in-law who was about Ramabai's age. She was very close to him.
**In this notorious case, Malharrao Gaikwad, the ruler of Baroda who had had a series of confrontations with the British Resident, was accused, in 1875, by the British government of trying to poison his brother. Consequently the British government was able to dethrone him and take over the state. There was widespread protest and M. G. Ranade appeared in court on his behalf, but they lost the case.

picious eye. Later, in order to suppress the movement, a new law was formulated for the Bombay Presidency. According to that law, a sub-judge could not work for more than three or five years at the same place. Our transfer to Nasik had been a direct outcome of this new law.

Part XIV, Chapter 1. Anasuyabainche Purana (Anasuyabai's Purana)

Around this time, a woman called Anasuyabai came to Pune. She was well versed in Sanskrit and was accompanied by her husband and old father. She used to read the Holy Bhagawata like Pandita Ramabai. She would set the verses to a tune and chant the text like a *puranika* (preacher) while she explained their meaning. She made a presentation once at our house, and later at several other houses too. One day a reading was arranged in the Vishnu temple, which was also known as Joshi's temple. It was usually women who went to this temple. Once the program was arranged, the women who were there decided on a plan of action. "We won't leave any place for the wives of the reform-ists to sit. We'll leave the assembly hall of the temple empty for them, but we'll occupy all the places in front of the sanctum. Then they will have to go and sit with the men in the assembly hall. And anyway, don't they sit together with the men when they attend those meetings? On chairs, too. As if they were their equals! Why would they need a separate place here?"

I learned of this plan from a couple of my friends. I normally used to mix both with the orthodox women and with the reformists. Nat-urally, I had friends in both camps, and did not like this plan to seg-regate us. I felt aggrieved and insulted. I would have easily upset their plan had I come to know of it a couple of hours earlier. But I had no such time. As it was, I got to the temple a little late. It was only then that I came to know of their plan. But by that time it was too late. The temple was already packed with people. I had no choice but to go and sit where Pandita Ramabai and the other reformist women were sitting. But I was unhappy. I kept thinking of going home. A place was made for Anasuyabai between the reformists and their wives.

Around twenty minutes after the reading began, I whispered in Pan-dita Ramabai's ear, "I am not well today. I feel rather giddy. I think I'll go home." Saying so, I left.

On my way home, I kept on feeling that I had acted very wisely, that I had done a very brave deed. And in that jubilant mood, I nar-rated the whole incident to Taisasubai, who was sitting outside on the veranda. I told her everything. I told her how the women in the temple were in league against us, how they had made us sit with the men and occupied all the places in the sanctum, how all this had angered me, and finally, how I had decided not to sit with the men and marched home.

I was speaking with great confidence and pride, as if what I had done was very commendable and would meet with everybody's approval. And Taisasubai was, indeed, pleased with me. She said in a very encouraging tone, "Well done! You should always use your reason like this. That is the proper way to behave in public life. Then people will not speak ill of you. These newly educated young men—what do they know of the ways of the world? They will ask you to do anything. But you should know better than that. You don't have to do everything that they ask you to. And don't worry if they get angry about it. Let them. Don't you fuss over them at such times because it is in their nature to get angry like that. Whatever the reason, they will always take it out on their women. Why, they seem to consider that heroic! God alone knows what makes them think that. It's beyond me!"

She spoke at length, encouraging me to "behave with reason" for the sake of people. Her affectionate words and concern for me made me feel gloriously happy.

But this glorious happiness of mine did not last even for two hours. And that wasn't all. I was to learn a major lesson of my life. And never did I dare make such a mistake again.

When in the evening he returned home, I went to him as usual, to help him undress. As soon as he saw me, he asked me, "What's wrong with you today?"

"Nothing whatever," I replied innocently.

And no sooner did I give this reply than I remembered that I had left the temple on the pretext of being unwell. I was terribly confused. What would I say if he demanded an explanation? Fortunately, he didn't ask me anything; but then he did not say even a word to me. I was waiting there to collect the clothes he had taken off. But instead of giving them to me, he hung them on the peg by himself. I stooped down to remove his shoes, but he quietly pushed my hands away and removed them himself. I stood there, rooted to the spot for some more time, but no conversation of any kind ensued. My heart beat faster with a strange sense of foreboding. All my pride just vanished into thin air and I grew extremely apprehensive. It was his custom to chat with me at least for some ten minutes after he came home. This routine would be interrupted only when he was accompanied by his friends or was busy with some urgent work. But today there was no such reason as far as I could see. "Then why does he behave like this?" I wondered. His behavior did not change during the meal either. Usually he told me whether he had liked or wanted a particular dish. But today, everything was indicated with gestures. Nobody seemed to notice this, but I certainly did! Immediately! And became even more worried. "If he doesn't like what I have done, why doesn't he scold me?" I thought. I would have preferred it had he scolded me, even if it was in front of the others. But his reticence was causing me so much suffering and I had to endure it mutely.

As usual, I went upstairs and began to read the book from the place I had left off last night. We used to receive these books from the Dakshina Prize Committee. Usually, I would be told to mark that particular word or sentence which I had read erroneously; but that night, the few mistakes that I deliberately made went without any comment. When he pulled the covers over himself, and turned his face to the other side, I knew that this was a signal to me to stop my reading. I put the lamp away and set the book down. The servant came with ghee as usual to massage his feet. I said, "Today you are not required to do it. Go away." I started rubbing his feet with the ghee myself. I wanted him at least to say, "Now that's enough!" But no, he went off to sleep as soon as I started rubbing his feet. Usually, after an hour's massage, he would extend his other foot and ask us to start working on that. But today, I don't know how, he did not forget his resolve of silence even in his sleep. He didn't speak a single word. And turning on the other side, he pretended to be fast asleep.

Up to this time, I was really dozing even while rubbing his feet. But when I saw him feigning sleep, I realized that the opportunity to speak was completely lost. I couldn't sleep now and felt absolutely miserable. I even cried for a long time. I was dying to say to him, "What's the reason for this silence? You've never treated me like this before." I wanted to beg him to forgive me, but the words just refused to come out. It is very difficult for the proud nature of youth to speak even though the mind has become meek enough to do so. I couldn't bring myself to utter a single syllable even though I resolved a thousand times to speak. Whenever I tried to speak, I realized that he, too, was awake, and then all my resolve would just melt away. The whole night passed like this. Both of us hadn't been able to sleep a wink. At the break of dawn, he got up and left the room. I was extremely disappointed and cried a lot at this unbearable punishment. Then I washed my face clean with cold water and went downstairs, but I was feeling absolutely wretched.

Why did I let the whole night pass by without saying that I was sorry? Why did I invite this misery with my senseless pride? Then I thought, "If only I could speak to him before the afternoon meal, I would feel well again." So I took my bath and did all my daily chores, like preparing the salads and the chutneys, and the buttermilk and so on. But I was still in my *sovle** clothes, and I would have to change to ordinary clothes to see him. I was worried about finding a pretext to change my clothes. Since I had started serving the food at the afternoon meal, all the senior women liked me to wait upon them. But they had a rule: I was not allowed to go anywhere else except the rest room, the kitchen, and the prayer room in my holy clothes, until the second round of serving and eating was over, that is, till the time the elder women had eaten their meals. If I went to the tank or to the backyard or upstairs, I would have to bathe again. Otherwise I wouldn't be allowed to serve the food. I was perplexed. I knew that it was time for him to come downstairs for his bath. I decided to use the pretext of a stomachache to get into ordinary clothes. With this intention, I said aloud to the other women in the house, "I am not feeling very well today. Can somebody please serve the food till I come back in a little while? I will have to bathe again."

My sister-in-law got very angry when she heard this. She said, "Oh yes, sure! So that by the time we have finished serving everything, her ladyship will step in to supervise us!"

All the other women started laughing at this but Taisasubai said, "Why do you say so? Doesn't she serve every day? She is not a proud woman at all. And she won't pretend to be ill. She has really been looking unwell since this morning."

The women forgot me and started chattering away among themselves. I too was looking forward to something else. So I took this chance to slip off upstairs to our room. He was busy arranging his office files. I went very close to him and said, "I made a mistake yesterday. I promise never to repeat it. I have been miserable since yesterday evening."

After some time, he said, "First, you behave stupidly. You yourself suffer because of it and make me suffer too. Who would like it if his own one didn't behave according to his will? Once you know the direction of my thoughts, you should always try to follow the same path so that neither of us suffers. Don't ever do such things again." Afterward he left for his bath.

---

*She was wearing ritually pure clothes, worn after a bath for cooking and worship.

I too hurried downstairs, and had a quick bath with the hot water Bajaba had kept ready for him. I went back quickly to the kitchen to stop any gossip that my absence might have occasioned.

The meals were soon over. I too ate with the senior women. Yet my whole day was gloomy. I resolved never to do anything that "he" would not like. And since my mind was convinced that there was no punishment more terrible than silence, I never allowed any such incident to occur again. And to be frank, nothing of this sort ever happened again.

Translated by Maya Pandit.

BINODINI DASI ————————————————

(1863–1941)   *Bengali*

Binodini Dasi is a legendary name in the Bengali theater. During a brief meteoric career, which lasted from 1874, when she was eleven, to 1886, Binodini was the Bengali theater's brightest star: she acted in fifty plays, including operas, farces, and tragedies, in which she took sixty different roles. Many of the great artists of her times were her friends and admirers. "Binod, you are the living goddess I have created," Girish Chandra Ghosh (1844–1912), the founding father of modern theater in Bengal, often told her. When she played Mrinalini, a character created by Bankim Chandra Chatterjee, he remarked that he had created a character in fiction, but it was left to Binodini to give it life. Her autobiography is a major document of the Bengali theater and among the earliest first-person records we have of a woman who remained single and worked for a living. In it we are taken behind the scenes of her spectacular reputation to witness what it cost this warm, courageous, and gifted actress.

Born in Calcutta into a family whose members were traditionally entertainers, but now also practiced prostitution, she grew up in an environment that she hated. She was married when she was very young, but her husband refused to accept her. When she was nine, an event took place that was to change the course of her life. The famous singer Ganga Baiji came to live with the family, and Binodini's mother encouraged her to learn music from this artiste of renown. Though she was carrying on an occupation traditionally handed down from generation to generation, Ganga Baiji worked as an independent professional, and took pride in her success. For the young Binodini, having Ganga as a model must have been as important as the accompanying change in her world, which suddenly opened up with many important people coming to listen to the famous singer. Soon there was a request from one of them that Binodini be allowed to perform on stage. She started at a wage of ten rupees a month, and made her first stage appearance in 1874 playing a small role in Haralal Roy's *Shatru Sanghar* (Destroying the Enemy). In the next production she played the heroine, and continued to do so throughout her career. The troupe not only performed in Calcutta but toured round Bengal, and life was far from easy for this beautiful young actress.

In 1877, Binodini met Girish Chandra Ghosh (whom she refers to as Girishbabu in her memoir), with whom she worked for the rest of her life. Ghosh, according to theater historians, was her mentor. He tutored her in acting, introduced her to the classics of Bengali drama, and shared with her his knowledge of the foreign theater. Of Binodini's contribution to Ghosh's career as a dramatist we have no mention, but we can surmise.

Binodini's autobiography, written in the form of a series of letters to Girish Chandra Ghosh, the first one dated, according to the Bengali calendar, 1 Sravan 1316 (1910) and the last, 11 Bisakh 1319 (1913), was published in 1913 when she was forty-nine. During the first phase of her career, Binodini tells us, she was living with an upper-class Bengali gentleman, whom she refers to as Au Babu. They were obviously very much in love, but Au Babu did not approve of her acting. He had promised her that he would never marry anyone else, but a few years later, he did. While she was still raw from the trauma of her broken love affair, Gurmukh Rai (Gurmukhbabu in her book) offered to help finance the theater that she and others were planning to build if she agreed to live with him. Binodini was torn by her loyalty to her earlier love, but under pressure from her theater colleagues, including Girish Chandra Ghosh, she agreed. These very colleagues later were to object to working in a theater owned by a "prostitute," and to refuse Binodini a share in it.

Early in 1884, Gurmukh Rai left Binodini and sold the Star theater as a result of pressure from his family. Denied a share in the new ownership by colleagues she had trusted, Binodini decided she did not want to live any longer as mistress of one man or another and would struggle to survive entirely on her own earnings. She kept herself active in the theater world but refused to share her personal life with anyone. For a period of one and a half years she attended rehearsals and performances, and lived quietly and alone at home. She found enormous peace in this existence, she says. But because of the differences between her and her colleagues in the theater, and also perhaps because now that she was no longer so youthfully attractive they had little use for her, she had to retire from the stage.

Shortly before then, she had developed a friendship with Ranga Babu, a married man with children. He provided her with a home and security and tried, according to her memoirs, to give her the "respect due to her." But Binodini's personal life continued to be fraught with tragedy. Her only daughter died in 1904 at the age of thirteen. Ranga Babu died in 1912. Once again Binodini was hounded out of her house, and she had no option but to return to the environment she hated most—the parts of the city where the prostitutes lived, and where she had spent her childhood. Now, she writes, she had "only death to look forward to."

We could find very little to tell us about her life after 1915. Another unfinished autobiographical piece, *Amar Abhinetri Jiban* (My Life as an Actress), appeared serially in *Rup O Ranga,* a literary journal edited by the well-known novelist Saratchandra Chatterjee, between January 1924 and May 1925.

The extract from *Amar Katha* chosen for translation is an account of her experiences of setting up what became the Star Theater.

◆

From AMAR KATHA
(My Story)
Star Theatre Sambandhye Nama Katha (The
Story of the Star Theater)

I decided to set up a theater. Why should I not? The people I had lived with all my life, together as brothers and sisters, those who still had such power over me, were right in what they said. If I were to build a theater, we could all live under one roof like one big family. When my mind was quite made up, I got Gurmukh Rai to support my scheme. I know this has been an age-old custom with us, to abandon one man's protection, only to fall back on another's; but it disturbed and pained me at the time. People might laugh at the very idea of our type displaying any sense of guilt or distress at playing false. Careful thought would bring home to them that we are women too. When the Almighty sent us to this world, he did not deny us the tender emotions of a womanly heart. He gave us all, and we lost all, by ill fate! But does the social order not bear any responsibility for this? The tenderness that our hearts were full with once can never be fully destroyed. As proof, take the way we rear our children. We too desire a husband's love, but where do we find it? Who is willing to give us heart for heart? There is no shortage of men who come in lust, and charm us with their talk of romance; but which of them would give his heart to test whether we have hearts too? Were we the ones who first played false, or did we learn to only after we ourselves had been deceived? Has anyone ever investigated that? It was a harlot like us who was sent to beguile that holiest of holy men, the immortal Haridas. But because of the way the Vaishnava treated her, she became a Vaishnavi, that is well known. If she did not have a heart, if she were completely devoid of feeling, never could she have dedicated herself to Vishnu. Money cannot buy anyone's love. We too cannot sell our love for money. That is what the world holds against us. The playwright Girishbabu in his poem "Barangana" (Harlot) portrays these unfortunate women very accurately. "She had a lotus heart like any other woman," he says. In many regions water turns rock-hard! That is how it is with us! Falling helpless victims of oppression again and again, our hearts grow hardened one day.

Let us not go into that now, however. To adjust to the changed situation I have described earlier, I and the rest of the theater people had to struggle greatly. Because when the aforesaid young gentleman came to know that I was planning permanent links with a theater under someone else's patronage, he tried putting all manner of obstacles in our way, whether in anger or through sheer cussedness I do not know. But those obstacles were none too easy to overcome! He called the muscle men from his own *zamindari* and had our house surrounded; Gurmukhbabu also hired big-time *goondas*. There were clashes, the police came, and a great commotion continued for some time.

At one point, there was even a threat on my life! One day, after rehearsals, I was asleep in my room—it was about six in the morning—when I woke up suddenly at a crashing sound and the heavy trudge of boots! There stood a young gentleman in military uniform, sword at his side, right in the middle of my room, saying, "Meni, why sleep so much?" I sat up startled, and he went on, "Look, Binod, you have to quit their company. Whatever money they have spent on you so far, I'll pay back. Here's ten thousand now; if it comes to more, I'll give that too." I was always a stubborn sort; if anyone acted tough with me, it made me so mad that I lost all sense of discretion! I would stick to my point, and nothing could make me give it up. What I would agree to do if asked nicely, with care and affection, I would refuse to do if forced or forbidden; it was not easy to bully me. Well, his highhanded manner made me so angry I said, "No, never! I have given them my word; I cannot go back on it now." He said, "If it's for the money, I'll give you another ten thousand." His words inflamed me even more! I stood up and said, "Here, keep your money! It is I who have earned money, rather than money having earned me! Fate willing, your ten or twenty thousand will come to me again several times over. You can leave now!" When he heard that, he went blazing mad, put his hand on his sword, and said, "Is that so? You think I'll let you off that easy? I'll cut you to pieces first! The twenty thousand I was going to give you I'll spend on something else, and let's see then." And he took his sword out from its sheath and aimed it straight at my head. My eyes had been on that sword of his, so the minute he swung out, I crouched down behind a table harmonium. The sword struck the top of the harmonium and knocked three inches off the wood! He lifted it off and hit out again, but luck favored him, and I was not destined to die, so this time the blow fell on the music stool. I rose up at once and caught his raised hand, and said, "What exactly are you up to? If you want to slay me, leave it for later; think what you will face in the end. How does it matter whether this tainted life of mine remains or ends? What will become of you? Think of your family, think of leaving this world marked and burdened forever, all for the sake of a despised harlot. For shame! Listen to me. Calm down. Tell me what you want me to do, but cool off now."

I had heard that when the first surge of fury subsides, people come to their senses. That is exactly what happened. He flung away the sword and sat down on the spot with his face in his hands. I was filled with pity at his distress! I thought, to hell with everything; let me go back to him again. But I was so thoroughly enmeshed by then with the theater people and Girishbabu that it was impossible for me to escape. Well anyway, I survived that day. He walked out without a word! Now the few of us who had formed a group left the Bengal theater we had been working for. Gurmukh Rai insisted that he would do nothing for the theater unless I submitted to his wishes fully and entirely. Therefore, to solve the problem, we debated among ourselves and thought it best for me to keep out of the way for some months. Sometimes Raniganj, sometimes some other town—I moved around constantly. In the meanwhile, the planning went on: what kind of theater we would build, how it would run, and so on. Later, when it was settled that we would lease Priya Mitra's place on Beadon Street, and what funds that would require, I came back to Calcutta again. A few days later, Gurmukhbabu said, "Look, Binod, forget about that theater and all its problems. You take fifty thousand rupees from me. I'll give it to you straight!" And he took out a bunch of notes. I used to love the theater, and that is why, in spite of being a contemptible harlot, I still rejected the tempting offer of half a lakh of rupees. When Amrita Mitra and the others heard that Gurmukh Rai was willing to pay me fifty thousand and not do a thing about the theater, they were worried indeed. They worked hard to dissuade me from accepting the money, but their efforts were not really necessary. I was determined to build that theater. So if he did not help us build it, I would not obey his bidding in any way. So it was on my initiative that the land on Beadon Street was taken on lease. Later Gurmukh Rai was generous in providing funds for its construction. . . .

The work proceeded with much excitement and joy. During this time, we would go for rehearsals at two or three in the afternoon, finish off there, and move on to the theater site; when the rest had gone, I would stay on to carry baskets of clay to fill the pit and the back seats area. Sometimes, to encourage the workers, I would pay them four *koris* per basket. The construction had to be completed as early as possible, so work went on into the night. No one knew how happy I felt in those days! With great enthusiasm, and with a lot of expense, the theater was finally ready. It must have taken just under a year. But along with this there is one thing I feel I just must mention. While the theater was coming up, they had all said, "This theater will have your name linked with it. So even after you die, your name will live on. In other words, 'B' Theater will be its name." That had made me happier still. But ultimately they did not keep their word—why I do not know. Right up to the point when the theater was to be registered, I thought it was to be named after me. But the day they went and registered it—all arrangements were complete by then, the theater was to open a week from that day—I asked them eagerly about the name they had given. Dashubabu cheerfully answered, "Star." When I heard this, I was so deeply hurt inside that I flopped down on the spot and couldn't utter a word for two full minutes. After a while I controlled myself and said, "Good!" I thought about it later. Had their show of love and affection been just empty words to serve their own interests? But what could I have done. I was helpless! I was totally in their hands by then! And I had never dreamed they could trick me like this, act in such bad faith. The time I refused the offer of all that money did not hurt me half so much as their behavior did. Though I never said a word about it to anyone, I couldn't forget it either. I remembered it all my life. Besides, I loved the theater so much, thought it so much my own, and a new hall put up, no matter how, was such a great happening that the matter could have received no importance in any case. But in later times too, after the theater was ready, I was not treated well! They tried to quote all kinds of rules to prevent me from staying there, even as a salaried actress. And they succeeded, so for two months I was forced to sit at home. After that I was back again, thanks to Girishbabu's efforts, and my own insistence on my proprietary rights.

Translated by Madhuchhanda Karlekar.

CORNELIA SORABJI ───────────────

(1866–1954)   *English*

When young Cornelia, "to [her] surprise," took first place in the Bombay Presidency (an administrative unit of the colonial government), in the final degree examination, and automatically obtained the Government of India scholarship for a course at an English university in 1887, her long battle began to open the public world to women. "In spite of the University Constitution declaring that women were as men, I was not allowed to hold any scholarship. The test had been the same, and all conditions fulfilled, but the Authorities said, 'No!' It was in fact impertinent of any woman to produce circumstances which were not in the mind of Authorities as a possibility when they dangled a gilded prize before eyes that should have been male eyes alone!" Cornelia had been the first woman to graduate from Bombay University; the next one did so only twenty-four years later, in 1911.

Similar experiences were to await her when she finally got to Oxford in 1889. She wanted to study law, but was told that no woman might do so. The warden of Somerville College suggested she read English, "the then most popular school for the nondescript." But Benjamin Jowett, the master of Balliol College, who seems to have been a friend and guardian to this young Parsi girl, intervened. She spent a term sitting in on law lectures before she was allowed to read for the B.C.L., "the best that Oxford had to give." The hazard of being the first woman to do this, Cornelia writes, "found me looking into the barrel of a pistol at the most crucial moments." She sat for the examination but it was not possible for her to actually qualify as a practicing lawyer until she had been "called to the Bar," and that she could not do until thirty years later, in 1923, when women were admitted there, and when Cornelia finally acquired the "label I had longed for all my life."

Though she kept a diary for most of her life, a richer record of her experiences is found in the letters she regularly wrote, initially to her parents in India, later from India to Eleanor Rathbone, the social activist and campaigner against child marriage in England, and finally from England to the Allahabad judge Harrison Faulkner Blair, with whom she had a close relationship from about 1900 to his death in 1907. Her mother, Franscina, "who never tired of sharing with others the Gospel as she knew it—the Good News—of Christianity, of Health, of Education, of Sanitation," and her father, the Rev. Sorabji Kharsedji Langrana, who "had in the manner of the early Martyrs of the Christian Church, at peril of death, changed his religion," Cornelia writes, "brought up" their six daughters and one son "English." Discipline and education were "written in rubric in the book of the Sorabji Home" and to this must be added, she says, "the teaching that we, as individuals, were our brother's keeper."

While she was in England, Cornelia moved among artists and dignitaries of various kinds. Among the people she knew well were the Max Müllers and the Toynbees. Benjamin Jowett sent her to call on the ageing Tennyson and on Florence Nightingale. She was even presented at Court. Queen Victoria, Cornelia writes, sent a message that "one of my pretty colours (not white) would be permitted."

On her return to India in 1894, Cornelia made a place for herself working with widows in purdah (most often royalty) who had, under the new legislation, become "wards" of the British government, under whose guardianship their estates now fell, and who had difficulty using the courts. Large sections of her memoirs, *India Calling,* 1934, describe with a wry wit her life between 1894 and 1923 helping these women. Her adventures with the Imprisoned Rani, which we have excerpted here, took place around 1904, when, after a great deal of effort on Cornelia's part, the government officially recognized her as lady assistant to the Court of Wards in Bengal. In her writing, she always speaks of her clients as "my *purdahnashins,*" and they come through in her narrative as superstitious but simple people, quite incapable of looking after themselves, but easy to help if one did not "upset their beliefs." She seems to have grown particularly fond of one of them, "the victim of a horoscope" who, Cornelia writes, when her "how many-th petition" for managing her own estates was refused by a British official, "who had carefully explained to her the difficulties a secluded woman would meet with in the process," retorted, "in my opinion I could not do worse with bandaged eyes, and hobbled feet, than you do with your eyes open and limbs unfettered." Her comment on Cornelia is even more vivid: "You are either mad or a *pujain* (a religious), or why should you live like a man or a tiger, eating out of the hand of none: eating only what you kill?"

She was a prolific writer and had incredible resources of physical energy and mental strength. She worked all day at court, and often spent the evenings responding to calls from her clients before she came home later to write. She published several books, the most important among which are her memoirs and her account of her younger sister, *Susie Sorabji,* 1932. Her first collection of essays, *Behind the Twilights,* came out in 1908. It was soon followed by *Sun Babies,* and in 1917 by *The Purdahnashin* and *Shubala:*

A Child Mother. She wrote regularly on matters of public interest, the law, politics, and women, for important British journals such as *Nineteenth Century* and *National Review.* In 1936 she published her last book, *India Recalled.*

Clearly a conservative both as a feminist and in politics, she dismissed the "new woman" in the West with patronizing contempt, but also consistently opposed the Swadeshi and the Gandhian movements. India was not ready for independence, she felt. She took issue even with the Labour leader Gladstone, who, she writes, "had but one defect—he supported Home Rule." Her continued belief in the rationality, the wisdom, and the good intent of the imperial government, even in the face of the discrimination that she herself had to face, both as an Indian and as a woman, is quite amazing. In the "Economics and Politics" section of her memoirs she describes nationalist politics as disruptive and as deceiving gullible people. Gandhi himself might have been "genuine in his social service aspirations," but was "exploited by his disciples." Of women activists she had even more scathing things to say: "Women picketers did the most harm to the country, because they set back the clock of progress in the orthodox Hindu and conservative regions where progress was vital, and where the move forward had just begun. Moreover, that women should lie flat in the mud in public streets, should scratch the faces of Indian tradesmen, set fire to their shops; should picket liquor shops and bandy words with the intoxicated" was unthinkable. It had a retrogressive effect in many areas: "We had begun to think that education was good, said orthodox Hindu purdahnashins, but if that is what it does to women, ignorance is better," Cornelia writes. The appeal of the nationalist movement "to the educated Indian woman, whom we older ones have relied on for the work which so terribly needs doing for women and children, has its psychological explanation, but is, nonetheless, the most bitter drop in our cup," she concludes.

Cornelia Sorabji's private life seems to have been extremely lonely. The years at Oxford provided many opportunities for interaction, but her memoirs mention no friends in India. She was clearly fond of the women she worked for, but the only friendship she maintained over the years was the one with Eleanor Rathbone. Around 1944, Cornelia grew very weak and left for England. For a few months she thought that blindness was imminent. Her physical condition improved with rest and medical care, but in March 1945 her mental health deteriorated. She rambled, spoke incoherently, was restless, and developed acute paranoias. Neither her solicitors nor her youngest sister, Dr. Alicia Pennel, could get her to grant a power of attorney to anyone. She hated hospitals, doctors, and nurses and when she was forced into a hospital in 1947, she simply refused to eat. The next seven years of life, documented in her sister's letters to Eleanor Rathbone, are a pathetic journey from hospital to hospital. It is a horrible, tragic end for this singular woman, who was both a fighter and a victim of her times.

◆

From INDIA CALLING

Part II (1894–1902), Chapter 4. The Imprisoned Rani [excerpt]

About this time my Brother had returned to India from his long sojourn in the West—Public School, Oxford, London. He was a Barrister and had decided to practise at the Allahabad High Court, United Provinces.

I went up North to help him settle into his house: and a thought which had for long been with me arrived at maturity. The work I was doing as a roving and privileged Practitioner of the Law was without doubt interesting: but it did not amount to beating out a path which other women could follow. It was too personal: Privilege might be withheld from my successors, curiosity sated: and to what practical purpose was the beginning of work so well worth doing, if provision were not made for others to carry on?

In the interest of professional posterity, then, a recognized title to practise at the Bar seemed a necessity: and to obtain this in British India would mean the best recommendation to confidence. Work in Native States could still be continued from any British-Indian centre as headquarters.

Allahabad differed from Bombay, Bengal and Madras, in that here there were no Solicitors. Barristers took instructions directly. As I have already said, I had in practice found direct contact with clients useful. This was another point in favour of Allahabad.

Practitioners in the United Provinces included Barristers, *Vakils* (i.e. Graduates of Law, of the Universities of any Presidency), High Court Pleaders (qualified by a Special Examination, held by the High Court), and in the Districts, *Mukhtars*, etc. (less well qualified). Barristers had pre-audience: and the High Court had just instituted the distinction of Advocate, i.e. eminent Vakils of long standing, who were, in consequence of being termed "Advocate," admitted by grace of the Court to the status and courtesies of Barristers in the Allahabad High Court. Tej Bahadur Sapru and Motilal Nehru were the Vakils so honoured.

As a Bachelor of Laws of the Bombay University I was entitled to be enrolled as a Vakil, and I made an application to this effect in 1897.

After consideration by the entire Bench—Sir J. Edge, C.J., presiding in what I believe was called "English Meeting," i.e. the Controlling and Administrative Department of the Court—I was told that as the University door was not their own special High Court door, the Court hesitated to make an innovation on the ground that I had cited. But if I would do the High Court Pleader's examination (their own creation) they would have power to act.

By this time I was sick to death of examinations, and this new one included proficiency in Shikasta. Now Shikasta (lit. "broken" writing, or writing "in ruins") is the running hand of the Persian character, and a nightmare to decipher. Dots and strokes, both so essential to the distinguishing of letter from letter, with other characterizations, are omitted: and letters are joined which are only recognizable apart.

Shikasta is used in Court documents, though the language of the Courts is now Urdu: and [the need for] its inclusion in the tests for this special High Court Examination was obvious.

Yes—I was thoroughly sick of examinations; but there could be no question of my not complying with the new condition—"one more river to cross"—and I buckled to the re-study of Hindu and Mahommedan Law, of the rubbish-heap of codified British-Indian Law, and the acquisition of Shikasta.

The bright spot of the adventure was my dear old Moslem Munshi who taught me Persian, Urdu and the reading of Court documents.

He was a character, and deserves a monograph. In due course I passed my Examination: but the High Court said, almost shamefacedly, that "on reconsideration" they felt it would be impertinent of an Indian High Court to admit women to the Rolls before England had given the lead.

It was a bad jar, and I could have said much in protest. After all, in matters of this kind, the advantage of India lay in the very newness to which I suppose the Court referred; in having, that is to say, unlike England, no traditions to outrage. She was therefore herself in the position of Leader; and it would have been fun if that particular Court had recognized this!

But protest would have been of no use. I was a single individual. At that time I could not produce even one other woman student of the Law: and I had no assurance that other women would want to follow my Profession.

There was nothing for it but to continue being a "rover," working from the end of a need to be met, not from that of an equal title with men to the reward of legal work.

And with this intention I set myself to collecting the opinions of experienced judges, lawyers, and administrators all over India.

I wrote first to such as I knew personally. I had found, said I, this or that—not stating my worst cases—instances where, although the most efficient of men lawyers were indeed available, Purdahnashins had no possible means of access to or contact with them, the result being needless hardship and injustice.

I kept the lights as low as possible.

The answers were most gratifying:

"Oh, but we know worse. . . ." They also added instances where the seclusion of women had prevented important evidence from being put before the Court, e.g. in property cases where the rights of women were in question.

Purdahnashins of the highest status, in strictest seclusion, are excused attendance as witnesses in Court. Their evidence is taken at their homes by a Commission. Judges and Lawyers both expressed a doubt on occasions as to the identity of the witness thus examined. The men might not see her for themselves. Again, how did they know that the witness spoke freely? They could not tell who were shut in with her behind the purdah: or what fears and coercions assailed her.

They might not even hear her voice—a third person being the medium of both question and answer.

When the witness attended Court, there was the like difficulty; she came in a palanquin accompanied by a male (claiming to be a relation) who acted as "carrier" during her examination, speaking to her through a slit in the doors of the palanquin and broadcasting her answers to the Court.

One of my correspondents, a Parsee Judge from Bombay (the least secluded of Provinces), told me an amusing story in this connection.

He had his suspicions during the progress of a certain case about the witness in a palanquin, and ordered the palanquin to be taken to his chambers for examination of the occupant by the matron of a hospital.

"You are quite safe," said the Matron, the palanquin duly deposited in the Judge's Chambers, behind closed doors. "Come out now."

She pushed back the palanquin shutters, and drew the curtain—a bearded old man stumbled to his feet and confronted her!

An experience of my own in later years was equally illuminating. The High Court of Calcutta appointed me Commissioner to take at her house the evidence of a Purdahnashin in the matter of an important reference then before the Court.

The requisite address had been supplied by the litigants and was on my commission.

I drove down to the house indicated, and it was evidently a surprise to the men who received me that I was a woman.

"Oh, well!" I said. "It's better still, is it not? I can go into the Zenana and examine the lady face to face."

"Oh, no! You would not like that. Zenanas are very shut-up places. You will get ill. Sit here, outside the purdah, on that red-plush chair we have put ready for the Commissioner."

I said I knew what Zenanas were like, and must go in, thank you.

But they were very reluctant to let me pass that purdah. So I said, "I'll return my Commission to the High Court, stating the reason why it has not been executed"—and I walked towards the door.

"Wait a moment," begged the men; and I waited while they talked together in a corner.

They came back to me. "Are you determined to see the lady?"

"Yes! I have told you that I must see her and be satisfied of her identity—or I go away, my work not done."

"Then," said the spokesman dejectedly, "she is not here. I will take you to her."

We drove twenty minutes before we arrived at the right house. I had been received by the representatives whose interest was in opposition to hers! Whom I would have interviewed behind that purdah, in the wrong house, I never discovered.

The "spotlight" case of this bit of the road was that of my "Imprisoned Rani"; and it came to me in a curious way.

An old priest appeared at my brother's house one morning. He said he had been tracing us from town to town. He did not know our name: but he was looking for "The Brother and Sister Ballisters."

His search finally narrowed to Allahabad, and he was directed to our yellow bungalow with the orange honeysuckle climbing over the porch.

The story he told was pathetic.

He was Chief Priest in a north-country Raj, which his ancestors had served before him, being rewarded with a grant of lands. His patron, the Raja, was sonless. He had two daughters, and consoled himself by educating the elder "as if she were a man," which meant, in their vernacular, the Hindi tongue. Her aptitude was so great that she even edited a Hindi newspaper from the Zenana, and her father, desiring to keep her beside him, deferred her marriage.

She was sixteen when her mother felt that marriage could be delayed no longer, and the Confidential Priest, complete with horoscope, was sent on a tour to find a suitable husband. At Benares, he met another priest on a like errand, looking for a suitable wife for the adopted son of the Dowager Rani of Amarpur.

"The lady must have brains and be educated," said he of Amarpur.

"The very thing," said the other. "My lady is cleverer and more learned than a man."

They compared their respective horoscopes, and found them to agree in essentials. The stars of each were favourable to the other, and marriage arrangements went forward.

Now the Amarpur priest had omitted some vital items of information. The prospective bridegroom was "wanting"—"God had made him a Fool"—as said his royal bride, later on—had said it in no accusation or bitterness, indeed as if speaking of one sanctified by the notice of God—even to his detriment.

And his natural father and uncle were Ministers of the Amarpur Raj. These men had plans other than the Dowager-Rani Adoptive Mother's.

They had in fact already bespoken a non-Royal bride, meaning to control the Raj upon the death of the Dowager. She was Purdahnashin, and they were all-powerful: so that on the marriage day two wedding processions made gay the streets of the town. First came the royal lady's. And, looking on her, her mother-in-law, the Dowager, so loved her that the _Runnumai, or "seeing-of-the-face money," which she gave her, was greater than was ever known in the history of the Family: and is spoken of to this day. The second procession, which the Dowager did not see, took place after an interval of a few hours; the Raja being married secondly to the non-Royal choice of his Ministers.

That his lady was however Pat (Chief) Rani was some consolation to the Confidential Priest who saw both *tamashas* (shows): but he felt terribly deceived, and did not know how to face his patron.

Custom in Amarpur shut the door on all connection with the Royal Bride's people instantly the marriage ceremonies were concluded. The Pat Rani was not allowed even the ministrations in her new "Chapel" of the Confidential Priest.

And her father in his northern hills had perforce to be content with custom. One comfort was that his daughter could write: and there was great rejoicing over the birth of her first son—rejoicing turned to mourning at report of his instant demise.

The letters of the Pat Rani were restrained: no details were given, and her mother might not visit her. It is contrary to general custom for an orthodox Hindu mother to go to the house of her son-in-law, even when her daughter is in trouble.

According to Raj custom elsewhere, the child might have been born in its maternal grandmother's house. But the Amarpur priests said that their own custom forbade that.

Soon letters stopped coming altogether, and the Pat Rani's parents were miserable. They could find no way of getting past that misfortune: and her father fretted at his helplessness. In about five years from the date of his daughter's marriage, he died.

But the Pat Rani about this time did write a letter, though not to her home. She wrote to the nearest British official, saying that she was again about to be a mother, and that she claimed British protection for the birth of her child. She said that two children had already been killed after birth: the first being stifled in tobacco fumes, the second strangled.

Her children were sons, the second lady's all daughters, and the Raj officials said that the Pat Rani had bewitched her co-wife. The Dowager had been very kind to her, but she had died within a year of the marriage, so that the poor little lady had been alone in her trouble, and was still defenceless within the Raj.

"I claim protection from the British Government for the birth of the Raja's heir," said the Pat Rani in her letter; and it was then she added, "The murders are not his fault: God has made him a Fool." She begged the British official to make his own investigations as to the truth of her story. He did so; and apparently found it correct, for he arranged for the removal of the Pat Rani to Sihur, a fortress five miles distant from Amarpur.

It was a fort in good repair, had a reliable wall loopholed for defence, a relic of early wars, and a very strong gateway. There were indeed two gateways with an inner and an outer moat. The British official put a guard on the Outer Gate, Indians from a British *Tehsil*.* That was wise, but he made one mistake—he allowed the Amarpur State to pay the wages of the guard.

The lady was to receive a maintenance allowance as long as she

---

*A *tehsil* is a division in the colonial administration. A *tehsildar (tahsildar)* is one who is in charge of the administration of a tehsil.—Ed.

remained in the fort. Had he known more about conditions in Raj estates, he would have made the guards' wages pass either through the hands of the Tehsildar at the nearest British outpost, or of the lady herself.

It was understood that there was no quarrel between the Raja and the Pat Rani; and that the Raja would visit her whenever he pleased. Apparently (as I heard later from the Pat Rani) he had "pleased" only once, when, while out hunting, he "lost his way" into the fortress through the guards' private wicket; and then after sitting looking at her for a while, said, "Let me go, lest I be moved to compassion and help you!"

The Pat Rani's third son was born in the fortress and stayed alive. . . .

The story thus far had filtered to the Pat Rani's people through the British Official: and had greatly reassured her old mother. But that was ten years previously. A new Administrator was now in charge of the District who knew nothing of the lady in the fortress, and said he could not interfere in the affairs of an estate not under his control.

The Confidential Priest had tried several times to get access to the fortress; but found unfriendly guards on the gate who threatened to shoot at sight any messenger from the "prisoner's" relations.

It was at this stage that the Confidential Priest—remorse for his part in arranging this marriage ever gnawing at him—heard of me, and came seeking.

"Would I go and see the Pat Rani, and at least bring news of her to her mother, taking whatever steps I might find necessary, according to her situation, thereafter."

The story of this adventure as it unfolded itself, I told at the time, August 1899, in letters to a friend in England, at whose instance the Letters were published.*

Here, I will only say, briefly, that I went by train and palanquin—a tortuous journey not without its excitements; that using a mixture of bluff and authority, I made my way into the fortress past the guard, and found the lady with her son, a boy of nine years of age; that they were in abject poverty, living on the terrace of the topmost story of the fort; their furniture two string beds and a chair; their provisions a little rice, and pulse and grain; no milk, no vegetables. The villagers just outside the fortress had been forbidden to supply her with anything. She never, of course, left the fortress, but a half-witted Brahmin brought her monthly, from a distant village, her meagre stores, and

---

*"Concerning an Imprisoned Rani," *Nineteenth Century and After,* October 1901.

drew water for her from the well in the courtyard. To eke out the stores, the Pat Rani herself ate only one slight meal a day. She cooked and kept the little terrace as clean as she could, sewed garments for the boy made out of her saris, and read over and over again all old newspapers which she could find at the fort.

("I should have gone mad if I let myself think," she said.)

One little thing which annoyed was a religious taboo; neither she nor the half-wit might use a broom (that would have been against caste rules). But she thought of a way out. The boy not having yet been tonsured, or given the sacred thread of initiation, was outside caste for the moment, and he was set to do the sweeping.

Every room in that fortress was the home of malodorous bats. The terrace, in reality a flat roof verandahed off where they slept, was at least airy, and the Pat Rani showed her intelligence in retiring to it when deprived of the servants whom the British official had seen accompanying her into her retreat.

The next deprivation was that of her maintenance allowance. For two and a half years she had had not a penny, and only the dry stores which the half-wit brought her.

Her supreme anxiety was for her son. He was still the only son—though girls came thick and fast in the Junior Rani's Zenana at the Capital.

And the nights were her terror. She decided not to sleep at all, and kept her vow, walking up and down armed with an old sword, while the child slept. Luckily the door which gave on to the staircase was iron-studded. She kept this barred and bolted always; and in the afternoons, the boy fed, her household work done, she repaired the sleepless night, while the child played beside her, and as it were guarded himself. For he knew he must wake her if a soul—whosoever—approached.

She was wonderful in her fearlessness.

Having got my facts and cheered her up, I returned to Allahabad, and arranged through British intervention for servants and food to be sent her. Later, after discovering how I could rightly serve her interests, I went back again with two empty palanquins to bring her and the boy to the guardianship of her mother in British India. Permission to take this course was given in response to an application put in by the mother, it having been proved that the Pat Rani was virtually imprisoned in circumstances originally designed for her protection.

The second journey was thrilling. I was warned that the Amarpur people had got wind of my programme and had planned to *dacoit* [ambush] us on the homeward journey and carry off the boy.

Two armed Tehsil peons had been provided by the British Administration for our protection, but we lost them, diverted by some trick of the Amarpur folk.

I determined to try and outwit the dacoits. I had my own servants with me, and sent my headman on by the regular route, telling him to sit by the village watch-fires at night and listen to the *gap* (gossip); though travelling quickly, so as to reach the fortress, in any case by the afternoon of the second day, when we were due to leave for Allahabad. I myself, with the other servants, the extra palanquin and a rabble of thirty bearers, went a short cut across country, arriving at the fortress only eight hours before we must again take the road. Would that space of time be long enough to dig the lady and her son out of their prison?

It all depended on how the great excitement of an escape affected my little lady.

It was indeed a ghastly day. She broke down, and was hysterical, presenting difficulty after difficulty. She could not travel except under the Gold Umbrella of Royalty in a heavy ancient Raj palanquin found in a godown near the Guardhouse. The poles of this relic were rotten, and the bearers refused to carry it.

Again, she could not travel apart from her son: he and she must be in one palanquin.

I conceded that.

And in the same palanquin must be put her *huqqa*, all her personal belongings, the food cooked for the journey, and her pots and pans and cooking vessels! I knew that cooking and eating vessels she must take, for not being a widow she might not use those found in her mother's house. But it would have been no use suggesting that *all* the luggage might go together in one of our spare palanquins. She was too upset to be reasonable.

So I contented myself, since time was racing, with persuading her to do without the Gold Umbrella, but (*baksheesh* [tips] making the bearers willing) I packed her and the son and the luggage into the Raj "relic."

"At least let me have the embroidered-*kincob* cover," she begged. And we threw it over the palanquin.

Quick then, past both moats, through the outer gateway.

Here my headman met us, breathless, and took me aside to give his news. We were to be dacoited at seven o'clock that evening on the regular route, the way he had come. I had to make an instant decision.

We must take the cross-country road in the opposite direction and start at once, for any moment our change of plan might be discovered.

It was extra important now not to risk the heavy worm-eaten "relic." So since hysterics could avail my Pat Rani nothing outside the gates, I turned the entire guard inside the fortress and shut the gates on them. We then put one of our light spare palanquins close beside the relic, covering both with the betraying kincob (it was useful now), set the doors between wide, and made the Rani and her son creep from the relic to the other, transferring also their impedimenta.

The kincob, having served its use as a purdah, I firmly folded up: my ayah (maid) I put into the second spare palanquin: and we started off in a long "line of march"—I first, and the Rani's palanquin between mine and the ayah's. The menservants and "relief" palanquin-bearers brought up the rear.

Every nerve was a-stretch throughout that devious journey: the fields of tall corn, on a pitch-dark night, which might conceal anything, a squad of dacoits for all we knew; the open spaces, where we ourselves were only too visible; rough ground where the bearers had to be encouraged every five minutes—and then the early dawn when things look gloomiest, and the long hot day that followed, though this was happily in safer territory.

But the journey had its humours in the songs made by the palanquin-bearers about the Rani and myself—personal descriptions, and conjectures (for instance) as to how much we ate! I was slim in those days. Also, my not being in purdah, had evidently greatly intrigued country folk unaccustomed to women of my race—Who could I be?

"She spoke like the Burra Lat Sahib (Viceroy) to the guard, turning the men in, shutting the gates on them. *And they obeyed.* Who can she be!" sang the leader.

And the Chorus chaunted—"Who *can* she be?"

"She wears garments of silk, but (contemptuously) eats only one bread a day."

The Chorus—"Half-a-bread! . . ."

We travelled from 5 p.m., when we had left the fort, all that night, and all the next day, with only one break for food for the Rani and the bearers—getting to railhead at 10 p.m. on the second night. Here a reserved railway carriage, next to my own compartment, was secured for my charges, and in due time she was delivered safely to her mother.

The end of the story was happy. A Lunacy Commission made suitable arrangements for the care of the poor Raja: the boy was put under

British protection and his estate administered till his majority should give him the *gadi* [power, status] of his inheritance.

LAKSHMIBAI TILAK ———————————————

(1868–1936)   *Marathi*

Literary historians speak of Lakshmibai's chatty, humorous autobiography more as a work of art than as a record of a life. Though Lakshmibai has written little else, her autobiography, which is one of the earliest in modern Marathi literature, ensures that she is among the few women writers unfailingly mentioned in mainstream histories of Marathi literature.

Some of Lakshmibai's tenacity, her independence, and her spirit of rebellion are often related to traditions of courage and resistance in the family. Her grandfather, Vasudev Bhagwat Joglekar, was hanged in 1857 in the aftermath of the Sepoy Rebellion. Part one of her autobiography, *Smriti Chitre* (Memory Sketches), describes the childhood of this spirited girl who was married at eleven to the poet Narayan Waman Tilak. Tilak had had a classical Sanskrit education and was well read in the poetry of the medieval Marathi saints. In Lakshmibai's writing he comes through not only as a warm, generous and impulsive person but also as one who rarely stopped to consider what his spontaneity might cost others. Though it was Tilak who secretly helped a young Lakshmi, terrified of the dark, to draw water from the well each night because her father-in-law insisted, it was also Tilak who pushed her roughly down the stairs when she was seven months pregnant because he was losing an indoor game they were playing together. Possibly because laughter was the most efficient strategy she could use, but possibly also because only the veil of humor enabled the chronicling of such experiences, Lakshmibai describes the incident as though it were a hilarious affair, though she also comments, in passing, "without doubt that day my infirmity brought me face to face with death. I was saved by so small a margin." The chapter concludes, "Tilak wrote a farce about his own temper. It was left half-finished." Most of her early married life was spent coping with the harsh idiosyncrasies of her father-in-law, who seemed determined to thwart and humiliate her constantly. Later she followed Tilak from Khandesh to Varhad, to Pune, to Bombay, to Vani, and to Murhad. Tilak changed his profession from *puranik* to *kirtankar* (a person who reads the scriptures aloud in public places and sings religious songs) to a printing press worker and ultimately to a schoolteacher. Often he disappeared for days on end, leaving Lakshmibai insecure and sick with tension. She invariably turned to her elder sister, Bhiku, and her husband, Pendse, who were constant supports in times of trouble.

Though Lakshmibai suspected it might happen, Tilak's conversion to Christianity in 1895 came as a surprise and a shock to her. Her subsequent breakdown and attempts at suicide are dealt with in a couple of short chapters in the autobiography, but it was five years before even she, a strong, resourceful person, was able to come to terms with the repugnance she felt for his new "unclean" religion and the social censure his action brought. She was torn between her love and her loyalty to her husband, in whose footsteps she had been brought up as a good Hindu woman to believe she should follow, and his (what seemed to her) totally unreasonable rejection of their religion and culture. Readers today have imaginative access to what Tilak's gesture must have meant in his time not only from Lakshmibai's reactions but from the responses of those around her. Clearly neither her sister, Bhiku nor Bhiku's husband, Pendse, her brother, Keshav, Tilak's younger brother, Sakharam, or even Tilak himself considered her disturbance, or her desire to kill herself, excessive or unwarranted. Finally, as much out of defeat as desire, she and their son, Dattu, went back to live with Tilak. In 1900, she became a Christian, though the changes in eating habits, life style, and association this involved continued to disturb her and sap her energy. Yet she coped, and in the process grew, as did the bond between this unusual wife and husband. The first extract reprinted here deals with this tumultuous period in her life and is taken from the much-acclaimed part two of her autobiography, which was translated in the early 1950s by Josephine Inkster and published as *I Follow After*.

It is mainly through Lakshmibai's writing that we get a sense of Tilak as a theologian and philosopher, and of Lakshmibai's own involvement in exploring their ideas and putting them into practice. When Lakshmibai wrote, "It is possible to say that the course of the thought of the Christian community was changed from the day of Tilak's baptism," she was not far wrong. Tilak regarded Christianity not as a religion but as yoga, and the universal love Christ preached, as identity with the ethical and religious foundation of life, in the true sense of the word. As can be seen in the poems and religious songs, the *bhajans* and *kirtans,* composed by this writer couple, and in Tilak's accounts of his conversion, they regarded Christianity as the fruition of the promise held in Hindu philosophy itself. Not surprisingly, they were, like Pandita Ramabai, to come into conflict with the more simplistic evangelical aspirations of some of their missionary mentors. Lakshmibai's own exasperation, which often borders on disdain for the narrow-minded irrationality of these missionaries, is clearly evident in the less well-known, posthumously published, part four of her autobiography, excerpts of which have been translated here. The mature, self-confident authorial self in this extract gives us a sense of how much this woman changed, intellectually and as a person, in the years after Tilak died in 1912.

Among Lakshmibai's writings are a collection of lyric poems entitled *Bharali Gagar* (The Filled Pitcher) and a long poem entitled *Christayan,* the life of Christ written in verse. Tilak, who started the work, wrote the first eleven *adhyayas,* or chapters, but the remaining sixty-one were written by Lakshmibai, who finished it after his death. Of the social novel that she writes so amusingly about in the autobiography, we have no evidence.

◆

From SMRITI CHITRE
(Memory Sketches)
Part II, Chapter 1. Devgharatha Basavile (I Am
Led to the Shrine)

Tilak forsook the house of the landlord of Chandori to walk up the front doorsteps of Dr. Justin Abbott. He left the train at Bombay, sought out the American Mission High School, and entered. . . . Tilak and Dr. Abbott had been corresponding for a long time. Tilak was taken in, and after they had made him study the Christian religion for four months he was baptized in the American Mission Church in the Bhendi Bazar, Bombay. It is possible to say that the course of the thought of the Christian community was changed from the day of Tilak's baptism.

The news of Tilak's baptism spread like wildfire on all sides. It was heard at once in Nasik. All his friends and relatives began to come in a steady stream to see Pendse, but Pendse arranged that no one should say a word inside the house. When people came they sat in silence. Some of them would turn toward me and Dattu, screw up their faces and wipe their eyes. When I saw this pantomime I fell into an indescribable state of mind. I wondered if Tilak had been killed in some terrible accident. "A man's own mind is his worst enemy."

Pendse sat stolidly leaning his head outside the window, his brow clasped tightly in his hands. We gazed at one another with vacant eyes. No one spoke. At the most we just wiped away our tears.

Dattu was in an extraordinary position. People were forever lifting him up, or giving him something to eat, but no one would speak. When I saw all this the strength in my hands and knees turned to water.

One day Pendse hired two bullock carts and sent the whole family off to see the Pandav Leni caves near Nasik. Only Bhiku and Pendse stayed behind. Next he sent a tonga to Jalalpur to fetch Keshav. He wanted to discuss freely with Bhiku and Keshav what should be said and done without letting me overhear anything. Pendse began, "Well, Keshav, what has happened has happened. What is to be done now?"

Keshav replied, "We are two brothers. We must look after her as if she were a third maimed, lamed brother, whom it is our duty to support."

Pendse said, "That is so, but we shall see presently what is to be done with her. First of all we must get reliable information about Tilak. I think you should go to Bala in Bombay, and the two of you can look for him. If he has really changed his religion it is another matter. If not, take this ring, drop it into his pocket or somewhere, and then inform the Police. The prosecution will be held here. We can see then what to do. Here are twenty-five rupees to take with you."

Keshav left at once. Bala was the son of Pendse's elder brother. The two men searched every Mission in Bombay. Finally they learned that Tilak was at Bassein, and at once followed him there.

Tilak met the pair of them, and asked them why they had come. Keshav replied, "We came to look for you."

Tilak said, "I have become a Christian. Look after your sister. The river Godavari runs by both Nasik and Jalalpur. See that she does not commit suicide."

"Whether she lives or dies you have now nothing to do with her." So saying Keshav and Bala left Bassein, their hearts very heavy. As he left Keshav saw that the sacred lock of hair on Tilak's head had been cut, and he sobbed aloud. However angry he had tried to appear, his eyes had been brimming over from the beginning, now the very last tear was drained out of his heart.

As soon as Keshav returned home he went and sat near the bed where Bhiku lay. He told her everything. She was nearly choked with tears.

"Tell Lakshmi anything you like," she said, "I cannot say a word to her." I was called upstairs. I was so overcome with apprehension I could not climb the steps. Like a small child, drawing myself up by my hands I came, and sat before my brother and sister. My brother began a sermon: how many chaste and dutiful wives had there been, Sita, Savitri, Tara and Draupadi, whose fame would last for ever. I broke in, "I know all the scriptures. Did you call me to give me a sermon? You went to Bombay to get word of Tilak. Tell me first, is he alive?"

"Yes, he is alive, safe, happy. He has got work as a teacher there but ... but. ..."

"Then why 'But'?"

"He is a Christian."

"Then let him be one! Enough that he is somewhere, and that he is well. Though he has gone he has not taken so much as a bit of skin off my forehead, or touched my fate written on it."

I spoke, rose, and descended the stairs in a hurry. Having reached the bottom, the strength flowed out of me completely. The rest of the women in the house were waiting anxiously by the door. They caught me, and made me sit down. They had all heard the news before I had, and now began to comfort me.

"Never mind if he has gone. God has given you a son of gold. One child is worth all the world. He will prove a dutiful son to his mother. You will enjoy as much happiness in the future as you endure sorrow now." The whole of this sermon was as water poured onto an upturned vessel. I had become as stone. I could not shed a tear. My throat was completely dry.

Most of our relations came to spend the night with Pendse. No one ate any dinner. No one spoke a word. One after another they came, spread on the floor whatever they could find and lay down to sleep where they fell. Not one said to another "Come in," "Sit down," "Eat something, drink something."

There was a large number of us sleeping in the house. I was in the middle. On one side lay Keshav and on the other Bhiku. Each of them had thrown an arm over me. At about one or two o'clock sleep began to weave her net. Everyone was caught in it except me. Very gently I drew off the arms encircling me from either side. Binding up the loose end of my sari tightly I looked for Dattu, but could not see him. I then retraced my steps. Going to the front door I began to lift the wooden-bar.

At that instant the night watchman's "All's well" fell on my ears, making a new thought master of my mind. If these men should catch me and take me to the Police Station, and if there were an inquiry on the morrow, the world would babble that I was the sister-in-law of such and such a man, and Pendse would be put to shame. It had been my intention to throw myself into a deep pool in the river, but I changed my mind, and went and stood by the household well. It was a very narrow well. Now came the thought, that if I committed suicide here my body could not be retrieved without infinite trouble; and at the Police investigation the next day Pendse would have to hang his head for me. My ears were buzzing. I could see no way open before me.

I returned to my bed, and lay down. In a little while I grasped Keshav's hand so fiercely that he woke in a fright, and roused Bhiku with, "Bhiku, look at what Lakshmi is doing." Everyone awoke, and sat up. They all began asking each other, "What has happened? What has happened?" Keshav managed to unclasp my hand, and with that it seemed that all the strength drained out of me. I was quite conscious. I knew all that was going on about me, but in no wise could I move.

Each one had a different remedy of his own to suggest. My jaws were locked. Some said I had had a shock, some that I had taken poison. Bhiku replied, "She has not a farthing. How could she buy poison?" Someone suggested that I had swallowed powdered glass. A new kind of glass bangle had just appeared on the market and my sister had bought nine each for Gharu and me. She at once counted mine.

A doctor was brought. He could not find my pulse, and he also gave the opinion that I had taken poison. They began to try to open my teeth, and pour a little medicine between them. I was aware of everything, but lay like a log of wood. My tongue was drawn together and covered with prickles which did not go away for a whole month. Bhiku's sickness vanished, and rolling up her bed she now spent night and day standing beside me. She had to wait on me hand and foot. I could only lie [down]. She even had to brush my teeth. From time to time I was given milk and butter milk. Many days later my strength returned a little, and I began to sit up in bed.

Now were the flood gates of my tears opened. I cried continuously. My tears could not be dammed, unless indeed there was respite in sleep. I spoke to no one. One day I went to the house of someone living in the same courtyard, and sat down weeping. Dattu spent all his time with Bhiku, but seeing me now sitting in a new place, he came up, and taking my hand led me to the shrine of the house, and made me sit down; then he said, "Mother, cry in my aunt and uncle's house. Do not cry in other people's. Tell me what you want. Do you want lots of jewellry like cousin Gharu, or bangles and bracelets like Aunty? Or do you want a beautiful bordered sari? Tell me, but do not sit crying!"

Bhiku was standing nearby. Clasping him to her breast, and weeping herself, she said, "Borrow a little of his good sense." Dattu's comforting words only increased my grief.

Part II, Chapter 2. Kortat Bhet (Divorce Indeed)

Gopal* heard in Nagpur that Tilak had become a Christian, and at once went to Bassein to see him; he then came on to Nasik to me. At the sight of him I burst out sobbing, and so did he. Through his tears he said, "Bai, look on me as your elder son and Dattu as your younger." Having said this he left. Immediately afterwards he sent me ten rupees from Panchwati, meaning to send the same amount every month, but my brothers and sisters did not approve, and let him know, though in such a way as would not hurt his feelings. He also wrote to say he would bring his wife and children to see me. This plan did not materialize either.

That hot weather Tilak went for the first time to Mahabaleshwar. Gopal also rented a bungalow there intending to take me and Dattu. For some unavoidable reason that I cannot remember this plan too came to nothing.

While in Mahabaleshwar Tilak began to write the first of his famous poems on flowers and children. Dr. R. A. Hume of Nagar, more or less kept him in his own house. There were Dr. Hume's children, his sister's children and all the wild flowers growing in Mahabaleshwar, and well did it suit Tilak's mood to write of them. His famous poem, "The brown hair flowing freely down her back," was written about that graceful child, Miss Fairbank. His alleged consumption vanished in this happy environment. When he left Mahabaleshwar, Tilak began to study in Nagar Theological College under Dr. Hume, and at the same time also began to teach some subjects as well.

Pendse was transferred to Pandharpur. Sakharam was already there, and I went with Pendse. Yet as I was, so I remained; that is, the tears never dried out of my eyes, and no speech fell from my lips. Everything had to be done for me by Bhiku and Vahini,—the widow of Pendse's brother.** She was the stepmother of Bala and a child widow. Dattu was very fond of her. From the colour of her widow's sari he called her Red Aunty. He had named all his aunts in this way. "Short Aunt," "Thin Aunt," "Red Aunt." And each aunt was amused when she heard her own name. Bhiku was fat, so she was called "Fat Aunty."

No sooner had we arrived in Pandharpur, than Bhiku engaged a master for Dattu. She thought that if Dattu could learn and make good,

---

*One of Tilak's students, son of a rich landlord, Appasaheb Buti, whose tenants Tilak and Lakshmibai were. Gopal was practically brought up in the Tilak household.—Ed.

**Vahini is an affectionate term for sister-in-law.—Ed.

all would be mended, she need have no more anxiety for her sister. She was forever urging him on to study. Pendse would protest, "Why worry him? Let him play. He is not so old yet. He will learn in time." But Bhiku never swerved from her set purpose. Pendse used to spoil Dattu. He would never sit down to a meal without him. Bhiku thought Dattu should not be present when his uncle was eating. When it was time for a meal she would say, "Dinner time," and Dattu would say, "I shall play outside Aunt." Pendse was always grieved to hear this suggestion and its answer. Bhiku was afraid Dattu would annoy him. Better, she thought, that Pendse himself should call for him. Nevertheless, not for one day did Pendse dine without Dattu. He used to call him Tilak, and as soon as he was back from his work he would look for him. "Where is Tilak? Call him for dinner. Tilak, ho Tilak! Here is a sweet for you." Then Dattu would come, and both sit down to dinner. This was the daily routine.

"Red Aunt" had to ask Dattu's advice everyday about what should be cooked for their light supper, and dishes were prepared accordingly.

I just lay on my bed. With difficulty I was forced to eat. Presently I began to tear my sari to pieces, and Bhiku thought I would lose my reason altogether. Better that I should die! Who would look after a mad woman after she, Bhiku, was gone? Tilak heard of the state in which I was, and a telegram came from him. Up to now we had not even had a letter from him, but at last I received one, and in it an addressed envelope. In absolute secrecy I wrote to him. I was not allowed to send letters, and I never wrote anything but poetry. I remember three or four lines of the one in my first letter.

Oh Friend, as cruel as a second wife,
My own thoughts make a burden of my life,
I have a sister, Hope, relief to bring;
Yet slave Anxiety hath words that sting.

One other poem I sent to him [was entitled] "A Husband." My new occupation brought back some semblance of life to me, but Tilak would not believe it was I who wrote and sent the poems.

Sakharam was also in Pandharpur and used to come and see me every day. There was a rumour in circulation that Sakharam sent Tilak a hundred rupees a month to spend. Even though Tilak was a Christian and she was very angry with him, Bhiku could not help feeling proud of him. When she heard the rumour she scolded Sakharam well.

One day he came when Pendse was at his dinner. A low wooden

seat was set for Sakharam. Bhiku came and stood before him saying, "Since when has your brother become no better than a barber?"

Sakharam completely failed to understand her action and words. He said, "I do not understand what you are saying."

"Why shouldn't you understand? Who will believe that you send your brother one hundred rupees a month when you do not even see that Lakshmi's saris here are in rags!"

Sakharam listened to all this quietly, his head bowed. The next day he sent me a sari and Dattu two shirts.

Another day Sakharam came and sat down beside me. Having talked of this and that he gently broached the subject of Tilak. I was lying [down,] giving only grunts in reply.

"Lakshmi," he said, "you are ill. See how many people there are to look after you. Do you think anyone is looking after Tilak? Tell me. If you give him a divorce, he will be free. There are plenty of people to care for you."

When I heard this I sat up promptly. "And was there no one to take care of him? Who keeps him away now? How can I give him a divorce? Have I run away? Or have I left him? I have no money, no education, my child is young, what can I do? Shall I not sit and polish pots for all of you till I die? Enough of your interference! Send him a letter saying, 'First get your wife married properly and then arrange for your own marriage.' Do you not realise to whom you are speaking?"

As I spoke, I stood up. Sakharam listened to it all with his head down.

I got a letter from Tilak every day, sometimes even three at a time. If I wrote at all, it was only a poem. I had nothing to ask of him, nothing to tell him. A wire to Pendse one day said, "I am coming to see Lakshmi." Pendse sent a return wire, "Do not come to my house."

The household fell straightway into the state we were in in Nasik. No one ate, no one slept, no one spoke to anyone else. I knew nothing of the cause of it.

At eight o'clock in the morning Tilak was in Pandharpur. By two in the afternoon there was still no answer from Pendse. Tilak was very annoyed to get no reply to so many letters, and in the end wrote this: "I have come on purpose to see my wife, because I hear she is not well. Since my arrival I have sent three or four conciliatory letters from here. You have not replied to one. I am very hurt. I shall not leave until I have seen her. I did not intend to go against you, but tomorrow I shall meet her in the court of law."

Part II, Chapter 3. Masteranchi Katpat (The Headmaster's Help)

The letter arrived. Pendse called Bhiku and asked her what way she could see out of the predicament.

"You must do what is right," she said. "I know no law, but rather than have a scene tomorrow let us take Lakshmi quietly to meet him today. Then he will go away."

"Do not be at all anxious about Lakshmi. I shall never let her run away with him. We shall send her for an interview. Vahini can go with her. I shall also provide two servants." Pendse then wrote to Tilak saying he would send me to meet him after nine o'clock at night. If he had time he should wait, if not there was no help for it. All I knew was that Tilak was in Pandharpur. I knew nothing of the commotion it had caused.

Pendse and Bhiku were in the sitting room talking, and I was stretched on my bed as usual, when Yesu came to call me. Yesu,— later the wife of Dr. Bhat of Yaola, was Pendse's granddaughter. She delivered her message that Pendse had sent for me. Accordingly I went and sat down before the two of them.

Pendse began, "Lakshmi, do you want to see Tilak?"

I said, "Yes," and at once he rejoined, "Then lay your hands on my feet and swear that you will not go away with him."

I touched his feet, and swore, "I shall not go with Tilak," then straightway retired. Bhiku followed me talking volubly.

"Out of sheer love have I given hospitality to my sister, and now we are faced with a court case." These words had an extraordinary effect upon me. I hardly knew myself what I was doing, but was afflicted with a desire for motion. From upstairs to the centre hall, centre hall to the flat roof, from the roof to my bed, back upstairs to recommence the round, I went. Bhiku was very upset when she saw me. "What insane behaviour is this? Go mad and complete the orphaned state of a son [who is like] gold. Your husband has lit a torch so you must start a bonfire!" I heard everything she said and understood too, but as I had begun, so did I continue till evening. Why I should have behaved like this I myself still do not understand.

Evening came and then supper time for all. I still had a great deal of doubt as to whether they would send me to meet Tilak or not. My whole attention was fixed on the tonga, horses and servants. I could not speak to anyone, because every one was keeping watch over me. I was besieged by the fatal nine constellations, office-servants, house-servants, women-servants, water-carriers, cook, sister, Vahini, Yesu, Pendse. I could not move from here to there for the strictness of their guard. I was pestered with questions from everyone. "What are you doing?" "What are you eating?" "Where are you going?" "What are you writing?" Though I only went out of the back door, someone was with me.

The clock struck nine, and my heart began to beat faster. I had doubts whether I should see Tilak or not, and my suspicion grew. I watched the courtyard below steadily. At last the horse was harnessed. Vahini threw her shawl round her shoulders, and her call of "Lakshmi" fell upon my ears. I came out as soon as I heard her, and seeing me, Pendse said, "Lakshmi, do you remember what I told you? Take care or I shall put the police onto you. You know who I am." I only nodded my head. Pendse having finished, Bhiku came forward. Her blow was on the other side: "Lakshmi have pity on this child." To her too I answered with a nod of my head. My mind was full of fear, and my heart aquiver at the thought of what was in store for me. I was trembling in every limb. My mouth was dry. All my life was in my eyes, and the end of my sari took its measure in tears from time to time.

Somehow or other I descended the stairs, then I was lifted into the tonga. We five people,—two servants, the driver, myself, and Vahini, with five mouths entreated God's mercy as we sped along.

Tilak was standing at the door of the rest-house for travellers, watch in hand. As soon as he saw the tonga he went inside. I was lifted down and placed before him by two men. He was standing. Straightway I laid my forehead on his feet. "Tell me in what I have sinned against you that you should behave so strangely, then I shall loose your feet."

"You have not sinned against me in anything," he said, and withdrew his feet. Done! That was all we said. Tilak was leaning up against a post. Neither of us could say any more.

Translated by Josephine Inkster.

Part IV, Chapter 2. Mumbai (Bombay)

Ever since I was a child of eleven, I had lived with and by the side of Tilak. We had lived apart for five years in between, but not for a single moment of those five years had Tilak moved from before my eyes, nor I from before his. What I am today is because of him. If he wished to reach a goal, I was there to help him to it; if he wrote a poem I was there to sing it; if he had to beg, I was there to carry the begging bowl.

We quarreled only when I found it impossible to keep up with the speed of his progress. I was like a cart tied to the Deccan Queen* in full speed, bumping and crashing along behind him. But when he slowed down to a speed I could manage and gave me enough time to understand which way he was going, then our carriage ran smooth on the rails. Tilak was like a steam engine, running on his own power, and I like a carriage that ran on the speed imparted by the engine. Once I had worked up momentum, though, there was no stopping me.

But now he who had held the strings of my life had left me. A new world sprang up around me. A new life began.

I could not live in Bombay by bhajans and kirtans. The missionaries offered me a job that was made for widows. Most women who lose the prefix "Saubhagyawati" (married woman) automatically become matrons of girls' hostels. I became a matron at forty-five rupees a month with spacious living space and permission to keep my family with me. I cannot describe my joy. It is true Tilak was no more; but at least I had my children, Dattu and Baby, and my daughter-in-law Ruth, with me. I was content.

And so I stepped into the kindergarten class. I began to learn the alphabet. I had to check accounts written in English. Dattu used to be out at work, Baby at college, and Ruth was away at her parents'. So they gave me a key to the accounts. They taught me numbers and showed me how I could recognize grocery items by their initial letters. C was coconut, S was sugar, P was potatoes, and T was tea. That is how I managed to check the accounts and sign for them.

One of my jobs as matron was to open the mail and read it before passing it out to the girls. I'd get Dattu or Baby to read out the English letters to me. The world had always been kind to me. Nobody had ever refused me help. Even here there were many who helped me. There were about 250 girls in the hostel. Some of the older ones had volunteered to take over some of my chores completely. They swept and dusted, dealt with the washerman and kept an eye on the *bhakri* makers.

Madamsahib** was in the habit of making two visits a day, though I

---

*A "superfast" train, running between Bombay and Pune, that had just been introduced when Lakshmibai was writing in 1936.—Ed.

**Madamsahib* is the term for the white "madam" in charge of the hostel. Lakshmibai deliberately does not use her name.—Ed.

wasn't sure why. I had never been in this kind of a job before. But I was told by the girls that the matron was expected to whisper complaints in madamsahib's ear twice a day. The whisperings might, for instance, be about the secret letter this one had received, or the secret glance that one had cast; about how this one had answered back or how that one was not on speaking terms with the other one. The whispering over, punishments would be meted out to fit every crime.

But how could all the girls be alike? Two hundred and fifty girls from 250 homes. Even children born of the same parents are so different from each other. And that is the fun of it. What would we have done with 250 Pune dolls? If there is no wickedness, how is goodness to be recognized?

Certainly, many of the girls were mischievous. They picked up pranks from each other. One evening during study time I thought I heard men's voices upstairs. I went up to investigate, but I only saw girls. As I came down, I again heard men's voices. I went back up and once again I could see only girls there. I thought I was going crazy. Finally one girl felt sorry for me and let out the secret. She even spoke in a man's voice to show me how.

By and large, though, the girls were kind to me, which is not to say that they didn't get difficult once in a while.

One day a girl asked me to let her see the mail. This wasn't allowed, so I didn't show it to her. She instantly made it the mission of her life to harass me. She carried her intention to the point of burning up my saris in a heap of dried leaves and twigs. I could smell cloth burning but couldn't think what it was.

I hadn't shown the girl the mail because it often contained anonymous letters full of obscenities. I used to burn these letters without showing them either to the management or to the girls for whom they were meant. If I had shown them to the authorities, the concerned girls would have been immediately punished. If I had shown them to the girls, their minds would have been adversely affected. So I thought it better to make burnt offerings of such letters. Not content with obscene letters, the fire god had demanded my saris as well!

Things had happened exactly as Tilak had wished. He had always said that he would not want anybody to mourn for him. He said he would leave behind money enough for a month and then each one would have to fend for himself. We came to Bawkar Hall a month after Tilak's death and we had just one rupee left by then. There was no time to mourn for anybody after that. It was work all day, and fear all night.

Bawkar Hall had a basement. It looked like a vault through the cracks in the floorboards. Cockroaches abounded. In the dead of the night, this cockroach army would march out through the cracks and pitter patter all around us. The girls' empty heads were stuffed as it [was] with ghost stories. The sound of cockroaches scampering around made them behave like crazed ghosts themselves. So, though the work was hard and long, there was never any paucity of excitement.

I carried out an experiment there, which turned out to be successful. I couldn't bring myself to hit the girls when they misbehaved. So I would make the smaller ones stand before me and I would cane myself instead. They felt terribly upset to see their granny punished and they would stop playing pranks. The older girls were made to stand in a corner. One girl whom I had punished in this way couldn't stomach it. She decided to pay me back.

I had kept hens in the backyard to help out with household expenses. I had ordered hens worth twenty-two rupees from Rahuri. Now this girl stole into the backyard at night and killed seven or eight hens by swinging them around and hitting them against the ground. The following day she felt terrible about what she had done. Her anger had drained away completely. She caught a dove and brought it to me. "See how big and lovely this dove is," she said. "It is for you."

I put the dove in a cage. He ate half a chapati at one go, had a drink of water and only then did he raise his head and look around him. Who knows how many days he had been starving. When Dattu got home in the evening, I showed him the bird. "I've always wanted to have a dove," I said. "Tilak used to say he'd get a Zanzibar dove for me one day. Now I have one."

"Ai, we are in such straits. How much did you pay for him?"

"Sixty rupees."

Suddenly the dove began to talk. He sounded just like a man. He even sang. But for the life of us we couldn't make out what language he was speaking and singing in. We were all astounded.

This dove stayed with us till 1932. He learned to imitate the voice and speech of every person in the house. I had always wished to have a dove for a pet. My wish had been granted.

Translated by Shanta Gokhale.

BANDARU ACCHAMAMBA ─────────

(1874–1904)   *Telugu*

Bandaru Acchamamba, the first feminist historian in India, begins her book
on great women in India by quoting a verse in Sanskrit:

> It is not the women imprisoned at home
>   by men who hold them dear who are protected.
> Only those women are truly safe who protect
>   their own souls.

Her book *Abala Saccharitra Ratnamala* (A Garland of Great Women's
Life Histories) was published in 1901, but had been serialized earlier in
the social reformer Kandukuri Veereshalingam's journal, *Chintamani*. Acchamamba had planned a magnum opus in three volumes. In the first, she
would research and write about the lives of great women in India; in the
next, about the women in the Vedas and the great epics; in the third part,
about the lives of great women in other countries. Her objectives in attempting this work, which unfortunately she did not live to complete, are
clearly stated. First, she wanted to demonstrate that women are naturally
possessed of dignity and a sharp intellect, and that the attempt to characterize them as inferior or cowardly was a result of prejudice. Second, she
hoped to prove that women would gain benefits through education and
that it was stupid to argue to the contrary. And third, she wanted to give
the sisterhood of women a major source of information that could be used
in their speeches and talks. The commitments of this massive academic
enterprise are evident. So is Acchamamba's clear analysis of women's issues and her own polemical engagement with the major debates of her
time. Acchamamba's death at the age of thirty, after a long illness, was as
much a loss to women's scholarship and history as it was to the women's
movement.

Acchamamba was born in 1874, in a village called Nandigama. Her father,
who was a diwan (a minister in the state government), died shortly after
she was born. She did not have any formal education, but, her biographer
Pulugurti Lakshmi Narasamamba tells us, like other girls in her day she
sat nearby as her brother was initiated into traditional scholarship. Along
with him she learned Telugu and Hindi and a little Marathi, and was, "in
fact, ahead of him always." When he left for Nagpur to continue with his
studies, she worked on her own, learning Bengali and Gujarati as well as

a little Sanskrit. This remarkable linguistic achievement was to stand her in good stead later.

Both Acchamamba's children died very early. Her biographer suggests that the pain of those losses became the driving force behind her decision to turn to serious study. She was never, however, a cloistered academic. Right through her brief adult life she played a crucial role in building up a women's movement. She started the Brindavan Stree Samajam (Brindavan Women's Association), the first women's association in Machilipatnam, with Oruganti Sundariratnamamba in 1902. In 1903, she traveled all over the state, setting up similar women's organizations. Acchamamba provided shelter to women who needed it, and there were always four or five orphaned children living in her house and going to school.

Acchamamba developed a reputation as one of those women who were so kind and generous that they could convert anyone, however extreme his or her opposition was, to her point of view. Her biographer quotes the example of Acchamamba's husband, who was initially quick to anger and believed in safeguarding the chastity of women by keeping them in strict seclusion. Acchamamba won him over with her goodwill and gentleness. In a period when it was impossible to move even an inch forward without the explicit cooperation of the husband, one finds many women who, like Acchamamba, repeatedly praise their husbands' generosity. Acchamamba dedicates her book to him with the line, "Without your mercy I could not have acquired the ability or the independence to write this book." She also acknowledges her brother, who encouraged her to write this history and helped her at every stage.

Acchamamba was a prolific writer of essays, stories, and poems, published in leading journals such as *Hindu Sundari* and *Saraswati*. Though her main work, *Abala Saccharitra Ratnamala,* is available today, some of her other work, especially a story called "Bida Kutumbam" (A Poor Family), 1904, and *Satakam* (A Cycle of a Hundred Poems), which the writer Lakshmikantamma mentions in her *Andhra Kavayitrulu* (Women Poets of Andhra), 1980, cannot be traced.

Acchamamba traveled all over India, collecting material for her books. She held discussions with scholars and drew on journals in local languages for her information, always carefully documenting her sources. The first part of her book, which took four years to write, contained histories of women from Punjab, Kashmir, Rajasthan, Gujarat, Bengal, Maharashtra, and Andhra. She had just begun work on the second part, publishing sketches of Sita and Draupadi in *Hindu Sundari,* when she died. The women writers she includes in her book are evidence of the range of her reading and the careful contact she maintained with what was happening in the rest of India in her field. But they are also evidence of how soon and how easily these figures were forgotten. Among the writers she includes are Pandita Ramabai, Hardevi, Kashibai Kanitkar, Kamala Sattianadan, and Kotikalapudi Sitamma, many of whom, of course, are also included in these volumes.

In the selection translated here, Acchamamba retrieves the story of Khana, who is mentioned in early accounts as the brilliant wife of the famous astronomer Mihira (some of whose calculations have not, to this day, been surpassed). Acchamamba puts together bits of information from various sources and reconstructs an account of the life of this distinguished couple in which Khana's scholarship and her work as an astronomer are given a new significance. Acchamamba also introduces, in passing, a theme of interest to contemporary feminists and those concerned with the relationship between knowledge and power. She suggests that popular knowledge held by the dark-skinned indigenous people was not only delegitimated and forgotten as the light-skinned Aryan invaders established their dominance, but often formed the hidden and unacknowledged basis of later authority.

◆

KHANA

Years ago Khana acquired great proficiency in astronomy and astrology. She had won fame as a poetess and her poems thrilled people of all ages, young and old. She was known far and wide through the country during her lifetime. But since recording history is not the practice in our country, it has not been possible for us to obtain a complete account of her doings and writings from any source. We have to regret this sorry state of affairs. We do not know who her father and mother were; they both died when she was very young. We know that she was brought up by a local person, one who was not an Aryan, who adopted her as his child. It was from him that she picked up her knowledge and skill in the occult science. The story appears quite strange, but it is believed that in ancient days, when urbanization was still on the distant horizon, the indigenous peoples were better informed than the groups who were beginning to raise their heads at the time.

Khana was a smart and intelligent girl who did not spend her time playing games like the other children. In a short period, she acquired a complete knowledge of astronomy! Her adoptive father admired her diligence and taught her all that he knew in the subject. Thus Khana became skilled in a branch of knowledge that many people shun. The intricacies of the subject were clear to her.

In the village where Khana lived, a brahmin boy, Mihira by name, was also being brought up by another family. The boy's adoptive father also took care to train him so well in astrology that his was the last word on the subject. When Khana and Mihira came of age, they were married with the blessings of their adoptive parents and set up a home of their own.

Though we know nothing regarding the parentage of Khana, we know a little about the family roots of Mihira. He was the son of Varaha, an astronomer royal and one of the nine great scholars in the court of the famous emperor Vikramaditya.* Varaha was the author of many great treatises on astronomy. When a son, Mihira, was born to him, he drew up the horoscope of the child calculating the positions of the different planets following the mathematical rules for them. Due to an unrecognized error that crept into his calculations, Varaha thought that the child's life span would be only ten years, though in reality it was a hundred years. Varaha reviewed his calculations a number of times. But because of an obsession in his mind, he came to the same conclusion every time. He visualized the misery and sadness he would suffer at the loss of his dear child after bringing him up affectionately for ten years, and he preferred to abandon the child straightaway. Accordingly, the child was laid in a box and put into a flowing river. A family of tribal people found him, adopted him, and trained him to be a master in their learning.

After their marriage, Khana and Mihira wanted to rejoin their elite Aryan community, and requested their protectors, who also were the administrators of the area in which they lived, to permit them to do so. Their protectors conceded the request, and chose a tribal woman as a guide to accompany Khana and Mihira, so that they could safely cross over into the Aryan territory. They also gave rare and highly specialized books on astrology to the guide, with instructions that she should observe the degree of skill acquired by Khana and Mihira by applying suitable tests. The guide was expected to bring the books back if she found the pair of young scholars fully proficient. If on the other hand she found the training they had received defective, she was to give the books as parting gifts to Khana and Mihira so that no deficiency would exist in their scholarship. An opportunity to test their skills occurred just when the party was nearing its destination. A cow was about to deliver its calf. With a view to testing the ability of the new scholars, the guide wanted them to predict whether the calf to be born in a short

---

*Vikramaditya was a ruler of the first century B.C., of legendary renown for his charity, patronage of learning, and association with the famed literary circle known as the *nava ratna*, or the nine gems.

time would be brown or white in color. Mihira made a quick calculation and declared that the calf would be white. But in a few minutes the cow delivered a brown calf. Since the knowledge acquired by Mihira was defective and incomplete, the guide presented the books to Mihira and left for home. Mihira threw the books into the river, which they were crossing at that moment to get into the Aryan territory. He thought in disgust and anger, "If I have not acquired enough knowledge and skill after many years of training, the study of these books will not help me." Khana could not prevent Mihira from throwing away the rare and precious manuscripts. But she did recover two of the books; the rest were washed away by the current.

Mihira and Khana continued their journey and reached a village. King Vikramaditya was camping in the village next to a forest, along with his party of hunters. Mihira met the king holding court, and exhibited his skill and scholarship. Vikramaditya was pleased, and appointed him scholar to his royal court. The hunting party returned to the capital. The king sent word to Varaha and entrusted to him the young couple, who were to be his guests of honor till they could be accommodated in a fitting manner. Varaha accepted the pleasant duty, and in a short time found out that the child he had abandoned years ago had come back to him as a grown young man along with his scholarly wife. Thereafter Varaha, Mihira, and Khana formed a trio of scholars, spending many sessions discussing problems in astrology and making many new discoveries. Mihira was equal to his father in scholarship. His skills were recognized by Vikramaditya and by everyone else in the realm. Although she never made appearances in the royal court or participated in public discussions on different scholarly subjects, Khana's fame as a scholar also spread over the land. The daughter-in-law of Varaha and wife of Mihira was a great astronomer in her own right, and when occasion arose, every scholar referred to her as a rare phenomenon!

One day, King Vikrama became curious to know the number of stars in the sky, and posed the question to Varaha: "Count the stars in the sky and let me know their number." Varaha realized that he was facing an insurmountable problem, and though he attempted to refer to books he had, he could not obtain the information. Counting the stars in the sky was plainly not possible! He consulted Mihira, his son. His skill and intuitive ability too were of no use in finding a solution. The very thought that they had to face the humiliation of admitting their ignorance made the father and son immensely dejected. Khana politely asked them the reason for their dejection. On learning of the problem, she immediately set to work. She worked for a little while and gave them the result of her calculations along with the basis of the formula she used. They felt relieved and with confidence went back to the royal court. Varaha surprised the king as well as the scholars who were assembled with the information he could furnish. After the presentation, which stunned the court, Varaha paid a handsome compliment to his daughter-in-law, whose scholarship was without match in solving this intricate problem. The courtiers assembled there also praised the excellence of Khana's scholarship. Vikramaditya announced that she, a scholar of such magnitude, would adorn his royal court forthwith as the tenth jewel, along with the nine scholars who were called the nava ratna of his court. She was requested to accept the honor and to attend the court from the next day.

The royal orders created a panic in Varaha. He felt women should live a secluded, sheltered life in their homes. Making their presence felt in public only degraded them. But if his daughter-in-law was not taken to the court, he would have to face the fury of the king, so Varaha decided to put an end to Khana's life, since he considered her responsible for the whole predicament. He ordered his son to cut Khana's tongue off. Mihira loved his wife and was not prepared to obey his father. Khana came to know of the predicament and offered to let her tongue be cut off in obedience to her father-in-law's order, and begged her husband to carry out his father's orders. Such self-sacrifice was possible only for Khana, and no one in history or in traditional accounts is known for such courage. Mihira turned his heart to stone, and cut Khana's tongue off. Khana left this world after a short while only to become immortal.

There is another version of this incident. According to a second version, Khana was the court scholar for some time. Her death, which came later, was due to natural causes. No one killed her. This second account seems to be more plausible, since it fits into the historical traditions of the period in which King Vikrama lived and ruled. Women did not live in seclusion at that time. There is ample evidence for that. If life in seclusion was the custom of the age, would a king like Vikrama appoint a lady as his court scholar? It is also difficult to believe that a loving husband like Mihira could be so heartless as to kill his wife.

When we sum it all up we find many unbelievable aspects to this story. Even if we were to set aside all those as fiction, we learn one indisputable fact.

We have many instances of women in ancient times who were interested in the study of astronomy as well as astrology and acquired a proficiency of the highest order, surpassing all men. Khana is only one such person. This example refutes all loose talk that, when compared to men, women are dull witted, weak minded, and endowed with brains smaller than men's in size. It is quite clear that all such statements are baseless, partial, and meant only to boost men's egos. Since women are brought up from childhood without any access to knowledge or education, they only appear to be ignorant, whereas in reality none of them is so. All of us must have observed that in childhood both boys and girls seem equally endowed with sensibility and intelligence for their age. Though girls never lag behind boys in intelligence, the parents do not provide any facilities for the education of their daughters, nor do they encourage the pursuit of knowledge. That is the reason why most of the girls lapse into ignorance and sometimes even lose their inherent capacity to discriminate. On the other hand, a boy who is dull witted as a child is put through the educational machinery and drilled and grilled in many branches of knowledge. As a result, he becomes successful and earns a name while his elder sister, who as a child was more capable but untouched by education, becomes a first-rate ignoramus. The same would have been the result had the boy remained without education. The gap that exists between the intellectual abilities of men and women is entirely our creation. It is not a result of a natural or inherent disability of girls. Therefore, we have no hesitation to affirm and conclude in this essay that only if men shed their selfish and partisan attitudes and decide to educate and encourage in women the desire to acquire specialized knowledge will women also display abilities equal to those of men, thus proving that they are "better halves" not merely in name but in reality.

Translated by Hari Adiseshuvu.

SAROJINI NAIDU ——————————————

(1879–1949)   *English*

Sarojini Naidu was the eldest of eight children of the poet Varada Sundari and the distinguished educator Aghorenath Chattopadhyay, who founded the Nizam's College in Hyderabad in 1878. She grew up in a household that was a center of learning and the arts. Poets, philosophers, alchemists (her father dreamed of solving what he called "the mysteries of alchemy"), intellectuals, and revolutionaries were regular visitors to the home, which "turned no one away hungry" and in which, she writes, she was brought up to be an *Indian* (not a Hindu or a brahmin) and a proud citizen of the world. And, as is clearly evident in her poetry, her speeches, and her political commitments, the young Sarojini was shaped as much by the rich Muslim culture of Hyderabad as by the traditional Hindu ethos of her family and the Western influences of her education.

Though she refused to speak English until she was nine, by the time she was eleven she had begun to write poetry in that language: "I was sighing over a sum in Algebra: it *wouldn't* come right; but instead a whole poem came to me suddenly. From that day, my 'poetic career' began." At the remarkably early age of twelve she matriculated, coming out first in the entire Madras Presidency (an administrative unit of the colonial government) and gaining instant fame. At fifteen she met and fell in love with Govindaraju Naidu, a doctor and a widower ten years her senior. No doubt also to defer what they thought might be a hasty decision on her part, her parents sent her to England to study. She spent three years there, first at King's College in London and later at Girton College in Cambridge. Biographers speak of her health "breaking down" during this time. She was initially sent to Spain to convalesce, but returned to Hyderabad in 1888. She married Govindaraju Naidu the same year in a controversial intercaste marriage: she was a brahmin, he was not. They had four children between 1899 and 1903: Jayasura; Padmaja, who was active in the women's movement, and governor of West Bengal in the early 1950s; Randhira; and Lilamoni.

Most of her poetry was written between 1895, when she was sixteen and published her first collection, *Songs,* and 1917, when her fourth and last volume, *The Broken Wing,* including "The Temple, A Pilgrimage of Love," came out. She published in 1905 *The Golden Threshold,* a book she dedicated to Edmund Gosse, the well-known British critic. *The Bird of Fame,* her third book of poems, which includes "Bangle-Sellers," came out in 1912. Though her poetry is widely read and even committed to memory by people who may not know other poetry in English but enjoy the delicate rhythm and the luxurious imagery of her verse, literary critics have characterized her work as sentimental and as offering an exotic image of India. The poems we have included here are among the most popular.

Though she may be remembered chiefly as a poet, Sarojini Naidu was deeply involved in politics, played a colorful role in the struggle for Independence, and had a talent for witty repartee. Her political interests, the seeds of which were planted in nationalist commitments of the Chattopadhyay home, grew more intense in the years after 1906, when she made a much-acclaimed fiery speech at a meeting of the Indian National Congress in Calcutta. She went on to participate in meetings and protest actions, emerging as a powerful and talented speaker and a sensitive organizer who was extremely popular with students and young people. The speech included here was addressed to students at Ahmedabad in 1922. In 1914 she met Gandhi and worked closely with him for many years. In 1925, she was elected president of the Indian National Congress.

Sarojini Naidu was among the few women who took part in the famous Salt Satyagraha in 1930. The British government had imposed a levy on salt. In protest, a group of people led by Gandhi set out from his ashram at Sabarmati to walk for twenty-five days, through the heartland of Gujarat, down to the sea to make and sell salt in defiance of the British government. Sarojini Naidu was imprisoned thrice: in 1930, 1932, and 1942. She is also remembered for the part she played in setting up the All India Women's Conference and demanding, as early as 1917, full franchise for women.

When India became independent in 1947, Sarojini Naidu was appointed governor of Uttar Pradesh, the largest state in the country. But the joy at having achieved the goal of a struggle to which she had given more than forty years of her life was marred by the partition of India and Pakistan. The dream she had of unity among Hindus and Muslims had been shattered. She died in 1949, at the age of seventy.

◆

BANGLE-SELLERS

Bangle-sellers are we who bear
Our shining loads to the temple fair . . .
Who will buy these delicate, bright
Rainbow-tinted circles of light?
Lustrous tokens of radiant lives,
For happy daughters and happy wives.

Some are meet for a maiden's wrist,
Silver and blue as the mountain mist,
Some are flushed like the buds that dream
On the tranquil brow of a woodland stream;
Some are aglow with the bloom that cleaves
To the limpid glory of newborn leaves.

Some are like fields of sunlit corn,
Meet for a bride on her bridal morn,
Some, like the flame of her marriage fire,
Or rich with the hue of her heart's desire,
Tinkling, luminous, tender, and clear,
Like her bridal laughter and bridal tear.

Some are purple and gold–flecked gray,
For her who has journeyed through life midway.
Whose hands have cherished, whose love has blest
And cradled fair sons on her faithful breast,
Who serves her household in fruitful pride,
And worships the gods at her husband's side.

From THE TEMPLE, A PILGRIMAGE OF LOVE

"My passion shall burn as the flame of Salvation,
The flower of my love shall become the ripe fruit of Devotion."

—*Rabindranath Tagore*

I

Were beauty mine, Beloved, I would bring it
Like a rare blossom to Love's glowing shrine;
Were a dear youth mine, Beloved, I would fling it
Like a rich pearl into Love's lustrous wine.

Were greatness mine, Beloved, I would offer
Such radiant gifts of glory and of fame,
Like camphor and like curds to pour and proffer
Before Love's right and sacrificial flame.

But I have naught save my heart's deathless passion
That craves no recompense divinely sweet,
Content to wait in proud and lowly fashion,
And kiss the shadow of Love's passing feet.

II

Bring no fragrant sandal paste,
Let me gather Love instead.
The entranced and flowering dust
You have honored with your tread
For mine eyelids and mine head.

Bring no scented lotus wreath,
Moon-awakened, dew-caressed

Love, thro' memory's age-long dream,
Sweeter shall my wild heart rest
With your footprints on my breast.

Bring no pearls from ravished seas,
Gems from rifled hemispheres;
Grant me, Love, in priceless boon
All the sorrow of your years,
All the secret of your tears.

V

If you call me I will come
     Swifter, O my Love,
Than a trembling forest deer
     Or a panting dove,
Swifter than a snake that flies
     To the charmer's thrall. . . .
If you call me I will come
     Fearless what befall.

If you call me I will come
     Swifter than desire,
Swifter than the lightning's feet
     Shod with plumes of fire.
Life's dark tides may roll between,
     Or Death's deep chasms divide—
If you call me I will come
     Fearless what betide.

VI

Forgive me the sin of mine eyes,
O Love, if they dared for a space
Invade the dear shrine of your face
With eager, insistent delight,
Like wild birds intrepid of flight
That raid the high sanctuaried skies—
O pardon the sin of mine eyes!

Forgive me the sin of my hands. . . .
Perchance they were bold overmuch
In their tremulous longing to touch

Your beautiful flesh, to caress,
To clasp you, O Love, and to bless,
With gifts as uncounted as sands—
O pardon the sin of my hands!

Forgive me the sin of my mouth,
O Love, if it wrought you a wrong,
With importunate silence or song
Assailed you, encircled, oppress'd,
And ravished your lips and your breast
To comfort its anguish of drouth—
O pardon the sin of my mouth!

Forgive me the sin of my heart,
It trespassed against you and strove
To lure or to conquer your love
Its passionate love to appease,
To solace its hunger and ease
The wound of its sorrow or smart—
O pardon the sin of my heart!

VII

O could I brew my Soul like Wine
    To make you strong,
O could I carve you Freedom's sword
    Out of my song!

Instill into your mortal flesh
    Immortal breath,
Triumphantly to conquer Life
    And trample Death.

What starry heights of sacrifice
    Were left untrod,
So could my true love fashion you
    Into a God?

PRESIDENTIAL ADDRESS AT THE
AHMEDABAD STUDENTS' CONFERENCE, 1922

My young comrades, if some fairy god-mother of destiny were to say to me, "Yet in time, now or in the future, which is the one supreme wish of your heart, what is the one supreme honour you covet, what would be the crowning glory of all your achievement—choose." Do you know what I would choose without hesitation, without doubt in my mind? For my opportunity I would choose to mould the mind of the young generation. For the supremest honour of my life I should ask for the love of the young generation. For the crowning glory and achievement of my life I should like it written on my epitaph—"She loved the young generation; she trusted the young generation; she worked with the young generation; she won freedom side by side with the young generation of Indians for India." That is the secret desire of my heart. So you can understand that if I stand before you today your chosen President, it seems to me as if the fairy god-mother were already, without my asking for it, almost without my knowing it, conferring upon me the boon of boons. Ever since I could speak articulately, not the language as one finds the language in the dictionaries of the world, but the language of the heart of youth and the imagination of youth, no matter in what tongue and in what country, my one thought has been always for the freedom of India; and my earliest service in that direction was the companionship of students always.

My first entry into public life was as a speaker in the colleges, the chosen guest of the students of the cities of India. To speak from larger platforms to larger audiences came much later but never brought to me the thrill that I still remember of those little audiences in attentively listening to me with avid faces and those burning eyes looking into the future and demanding an answer from the Time Spirit. Today I stand amongst you once more, representatives of the spirit of India. You have come from North and South, East and West and the central heart of India,—you who represent many races today, many creeds today, many sects today, all times of civilization, all kinds of traditions, all kinds of conflicts, and yet united by the one burning desire to serve your country, to sever her from bondage, to enthrone her among the stars,—you who have come together at that call of the nation,—you who have made a response to the voice that has trumpeted forth, saying "Stand forth, you, young generation, and break the shackles of your mother." What is the message that I can deliver to you? What is the strength that can be mine that will guide you aright today on the difficult pilgrimage towards freedom? Those of you who were here the other day must remember with a thrill the words that I read from Deshbandu Chitta Ranjan Das' message in which he speaks of the students. There he says in words that are written in fire:—"Let me not forget the students. They are the inspiration of the movement. They are the torch-bearers on the path to freedom. They are the pilgrims on the road to liberty. If theirs has been the sacrifice, then victory is their due." This is the message which the chosen President of the National Congress wrote for the students in whom he has faith, in whom his generation has faith. And I, representing his generation, deliver to you the message of his generation and mine, asking that you will fulfil the pledges that we have made to the world, because you and you alone are not only the heroes of all our greatness but the fulfillers, the completers of all our imperfections, all our shortcomings, all our weaknesses. You are to wipe out the stains upon our generation. You are to blot out with your prayers, with your sacrifice, all the stains, the scourges, the follies, the back slidings, the curse of our generation. This is the message that I bring you today.

You want to know what India demands of you. Turn over the pages of the history of the nations that have found freedom, and you will find in page after glorious page, not the record only of battles fought and won on the open fields and under the stars; no, the most inspiring pages are not there. But the inspiring pages come where name after name of young men in their serried ranks fill up the gaps as soldiers fall, the young serried ranks that urge into their trenches and with the cry of victory win the liberties of nations. You are in that position today. Greece in her glorious days could show no more radiant page of achievement. Rome with all her imperial purple has not a passage more glowing than you can show today to the world. Nay, the history of your country, the history of such supreme sacrifice, such glorious achievement can show no page more lovely with sacrifice, more burning with the fire of prophetic zeal than you today in whose hands the writing and the illuminating of the history of Empire lies. The call to students came last year, but the call came with a rather hesitating voice because still the nation was not aware of its own peril. Nor was it so imminently and urgently aware of its need, its power, its great unity, its strength to sacrifice, its power to endure, its capacity to hurl back to an imperious bureaucracy the challenge of an invincible hope and an invincible resolve. Today the call is not of an answering voice, the call is rising not from the mountain tops, but from the secret valleys of your own hearts and souls. If the voice of Mahatma Gandhi speaks to you, he is but the flute-call of your own hearts. He is not the Sri Krishna. He is the flute of Sri Krishna that is within your own hearts and souls. So, my young comrades, your duty today is clear before you. Sacrifice! Sacrifice! Sacrifice!

One year ago I did not believe in the wisdom of young men turning their backs upon their colleges, shutting the pages of their textbooks, denying to themselves the inviolable right and privilege of knowledge and culture. But today after the agony of nearly one year's experience of the bitter need of India, the bitter peril of India, I stand up to say, though it hurts me still so to feel, that the young generation must turn its back upon the colleges, must deny to itself its own inalienable heritage of the right to learn, the right to know, the right that enriches the mind and the spirit with the garnered treasures of ages. I nonetheless say that freedom is worthy of even so valuable a sacrifice. Why shall men barter all their wealth to buy one pearl of great price? Shall men sell their lands and kingdoms to satisfy one passionate whim of theirs, and yet the youth of the nation not offer itself up in a flaming sacrifice for the sake of the freedom of India? In 1914 when the great battle-cloud broke over Europe, when the sky of August was stained blood-red with the menace of war, when the boom of the thundering cannon roared in the great cities of Europe, did I not see young man after man in their hundreds of thousands pouring out of their colleges at Oxford and Cambridge, from the London Colleges and the Welsh Colleges and the Scottish Colleges and the Manchester Colleges and marching to the music of their own brave youths to victory or to doom? Is today so different from that day that needed the sacrifice of the youth of Europe for the sake of Europe's peace? Is not our plight more tragic? Is not our need more terrible? Is not our case more vitally urgent? Is not our peril the peril not merely of lands that may be lost, of lives that may be lost, but of the nation's soul, the nation's honour, the nation's right to live among the living nations of the world? Therefore, I ask you, my young friends, you who are today the representatives of hundreds and thousands of young men and women all over India, pour forth in your uncounted numbers. Pour forth to battle, not to the battle of those that wade across seas of blood towards victory, but the battle of those who wade only across the blood of their own hearts—not the blood of their enemies' hearts.

The difference between our warfare and the warfare of Europe, the warfare of the West, the accepted warfare of the world, is this, that whilst nations of another land win their victory slaying their enemies we win our victory by slaying only our sins. It is the great battle of self-purification. It is the great battle of self-sacrifice. It is the great battle of self-devotion. If in the years to come when the Swaraj flag flies over our own national assemblies, in the summing up of the achievement of the great battle for liberty we count up the gains and the losses and among the losses irreparable, incalculable though they may be, we find that the youth of India has perforce to remain ignorant, bereft of that knowledge, that wide culture, that noble learning that is the inheritance of the young generations of the world, shall we have time to bemoan that ignorance? Shall we have time to lament that loss? Or shall we not say "Set against this loss, this lack, irreparable, incalculable though it is, the one thing which is worthwhile having, the one thing for which the young generations have not sacrificed their all for nothing." There is on the one hand a few years of sacrifice, on the other, the imperishable legacy of freedom to a land set free for ever by the sacrifice of the young generation.

I want you all to realize that today you are the recruits in the great army of freedom. You are the new soldiers in the army of peace. I want you to understand the implications of that remark. I want you to realize in all its manifold bearings, in all the terrible responsibilities the meaning of that word. What does it mean to be a volunteer? What does it mean to be a non-cooperating student? What does it mean today to sign that pledge which you heard proclaimed yesterday in tones, solemn and moving from the lips of the apostle of freedom? It means this, my young friends, not merely that you will learn to parade and drill and fall into line and salute your superiors and have ranks in the army and march singing national songs. These are the details, the outer trappings, the true symbols that count for nothing. But to be a soldier in the army that Mahatma Gandhi leads is to be reborn pure and flawless in the flame of sacrifice. It means the cleansing out of every secret sin from the secret recess of your hearts. It means the purging of every fibre of yours from every evil thought, passion and desire that still might be lurking unsuspected in the crevices of your being. It means that you pledge yourselves not only to the world that can see the outer things and judge you, but it means that you pledge yourselves to your Self, to the being seated in the midst of you, that you will abstain in thought and word, desire and deed, from every low, evil, vicious, cancerous, leprous sin. That is what I want to impress upon you. That is what I want you to realize. It means the discipline of perfection, the discipline of the mind, the heart, the senses, the desire; not merely the obeying of the orders of that captain that is in every man's heart and is called conscience by many tongues. It means that you will learn so to conquer yourself, your selfish desires, your selfish needs, your selfish pride, that you will endure, without retaliation, without resentment, all the indignity, humiliation, suffering, losses, penalties,—if necessary, floggings and torturings and death—for the sake of the cause to which you are pledged today.

That is really the message I have for you. If you have understood what the pledge stands for, if you have understood why the hand-spun and hand-made outer symbol, that your garment, is the true symbol of your inward regeneration, if you have understood that you cannot ask for freedom for yourself, if within one single heart amongst you there still remains that shrinking from your neighbour because he is not born like yourselves within the mantle of the four-fold caste—if you have understood all these things, you have understood the meaning and the purpose of Swaraj. But if you have still within you the feeling that there are barriers between Hindu and Hindu within his own caste, between Hindu and Mussalman, between Mussalman and Parsee, between Parsee and Christian, if we still define ourselves in terms of sects and provinces and castes and divisions, there is no Swaraj for us; there is no Swaraj for the young generation. Therefore, my purpose today is to make clear to you the meaning of that great pledge. But the young generation does not need my interpretation of the gospel of freedom. I want you, therefore—I know you will—therefore, to join in your hundreds and thousands and become yourselves the young apostles of your own deliverance. There should be no peril that is too great for you to face, no difficulty too difficult for you to overcome, no death too terrible for you to master, no destiny too exalted for you to achieve.

But my young friends, my young comrades, Oh pilgrims on the road to freedom, as said the other pilgrim who is in the half-way house to freedom in the prisons of Bengal, I charge you, "remember the sacred duty that will bow these young shoulders, the terrible burden that will bow those young heads. But though your backs be broken and your heads be bowed, I charge you, let your hearts be never bowed or burdened. For, no matter how heavy the burden, let your own courage be the torch in your hand; no matter how steep the path, let your own hope be the pilgrim's staff in your hand; no matter how far the goal, let your young strength give you wings to reach the goal. When the goal is reached and you stand high up on the peaks and look back across the difficult way you have come, comrades, remember; let there be nothing that you see on the road you left behind save your own follies and weaknesses and sins and nothing of value, nothing of abiding worth or beauty; take it all with you for the enriching of the temple, that is the temple of liberty. March with me to the temple of liberty. I carry the standard in my hands. Comrades, march with me till we reach the goal."

ROKEYA SAKHAWAT HOSSAIN ─────

(1880–1932)   *English*

In her witty utopian fantasy, "Sultana's Dream," 1905, probably the first such work in Indian literature, Rokeya Sakhawat Hossain describes a world where men are confined to the *murdana* and women have taken over the affairs of the country.* War and crime are unheard of in this tastefully ordered world, where cooking is so simple that it is a pleasure, horticulture is a serious business, and science is used in the service of humanity. Her husband, Sakhawat Hossain, proudly remarked that the story was "a terrible revenge" on men.

This courageous feminist writer and activist who worked all her life to remove what she called the "purdah of ignorance," was born in Pairaband, a village in what is now Bangladesh. Her father, Mohammed Abu Ali Saheb, was a rich landlord and an orthodox Muslim. Of her mother we know very little. Rokeya's two brothers were educated at St. Xavier's, one of Calcutta's most prestigious colleges, but she and her sisters, Karimunessa and Humaira, were not sent to school, though they did have a traditional education at home. Karimunessa, Rokeya writes in a warm tribute to her sister, painstakingly taught herself to read Bengali. Even though Muslim girls commonly learned to recite the Koran and picked up enough Urdu to read books, such as Maulana Thanawi's *Bihishti Zevar* (Heavenly Riches), that were popular prescriptions for feminine conduct, they were not usually encouraged to learn Bengali. When Karimunessa's interests, especially her love of Bengali literature, were discovered, she was sent to live under the close supervision of her grandparents and soon married off. Rokeya was luckier. With her brother Ibrahim Saber's support, she was able to learn English and Bengali, though she had to do so secretly, at night after everyone in the house was asleep. In her essays Rokeya speaks

─────────

*The *murdana* is the men's quarters in the household. The section to which women were restricted was the *zenana*.

warmly of the support she always received from her brother and sister. "If society had not been so oppressive, Karimunessa would have been one of the brightest jewels of this country," she once wrote.

Rokeya was married when she was eighteen to Syed Sakhawat Hossain, a widower who was then a district magistrate in Bihar. His first wife had died after their daughter was born. Of Rokeya's children, none survived. Sakhawat Hossain believed that women's education was the best cure for the evils that plagued his society. He encouraged an only too willing Rokeya to write. Enthused by his young wife's interest in women's education, he set aside ten thousand rupees from his savings to start a school for Muslim women. When he died in 1909, just eleven years after they had been married, Rokeya started the school in Bhagalpur in his memory. There were only five students, but she was undaunted. A quarrel with her stepdaughter's husband over property, however, similar to one she describes in the long essay "Griha" (Home), forced her to abandon her house, close the school in Bhagalpur, and return to Calcutta, where she lived until her death. There she began again in 1911. This time the school had eight students but she worked hard, at great personal cost and in the face of much opposition, to build it up. She also took great interest in civic affairs and was a member of the Anjumane-Khawatin-e Islam (the Association for Muslim Women), to which Sughra Humayun Mirza of Hyderabad also belonged, and was involved in many activities designed to help other women. At Rokeya's invitation, an annual session of the newly formed All India Women's Conference was held in Calcutta.

Many of Rokeya's essays, which were written in Bengali, sought to elicit support for the cause of women; they were published during the twenty years or so she spent in Calcutta after her husband's death. Writing from Bangladesh where Rokeya has received more recognition than she has in India, the scholar Roushan Jahan, who has translated some of her work into English, compares the essays in the two volumes of *Motichur* (Pearl Dust) to the work of the eighteenth-century English feminist Mary Wollstonecraft in *Vindication of the Rights of Woman*. Though it is very unlikely that Rokeya would have known about or read Wollstonecraft, in December 1932, shortly before her death, she was at work on the essay "Narir Adhikar" (The Rights of Women), which remained unfinished.

In one of her earlier essays, Rokeya had argued that if the main object of wearing ornaments is to display a husband's wealth, "I could tell you a few ways in which you could do this. Why don't you decorate your pet dog with your necklace? When you go riding on your horse carriages, deck your horse with your beautiful ornaments. You could use your bangles and bracelets as curtain rings in your drawing room. That would be the proper way of being extravagant with your husband's, the Nawab's, money. . . . If men want their wealth displayed, do it in the manner I have suggested. But why display their wealth on your body? That is nothing but a symbol of your slavery." "Prisoners," she adds, "wear handcuffs made of iron, we wear bracelets made of gold or silver." This witty and imaginative polemic was typical of Rokeya's writing. In *Avarodbhasini* (Secluded Women), a series of articles published in the *Muhamadhi* between 1928 and 1930, she presents a sequence of predicaments, sometimes moving, occasionally pathetic, but mostly ridiculous, that the practice of purdah resulted in. Many of the essays in the two volumes of *Motichur,* 1905 and 1921, and in *Pipasa* (Thirst), 1922, are similarly anecdotal and argue a case, citing incident after incident, each vividly and humorously described. Rokeya also wrote one novel, *Padmaraga* (Ruby), in Bengali. "Sultana's Dream" was first written in English and then translated by the author into Bengali.

Like her contemporary Pandita Ramabai in Maharashtra, Rokeya had to face much criticism. Her writings were constantly attacked by some who wished to protect religious orthodoxy and others who considered her antinational. To her, one critic complained, "everything Indian is bad and everything Euro-American good."

Rokeya died when she was fifty-three, suddenly, of heart failure. At a memorial service organized at Calcutta's prestigious Albert Hall, Kazi Abdul Udud asked, "If such intelligence, culture, and independence could have been reared in a person who grew up and lived in the dark confines of the home with its many restrictions and suppressions, what have Bengali Muslims to be fearful about?"

◆

SULTANA'S DREAM

One evening I was lounging in an easy chair in my bedroom and thinking lazily of the condition of Indian womanhood. I am not sure whether I dozed off or not. But, as far as I remember, I was wide awake. I saw the moonlit sky sparkling with thousands of diamond-like stars, very distinctly.

All of a sudden a lady stood before me; how she came in, I do not know. I took her for my friend, Sister Sara.

"Good morning," said Sister Sara. I smiled inwardly as I knew it was not morning, but starry night. However, I replied to her, saying, "How do you do?"

"I am all right, thank you. Will you please come out and have a look at our garden?"

I looked again at the moon through the open window, and thought there was no harm in going out at that time. The men-servants outside were fast asleep just then, and I could have a pleasant walk with Sister Sara.

I used to take my walks with Sister Sara, when we were at Darjeeling. Many a time did we walk hand in hand and talk light-heartedly in the Botanical gardens there. I fancied Sister Sara had probably come to take me to some such garden, and I readily accepted her offer and went out with her.

When walking I found to my surprise that it was a fine morning. The town was fully awake and the streets alive with bustling crowds. I felt very shy, since I was walking in the street in broad daylight, but there was not a single man visible.

Some of the passers-by made jokes at me. Though I could not understand their language, yet I felt sure they were joking. I asked my friend, "What do they say?"

"The women say that you look very mannish."

"Mannish?" said I, "What do they mean by that?"

"They mean that you are shy and timid like men."

"Shy and timid like men?" It was really a joke. I became very nervous, when I found that my companion was not Sister Sara, but a stranger. Oh, what a fool had I been to mistake this lady for my dear old friend, Sister Sara.

She felt my fingers tremble in her hand, as we were walking hand in hand.

"What is the matter, dear, dear?" she said affectionately.

"I feel somewhat awkward," I said in a rather apologising tone, "as being a purdahnashin woman, I am not accustomed to walking about unveiled."

"You need not be afraid of coming across a man here. This is Ladyland, free from sin and harm. Virtue herself reigns here."

By and by I was enjoying the scenery. Really it was very grand. I mistook a patch of green grass for a velvet cushion. Feeling as if I were walking on a soft carpet, I looked down and found the path covered with moss and flowers.

"How nice it is," said I.

"Do you like it?" asked Sister Sara. (I continued calling her "Sister Sara," and she kept calling me by my name.)

"Yes, very much; but I do not like to tread on the tender and sweet flowers."

"Never mind, dear Sultana. Your treading will not harm them; they are street flowers."

"The whole place looks like a garden," said I admiringly. "You have arranged every plant so skilfully."

"Your Calcutta could become a nicer garden than this, if only your countrymen wanted to make it so."

"They would think it useless to give so much attention to horticulture, while they have so many other things to do."

"They could not find a better excuse," said she with [a] smile.

I became very curious to know where the men were. I met more than a hundred women while walking there, but not a single man.

"Where are the men?" I asked her.

"In their proper places, where they ought to be."

"Pray let me know what you mean by 'their proper places.' "

"O, I see my mistake, you cannot know our customs, as you were never here before. We shut our men indoors."

"Just as we are kept in the Zenana?"

"Exactly so."

"How funny," I burst into a laugh. Sister Sara laughed too.

"But dear Sultana, how unfair it is to shut in the harmless women and let loose the men."

"Why? It is not safe for us to come out of the zenana, as we are naturally weak."

"Yes, it is not safe so long as there are men about the streets, nor is it so when a wild animal enters a marketplace."

"Of course not."

"Suppose, some lunatics escape from the asylum and begin to do all sorts of mischief to men, horses and other creatures, in that case what will your countrymen do?"

"They will try to capture them and put them back into their asylum."

"Thank you! And you do not think it wise to keep sane people inside an asylum and let loose the insane?"

"Of course not!" said I laughing lightly.

"As a matter of fact, in your country this very thing is done! Men, who do or at least are capable of doing no end of mischief, are let loose and the innocent women shut up in the zenana! How can you trust those untrained men out of doors?"

"We have no hand or voice in the management of our social affairs. In India man is lord and master. He has taken to himself all powers and privileges and shut up the women in the zenana."

"Why do you allow yourselves to be shut up?"

"Because it cannot be helped as they are stronger than women."

"A lion is stronger than a man, but it does not enable him to dominate the human race. You have neglected the duty you owe to yourselves and you have lost your natural rights by shutting your eyes to your own interests."

"But my dear sister Sara, if we do everything by ourselves, what will the men do then?"

"They should not do anything, excuse me; they are fit for nothing. Only catch them and put them into the zenana."

"But would it be very easy to catch and put them inside the four walls?" said I. "And even if this were done, would all their business—political and commercial—also go with them into the zenana!"

Sister Sara made no reply. She only smiled sweetly. Perhaps she thought it useless to argue with one who was no better than a frog in a well.

By this time we reached Sister Sara's house. It was situated in a beautiful heart-shaped garden. It was a bungalow with a corrugated iron roof. It was cooler and nicer than any of our rich buildings. I cannot describe how neat and how nicely furnished and how tastefully decorated it was.

We sat side by side. She brought out of the parlour a piece of embroidery work and began putting on a fresh design.

"Do you know how to knit and do needlework?"

"Yes; we have nothing else to do in our zenana."

"But we do not trust our zenana members with embroidery!" she said laughing, "as a man has not patience enough to pass thread through a needlehole even!"

"Have you done all this work yourself?" I asked her pointing to the various pieces of embroidered teapoy cloths.

"Yes."

"How can you find time to do all these? You have to do the office work as well? Have you not?"

"Yes. I do not stick to the laboratory all day long. I finish my work in two hours."

"In two hours! How do you manage? In our land the officers, magistrates for instance, work seven hours daily."

"I have seen some of them doing their work. Do you think they work all the seven hours?"

"Certainly they do!"

"No, dear Sultana, they do not. They dawdle away their time in smoking. Some smoke two or three cheroots during the office time. They talk much about their work, but do little. Suppose one cheroot takes half an hour to burn off, and a man smokes twelve cheroots daily; then you see, he wastes six hours every day in sheer smoking."

We talked on various subjects; and I learned that they were not sub-ject to any kind of epidemic disease—nor did they suffer from mosquito-bites as we do. I was very much astonished to hear that in Ladyland no one died in youth except by rare accident.

"Will you care to see our kitchen?" she asked me.

"With pleasure," said I, and we went to see it. Of course the men had been asked to clear off when I was going there. The kitchen was situated in a beautiful vegetable garden. Every creeper, every tomato plant was itself an ornament. I found no smoke, nor any chimney either in the kitchen,—it was clean and bright; the windows were dec-orated with flower garlands. There was no sign of coal or fire.

"How do you cook?" I asked.

"With solar heat," she said, at the same time showing me the pipe, through which passed the concentrated sunlight and heat. And she cooked something then and there to show me the process.

"How did you manage to gather and store up the sun heat?" I asked her in amazement.

"Let me tell you a little of our past history then. Thirty years ago, when our present Queen was thirteen years old, she inherited the throne. She was Queen in name only, the Prime Minister really ruling the country.

"Our good Queen liked science very much. She circulated an order that all the women in her country should be educated. Accordingly a number of girls' schools were founded and supported by the Govern-ment. Education was spread far and wide among women. And early marriage also was stopped. No woman was to be allowed to marry before she was twenty-one. I must tell you that, before this change we had been kept in strict-purdah."

"How the tables are turned," I interposed with a laugh.

"But the seclusion is the same," she said. "In a few years we had separate universities, where no men were admitted.

"In the capital, where our Queen lives, there are two universities. One of these invented a wonderful balloon, to which they attached a number of pipes. By means of this captive balloon which they managed to keep afloat above the cloud-land, they could draw as much water from the atmosphere as they pleased. As the water was incessantly being drawn by the University people, no cloud gathered and the in-genious lady Principal stopped rain and storms thereby."

"Really! Now I understand why there is no mud here!" said I. But I could not understand how it was possible to accumulate water in the pipes. She explained to me how it was done; but I was unable to understand her, as my scientific knowledge was very limited. However, she went on,—

"When the other university came to know of this, they became exceedingly jealous and tried to do something more extraordinary still. They invented an instrument by which they could collect as much sun-heat as they wanted. And they kept the heat stored up to be distributed among others as required.

"While the women were engaged in scientific researches, the men of this country were busy increasing their military power. When they came to know that the female universities were able to draw water from the atmosphere and collect heat from the sun, they only laughed at the members of the universities and called the whole thing 'a sentimental nightmare'!"

"Your achievements are very wonderful indeed! But tell me, how you managed to put the men of your country into the zenana. Did you entrap them first?"

"No."

"It is not likely that they would surrender their free and open air life of their own accord and confine themselves within the four walls of the zenana! They must have been overpowered."

"Yes, they have been!"

"By whom?—by some lady-warriors, I suppose?"

"No, not by arms."

"Yes, it cannot be so. Men's arms are stronger than women's."

"Then?"

"By brain."

"Even their brains are bigger and heavier than women's. Are they not?"

"Yes, but what of that? An elephant also has got a bigger and heavier brain than a man has. Yet men can enchain elephants and employ them, according to their own wishes."

"Well said, but tell me please, how it all actually happened. I am dying to know it!"

"Women's brains are somewhat quicker than men's. Ten years ago, when the military officers called our scientific discoveries 'a sentimental nightmare,' some of the young ladies wanted to say something in reply to those remarks. But both the Lady Principals restrained them and said, they should reply, not by word, but by deed, if ever they got the opportunity. And they had not long to wait for that opportunity."

"How marvellous!" I heartily clapped my hands.

"And now the proud gentlemen are dreaming sentimental dreams themselves.

"Soon afterwards certain persons came from a neighbouring country and took shelter in ours. They were in trouble having committed some political offence. The King who cared more for power than for good government asked our kind-hearted Queen to hand them over to his officers. She refused, as it was against her principle to turn out refugees. For this refusal the King declared war against our country.

"Our military officers sprang to their feet at once and marched out to meet the enemy.

"The enemy however, was too strong for them. Our soldiers fought bravely, no doubt. But in spite of all their bravery the foreign army advanced step by step to invade our country.

"Nearly all the men had gone out to fight; even a boy of sixteen was not left home. Most of our warriors were killed, the rest driven back and the enemy came within twenty-five miles of the capital.

"A meeting of a number of wise ladies was held at the Queen's palace to advise [as] to what should be done to save the land.

"Some proposed to fight like soldiers; others objected and said that women were not trained to fight with swords and guns; nor were they accustomed to fighting with any weapons. A third party regretfully remarked that they were hopelessly weak of body.

"If you cannot save your country for lack of physical strength, said the Queen, try to do so by brain power.

"There was a dead silence for a few minutes. Her Royal Highness said again, 'I must commit suicide if the land and my honour are lost.'

"Then the Lady Principal of the second University, (who had collected sun-heat), who had been silently thinking during the consultation, remarked that they were all but lost; and there was little hope left for them. There was however, one plan which she would like to try, and this would be her first and last efforts; if she failed in this, there would be nothing left but to commit suicide. All present solemnly vowed that they would never allow themselves to be enslaved, no matter what happened.

"The Queen thanked them heartily, and asked the Lady Principal to try her plan.

"The Lady Principal rose again and said, 'before we go out the men must enter the zenanas. I make this prayer for the sake of purdah.' 'Yes, of course,' replied Her Royal Highness.

"On the following day the Queen called upon all men to retire into zenanas for the sake of honour and liberty.

"Wounded and tired as they were, they took that order rather for a boon! They bowed low and entered the zenanas without uttering a single word of protest. They were sure that there was no hope for this country at all.

"Then the Lady Principal with her two thousand students marched to the battlefield, and arriving there directed all the rays of the concentrated sunlight and heat towards the enemy.

"The heat and light were too much for them to bear. They all ran away panic-stricken, not knowing in their bewilderment how to counteract that scorching heat. When they fled away leaving their guns and other ammunitions of war, they were burnt down by means of the same sun-heat.

"Since then no one has tried to invade our country any more."

"And since then your countrymen never tried to come out of the zenana?"

"Yes, they wanted to be free. Some of the Police Commissioners and District Magistrates sent word to the Queen to the effect that the Military Officers certainly deserved to be imprisoned for their failure; but they never neglected their duty and therefore they should not be punished and they prayed to be restored to their respective offices.

"Her Royal Highness sent them a circular letter intimating to them that if their services should ever be needed they would be sent for, and that in the meanwhile they should remain where they were.

"Now that they are accustomed to the purdah system and have ceased to grumble at their seclusion, we call the system 'Murdana' instead of 'zenana.' "

"But how do you manage," I asked Sister Sara, "to do without the Police or Magistrates in case of theft or murder?"

"Since the 'Murdana' system has been established, there has been no more crime or sin; therefore we do not require a Policeman to find out a culprit, nor do we want a Magistrate to try a criminal case."

"That is very good, indeed. I suppose if there were any dishonest person, you could very easily chastise her. As you gained a decisive victory without shedding a single drop of blood, you could drive off crime and criminals too without much difficulty!"

"Now, dear Sultana, will you sit here or come to my parlour?" she asked me.

"Your kitchen is not inferior to a queen's boudoir!" I replied with a pleasant smile, "but we must leave it now; for the gentlemen may be cursing me for keeping them away from their duties in the kitchen so long." We both laughed heartily.

"How my friends at home will be amused and amazed, when I go back and tell them that in the far-off Ladyland, ladies rule over the country and control all social matters, while gentlemen are kept in the Murdanas to mind babies, to cook and to do all sorts of domestic work; and that cooking is so easy a thing that it is simply a pleasure to cook!"

"Yes, tell them about all that you see here."

"Please let me know, how you carry on land cultivation and how you plough the land and do other hard manual work."

"Our fields are tilled by means of electricity, which supplies motive power for other hard work as well and we employ it for our aerial conveyances too. We have no railroad nor any paved streets here."

"Therefore neither street nor railway accidents occur here," said I. "Do not you ever suffer from want of rainwater?" I asked.

"Never since the 'water balloon' has been set up. You see the big balloon and pipes attached thereto. By their aid we can draw as much rainwater as we require. Nor do we ever suffer from flood or thunderstorms. We are all very busy making nature yield as much as she can. We do not find time to quarrel with one another as we never sit idle. Our noble Queen is exceedingly fond of Botany; it is her ambition to convert the whole country into one grand garden."

"The idea is excellent. What is your chief food?"

"Fruits."

"How do you keep your country cool in hot weather? We regard the rainfall in summer as a blessing from heaven."

"When the heat becomes unbearable, we sprinkle the ground with plentiful showers drawn from the artificial fountains. And in cold weather we keep our room warm with sun-heat."

She showed me her bathroom, the roof of which was removable. She could enjoy a shower bath whenever she liked, by simply removing the roof (which was like the lid of a box) and turning on the tap of the shower pipe.

"You are a lucky people!" ejaculated I. "You know no want. What is your religion, may I ask?"

"Our religion is based on Love and Truth. It is our religious duty to love one another and to be absolutely truthful. If any person lies, she or he is—."

"Punished with death?"

"No; not with death. We do not take pleasure in killing a creature of God,—specially a human being. The liar is asked to leave this land for good and never to come to it again."

"Is an offender never forgiven?"

"Yes, if that person repents sincerely."

"Are you not allowed to see any men, except your own relations?"

"No one except sacred relations."

"Our circle of sacred relations is very limited to, even first cousins are not sacred."

"But ours is very large; a distant cousin is as sacred as a brother."

"That is very good. I see Purity itself reigns over your land. I should like to see the good Queen, who is so sagacious and farsighted and who has made all these rules."

"All right," said Sister Sara.

Then she screwed a couple of seats on to a square piece of plank. To this plank she attached two smooth and well-polished balls. When I asked her what the balls were for, she said, they were hydrogen balls and they were used to overcome the force of gravity. The balls were of different capacities to be used according to the different weights desired to be overcome. She then fastened to the air-car two wing-like blades, which, she said, were worked by electricity. After we were comfortably seated she touched a knob and the blades began to whirl, moving faster and faster every moment. At first we were raised to the height of about six or seven feet and then off we flew. And before I could realize that we had commenced moving, we reached the Garden of the Queen.

My friend lowered the air-car by reversing the action of the machine, and when the car touched the ground the machine was stopped and we got out.

I had seen from the air-car the Queen walking on a garden path with her little daughter (who was four years old) and her maids of honour.

"Halloo! you here!" cried the Queen addressing Sister Sara. I was introduced to Her Royal Highness and was received by her cordially without any ceremony.

I was very much delighted to make her acquaintance. In [the] course of the conversation I had with her, the Queen told me that she had no objection to permitting her subjects to trade with other countries. "But," she continued, "no trade was possible with countries where the women were kept in the zenanas and so unable to come and trade with us. Men, we find, are rather of lower morals and so we do not like dealing with them. We do not covet other people's land, we do not fight for a piece of diamond though it may be a thousand-fold brighter than the Koh-i-Noor, nor do we grudge a ruler his Peacock Throne. We dive deep into the ocean of knowledge and try to find out the precious gems, which Nature has kept in store for us. We enjoy Nature's gifts as much as we can."

After taking leave of the Queen, I visited the famous universities, and was shown over some of their manufactories, laboratories and observatories.

After visiting the above places of interest we got again into the air-car, but as soon as it began moving I somehow slipped down and the fall startled me out of my dream. And on opening my eyes, I found myself in my own bedroom still lounging in the easy-chair.

BAHINABAI CHAUDHARI ⎯⎯⎯⎯⎯⎯⎯

(ca. 1880–1951)   *Marathi*

"It was like treasure buried in a field when Maharashtra discovered Bahinabai's poetry last year," P. K. Atre wrote in the preface to the first edition (1952) of the poems of this cotton farmer from the Jalgaon district.

Bahinabai's songs/poems are composed in the *ovi* meter traditionally used in rhythmic accompaniment to the grinding of grain on the *chakki* (hand mill) and in lullabies. But like grinding or pounding songs, work songs, or lullabies in all Indian languages, they range widely in theme, mood, and tone. She uses a mixture of two dialects prevalent in the northern cotton-farming districts of Maharashtra: Khandesi and Varhadi. She was not literate, but as is obvious from her philosophical poetry, she was far from uneducated. In one of her poems she declares that Ram was her school and Saraswati her teacher. She is obviously referring to the rich oral tradition of religious literature recited in the *katha kirtans,* but to that she might have added her experience as a cotton farmer, a woman, a mother, and a friend.

The story of how these poems came to be written and later published is worth recounting. Her son, Sopandev Chaudhari (1907–1982), a poet himself, once read the story of Savitri and Satyavan to her from his primary school textbook. By next morning she had transformed the tale into a song in the ovi meter. Sopandev, struck by his mother's talent, wrote down some of her songs in a notebook, but they were set aside and forgotten. Several years later, after her death, when he was sorting out her things, he came across the notebook again. The story is now taken over by Atre. Sopandev, he writes, "was a shy man. He must have thought that the 'educated and cultured' reader of Maharashtra would not appreciate the beauty of his mother's Khandesi dialect. He happened to visit me last Diwali. In the course of a conversation, he opened a small notebook and read out to me, very timidly, one of his mother's poems. When I heard it I literally pulled the notebook out of his hand and greedily read the remaining poems. I had no problems at all with the dialect. 'But this is pure gold,' I shouted. 'It would be a crime to hide this from Maharashtra.' " Many of her poems have been lost, but 732 of them have been preserved. What we have, in the writer Shanta Gokhale's words, "give some clue to Bahinabai's wide-ranging mind, her compassion, her toughness, the freshness of her vision . . . in her own earthy, deeply sensitive language." Bahinabai's poetry is reflective, sometimes abstract, but her imagery is a startling mix of traditional icons and realist detail.

The first of the two poems translated here, "Ata Maza Male Jeeva" (Now I Remain for Myself), written after her husband's death, is one of the few in which Bahinabai speaks about herself. Among the outer symbols of marriage she, as a widow, will no longer use is the *mangalasutra,* a cord on which the token of marriage, usually fashioned in gold, is worn. The other poem, "Mun" (The Human Spirit), is more philosophical and difficult to translate, for the term *mun* includes the cognitive as well as the affective and imaginative dimensions of the human intellect. There is no English word that encompasses all these; "the human spirit" is a rough approximation.

◆

ATA MAZA MALE JEEVA
(Now I Remain for Myself)

There was no end to the tears
flowing from eyes.
I have cried so much.
Now tears have run out;
sobs remain.

Tears have run out,
giving me some respite.
Don't cry without tears,
O my Heart.

Tell me, O Mother Earth,
how did it all happen?
How did the tree vanish
leaving its shadow behind?

The gods have gone
to their heavenly home;

two golden boys smile
before your eyes.
Don't cry, O Heart.

Don't cry, O Heart.
Crying to you is second nature.
Make your tears laugh a little!
That's what gives life on earth
a bit of taste.

The vermilion mark
is wiped off my forehead;
only the tattoo remains
to welcome fate.

The bangles are broken,
but the wrists can still
wrestle with fate.
The mangalasutra
no more graces my neck;
but the vows taken,
hand on the neck,
still endure.

No, my sweet women,
do not weep for me.
I am now at peace;
now it's all between
my heart and me.

Translated by Vilas Sarang.

MUN
(The Human Spirit)

The human spirit comes back, it comes back,
Like cows to full-grown corn.
You may drive them, drive them away,
They come back, they come back to the corn.

The human spirit runs free, it runs free,
Finding paths, some here, some there.

It runs on like the waves upon water,
Driven on, driven on by the breeze.

The human spirit has its whims, has its whims,
Who can dare, dare to fasten it down?
It will wander, will wander untamed,
Like the wind in a gale or a storm.

The human spirit is poison, is poison,
Unknowable its deeds and its ways,
Far better the snake, the scorpion,
Their venom might answer to charms.

The human spirit is a bird, is a bird,
Who can truly describe its flight?
Right now it was here, on the ground,
Now it's gone, gone into the sky.

The human spirit is so quick, is so quick,
It knows not what patience is.
It streaks like a flash of lightning
From the sky to the earth as it will.

The human spirit is as small, is as small,
As the seed of the poppy flower.
And how vast, and how vast is that spirit?
Too vast for the heavens to hold.

Dear Lord, you have fashioned the human spirit
Unlike anything else in the world.
A miraculous maker you are—
And miraculous too are your works.

What is this thing called spirit
And with what skill have you wrought it so?
Was it, perhaps, a strange dream
That you dreamt with wide-open eyes?

Translated by Shanta Gokhale.

ANONYMOUS _____
(1881, 1889)   *Marathi*

Two rare early pieces—a speech and a newspaper article—have survived
because they were reprinted by Baba Padmanji (1831–1906), the first Marathi novelist, as appendices to his novel *Yamuna Paryatan* (Yamuna's Journey), 1857. The novel was subtitled "An Elucidation of the Condition of
Widows in India." Yamuna, the main character, undertakes a pilgrimage
and travels to different holy places. At another level her journey takes her
from Hinduism to Christianity. Baba Padmanji included these two essays,
he writes, because "there can be no substitute for a description of women's
woes and anxieties made by women themselves." The true value of his
novel, he thinks, would have been enhanced a hundredfold had it been
written by an educated Yamuna on her own.

The speech reprinted here was read by a woman at the meeting of women
organized by the Prarthana Samaj, Bombay, and printed in the *Subodh
Patrika* of 7 August 1881. The article, entitled "The Plight of Hindu Widows as Described by a Widow Herself," first appeared in *The Gospel in All
Lands,* April 1889. These pieces are of special interest for several reasons.
The question of the inhuman treatment of widows and the movement for
widow remarriage was a major focus of reform in the second half of the
nineteenth century. Among the first novels in nearly every Indian language were stories that, like Baba Padmanji's, placed at the center of their
plot a young Hindu woman, often a widow. The narrative posed her life
as a problem, which the author proceeded to elaborate, complicate, and
then resolve. Invariably the story also argued the need for her independence, and advocated women's education. Sometimes conversion to
Christianity was suggested as a fit resolution to the problem of the Hindu
woman. Krupa Sattianadan's *Saguna* and *Kamala* are novels that are thematically and structurally similar, as is Hannah Catherine Mullens's *Phulmani O Karunar.* Within the obvious constraints of the genre, however,
many other questions of more interest to women opened up. The issue of
young widows and their remarriage was of course not restricted to fiction.
Many of the principal activists of the social reform movement, notably
Iswarchandra Vidyasagar from Bengal and Kandukuri Veereshalingam
from Andhra Pradesh, gave their lives to the cause. In the second half of
the nineteenth century, widow remarriage became *the* issue around which
the women's question as a whole was focused, much as sati had been in the
first half of the century. It is often difficult for us today to appreciate

the passion with which those reformers, women and men, worked, or indeed the insistent need they felt for action on that front.

These unusual texts give us a vivid sense of what women went through and how the horrors inflicted on widows, often small children, served to reinforce women's dependence on men.

◆

MUMBAITIL PRARTHANASAMAJSAMBANDI STRIYANCHYA SABHETA EKA BAINE VACHLELA NIBANDHA
(A Speech Made by a Woman at a Women's Meeting Organized by the Prarthana Samaj, Bombay)

See how terrible is this custom of not allowing widows to remarry. Women have to suffer great misery because of this. Besides, incidents like infanticide are extremely common, for widows are tremendously scared of the social stigma. I confess that I am not competent enough to talk about all the miseries of the Hindu women, yet I would like to talk about a few that I have been thinking about these days. The woman whose husband dies is considered to be totally inauspicious and polluting. We consider it an ill omen to see her face first thing in the morning. So the poor thing is forbidden to walk around in the house. After the husband's death, her hair is shaved off and widowhood is permanently stamped upon her, even if she is just fifteen years old. She has to spend her whole life thus. She cannot wear pretty saris, or ornaments, she cannot mix with people, cannot attend religious ceremonies, and has to spend all her time sitting in a corner. Even after enduring all of this, however, she is not loved by anyone. Even her parents seem to consider her like grit in the eye, and they say, "Why was this wicked girl born in the first place? And if she was born, why didn't she die after birth? If our son-in-law had been alive, we would have given him our second daughter." Now, dear sisters, please try and imagine what [that] woman must feel when her own parents wish their daughter dead and the son-in-law alive. The poor soul must be eating her heart out, thinking, "Why was I ever born? What's the point of being alive? I'm not yet fifteen—and look at what a terrible condition I am in! No good clothes to wear, no mixing with people, no permission even to talk with anyone! Even my parents hate me. People frown when they see me. What's the point of having been born? It would be far better to die than live like this." We all know that these are only a few of the hardships a widow has to endure. There are many more. No amount of writing could cover them all. Isn't it a great injustice that if one wife dies, the man can marry another, and if that wife also dies, then he can marry a third one? He can eat, drink, laugh, roam around, and has no restriction whatever of any type. He is entitled to every pleasure, but the poor widow isn't allowed even one of them. When God created them, he created them as equals. Can it be called God's justice that one is allowed every freedom while the other is forbidden to have any? This great injustice is really a result of the ignorance of our people. My dear ladies, don't you damage your own cause yourselves. I have already told you about the miseries of widows. So, now, if you see any widows around, encourage them to remarry, and if some widows are getting married, don't create problems for them. Try to help them as much as you can. Just watch and see how things will change for the better after widow remarriages take place. Infanticide will decrease and the lives of women won't be wasted. Now, when the wife of an old man dies, he marries a young, ten-year-old girl, and often by the time she grows up, he dies. Obviously this is a widowhood that her parents actually invite for her. It is not her unchangeable fate. Marrying young girls to old men results in an increasing number of young widows. As opposed to this, if we have the custom of widow remarriage, the number of young widows will go down and there will be several other advantages. So my sisters, my last request to you is this. Let us all help this cause as much as we can.

Translated by Maya Pandit.

HINDU VIDWANCHI DUKHIT STITHI: EKA VIDHWA BAINE VARNILELI
(The Plight of Hindu Widows as Described by a Widow Herself)

There are four major castes among the Hindus and I was born into the caste known as kayastha, which is the third in the hierarchy and most infamous for its maltreatment of widows.

Widows anywhere have to suffer, but the customs in our caste are too terrible. The people in the Punjab don't treat their widows so strictly. But we do not belong to the Punjab. Originally we migrated from the northwest and settled there. And since ours is a well-to-do, why, even wealthy, caste, our regulations in this regard are extremely strict.

Once the husband dies, the torture of his wife begins, as if the messengers of the death god Yama themselves have come to take away her soul. None of her relatives will touch her to take her ornaments off her body. That task is assigned to three women from the barber caste. Their number varies from three to six. No sooner does the husband breathe his last than those female fiends literally jump all over her and violently tear all the ornaments from her nose, ears, etc. In that rush, the delicate bones of the nose and ears are sometimes broken. Sometimes while plucking the ornaments from her hair, tufts of hair are also plucked off. If she is wearing any gold or silver ornaments, these cruel women never have the patience to take them off one by one; they pin her hands down on the ground and try to break the bangles with a large stone. And many a time her hands are severely wounded in the process. Why, these callous women torture even a six- or seven-year-old girl, who doesn't even know what a husband means when she becomes a widow!

At such times grief crashes down on the poor woman from all sides. On the one hand she has to endure the grief of the husband's death, and on the other hand, no one comes near her to console her. On the contrary, those who had loved her from her childhood, and had brought her up tenderly, even they shower curses on her. In our caste, it is the custom that all the women accompany men when the corpse is carried for cremation. Everyone has to walk even though they are wealthy and have carriages. The menfolk walk in front and women follow them, clad in veils. And the poor widow follows them all. She is supported by the barber women. There has to be a distance of two hundred feet between her and the rest of the women because it is believed by our people that if her shadow falls over a married woman, she too will become a widow. It doesn't affect the barber women, who torture her, however, in the same fashion. Because of this stupid superstition, even a relative whose heart melts at the sight of her doesn't dare to look at her. But people are not satisfied even when they have tortured her so much. They brand her heart further as if with red-hot irons. Several men keep on shouting in that procession, asking people to stay away from her, and the barber women literally drag her along throughout the walk.

The place for cremation is usually on the bank of a river or a lake. When the procession reaches the site, the widow is pushed into the water. She has to lie there till the corpse is burned to ashes and all the people have had their bath and dried their clothes. When people are ready to go home, they pull her out of the water. Whether the water is cold as ice or the sun scorches down fiercely, she has to stay there until everyone has finished. Nobody takes pity on her. Even on the way back home, she is dragged along throughout. Because of such things, women prefer to burn themselves on their husband's funeral pyre. If the poor woman falls ill on such occasions, nobody even thinks of giving her medicine.

Once, before I became a widow myself, I had been in one such funeral procession. The place of cremation was nearly six miles away. It was summer. It was three o'clock in the afternoon by the time we reached home after having completed all the rites. I will never forget how the scorching heat of the sun was literally burning us on our way. We used to halt at regular intervals to rest a while and drink water. But that poor widow did not dare to ask for water. Had she asked for it, she would have lost her honor. The women with her could have given her some, but they felt no pity for her. Finally she collapsed unconscious. But even then her torturers continued to drag her throughout the road. On top of it, they kept nagging at her, saying, "Are you the only widow in the world? What's the point of weeping now! Your husband is gone forever!"

Later on, when this poor forsaken woman did not even have the strength to crawl, she was tied up into a bundle as if of rags, and then dragged off. This woman was one of our relatives; but none of us dared go anywhere near her. Had anyone done so, she would have been showered with curses. But even then, one woman somehow managed to take her water in a glass. On seeing her the widow ran to her like a wild beast. I cannot even bear to describe her behavior then. First of all, she gulped down the water, which revived her a bit. Then she fell at the feet of the woman who had given her the water and said, "Sister, I'll never forget what you have done for me. You are like a god to me. You have given my life back to me. But please go away quickly. If anybody comes to know of what you have done, both of us will have to pay for it. I, at least, will not let this out."

It is the custom that a widow should eat only once a day for a year after her husband's death; apart from that, she also has to fast completely on several days. Other relatives also eat only once a day. But only for fifteen days. After returning from the cremation ground, she has to sit on the ground in a corner, without changing her clothes, whether dry or wet. Nobody, apart from the barber women, visits her. If her own relatives are poor, even they don't come to see her. She has to sit alone. Oh, cruel corner, all of us widows know you so thoroughly well. And we never remember you unless we are grieved.

A woman whose husband is dead is like a living corpse. She has no rights in the home. In spite of her grief, her relatives brand her with frightening words and gestures. Though she is all alone there and not allowed to speak to anyone, her relatives go to her and pierce her with sharp words. Her mother says, "What a mean creature! I don't think there is anyone more vile than she. It would have been better if she were never born!" Her mother-in-law says, "This horrible snake bit my son and killed him. He died, but why is this worthless woman still alive?" There are even other widows among the women who speak cruelly to her! They feel that if they don't speak so, people, and God too, would think that they actually pitied her. The sister-in-law says, "I will not cast even a glance at this luckless, ill-fated creature! I will not even speak a word to her." Those who come to console the relatives of the dead say to the mother of the dead man, "Mother, this monstrous woman has ruined your house. She must be cursed. It's only because of her that you have been thrown into the ocean of grief!" And to the widow they say, "Now, what do you want to live for?" If she wails aloud, they say, "What a shameless woman! How callous! She cries because she wants a husband." Thus, she has to spend those thirteen days of grief in that alcove. What an unendurable state! No one can understand how painful it is unless she experiences it.

On the eleventh day, the brahmin comes. He comes like a policeman to arrest a convict. And then he authoritatively demands money or oil and so on. The widow has to pay him even if she is very poor; if she cannot pay immediately, she has to promise him that she will pay in future. Even if the widow is exceedingly poor, she has to pay at least thirteen rupees. Other brahmins demand other things. They demand more if the family is a rich one. Sometimes the widows have to work as servants doing household jobs, to earn money to pay these brahmins their dues.

Thus, there is nothing in our fate but suffering from birth to death. When our husbands are alive, we are their slaves; when they die, our fate is even worse.

The thirteenth day is the most fateful, the worst day for the widow. Though on this day she is allowed to change the clothes she has been wearing since her husband's death and have a bath, people continue to condemn her. Her relatives gather around her and place some money before her. This is supposed to be for her keep. They curse her a million times while doing so. If the money gathered is a large sum, one of her relatives takes it into his possession and doles it out to her in small installments.

Then the brahmin comes again to demand money. The brahmin and the barber women have to be paid again when the widow's head is shaved. After six weeks, she is again given the very clothes she had been wearing for the first thirteen days. When she sees those clothes again, she shudders from head to toe, as if she has been widowed again. Then she is sent on a pilgrimage to the Holy Ganges, and those clothes are thrown into the river after she has taken a holy dip in it.

After one year, if the widow is staying with her parents, she may be allowed to wear some ornaments. If asked about the reason, the parents say, "How long can our daughter continue not wearing ornaments? How can we bear to see her sit like that before us, wearing none, when we ourselves wear so many?"

Those widows who have lost their parents, however, have a terrible fate. They have to remain as slaves to their brothers' wives or even sons. People feel there is no need to employ a servant if there is a widow in the house. If the widow has a sister-in-law (her brother's wife), she has to suffer harassment at her hands. They constantly quarrel. Her fate isn't any different in her husband's family. Her mother-in-law and her sister-in-law hate her and often beat her. If she decides to separate and live independently because of the frequent quarrels, her honor is maligned. If she has any children, she has to toil hard for their upkeep. And when they grow up and get married, she becomes a slave to their wives. If a widow does not have any children, her relatives make her adopt a male child. He becomes heir to her property. And when he grows up and gets married, he is ruled by his wife and provides his adopted mother only with food and clothing. The widow has no right whatsoever to any property she may have. In such a condition, it is better for her if she earns her own living by working for others as a domestic servant.

In our caste, a woman does not have a right over even a piece of her father's property. It all goes to his relatives. Similarly, widows do not get a share in their husband's property either. They can claim only that which someone is kind enough to offer them. If they get any cash, they know neither how to keep it safe nor how to spend it. If a woman dies when her husband is still alive, her body is decorated with ornaments and new clothes, and then cremated. But when a widow dies, her body is just wrapped up in plain white cloth and cremated. It is reasoned that if a widow goes to the other world in ornaments and new clothes, her husband will not accept her there.

Thousands of widows die after a husband's death. But far more have to suffer worse fates throughout their life if they stay alive. Once, a widow who was a relative of mine died in front of me. She had fallen ill before her husband died. When he died, she was so weak that she could not even be dragged to her husband's cremation. She had a burning fever. Then her mother-in-law dragged her down from the cot onto the ground and ordered the servant to pour bucketfuls of cold water over her. After some eight hours, she died. But nobody came to see how she was when she was dying of the cold. After she died, however, they started praising her, saying that she had died for the love of her husband.

Another woman jumped from the roof of her house and committed suicide when she heard that her husband had died away from home. I and many of her other friends knew that this woman had never gotten along well with her husband. They used to quarrel often. Yet people praised her for committing suicide. If all these tales are put together, it would make a large book. The British government put a ban on the custom of sati, but as a result of that several women who could have died a cruel but quick death when their husbands died now have to face an agonizingly slow death.

Translated by Maya Pandit.

NIRUPAMA DEVI _____

(1883–1951)   *Bengali*

Nirupama Devi wrote in snatches between the onerous domestic chores generally assigned to widows and the religious rituals she carefully observed right through her life. The kitchen pantry, where she spent most of her time, was her study.

Yet, in the character of Suroma, the protagonist of her best-known novel, *Didi* (Elder Sister), 1915, Nirupama created a figure that was, in one form or the other, to grip the Indian cultural imagination in a powerful and continuing hold and reappear in the work of several other writers. Suroma embodies the idea that a woman who derives her spiritual strength from tradition can transform her world and redeem society through her exemplary compassion. The novel subtly inflects each of these abstractions, pulling the novel away from its conventional moorings to grapple with the new demands of a changing society. Suroma's influence, for instance, does not arise, as it might have done earlier, from the stern authority of her principles, nor from the power of her suffering, but from what would have been far more appealing to the contemporary reader, her compassion, her vitality, and her self-respect.

The emphasis is not, as one might expect, given that the Swadeshi phase of the national movement for Independence was at its height in Bengal at the time, on nationalist politics, but on mending a frayed social fabric, which in turn meant revitalizing the individual's inner life. The life of the *bhadralok,* the rich landowning classes, who like Nirupama Devi's hero, Amarnath, were taking up professions and moving into the cities, is presented as if this class lived in a political vacuum. The effect is initially disconcerting. But only so until we realize that the new image Nirupama Devi fashions in Suroma, of a woman who is powerful, modern, even individualistic, yet also deeply traditional, is one that we repeatedly meet and that sustained the nationalist imagination for several generations.

The philosophy is conservative, but in contrast to similar images that were emerging in the novels of Saratchandra Chatterjee (1876–1938) and other writers who took their lead from him, Suroma stands out as one who at her own initiative, and in her own interest, chooses the traditional way. In the novel, her choice is a strategy that allows her not only survival but also the possibility of self-fulfillment.

Nirupama Devi was born in Behrampore into a wealthy family. Her father, an employee of the imperial government, was at the time a subjudge in the Alipur court. She was married early, but her husband died when she was fifteen and she returned to Bhagalpur to live with her parents. While she was at her marital home, however, she had met Anurupa Devi (1882–1958), the writer with whom she was to enjoy a close and lifelong friendship. In Bhagalpur, Nirupama Devi lived the austere life of a widow—but she also wrote poetry. Around that time a literary circle had formed itself in the town around the popular novelist Saratchandra Chatterjee. As a woman and a widow, Nirupama could not participate in its activities, but she sent her poems to the literary circle through her brother, who was an enthusiastic member of the group. She cherished Saratchandra's comments, which inspired her and were a real support. It was he who first suggested she should try her hand at prose. Daunted by the reputation of this great writer of prose, however, Nirupama did not do so until her two writer friends, Anurupa Devi and Surupa Devi, persuaded her to try. Her work, which created a stir when it first came out, has always been extremely well received. Among her other novels are *Annapurnar Mandir* (The Temple of Annapurna), 1913, and *Shyamali,* 1919, the story of a mute half-wit who blossoms into an intelligent, warmhearted woman. Many of her poems were published in leading journals. Nirupama Devi received considerable recognition in her own times. In 1937, the novelist Sailabala Ghosejaya hosted a reception in her honor at the Burdwan Sahitya Parishad, an important literary organization. She received two major awards from Calcutta University: the Bhubanmohini Swarnapadak in 1938 and the Jagatarini Swarnapadak in 1943. In 1939 she chaired the sessions on prose writings at an important writers' conference held in Calcutta.

Though she was a shy and retiring person, Nirupama actively involved herself for a time in welfare work for women. She helped found the Mahila Samiti, a women's organization at Behrampore, and was its secretary for a number of years. It was at her initiative that a girls' school was established in the town. Throughout her life, however, she strictly observed the rituals of widowhood. She often went on pilgrimages and later became an ardent Vaishnavite. Toward the end of her life she spent a great deal of time caring for her ailing mother and going with her to Benares and Brindavan on pilgrimages. She herself died a little more than a year after her mother passed away in 1949.

The early part of the plot in the novel *Didi,* which we have excerpted for translation, deals with the marriage of the principal character Suroma with Amarnath and his subsequent involvement with another woman, Charu, whom he later marries. Amarnath and Charu go off to live in the city while Suroma assumes responsibility for her father-in-law and looks after his household. Just before his father dies, Amarnath returns to the family home and settles there. Charu takes an immediate liking to Suroma. The novelist portrays the younger woman as a simple, openhearted person who does not feel threatened or perturbed by the complexities of the relationship between her and Suroma. Suroma responds warmly and takes Charu under her wing, but she cannot forgive Amarnath. She continues to manage the household, however, and even advises Amarnath on the running of his estates. She makes it clear that Amarnath is Charu's husband, and has no connection with her. But gradually her behavior toward Amarnath grows more relaxed and she begins to treat him as a friend. By changing the relationship to one of friendship, she is able to deny her other relationship with Amarnath more emphatically. Suroma's intelligence, strength, and personality attract Amarnath, who realizes that he is in love. Suroma feels the same, but is afraid that all the years she has exercised self-control in her relationship with Amarnath will come to nought if she yields. She leaves her husband's home and returns to her parents. Before she leaves she tells Amarnath that no relationship with him is possible in the present or in the future. But taking leave of the bewildered Charu is much harder.

In the second part of the book we find Suroma in her parental home. The author uses a minor incident to highlight Suroma's strength and her practical common sense, and build the "traditional" proportions of this character. Observing the beginnings of a relationship between a child widow, Uma, and a young man from the village, Prokash, Suroma takes Uma away on a pilgrimage and arranges for Prokash's marriage to another girl. Prokash, who is very fond of Suroma and admires her strength, cannot understand her harshness. To Suroma, however, the matter is clear. Uma is a child widow in an era when remarriage is taboo. In order to save Uma the heartbreak and trauma she is likely to face, Suroma puts an end to the budding relationship. Given the lines of its development, *Didi* ends on a surprising note when after several years of restraint, Suroma sets her hurt aside and accepts Amarnath.

◆

DIDI
(Elder Sister)
Chapter 2

Amarnath returned home and felt at peace with himself and with the world because his father had behaved so affectionately toward him. But that was only a prelude to his father's announcement that his marriage had been arranged. The would-be bride, Suroma, was the only granddaughter of Sri Radhakishore, a zamindar of Kaliaganj. She was beautiful, the father added, though somewhat above what was considered the marriageable age for girls. Haranathbabu, Amar's father, had personally visited the family and finalized the match. Shyamacharan, the family dewan, gave Amarnath more details of the arrangement and added almost parenthetically, "She is a very intelligent girl, a very good girl."

Amarnath wanted to laugh. He had a good mind to ask them whether they even thought she was capable of keeping the accounts and looking after the affairs of their zamindari. He refrained from joking with the old man, afraid of hurting his feelings.

Amarnath lost his peace of mind. There was a nagging feeling that this was not what he wanted and yet he could not articulate what his real objections were. After all, his father had arranged the match and he could not object to that. At times he felt that the whole thing had happened too hurriedly and too early in his life. But he was embarrassed to speak frankly to his father regarding such trivial doubts. What objections could he put forward to this match; the other party was well-off and his father had not rejected some poor girl's family for this one. If that had happened, perhaps there would have been some cause for contention. But under the circumstances his vague discomfort did not seem to him to be an adequately rational reason for disagreement with his father.

The few days of the month of Kartik flew by and the auspicious day arrived in the month of Aghrayan. Amarnath was married. Since both families were well-off, they outdid each other in the preparations, pomp, and grandeur of the occasion. Amarnath, however, did not inform his best friend Deben about his wedding. He was not quite sure why he did not do so. He was ashamed to inform Deben, almost as though by admitting his marriage, he was betraying a pledge.

The ceremonies over, the bride and groom spent their first night together in a room bedecked with flowers. Amarnath lay stiffly at one end of the bed with great unease and somehow went through the ceremonial night. He was embarrassed. His bed companion was not a child but a grown-up lady of about fourteen years of age. Amarnath was himself hardly past his teens. The few days after the marriage, during which the bride stayed in their house, Amarnath spent most of his time outdoors.

When the bride returned to her father's home, Amarnath took leave of his father and returned to Calcutta.

Amarnath received a number of letters from his friend Deben, asking him to visit him at his village. But he did not reply. During the puja vacation he returned home to learn that his wife's mother had died and so she could not come during this period to her in-laws' house. Amarnath considered writing her a letter, to express his grief or at least to say something consoling. But he found it impossible to write to somebody whom he had never talked to. He decided to wait till he was properly introduced to her.

A year and a half went by since his marriage and Amarnath was making preparations to go home to visit his father when he received a letter from his friend Deben asking him to come to his village. The urgency of tone prompted him to change his plans and make the trip to Deben's village instead.

On enquiring from Deben as to what was the urgency, his friend replied in a lighthearted manner, "It's nothing that urgent. It was only a way to get you here, since you never visit us."

Amar was taken aback. "What kind of child's play is this? It was very wrong of you."

Deben paused a while and then said jokingly, "Come now, you have nobody at home as yet to whom you have to be accountable."

Amarnath blushed with embarrassment but still could not bring himself to tell Deben what had happened in his personal life.

That evening Deben suddenly asked, "Do you remember that girl Charu?"

Amarnath felt ill at ease and finally asked in low tones, "Why, what has happened? Is the girl dead?" As he spoke about her he could faintly recall the thin, emaciated face with the smiling, innocent eyes. Realizing that Amarnath was lost in his own reveries, Deben hastened to reassure him. "No, the girl is not dead. It's her mother. She is on her deathbed. I am treating her. Would you like to visit them?"

"Okay, let's go. Poor thing. Is she married yet?"

Deben replied, "Married? No, she is not married. Don't you realize that it takes a lot of money to get girls in your caste married? Since you had assured us that you would fix up a match for her, we have been relying on you."

Amarnath felt very guilty. He had forgotten that he had made such a promise.

They entered the crumbling and decrepit home that housed the mother and daughter. The ailing widow, Molina, was lying on the bed; the daughter, Charu, sat on the edge of the bed. There were deep circles under her smiling eyes and she looked thin and worn out. Amarnath was consumed with pity on seeing her. The girl shifted her position and sat in a self-conscious manner. Her eyes betrayed her embarrassment. Is the girl so unfeeling and so simple that even in these circumstances she feels embarrassed, Amar wondered.

After a while Deben spoke loudly to the prostrate figure, "Kakima, Amar has come." The widow whispered, "Where?" Deben pushed Amar toward her, saying, "Here he is." The sudden expression of joy on the dying face astounded Amar.

She caught hold of his hand with her last dying strength and declared in hoarse whispers, "I give her to you. I give you my daughter Charulata. May God bless you both."

Amar sat there stunned and frightened. His hand, which held the fragile fingers of the widow, seemed paralyzed. Her tears dropped onto his hand and shone like pearls.

Amarnath recovered his power of speech and hastened to remonstrate, "What are you saying? Do you know that—"

He was interrupted by Deben. "Hush! She is just falling off to sleep. Let her rest."

Amar persisted in an agitated manner. "I must explain. I have much to say. I am—"

Deben stopped him. "Later, later, Amar. How can you be so heart-less?"

That night the widow's condition deteriorated. Amar realized that she did not have much longer to live. He thrust aside the grief-stricken Charu, prostrate on her mother's breast, and said in loud, clear tones to the dying woman, "I am married. Do you hear me? I am married." It was too late. The widow was unconscious.

Deben was shocked. "What did you say, Amar? You are married? I didn't know anything about this."

Amar replied, "Certainly you didn't know. I didn't write to you. But look at the situation you have got me embroiled in. While she was still conscious you didn't let me tell her. Against my will I am now the victim of her last wishes. What have you got me into, Deben?"

"God be my witness. I am not at fault. I thought you were unmar-ried and so kept the widow's hopes alive. I thought you were trying to tell her that your father would not agree to the match."

The widow died in the early hours of the morning. Deben collected the village folk together and performed the last rites. Amarnath did not know how to console the grief-stricken daughter as he sat quietly next to her. The homeless, helpless girl lay on the floor weeping in-cessantly. Perhaps she had never appreciated fully the extent of her own helplessness. The whole world seemed clouded through her tear-ful, unseeing gaze. Amar wondered whether there were other things adding to her grief besides her mother's sudden death.

Days passed. Amar asked Deben, "What shall I do? Where is the way out?" Deben replied, "I don't know."

"Can't you people keep her here and get her married?" Amar asked.

"Where can we find a groom who will be willing to marry her without a dowry," Deben responded.

"I will give you the money," replied Amar.

"I can't keep her in my house against my mother's wishes. We be-long to a different caste. She has no alternative but you, Amar. The only way out I can think of is that you take her with you and get her married. What guarantee is there that you will remember your respon-sibility toward her once you leave here?"

Irritated and agitated by Deben's last jibe, accepting that now this was his fate, Amarnath left the village, taking Charu with him.

Chapter 4

It was a well-decorated, brightly lit room. The smell of flowers wafted in through the open windows. The faint melodies of the *shenai* being played in the temple floated in, creating an environment of peace and solitude. Amarnath lay half-reclined on one of the couches in the room.

Amarnath had arrived home that very day. He had left Charu in Calcutta after explaining the situation to her. Now all that was left to be done was to convince his wife and father about the seriousness of the pledge that he had undertaken. He felt that in this matter his wife's permission was the most important, and he needed to talk to her before speaking to his father. He was waiting for his wife to come and talk to him.

The door opened quietly. A young woman with her head covered walked silently over the heavy carpets and stopped suddenly near the couch. Then slowly she approached the couch where Amarnath lay sleeping, and stood still. Amarnath awoke and found himself face to face with an unfamiliar figure, whose large, dark, bright eyes looked steadily at him. Amarnath sat up. Half-consciously and involuntarily he asked, "Who are you?"

The young woman lowered her eyes, pulled her sari over her head, and said in a soft tone of voice, "It's me." She stopped, looked at Amarnath, and announced clearly, "I am Suroma."

Suroma! That was his wife's name. He was meeting her for the first time since the ceremonial first night. She had grown up. Amarnath sat up. Amarnath felt agitated like one who awakes from a dream and finds exactly the opposite happening to him. All this time, half in a dream and half awake in this beautiful room with its scent of flowers, he had imagined a shy, embarrassed bride approaching him. But he found himself instead confronted by a confident young woman who was not the least embarrassed, whose gaze held him, and who stood with the confidence of one who belonged there—erasing the vision of the shy bride come to meet her lover.

Amarnath sat down with a serious expression. Suroma waited awhile and then moved toward the well-decorated table as if to tidy it up. Having moved some pieces on the table, she proceeded toward the door. Amarnath called out to her, "Listen." Suroma came closer.

"Sit down."

Suroma looked around for a place to seat herself and finally sat at the edge of the couch on which Amarnath was himself seated. After a long time, and many moments of silence, she finally asked, "Did you send for me?"

Amarnath still remained silent.

Suroma prompted, "Do you want to say something to me?"

"Yes," said Amarnath.

"What is it?" asked Suroma.

Again Amarnath lapsed into silence.

Suroma waited awhile and continued, "Is it something that embarrasses you?"

Amarnath finally found his voice, "No, I don't feel embarrassed."

"Well then, is it something that I should be embarrassed by?"

"No, it's not about you. It is something that concerns me. But it is not so much a troublesome matter as one of obligation and duty. Listen carefully and try to understand."

"Yes . . ."

Amarnath began cautiously. He related at first only as much as he felt he could tell her. He spoke about his first visit to Deben's village, when he was able to save Charu from a serious illness; his second visit during the puja holidays and the conversations he had then; his marriage to Suroma on his return; the illusions that Charu's mother and Deben had fostered in the village regarding him and Charu; and finally Charu's mother's deathbed request, against which he was unable to protest. Incident by incident, Amarnath told his wife the whole story.

Suroma listened in silence. When Amarnath ceased his narration she asked, "Where is this girl?"

"The girl? Charu? She is at my house in Calcutta."

"That means she has been there since the month of Jaishthya. How is it that we were not informed all this time?"

Amarnath was annoyed. Suroma's tone seemed to hold both responsibility and reprimand.

"There was nothing wrong in not letting you know at that time. What difference would it make whether I told you then or today?"

"It is not the same thing. Charu—isn't that her name?—you could have brought her here and left her here with us."

Amarnath said in agitation, "Whether I kept her there or here, it's the same thing."

"It's not the same thing. In this house you have a father and your wife lives here also."

"There is nothing wrong in keeping a woman whom I intend to marry with me."

"Of course it's wrong. But let that pass. Is your decision to marry her final?"

"This is not a matter to be decided now; it was already decided then. Under these circumstances, is there any other way to fulfill one's duty except by marrying her?"

"Now it is your duty to marry her. At that time a match could have been arranged for her."

"What is the difference between then and now?"

The woman fixed her bright gaze on him, "Now you love her."

Amarnath sprang up. He retorted furiously, "You speak like a selfish woman. I . . . I may love her, but it was my duty then as it is now to marry her."

"All right. Then, have you come here to seek my permission? Is this also your duty?"

"I am not so stupid. But it is my duty to inform you."

"Good! I presume you have not told your father yet; that too is part of your duty."

"I don't need you to remind me about my duty to my father."

"You expect that he will agree?"

"Even if he does not, I have to do my duty."

"Even if he does not permit it, you are sure about your obligation?"

"Of course."

"All right. Can I go now?"

"As you please," said Amarnath, and flopped down on the couch. Suroma stood for a while, thinking. Then slowly, she left the room.

Chapter 17

The family returned home from their holiday at Monghyr. After that Suroma tried to be more careful. She had understood her mistake; she should have maintained her distance. Her closeness to Amar and friendship with him or any demonstration of affection would inevitably result in what she had always avoided up to now. She had not realized till now that any relationship with him was inadvisable. Her fate had determined that she could not take the easy way out; she would have to live alone and independently of everybody. She was hopeful that if she behaved with her former disregard toward Amar, his momentary weakness for her might dissolve of its own accord. Suroma grew more firm in her decision.

She stopped meeting Amar and even talking to him. She avoided the pleasant chats she and Charu had grown accustomed to having in their afternoon leisure. She thought up, and kept herself immersed in, new household duties every day. It was only when her son Atul came running up to her and hugged her that she had to relent. Charu kept complaining about her behavior. Suroma tried to laugh it away by saying, "Household duties need a lot of attention. Otherwise things do not work properly." If Shyamacharan approached her for advice about the property, she would reply, "Don't drag me into it. If you can get the work done, well and good. If you can't, let it be." Shyamacharan understood that Suroma was confused and troubled, and stopped going to her for advice.

Suroma did her best to develop feelings of distaste and dislike for Amar in her own mind. She felt that Amar's behavior was indecent and in bad taste. If a person cannot be determined and strong, then why should he be considered a human being? When Amar had dared everything earlier for his love of Charu, why were his feelings toward her today so disguised? His visible sentiments for Charu were obviously false. He had betrayed her even by entertaining in his mind affectionate sentiments for another woman who was not his wife. Suroma tried to conjure up Amar's image and reprimanded him in her imagination for his baseness.

When one is young and spirited, one dares to bet one's life on a single principle. One does not weigh the pros and cons. The victory of the spirit against all odds is considered in youth to be the highest necessity. But as one grows older and mellows, one realizes that what has been discarded as a trifling constraint to the realization of an objective was perhaps not such a trifling matter. There comes a time in one's life when that which was discarded as a trifle gains in importance and consumes one's life. Although Amarnath was not old enough to be suffering from ennui, and his affection for Charu remained, he realized that in having done what he did to uphold his principles, he had stepped heavily on the side of God's balance and it was time to restore the balance. This was God's revenge and it was beyond the powers of a human being.

If all were to be considered, could Amarnath be faulted for his present state of mind? Was not Suroma also involved and to some extent at fault in helping create this state of mind? (Amar could only be faulted for not having been able to gauge Suroma's power.) She was beautiful, learned, intelligent, and, what is more, magnanimous—these were her faults. If on earth these qualities exerted a divine power to attract ordinary mortals, then it was not the fault of the mortal to be drawn to it but the powerful magnet of these divine qualities personified in a human being. The person who had provided nectar to the flowering relationship between a man and wife was at fault. What man could not be attracted to a wife who had been his companion in happiness and sorrow, in dejection and hope, and yet did not enjoy the rights and privileges of a wife. This attraction had not occurred in one day. It grew gradually, day after day, month after month, and year after year, while he was encircled by this extraordinary, affectionate, loving, mysterious personality. Its influence had seeped into his blood, his very being, and he had grown involved and expressed his weakness for her. The calm affection he enjoyed with Charu had no connection with the challenging, highly emotional and disturbing sentiments he felt for Suroma. It had to be conceded that this was really his first experience of such love. He had no notion that such a person could exist in the world. He had read about such characters in novels and poems but could now feel its reality in his inner being.

Suroma found that her change in behavior did not bring about the desired result. Although she had stopped talking to Amarnath, his feelings for her were betrayed in his glances and expression. Amar spent very little time in the house, and did not go out on *shikar;* nobody could fathom the preoccupations that kept him away from home for such long periods. Charu complained to Suroma, "Have both of you deserted me?" And Suroma sought ways to extricate herself even further.

That evening Suroma went in search of Charu and found Amarnath in the room. Suroma withdrew, feeling uneasy.

She heard Charu say, "What has happened to you? What is all this work that keeps you from the house?"

Amar laughed, "Nothing, really."

"Then why don't you stop for your usual evening chats?"

Amar remained silent for some time. "I don't feel like it. Why, do you miss me?"

"Never mind that; tell me why you don't come?"

"Charu, would you like to go on holiday?"

"Where to?"

"Oh, anywhere. To some other place. Then I can spend day and night with you."

Amar was not suggesting the trip to try and escape from his worries. He had attempted this before when the seeds of his anxiety were germinating, but had returned without being relieved of worry. At present he did not want to be liberated. His only concern was that Charu should be happy and that is why he wanted to go away somewhere with her.

But Charu did not agree.

Amar left the room. Somebody called out to him. It was Suroma. "Please, come here, I have a few things to say to you."

Amar was suffocated by the sudden rush of blood in his veins. He curbed his excitement and followed Suroma. Suroma said, "Do you want to take Charu away somewhere?"

"Yes," Amar replied without raising his head.

"This is not a bad idea. Why don't you go? But before you go I have a few things to say."

Amar waited awhile, looked at her expectantly, and said in a soft voice, "Why don't you proceed?"

Suroma had her eyes downcast all this while, but when Amar spoke she looked up in surprise.

She waited awhile and then with a clear gaze confronted Amar. "And after that? When you return to this house and to me, can I expect to see you cleansed and pure?" Amar did not reply; he fixed his gaze on the ground. "Tell me. I want an answer. If you cannot come back chaste of mind, then this travel abroad will have been of no use. Tell me, can you do it?"

Amar raised his face. In an emotional voice he replied, "Really, Suroma, going away is a punishment. I am not going away for that reason."

"Then why are you going?"

"In case I can do something to help Charu."

Suroma's tone grew harsh. "And at present do you think you are doing justice to her? Since you are hers, if you entertain any thoughts of anyone else, you will have done her a wrong."

Amar replied in a lowered voice. "To her this mistake of mine is absolutely unforgivable. And what I have done to you, is that forgivable?"

"But I have forgiven you."

Amar's voice was choked. He enquired, "Why? I did not ask for your forgiveness. I would now like to do penance for what I have done to you. You must give me that time. I will not come near you; let me do this penance from afar.

"Although I have no right to say anything to you, I still want you to know I want to bear this punishment, go through this retribution with all my heart, Suroma. My happiness today is dependent on being able to undertake this retribution. Give me this little happiness. This small right."

"You want to perpetrate one wrong by doing penance for another?

Don't even imagine I will give you the opportunity to clear your conscience. Do you know why I forgave you? I didn't forgive you for yourself. I forgave you because of Charu. You are nobody to me, you never were, you still are not."

Amar was stunned. He felt as if the firm earth under his feet was suddenly shaken. He had never been hurt in this manner. Hesitatingly, falteringly, he could only say, "Nobody can be so cruel to one's face. Whatever else you do, I beg only—"

"Should I say it less hurtfully? Have I said it too harshly? In the first years of my life, did you show me even this much softness? Did you ever consider then how hurtful even ordinary words and incidents could be? At that time did you ever think of me and my feelings? It's a good thing you didn't. I respected you for that. I concluded that you were upright and honest in your love for Charu, and that is why you could not see me as your wife. But today? Today, even that respect has been shattered."

Amar slowly crept onto a seat on the floor, stunned into silence. Suroma watched him for some time, motionless. Then suddenly she went nearer to him and said in a plain tone of voice, "Please forgive me. I have said many things I should not have. I did not wish to hurt you in this manner. It's my fate, a fault in my personality that I cannot stop myself from saying what I want. Please forgive me. I trust you, think of you as a friend. You are Charu's husband. I don't wish to hurt you."

Amar hid his face in his hands and cried out in grief. "That's enough, quite enough. Don't give me this pity; forgive me instead."

Suroma was not silenced. "I did not speak so harshly to you because I bear you any grievance or wanted to take revenge on you. I want you to be as before—completely devoted to Charu."

"You are cruel. Why can't you concede this much? Why can't you say that since you never got what was rightfully due you, I, too, have no right to get my due. Am I even unworthy of your insults? Do I not have the right to your hurt feelings—or did I never possess this right? Recalling the incident that day—"

"Why should I be hurt by what you say? I never had any relationship with you."

Amar got up and left hurriedly.

The family learned that Suroma was going to her father's house. Everybody understood that this was forever.

"What are you doing?" Shyamacharan asked.

"Why should I allow Atul to be disinherited?"

He noticed that Suroma had made up her mind and held his peace.

He told Amar, "So you are effectively putting an end to my ambition to go on a pilgrimage to Benares?"

"No, you should go. I have learned a lot. I don't want to prevent you from performing your religious duties. I have no wish to prevent anyone in the world from doing what they want to do," Amar replied.

Charu embraced Suroma. She could not speak; her tears flowed over Suroma's breast. Suroma could no longer hold back her tears. Finally she said, "Charu—my dear sister—please forgive me. Please don't weep like this."

"Didi? Are you a sister? You are so cruel."

Suroma lifted Charu's face to hers and wiped her tears. She said, "Don't say I am cruel. Let the others call me names, but when you say I am cruel, it breaks my heart."

Charu embraced her again and said, "Then why are you leaving us, Didi? Please don't go."

"Please don't ask me to stay. I can't do it. Just to know that you would prevent me from leaving makes me grieve."

"Why have you suddenly made this decision, Didi? You haven't gone to your father's home all these years."

"It's God's wish, Charu. Only he knows why I must go. My father has no one—think about that too. And why should I give Atul's inheritance away to someone else?"

Charu tried to stop her. "Atul does not have any wants. And besides, how will he live without you?"

"What can I do, Sister? I am helpless," Suroma replied.

"Then when will you return?"

"When Atul has children, I will come to take my share."

"Didi, will you be able to live without us? Is your heart so hard?" Suroma managed a wan smile in reply.

"Didi, I have been meaning to ask you a question but I have never dared. Can I ask you today? Is your husband nobody to you?"

Suroma laughed, pinched Charu's cheeks, and said, "Why should he be nobody to me? He is your husband."

"Don't you have any responsibilities toward him?"

"No, those I gave to you."

"Didi, forgive me, I have something more to say that I have never said before. Since he is your husband, why have you always deprived yourself of the rights that you were entitled to? He wronged you. I know you have forgiven him, so why are you again forsaking us? I want you to keep your position in this household. I will live in the shadow of your affection and his love. Don't leave us."

"Charu, if you love me even a little, please don't prevent me from going. You have always thought of me as your sister. Why is it, then, just as I am departing, that you think of me as your co-wife? I am your loving sister, not your co-wife."

"Forgive me, Didi. I am really stupid, forgive me."

"Then don't ask me to stay."

The day of Suroma's departure arrived. Suroma kissed Atul good-bye and said, "When you grow up, come and see me."

Charu said in a broken voice, "Take him with you now."

"No, let him grow a little older. I am going, Charu. . . ."

Charu hid her face in her hands. Suroma lifted her face, kissed her on her brows, and put her hand on Charu's head for the final blessing.

Translated by Maitrayee Mukhopadhyay.

SUGHRA HUMAYUN MIRZA ─────────

(1884–1954)   *Urdu*

In one of Sughra Humayun Mirza's novels, the heroine, Mohini, a princess who has renounced her inheritance and set out to seek the truth, is transported in a dream to the world of the dead where she meets a curious assortment of well-known Persian poets and erstwhile reformers, such as Amir Ali and C. R. Das. They are in conference discussing the question of women, and among them is a spirit who represents the Prophet's daughter, Hazrat Fatima. Everyone speaks in favor of divorce for oppressed wives, remarriage for widows, and a woman's right to choose her husband. Fatima's spirit expresses her displeasure at the oppression of women in the world of the living. All of them, including, for some reason, Napoleon, who is there with his two wives, condemn the practice of purdah.

For this activist and writer, fiction and poetry were modes to express her reformist views in an entertaining way. Born in Hyderabad into a well-placed family—her father, Haji Safdar Ali Mirza, a surgeon in the state army, was a man of learning and pious Sufi leanings—Sughra Begum did not go to school, but studied Urdu and Persian under private tutors. She married Syed Humayun Mirza, a barrister from Patna, who came to live in Hyderabad after their marriage. Sughra continued with her writing and her work for the rehabilitation of destitute women. With her husband she traveled extensively in India, and visited several countries of Europe in 1924.

Sughra Humayun Mirza was a fairly prolific writer and her works include several *safarnamas* or travel accounts, novels, short stories, poetry, and reformist writing. Of the fifteen books she published, six were safarnamas. Her five novels are *Mohini,* 4th ed. 1955, *Zohra, Bibi Turi ka Khwab* (Turi's Dream), *Awaz-e-Ghaib* (Voice from the Unknown), and *Safina-e-Najat* (The Barge of Liberation). Her reformist writings appeared mainly in the women's magazines she edited, including *Musheer-e-Niswan* (Woman's Counselor), *Al Nisa* (The Woman), and *Zaib-un-Nisa* (Women's Adornment). She wrote poetry under the pen name of Haya.

Sughra Humayun Mirza was not principally a writer. She was one of the first women activists of Hyderabad. Though she faced a great deal of opposition at every stage, Sughra Begum never gave up her battle to help women discover their rights and live a life of dignity and self-confidence. In 1913 she became the secretary of Anjuman-e-Khawatin-e Islam (Association for Muslim Women), started by Tayyaba Begum, an all-India association to which Rokeya Hossain in Bengal also belonged. In 1919 she became the president of another women's organization, Anjuman-e-Khawatin-e Dakkan, which ran institutes for women where trades and crafts were taught. The Anjuman invited several eminent persons to speak on social evils, including purdah. Sughra Humayun Mirza started similar organizations in other cities of India such as Madras, Delhi, and Aurangabad. At a time when it was still extremely difficult for women to go out of the house, she opened a school for girls, the Madrasa-e-Safdaria in Hyderabad, for which she donated a large part of her property.

Sughra Humayun Mirza's fiction is difficult to excerpt. We have chosen instead a poem that captures a momentary regret that many of the women involved in the social reform movements must have felt, given the odds they had to battle against.

◆

[Who will care to visit my grave when I am gone]

Who will care to visit my grave when I am gone,
Only the wind will raise its dust when I am gone.

No one knew my worth while I was alive;
No one will shed tears for me when I am gone.

The regret remains that my people ignored me,
But a voice will rise in protest from my grave when I am gone.

During my life I found no return, no reward,
Lord! May my work find acceptance when I am gone.

My last wish is this, that those who care for me
May strew a few flowers on my grave when I am gone.

Translated by Syed Sirajuddin.

NANJANAGUDU TIRUMALAMBA ———

(1887–1982)   *Kannada*

After Nanjanagudu Tirumalamba became a widow at the age of thirteen, her father encouraged her to study. She read classical poetry and religious texts at home, and soon started writing herself. Her first poem, in three stanzas, "Bharati Poreyennanu" (Bharati, Protect Me), came out around 1902. By 1911 she had moved into what might be considered the period of her mature writing. Her first novel, *Sushile,* appeared in 1913. Twelve more came in quick succession, notable among them *Nabha,* 1914, *Vidyullata* (The Vine of Learning), 1914, *Viragini* (The Dispassionate Woman), 1915, *Dakshakanya* (The Capable Girl), 1916, and *Matrunandini* (Daughter of the Motherland), 1916. She also wrote several plays and some lyric poetry. Her themes were the problems of widows, dowry, and child marriage. In all her writings she argues that women should have access to formal education.

Apart from being the first major woman writer in modern Kannada, Tirumalamba was also an activist. She believed that women's intellectual and spiritual life needed to be revived, and in 1916 started *Karnataka Nandini* (Daughter of Karnataka), the first magazine for women in Kannada. For three years she ran it almost single-handedly. She also started a publishing company, Satihitaishini (Well-wisher of Virtuous Women), which not only published her books but also featured translations from other Indian languages and collections of poetry and plays by other Kannada writers. For some time she taught young children, ran a children's magazine, and wrote and directed a series of plays for them. She was also a practitioner of folk medicine and treated the people in her village, especially during the plagues that ravaged parts of Karnataka during the early twentieth century.

As was common in her time, she advocates education for women and analyzes the problems of widows, from a traditional position. Widows in her novels fight for dignity and work to serve society, but oppose remarriage and renounce worldly pleasures. Widowhood, she believed, was the result of evil deeds in a previous life. Education was necessary because it would help women become better wives and mothers, and a good wife was one who obeyed her husband's demands implicitly and considered him a god. But in spite of this, Vijaya Dabbe comments, Tirumalamba's defense of women's capabilities, their intellectual powers, and their right to a dignified life is remarkable. Beneath her traditional stance, we see the awakening of a feminist consciousness. Tirumalamba also opposed child marriage, the tonsure of widows, dowry, and ostentatious expenditure, especially at weddings.

In the novel *Nabha,* from which the episode translated here has been taken, the heroine loses her only parent and also becomes a widow. She has to move in with an aunt, who gives her shelter but takes away her few possessions and insists on shaving her head in case she gets into trouble and ruins the family name.

◆

From NABHA

Chapter 3

The setting sun indicated that the sun of Nabha's fortune was going down as well. The skies darkened, and a dark shadow of worry engulfed Nabha. Ten days had gone by since the death of her mother. Though it was past nine o'clock, Shankarnath had not returned that night. Sharavathi, his wife, stands by the door, waiting for him. In the small room at the back of the yard sits Nabha, unadorned. She shows no sign of calmness or enthusiasm. She had given up all her wealth to Sharavathi by means of a transfer deed on the third day after her mother's death. Will and determination were the only jewels she possessed now.

Learned reader! Do those gripped by the desire for wealth ever respect their gurus, their parents, their kith, or kin? Do they think of evaluating anything in terms of justice and injustice? The power of money can render a guilty person innocent, an ignorant man knowledgeable. Small wonder that our elders said, "Money can make even a dead man talk."

Until now, the last rites of Nabha's mother had been performed without a misstep. Yet, the question of Nabha had not been settled. Sharavathi, who was capable of nourishing a poison tree in her heart, now forcefully expressed her desire. A decision had to be taken about shaving Nabha's head. Nabha waited anxiously to know what would happen. Sharavathi's gaze was on the road . . . Shankarnath returned home at last. As he entered, Sharavathi fixed him with a hawklike glare and spoke sharply. "Are you done with roaming around the town? You're fit to do nothing else!"

Smiling, Shankarnath said, "It looks as if the mistress is in a fine temper! Who's provoked your anger today?"

Sharavathi: "I'm angry at nobody—what right have I to do that? You carry on with your activities. It's you who'll suffer in the end."

Shankarnath laughed. "Why are you in such a rage? Each sentence of yours is turning into a sharp arrow."

Sharavathi: "That's the way I am. Why tease me when you know it?"

Shankar: "It's only natural that you make demands of me and that I pull your leg."

Sharavathi: "I don't want any fooling around."

Shankar: "Why not?"

Sharavathi: "You never listen to me."

Patting her back placatingly, Shankarnath said, "All right. I understand now. According to you, I've done something wrong today. I should have come home sooner. It's true. But I was delayed because I was getting some things for tomorrow's rites. Forgive me. Speak now and I'll listen. I'll carry out your bidding."

Turning away, Sharavathi said, "What should I say—and what will you listen to? Isn't this indication enough?"

Amazed by her talk, Shankarnath assured her, "I promise to do as you wish." He led her to a small room off the veranda.

Nabha, a witness to this exchange, thought, "What? Can a wife demand so much of her husband? Isn't he to be treated as a god? O Lord Rama! How cruel are the ways of the world! I for one cannot accept today's values, practices, talk. . . . But I must listen to their conversation today; they are bound to discuss me." Standing by the door she listened.

Shankar: "True, it's nine days now. So what?"

Sharavathi: "What arrangements have you made for the next task?"

Shankar: "What task is this?"

Sharavathi: "About the girl . . ."

Shankar: "What about her?"

Sharavathi: "Her adornments should be removed."

Shankar: "But what's left on her that we can remove?"

Sharavathi: "Her hair . . ."

Shocked, Shankarnath fell silent. His head started spinning.

Sharavathi: "What does your silence mean?"

Shankar: "Can't we let the hair be?"

Striking her forehead, Sharavathi exclaimed, "A curse on you! Why has God given you such ideas? Can we let a woman who's lost her husband keep her hair?"

Shankar: "She's still young, poor girl, and grieving for both her mother and husband. How can we bring ourselves to punish her like this?"

Sharavathi: "You think we shouldn't do it. But you are a man and may do what you please. Still, what about us? What about the fire consuming us?"

Shankar: "What do you mean?"

Sharavathi: "Why do you keep asking the same question? What adorns a woman best? Isn't it her hair? If we allow the hair to add to her youth and beauty, one can only imagine what will become of her. Vile practices are only helped by long and plentiful hair. Think about the effect it'll have on the family, on your lineage. Still, what does it matter once the husband himself is gone? How does morality matter, or our customs?"

Shankar: "All right. But not straight away. There's time enough for all that."

Sharavathi: "Why not now?"

Shankar: "Give her another five or six months at least."

Sharavathi: "But why not now?"

Shankar: "We've managed to snatch away all her property. Why be charged with having had her hair removed as well? No, I can't possibly do it."

In a rage, Sharavathi said, "In that case, you must face the music. But just know that what you're doing will bring a bad name to the family."

"Don't shout."

"Yes, I shout all the time. I'm ignorant. But you, you're all-knowing. Do as you please." She walked away in a rage.

Nabha overheard the whole conversation and moaned as she returned to her corner: "O Lord! Is this my destiny? But, as the elders say, we must suffer our sins. Yet, Lord, dear Lord! What have I done to deserve this?"

Translated by Seemanthini Niranjana and Tejaswini Niranjana.

JANAKI BAI

(1889–?)   *Urdu*

Janaki Bai was born in Allahabad. Her father, Shiv Malik Ram, and her
mother, Manaki Bai, had moved from a nearby village to the city where
they had opened a sweetshop. We know very little about Janaki Bai's
childhood or education, or indeed how she trained to become a singer and
dancer. But we do have evidence that in her day she was a highly sought-
after composer and singer of ghazals (see our discussion of Mahlaqa Bai
Chanda). Reviews comment on her haunting voice and her extraordinary
beauty. In the 1920s and early 1930s when her career was at its height,
she was able to demand a much higher fee than other artists for a performance. The *Pioneer* of 10 September 1928 compares her dancing to that of
a peacock and comments on the splendor of the sets that were used. It is
said that one of her admirers, Raghunandan Dubey, wanted her exclusively to himself. Janaki Bai's mother would hear of no such thing. Infuriated, he came to their house and stabbed the singer fifty-six times. After
that she was popularly known as Janaki Bai Capancuri (Janaki Bai, of the
Fifty-Six Knives).

   The only extant collection of her writings, *Diwan-e-Janaki* (The Poems
of Janaki), was published in 1931.

◆

[I remember the days of love's first flowering]

I remember the days of love's first flowering,
When the heart was in its place and your secret locked in the heart.

The double mystery is now revealed to me at last;
Magic and miracle both meet in that bewitching eye.

How can I hope to escape suffering and grief
When I've given my heart to one so treacherous?

To this day the lament in my heart hasn't reached my lips;
My plaint perhaps holds the secret of one who is veiled.

Why ask me, why not ask yourself
How love began, what it has ended in?

In the vale of love they all went their ways,

My heart alone remained with me, my companion and friend.

What grief, what pain has come to Janaki from one
Of whose kindness and favor she was once so proud.

Translated by Syed Sirajuddin.

INDIRA SAHASRABUDDHE ―――――――

(ca. 1890–?) *Marathi*

We have been able to locate very little biographical information about this important feminist novelist. Her short, thought-provoking articles started appearing in reformist journals such as *Manoranjan, Navayug,* and *Udayan* from about 1910, the year in which her first novel, *Godavari,* was also published. The novel speaks of the way a child-bride is insulted and ill treated. Indira Sahasrabuddhe, who says in the introduction that the book holds a mirror up to the institution of marriage, compares the husband's house to a prison and the young bride to a prisoner. In what was undoubtedly a revolutionary gesture, she describes the first night of this nine-year-old bride. Godavari thinks of the flowers, the bed, and the other paraphernalia as a vicious trap. Unlike other novelists of this time, who preached widow remarriage but portrayed characters who always stopped short of it, Sahasrabuddhe's Godavari marries her childhood friend after her husband dies.

The issues *Godavari* dealt with were the major reformist issues in Maharashtra at the turn of the century: child marriage and widow remarriage. Indira Sahasrabuddhe's second novel, *Keval Dhyeyasathi* (Exclusively for the Higher Life), 1924, was bolder, and the position she took, unprecedented. She not only criticized the institution of marriage but also called it redundant. The heroine, Shaline, the preface says, "knows, and we all know, that marriage is a legal ban on love. Shaline is an idealist. People might call her an immature idealist. In our country where people are still hotly discussing whether a girl's age at the time of marriage should be fourteen or sixteen, this novel will not be given even a patient hearing." The preface continues, "Significantly even the Western-educated characters in the novel cannot appreciate that women may want more than home, marriage, and motherhood." Her third and last novel, *Balutai Dhada Ghe* (O Girl Child, Learn a Lesson), published in 1931, is cast in the form of a long autobiographical letter written by a mother to a daughter. As she tells the story of her life, the mother exposes the newly educated brahmin families. Their modernization, she knows, is only a veneer, their commitment to women's education halfhearted. The protagonist, who takes seriously the promises of freedom and self-determination that were held out by the reform movement, is betrayed and attacked. When an early relationship is broken up and she is forced to marry a man of her father's choice, she speaks of it as her *re*marriage. Women's slavery, the mother tells the daughter, continues. Since it also raises the question of sexual relationships in marriage and of a woman's right to choose whether she wants to be a mother or not, the book was very controversial.

Indira Sahasrabuddhe is a name unfamiliar to students of Marathi literature, but she, together with Geeta Sane and, somewhat later, Vibhavari Shirurkar, were the formative voices in what might be considered a feminist tradition in Marathi literature. Their work is all the more important because they pose many of the issues that emerged in the nineteenth-century reform movements more radically, exploring the implications of freedom and the right to self-determination for women.

◆

From BALUTAI DHADA GHE
(Learn a Lesson, Balutai)
Chapter 14. Sonucha Punarvivaha (Sonu's
Remarriage)

When he saw that I had stayed home that night, Baba was happy and relaxed.

I was married the next evening as scheduled at the auspicious moment of the day. The arrangements were grand, and spoke well of our financial status.

My father and my mother were so delighted that no one needed to ask how happy they were. All the guests were pleased too.

I was the only one who was unhappy.

But nobody was worried about me!

My mother thought that I must be happy because I had rich, brocade saris, clothes made out of expensive, finely woven cloth as well as gold, pearl and diamond studded jewelry.

Poor Mother! How could she understand what I was going through? In fact, when I looked at the jewelry, all it reminded me of was my slavery. It was to this jewelry that Father had sold me. Because of this jewelry I had lost my freedom and become someone's slave. God! Would my mother ever realize the importance of freedom?

Freedom is of no value to us. We are born only to serve—father or husband—that is what she believed. That is why the very things that grieved me must have made her happy. What a huge difference between the views of the two generations.

We women have got used to depending excessively on men. We can't even do the most minor things without their help. That is why we have become the weaker ones, and are denied the freedom to choose our life partners.

Compared to the happiness I would have had with a plain cotton sari from Bhasker, what I got from this jewelry was nothing. I wept all through the Laja-Hom*; but I pretended the smoke had irritated my eyes. Five or six days later the marriage rituals were over and it was time to leave with my husband, Tatyasaheb. Fortunately Tatyasaheb had made a good impression on me. He looked very gentle and affectionate. So I was not at all afraid to go with him.

Mother began to weep because I was going away to my husband's house. That really made me want to laugh. Baba and Ai had together pushed me out—and now they were upset about my going!

I had had enough of my father's house. The very father who had given me so much freedom as a child had now thrust this slavery on me. He had put chains around my legs and had finally destroyed me. And that is why I did not feel sorry in the least to leave him.

All the same I felt heavy in my heart when I thought of Mother's unstinting affection and of my innocent brother Madhu.

Only Madhu cared about me. Sometimes when he found me alone he would come up and ask, "Tai, is there anything you want me to tell Bhasker?"

Those moments really endeared Madhu to me. I was dying to know what Bhasker was going through, but I said, "Madhu, what connection do I have with him now? Father has broken the tie between us. He has snapped it and burned it down. Now I must learn to forget Bhasker—and if I can do that, it will be an achievement. In fact, if that happens I would consider life's duty fulfilled."

Madhu was surprised—and disappointed—at my resolve not to mention Bhasker again, yet it showed me how much Madhu himself approved of Bhasker.

Laja-Hom is the ceremony when popped rice is thrown into the sacred fire.

Chapter 24. Khara Parapurush Kona? (Who Is the Real "Other" Man?)

Baba and Ai were both surprised when we suddenly arrived at their house, but they were happy. Then, since we did not appear to share their happiness, they were perturbed.

Having accompanied me to my father's house, Tatyasaheb left immediately for a friend's house. He left from there, that very night, for Bombay.

All that he said to my father as he left was, "Your daughter and I don't get along with each other. So I don't want to be responsible for her."

Baba was flabbergasted when he heard that. He urged Tatyasaheb to explain everything before going away. But Tatyasaheb would not listen to him. He ignored Father's entreaty and left. Father sent for me immediately.

When I was called I knew I would have to answer his questions, and I went determined to speak boldly.

He was sitting in the hall, leaning against a large cushion, engrossed in thought. When he saw me he asked me to sit down beside him and began, slowly, to ask about me. This was the first time we had met since my wedding. After a while Father said, "Sonu, we didn't imagine that you would forget us so quickly after marriage. I wrote many times to Tatyasaheb, asking him to send you over because Ai kept asking for you. But each time he wrote back to say that you did not want to come to Pune. So we thought you must be very happy in your new world. In fact, once we almost decided to come and visit Bombay so that we could see for ourselves. But your mother said, 'How can we go unless we are invited?' That's why we didn't come. When I heard what Tatyasaheb said this morning, I was really alarmed. I had not imagined that there would be problems between you and Tatyasaheb. What is it that you lack that Tatyasaheb has abandoned you like this? And if he has no just reason we shall not hesitate to go to court."

I wanted to laugh. I said, "Baba, in matters such as marriage force is of no use at all. First, I must explain that Tatyasaheb is not at fault at all. In a way what he has done is right. Now, whether I take shelter here or not, whether you take me in or you don't, is an altogether different issue. But in this whole affair Tatyasaheb is not to blame at all. If anyone is to be blamed for these misfortunes, it is you. . . ."

"Me? Me to be blamed? Why? I haven't been eating his bread. On the contrary, he should thank me because he got my beautiful, educated daughter for his wife."

"All that is true. But I feel you still haven't understood your own daughter's nature. How does it matter in any way whether one is beautiful and educated? In a marriage what really counts is the harmony between two people and the pleasure one gets in the other's company. And that is precisely what is totally missing with us. Right from the very beginning, because I had Bhasker in my mind, whenever Tatyasaheb and I were alone, I felt like leaving on one excuse or another. How could there be any talk of love? I really tried, but I can't do it. I cannot make him happy."

"Is he a bad character? How does he ill-treat you? Does he beat you?"

I shook my head. That made Baba furious. He shouted, "Then what do you mean by saying you don't get along with him? Can't you run his household? Was all the education, all the careful upbringing we gave you useless?"

I sighed deeply. In order to make things clear to him I said, "I don't understand your idea of marriage, Father. In a marriage it is not enough that a man be good. There are many good men in the world, but we do not consider marrying them. I agree that Tatyasaheb is a good man. He really treats me very well. And I respect him. He has many good qualities. Yet, I cannot be a wife to him. I tried to conform, and for the sake of your name I tried to behave. But I felt repulsed. I felt there was no difference between me and a prostitute. If there was any difference at all, it was because they sell their bodies to a dozen different men, while I sold mine only to one."

"What do you expect me to do? Applaud?"

"What use is it to react like this, Baba? One cannot just ignore such grave questions. You may applaud me, or condemn me, or consider me a fool—as you wish. But I don't want to be responsible for giving birth to children under such disgusting conditions. I managed somehow to live with him until today, trying to make up for my faults— but that was a mistake."

"Well," said Father, letting out a deep breath. "Did you share these ideas with Tatyasaheb too? Did you tell him that you do not want to live with him?"

"No, I did not say anything. When he realized that I loved Bhasker, he got angry and brought me back here to hand me over to you. I think he feels a woman must always be in the custody of a father, husband, or brother!"

"He did the right thing. One should never give such notions of freedom as you have any scope."

"Then why did you allow me this freedom when I was a child? Why did you educate me like a boy?"

"Because I didn't expect you to abuse your education like this."

"To think independently, Baba, is not to abuse education. The whole purpose of education is to think independently and then reform the world."

"I don't need *you* to teach me this. Education can be used for both purposes: good as well as bad."

"But what am I doing that is bad?"

"Bad? What can be worse or more contemptible than a woman from a good family whose eyes fall upon other men with desire?"

"How can I help it, Baba, if for me Tatyasaheb is the 'other' man? You knew everything about me. You knew how deeply I loved Bhasker. And yet you chose to ignore it. In fact you forced me into this marriage. If you had actually given me the freedom, I would never have married Tatyasaheb."

"Okay. It was good of you to comply with my wishes at that time. Perhaps now too you will go back and live honorably with him."

"No! That is impossible. What can I do if I just can't forget Bhasker? I can't behave like a wife to Tatyasaheb when I love somebody else. Besides, I don't want to give birth to any children in these disgusting circumstances."

"On the contrary, I think that if you have a couple of children, you will begin to love Tatyasaheb because of them."

"Perhaps. But how can that be called love? That is just a materialist way of thinking. What you are actually telling me is that I should take whatever Tatyasaheb offers me, do what he bids me to, and keep bearing his children. And then, for the children's sake, start loving him."

"Huh! What a meaningless rigmarole all this is. Enough! It's better to plug my ears than listen to such things."

"What is the use of plugging your ears, Father? Tell me what is wrong with my way of thinking?"

"There is no point arguing with you. You are an insane woman. All that I know is that I must do something in order to bring you back to your senses. Go! I need some quiet to think things through."

Translated by Jayant Dhupkar.

NAZAR SAJJAD HYDER ─────

(1894–1967)   *Urdu*

Though her family originally belonged to Lucknow and Moradabad, Nazar Sajjad Hyder was born in Kohat, in what used to be the North-West Frontier Province, where her father, Khan Bahadur Nazrul Baqar, was posted as a supply agent to the British army. His sister, Akbari Begum, was also a writer who published her first novel in 1898. Her second, a much better written reformist novel called *Goodar-ka-Lal* (A Gem in Rags), came out in 1908. It was immensely popular and soon became a standard part of a bride's dowry.

Nazar Sajjad Hyder, still often referred to by her maiden name, Bint-e-Nazrul Baqar, started writing at a very young age. Her stories and articles were published in such prestigious literary magazines as Abdul Qadir's *Makhzan,* which was published in Lahore. She was also honorary editor of *Phool,* the now legendary Urdu weekly for children, and contributed to epoch-making women's magazines such as *Khatoon* (Aligarh), *Ismat* (Delhi), and *Tehzib Niswan* (Lahore), in which the piece excerpted here was first published in 1937. She was among those who brought up the idea of the All-India Muslim Ladies' Conference which was founded a little later.

Nazar Sajjad Hyder designed and popularized the *burqa* (as it is worn today) and simplified the heavily pleated, trailing *gharara* worn by upper-class Muslim women in northern India. She herself took the bold step of discarding purdah in 1923 when she joined the freedom struggle.

Her best-known novel, *Akhtarunnissa Begum,* came out in 1910. In 1912 she married Syed Sajjad Hyder Yildirim (1880–1943), a pioneer of the modern Urdu short story and a champion of women's rights. She published her second novel, *Ah-i-Mazlooman* (Sigh of the Oppressed), which highlighted the miseries created by bigamy, in 1913. Another novel, *Suraiya,* 1933, dealt with forced marriages. *Najma,* 1939, depicted the harm extreme Westernization brought to Indian society. According to her daughter, Qurratulain Hyder, who is a distinguished writer herself, all her heroines "were independent, courageous women who fought against orthodoxy, without giving up the basic values of their own religion and culture."

Nazar Sajjad Begum opened girls' schools in various cities of the United Provinces, now Uttar Pradesh. Like her aunt, Akbari Begum, she was deeply involved in issues of social reform. She helped Sheikh and Begum Abdullah, founders of Muslim Girls' College, Aligarh, and assisted the management of Karamat Hussain Muslim Girls' College, Lucknow. She boycotted English cloth and wore the homespun khadi during the non-cooperation movement of the 1920s and 1930s. Her novel *Jan Baaz* (The Valiant), 1930, was written against the background of that struggle. She socially boycotted bigamous men, and as a result of her quiet influence and encouragement, her daughter writes, many north Indian Muslim families sent their daughters to colleges and universities, and gave up purdah. She was a brilliant conversationalist and was known for her wit and sense of humor.

Her work seems sentimental and stilted today, and all her books except *Najma* have long been out of print. Her *Diary,* which provides valuable social history from 1908 onward, was serialized in *Tehzib* and *Ismat* from 1942 to the last years of her life, and was avidly read.

◆

PURDAH

Such is the diligence and industry required of a man today, to fulfill his duties whether in business or employment successfully, that he is forced to expend more and more of his time at work. Consequently the time he can devote to his home and household requirements is diminished.

In such a situation it is evident that the ordinary requirements of the house lie neglected without him, causing his wife and children great inconvenience. Put aside the larger problems and requirements, just consider this much. Say that the children's shoes are worn out, or that winter has come and the children have no winter clothing. The husband, who gets no relief from his work till the evening, returns home tired and exhausted and has no energy left to go to the bazaar. This small but necessary chore gets postponed from day to day and the little children wander about enduring the winter in barely sufficient clothing.

It is certainly worth considering what loss would be incurred if the woman of the house ventured forth wearing her burqa, and set out in a curtained carriage, accompanied by her children, to the bazaar and purchased the needed shoes and clothing. She need not even alight at the shop after all; the servant or her children can bring the goods from the shop to the carriage and show them to her. But even to do this much, these wives are not permitted.

Why on earth not? At this point I shall write without mincing matters even if it means displeasing the men. It is but mere empty words when they say, "We are willing to give freedom to a certain extent. But what can we do? We must respect the times. One holds the elders of the house in awe. If women go out, these people will say that respectable wives have begun to roam the bazaars. The men have grown shameless and wear bangles."

The truth, however, is this: that their hearts do not desire that their wives should come or go anywhere beyond their controlling vision. Even if there are a hundred thousand purdahs, they fear that another's look may fall upon them. Who knows? If the curtain of the carriage flies up, if their wife's voice is heard by another, that would be disaster indeed!

Mostly it must be this fear that, when she who has been a prisoner for ages leaves her prison, then the desire to see the world will certainly stir in her, and she will peep out of the carriage, look at the shops, and many faces will pass under her eyes. They do not like such things under any circumstances. As a result of these fearful thoughts, women are not given freedom. A noble inheritance, blue blood, the restrictions of tradition are but mere excuses for this. Man has for ages been master of his life and in control of his actions. Outside the home, whatever he does, there is no one who can question him. If any wife should object to his flouting the decorum of the household, then the control on her is tightened so that no news from the outside world reaches her. She is not even permitted to meet his friends' wives lest they teach her something new.

Because they take undue advantage of their own liberty, nay, it would be more fitting to say ill advantage, men fear that if the women are given freedom, they will also become like them. Therefore, [men conclude] it is wise to keep the women confined.

From this mode of reasoning men arrive at these results, and use such increased control on women imprisoned with no thought of their health. Women do not even have the license to walk out in the night, if not in the daytime. One sees that some husbands do take their wives out at night, but that is only if they are so inclined and find the time, otherwise not. The wife does not have permission to go out accompanied even by another male relative or a servant.

This severe confinement causes such social and national waste that it is not even necessary to elaborate on it here. Now the time has come to focus one's thoughts with a great deal of sharpness on this issue. Discussion must now take place on what is the real extent of loss in giving such appropriate freedom to women and on how much advantage has actually been gained from such imprisonment.

Translated by Vasantha Kannabiran and Rasheed Moosavi.

KALYANAMMA

(1894–1965)   *Kannada*

Born into a traditional family, the second of eight children, Kalyanamma
was brought up and educated in Bangalore. She was married at the age of
ten. Three months later her husband died. Though her family was not
very enthusiastic about it, she continued at school and in 1906 passed her
lower secondary examination. Her mother tongue was Tamil, but she was
educated in a Kannada school and wrote in Kannada. Soon she began
publishing short stories, articles, and translations from Tamil. In spite of
the long hours of domestic labor she had to put in as a widow living in
an extended family, she made time to read and write. She worked in the
face of opposition from her family, especially from her elder sister, who
was also a widow and fiercely opposed to Kalyanamma's activities. It
would seem that her mother also tried to discourage her. To make matters
worse, the family was poor and Kalyanamma suffered from epilepsy. But
she continued working until the end.

Unlike her contemporary Tirumalamba, who was principally a writer,
Kalyanamma took on a whole range of social activity. Perhaps it was
easier for her to do so because she lived in a city. She started a women's
organization, the Sarada Stree Samaj, in Bangalore and worked as its secretary until 1926. She also began an association for children and ran a
magazine for them; later a section of *Saraswati* was reserved for children.

Saraswati was undoubtedly Kalyanamma's major achievement. She
launched it in 1921 as a slim volume of forty pages with three hundred
subscribers, but it became very popular and the circulation soon grew to
two thousand. Though she was encouraged initially by some well-known
social workers and administrators in Bangalore, in reality she ran the
magazine single-handedly. She was editor, proofreader, contributor, and
advertising agent. The magazine's reputation and influence grew. The
governments of Mysore and Bombay recommended it for their school
libraries and many well-known authors—women and men—began to write
for it. The range of subjects in *Saraswati* was broad—politics, fine arts,
current affairs all came within its scope—but its principal objective was
the all-round development of women. It called upon them to become more
useful members of society. When G. R. Lalita became the publisher in
1955, Kalyanamma was relieved of the financial and administrative work
of the magazine. She continued as editor until 1963 when, on Lalita's
death, the magazine closed for want of a publisher. Apart from the short

stories, plays, essays, and biographical sketches she contributed to the magazine, she wrote several novels between 1918 and 1935, which deal with the question of child widows. Notable among them are *Indire Athava Nirbhagyavanite* (Indira, or the Unfortunate Lady), *Priyamvada, Sati Padmini* (Padmini, the Virtuous Lady), *Sukhalata, Madhavi,* and *Bhaktamira* (Mira the Devotee). She also wrote stories for children.

Like other writers in her time, Kalyanamma opposed the giving and taking of dowry and discussed the problems of widows. Unlike many other writers including Tirumalamba, who stressed the spiritual regeneration of women, she was more interested in the economic and social advancement of women. It is interesting that when the Sarada Stree Samaj opened a badminton court for women, Tirumalamba opposed the move, but Kalyanamma encouraged women to play.

The piece included here demonstrates a keen feeling for the pressures on women in the context of a growing nationalist spirit, but also a sense of how this nationalism was focused in terms of Hindu solidarity against the "alien" Mughals. The name Rana Pratap (1540–1597) personified chivalry, self-sacrifice, and dedication to the cause of liberty. In 1576, despite a spirited resistance, he lost the battle of Haldigatti to the famous Mughal emperor, Akbar.

◆

SURYASTHAMANA
(Sunset)

Most readers of *Saraswati* must know the history of Rana Pratap, the light of Mewar. Toward the very end of his reign some traitors in his kingdom joined the Muslims and plotted to overthrow him. Although Rana Pratap despised the thought of an alliance with the Muslims, there were many who deemed it noble. One such was Raja Mansingh, around whom this story revolves. Mansingh had earned the goodwill of the emperor Akbar by giving his sister Jodhbai in marriage to him.

One day as the sun set at the foothills of the Aravalli Ranges in Rajasthan, Mansingh paced up and down recalling his brave deeds and glowing over his own achievements.

Mansingh: Your star is at its height now. Everyone admits the extent of your power. Tales of your valor are told from Kabul to the Bay of Bengal. You are the chief pillar of the Mughal Empire. The emperor himself trembles at your growing success. Your name and your fame echo from corner to corner. What more do you want? What else do you desire? Desires? Ah! There are so many! Is there an end to my desire? People still scoff at me. They jeer at me because I gave my sister's hand in marriage to a Mughal. Pratap! Pratap! Just wait and see. If not today, tomorrow your fame will be trampled into the dust— by the people themselves. You are my Rahu—the source of my shame— darkening my bright name.* But you will answer for this—and soon!

[looking up.] Who could this beautiful woman be? Her step is as soft as blossoms blown by a thunderstorm onto the thick dew-laden grass. How soothing to behold her gentle walk in this forest ravaged by the rough march of soldiers' feet. Strange! She seems to be coming toward me. Is she the goddess of the forest? Who is she? She seems to be overwhelmed by the goddess of sorrow and yet the sorrow but adds to her beauty!

After thinking along these lines for some time Mansingh spoke to her.

Mansingh: O woman! Draw closer and have no fear. I am a Rajput who knows how to respect women.

Woman: That is a lie!

M: You woman! You audacious woman! You dare call Mansingh a liar to his face!

W: Why just that? I can say much more.

M: Your boldness surprises me. But anyway, you are safe, for Mansingh's sword will never be drawn against a woman's body.

W: Isn't your sword already stained with your brother's blood? Isn't that worse?

M: You speak in riddles, beautiful woman. I do not understand your meaning.

W: [vehemently] Never! Haven't you crossed swords with your brother Rajputs? Haven't you joined the Mughals to fight the Sun of Mewar, Pratap, the sacred jewel of all Indians? What more do you want?

M: If you mention that name to me again, I may forget that you are a woman! Beware!

W: [laughing] Small wonder! How can a woman's life be sacred to a traitor betraying his own motherland?

---

*Rahu is the postvedic name for the demon that was responsible for the eclipses of the sun and the moon; Rahu *kalam* is an inauspicious period.

M: Stop! Don't fuel the fires of my anger anymore! [Draws his sword from its sheath.]

W: Your sword does not frighten me. Just look at your shining sword. It is still stained with your mother's blood.

M: Mad woman! What did you say?

W: What did "I" say? Every brave deed of yours, every noble favor shown to the Mughals—what is it but a cruel betrayal of your motherland? Can a mother ever forget such treachery?

M: Silence! Do you think that your beauty can always save your life? I am not a Mughal to set you free, seduced by your looks!

W: [surprised] Ha! So you despise the Muslims? Then why have you given your sister in marriage to one of them? Why do you help the Mughals? What wrong has Pratap done you that you behave thus? Is it because he is far above your evil and treacherous ways?

M: [turning to her with sword drawn] Witch! Prepare to die!

W: [courageously] A Rajput woman does not fear death.

M: [surprised] What? A Rajput?

W: Oh yes . . . I was once that.

M: In the past? But not now? Come forward. I'll pardon your boldness. Come here into the light and let me see your face, so shrouded in mystery. Your voice sounds familiar. Who are you—capable of disarming me, Mansingh, whom even Akbar fears?

W: [fearfully] Alas! . . . say, "whom Akbar too hates."

M: Has he the courage to do that? After all, he knows that I am the support of his throne and his kingdom. Who else can he respect?

W: A victorious king never respects those whom he has vanquished. You are mistaken if you believe that he will respect the one missed by his arrow. Though he may pat you on the back, deep inside he has far greater respect for his gallant enemy.

M: [in a rage] Stop it. You try a man's patience too far. You must be a spy of Pratap, surely. According to the law spies deserve to be punished. [As he prepares to strike, the woman draws aside her veil.]

[amazed] Ha! Jodhpuri! My sister! Am I dreaming? Or is this an illusion?

W: Yes, it is your sister—Jodhpuri.

M: Dear sister! Queen of Delhi! Mother of future emperors! Forgive me . . . but why do you seem so sad?

Jodhbai: Don't you understand anything?

M: Dear sister! Your words amaze me. You, whose word can make the country march . . . you, who are drowned in wealth and riches—how can these words come from your lips?

J: You have sacrificed me to Agni, O Prince.

M: Don't be so perturbed. Sister! Be calm! Your mind is saddened. Soothe your spirits and explain your meaning clearly. I don't understand you.

J: Meaning? Listen then. Why did you arrange my marriage with that alien?

M: Dear sister, for your happiness.

J: [angrily] My happiness? Or did my marriage help you consolidate your power?

M: Fair enough . . . but what is wrong with that?

J: You sought to further your own interests selfishly. Did you ever spare a thought for your poor sister's happiness? Curse your selfishness.

M: [sarcastically] The queen of Delhi, "poor"—how sad!

J: Why? Is wealth the only thing in life? If it is, why wasn't I brought up to believe so? Why was I born into the Hindu fold, which condemns material wealth?

M: The essence of all religions is one, Sister. The emperor himself believes and practices it.

J: I am not learned enough to discuss such matters with you. But my earlier training rebels against what I see today. What you call happiness is gradually destroying my soul,—like termites destroying a building. Why didn't you give me in marriage to some poorer Rajput in your own kingdom? How could you sell a Rajput woman—brought up to worship her motherland, taught from a tender age to worship Lord Shiva devotedly—to an outsider in exchange for riches and power? Will you ever understand how that touch sears me?

M: Sister, why didn't you speak out earlier? I understand now.

J: Even now it's not too late to repent and pray to God for forgiveness.

M: Forgive me, Sister [kneeling, he implores her].

J: I may forgive you, but will your kingdom ever forgive your crime?

M: [eyes filling with tears] What am I to do now? Have I written my name on sand then?

J: Yes, and Pratap's name is engraved on every rock.

M: [bitterly] Oh, cruel fate! Will all my great deeds end like this?

J: Need I reply? History will tell all, adequately.

Mansingh grew quiet and began to pace up and down again. Jodhpuri quietly turned to the western sky.

J: What a wonderful streak is sinking into the earth! Every valley in Rajputana is bathed in its light. The bleak night will soon wipe out this splendor. Only Pratap's fame, the Sun of Mewar, will shine alone in the coming night. Will the ancient glory ever be revived?

She spoke in a low voice. Mansingh heard her.

M: Alas, it is against the laws of nature. The bright morning light shines steadily during the day and into evening; the sun sets with a glorious burst of light. In the end the dying reflections of the bright image enshrined in our hearts are extinguished by the pervasive darkness, plunging us into infinite despair. Ah! What worthless utterances, worthless hope, and yet how sweet, how wonderful.

[The valiant part played by Rajput women in correcting the errors of their brothers, father, or sons and in guiding them along the right path is evident from this small episode. Although we are also women like them, we have lost our courage and become puppets in the hands of fear. Evidently supporting this God of Fear, men have pushed us further and further aside. If only we had retained the courage and fortitude of the women of our past, many brave men like Rana Pratap of Mewar would have been born. Instead of returning to Manu's dictum that "women are unfit to be free" and reducing women to uselessness, men should help women to extend their knowledge and understanding. A return of that courageous spirit of the Rajput women will mean a reawakening of India's glory through the birth of many more like

Rana Pratap, Shivaji, Ahalya Bai, Jhansi Lakshmi Bai, and Tarabai.
Let us pray together with folded hands for such a transformation to
come soon.]

Translated by G. Rajagopal.

TALLAPRAGADA VISWASUNDARAMMA —
(1899–1949)   *Telugu*

"It is rare that patriotism, imagination, and the ability to write poetry are
combined in one person," Cherla Venkata Sastry wrote of Tallapragada
Viswasundaramma, who is spoken of as the first woman poet of modern
Telugu literature. Inspired by the nationalist movement as well as by the
ideals of the earlier social reformers, she wrote nearly sixty poems between
1920 and 1935, many of which can be found in her *Kavita Kadambam*
(Garland of Poetry), 1973, collected and published posthumously by her
brothers.

Viswasundaramma was born in Undi, a village on the east coast of Andhra
Pradesh, the eldest of three children. Her father was a schoolteacher who
opened a middle school in the village as early as 1900 with much difficulty.
One of her brothers later became a poet and the other a minister of education in the state government. As a child Viswasundaramma, we are told,
constantly interacted with her father and learned Sanskrit and Telugu. By
the time she was twelve, she had read the *Ramayana* and the *Mahabharata*
as well as the writings of the influential social reformers Veereshalingam
and Chilakamarti, whom the family also knew personally. They were all
influenced by the Brahmo Samaj, and when she was nine, Viswasundaramma was married to a fellow Samajist, Tallapragada Narasimha Sarma.

Initially she and her husband worked as supervisors of the widows' home
run by Veereshalingam, but in 1923 they started an ashram, Anand Niketan. In the ashram, set on the banks of the Godavari, the rules of the
caste system were not practiced, and women's education and advancement
were encouraged. Around 1920 Viswasundaramma began getting involved in the national movement. She took part in the noncooperation
movement, and in 1930 she led the women of the West Godavari region
in the Salt Satyagraha, was arrested in Eluru, and imprisoned for six
months. Again in 1932, she was arrested for presiding over a Congress
meeting that had been banned by the imperial government. Police broke
up the meeting and Viswasundaramma was sent to jail. In 1942, during
the Quit India struggle, the government confiscated Anand Niketan.

Poems such as "Sarkaru Doratanamu" (The Ruler's Autocracy), "Streela Cherasalalo" (In the Women's Prison), "Angla Gouravam" (The Greatness of These Englishmen!), "Simon Commission," and "Lathi Rajyam" (Baton Rule) describe her experiences. Her poems were published in the leading journals of the time, but she first came to notice as a poet when four of her poems were published in an anthology, *Vaitalikulu* (Pioneers), in 1935.

For one whose public life is recounted in such glorious terms, she left surprisingly little information about her private life, and indeed about her relationship with other members of her family. But there is evidence that she was lonely and disturbed. Cherla Ganapati Sastri writes that "she was always engrossed in her own world, talking to herself, making gestures, and so on." She was ill for a long time and went into a severe depression. In 1949 she committed suicide. The poem translated here was actually written in jail, but in the context of what we know about her personal life, it takes on other symbolic meanings.

◆

JAILU GADIYARAMU
(Jailhouse Clock)

You need no money
    to enter this mighty kingdom
Without a copper coin or measure
    to meet your daily needs
You can shed the weight of responsibility
    to live your life out here
You need no wage or money
    to avail of service here
Everything goes by this clock
    that moves with such awesome precision
This magic clock that has no stop
Time in this jail goes on and on.

Translated by Srinivas Rayaprolu.

MARY JOHN THOTTAM ─────────────

(Sr. Mary Begina, 1901–1985)   *Malayalam*

Many women in Kerala who would not regard themselves as readers of poetry would have read, and perhaps committed to memory, Mary John Thottam's 1928 autobiographical poem "Lokame Yatra" (Farewell to the World). In the subtle blending of pain with a stoic strength and a quiet but determined self-assertion, the poem speaks of survival and even hints at victory despite the harshest of circumstances. As the poet takes her protracted leave of her family, her friends, her past life, her physical surroundings, before she goes into a nunnery, she speaks of the loss she will suffer, but she also underscores the loss the world will suffer after she has gone.

Mary Thottam was born into the Thottathil family in Ithikara, a village in central Kerala. She was the eldest daughter and started writing poetry when she was a child. Her first collection, *Geethavali* (A Bunch of Poems), was published in 1927. The next year, apparently after an unhappy love affair, she renounced the world to become a nun. In Kerala the Christian community is popularly traced back to the conversions made in the first century A.D. by Saint Thomas, the Apostle of Christ who, it is said, traveled in India. Scholars today question the validity of that claim, but agree that there is evidence to date Christianity in this southern tip of the subcontinent to the fourth century A.D. when another St. Thomas, a missionary of the Church in Syria, came to Kerala. The Catholic tradition to which Mary John Thottam belonged was grafted onto these earlier Syrian traditions. But as perhaps was also the case in other parts of the world at the time, in the 1920s, when she took her vows, becoming a nun meant a far more radical and awesome severance of ties with the family and secular life than it does today. Outside that context, the protracted farewell in the poem, written in 1928, may seem unduly sentimental.

As Sr. Mary Begina, she continued to write, publishing in 1929 *Kavitharamam* (The Garden of Poetry), in 1934 *Eesaprasadam* (The Blessing of Jesus), and *Athmavinte Sangeethum* (Love Song of the Soul) in 1936. *Anthinakshatram* (Twilight Star) came out in 1968 and the epic *Mar Thoma Vijayam* (The Victory of St. Thomas) in 1970. An index of the popular appeal of her poetry is the appearance of the nineteenth edition of *Kavitharamam* in 1952.

Her poetry is essentially Romantic. She describes nature as a living reality, reflecting and sharing the feelings of human beings, but the principal theme of her work is the arduous journey of the spirit from the sensuous love of

402   ◆   REFORM AND NATIONALIST MOVEMENTS

the earth and its beauty toward an understanding and acceptance of its metaphysical relevance. The poems maintain a fine tension between the philosophical tenets and the imagery of Vedantic Hinduism, which she draws on to elaborate her metaphysical longings, and the Christian faith she professes. One of her best-known poems, "Sayannathile Ekanta Yatra" (The Lonely Journey at Dusk) is set in the cemetery in the evening; its message is the passing of worldly riches, the vanity of a life that is merely of this world.

◆

LOKAME YATRA
(Farewell to the World)

1

From the day I was born you cherished me with fond regard.
And gladly met my every need; now, O World,
Goodbye—I take my leave of you to court a future
That's unaffected by the frown of evil fortune.*

2

Why now that puzzled look upon your face?
Truly my friend, we bear no mutual grudges;
Nor have I forgotten all those days
We lived as if never to be parted.

3

Although you are still my friend, I realize
No values of a lasting kind are found
In you—and that alone's the reason why
I venture thus to part and go away.

4

Why should I worship you who never can
Bestow on me a single gift that lasts?
Is the noble human life like that of beasts,
Which live to daily riot and gorge themselves?

---

*Literally, "by the blight of Saturn," alluding to the popular convention that the worst tragedies in one's life happen during the astrological phase of Saturn.

5

That everyone who is born must die is a truth
That none would question; but remember
It's our distinction that we do embrace
After death a life that never ends.

6

Laugh not, O World, deride me not as daft—
Perhaps you do not understand, as yet;
One day, for sure, the truth of all I say
Will stare you in the face—and then you'll believe!

7

What in the end befell the great ones of the past
Who won renown for wit—have you not heard it told?
The skills they learned of no avail, bereft of soul,
Their rotting bodies soon returned to dust.*

8

The brilliant Caesar, the celebrated Homer,
And savants like the peerless Solomon,
If all were by the whirling wheel of time brought low,
What question then of us? The die is cast.

9

Fare forth we must, one day, departing from this body
And the world—demurs will be of no avail—
Upon a pilgrimage without return; so then, we must,
Before we cross the borderline, surrender all we hold.

10

Earthly riches, fame, and noble birth—
One goes not bearing these upon the final journey;
Holy deeds, unsoiled by pride of self,
Alone will bring one profit in the life beyond.

---

*Literally, the five elements.

11

I leave to gain true riches that will help
Me live that endless life, released from pain;
The glowing, glittering snides that tempt
Are not for me; to them I shall not yield.

12

Forsaking all, I'll follow in the steps
Of fearless ones who found peace beyond desire.
May the world forgive this rashness and let me strive
For the noblest ends of human life.

13

Trimming my lamp here, I step out upon my way;
In vain shall people call, I shall not turn to look.
These garish scenes I'll leave behind, depart
To live in deep contemplation and peace of mind.

14

They will not find, who range abroad to seek for me;
Those who write in anxious care won't hear from me.
Although I may thus disappoint many friends,
Do not, I plead, mistake that for ingratitude.

15

It is not with ease I leave and lose the ones
So joined to me with guileless deep affection;
I am not possessed of superhuman strength;
This truly is the time I take my measure.

16

Can I, of immature mind, e'er hope to break
The roots of desire,★ this world the wizard weaves?
Austere ascetics find such parting hard;
My heart is not just scorched, it's burning up.

★Actually, "banyan tree." The sprawling banyan tree, "without beginning or end,"

17

Listen, circle of my friends, I say good-bye
And go; let's stay thus parted for a while;
And then, I give my word, we'll meet again
To be united for eternity.

18

My teachers, at your hallowed feet, I bow,
You who yearned and strove to see me prosper,
Beginning from that day you held my finger
And helped it draw a letter shape in rice.

[In stanzas 19–23 she bids farewell to her classmates, other poets, and
the students she taught before she turns her attention to her home.]

24

There, with broken heart, her body languid
On the ground, she weeps, the one who gave me birth;
Brothers' tears roll down to ground; my noble-hearted
Father, watching, lays his hand upon his breast.

25

I'm at a loss to know what I should say,
Or what I can do—I am sore perplexed in truth.
Step out and leave? It is far from wise; I'll speak
A few consoling words, with reverence.

27

Take courage, my dear parents, I do pray;
I am setting out to trample under foot
The dark, mysterious sea of cosmic flux—
Should that not greatly gratify your hearts?

––––––––––––

"with roots above and branches beneath," is a well-known symbol of the mysterious world of *maya* (illusion).

28

Why feel dejected that we're parting?
What bond is there on earth that's never broken?
Although we grieve o'er children who are dead,
Could we e'er bring them back to gain relief?

29

These sorrows are of no import—this is the way
The world of sense does drug us mortals.
Revered parents, do not weep, your daughter pleads,
Making obeisance at your lotus feet.

30

Place your hands upon my head and bless me—
That is my only plea; now let me leave.
In another clime where light of setting suns ne'er falls,
Ungrieving we shall joy—there we shall meet again.

31

My little brothers, sisters, motionless
You stand, the sorrow of your guileless hearts
Writ large upon your faces, brighten up,
Take comfort, dears, and give me leave to go.

32

My little brother, with your arms a tender pair
Of climbers, tightly winding round my waist, weeping,
The time is come for me to leave; here I press
A kiss upon your face. Let go, my dear, and let me go.

33

My house, I who was born upon your floor
And breathed your air, slept under your lofts,
And lived with greatest joy up to this day,
I am setting out, I am leaving you for e'er.

34

This door hereafter will not open for my sake,
The lamp for me will not be lighted in this room,
No mattress ever spread for me; and with my dearest,
In this house I'll ne'er sit down to eat.

35

Here, I am setting out, treading across
This kindly floor that from my earliest days
Cherished the pressure of my infant feet;
I will not turn or once look back on aught.

36

My pen, that's ever companioned me, turn back;
Why want to come with me upon this journey now?
Desirous still of public life—can you e'er rest
Or feel at home within a tranquil hermitage?

37

But if you're bent on coming, do, my friend,
I'm not inclined to harshly turn you off.
Have but a care to cause me no offense,
And nothing untoward, then, need we fear.

38

There no doubt you will have to undertake
Many works of noble character;
So, free from sense of self or lust of fame,
In secrecy you must fulfill those tasks.

39

And now, moving on, O great wide world;
I'm passing through, O home town and its people dear;
Though I can't return, restrain me not, I pray.
I make obeisance, and seek your farewell in blessing.

40

Distancing everything behind, my ship sails onward now,★
Over these rolling surges will I speed with heart unflinching;
O'er the horizon will I post and range; and my arms
Stretch out for that golden-tress'd Sun, the Soul of Felicity.

Translated by P. T. George.

SUDHA CHAUHAN ——————————————

(b. 1924)   *Hindi*

Sudha Chauhan's major work for adult readers, *Mila Tej Se Tej* (As Strength
Met Strength), from which we have excerpted and translated these accounts of her mother Subhadra Kumari Chauhan's life—a writer and an
activist loved and admired by many—is as much a history of India's struggle for Independence and what it meant at the level of everyday life as it
is a biography of her parents. Born in Jabalpur when her parents were in
the thick of their early involvement with the movement, she grew up in
the midst of political and literary discussions, arguments, protest marches,
and the constant risk that one or both of her parents would be arrested or
badly hurt as they took part in Congress processions and strikes. She
developed into "an avid reader and an occasional writer," and graduated
from Nagpur University in 1944. In 1945 she was married to Amrit Rai
(son of the distinguished Urdu novelist Premchand) in one of the celebrated intercaste marriages of the time. She took her master's degree from
Benares in 1956.

   Though this biography was written in 1975, we have placed it here
because it provides a backdrop to Subhadra Kumari Chauhan's work and
because it fleshes out the history of the 1930s. Though several women
were involved both in the Congress-led struggle and in the peasant movements of the time, very few of them wrote about their experiences or
about the public events of the period.

   As a writer, Sudha Chauhan is best known for her children's poetry: "I
love to write for children. . . . Four books of these poems have been published so far and many more await publication."

◆

———————————

★This concluding stanza uses a longer and statelier meter, a common device in
   Malayalam poetry, intended to create the effect of a grand finale.

From MILA TEJ SE TEJ
(As Strength Met Strength)

The origin of most of Mother's stories could be found in some real-life incident but her imagination transformed it and wove it into something quite different.

There was one story called "Cada Dimag" (Vanity) in which an editor inadvertently mixes up the envelopes of letters written to the writer and to another person, and the writer receives the letter written to the other person. In it the editor complains that the writer does not reply to letters and has not been sending in any stories. This story is based on a real-life incident. When Sri Ilachandra Joshi was the editor of *Vishwamitra* he had sent a letter meant for Mother to Narmada Prasad Khare and she had got the letter meant for him. The description of the misunderstanding and confusion it caused was also drawn from her own experience.

Similarly the account of the brahmin child widow in Ekadasi is based on a person from real life and the doctor in that story is possibly Dr. George D'Silva. He was not only an able medical practitioner but was also a dedicated and fearless Congress worker from Jabalpur, who, perhaps because of these very qualities, never found a place in the ranks of the Congress leadership.

In most of Mother's stories, the dependent woman, bound by the harsh discipline of the family, or the rebellious woman, ready to take on society and her helpless anger, both find a voice. The heroine can challenge society to demand respect for her selfhood and can have a relationship of equality and friendliness with men. But in many stories this rebellious woman is defeated and broken by the injustice she has to bear and either goes mad or is forced to commit suicide.

One story—"Manjli Rani"—begins like this: "Who was he to me? What can I say? Well, if you consider it seriously he can be nothing to me. How could he? I, a brahmin; he, a kshatriya; I, a woman; he, a man. He could not be a relative, nor could he be a friend. Oh, what have I said! Friend! As if a woman can have a man as a friend, and if so, would society tolerate it? If a woman has any interaction with a man, if she talks to him in a friendly way, then that woman must be depraved or of weak character."

A woman's struggle to establish her identity and selfhood is at the core of many of her stories. In her own life her husband had encouraged her to grow and assisted the development of her personality. The experiences of her women characters should not, therefore, be regarded as what she herself went through but as what she knew in general. They should be read as her response to the injustice meted out to women, of which she herself was a victim.

Srimati Shakuntala Srivastava, who had been a close associate of Mother's in the Congress before she got married, wrote to me, saying, "He [Lakshman Singh] never insisted on Subhadraji observing purdah. In fact he gave her opportunities to go freely out of the house and meet people. It would not be an overstatement to say that it was due to his encouragement that Subhadraji could develop her literary talent and could involve herself in politics. The atmosphere of the town was conservative and she had become a talking point because of her activities." In spite of finding so much support and sympathy in her personal life, Mother must have had to struggle and fight against social pressures all the time. Around 1920–1921 when illiteracy and purdah were enormous realities for women, to cast aside purdah and go out courageously roused enough comment to break a weak person's resolve. But it merely made Mother more rebellious. It was inevitable that her stories reflected anger against unjust social strictures because she herself was a victim of their excesses. The one point difficult to comprehend in her stories is that it is the husband who most often takes on the role of oppressor as a representative of a larger social reality. Her own husband was a man of liberal views who had a very modern outlook toward the question of respect for women and equal rights for them. Even in the present day there are few men who are so truly progressive, both within and without; fifty years ago such a person seemed to belong to the world of imagination alone. It was perhaps Mother's attempt to paint the picture of a larger social reality rather than express the truth of her personal life that accounts for the men in her stories being so oppressive and suspicious.

This is not to say, however, that Father and Mother never disagreed. Their biggest difference, which sometimes led to a quarrel, centers around Grandmother. Father had a weak spot in his heart for his mother. She was an old-fashioned orthodox person. Often Father would say to Mother, "You are educated and intelligent. You should not argue with Mother." He said this even though he did not agree with his mother's views about not breaking traditions. It was always Mother who bore the brunt of her mother-in-law's ire. In "Dristikon," one of Mother's stories, the heroine wishes to give shelter to a child widow who is five months pregnant, who is sitting on the roadside after being abandoned by her family. The heroine has to bear the diatribe of her husband and mother-in-law, but her sympathy for the luckless widow does not waver. I don't know if this story draws on experience for its plot but undoubtedly in any such situation, if Grandmother took an opposing stand, Father would simply ask Mother to give in. He would unhesitatingly provide moral support and financial help to such an unfortunate person, but he would consider it better to avoid doing anything that would add fat to the fire of his mother's temper.

In our neighborhood there were three or four Rajput families, but except for us, all held government jobs. There was a deputy commissioner, a police station officer, or *thanedar,* a doctor, and a senior clerk in the police department. These were our neighbors; there was some interaction between us but there was neither attraction nor enthusiasm to increase intimacy. But marriages were another matter. When the thanedar's daughter was married, all the neighbors were invited for a meal. A row of women sat down to eat. *Kaca kana* was being served.*
A young girl, the daughter of one of his tenants who was a schoolmate of the thanedar's daughter, came and sat alongside the others. There were many conjectures about her origins. People said that her mother had been "found" by her grandmother, and that her parents had lived together without being lawfully wedded. Her mother had since died and her father had returned to his family, so the orphaned child was being looked after by her grandmother. The feast had not yet begun. The lady of the house came down the row serving something, and as soon as she saw the girl, she pulled her up by the hand and said, "You sit and eat outside." The young girl of ten did not know why she was being asked to get up, but felt hurt enough to burst into tears. Mother could not bear this. She left the feast and brought the girl home. Food was cooked, and they both ate from the same plate. It is not difficult to imagine the criticism and the innuendo such behavior would have excited in the community. But Mother felt she had been gifted with another daughter and she maintained this relationship throughout her life.

Her patriotism was also part of this larger humanity of hers. She regarded the poverty and illiteracy in the country as a result of colonialism. Her love of her country was synonymous with courage and sacrifice, and was based on the solid ground of idealism. Her being an idealist was deeply interlinked with her being a true Gandhian, but she was not unaware of the growing bureaucratic mentality and ever-

---

*This is a nonfried cooked food that carries with it the possibility of ritual pollution through the touch of a person of a lower caste.

increasing power struggles within the Congress. She discusses it in her story "Manjli Rani." Manjli Rani's father-in-law turns her out of the house on suspicions of her moral character. A woman bereft of the protection of her home after marriage does not find refuge in her father's house either. Mother writes, "A woman who was the queen of a palace until yesterday did not have a place to stand today. I thought long and hard. The satyagraha struggles for the country's freedom are on. Why shouldn't I join it as a *swayamsevika* and spend the rest of my days in the service of my country? I asked many people for directions and reached the Congress party office. There were three people sitting there. They asked me to produce a letter of recommendation from a Congress committee, and when I said I did not have one, they refused to register me as a volunteer."

Whether it is with the Rai-sahibs and seths who supported the foreign rulers or the patriotic freedom fighters, a poor person finds no place in either social setting. He or she is scorned everywhere. Mother's stories, which show a patriotic feeling, carry a deep empathy for the poor and downtrodden as a necessary element of patriotism. . . .

In the beginning, for a long time, we did not get any news of Mother or Father. Neither did they get to hear about us. We were young and were roused and excited by the arrests made by the government as well as by the general unrest. Living alone without our parents, we felt that we were also doing something toward the attainment of the country's freedom. So we weren't very upset or worried. Youth is such a time of energy and enthusiasm that the tired footsteps of anxiety cannot keep pace with it for long. But our parents were cut off from the dailiness of life, incarcerated within the high walls of jail and without news of the movement outside or of their children, whom they'd left alone. And whatever they heard from the new prisoners was not very encouraging. One can well imagine what a time of deep anxiety those early days must have been for them.

After a few weeks we received letters from Mother and Father. Both of them said that they were well over there and we were not to worry about them. I was the eldest so I was told to take care of my brothers and they were instructed to obey me. From the letter we gathered that they were still in the Jabalpur jail and that we could write to them four times a month. This was the first time that I, a completely inexperienced callow girl, had had the responsibility of managing the house. I heard that among other things postage would cost more soon. I thought to myself that there will be letters to write to Mother and Father every week so why don't I buy several postcards and envelopes before the rates rise. As a result for many months we had to post letters with additional stamps!

In the individual satyagraha program of 1941, Mother had been the only female political prisoner, but this time there were many women with her. All the female political prisoners from Madhya Pradesh were in the Jabalpur Central Jail. There were only two women in the A class category. Jamnalal Bajaj's daughter, Om, and his eldest daughter-in-law, Savitri Bajaj. In the B class there were many other women along with Mother; there were at least twenty to twenty-five women from Wardha Mahilashram and their superintendent, Kamla Tai Lele. There was a Maharashtrian woman who had a son about as old as our youngest sister, Mamta, whom Mother had taken along with her. There were some women with young children in the C class also. One such C class prisoner told the story of her arrest to Mother. Her husband had been arrested in August as soon as the movement had begun. She and her two children were left without any resources. Police repression was at its most brutal, so the neighbors not only did not help her, they were scared even to talk to her. She had no close relatives and the distant ones became even more so in times of such trouble. This illiterate and destitute woman could see no support in the whole wide world for her and could think of no means to feed her two children. She then began, very deliberately, in full view of a policeman, to hammer at a letter box with a stone. She was immediately jailed along with her children. This was her objective, because here she was secure and her children would be fed. The simple woman to be found in the C class did not don robes of idealism, neither did she know how to weave a web of high-sounding words.

Leaders talk of socialism and trusteeship on the dais but it seems as if, like caste prejudices, class differences have seeped to our bones and are unwittingly revealed in our daily behavior. For the entire conglomeration of imprisoned freedom fighters this categorization of A, B, and C was not just a classification imposed by the state. It was a division that their own hearts and minds responded to and accepted. And so the behavior of A and B class women prisoners toward the C class women was not particularly admirable, although they did fondle their children occasionally much as policemen show concern toward the people during a goodwill week.

The Maharashtrian woman's good-looking child became a plaything for all the other women. They had all left their homes and families behind and the presence of the child evoked their maternal feelings.

Mamta could not speak clearly because of a defect in her palate. Mother had been taking her to Bombay for the operations she needed every three months. During the 1941 satyagraha she had had to delay her participation because of the operation, but in 1942 she had no alternative. Mamta's life and future were Mother's greatest anxiety, but they too fell a little below the call of the struggle in the country. If Mamta's future had been a greater concern than the country's problems, she could easily have assured the government of her dissociation from the movement, and she would have been immediately set free. But how could such a thing happen when the freedom of the country and the self-respect of her countrymen were at stake? Who could think only of one's own children and family at such a time? It is not as if Mother did not feel torn between the two, but after considering the matter carefully, she put her country before her family's happiness. Whatever Mother did was well thought out. She took a clear decision and went to jail, but her daughter Mamta was still a child. What did she understand of it all? Only that her Mother and Father were both in jail, and that Mother had only arranged for some flour, rice, and lentils to make sure that her brothers and sister did not starve. Who was there to send her fruits and sweets and toys from home? The A class prisoners were given many facilities and there was no dearth of relatives to send them things. The other women had all left affluent families and homes behind and so the other child never wanted for fruit or sweets and playthings. He had thirty guardians. Mamta was usually ignored. The love and affection of all the women were showered on the other child. Mother noticed this partiality, but how could she say, "My child cannot speak but she is dearer to me than the whole world. Please show her a little affection too; you have nothing to lose by it." Mamta would often come crying, saying Bhabhi had given Baba a toy or a picture book or sweets. All her mother could do was to assure her she would also get everything for her sometime. The little daughter who was gifted with a fine intelligence would not throw any further tantrums.

There were two or three guava trees in the compound of the women's ward. Mother would sit with Mamta under the furthest tree and then mother and daughter would talk of Father, of her sister and brothers, of all those who loved Mamta very much and would send her lovely things. Both would thus lose themselves in the memory of their home, where there was plenty of love and a sharing of whatever little was there to be shared. . . .

Mother could do her reading and writing only in the dead silence of the night. The consequence of having sufficient oil for just one hour of light was that in that ten-month period of imprisonment she managed to write just a few pages of her diary, whereas when she was in jail for a month in 1941 she had produced nearly fifteen stories. Keeping a diary at the least may have reduced her feeling of helplessness—she knew it was impossible to talk about her problems. There was nobody to share her pain and there are limits to bearing repression, which is why it is sometimes cathartic to keep a diary. But very often we came across passages like this: "There is no oil in the lantern so I will not be able to write," or, "I want to write something very quickly because the lantern will soon go off!"

Long periods of proximity had created a sense of kinship among the women. Mother would never sit idle. She had had a large household, five children, her own home, a small garden, cows, and buffaloes. Besides, the problems and anxieties of all the people she knew became her own. Outside the prison there was hardly a moment during the day when she was not busy. Except for the men's trousers and shirts, she would stitch our blouses and Father's garments herself. Her Singer machine was a daily companion. In prison, it was an inactive life. Reading and writing at night were impossible because of the absence of light. She wrote to me, *"Beti,* if you need petticoats and blouses, send me the material and I'll stitch them for you." She wanted the authorities to allow her to get her own sewing machine, but she was not granted permission. Then she stitched my clothes by hand. After that all the girls of Mahilashram asked to have their blouses stitched by her. Mother was very good at both knitting and stitching. She was not fond of embroidery but in jail she even embroidered pillow covers so that the hours would pass. She also liked to compose doggerel verse to amuse the others. Her relationship with the other prisoners was one of openness and friendliness. Once they all decided to celebrate Holi, the spring festival. Colors were prepared inside the jail and everyone threw color with abandon. On Vijay Dashmi they put together an entertainment program. The ones who could, sang, others produced a play. The girls pursued Mother and made her recite her poetry.

At this level the contact was fine, but the occasional shallow pretense of sticking to a principle would pain Mother greatly. Meals for the Mahilashram women came together and invariably a little would be left over, which was sent back. There were one or two pregnant women in the C class who found their food unpalatable. Mother then suggested that instead of sending the B class food back, it could be given to these women instead. How could the women who had taken a vow of truthfulness do something that was illegal! As a result of this, Mother had to give them something out of her own meal. The jail authorities were generally annoyed with her behavior and would punish her when they pleased by not allowing her to write or receive letters.

There are other incidents that reflect the contrast between Mother's way of looking at things and that of the Mahilashram women. Once the matron locked some C class women out of their barracks as a punishment and went away. Their bedclothes were all inside and some of the women had young children with them. The women might manage somehow, but how would the children manage? Mother could not give away all her bedclothes because she also had her daughter to think of. She went to the women from the Mahilashram. They had long strips of jute on which they sat to spin the *charka* and in the evening these strips were used for prayers and the singing of hymns. Mother asked them to give these jute strips to the women, who could use them to lie on on the floor. But what about those who had been punished by being kept from their beds? Would it not be a danger to truth and *ahimsa* to violate the law and provide beds for them? So the other women refused. Disappointed, Mother gave away a *dhurrie* and a blanket from her own bed and had to bear the brunt of the anger of the jail authorities for this crime. . . .

Conditions were not the same for all the women. The younger ones had left no responsibilities behind; for them this prison sojourn was more like an uninterrupted vacation, which they could put to productive use by exercising to keep their bodies fit or to improve their skins. But not all of them were so fortunate. Mother used to worry constantly about her four children who were outside: "Today there was no letter from the children and now I will not get one for a month. God is there. He will protect them and give them the courage and strength to bear suffering. God, you alone can look after my blameless young children. O Divine Spirit, they are young, look to their needs. God, you who look to the welfare of everybody, cast one look toward my four children after that. That will be enough for them. I have done no virtuous deeds that I can beg for your favors, but the father of the children! He is like a *devta*.* Think of him and look after the children, O Lord!"

To knowingly give up writing and receiving letters from the children—for whom her heart was torn asunder—in order to fight injustice

---

Devta refers to a minor god or a god on earth; distinct from a *deva,* one of the gods in heaven.

testifies to her enormous moral courage and her deep devotion to the values she held important.

Naturally maternal, Mother endured an anxiety for her children that knew no end. To console herself she could turn to nobody but God. One daughter was with her, and by looking after her and showering affection on her she could try and divert her mind, but that too was not possible. In jail, unthinking hurtful behavior on the part of any person can deeply wound another's sensitive spirit and Mother often had to bear this. But there were occasions when some incidents acted as a soothing balm. The jailer took Mamta to the men's ward and Father was able to play with his daughter and this made Mother feel very much better.

Once either in jest or in the spirit of an experimental joke and perhaps to test his character, the chief jailer said to Father, "I'll go to Subhadra Kumari today and say that Chauhan Sahib says that the children are alone so she should seek a pardon." Father had no doubts at all on his wife's account. He believed that she would not do anything that would go against their self-respect. He told the jailer, "Go and say what you like." The jailer came to the women's ward and said, "Chauhan Sahib says the children are all alone at home and that you should apologize and go home to them." Mother shot back, "Tell him if he is worrying about the children so much, he can apologize and go free." The jailer, despite being a servant of the British, was touched by her strength and self-respect. He told Father happily the next day, "Do you know, Chauhan Sahib, Subhadraji is a real *kshatrani* (a woman from the Warrior caste). What did she say? She said, 'Go and tell him if he is so worried about the children, then why doesn't he apologize and free himself!' " Father knew that this would happen. Even so, hearing it from the jailer pleased him very much.

The occasional news that one received of the other simply because they were in the same jail also ended soon, because Father and many of his associates were sent to Nagpur. We only knew of his transfer when we started receiving his letters from Nagpur. When he was being sent, somebody who had seen him at the station had told us that our Father was being sent out of Jabalpur. But we did not know where.

Translated by Manisha Chaudhry.

SUBHADRA KUMARI CHAUHAN ————

(1904–1948) *Hindi*

One of the poems every schoolchild in India is likely to have read, and perhaps learned by heart, is Subhadra Kumari Chauhan's "Jhansi Ki Rani," a poem written in ballad meter in which the famous queen's valor in fighting the British in the Rebellion of 1857 and her unswerving patriotism are rousingly extolled. Subhadra Kumari's own public involvement in nationalist politics goes back to March 1923. Following the orders of the imperial government, the police pulled down the flag Congress workers had hoisted on the Jabalpur municipality building and, in an excess of zeal, trampled on it. In the protest that ensued Subhadra Kumari led a procession, defying prohibitory orders. She later became the first woman *satyagrahi* in the country. A *satyagrahi* is literally one who persists in the struggle for truth. *Satyagraha* was the term used for the nonviolent resistance to British rule that began in the early 1920s. Thousands of satyagrahis courted arrest in these campaigns. Reports have it that it was only as a result of her persistent requests that she was allowed to take on what was considered a task too dangerous for a woman. She was arrested and jailed twice, once in 1940 and again in 1942. The second time her youngest daughter, then a toddler, went with her.

Subhadra Kumari was born in Allahabad into an orthodox Rajput family. Her father was a strict disciplinarian. The family practiced untouchability and the women observed the rules of purdah. All the daughters in the family were educated, however. Subhadra Kumari studied at Crossthwaite Girls' School, where she was a few years the senior of the poet Mahadevi Varma. Drawn by their mutual interest in literature, they formed a friendship that lasted right through Subhadra Kumari's life. She passed the middle-school examination when she was fifteen and was married the same year to Lakshman Singh Chauhan, who later became a lawyer. She then joined the Theosophical School Annie Besant had started in Benares as part of the national education program. In 1921 when the noncooperation movement began, she discontinued her studies and went back to Jabalpur to join her husband, who was deeply involved in the Congress-led freedom movement.

Unlike her contemporary Sarojini Naidu (1879–1949), who set aside the writing of poetry as she moved into the nationalist struggle, Subhadra Kumari wrote much of her soul-stirring poetry in the thick of it. The commitments that run through all her work are an intense patriotism, a need to secure equal rights for women, but above all, it would seem, a desire to break down the barriers of caste and religion that divide people. Among the writers she admired were Makhanlal Chaturvedi (1889–1969), a writer known for his passionate nationalism, and Munshi Premchand (1880–1934), a master of the realist novel.

Her most famous collection of poems, *Mukul* (Flower), came out in 1930. *Bikhre Moti* (Scattered Pearls), 1932, was followed by the collection of short stories, *Unmadini* (The Intoxicated Women), 1934, and *Seedhe Sade Chitre* (Simple, Straightforward Stories) appeared in 1946, after her death. Her touching if somewhat sentimental poems for children were published mainly in journals.

Subhadra Kumari is often remembered today as an unassuming, warm-hearted person who walked around barefoot most of her life; this is how she comes across in the biography her daughter Sudha Chauhan wrote of her.

The story translated here, "Ekadasi" (A Woman's Fast), is set against the backdrop of the widespread nineteenth- and early-twentieth century religious reform movements such as the Arya Samaj, founded by Swami Dayanand Saraswati (1824–1883), which gained strength in the 1880s and 1890s. The Arya Samaj combined a critique of many Hindu practices including polygamy, child marriage, the taboo on widow remarriage, and untouchability (which it claimed were later accretions on vedic practices and undermined the strength of Hinduism) with an aggressive assertion of the superiority of Hinduism over other faiths, an approach not unlike that of the Christian missionaries. By the first decades of the twentieth century, they revived, amid a great deal of controversy, *suddi,* a purification ritual designed to integrate the lower castes into the mainstream of Hindu society and convert others to Hinduism. Subhadra Kumari Chauhan's story frames an important new female figure that emerged in the context of the ideological turbulence of those times. This woman's strength lies in the intense personal commitment, a commitment that goes far beyond the call of duty or form, which she invests in traditional practices. The woman in the story is a Hindu child widow who later marries a Muslim, but her power lies not in these outer forms but in the tenacity with which she holds onto her beliefs. The strength that consequently glows from within can be recognized anywhere, the story seems to suggest, and is so compelling that it will convince any genuine seeker of truth, however skeptical he or she may be.

◆

EKADASI
(A Woman's Fast)

There was no doctor in the whole city who could be compared to Dr. Misra. He had a good practice. He was also a jovial, affable and generous person. His pleasant nature and lively manner of speaking could even bring the dead back to life! Even a man groaning with pain would start laughing. He was so easy with his patients that it seemed as though he were a relative or close friend. Sometimes in order to drive despair away and instill confidence and hope instead, he would spend hours with a sick man, talking of all kinds of matters.

He was especially fond of children. This was why, whenever he appeared on any of the streets, the children would come running out to hold his hand. Besides, he had with him an added attraction—one that drew the largest crowds—a pocketful of sugar pills, which he kept solely for the children. He was a homeopathic practitioner. And once the children spotted him they wouldn't rest content unless they had tasted the pills; this is why he always had to keep some plain unmedicated pills with him.

One day as usual some children surrounded him. On this day he had with him in the tonga some fruits and sweets given him by a patient. So, instead of sugar pills, the doctor began to give the children the sweets. Among them was a ten-year-old girl whom the doctor had not seen before. Her face had a certain innocence and her eyes in particular, had a piercing glow that made her unforgettable. The doctor stretched his hand out to offer her a sweet, too. But the girl drew back awkwardly and shook her head shyly in refusal. A child refusing sweets; that seemed rather strange. The doctor took out two *laddus* instead of one and affectionately coaxed her to take them. The girl shook her head again in refusal. The doctor asked, "Why, little daughter, why won't you take the laddus?"

"Today is Ekadasi. How can one eat sweets on this day?"

The doctor started laughing and asked, "What about all these other children who are eating?"

"Men can eat, women do not. My grandmother says that on Ekadasi we should not eat any kind of food."

"So you keep the fast of Ekadasi too?"

"Why not? My grandmother says that we must always observe religious customs."

The doctor visited several sick people that day and was, as usual, mobbed by children on the streets. So he had quite forgotten the girl.

SUBHADRA KUMARI CHAUHAN　◆　421

But at bedtime when he put out the lamp and lay on his bed, he remembered her again. The image of her shy eyes, the innocent yet determined face, and the way she refused the sweets came back vividly before his eyes.

Later the doctor learned that she lived in a housing colony some distance away. Her father was a poor brahmin who worked as a priest in a nearby temple. Only two years earlier the girl had been married, and only six months later, widowed. Her head had been shaved according to the old customs. That was why she was bald. In that family there were two widows. One was the priest's aged mother, the other this unfortunate girl. For one, life was a past filled with darkness through which a few happy memories glimmered like stars on a foggy sky. For the other, life was a future filled with darkness. One could only be glad that the girl was as yet unaware of it. The daily routine for each widow (one aged sixty and the other aged ten) was the same—abstinence and rigor. The poor girl was not aware that soon there would be a battle between abstinence and youth in her life.

Ten years passed after the doctor first met the girl. He had, during that time, felt the city to be inadequate for his practice and moved to another, larger city. There his professional skills shone even more. The poor and rich alike knocked at his door.

It was a large city. All kinds of organizations and societies flourished there and every organization wanted men like Dr. Misra to join it. But Dr. Misra, with his busy schedule, continued to avoid these involvements.

Around the same time there was a great deal of debate about the ritual suddi and the effort to unify Hindus. A people who had not moved for centuries suddenly noticed that their numbers were decreasing day by day and those of other religions, particularly Islam, were increasing. Hindus feared that if the trend continued, in another hundred and fifty years there might be a few Hindu-sounding names but hardly a trace of a practicing Hindu. One would probably find only Muslims. Most Hindus acknowledged the importance of the efforts to create awareness among wayward Hindus and to convert non-Hindus. The Arya Samaj had already held large rallies and had even performed five or ten suddis. Among Hindus, some were happy about the activity, but other, more orthodox ones felt that all these efforts were of no use.

The Muslims had also begun to emphasize organization and preaching. But none of this influenced Dr. Misra. People from both communities consulted him, and he treated all his patients with equal care and dedication. Besides, he loved the children of both communities. According to him, the suddi ceremonies of the Hindus and the excited preaching of the Muslims were equally meaningless.

One day while the doctor was in his clinic a frightened, ordinary-looking Muslim came and asked the doctor to accompany him immediately. He explained that his wife was very ill. About a year ago she'd given birth to a child when she was with her parents. Not being able to get proper treatment in the village, she fell ill, so Rahman brought her back to the city. But day by day her health deteriorated. The doctor set out in a tonga with Rahman to examine the sick woman. At the turning of a narrow lane the tonga stopped. Here, just a short distance from the canal, was Rahman's house. The house was a humble mud one, a piece of sacking served as a curtain at the entrance. The curtain was torn in a couple of places. There was a mud-red stain on it where someone had spit out betel juice. Just beyond the entrance was a small porch, which led to a room. This was Rahman's main room, which also served as the kitchen. Rahman earned his living by rolling *beedis.* On rainy days this room would serve as Rahman's work-shop as well, since it would be difficult to work on the porch with rainwater splashing in. A door at the other end of the room led to another small room, which served as the latrine. It smelled foul. Rahman went into the room first and Dr. Misra waited at the entrance. He went inside only when Rahman called him. As he entered the room a hen, clucking with fright, flapped its wings and fled, running between his legs. Rahman offered the doctor a stool to sit on. His wife was lying on the cot. The filth all around and the stuffy air filling the room worried the doctor. He examined first the pulse and then the chest of the patient. He could detect no illness other than weakness.

He said, "She's not suffering from any illness; she is just very weak. Do you feed her broth?"

"If only she would eat broth! I am tired of persuading her. She does not eat anything except a porridge of sago and milk. Is there any strength in that?"

The doctor asked, "Why, is there any reason why she won't eat?"

"What reason could there be, Doctor? She says she cannot digest it at all."

The doctor laughed and asked, "Come now, why can't it be digested? I assure you, everything can be digested."

"Doctor, please do me this one favor. Feed her some broth yourself, because I know she will not listen to me."

The doctor turned toward Rahman's wife and asked, "Will you, if I ask, drink a little broth? I'll take the responsibility for your digestion."

She did not reply. She merely shook her head. She turned her face to the wall. It was clear that she did not want to look at the doctor. "You must eat a little broth while I'm here today; you will certainly feel better after that," the doctor repeated.

She still shook her head in refusal and didn't utter a word. The doctor would not give up so easily, though. He asked Rahman to bring him some broth if it was ready.

Rahman eagerly picked up a bowl and went out into the yard to clean it. At this moment Rahman's wife raised her eyes pleadingly to the doctor and said, "Doctor, please forgive me, but I cannot drink the broth."

The voice sounded familiar and her eyes had something so special about them that the doctor felt a bit giddy. A faded memory reappeared before his eyes. Involuntarily his lips formed the question, "Why?"

With overflowing eyes the woman answered, "It is Ekadasi today."

The doctor was shaken. Wide-eyed, he remained staring at her. From that day onward, Dr. Misra became a supporter of suddi.

Translated by Indira Raghavan.

VIBHAVARI SHIRURKAR ————————
(Malatibai Bedekar, b. 1905)   *Marathi*

When *Kalyanche Nishwas* (The Sighs of Buds) was published in 1933, it raised a storm in Maharashtrian society, for the short stories in this book were about the lives and aspirations of educated women, most of whom were single and working. The stories dealt with the pressures these women were victim to, and even discussed their sexuality. They portrayed the male ego as deeply destructive of women. Implicit also was a critique of the double standards and rigid norms of Indian society. A contemporary critic called the book a "clear demand for justice."

In one of the best-known stories in the collection "Babanche Sansar Maza Kasa Honar?" (How Can My Father's Family Life Be Mine?), the protagonist, an unmarried working woman, wants to set up house on her own, but cannot. Even an educated woman who is economically independent does not have the freedom to make her own decisions. In "Tyag" (Sacrifice) a girl who wants to get married cannot because she has to work and support her family. In another equally well known story Shirurkar writes of middle-class girls who may be "shown" to a hundred prospective bridegrooms. Each time the girls pin their hopes and build their dreams on a person who may well reject them on a whim. Yet society considers this blatant auction, which makes the woman so helpless and destroys her self-esteem, the purest way of deciding on marriage.

It is not surprising that a woman writing so frankly about women's experiences shocked society at large and critics in particular. But she also delighted many. She was accused of obscenity, of indecency, of not considering the interests of society as a whole when she depicted women, of being self-centered. Her heroines, they said, were always weak and tearful. There were several threats against her life. The more astute and sympathetic response of S. V. Ketkar, a writer himself, but better known as the initiator of the famous Marathi encyclopedia *Dnyanakosh,* is a better measure of the effect her writing had. "Men and women," he declared after reading Vibhavari's stories, "are two different castes. Men will never be able to understand women's minds using their own logic. For society to understand women's minds, women must speak." Other critics too, notably, R. D. Karve and Narayan Kale, praised her writing for its courage and honesty.

She wrote these stories, Vibhavari Shirurkar tells us, because she was interested in the changes that were taking place as women became educated and so altered their lives. They were drawn to ideas of romantic love and exposed to new relationships. (She mentions lesbian friendships and platonic love between men and women among the new possibilities that emerged.) Though writers did take note of the many changes—religious, social, and political—that were taking place, literature was silent about the changes in a woman's life. Women's experiences were never portrayed or explored. Besides, writers and critics alike seemed to have taken it for granted that women had no sexual desires or emotions, and that the stone-like existence they were forced into was only a reflection of their real nature. Her writing, she claims, was simply an effort to refute this. *Kalyanche Nishwas* was soon followed by the novelettes *Hindolyawar* (On the Swing), 1933, and *Virlele Swapna* (The Dream That Has Faded) in 1935. In the next fifteen years she published only a few short stories though she remained in the public eye. Since she had been publishing under her pseudonym, there was much speculation about *who* this Vibhavari Shirurkar actually was. It was only in 1946 that she revealed her real name: Malatibai Bedekar.

In 1950 she published a novel, *Bali,* which was set in a "criminal" community. *Bali* was highly applauded. Another novel, *Sabari* (the name of a woman; the tribal woman in the *Ramayana* was called Sabari), charts the consciousness of a married woman over many years. It explores, writes

Maya Pandit, "the closure formed in the mind of the woman by the institution of family and reveals the various inherent contradictions within the relationship of husband and wife as well as within the ideological unit that is the family." Vidyut Bhagwat, however, feels there has been a change in Vibhavari's position: "In *Sabari* she places the responsibility for a broken marriage on the woman and concludes the novel with a cautionary note: a woman should be patient and balanced, she seems to say." A collection of her literary essays, *Manasviniche Chintam* (Reflections of an Independent-minded Woman), came out in 1971.

Malatibai Bedekar was born and brought up in a small town in rural Maharashtra. Her father was a primary school teacher who took pains to encourage his daughters to study. Her mother, who by and large remained confined to the household, toiled hard to look after the home and the children and work in the family dairy. Later Malatibai joined the Karve University in Bombay, where she earned the degree of Pradeyagamma. From 1923 to 1933 she worked as the principal of a girls' school and from 1937 to 1940 with the Department of Education and Welfare. It was this work that took her among the tribes branded "criminal." In 1938 she married the well-known novelist and filmmaker Vishram Bedekar. In spite of all the controversy it aroused, Vibhavari Shirurkar's fiction is generally recognized today as having introduced a strong, new feminist note in Marathi literature.

The short novel, *Virlele Swapna,* excerpts from which are translated here, is structured as a series of five monologues, or diary entries, addressed sometimes to the Self, sometimes to the Other. Rohini and Vaishakh are the alternating headings. The monologues are further divided into sections, beginning with number one. We have translated some sections and have retained the original numbering.

◆

VIRLELE SWAPNA
(The Dream That Has Faded)
Rohini

2

I feel like laughing when I see young boys and girls in love. And I also think I would never be as blind as they. Yet, even as I think this thought, another cannot help rising in my mind. Each one of us thinks our love is sighted. Each one of us thinks our experience of love is different from everybody else's.

I too feel that my Vaishakh is different from others. There is something in our yearning for each other that is more enduring than mere emotion. The everlastingness of the love that brings two incomplete lives to completion arises not out of shared emotion but out of shared thought. That alone can make love last through life; else, the bonds, rotted away with emotion, will break, and the two lives will once again suffer the pain of incompleteness.

To play with love is to play with fire. If you cannot play with sufficient skill, you cannot escape being burned, consumed by it. It is often better, therefore, rather than giving oneself over to it totally without thinking, to study instead, in a practical way, unemotionally, the merits and demerits of the other, and only then to allow one's emotions to be involved.

5

Vaishakh! You needn't talk about it. Needn't tell me of it. But your eyes speak of your involvement. Sometimes I want to see some external expression of that involvement. But then I decide I'd rather not—better to let my dreams of happiness stay intact. A day will come when this involvement, which you hold suppressed in your heart, but which speaks through your eyes, will break all barriers and find a voice. How unnaturally you behave! It makes me laugh. You seem to intentionally avoid all situations in which you would have to move and talk in an easy, natural manner. That makes me suspicious. But however you drift away from me, your glance stays back, circling around me like a hawk's—is it possible that I could be deceived? Then who is to break through this deadlock? Are you afraid? I am not. I remember a certain discussion. You said to somebody, "Huh! You should have known as much. Flatter a woman and there is no way you can escape her contempt."

Vaishakh! I don't want flattery. But why do you avoid ordinary conversation? I shall talk to you. You won't feel contemptuous of me, will you?

7

The heart often grows fearful when it paints pictures of the future. What am I to do with this future? I suppose I will study. If an opportunity comes along, I will teach a bunch of girls, somewhere; fill in the hours and days, somehow. Or else, stand around forever and ever holding a garland in my hand ready to drop it, with closed eyes or maybe even open eyes, round the neck of the first man who comes along and so settle down to conjugal life!

VIBHAVARI SHIRURKAR ◆ 427

And what, pray, does this conjugal life amount to? I see so many girls of my age broken under the strain of marriage. The wife cooks and breeds. The husband, having brought home the money, is free to wander around in the world outside, quenching his intellectual thirst with intellectual relationships! I am certain that people who come together to share their lives in this way are flung apart with the very first steps they take. But perhaps my mind, which is so intensely conscious of the education I have received, unreasonably conjures up false images of people ruined by marriage.

Vaishakh

1

I have asked you many times why you feel drawn to me. You say it is on account of my qualities. When you say this, I feel a kind of shock. Rohini, I think you are looking at me blindly. I don't think a genuine assessment of anybody's qualities is possible yet in the marketplace transaction we call marriage. For I can see quite clearly that merit garbed in the rags of poverty is not even noticed because of the great disparity in wealth. Whereas those who are totally without merit are yet accused of possessing it because of their gilded skins. In society every virtuous human being makes an honest attempt to hold his head high. Yet those who are virtueless but rich leave such people far behind by standing upon their shoulders in order to be noticed by society. Could this be true in your case? Real competition, a real test of comparative merit can only occur between those who enjoy a similar economic status. What do you see in me? My merit? I often think you are attracted to me, not for my merit, but by a deceptive appearance of merit.

3

Rohini, I quite honestly feel that if you consider the constraints we are surrounded by, your ideas about "greatness" will also collapse the way mine have. You say you crave a life of principles. Tell me, what could my principles in life be? And what are "principles" in any case? Do you think that people we call idealistic hold clearly defined principles all their lives?

I for one feel that all our ideas are initially quite nebulous. Even the idealist does not see his ideals in a clear, perfectly chiseled, molded form. It is we who think he has always seen them clearly. Every human being struggles to the end of his days to give shape to his ideas, to breathe life into them. Some manage to do so and are acknowledged as idealists. But those who, despite pouring their lifeblood into the struggle, have still not been able to shape their ideas clearly in the eyes of others are labeled unprincipled. Call me a pessimist if you like, but do the ideals of idealists remain intact forever?

Take a look at the histories of organizations and individuals whose work has been based on firm principles. I see their principles changing and shifting as imperceptibly as does treasure buried underground, or a stream changing course.

5

Man's life is like a pole, tied and pegged down on all sides by thick ropes of love and faith. The man who is held upright by love of mother, father, and friends, and by faith in tradition and customs, sways uncontrollably in his place when these bonds are loosened. He neither loses his balance and falls, nor is he able to hold himself firm. Instead, he bends this way and that, uncertainly, always afraid he will fall. I don't want this to happen to me. One should cut away these lifeless bonds, or root oneself firmly and live with confidence in one's own firmness.

Perhaps, at times, there is joy in that uncertain swaying; but for how long? You can't live on visions of the past or of the future when you can see every moment that the ropes of love and faith that hold you down are worn thin, and you can no longer believe in their support. The heart grows restless then, wanting to weave new ties.

I do not feel I would be able to hold myself firm on the strength of the present bonds. That is why I feel restless and bewildered all the time. All the bonds have grown weak, some through contact with the strength of my skepticism; others through their own ancientness. Rohini! At such times I think of you. If I am to break all these weakened bonds and create new ones, based on another faith, it could only be with your support and help.

Rohini

6

All women must want to see their husbands as distinctive in their own universe. Else they wouldn't eagerly talk to other women about their husbands' particular likes and dislikes in a way that would make them out to be distinctive. Whenever I grope around my own heart, I can't help noticing how beloved a spot this wish has acquired for itself in me.

When I see Vaishakh stand up in my circle, I see other eyes lowered under his gaze. I see everybody's attention turned toward what he is saying. I see the atmosphere overwhelmed by his intellect. And then I feel my ambitious heart would be happy only in the company of such a man.

But then there are times when I suspect that all these are games that my mind is playing. That I am allowing my mind to paint only with the colors that it fancies. Yet how could that be?

For years I have heard his name pronounced with respect in every field. No, this can't be self-deception. And then again I feel that there is a sharpness about Vaishakh's attitudes that might goad me continuously. So then, what do I want?

Vaishakh

1

Let this restlessness, this struggle remain in my spirit forever. When this restlessness, this struggle subsides I shall say to myself I am dead alive. I see so many around me who appear to me like cold embers. I get the feeling that people die in their thirties. They all look dead to me. When people who have settled down in family life think they have now "found their way," "found a direction for their lives," look upon a man like me as a ne'er-do-well I feel a little confused. Yet I feel I am the one who is really alive, and they are the ones who are half-dead. I don't feel one bit tempted by their mechanical lives, lives that have grown insipid with being immersed in the same routine. How unnaturally they live! Their years after the midthirties are an exact image of the lives they have lived till then. What kind of life is it where you continue to reproduce the same deeds and words that you have earlier done and said?

Rohini, will you fill this life of mine that seems so empty? Sometimes when you talk to me in that restless way of yours, I feel that you are grappling with precisely the same kind of discontent as that which has been churning up my life. The intensity of this discontent makes us want to destroy everything around us that is near to collapsing and raise something totally new in its place. When such feelings boil over in me, I think I will feel lighter only if I talk to you. You say you don't want our life together to be like that of crows and sparrows. And I don't want to own a plastic doll. Or a slave. I want someone who can think. Rohini! I so often feel, when I look around at girls, that they are wandering sirens waiting to claim male sacrifices with their delicate coyness. I have never found this coyness irresistible. When I see hundreds of young men deadened by the routine of family life, I feel a great rage against these sorceresses who have first put them under a spell with their exquisite attractions and then cut the very vein of their humanity. That is all they do—cast their spells on men! Rohini! When I see your struggle, I feel certain you won't let me fall into this kind of stupor. That you will fight to keep the humanity in me, and in you, alive. That is the kind of battle I want.

5

When I envisage a home, I am horrified by what I see. However little faith one may have in these things oneself, circumstances and society do exercise their pressures. And so a woman who is capable, but fearful and docile, must rot away with cooking, children, and religious rituals! Is there a man alive who thinks such a life is respectable? If he has any feelings about it at all, these feelings have nothing to do with respect, but with his desire to ensure his own comforts. In a life such as this, the woman closes all doors and windows. Because her humanity, her personality are stunted, because her eyes are dazzled by the bright light of the outside world, she locks herself up for life in her darkened home. Surely the man, who inhabits the growing light in the outside world, does not feel very happy to see, when he returns home, a woman who is gradually growing blind in this way. But he too has no choice, and so he continues to suppress his feelings. If these are the sorrows of self-aware men and women, then certainly those others, who are not aware and do not wish to be so, live lives even more deprived of human values.

A man is not excited by a woman's ignorance. When he uses woman merely to satisfy his physical desires, that woman too is like a python swallowing a goat who, being stunned, allows her to devour him whole. That is the single task of women from the time they achieve understanding up to the time they collapse. However much they educate themselves, whatever new life styles they adopt, their entire life and all the skills that are in them are trained toward one goal—the flattering of men, initially to win them, and then in order to survive. And the goal of all men is, initially, to lose their senses over women and then to kick them around and out of their homes! This is what our homes and family lives are.

From the time they come of age, girls and boys are desperate to build such homes for themselves. Everybody around them also sets up a great hue and cry to persuade them to make such homes for themselves. Yet if those wounds that are covered when they speak were to be laid bare, if they were compelled to reveal these wounds, then their voices would take on the vengeful edge that comes of despair. The hope or joy with which they entered their nests has long ago turned into a barrenness. And they remain full of pain. There are so many who stay where they are, consumed in the fire of this pain. And many who, unable to bear it, break through the constriction of these homes.

10

Those immense rallies! The thrilling struggle in them! Often they create such tensions in the mind. And then, just as often, when you have emerged victorious from the meeting, you are filled with the deepest joy. When I get back home at all hours of the night, I crave to hear a loving voice call out to me as I open the door of the room. I want a partner to share in my joy, the joy that is overflowing both banks. When my heartstrings seem to snap one by one, I yearn for a friend. Then I want to run to you. But soon, upon the heels of this urge, comes this thought: of what use would it be to tell you? I would not be satisfied if you, in order not to spoil my joy, made a pretense of smiling appreciation. I must admit, though, that the craving for woman's love and nearness is irresistible. To suppress it calls for a gigantic effort. When I am idle, too often the heart is so filled with desire that the spirit trembles in fearful anticipation of all one's dearest ideals collapsing before the strength of this emotion. It suddenly seems as if the world is empty if I cannot be near you. That seems to be the only meaning life has. To emerge from the intensity of this passion is like coming out unscathed from a house on fire.

An awareness of the incompleteness of life burns so intensely into the heart that I grow helpless with wondering how I am ever going to get out of it.

What a tornado it is! Will my skull split with it! Why not give up all this and seek only Rohini's love! At least for this moment.

Rohini

1

There is no doubt that your ideas of women's emancipation entice me. I see that the very reasons for which my heart fears marriage are non-existent here. But I shall remain wary. I often feel that a man who sets out to conquer unerringly finds ways to persuade and coax. He notes the woman's views and inclinations, and makes it known that his own opinions, likes, and dislikes are in line with hers. If a woman allows herself to be taken in, she might very well repent later. Therefore I shall neither speak nor open my heart. Not to give the slightest clue to what my ideas are would ultimately be in my interests. I'll let you speak. And if I find that the ideas you spontaneously express as yours are at variance with mine, it will be easier for me to keep myself in check.

To play the game of love blindly is to play with life blindly. I am aware that the very nature of this emotion is such that it puts blinders on the eyes of the most rational people. This mirage that enters slyly into the minds of two people and gains control over them causes them to play games of deception with the world. When they play such games they are intoxicated with a sense of their own power before which the power of the world is as nothing. Soon harsh reality works its own magic and the mirage escapes as slyly as it entered. Then the two wretched creatures wake out of their daze and helplessly look to the world for help.

2

"Men earn money and feed their wives and children. I see this differently. There is no reason why a woman should feel enslaved. She is independent. She runs his home for him and he pays for her labor. Often what he pays doesn't match the work she puts in. If every man and woman would only keep this principle of the division of labor in mind, neither would look upon the other as either superior or inferior. Both must believe that they are living by their own, independent labor. Only when our women become conscious of this, will they acquire the strength to think independently." This is the kind of thing you often say. I am shocked by the bitter truth of what you say. It has erased from my mind the old, poetic picture of married life. And it has weakened the old insistence on women serving somebody and deluding themselves into believing that they have achieved economic independence.

Though your view of married life is acceptable to a person like me, I often feel that this business of paying, or being paid, for every piece of work, this attitude toward work itself, turns the sweetest sentiments shared by men and women into poison—sentiments that impel people to self-sacrifice and to doing deeds without seeking returns. They are so delicate in nature that it would be impossible to assess them in terms of money. But while they may not be assessed, they are intensely felt in the heart, and they keep the heart tender and moist. It is these precious feelings that bring warmth to the harsh life of human beings. The day man begins to assess and evaluate these feelings in a commercial manner he will discover that his life has become unendurable.

What! To accept marriage as a business transaction! What an ugly thought! I wouldn't like to admit it is so even if I were convinced it was. I am happier to think that marriage is one area in which you need to be selfless and to work without anticipating rewards. I'd rather be blindly faithful than have my illusions shattered.

If this principle of shared labor in marriage, which you espouse, is consciously applied, it could quite easily happen that one person's labor will stop giving satisfaction and so another laborer will be appointed. If a man finds that a woman's work isn't worth the pay he gives her, he might very well pay her for the days she has worked and ask her to leave. Similarly, the woman might decide to leave.

Your ideas about morality and society appeal to the mind but not to the heart. And yet you say that it is these ideas that will ultimately protect our feelings! I feel thoroughly confused when I think about these things.

Do you have any idea at all of how painful your despair is to me? When I see that you have no faith in anything at all, I fear you might have just as little faith in marriage. You might merely play around and then escape as you have played around with other things and escaped. You might very well say to me one day, "Rohini, look at marriage. What sense is there in it? Why enter into it and get bored? Why not be happy with the imagined thing?" I doubt very much if your mind, which bitterly tears everything to shreds, will continue to contemplate marriage with blind eyes.

How is it that you have no faith in anything at all? Anything in the present? You have no love for anybody. No individual or ideology, not Gandhi, nor Kelkar, nor Malviya; not the councilists nor the reformists nor conservatives. None has escaped your vicious attacks. What, according to you, is good then? I feel terribly confused at times.

Would I accept a Vaishakh who is always going to be different from everybody else? Who regards fame cynically? I don't know. I am an ordinary woman who is happy walking the beaten track. I don't understand all these ideas of yours.

Vaishakh, I think you and I are two opposites. How could I have ever felt that our thoughts were similar? Trying to fathom the mind is, I suppose, like trying to fathom the vacuum of the sky. The mind is always playing new tricks. Can one ever understand another's mind completely? However direct and clear one is, many ideas and thoughts remain unexpressed in words and deeds. It is these that cause differences to arise between one person and another.

It is true that there are immense differences between you and me. But I still feel tempted to continue the way I am, eyes closed, half-asleep. The idea of facing our differences lacerates me. My heart has become so tender now that I would not have the strength to bear that. Vaishakh, could one live one's entire life with closed eyes? If that were possible, then one could escape the anguish of awareness. But it cannot last. I am being dragged back and forth all the time through the fires of thought. These turbulent thoughts destroy my peace, just as boiling water attempts to throw the heaving lid off.

7

When the first loving tears that the clouds shed upon the parched earth touch her, the sigh of happiness that arises from her spreads into and fills all space. But if, seeing this, the clouds continue the downpour, it turns to poison upon the earth. I think all women are like that. They are parched without love; but when they receive love in abundance it turns to poison in them. Perhaps it is for this reason that marriages lose their savor. Yes. Stay away from me as you have been doing. Let my soul burn in anguish and let the moistness of your love touch it only once in a while. The warmth of half-given love will bring more joy to life than an unending stream.

9

Yes, Vaishakh! My ideas of "greatness" are as narrow as my mind. I can see now that I measure all greatness by tangible, material values. I had no idea of the hidden power of your spirit. Will you not rein yourself in? You are running too fast. Why do you want to turn the universe upside down? When will you come back? And how long shall I wait for you? I feel a gnawing fear within. What if the reins snap? You will ride the winds unchecked. Vaishakh, you'll be thrown. People are singing your praises now when you are in full gallop. What when you are thrown? When you have flown this mortal body? They will sing elegies then, for a little while. But I will have lost you for all time, Vaishakh. Yet I do not have the strength to go with you. To follow you is agony for my spirit. Vaishakh! You will hold me in scorn. You will grow tired of me. I have dared to throw a lighted match into a cellar full of pure alcohol and now my ears are deafened with the explosion of my deed. The earth shakes with the shock of it. My feet are unsteady on the ground. Such timidity will fill you with contempt. But what is this? Vaishakh, you aren't anywhere near me. You've already moved far away from me.

I look upon you with wonder and admiration. With wonder and admiration—certainly—and with love too. . . . I will always look upon you thus, wherever I go. But always from afar. I do not have the courage to come closer to you as one who belongs to you. Is the instinct for self-preservation the sharpest in all women, as it is in me? Who knows! I can only speak for myself. And as I speak, I feel ashamed—even scornful—of myself. What can I do? There is no way I can live without trying to protect myself. I am afraid. What would I do if you walked out on me, out of our home? I would not be able to live merely on the knowledge of the unlimited strength of your love for me and mine for you. I have more fears than this. Suppose there is another tender life that is ours to look after? How could I bear to see it neglected? What would I feed it with? The nobility of love stirs me profoundly. Yes. But then the compulsions of this mortal body dig their spurs into me and wake me up.

16

Dear heart! It was you, wasn't it, who built these massive temples to love? Massive and yet invisible. Nobody will ever see them. These temples, which took years to build, working through every moment, day and night without rest. Why did you take such pains? For whom? Dear heart, there is no foundation to them. They will be blown away with a single breath. Temples built on a diet of blood from the heart. All of them useless! And useless the labor that went into them. They are but painted theaters. I have no desire to enshrine anybody in them as a god. I am angry. What foolishness this is. Why did you build them? On what basis? Now pull them down. Go. With more energy than when you built them. I don't want them before my eyes.

If you have grown weak and barren, draw sustenance from my moist blood and go to work. Pull them down. Let me suffer to see them fall. There was pain when they were built. Now there is pain when they are pulled down. But remove them from my sight. Let them vanish from memory. My heart! Dear heart! Foolish heart! For whom did you build? For a god? No, my dear. He was no god. A man. A man who is galloping ahead at fearful speed. Was it for him that you took such pains?

Translated by Shanta Gokhale.

HOMVATI DEVI ————————————

(1906–1951)   *Hindi*

Homvati Devi, Kamla Chaudhry, and Subhadra Kumari Chauhan, all of whom published their initial works in the 1930s, are among the first women writers in Hindi. Born in Meerut of well-to-do parents, Homvati was an only child. Married when still quite young to Chiranjilal, a physician, she lived the traditional confined life of a housewife in Uttar Pradesh and hardly ever left the house. Though as a child she was drawn to literature and wanted to write, she did not pursue either interest seriously until several years later. The few things she tried her hand at were brief sketches about the strains and tensions within the household. None of them was published. She felt handicapped by her lack of formal education and had little time to spare after the many duties she had as the wife of a man of high status. Things took a different turn when her husband suddenly died in 1929. Homvati was then twenty-three.

With the encouragement of Krishna Chandra Sharma, a Hindi writer of some standing, she began to write more seriously and in 1939 read her first story to an audience of fellow writers at the Nauchandi Mela held in Meerut. Her home soon became a gathering place for writers and intellectuals, who came even from other cities to discuss Hindi literature and read their work. Some of the debates that took place on the lawns of her house may have well changed the course of Hindi literature.

Homvati Devi's writing is marked by an eye for detail and a feel for the everyday pains, the unexpected joys, and the searing humiliations a middle-class woman experienced. The stories may seem sentimental to us today, but their value lies also in the realistic account they provide of the law, and of other institutions of the state, as women experienced them. Before the Hindu Succession Act of 1956, according to some schools of Hindu law property was passed on along a line of male descendants. A widow was entitled only to maintenance, and could be disinherited totally on grounds of unchastity. "Apna Ghar" takes up the issues of a movement for reform that was sustained over two decades.

We have been able to locate four of Homvati Devi's stories, each published independently: "Apna Ghar" (Our Home), circa 1935, "Swapna Bang" (The Lifting of a Dream), 1948, "Nisarg" (Creation), no date, and "Ardh" (Half), no date.

◆

APNA GHAR
(Our Home)

I

When Uma shed all her obligations and, carrying the weight of her sorrow and widowhood, returned to her natal home, she realized that there was nothing for her there. She had been brought up amid great luxury and wealth. The riches were still there in abundance, but for her there was nothing except disdain. All the affection, respect, and her right to anything had gone up in smoke on the pyre of her mother and father. She had no brother. She had been an only child and now her ill fortune had brought her to the doorstep of her uncle's son for succor. She had never imagined that every morsel of food she received in this house would increase her exploitation and humiliation. She would have preferred to toil as a laborer or be a teacher to little children to feed herself and her ill-starred child. She was constrained to stay alive only because she felt bound to him like one does to a curse.

He too was neither old enough to understand all nor so young as to sense nothing. He was in his seventh year. He set himself up to compete with his uncle's children in everything. I'll sit in the car, I'll go for a drive, I will also drink milk, why was I not given an orange? These shoes are old, I want a new pair, I also want new clothes. . . . His demands constantly vexed Uma. She would think of ways to keep him quiet. Should she strangle him and then kill herself? Thinking in this vein, her extreme sensitivity and distress would drive her into some corner, and casting aside the work at hand, she would shed tears to lighten the burden of her heart.

She had chosen to live with her in-laws, her marital home. But whom could she stay with? Her husband's brothers had already begun to wrangle for the few thousands due from the insurance and the company had deferred payment until the dispute was settled, even though the true heir was her seven-year-old Neelam. All this had put Uma in a real quandary. She had seen the same thing happen once before. She had been disinherited from her father's immense wealth even though she was the only child. Arguing the case of joint families and joint ownership, her cousin had appropriated all the money, and she was now reduced to dependence on him for her survival.

She felt diffident about finding a job. What would she introduce herself as? Besides, she was young and extremely beautiful. Destiny had led to her birth in a wealthy family and its caprice had also carried her to an ordinary life. And today even that was threatened. She had forgotten herself and everything in the love and contentment her husband had given her, but now all her wounds were raw and she was ashamed to expose them, but they were also too painful to cover.

And suddenly, as if to get away from herself, she slapped Neelam and said threateningly, "Go and get your book, and let me hear the lesson I taught you yesterday." And she cursed him silently, "I wish he were dead; then I would be free. I should have put him on the pyre with his father and not had any bonds." And large tears fell from her lovely eyes. She quickly wiped her face and began preparing the vegetables. From the background the maidservant who was kneading the dough said, "Don't push him so, Bibi! Times change. If he lives, your good days will come again. He is a child after all. If he picked two flowers from the garden along with the other children, what does it matter? And these are people of status . . . What can one say if their children are like this. . . . They immediately came and told on him . . .

See!" Uma was not in the least comforted by the servant's sympathy. Her heart was in fact cut to the quick. People of status . . . their children . . . and this servant . . . and she . . . and Neelam. Oh! She got up instantly and went to the terrace, where sitting under the hot sun Neelam was trying to memorize yesterday's lesson.

II

"When Seth Kanhaiyalal died, Asharfi Bibi must at the most have been around thirty, but from that day she gave up wearing saris with an edging and had only one meal a day for a year and that too without salt." Saying this, Uma's sister-in-law, who had been a child widow and was now over forty, peeled two litchies and popped them into her mouth. Uma stopped stitching and looked at her sister-in-law, her eyes moving from head to toe and pausing on the green broad-bordered sari and the blue printed blouse. In that very instant she also thought of her zamindar cousin, himself a widower, who had given this lady, his second wife, the right to say anything she pleased to anybody. Then she decided: the next morning she would tear off the borders of all her saris and stitch the edges on the sewing machine. That evening she did not eat her usual meal and nobody bothered to find out why.

On the next day Neelam's school moved into a morning shift. As on all other days, Uma got up very early and served breakfast and milk to the children and put some milk out for Neelam also. She thought, "He's a child. How will he remain hungry until noon?" Neelam arranged his school bag. The milk was kept on the low table on which the other children were also eating when a crow came and knocked over the poor child's milk. The children began yelling. The mistress of the house drew her brows together and said, "Of course, you want enough milk to drink and to spill. Where will it all come from? We've got cows and buffaloes in the house, but does that mean that milk can be thrown about like water?"

Uma and Neelam stood rooted to the spot like criminals in the dock. Neither could the mother find the courage to serve fresh milk, nor the child to ask. He merely said, "I won't drink any milk, Amma." And tucking his bag under his arm he went out.

That night it rained heavily and it did not stop until the morning. All the children got ready and sat in the car. Neelam also went and stood there with his bag. Just then the zamindar Babu's elder son spat out, "There is no place in the car. You can walk."

"I'll get wet, Bhaiya," said Neelam. But as he walked toward the car, it started off. Neelam walked slowly in the rain.

When he returned at noon, he had a high fever. His clothes and books were soaked. When Uma asked how it had happened, he burst into tears. "Amma, let us not live here anymore. Let's go home to Father."

Uma's heart broke when she heard this. Home—there is no home. Father—he will not come back now. Where should I take you? You study hard and grow up fast; only then will we have our own home. And she was lost in painting a vision of the future. Neelam, his wife, his children, servants, cows, milk, curd, and . . . our home. All this began unfolding like a series of moving pictures in her imagination. It touched her pain. Some strand of hope for the morrow transported her to another world. It was as if she were not the young woman of twenty-two but a fifty-year-old mistress of a prosperous household. And she was bathed in the glow of love and contentment . . . when Neelam said, "Amma, I'm cold."

Uma's reverie was broken. Back to the real world. She dried his body, changed his clothes, and laid him on the bed. She put her head on the plank but then stood up alert as she heard the sound of Zamindar Babu's wooden clogs. She still had not arranged the plates, the chutney had not been ground, nor the curd seasoned. Her heart sank with fear and nervousness. Neelam said, "Amma, get me an umbrella. I will not sit in their car." She said, "Yes," and went toward the kitchen.

III

Uma gave her silver collyrium bottle and mirror to the Munshiji and said, "Don't let anybody know, Munshiji. Sell these and get an umbrella, one pair of shoes, and material for a few shirts and pajamas, and put it all in this room and I'll take it from there."

Weighing both things in his hands, Munshiji said, "Let's see what price these will fetch."

Uma calculated mentally. These things were twenty tolas and her mother had bought them to give in her wedding. One should get at least twenty rupees. The rate of silver is very high, I've heard. She then said to the Munshi, "About how much will the umbrella cost, Munshiji? If not a pair of shoes, then at least sandals."

The Munshi replied gravely, "Everything is selling at four times the price, Bibi. I'm not going to make any profit out of this."

And then Uma said no more and came back into the house crest-fallen, looking like a creeper shriveled in the frost. Her sister-in-law asked sarcastically, "What did you go out for?"

"I wanted an umbrella for Neelam. His shoes are also in bad shape," Uma replied and began culling the greens.

"Hm . . ." said Harnandi after casting a sharp look at her sister-in-law, but she was not satisfied yet. She was not used to being cut short in conversation. She said, " 'He' has been saying that Neelam is quite old now. Why must he sleep in the women's rooms? He should sleep outside; the other children also sleep there."

Uma felt she was plunging from the sky. "Neelam has only turned seven. He's too young to sleep outside . . . he's younger than all the other boys of the house. He's never slept away from me." But what could she say? She bowed her head and listened in silence. The mistress of the house felt that her statement had not been taken due notice of. Nobody in the house dared to remain silent when thus spoken to. And so releasing a sharp, fearful arrow, she returned to her room. Uma sat there calmly, busy cutting vegetables.

That evening Uma's sorrow and amazement knew no bounds when she saw that the servant had come to take away Neelam's bedding. Gathering her courage together, Uma asked, "Who asked you, Kalicharan, to take Neelam's bedding?"

"The master," was the answer.

And Uma was left wringing her hands helplessly. What more could she do? But that night neither she nor Neelam slept much. In the morning he buried his face in his mother's breast and cried, "Amma, I don't like it here. Let's go," and he ran such a high fever that he was unconscious the whole day. It was then decided that he should be examined by the doctor the next day. The doctor diagnosed typhoid. He should be kept apart from the others. This is a highly contagious disease.

The hours turned to days and the days to weeks and two months passed, but Neelam's fever did not break. It would go down briefly only to shoot up four times higher. He was now just a bag of bones. His eyes receded deep into their sockets and his limbs were thin and wasted. He would neither hear nor speak. If at all he spoke, it was in a delirium. Everybody would watch and make hopeless gestures before going away. Doctors would arrive and heave a sigh of futility, glance toward Uma, and leave. Uma herself, half-dead, sat like a statue of stone, thinking about God alone knows what. She neither ate nor drank—it was as if she were the very figure of compassion and pity.

"Neelu—speak little one—it's been more than two months since I heard your voice. Neelam, open your eyes once, my dearest. Where are you preparing to go, my son? Don't go alone, Neelu! I can't manage without you, and you can't without me." Saying this, Uma banged her head against the bedpost. The world grew dark before her eyes. Her tears had gone dry and they would not flow, or else she could have wept away some of her suffering.

It was the height of noon. There was a furnace burning in the mother's heart. She had been weeping for a long time. The head of the house entered quietly. Every sentence that Uma uttered today had pierced his heart. He felt there was no penance for this, felt as if he was the reason behind this young woman's ruin. He had reduced her to the existence of a beggar on the streets. Her golden frame was turning to mud. He remembered the day when he as a brother had seated her in the bridal palanquin all decked out in her finery. Her parents had brought her up with such tender care and affection. Now the zamindar Babu felt that Uma's parents had returned and were staring at him accusingly like avenging ghosts. His heart sank. Uma raised her head and looked at Neelam again.

Babu gathered courage and took two steps until he was right behind Uma and said, "You have won the case, Uma. There has been a telegram. You will get the money soon."

But Uma did not understand. She stirred restlessly and put her head on the feet of her cousin brother and said, "Save Neelam, Bhaiya. He's slipping away from me quietly. He doesn't even open his eyes now. His spirit wants to be released. He docs not like to be bound. Find me a corner that Neelam can call his home, where he is not humiliated, where nobody can separate us. And if he is to die, then at least he can die in peace."

There was a stream of tears flowing from Uma's eyes as she said this. She felt that after ages she had found a slender support. Somebody was at least listening to her. Her bonds were loosening a little. Somehow a few words found their way out. Her cousin helped her up. "Stop now, Uma. Whatever you wish will be done. Neelu will be well. I'll call another doctor immediately."

He went out. The stone melted under the sharp heat of the fire of compassion. Uma wiped her tears and stroked Neelam's head. She then folded her hands in thanksgiving to some unknown force. Neelam turned his eyes toward her and in a very feeble voice, said, "Amma—water."

The sound was like nectar to Uma's ears—it was as if the moon had suddenly dropped in her palm from the skies. She put a spoonful of water in the child's mouth and said, "Get well soon, Bhaiya. Then we'll go home."

Translated by Manisha Chaudhry.

GEETA SANE —————————————

(b. 1907)   *Marathi*

This significant but relatively unknown feminist writer, who worked mainly in the 1930s and 1940s, was a contemporary of writers such as Vibhavari Shirurkar, Kusumavati Deshpande, and Indira Sahasrabuddhe. Like them, Geeta Sane focuses on the contradictions that arose for women in the first decades of this century as they reached out for the new education and the promises it made. Again and again, her heroines discover that the much-vaunted liberal ideals of the time—ideals of individualism and personal fulfillment—stop strangely short of women's lives and women's desires. In her first novel, *Nikalele Hivakani* (The Dislodged Diamond), 1934, Achyut, a wealthy young man, assumes that his wife, Krishna, will always be sexually available when he desires, and he imposes himself on her quite insensitively. Krishna is nauseated by his rough and thoughtless behavior, and when she becomes pregnant, she feels motherhood too has been forced on her. She cannot bear to live with Achyut in what she regards as a "sinful" life, because their relationship is not based on love. The child dies at birth and Krishna goes into a depression. Only in Ratna, the nurse she meets in the hospital, does she find any sympathy or understanding. "Our pandits sleep quietly though they know that there is so much pain and injustice going on within our marriages," Ratna says. "Yet they criticize any woman who decides to marry into another caste. If a widow takes one wrong step, they will immediately call her a fallen woman. There is no one to take our side. Even our mothers do not really belong to us. Ours is the freedom only to cry or to commit suicide." But Krishna fights. She leaves Achyut (but not without explaining her position and arranging another marriage for him), goes back to school, and works until she gets a master's degree. Then comes the blow that cripples her. No college will give her a job because she is considered a "bad woman." As the novel ends, she goes insane and dies.

Related themes run through each of Geeta Sane's other novels. In the preface to *Vathalela Vrksha* (The Stunted Tree), 1936, published in the same year as *Hirvalikhali* (Under the Grass of the Green Lawn), Geeta Sane writes, "Marriage is a riddle. People give up their lives solving this problem. Whether you consider it a mere contract or something that binds one for seven lives, it creates problems." The protagonists are modern young people who choose each other as life partners but, over a period of time, develop in different directions. The woman is drawn to socialism, the man to fasting and theosophy. Tired of the strains between them and unwilling to face the daily tensions, the woman leaves the house and takes a job as a teacher in another city.

Not only in her resolutely uncompromising endings is Geeta Sane's writing revolutionary. Her sense of how feminist issues are related to other social and political questions of the time sets her work apart. *Dhuke Ani Dahiwar* (Mist and Dew Drops), 1942, published when the Congress-led national movement was at its height, explores the different ideological strands in the freedom struggle, especially the Gandhian. The protagonist, Ujjwala, dreams while she is in college of marrying the man she loves and settling down, but moves, at his suggestion, into public life. The crèche she sets up for poor children draws her into a strike of women beedi rollers. Her discussions with a Marxist doctor, who works in the area, help her understand the limitations of an approach based on charity. She is shocked by the violence with which "nonviolent" Gandhians put down the strike. The novel is ultimately a debate about the social and political issues of the time and their effect on women's lives. An earlier novel, *Avishkar* (Expression), 1939, had explored similar problems. Among Geeta Sane's other works are *Pheriwala* (Hawker), 1939, in which the protagonist struggles in a time of great unemployment to find a living, while the woman he loves has to take up prostitution, and *Deepastamba* (Lighthouse), published in 1950.

Geeta Sane was born in Umravathi, a town in northern Maharashtra. Her father was a teacher who later trained to become a lawyer. Her parents had to leave the joint family home because her grandmother objected to the esteem her mother, the youngest daughter-in-law, received because her husband was a lawyer. Geeta Sane still remembers how cramped their new home was and how difficult it was for her parents to manage entirely on their own. Her father started a legal practice, but had to discontinue because he got deeply involved in the Home Rule movement led by Lokmanya Tilak. Her mother, Geeta Sane says, had an engineer's mind. She invented new kinds of *chulas* (charcoal/wood stoves) and constantly experimented with other appliances. In what was a revolutionary gesture at the time, her parents decided that none of the daughters was to be married before puberty. Their weddings were conducted without religious rituals. "They must have cost my father only a rupee and a half each," she adds.

Geeta Sane herself chose to study science and later taught mathematics. She started writing in 1927, her first piece an angry response to the turmoil caused by the Khan-Panandikar affair. The furor over this marriage between a Hindu and a Muslim, both students at the university, started up following a news items in the *Pune Vaibhav.* While a few people like S. V. Ketkar supported the couple, others strongly opposed it. Since then she has written regularly on social issues. Most of her articles were published in *Stree,* which for many years was edited by the writer and feminist Vidya Bal. When she was twenty-six, she married Narasimha Dhagamwar. He also took active part in the freedom movement and was one of those charged in the famous Meerut conspiracy case of 1929. In an attempt to defuse the growing unrest among workers and the increasing influence of the left in the labor unions, the British government arrested thirty-one leaders and charged them with conspiracy. Geeta Sane's daughter, Vasudha Dhagamvar, is a well-known civil liberties activist, lawyer, and journalist.

◆

From HIRVALIKHALI
(Under the Grass of the Green Lawn)
Chapter 4. The Chains of Slavery

"Even you may not believe that until recently I had never even witnessed a sunset. . . ."

Vanita did not respond. But today I was in the mood to unburden myself. It was a beautiful, moonlight night. It was almost ten o'clock and silent all around. But it was rather warm. Vanita and I were sitting on easy chairs on the terrace. After a great deal of persuasion she had managed to get me to go to the Haldi-Kumkum ceremony that day.

"You think I am cowardly and useless. You are quite right. When I see your courage, your initiative, your thoughts, I feel ashamed of myself. I feel my whole life has perhaps been a waste. But what is the use of blaming girls for all this waste?

"Independence is something we have never been familiar with. No one seems to need the daughter of the house even as much as they need the cow. She gets her food as a matter of right; the women fast twice a year, invoking her name as the holiest of holy ones. There are still riots when a cow is killed. But what about a girl? No one cares about her. She is only the evil witch who seduced Brahma the Creator with her wiles.

"The moment a daughter is born, the parents are saddled with a burden. The elders begin to think about her marriage even before the babe opens her eyes. Strife begins in the house because of her while she is still a child—when she should be laughing, playing, and enjoying her life.

"Vanu, I cannot think big like you. We grew up like unwanted cattle. But I have experienced the treatment meted out to the likes of us and it has hit me where it really hurts. You were so upset because a young girl like me entered wedlock with my eyes shut. But are you concerned about the thousands of injustices perpetrated upon girls everywhere? It is possible the situation is somewhat different in the educated, cultured households. Perhaps educated parents think differently. But what about most girls?"

"My life has taken a different path," Vanita observed. "My parents are loving and understanding. They made no distinctions between a son and a daughter. I was fortunate to find equally loving parents-in-law. Even Shreesh is good-natured. No one has ever tried to crush or subdue my personality. It is society that has created the thorns in the path of my life, not any individual."

"The responsibility for our maltreatment, too, is upon society. What is our value in society? Nothing! There was a story I heard time and again when I was a child. It went, 'Sakhu will leave for her husband's home. Baku will go to her spouse's home. It is only my Jubrya [son] who will be of use to me!' At the back of her mind every mother carries the same thought. Because the daughter will eventually go to someone else's house, the mother couldn't care less; because a daughter-in-law is someone else's daughter, the mother-in-law couldn't care less. And men by virtue of being men will lord it over them! Why then be surprised if girls turn into dolls? Will a creeper ever grow if we prune it every day?"

Vanita took my hand and held it. "I admit that the circumstances are against us. The winds are blowing in the opposite direction. Is there any bravery in turning your back to the enemy and retreating?"

I smiled a little. "The men show enough courage. There is no need for women to show it too."

I knew that Vanita had a sharper intellect than mine; and because I felt so inferior I usually avoided arguments with her. Today, encouraged when I saw that she agreed with my ideas, I spoke seriously.

"Ever since I can remember I have been hearing, seeing, and learning that a woman shouldn't try to compete with a man. Even before we could distinguish between men and women, we were taught: 'I am a woman. I should suffer all the injustices perpetrated by men without complaint.'

"Our father was a teacher in the A. V. school. He started on a salary of twenty rupees. Both Grandfather and Grandmother were still alive. God alone knows how a family of four survived on twenty rupees. To add to the travails, since my parents' first children had been prey to infant mortality, my mother gave birth every year regularly. Apart from this, every religious observance or ritual had to be conducted in the appointed way. As a result, both Father and Mother became extremely disciplined; the month's expenditure had to be planned out. Budgeted things were purchased in budgeted quantities. If there happened to be a shortage of a particular thing in a given month, one had to do without it. They had no option. If they had not behaved as they did, they would have gone bankrupt.

"They performed many religious rituals and fasts so that their offspring might live. At last, as a result of the blessings of a holy man, Bhau [her brother] lived. And because this holy man worshiped Jagadamba as his deity, my brother was named Devidas, or the servant of the goddess. The rituals for thanking various gods for the granting of a healthy child continued till it was time for Bhau's thread ceremony. I was born two years later, and at the instance of the same holy man I was named Mahadevi, the great goddess. Bhau shortened it to Madhu. You know of course that Mother calls me Manu. . . . I cannot remember when my grandparents died. But Father became even more religious after Bhau's birth and continued to be so till the end.

"Though Father was poor, he indulged Bhau in every way he could. That is why Bhau became so spoiled and stubborn. As a child he never touched the coarse millet-flour *bhakris* we ate. Mother used to make two fine light chapatis of wheat flour for him. Any chapatis left after Bhau was satisfied went to Father. I would get a glimpse of a chapati only on festival days. Childlike, I pined for a chapati and would sometimes say, 'Mother, will you give me a chapati today?'

" 'Why do you behave in this greedy fashion? Have you ever seen a chapati without craving for one? You are born a girl and yet you hanker for light chapatis and sweets?' This would be accompanied by a slap or a rough pinch on my cheek.

"It was only rarely that a sweet was made or brought into the house. And even on such occasions the first claim was Brother's, then Father's; after them maybe I would get the minuscule quantity that was left. My mother never kept anything for herself. But nobody worried about that. Not only that, they even thought it natural that this should be so. As children we were taught the principle of 'giving the rice to those in power and drinking the water that remained.' But as a child I hankered for these things. I used to sit at a distance and watch Father and Bhau eating. If my mother caught me at it, she used to shout, 'Why are you staring like a greedy person? Get up. They will not be able to digest what they are eating with you looking on like that!' Helplessly I used to get up and go out, tears of frustration filling my eyes.

"Sometimes if it happened that Mother or Father was not around, I used to plead with Bhau. But he only boxed my ear and complained to Mother. 'Look at this Madhu, always asking me for this or that.' And then there would be a flood of tears in my eyes when Mother spanked me. Bhau was always given better clothes to wear. Many times I was just tempted to touch and feel his clothes, but Bhau used to hit me if I did that. Mother of course always took his side.

"Every expression of a girl's spirit was squashed in a thousand ways. Bhau used to get toys from the fair. I only had the satisfaction of looking at them. Bhau was picked up and tossed by all Father's friends. I always stood watching behind the door, envying him. Bhau had a little mattress to sleep on. I used to sleep on a thin quilt handmade from my mother's old saris. Father and Bhau used to eat their meals together, but until quite recently it was taken for granted that I would eat afterward from Bhau's used plate. Mother ate what was left over. As poor people we didn't dream of throwing food away.

"But all this did not mean that Mother or Father did not like me or want me. They were so poor. They were not able to look after two children, so they discriminated. They were also under the pressure of the old culture. Their way of expressing their love was different. Bhau was their heir, their support in old age, and the son who would put the holy water in their mouths when they died. And what about me? After eating free meals in their house I would go to someone else's house. They understood the simple meaning of love. They were not people in a novel singing praises of some heavenly love. Once, when I was perhaps eight years old, my parents were talking and I, half asleep, overheard them. 'The lawyer's wife next door wants Manu to live with them during the four holy months of the year.'

" 'Hum!' Father replied as was his way.

" 'I think we should let her go. She never gets anything she wants in this poor house. At least for these four months she will have four square meals a day and feel satisfied.'

" 'All right. If you think she is a good woman, let Manu go.'

"And during those four months I used to eat at the lawyer's house. I would get at least a spoonful of *kheer** every day. I had chapatis every day and ghee in the *dal* curry. I was very happy. When the four holy months were over, they stitched me a long skirt and blouse of Dharwar material. I was given silver toerings and a gold ring for my nose. My joy knew no bounds. After that Kaku, the lawyer's wife, seemed a goddess in my young eyes.

"Tell me, Vani, why should my mind and my sensitivity not die out? Right from my childhood it has been these words, this treatment, and this behavior. Why? Because I had committed the cardinal sin of being born a girl. It was clearly etched on my face. My mother was not a stepmother. Neither was she wicked. But she had the bad fortune of living in poverty. Don't you think it is unjust to expect girls constantly bruised like this to become strong? Even a stone baked in a hot oven turns to lime!

"When I entered my eleventh year, there was a hurry to get me married. My horoscope showed a malevolent Mars. My father could not afford a dowry. Groom hunting became an onerous task. They did not want to marry me off to a widower. A prospective groom would first ask, 'Is the girl educated?'

"Fortunately, my parents had not objected to my attending school with the other girls in the neighborhood after I had finished the housework. And since I was fairly clever, I passed every year and completed the fourth standard. Since education was being discussed everywhere, it was decided to keep me in school for a couple of years more—until I got married.

"The second question to crop up would be of age. Everybody thought that a girl of eleven was too young to be married. As a result the age at which boys married was also going up. Conversely, the parents of girls were in a hurry to get them married. But a boy marrying at twenty-two wanted for a bride a girl who was at least thirteen or fourteen.

"The third question was always about the dowry. A bridegroom who was 'matric pass' and earned twenty-five rupees a month expected

---

*Kheer is a desert made from rice, milk, sugar, and almonds, often flavored with cardamom.

a dowry of between five hundred and a thousand rupees. Even these types were not so easy to come by for me because of the malevolent Mars in my horoscope. My age kept rising. My father was tired of looking for prospective grooms. When I turned fourteen, Father was sick with anxiety. He used to go and inquire whenever he learned about a groom who had a Mars-oriented horoscope, and was really frustrated when the whole thing fell through for one reason or another. It is not surprising that that frustration turned to anger against me. I tried to keep out of his way altogether.

"Not many families came to test me as a bride, and those who came stuck to the conventional frames for such occasions. The first occasion was when I was twelve. When I saw my married friends, even I wanted to be married. My idea of marriage was clouded with grand saris, lots of jewelry, lots to eat, and a continuously playing band. That's why I also accepted the dream world of being looked at—approved—and married.

"I wore my mother's special *erkali* sari. Have you ever seen the special-occasion saris preserved by poor women? It had not been washed once in twelve years. The gold thread in the border was not crinkled, it had never been aired or sunned. It was still new. I wore it happily. My mother gave me her broad gold bangles and pearl earrings. I wore the neighbor's pearl necklace and put my hair up tightly in the traditional way with a gold flower pinned into it.

"Shyly I took the tea out and stood with my eyes cast down at my toerings as my mother had taught me. . . ."

Translated by Jyoti Kanitkar.

DARISI ANNAPURNAMMA ⸻⸻⸻⸻

(1907–1931)   *Telugu*

Darisi Annapurnamma lived only for twenty-four years but in that short span achieved many things. She was born in Bellary, a small town in Andhra. An educated woman was very rare in those days, more so among the vaisya community to which she belonged. But her mother, who was inspired by the social reform movement, encouraged her to study. A remarkable woman by all accounts, her mother was also the first person in the community to delay her daughter's marriage until puberty.

Annapurnamma studied in several schools in Andhra. Even as a child she showed interest in philosophy and mastered Telugu, English, and Sanskrit. Later, she lectured on different aspects of spiritual life and became known for her willingness to answer questions from the audience. When the first Arya Vaisya Conference took place in Madras, Annapurnamma won a gold medal in the competition for extempore speech. It was while she was studying at Sarada Niketan in Guntur that she met Darisi Chenchayya, who was also a writer, and married him. She was then fifteen. She married him, he writes in his autobiography, *Nenu Nadesam* (I and My Country), 1952, because she felt that he would support the work she wanted to do for society. She was intensely involved, he writes, with the idea of building a woman's movement. She worked for the betterment of nautch girls and supported widow remarriage. Many destitute widows found shelter in her house. Unlike many of the others who took up issues already raised by the reform movement, Annapurnamma supported the idea of divorce. She felt it was better for the incompatible couple to separate. She personally encouraged many women to get an education and fight against caste discrimination. She was one of the representatives from Andhra at the 1929 All India Women's Conference, and one of the few women who participated in the famous Salt Satyagraha led by Mahatma Gandhi in 1930.

In 1931 Annapurnamma went to Bandar to attend a widow remarriage, but came back with a case of pneumonia, from which she died, leaving behind two small daughters: one three, the other five.

Like many other writers of the period, she also wrote on issues that had been raised by the social reform movement. Her articles deal with the rights and duties of Hindu women, the law of divorce, purdah, women's education, and nationalism, while her stories, written in a humorous colloquial style, are about superstitions and blind belief, the woman's place in the family, and male domination. The story chosen for translation exposes charlatans who pose as holy men and exploit gullible people. This was a topic popular in the literature of social reform, but Annapurnamma encrusts onto the narrative women's frustration and helplessness—and male folly. Again, in her story, the men are simpleminded and obtuse, for they reject the knowledge of the senses and of experience for the wild promises made by these "holy" men. The women, on the other hand, are more astute, but helpless—unlike the protagonist, Gnanamba, who objects.

◆

GNANAMBA

After several miscarriages and the loss of many children in infancy, Lakshmamma was left with five daughters and five sons. The brothers were called Keshava, Narayana, Madhava, Govinda, and Vishnu. The family was quite prosperous and owned several head of cattle. After the death of the parents, the keys of the treasury passed into the hands of the eldest son, Keshavaiya. The younger brothers conducted themselves according to the wishes of their elder brother. Among the women there were disputes, but there was no one to pay any heed to them. When the men appeared a furlong away, the wife and other women would vanish from sight. Remarks such as "You there! Why don't you answer? What are you doing?" and a few well-directed glances were enough to secure the men all the services they required—systematically and respectfully. When anything seemed amiss, the proverb "A sound blow is a sounder teacher than God himself" was always handy. With the first crow of the cock the women would rise and start on the chores that were allotted to them—cleaning the house, scrubbing the pots and pans, washing clothes, and cooking. In the afternoons they were busy grinding the grain on the hand mill and pounding rice and pulses and chili and turmeric, and preparing other things needed in the house. Neither the women nor the men had a moment's leisure from dawn to midnight. It was not like modern times when if the husband earns as much as twenty rupees they immediately hire a woman to cook, another to dress the hair, one to cut the vegetables, and yet another to scrub the pots and pans.

Keshava Rao was a God-fearing man. Most important was that he revered all saintly men, ascetics and scholars. If he so much as saw a man in ocher robes coming down the street, he would immediately prostrate himself in front of him and pray, "Swami, please bless me by visiting me and partaking of my humble hospitality, and help rid me of my sins by talking of holy matters." His credulity was so great that it was like offering a bed to a man who is weary. Soon enough his house became a veritable haven for loafers and lazy men who went about pretending to be men of God. Not only were they fed with the best, but they were also given foodstuffs to carry away with them. In addition all the men and women in the house attended on the "holy" guests so that they did not have to stir hand or foot.

Holy men are of many kinds. Some of these ascetics used to extract money from Keshavaiya on any excuse, citing a need such as a pilgrimage or puja. The caste gurus often refused to visit Keshavaiya's house for an auspicious occasion unless he offered them five hundred rupees.

Then Keshavaiya used to go to the guru with friends and family and plead, saying, "Sir, this year business has been very dull. So kindly accept three hundred."

But the guru would reply, "The whole town has been talking of the profit of ten thousand you have made and you are talking like a petty miser."

"Believe this poor disciple, sir, even for this auspicious occasion out of the ten thousand rupees needed I have utilized the profit of five thousand and in addition had to withdraw the rest from my capital," Keshavaiya pleaded in response. Finally accepting four hundred, the caste gurus would proceed to Keshavaiya's house in great pomp accompanied by music and drums.

Yet another kind of holy man would say to Keshavaiya, "I've heard that your brother's son has died. Poor fellow, all his three offspring have withered away like this. How can you, as an elder, remain so indifferent? An expense of a mere two thousand and you can perform a propitiatory puja to the holy cobra. And all the children of your house will live long." And Keshavaiya would immediately accept the brahmin's words as more important than even the Vedas and perform all the sacrifices.

Yet another would persuade him that only one initiated by a guru could attain salvation, and only the worthy could be initiated. But Keshavaiya was truly worthy. Keshavaiya then would be initiated, for a price, with some meaningless mantra in all secrecy, and later he would discover that the very same guru had given the very same initiation secretly to all members of the family.

Keshavaiya once went on a pilgrimage to a holy place in the Himalayas accompanied by his guru. He spent a great deal of money on his gurus out of sheer devotion. These gurus went about with long beards and ash-smeared bodies; they smelled rank because they had not washed or bathed for months on end. They smoked opium and hashish perpetually and spent the day loudly singing their lewd songs. Keshavaiya, who thought he did not understand the songs because of his ignorance, pleaded with the gurus to reveal the hidden essence of these songs to him. They would then explain the meaning in even more obscure terms and in meaningless jargon that could not be found even in a dictionary. And thus they passed months and years in Keshavaiya's house explaining the Vedanta to him. They then decided that the best way to ensure an easy supply of hashish for themselves was to get Keshavaiya addicted to it. So they said to him, "Merchant, even if you serve brahmin gurus for a thousand years, you will not achieve self-realization. But if you smoke hashish with dedication for a month, you will achieve it. If this does not happen then we swear we will give up this ascetic life and become family men." Keshavaiya, because his blind faith did not allow him to use his critical faculties to distinguish right from wrong, gave in to his gurus' orders. Soon enough he excelled his gurus in smoking hashish and achieving self-realization. Since business was flourishing, by some chance his younger brothers also began to follow his example. Hindu women learn from birth that there is no greater sin than to disobey a husband even if he is addicted to hashish. And so Keshavaiya's wife and the rest of the women began to serve the gurus, massaging their legs, applying sandal paste on their bodies, and decking them with garlands.

Soon enough the word spread in the neighboring towns and villages that there was no match to Keshavaiya's devotion. The gurus usually traveled across the country and wherever they went, they praised Keshavaiya's devotion so greatly that his fame spread far and wide even though there were no newspapers in those days. And just as if one says, "There! a tiger!" another adds "and here is the tail!" Keshavaiya was soon believed to be a god. And several meat-eating and liquor-drinking gurus sought to enjoy Keshavaiya's hospitality. The new gurus suggested that they set out for Bhadrachalam and worship Rama at the temple there. Keshavaiya promptly set forth with a retinue of his family, followers, friends, and gurus. They traveled by bullock cart. The provisions and people together filled fifty carts. Since he had undertaken many such pilgrimages earlier, Keshavaiya was well prepared with tins of ghee, oil, rice, lentils, and plenty of sweets and other delicacies. Wherever there was water they stopped and cooked their meals. After the holy men had eaten, the followers were permitted to eat the morsels left over on their leaves. These were treated reverently as consecrated offerings to the gods. There is a saying that the temple is a safer spot than the home. Now although these holy men were getting far greater comforts in the forest than they did at home, they were dissatisfied because they missed their meat and liquor. Suddenly one of them started shaking his locks and, with reddened eyes and gnashing teeth, started shouting that he would destroy them all. The rest said that he was possessed by the spirit of Rama and that something had gone wrong with the arrangements. Keshavaiya implored forgiveness. He lighted camphor and incense, used flowers and turmeric and sandal to propitiate the angry spirit, who then declared that he had not been fed with meats and wines. Keshavaiya promptly gave the other gurus money and requested them to satisfy Rama's spirit.

Then Keshavaiya's daughter-in-law Gnanamba hesitantly said, "But Mother, I have read in the holy texts that it is only demons that ask for meats and not gods." But the older matrons tweaked her cheeks and asked her to hold her tongue. There was a whispering among the women. One said, "How proud she is!" Another said, "That is why they say that women should not have any learning." And all of them pecked at Gnanamba like a bunch of crows. As soon as the puja was over, the gurus ate a bellyful of meat and drank the toddy. They handed the leftovers to Keshavaiya and asked him to distribute them as sacred offerings. Everyone accepted the offerings reverently, except Gnanamba, who threw hers away behind a hillock. A guru discovered this, seized some ash, and raised his hand to fling it at her to curse her. Everyone was frightened. They scolded Gnanamba and threw her forcibly at the guru's feet to beg his forgiveness.

They camped for a month at Bhadrachalam. Every day liquor flowed freely and each day a goat was sacrificed. During the day, as they roamed the forest, the gurus pointed out the paths that led straight to heaven, the caves that led to holy Benares, the place where Sita and Rama had lived, and so on. The followers were exultant. Keshavaiya's youngest brother was so moved that he wanted to go to heaven straightaway through one of the valleys that the gurus had pointed out. Afraid that his brother would object, he left a letter and set off, entering a cave alone. Thinking he was lost in the forest, they began to search for him and finally found his corpse lying in a dirty ditch. Assuming that he must have taken a careless step and fallen to his death, they performed his last rites. After a few days they found the letter. Keshavaiya then asked the gurus why his brother had died instead of arriving in heaven as he had wanted to. "He was punished," the gurus replied, "for not having asked our permission to embark on such a venture."

Gnanamba's disgust with the gurus increased day by day. They piously intoned, "What matter if it is stale rice or sweetened rice?" but demanded royal feasts each day. They preached that women were obstacles to wisdom and claimed that only he who had rejected the family could attain salvation. Like an earthworm, which lives in slush and mire but is not soiled by its surroundings, Gnanamba resolved to remain untouched by the superstition and blind belief that surrounded her. Her father-in-law and mother-in-law were determined to see that she grew as devout as they were. If she sat for her worship in a clean silk rather than in the ritually pure, wet clothes, her mother-in-law would pour a pot of water over her. She poured out her complaints to her son, Vikram Rao, when he came home, and he saw to it that Gnanamba got a sound thrashing. Gnanamba felt it was ridiculous to get beaten for such trivial things and so she conducted herself according to her mother-in-law's wishes. Believing that she had been tamed, Keshavaiya set her the task of fanning the gurus. Gnanamba then pleaded with her father-in-law that unless one had enough devotion, it was improper to perform such services. He yelled, "Traitor, you have been in my house ten years and you still shamelessly admit your lack of devotion? You will bring dishonor and disgrace on the family name! You are unfit to be even a servant in this house. Vikram, if you so much as look at this woman you will be committing a sin as grave as killing your mother!" Vikram Rao, who trembled at even a glance from his father, obeyed his father without question. He immediately confined his wife to the backyard. Though she grumbled and scolded, her mother-in-law secretly carried food to the backyard and fed Gnanamba at least once daily. "Where can the women go if the men are angry?" she said.

When Keshavaiya came to know of this he was wild. "Hey you! Will a woman who has her belly full listen to anything?" he shouted. "It is your leniency that has brought her to this pass. Disobey me any further and you will share her fate," he threatened his wife.

So Gnanamba was not fed for three days. Troubled and weak, she returned to her parents' house. Seeing her daughter in this state, the mother burned with anger. She bathed her daughter quickly and fed her some rice. Gnanamba could not swallow even a morsel. So her mother fed her a thin gruel. After three days she began to recover. It was a month before she regained her health. The father then tried to find an auspicious day to take his daughter to her mother-in-law's house.

With the mention of her mother-in-law's house, the young girl's knees turned to water again. She decided that it was no use pining in secret and so told her father what she felt. "Father! Their customs are extreme. From dawn to midday, you have to perform the gurus' pujas in wet clothes. No matter who he may be, or to which sect he belongs, the most villainous man who wears ocher robes is given all honors there. I, who do not believe in these gurus, am also forced to serve them. Because of their blind faith they waste huge sums of money on such things. If I give alms to a blind man or a cripple, they accuse me of emptying their coffers and destroying the house. Once the housewife next door was in dire trouble and had nothing to eat. I gave her a little rice and my mother-in-law beat me up for that. When I was free, I used to read the *Ramayana* and the *Mahabharata*. Saying that women reading was an insult to manhood, they did not allow any books into the house. During my monthly periods I suffered greatly.

During all those four days, thanks to their orthodoxy, if I got two meals I was lucky. All these troubles I faced patiently as only a woman can. But of late they have taken to eating meat and drinking liquor. They torture me because I do not follow their path. When I came away I thought that God had rescued me from a terrible sin and rejoiced greatly. Is it just on your part to send me back to that sinful world?" Gnanamba wept bitterly as she questioned her father.

"Daughter! The only permanent place for a woman is her husband's home. They will gossip and say that you plucked off your marriage thread and went back to your parents' home. You are my only child. Any fame or dishonor that comes to me depends on you. No woman can do anything independently. It is men who are responsible for sin or salvation. Not women. You can return to your mother-in-law free of all these worries and that will be best for all of us," said Gnanamba's father. She did not take any comfort from her father's words. She firmly believed that whether man or woman, each individual was responsible for his or her own good or evil deeds. She believed in the ahimsa that Lord Buddha had preached. But when her father, who could easily have supported a thousand brothers and sisters if she had had them, insisted on her going back, she prepared herself for the journey.

After pleading with Keshavaiya, and telling him that it was not right to ill-treat his daughter-in-law so, Gnanamba's father returned to his home.

At midnight the police subinspector's wife woke him up and said that a murder was being committed next door. The inspector said, "It must be Keshavaiya thrashing his daughter-in-law. That is a family matter and it is not just to interfere. If you can't sleep here let us move to another room." Then Suvarnamma pleaded with her husband, "It seems as if the beating is very brutal. Why don't you use your office to help Gnanamba?" Since that was a time when people quaked at the sight of a policeman, the inspector rescued Gnanamba, who was unconscious, and informed her parents of the circumstances.

Years passed. With her father's death Gnanamba inherited property worth a couple of lakhs. Since she was interested in helping people, she started charitable hospitals; she provided a livelihood for blind, crippled, and other men who could not earn a living, without making any distinctions according to their caste. She had wells and tanks dug in places that had no water. She set up the kitchens when there was famine. She felt that she could not live in comfort when the people were suffering, and so she ate only gruel.

Keshavaiya showed no mercy to the poor even during the famine.

The poor broke into his house one day and threatened him, asking him to reveal where he kept his wealth. They tortured the members of the household when he did not give in. Vikram managed to escape alive and came to his wife. She tried various measures to improve her husband's health but to no avail. When death was certain, he gave his wife the lakh of rupees that he had brought secretly with him, and asked her to adopt a boy so that the family line would not die out. Then Gnanamba spoke to him, saying that it was not fair to spend a lakh of rupees on one man's whim. She also said that setting up a charitable house for the poor would be a far better way of ensuring the permanence of his name and fame. Realizing at last the extent of his wife's intelligence and wisdom, he permitted her to do so.

Translated by K. Lalita and Vasantha Kannabiran.

MAHADEVI VARMA ─────────────

(1907–1987)   *Hindi*

Poet, painter, feminist, nationalist, and philosopher, Mahadevi Varma was easily one of the most distinguished and influential figures in modern India. She is best known in literary circles as one of the Big Four in the Chhayavad movement in Hindi poetry and as a writer of brilliant, chiseled prose sketches and essays. Chhayavad was a movement in Hindi poetry of the 1920s and 1930s, broadly Romantic but shaped also by a commitment to a cultural renaissance in India, to freedom from bondage, and to human dignity. It rejected the formalism of traditional poetics and broke with the earlier narrative school of poetry. Mahadevi Varma's initiative in, and lifelong commitment to, women's education is no less significant. Born in Farukhabad, now in Uttar Pradesh, into an orthodox family, Mahadevi was only nine when her grandfather, whose word was law to her parents, decided that it was time she was married. As was the custom, however, she remained in her parental home and continued her studies at the famous Crossthwaite Girls' School in Allahabad, taking active part in its many literary activities. It was here she met Subhadra Kumari Chauhan, some years her senior, who was also to go on to become a distinguished writer. In an unprecedented move, Mahadevi declined to go and live with her husband even after she graduated in 1929. The family was aghast, but she had her way. She considered becoming a Buddhist nun but the plan did not materialize and she went on to study Sanskrit for her master's degree, which she took from Allahabad University, specializing in Buddhist and Pali literature.

Allahabad was one of the centers of the Gandhian civil disobedience movement of the early thirties. There is no evidence that Mahadevi Varma took part in the processions or public campaigns, but she was involved in what was called constructive, as against political, work. She started teaching, along with several others, in village schools and continued to do so for several years (1930–1947, or so). Even before Gandhi gave the call, she forsook wearing jewelry and took to clothes made of the homespun khadi. Inspired by nationalist ideals and following Gandhi's example, she gave up speaking English, with the result that she developed a facility of verbal expression in Hindi that was rare among the Hindi-speaking intelligentsia. It was while she was teaching in the villages that she began writing the short personal sketches about people from the lowest and most-oppressed sections of society that are now so well known. A combination of biography, memoir, personal essay, and fiction, these sketches introduced a new genre into Hindi literature.

The second decade of the twentieth century also saw a growing interest in women's education in different parts of the country. D. K. Karve's women's university had been started in Bombay in 1915, and in 1922 the Prayag Mahila Vidyapith, of which Mahadevi Varma later became the principal, was established. The Vidyapith was initially little more than an examining institution, but even so it played a revolutionary role. The medium of learning throughout was Hindi (whereas in the main school system it was still entirely English after the primary school level); textbooks were carefully chosen or commissioned, to ensure an emphasis on a consciously national education. The Vidyapith also recognized that many girls and women were bound by purdah and had heavy domestic responsibilities, and therefore needed an education with easy physical access, which would proceed at a pace convenient to them. The system of private study, followed by formal certification, offered them the opportunity of an education that did not demand a total disruption of their social and cultural universe yet supported their own efforts at education.

Under Mahadevi Varma's committed leadership the college maintained its nationalist ideals and Gandhian simplicity. It also took active part in encouraging literary and other cultural activities, especially among women. Conferences of women poets, or Kavi Sammelans, were organized on several occasions, and in 1936, Mahadevi organized a Galpa Sammelan, or short story writers' conference. Sudakshina Varma, who presided over the conference, said, "As writers of short stories, women are only beginning to enter the field of Hindi literature. But women in India have, over the ages, been telling stories to children. Making up stories and telling them are part of women's nature and the best creators of stories have probably been women." Their theme was the need for women to write out of their own experience and not imitate the style and subject matter of men.

"This emphasis on the validity of women's experience, and the need for women to take pride in being who they are, was central to Mahadevi Varma's own thinking . . . it was implicit in her whole approach to educating young girls and women," Karine Schromer comments in her biography of Mahadevi Varma. The major source of Mahadevi Varma's feminist writings, however, is the editorials in *Chand,* the magazine she edited, wrote for, and illustrated over several years. In one editorial entitled "Sahitya aur Usmen Striyon Ka Stan" (Literature and the Position of Women in It), 1935, she made a careful survey of the women who had been writing in Hindi since 1920 or so. The problem for women writers, she argued, was not so much the objective disadvantages they suffered, but their lack of confidence in themselves and the value of what they had to say. Many of these essays were reprinted in *Srinkhala Ki Kariyan* (The Links of Our Chains), 1942.

A certain amount of disservice has been done to Mahadevi Varma's work and her writing by the mystique that has grown around her as a modern-day Mirabai. As a result her poetry has been discussed mainly in devotional terms, the critical emphasis placed on its Romantic agony rather than on the cultural renaissance it augured or indeed on the explicit and vigorous feminist concerns it embodied. Her position as a major feminist philosopher of our times has also been sadly unexplored. The emphasis on the personal and the obvious lack of social and political commitment in her writing were repeatedly criticized by leftist or progressive writers in Hindi. Though she was sympathetic to many of their ideals and agreed with them about the social responsibility of the writer, Mahadevi Varma never gave in on the issue of subjectivity or the liberal idea of the free and responsible individual consequent on it. Subjectivity, she insisted, had to be the basis not only of lyrical poetry but also of a scientific outlook.

In 1983 Mahadevi Varma won the nation's most prestigious literary award, the Bharatiya Jnanpith. She is the author of a large body of poems, essays, and personal sketches. Among her more important collections of poetry are *Nihar* (Frost), 1930, *Rashmi* (Ray), 1932, *Niraja* (Born of Water), 1934, and *Dipsikha* (The Tip of a Flame), 1942. *Atit Ke Chalchitra* (Live Images of the Past), 1941, and *Smriti Ki Rekhaen* (Memory Sketches), 1943, are two well-known collections of personal sketches.

◆

LACHHMA

With her old black skirt faded from repeated washing and tucked up in a strange manner, her torn and dust-stained veil wrapped tightly around her waist, and a large sickle in her hand, Lachhma leapt down onto a heap of grass and leaves that lay below, and burst out laughing. In a mixture of Pahari and Hindi, she said, "Why do you worry about me? Do you think I am a human being like you? I'm an animal! Look at my hands and feet! Look at the work I do!"

I now know why I am so fond of this young hill woman who overflows with spontaneous laughter, her suntanned face like an unripe apple roasted in the fire. Her eyes, liquid beneath their dried lids, look as if they are swimming in fathomless depths of unshed tears but have been dried on the surface by the sunshine of laughter.

Her teeth are white and even but her lips have turned blue with continual exposure to cold. Her soles have grown hard with climbing over rocks day and night, her hands rough with cutting grass and breaking sticks. Damp mud and cow dung are the only softeners they know.

Like a mole on the breast of a mountain, Lachhma's small grass hut stands perched on a rock. Her father's eyes are weak, her mother's arm broken. Her niece and nephew have lost their mother to death and their father to asceticism. So Lachhma is the only one strong enough to support these helpless beings. In this wilderness, what work can Lachhma find to keep so many people alive? That is her perennial problem. They have one buffalo, a memorial of better days. Lachhma gathers grass and leaves for it. She does the milking, sets curds, and churns whey. In summer, she sows a few potatoes around the hut. But this does not make up for the lack of grain, nor does it solve the problem of clothing.

Lachhma's life story is so wet and heavy with tears that even the most tireless storyteller and the most patient listener will find it difficult to listen to.

She was married into a village that lies sixty miles distant from the abodes of civilization. Her in-laws were thriving cultivators with plenty of land and many cows, buffaloes, oxen. Her husband could not be called mad but his mental development was no greater than that of a child. Parents-in-law may grow fond of a retarded son's intelligent and hardworking wife, but to her brothers-in-law she can only be a nuisance. Her presence means they must give the brother a share in the property; in addition, they have to restrain themselves from laying hands on her.

When all the tortures inflicted on her failed to make Lachhma relinquish her rights, she was beaten so severely that she fell unconscious. Thinking she was dead, they threw her into a pit. It would be hard to describe how she came to consciousness and, though suffering unbearable pain, managed to drag herself across the valley to the next village. Not a word escaped her lips about what she had suffered because, she thought, to talk of it would mean a loss of family honor. Again, how could Lachhma, self-respecting as she is, say that she had been beaten nearly to death. The story she invented, of having suddenly fallen from a high rock, bore testimony to a courage that one would not have found in the true brutal story of what actually happened.

On the way, for three days, she had no food. Laughing, Lachhma says, "When I felt very hungry, I would make a ball of yellow mud, put it in my mouth, close my eyes, and tell myself, 'I have eaten a laddu, I have eaten a laddu.' Then I would drink lots of water, and everything would be all right." When her family saw Lachhma thus returned from the mouth of death, they wanted to teach her husband's family a lesson, but she insisted they shouldn't, and managed to avert an epic war.

Sorrow seems to have taken up permanent residence in the shadow of this unfortunate woman. As soon as she reached home, her brother's wife died, leaving behind a little girl and a month-old baby boy to be cared for by Lachhma. Her body may be broken with toil, her fate severe, yet Lachhma has a whole and healthy heart, on the strength of which she took on this bittersweet duty. But what did she know of child care! There was no nursing mother to be found in the vicinity and the baby was not yet able to drink milk from a vessel. Lachhma had an idea. She managed to beg an empty oil bottle from somebody, and loosely tied a cloth around its mouth, like the wick of a lamp. With this, she fed the baby watered-down buffalo milk. Every bone in Lachhma's body is feeble with the tortures she suffered at her husband's house. If she sits still for a while, her spine begins to ache unbearably; if she remains standing, her knees begin to hurt. Yet, waking by night and toiling by day, she fulfills her sister-in-law's trust single-handedly. Today, that baby is old enough to follow his aunt around like a pet animal, mutely imitating every action.

When I first met Lachhma, I thought of taking her to Prayag and educating her there. When I made the proposal, Lachhma merely looked toward her fragile hut, and then bowed her head. In whose care could she leave those beings? There was still hope at that time that her brother, who had been severely shaken by his wife's death, might yet return and do his duty. But even when that hope proved vain, Lachhma's radiant laughter remained unshadowed by despair. With an unforced smile she says reading and writing are of no use in the forest. Here, one must know how to climb trees, how to pluck leaves and chop wood. When her old parents are no more and the children grow up, why should God keep her in this world any longer? Her next birth will definitely permit her to stay with me and to study, without neglecting her duty.

To educate her, I must wait at least until the next birth—if this strange statement did not speak of such dedication to duty and such simple faith in life, how could one avoid laughing at Lachhma's peculiar madness?

If friendship is defined as the free exchange of joy and sorrow on a level of equality, then I lack friends. I express my joy not only in art but also in the company of birds and animals, trees and plants. Sharing my gladness with them satisfies me completely. As for the expression of sorrow, I do not like to burden another with even a fragment of my sorrow. When someone is happy, I feel a kind of freedom from anxiety about that person, so I stay at a distance; my relationship to the grief-stricken is one of tenderness.

But my primary feeling for Lachhma, with her bramble-torn hands, her stone-bruised feet, and her radiant laughter, is one of respectful friendship. She is not so unstable in her distress nor so light as to think that she requires my support. On many occasions, I have found her far wiser and greater than I am.

Lachhma too, unlike other hill women, behaves as my equal. She fills the gap between us with her simple sense of equality, so I do not have to make any effort to reach her.

She knows that I can eat choice dishes, yet she goes out of her way to bring me foodstuffs that are found in the forest. One day, she came running with some fresh honey in a waxy piece of honeycomb, and insisted that I eat it at once. I am not fond of sweet things, and the sight of honey always calls up a vision of bees that takes away my appetite, but for Lachhma's satisfaction I had to taste it.

Many people keep bees and trade in honey, but Lachhma could not buy a wooden hive, nor were the walls of her house built to accommodate bees. When I asked, she told me that one wall of the hut had split open. Lachhma wanted to rear bees in the crack. But why should bees consider it worth their while to live there? Tired of waiting for them, Lachhma began to catch bees and transport them to the crack. Several times they stung her and her hands swelled up; several times they rejected the narrow crack and flew away. Finally, some generous bees obliged Lachhma by settling there. It was the first honey from their hive that she had brought me.

Similarly, one day, when I was leaving, she wandered far and wide to get a bunch of black grapes as a parting gift for me. When the buffalo yields milk, Lachhma comes running with milk in a wooden cup, curd in a leaf cup, or butter on a leaf, and making muddy pictures on the dry floor with her wet feet, she reaches my kitchen and insists that I eat a little.

Throughout my student days, I lived in a hostel. When I went home for vacations, my mother used to feed me with special care, but her care always seemed an exception to the rule, so I am not used to such care. As soon as I completed my studies, I accepted the duty of caring for a number of students, so I have not had anyone insisting that I eat. Lachhma's insistence does away with my alleged and imagined adulthood, and carries me back to the easy and natural state of childhood.

She is simple in her motherly love. Irritated by constant interruptions in my work, one day I said to Lachhma, "Next time I come here, I will make a hut on that lonely mountaintop and live there, where nobody will be able to disturb me."

Through constant worry about feeding everyone, she has come to realize that the problem of food is not easily solved, and without solving it, no work can be done in this world. Fearing that I too might be beset by this problem in the wilderness, she put forward a proposal that was truly characteristic of her. Lachhma suggests that I go and live on the high mountaintop when her two-year-old buffalo calf turns four and starts giving milk. Then the milk of one buffalo will suffice for the old people and the children, and the milk of the other for me. She will come every day and bring me a seer of milk, a seer of curd, a couple of potatoes, some wood, and water. She will not speak a word, she will not even look at me. She will just leave the things at the door and come away. Then, when I have finished writing my fat book and when I get bored with staying alone, I will just have to call out, "Lachhma!" and she will immediately come up, and will carry all the stuff down, even the thatched roof of the hut. When Lachhma made this weighty proposal, looking at me with a pleading gravity, I was too taken aback to say a word. Solitude and quiet can easily be obtained, nor is it difficult to write fat books, but one will look far to find a helper so inexplicably loving and caring as Lachhma.

Lachhma is not far from the truth when she says that she lacks good fortune, not good understanding. One day, as she watched me painting a picture of the Himalayas, she suddenly said, "If I had the materials;

I would paint the snow exactly as it appears." Jokingly, I asked, "What materials would you want?" With a strange combination of gestures and words, she explained that she wanted a big blue paper and some white and green colors. Then she would climb a very high mountain, spread her blue paper on a flat rock, and sit there all day, drawing the mountains, some of them upright as a wall, some spread out like a thatch, and some domed like a temple. The blue paper would be the sky, the white color the snow, and the green for deodar trees. I was amazed at this vast proof of little Lachhma's intelligence. The sight of my struggles to paint a blue sky on a white paper must have led her to think of a blue paper.

When I inquired, I found out that though Lachhma had never been taught the art, she was so fond of drawing flowers and leaves, plants and creepers that she had covered the walls not only of her own but also of her neighbors' houses with *geru* and rice colors. Her pictures may not hold much meaning, but the unskilled labor of the artist's fingers and the lack of means are clearly visible.

In the same way, by watching others she has learned to knit, but since she did not have wool and needles, she could not knit the sweater she wanted for her old father. When I heard about it, I got her the materials but I am convinced that she would have run away, leaving them behind, had the question of protecting her father from cold not been involved. She has a great deal of affection for me, but she would never think of using that affection to fulfill even the smallest of her own desires.

In general, the numberless discomforts and the many hardships of hill life make selfishness obvious, but I found Lachhma's life exceptional in this regard. I have to look for the tears hidden beneath her natural laughter, and then find out the causes hidden beneath those tears. And finally, Lachhma never fails to render my efforts vain by saying, "Oh, I am just a jungly [a person from the wild], what do I need?"

Lachhma, who is so pure in heart, is forced to remain unclean in outward appearance. Sometimes, she gets annoyed at her own uncleanness and says, "How dirty I am! Don't let me come inside the house. Stop me at the door. See how the whole house gets spoiled when I come in." These outbursts are addressed to herself, because she immediately starts exonerating herself to me: "I scrubbed my feet and washed them this morning, but when I was halfway here, I had to turn back to give the buffalo grass. I beat my skirt on a stone and washed it yesterday, but the children wiped their muddy hands on it. The day before yesterday, I washed my veil in the stream and dried it, but I had to tie it round the bundle of grass because the string suddenly snapped."

In some distant past, Lachhma had possessed a wooden comb. Ever since she lost it, she does her hair by washing it in the stream and then pulling out the more matted parts. The gift of an old black comb was a great event in her life. Having tucked it in her waistband along with her knife, she used to perform her toilet in the forest, washing at mountain rivulets. Her strange happiness at being able to do her hair could only bring tears to one's eyes.

What name should one give to the misfortune of a woman for whom such a minor object is a rarity, even in the twentieth century with its countless unprecedented beauty aids?

The other women once told me that Lachhma was in the habit of burning incense and wishing ill on their children. When I asked her, she said that she wished ill not on children but on the eyes of certain people. There is an old, moth-eaten picture of Durga in her house. Morning and evening, she puts lighted coals and perfumed, dry leaves before it, and prays that the eyes of those who look on her with evil intent may be burned to ashes.

I did not find it easy to explain to her the truth that purity cannot be protected by wishing ill on anyone's eyes, because the test of true purity is that the most impure vision is cleansed by contact with it, but Lachhma had no difficulty in understanding the subtlety of what I was trying to say. Ever since, she prays only for well-being—her own as well as that of others.

This daughter of the mountains is as determined as she is fearless. Just as she finds her way through the darkest night with the help of her sickle, so she also stands resolute and unmoved in the face of the fiercest opposition.

Some years ago, some of her in-laws' relatives heard that she was alive, so they brought her unknowing husband along, and asked Lachhma to go back with them. She asked her childlike husband to hand over everything to his brothers and to stay with her. She would sleep in the buffalo's shelter but she would provide a clean hut for him. Even if she had to lie on dirty, foul-smelling grass, she would procure a string bed from the villagers for him. Even if she went hungry, she would labor night and day to provide food for him. She told him that since she was married to him, she was willing to stay with him, all her life long. But she was not willing to go to his house because his people would kill her, and her parents, nephew, and niece would, in that case, die of hunger.

Her husband's relatives refused to leave him there, because they did not have confidence in the good faith of this magical woman who had risen from the grave. A wave of discontent with Lachhma's behavior swept through the surrounding areas, and she became the target of all kinds of gossip. The psychology of society is the same in the hills as it is on the plains.

If they so much as imagine that injustice is being done to a man, all men rise up to take revenge on the women concerned, but even after seeing clear evidence of cruel injustice done to a woman, women are ready to add to her unjustified punishment.

Thus a woman who does not solicit male help at every step is put in a strange position. As she moves beyond their reach, men get increasingly exasperated, and their exasperation usually expresses itself in false accusations. This is natural, because we find satisfaction in proving our possession of that which we cannot possess, whereas we feel no need to declare our hold over that which we have.

Is it surprising if they who are standing upright but keep hearing proclamations of their having fallen down begin to consider the effort of standing up futile? Until a woman becomes strong enough to stay unperturbed by false accusations, her situation remains insecure.

I saw in Lachhma the strength to stay unperturbed and also the generosity to forgive her accusers. Neither does she demean herself by criticizing others, nor does she diminish her self-confidence by justifying herself. Her mind, like a mirror, is evidence of its own purity. Once, while a certain gentleman was sitting in my house and enumerating to me her various imaginary faults, she was standing outside the door and making faces at him, like a small child.

Even when the wickedest men in the village are mentioned, she only says in her simple way: "Apne aap rahega." In the vocabulary she has framed, this means, "Let it go; he will be what he is."

When respectable people pass Lachhma on the road as if they see no difference between her and the buffalo she is grazing, this does not anger her. She justifies their behavior, saying, "I am not like a human being. They are very good. How can they talk to me? You talk to me—that is not very good. But you talk nicely to me; that is why I don't leave you alone." It is not easy to grasp all the implications of Lachhma's broken sentences, but one can understand that she has no place for ill feeling toward anyone in her heart, which has shrunk into itself at the thought of her own smallness.

The day I leave is a painful day for Lachhma. She comes running to see me after she has milked the buffalo. She comes again after filling water and once again after feeding the children. As my packing proceeds, each joint in her body seems to shrink and shrivel.

She always walks the first mile with me. When we reach the second milestone and I tell her to go back, she stands, looking lost, wiping her eyes, and watches me go on.

Hill paths are not broad and straight like our roads. They turn and twist; sometimes a tree blocks the way, sometimes a rock. Long after she has disappeared from view, I hear her tearful voice calling after me: "Go carefully, come back soon all right."

These days, Lachhma does not have to face the prospect of starvation. The apple orchards are heavy with fruit. The unripe and sour apples lying beneath the trees wither or rot there, so no one is forbidden to gather them. These days, Lachhma sits down under any tree and eats a half or three-quarter seer of sour, inedible apples. Then she works two days without eating anything.

But gradually winter approaches, when snow will lie three feet deep like a burden of sorrow on earth's heart, when people will sit around the fire at home, telling old stories after a new fashion, when the rich and the poor will live on their stored-up grain and mock nature's cruel game, when some animals will be sent to the warmer villages below while others will be secured in their shelters and fed dry grass. What then will Lachhma do with the disabled old people, the small children, and the unsheltered animals?

It is true and yet not true that I get no news of her. When I tell her that if she were literate she could write me letters, Lachhma, with strange gestures, says in her broken language, "I write in my own way. I sit on a rock and think I have written this, I have written that, that should not have been written. When I think that the letter has been sent, then I get up happily and cut grass or chop wood. All that I write—does it not reach you?"

Who can help laughing at the idea of a letter written without paper, ink, pen, or alphabet, and sent without the help of a post office?

But when, suddenly, in winter I am seized by the desire to leave my warm room and go to those mountains lying buried in snow, or when in summer I disregard all the fashionable, beautiful hill resorts in my eagerness to reach that silent, anguished corner of the mountains, who can say that I do not receive illiterate Lachhma's letters?

Translated by Ruth Vanita.

KUNTALA KUMARI SABAT _____

(1908–1938) *Oriya*

Many people regard Kuntala Kumari, the first modern woman poet in Oriya, as Oriya's first feminist writer. She was born in Burma, to Christian parents, Daniel and Mani Sabat, but came to India with her parents when she was nine. They made Cuttack their home. Despite having spent a large part of her childhood in another country, Kuntala Kumari had such a fluent grasp of Oriya that she began writing in that language when she was still in her teens. Her first collection of poems, *Anjali* (Offering), came out in 1923, soon followed by *Uchvasa* (Surge of Emotion), 1924. Also in 1923 she published her first novel, *Bhranti* (Misconception).

Kuntala Kumari tried to bring reforms into what she saw as the superstition-ridden Oriya society of her time. She was deeply sympathetic to the nationalist struggle and like her contemporary, the Hindi writer Subhadra Kumari Chauhan, she wrote patriotic lyrics that were set to music and are popularly sung even today. Many of these are collected in *Sphuling* (Spark), 1929. She also struggled, all her life, for the advancement of women's education in Orissa. Among her other collections of poetry are *Archana,* 1927, and *Prema Cintamani* (Love Song), 1931. *Odianka Kandana,* 1936, is a collection of folk lyrics sung when a bride leaves her parental home. Kuntala Kumari's poetry has been praised for its cadenced language and intensity of feeling.

Kuntala Kumari was also a gifted storyteller. She wrote several novels; best known among them are *Kalibohu* (The Dark Bride), 1925, *Naa Tundi* (The Gossip), 1925, and *Parasmani* (A Very Precious Gem), 1940. She also wrote in Hindi and was a contributing editor to several magazines. She was chairperson of the All India Women's Conference in 1931.

The poem translated here is commonly found in school textbooks in Orissa today.

◆

SHEFALI PRATI
(Verses to the Shefali Flower)

Shefali,
Frail is your body, but alive with nectar
Unimaginable; the Creator's work, beyond reason, its wonder
Blossoming unknown far away, deep in the leaves' recesses.
But my heart yearns still for your windswept fragrance.
Reveal to me, distant flower, whose hands have made you so.

How tender, how enchanting, how fair is your face,
And how harsh and dark loom the forests around.
With such grace you bloom in the leaves' coarse spaces,
Startling this earth with your scent in the breeze,
For God's will it is to rear the high inside the low.

See with what care His lotus blooms in the slime,
In the seashell's womb the priceless pearl is born;
How the lightning gleams in the dark clouds' embrace
And the *koel*'s haunting voice brims with sweetness;
Nothing is so lowly in this world that it bears no perfection.

Shefali,
Does your face come floating into my dreams?
As I revel to my heart's delight
Immersed in your perfume for just one night—
If for one brief moment you radiate nobility
Why then should I despair of my insignificance?

Small as I am in this world of atoms and dust,
I can never imagine the vastness of the universe.
Insignificant I am, but my birth not without reason;
Annihilation for all time isn't written in my stars—
Only to bloom for a night, and drop when morning comes.

Translated by Jayanta Mahapatra.

KAMLA CHAUDHRY ─────────────

(b. 1908) *Hindi*

Throughout the 1930s and 1940s while she was actively involved in nationalist politics, Kamla Chaudhry was writing fiction with a distinctive feminist edge on a range of themes. If the short story "Ankhe Khuli" (Realization) depicts the discrimination in the way parents treat their sons and daughters, "Suriya" deals with the lives of peasants and itinerant laborers who are underpaid and exploited by powerful landowners. "Swapna" (Dream) and "Rup" (Face) explore the problems of widows, and "Sadhana Ka Unmaad" (The Passion for Fulfillment) is about a wife's longing for love, which, long suppressed and unfulfilled, turns into morbid depression. Many others deal with the psychological results of the pressures women were victim to in society. Kamla has published four collections of stories: *Unmaad* (Passion), 1934, *Picnic,* 1936, *Yatra* (Journey), 1947, and *Bel Patra* (Leaf Letter), n.d.

Kamla Chaudhry was born into a well-placed family in Lucknow. Yet it was a considerable struggle for her to continue with her studies and take the Ratna and Prabhakar examinations in Hindi literature. Though both her father and grandfather remained "loyal" to the imperial government, young Kamla joined the nationalists. She took an active part in the civil disobedience movement launched by Mahatma Gandhi in 1930, and was imprisoned several times by the British. She continued to work with the Indian National Congress through the rest of her long and politically active life. She was vice-president of the All India Congress Committee in its Fifty-fourth Session. From 1947 to 1952, she served on the committee that drew up the Constitution of India and, in the late seventies, was elected a member of the Lok Sabha.

Kamla Chaudhry's better-known fiction delves into women's inner worlds, but she has also written stories about the historical and cultural emergence of India as a modern nation and has published a popular book of humorous poems.

◆

Kartavya
(Duty)

I

Usha's husband loves her very much. All the women in the neighborhood talk about it all the time. Usha also considers herself luckier than other women. She sees no other husband who cares for his wife or respects her as much as her husband does. She thinks, "My husband does not ever neglect me. He is never thoughtless about fulfilling my desires."

He wishes his Usha to be always well turned-out. He buys fine things and toilet articles for Usha and really likes to see her dress well. He takes her out with him often, and they also go to the cinema. Usha's friends say to her, "How have you bewitched him so, tell us your secret."

Then Usha's heart swells with a sweet pride. She laughs and of course says, "Oh, don't talk as if there is anything extraordinary in my life. Your husband also cares for you in every way." But in her heart she thinks that there is some truth in what her friends say: the excessive, intense love that Usha enjoys and her friends do not. Because of this love, Usha's husband never lets her go to her father's house. Since he cannot bear to be separated from her even for a day.

II

The fair at Harihar is an important one in Bihar. No other cattle fair is larger than this. People come from miles around to take part in it.

It was the third day of the fair and an enormous crowd had gathered on the banks of the Ganges. There was a virtual flood of boats in the water. Still, it was difficult to find a free boat, and since it was evening, people were eager for the pleasure of boating.

Usha also climbed onto a boat with her husband. The ferrymen protested against so many people clambering on, but who pays heed in a crowd? By the time it was ready to draw away, the boat was choked with people. The strength of the oarsmen failed in the face of the load. In midstream the boat was caught in a whirlpool. The oarsmen shouted to signal its sinking, and everybody jumped into the water to save their lives.

One by one everybody jumped off. Even the ones who were not

expert swimmers thought that if one had to die one had to die bravely, and they made attempts to stay afloat and save themselves.

Usha and her husband were the only ones left on the boat. Her husband tucked up his dhoti, and prepared to jump. Usha looked up at him like a frightened deer. Her heart beat fast as the boat rocked violently, signaling its imminent descent into a watery grave. The wind was very high and Usha closed her eyes in fear. She felt that this was *pralaya,* the very end of time.

She had been praying silently all the while for the safety of her husband, and now she wanted to hold him tight and forget the world. In her last moments she did not wish to be parted from her beloved, the one who was her very heartbeat.

Usha stretched her arms and tried to hold him, but to no avail! He did not even spare a look for Usha, and was jumping off the boat to save his life.

She closed her eyes, threw herself down in the boat, and called for death. From the shore, the eyes of thousands of people took in the scene. All prayed for the life of the drowning woman.

III

God himself could not ignore the prayers of so many people. Divested of its load, the boat did not sink but drifted toward the shore. Some heroic souls had already jumped into the water to save Usha. They brought her to the bank, unconscious with fear.

There was a wellspring of sympathy for her in so many hearts. There were crowds to help revive her. They praised God's mercy and cast ironic smiles in the direction of her husband. Some of them even went to the extent of reproaching him: "You seem to be a good swimmer; it was your duty to try and save the woman who was with you."

Poor Usha stared at her husband. What could she say in front of so many people? If they had been alone, she might have ventured a reproach! At that moment she felt somehow that she had fallen in her own eyes. She had no worth at all now. God had saved her for no reason. It would have been better had she died.

But now that she had been rescued, if only God would be so kind as to keep this incident from becoming common knowledge. She raised shamed eyes. Was there anybody here who knew her? Not just one or two—there were many who did. She looked down again.

In a flash many images of her future came to her. Those who were envious of her love would be happy. Her friends would discuss the matter and say, "Is this the husband who would not let Usha go to her father's house? He used to say 'Usha, how will I live without you in the house?' " Where or what was this great love of his? If Usha had died, would he have been heartbroken? It is possible to live alone in the house, but if it grew unbearable even for a day, there was a way out. After a decent interval and after observing a few social niceties, he would have married again. That foolish woman also would believe that her husband loved her very much. But what of it? Why was Usha thinking of such things? God had been so merciful that her husband had been saved from a terrible accident. She should thank God a million times and celebrate her good fortune. She should get him to make ritual offerings to the Ganges. God had averted a great calamity.

It was not right to cast aspersions on anybody. Who was there in this world whose love did not cast a shadow of selfishness? But what of duty? Yes, this social structure was held together by the chains of duty. But so what? Saving oneself was also a duty.

Woman, Man, Father, Son—all this is an illusion, a mere web of attachment. Nobody actually belongs to anybody else. Entangled in this web, not trying to save oneself even if one can is also a sin. After all, suicide is also a sin.

Some time ago, Indian women thought it their duty to burn with their dead husbands. That was their ideal, but was that form of suicide not also a sin?

Usha was shaken, grappling with all these ideas. These deep questions were not for her to resolve. Only the scholars of the *Gita* could say.

For a woman, what could be greater good fortune than that God had saved her husband from a terrible fate! A woman should be satisfied with so much.

She stilled her heart and with happiness in her eyes stood up. Trying to mitigate her husband's embarrassment, she said, "Come, let's go home. The Almighty has been merciful and saved our lives. Why do you worry?"

Translated by Manisha Chaudhry.

ASHAPURNA DEBI

(b. 1909)   *Bengali*

Ashapurna Debi is perhaps the most prolific and popular of contemporary writers in Bengali. In a writing career that now spans half a century—her first short story was published in 1936, though she had been writing since she was thirteen—she has published 150 novels and a large number of short stories and poems, many of which have been collected into books. Her works run into several editions and have been translated into other Indian languages. The profile of her career reads so much like that of a writer of popular romances that we must emphasize that she is not one. The setting of her well-crafted stories is the family; her principal characters, women; her themes, most often their struggles—subterranean, indeed invisible, if one has not lived the life of a middle-class woman. And Ashapurna portrays all this with a sympathy and understanding that imbues the most broken and rejected of characters with a certain dignity.

Barring notable exceptions such as the scholar and writer Nabaneeta Deb Sen, critics have either dismissed Ashapurna Debi's writing as "domestic" or ignored it totally. Obviously a critic trained—or indoctrinated—into the perspectives of the "mainstream" is not sensitive to the questions, however broad their import, that arise in a woman's world, or appreciative of what is at stake in the struggles and victories that take place within it. Where Ashapurna Debi is concerned, however, the critical dismissal is also a result of the apparently conservative posture her narratives promote. Rebellion, deviance, anger, resentment, and passion are portrayed and evoke our sympathy. But as in Nirupama Devi's fictional work, order, somewhat chastened no doubt, but the old order all the same, is always carefully restored. It is as if, given the scheme of the Ashapurna world, a rebellion that stubbornly insists on its fruits is an escapist dream—and this may explain her impatience with present-day feminism.

Pratam Pratisruti (First Promise), 1964, the initial volume in a trilogy that includes *Subarnalata,* 1966, and *Bakulkatha* (Bakul's Story), 1973, has, however, received critical acclaim. Conceived on a scale of epic proportions—forty-eight chapters and more than fifty characters—*Pratam Pratisruti* takes us back four generations to the early struggles of women for education and personal independence. The heroine, Satyavati, is a vivacious girl who "laughs out loud," romps around with the boys in the village, "hates being defeated," and composes verse. As Satyavati begins to question things, she exposes centuries of oppression, humiliation, and neglect. Her future holds a denuding marital relationship and several years of battling with a quarrelsome mother-in-law, a debauched father-in-law, and a spineless husband. But she survives, spirit and body, and opens a school for girls. Her dreams center on her daughter, Subarna. Satyavati hopes Subarna will have opportunities that she and other women never had. But her husband and her family conspire to marry Subarna off without Satyavati's knowledge. When she reaches the village, the ceremony is almost over. Furious inside, but in total control, she does not enter the house; she remounts the bullock cart that brought her and leaves—this time forever. She is going to Kashi, as women, perhaps for centuries, have done in protest. Her parting words are, "I have accumulated a pile of questions over the years. First I shall go there to demand answers."

After *Pratam Pratisruti,* the resigned tone of the sequel, *Subarnalata,* comes as a shock. Subarna measures out the days of her life in the confines of a small house, asking for little, with her hopes, toward the end of the book, pinned on the balcony her husband finally promises to build for her in their new house. When the house is done, Subarna walks through, looking for the promised balcony, her access to the outside world—but it isn't there. He has forgotten about it. Perhaps Ashapurna Debi feels that the rebellions and demands that were feasible in Satyavati's time are no longer permissible a generation later.

Ashapurna Debi was born into an orthodox brahmin family. Her father was an artist and her mother a housewife with a great interest in literature. Since her grandmother was convinced that women should not go to school, Ashapurna did not have a formal education. Her mother taught her to read and write. She was married young, into another conservative family, but her husband encouraged her interest in literature. Her first novel came out in 1944. She has won several awards, including the Rabindra award from Calcutta University in 1966 and the prestigious Bharatiya Jnanpith award in 1977 for *Pratam Pratisruti.* "Why are women so deprived of rights? Why do they have to spend their lives in the suffocating atmosphere of suppression?" she asked at the award ceremony. "I have thought and written mostly about women because I have seen their helplessness and that is what I know best. Over the years, great clouds of protest have accumulated, unexpressed, in my mind. And, Satyavati, the heroine of my novel, is the expression of that protest." The lighthearted short story translated here is the choice of the author, a story she insisted was "just right" for these volumes.

◆

Ja Noy Tai
(On with the Show*)

Gayatri stood before the mirror a long time, carefully examining herself—front view, side view. What was it she had? Was there anything so special about the way she looked that the whole male race should be ogling her, as Sripati so weirdly imagined?

How could one rid him of this absurd notion, which was searing Sripati's mind and grating on Gayatri's nerves every moment?

Of course, being considered alluring by men did give one a sense of deep pleasure—shameful it might be to admit as much; but denying it would be equally a lie. Gayatri could make no claims to such allure, however; she had sense enough to see that.

Did Sripati not see it too? Was he blind? Why was he so bedeviled night and day? What did those men do, who had truly beautiful wives? What violent fires must be consuming their tortured hearts?

Gayatri felt angry. Insulted. And sad too.

What reason had Sripati to burn so incessantly? Whenever a male relative visited their home, all Sripati's plans for the day would be immediately shelved! No matter how important the work he had in hand.

He would not even stop to consider how old or young their visitor was, it was such a fixation.

Why, only the other day, he was on his way to the eye specialist. When her cousin-in-law Rajen dropped in to invite them to his daughter's wedding, Sripati immediately stopped in his tracks.

Now Rajen was a great talker. He rattled on about the current market for bridegrooms, their relative prices, and so forth, showing no signs of hurry. And Sripati too stayed put. Yet his appointment time had been fixed.

In the end, the trip to the doctor was dropped.

To hell with his eyes. How could he leave behind the apple of his eyes when that other pair of lustful eyes was on her, swallowing her whole?

Apart from her father and brothers, all other male relatives were debarred from entering this house. It had become an unwritten rule. Many of them had been frequent visitors at first, in those first few months when Gayatri had still been newly married. But not now. Sri-

---

*The Bengali title means, literally, "not what it seems."

pati's expression of silent disapproval had worked better than an out-right notice of eviction.

Well and good. Gayatri had become adjusted to this state of affairs.

Whatever people might make of it, they had kept their thoughts to themselves. But the deep flaw in Sripati's character had never been made so amply evident as had happened the day before.

And yet the same drama was to be reenacted again this day.

What had happened was this. In her school life, Gayatri had made quite a name as a dancer and singer: she had given several recitals before she was married. But that was another Gayatri, now long buried. Now, eight years later, a horde of young people had descended on her suddenly, determined to unearth her buried talents.

Some of the ground had been cleared the day before, and they were coming back again today. The boys were from her old neighborhood, near her parents' place.

When Gayatri was married, these boys had been in shorts, still playing marbles. Now they were all responsible young men running a voluntary service society—the Benevolent Brethren of the Distressed, or some such mouthful of a name it had. A charity show was being put on by them, a variety program of sorts, for which tickets would be sold, proceeds to go toward the "alleviation of hunger." A worthy cause!

So far so good. If they had come to sell her expensive tickets, Gayatri would have willingly agreed. Sripati was neither poor nor miserly.

But that wasn't it. Their demand was more forceful.

They wanted Gayatri in person! According to them, Gayatri's voice in itself was more valuable than any donation she could make. They had roped in old Rekhadi as a veteran hand, and had come along in a body to persuade Gayatri to join them too.

Gayatri had simply laughed off the idea at first. "Sing in public? Are you crazy? Just as well you didn't say dance too! Isn't that on your program too? Sorry, but I've forgotten how to sing."

"What rot! Once people learn something, they never forget."

"Don't they? But they do when they get old." Now all the boys burst out laughing. "Old! You? Then what would you call Rekhadi? Decrepit?"

"Rekhadi?" Gayatri glances toward the lady, smiles faintly, and replies, "Oh, she's not to be counted. Rekhadi will be eternally young."

The lady had somehow squeezed her almost cubical frame into a chair, and was busy catching her breath all this while. Now she came out in full form: "Of course, I will! Not like you, my dear, old before your time! Tsk, tsk. What have you done to yourself, eh? Good lord, we all get married, surely. But whoever goes under the way you have! Forgotten the world, you're so immersed in each other!"

"Now stop it, Rekhadi! You're just the same as ever!"

"Why ever not? Expect me to change completely, like you? Anyway, let's drop all this nonsense. Just come along now!"

A peal of laughter from Gayatri.

"Come."

"What do you mean? Where to?"

"Where to? To hell, that's where! Honestly, the way you carry on! The boys were right, after all. 'Will she agree to come, if we go on our own?' That's why they dragged me along. And I've come with my mind made up: you're coming with us, even if I have to drag you by the hair, you rotten girl!"

Go with them! Gayatri wouldn't dream of it. How could she, in Sripati's absence, traipse off with a bunch of neighborhood boys to some club office or other? She could forget about reentering the house then; that was the horrible reality. But since she couldn't very well tell them so, she tried to make a joke of it: "This is a lawyer's house, don't forget! You could be arrested for 'trespassing,' 'use of violence,' 'plunder and theft,' and a heap of such charges!"

"Lump your lawyer! A fig for such small fry! I, Rekha Bhattacharji, can spin circles round even a High Court judge! Bijoy, ask them to start the car. Gayatri, look snappy. I'll give you just one minute to powder your nose."

All Gayatri's attempts at finding excuses were simply swept away by a torrent of words. Rekhadi just would not accept that leaving the house for a couple of hours could cause so many problems.

"Bone lazy, that's what you've become, my girl. That's all the more reason why you have to come out. Not as if you have such an enormous establishment to run anyway. Just the two of you, lord and lady. So why all this fuss? You should be gallivanting around all day! Now, take me; I have four minimonsters to tackle, and I still have more time of my own than you."

Impossible to withstand such an onslaught.

Still Gayatri made a last feeble effort: "That's exactly what the problem is, there being just the two of us. If he comes home and finds the bird flown, he'll pass out."

"Let him, just let him! You can fan him back to his senses when you get back and do your good deed as a virtuous wife! Oof, how marriage can ruin someone so! No one else has ever had a husband, of course.

And no other man has ever loved his wife! Hmph! Now where's that maid of yours? She was hanging around all this time! Hey girl! Come here. Listen, I'm taking your missus or madam, or whatever you call her, off with me. When your master comes home, tell him a gang of dacoits and their lady chieftain have kidnaped her!"

"Aw, you're quite impossible, Rekhadi! Okay, I'll join you tomorrow. Forget about today, there's nothing arranged."

"Hang your arrangements! You'll have to start rehearsals with those girls tomorrow. That's what we have to decide today. It's fine for these boys to say, 'Rekhadi, we leave everything to you.' They can relax and twirl their sweet young whiskers and leave all the headaches to me. Like it's my own mother-in-law's funeral! And with just four days in hand!"

There was nothing Gayatri could do but agree. But she got into the car only on one condition: that she could get back home by five o'clock.

"Yes, yes, agreed! Oh dear, she's such a heavy weight! Almost impossible to budge. Lord, may I never in any afterlife, ever be a lawyer's wife! What conceit!"

So Gayatri explained the matter carefully to the maid, and came away most reluctantly.

"So much effort spent on just bringing you out of the house, Gayatri. Far easier to move a mountain perhaps!" Flushed with joy at their success, one of the boys ventured this cheap crack.

Gayatri smiled weakly. "Well, it served as a test of your capabilities, didn't it?" she said.

Her heart was thumping madly now. The only thing was to get back home before Sripati. But even that was not to be!

It was the usual scene. The benevolent brothers became so engrossed in conversation that anybody listening from outside might have thought it was a wedding party. All kinds of fantastic ideas were thrown up. Imagination ran riot for hours. And then it all had to be pruned down more practically. Finally, when it was dark outside, the meeting had to break up. Gayatri realized suddenly that it was past five o'clock—ninety-five minutes past the hour!

She stood up agitatedly.

And even then, more time passed before they could finally disperse.

They extracted a promise from her to come back the next day before they let her go.

"Who's dropping her back?"

One of the boys answered Rekhadi's question: "Shivajida's already waiting near the car. Shivajida!"

Now who was that? Gayatri hadn't met him! And the *da* would mean someone older than the boys here. Oh hell! How much older? Gayatri's heart shuddered. These young boys with hardly a faint down on their lips, even they could have upset Sripati. Thank God he hadn't seen them! Imagine his reaction to an older escort!

"Hell's bells," she thought.

She said hurriedly, "Couldn't one of you drop me instead? Why bother the other gentleman?"

But as luck would have it, the gentleman in question walked in just then and answered her himself. "This poor gentleman has explicit instructions: twice every day, until the show is over, he must accept the bother of picking you up and dropping you back! So come along now. You needn't feel embarrassed."

It was a straight and simple enough request. How was he to know the cause for Gayatri's embarrassment? It was not just politeness, was it?

How lucky Rekhadi was. Such a free and uncomplicated life, it made Gayatri envious.

How could she let these people in on the demeaning secret of her own life? How could she tell them how petrified she was at the thought of driving home alone with Shivaji? As if the sky were crashing on her head!

No, that she couldn't.

So regardless of the impending calamity, she had to get into the car.

"So you're coming again tomorrow?"

Gayatri thought this question from Rekhadi gave her a good opportunity to back out. She made a show of annoyance and said, "What's the use of my coming? Is any work ever done? All we did is chat! No fears, I'm not coming again!"

"You think they'll let you off so easily?" Shivaji chuckled. "You don't know these benevolent brothers then!"

Gayatri just smiled quietly for want of a suitable reply. And anyway, she was too distraught now to make polite conversation. God alone knew what lay in store for her that evening.

What one dreads most inevitably happens.

At the moment she got out of the car, she saw Sripati waiting there in person. So even a little subterfuge like "Rekhadi dropped me back" was out of the question.

Yet Shivaji was no monster after all. Just a very ordinary young man, looking a few months younger than Gayatri perhaps.

Sripati was pacing up and down the road.

He had come home and been told of the whole incident by the maid. And for the last two hours he had been pacing back and forth like a caged beast.

Not a drink of water, not even a washup.

"Who was that smart aleck? Quite a Romeo!"

Gayatri was steeling herself mentally. She said with annoyance, "What kind of language is that? Just a young fellow—"

"Oh yes! A little bottle-fed toddler, wasn't he? So where was it you went?"

"To hell," Gayatri would have liked to reply. But no, Sripati's temper was very uncertain; no knowing where it might lead.

So she swallowed her anger and tried to sound natural instead. "Awf, you can't imagine! What a shindy in the middle of the afternoon! Rekhadi arrived out of nowhere and she wouldn't take 'no' for an answer. I just couldn't shake her off!"

"Now that's something I just can't believe. If one really wants to avoid something, one can. What was it all about anyway? Why this sudden overflow of affection on Rekhadi's part?"

"There's always a reason, of course." Gayatri sounded a little irritated.

"Now tell me, who gave you permission to ride off with a bunch of loafers?" Sripati's words were loaded with acid. He was never so openly harsh, normally. But then, Gayatri had never given him such an opportunity before. She hardly visited her parents' home. Not even a passing vendor had she ever ventured to hail.

"So I'm just a slave. I hadn't realized till now." And she walked away to the window to cool down.

"That's it! Try a lot of big talk now! When you know very well that I dislike such things. So what did Rekhadi want, may I know?"

Gayatri, now desperate, rattled it all out in one breath. "Not Rekhadi. It's those boys from my old neighborhood. They're putting up a charity show and they want me to sing for it."

"Oh really! Just sing? Not dance too?" Sripati gave a sneering laugh. "They couldn't find another singer in the country, yes?"

"Well, maybe not anyone as good as me!" And Gayatri smiled in triumph.

But Sripati was in no mood now to be won over by smiles. There was an ugly leer on his face. "Go sing and exhibit yourself in public for money; it's the done thing in respectable families!"

"Mind your language," Gayatri said. "The maid's standing there listening! Look, you're saying that, but isn't it true that everyone's doing so these days?"

"Everyone? Not everyone! Just half a dozen shameless females from those ultra-fashionable families. And they've dazzled the rest of you! Well anyway, just let those fellows know they can't try such nonsense here. And that's that!"

"Can't say that now; I've given them my word."

"Given your word? So what? Your head's not at stake! Pack them off when they come tomorrow. Tell them, my husband doesn't approve."

"How can I say a thing like that?"

Now it was Sripati's turn to look amazed.

" 'My husband doesn't approve.' What's wrong with saying that? Is every man supposed to approve of his wife singing and dancing around in public?"

"If you put it like that, it does sound bad. But I don't see anything wrong in it really." Gayatri was trying her best to gather some courage.

"You may not, but I do, that's all! There's nothing more to be said."

But that couldn't put an end to the topic. The verbal battle carried on, shot for shot.

His wife was not such a beauty, but she seemed to keep Sripati's heart constantly afire. Now the sparks from those flames flew out in his words. He said, "What a time to visit a gentleman's home! Mid-afternoon. Such innocent babes—how would they know! They wouldn't dare face me, or I'd show them!"

"How would you do that? Throw them out by the neck, I suppose?"

"Sure, if it came to that! 'By the neck' is putting it mildly. They should be horsewhipped, the twerps!" And so he carried on and on, till he was so worked up that he lost all sense of proportion. For what he said was quite devastating. If any woman felt embarrassed to make the simple statement, "My husband doesn't approve," Sripati had nothing to say about her character, and the only way to straighten out such women was with the boot! Those were his final words!

Gayatri was in no state to answer that.

But she lay awake in bed for hours, trying to work certain things out. Would half a bottle of spirit do to soak a whole sari? Was it impossible to get hold of a strong rope? Was the distance from the second-floor balcony to the pavement below long enough? What could one do to fulfill a sudden death wish at midnight? Take iodine?

All this was yesterday. Thoughts churned in her head while her blood was still boiling, until she finally fell asleep.

Next morning, she was up and about as usual. There was plenty to do around the house, there being no cook or any servants. This was not a necessary economy, but simply Sripati's driving sense of "morals." So she went about her work in a mood as heavy as the monsoon sky. She had made up her mind. Her life had so little worth anyway. What room was there in it for things like form and propriety? She would tell them it was impossible for her to go, that's all.

Even the maid had dared to come and say to her earlier that morning, "What a scene the master created last evening! And no surprise! Once they develop this fixation, it can be terrible, I tell you! I've gone through it myself, so I know. He'd beat me to a pulp at the slightest suspicion! At least in your middle-class families they don't raise their hands so easily."

And she had swallowed that insult, too, without a word. What else could she do? Contradict her? Scold her? That would have made it worse.

Sripati too had not said a word all morning. It wasn't from anger, but more from a lack of courage. He didn't like the expression on Gayatri's face. Well, perhaps he really did sound a bit too harsh last evening.

And of course he was feeling bad too. His love for her was genuine enough, but it was so all consuming; that's what caused all the problems!

On his way out to work Sripati picked up his courage and said, "I suppose those boys will turn up to pester you again today? Well, simply tell them you're not well. That's all." And he went off, asking the maid to shut the door after him.

As soon as Sripati turned his back, Gayatri asked the maid to have her meal, and went off to bed. She slept a long time, and woke up only when the maid grew anxious and started knocking.

"It's very late, ma'am, aren't you going to eat?"

"No! I think I told you so. Go, have your lunch now."

She got up then, and her eyes fell on the large mirror. Gayatri examined herself in it for a long time. Front view, side view. What was so special about her looks that kept Sripati on tenterhooks all the time? Far better to have been really ugly. It would have spared him the torture of suspecting the whole world to have designs on her. And Gayatri would have been spared too!

Suppose she caught smallpox now, became horribly disfigured over-
night? A virulent pox, that's it!

Chatter-ratter-rat!

Was it a bolt of thunder breaking into her thoughts? No, it was
someone at the front door.

Who could it be?

Must be Shivaji!

She brushed off all poxy thoughts, ran a quick comb through her
hair, changed into a fresh sari, and hurried down.

The maid had answered the door by then. And Shivaji was not alone.
Rekhadi had come too. Now how could she say to these people, "No,
I can't go because my husband doesn't approve?" She couldn't bring
herself to say it, not even under pain of death!

Rekhadi's voice reached a pitch the moment she came in. "So Her
Majesty has arisen at last! Our hands were nearly falling off rattling
that knocker so long! So, will her ladyship deign to make her way
now?"

Gayatri shook her head and laughed like a child. "If I don't, would
you leave me in peace! I used to so enjoy my little afternoon naps;
now there they go. How did this savage invasion happen? You know
when I got back last evening how absolutely mad he was? No tea for
him, and nothing to eat. Thank you, no. And that won't be necessary.
How he carried on! Today I had better be ready for a regular thrashing.
Or if not, at least the door slammed in my face!" Gayatri was in peals
of laughter. "Let's go now. And trust to luck." And she asked the
maid to lock the door.

She would have to have that door opened again in order to get in.
Or would it be closed to her forever? Would Sripati really not let her
in? Would he thrash her? Nothing was impossible. "Middle-class men
don't beat their wives." The maid had been wide of the mark there.

Not just one day, not even once in a while, but for Gayatri to go
out every afternoon to give singing lessons! And then go on stage and
perform! With hundreds of men watching her! If that didn't make Sripati's blood boil, what would?

And yet, what else could Gayatri do?

She had promised herself all morning to turn them away, to say,
"I'm helpless. I have no freedom; you see, my husband doesn't approve."

But the words had stuck in her throat.

How could she so lower herself in people's eyes?

Better to be beaten by Sripati in private than face such indignity in public.

Maybe this is what she would do all her life: put up with reproaches, insults, even the boot! But she would not throw open to public view the ugly scenes of her home life to outsiders. She would paint that life in the gaudiest colors—to dazzle their eyes.

What else could she do? What other means did she have? Should she rebel?

Are you crazy? Gayatri was no fool! An open rebellion would lower Sripati in men's eyes; how could Gayatri then hold her head high and move up in society?

A woman who was unable to put her husband in her pocket might be an object of pity, never of respect.

So what else to do but pretend a bulge in that empty pocket and put on a big show for the whole world to see?

Translated by Madhuchhanda Karlekar.

LALITHAMBIKA ANTHERJANAM ⸺

(1909–1987)   *Malayalam*

Addressing a seminar on feminism and literature only a month before she died, Lalithambika Antherjanam said, "I'm very glad we can have a discussion like this today.* It should have really happened a hundred years ago. . . . It is good that we can, at long last, talk about so many things today, but there are many more of which we still cannot speak." Coming from one who for more than half a century had been a courageous and outspoken critic of the oppression of women in Namboodiri society and of the blatant double standards of sexual morality it practiced, these words were chastening: there was a long way still to go on the journey she and others had begun.

The Namboodiris were powerful feudal aristocrats famed for their stern adherence to tradition. In her award-winning novel, *Agnisakshi* (Witness by Fire), 1976, set in the early twentieth century, Lalithambika Antherjanam gives us a glimpse of this world as she tells the story of two women

---

*Antherjanam, the term for women in the Namboodiri brahmin caste, literally means "people who live inside."

who rebel in different ways against the soul-destroying restrictions of the life laid down by their tradition. "My husband does not seem to know how to love anyone. He's afraid of everyone and everything—of Father, of Mother, of custom—why, he's even afraid of God. Brother was right. If I live too long in this house, I might also lose my senses out of fear," one of them says.

Women in this community were kept confined to the household. The major source of their hardship, however, was the custom that only the eldest son in a family traditionally married within his own community. Younger sons made alliances with the Nairs, who were a lower caste and matrilineal. The tradition was evidently designed, on one hand, to consolidate landholdings and, on the other, to extend the community's power and influence, but it also meant that Namboodiri women, who were not allowed to marry into lower castes, found it difficult to get husbands. Large dowries had to be paid and it was not uncommon for an eldest son to marry many wives or for a young girl to be married to a much older man. Many of Antherjanam's best stories deal with the sufferings of women confined in the *mudupadam,* or traditional household, and the profligate, irresponsible behavior the same society condoned and even supported in the men. A recurring theme is the callousness with which female desire is crushed to appease custom or male whim.

The central figure in "Confession of Guilt," one of Lalithambika's most powerful stories, is the victim of an exchange marriage. She was married to an elderly Namboodiri with four wives and forty *sambandams* (wives outside the Namboodiri community), and her father returned this favor by marrying her husband's sickly daughter, who had turned thirty. She saw her husband's aging face only once, and although her grandmother tried to make her go into his room, she never obliged; nor did he try to persuade her. Soon her stepdaughter, who was also her stepmother, died, and her old husband began to mistreat her. She returned to her own house where life was more comfortable because her mother was still her father's favorite wife. One day she saw her mother beating her chest and crying aloud; she was dragged away from her playmates into a dark room. The red *sindooram* on her forehead was wiped off and the *thali charadu,* the cord on which the *thali,* or token of marriage, usually of gold, is hung, cut. She could no longer join in any of the ritual pujas or festivities—her husband had died. Later, after her parents have died, and her brother's marriage made life in that home intolerable, she returns to her husband's house to share her frustration with her unmarried stepdaughters, who are older than she is. This long background of sexual suppression is the prelude to her love affair and the subsequent trial and excommunication at the hands of the *smarta,* or communal court. As she confesses her forbidden liaison with the young man in the family temple who reads and interprets the story of Krishna, she unveils a horrifying world of cruelty to womanhood. In this richly textured story, Lalithambika's rhetorical style acquires enormous power.

Lalithambika was born into a family of writers deeply involved in the early twentieth-century movements for the reform of Namboodiri society. The family home, which was a treasure house of books and journals, functioned as a forum for heated discussions in which many important writers of the time participated. Lalithambika was the first girl from the Namboodiri community who dared to wear a skirt and blouse, and adorn her ears with small studs, as against the heavy dangling earrings of gold that were traditionally worn. She was educated at home in Malayalam and Sanskrit, and started writing when she was fourteen. Inspired by the freedom fighters and especially Mahatma Gandhi, who was then in jail, she wrote a short piece and sent it to the publisher without letting anyone else in the family know. The magazine that carried her article first reached her father, who was immensely pleased to have discovered his daughter as a writer, and encouraged her to continue.

In 1926, Lalithambika was married to Narayanan Namboodiri. "He makes a living with the hoe and I with the pen," she once quipped. His encouragement, she says, played a significant role in her literary career. She has seven children. Marriage transplanted her from the free and intellectually stimulating atmosphere of her own house into the closed, custom-ridden setup of the traditional Namboodiri household of her husband's family. "Life in those corridors of darkness" shocked her. She refused to give in: "When the door to the outside closed, the door inside opened. . . . I saw many things at close quarters. I listened, touched, and felt. . . . Crying without tears, life without breath, rooms in which no blood was spattered but within which, not human beings, but shadows and statues moved. Their smiles and tears were alike."

She once replied in response to a query, "How can there be no conflict between a literary life and family life?" In her view, "both require complete involvement. A housewife has to look to the welfare of her husband, her children, and all the other members of the family circle. Besides, there is the kitchen, the cattle, and the servants—and isn't the physical and mental development of the children also totally her responsibility? . . . Creative writing too requires continuous reading, thinking, observation and training, concentration, time, leisure for examination and correction, and hermitlike meditativeness. Just try and imagine how difficult it is for the wife of a farmer in Kerala to succeed as a writer—and that too one with a sense of responsibility." Yet Lalithambika did. She wrote mostly at night, often rocking two children in the cradle at the same time and working till dawn. Her health was badly affected and her eyes began to trouble her. When the problem became acute, she wrote with her eyes closed.

Lalithambika's first books are collections of poetry, though she soon moved into writing her passionately committed fiction. Among her well-known collections of short stories are *Adyathe Kathakal* (First Stories), 1937, *Takarna Talamura* (Ruined Generation), 1949, *Kilivadilude* (Pigeon Hole), 1950, *Koddunkatil Ninnu,* (From a Whirlwind), 1951, *Mudupadathil* (Behind the Veil), 1955, and *Agni Pushpangal* (Flowers of Fire), 1960. She has also written a feminist critical commentary, not unlike Irawati Karve's Marathi classic *Yuganta* (The End of an Epoch) in its conception, on thirteen women characters in the *Ramayana* and *Mahabharata.* The book, *Seetha Muthal Satyavathi Vare* (From Sita to Satyavathi), 1972, according to the critic Jancy James, "adds a deeply feminist dimension to these thirteen female symbols of Indian culture."

The story we have translated was written in 1938 and is based on a historical figure, Kuriyedathu Tatri (1885–?), whose name has become in Namboodiri society a symbol for the anger of the wronged woman. No Namboodiri woman dared speak about Tatri, and Lalithambika was breaking this silence when she wrote. Tatri's story, including the *smarta vicharana* or traditional trial, caused such a sensation that it was prominently reported in the *Malayala Manorama* and the *Deepika* of 5 June 1905. At the trial Tatri turned the tables on her accusers by naming the men who had used her—many of them eminent people, some of whom were present at the trial. There was an uproar and Tatri was not allowed to continue after she had listed sixty-four names. All the documents relating to the trial have been destroyed by her husband's family.

◆

Praticaradevatha
(The Goddess of Revenge)

It was nearly midnight. I was sitting alone in the room where I usually did all my writing. The compassionate goddess of sleep stood by me, waiting to enfold in her caress the wounds that my spirit had accumulated in the course of all the hard work I had been doing. But I knew that if I threw down the pen and paper I had taken up to write my story, I would not be able to touch them again till this time tomorrow. And the same obstacles would present themselves tomorrow. I sat there, wrapped in thought. Silence lay deep around me, interrupted now and then by the sounds of two rats engaged in love talk in the attic above, or the snores of the children sleeping in the next room. The light from the lamp on the table crept out through the window and threw fearful shadows onto the thick darkness outside. The hooting of the many owl families that were my neighbors sounded like a warning in my ears. I must confess: I am a coward by nature. Especially at this deceptive hour of night.

I closed and bolted the window. And raised the wick of the lamp. I checked whether any of the children were awake or whimpering, then came back to my usual place. I had to finish writing today, come what may, but what was I going to write about? How was I to begin? Now that I had sat down to write, all the attendant problems rose up to confront me. Story writing is not a pleasant task. Especially for a woman like me, who nurtures her ideals on a sense of status and prestige, on an awareness of being nobly born. When fictional characters come to life and argue heatedly about contemporary issues, the author has to face opposition from many quarters. If an opponent were to use the weapon of obscene language against me, would I be able to defend myself with a like weapon? And then, the subject of caste distinctions was taboo, and religious restrictions were to be avoided at all costs. Indeed, we have arrived at a point at which writers have perforce to decide well in advance which particular literary theorist's recriminations they will have to face. It was all very distressing. I suddenly wanted to give it all up.

I threw my pen onto the table, filled with an obscure sense of anger, and closed my eyes. Innumerable characters passed through my mind as I sat there: people I had seen and not seen, people who were still alive and those who were dead. Women and men. Creatures tormented by pain. Those who had lost their voices, though their throbbing hearts thudded like thunderclouds, flashed like lightning. Were they demanding to be transcribed? I was afraid. But also inspired. Suddenly, I heard the sound of footsteps coming toward me, from the next room.

What could it mean? I sat up, startled. I had closed the door, bolted it securely, and locked it. And I had not even heard it being pushed open. It was midnight. Although I did not believe in ghosts, I trembled in fear. My head began to spin. My eyes closed tight. The footsteps grew firmer and firmer. They came and actually stood next to me, but I could not move.

The seconds ticked by. Did five minutes pass, or a whole hour? I can't say. Time stopped for a long while. Then I heard a woman's voice just in front of me, a firm, yet fine and delicately modulated voice:

"Are you asleep? Or afraid?" she said.

I remained very still. I did not have the strength to move, anyway. The voice went on, its sweetness tinged with a shade of mockery.

"When I heard that you wrote stories, I did not imagine that you would be such a coward. After all, a good writer usually witnesses so many scenes of agony and terror."

The eagerness to know the identity of this person, who had made such detailed enquiries about me, drove my fear away. I opened my eyes. In front of me, the figure of a woman took shape from the surrounding texture of dream. A woman . . . not a young girl. Not bold or proud. Not old either. All I can say is that she seemed a wonderful manifestation of meaning itself. Sorrow, a certain austerity, disgust, disappointment: all these mingled in her expression. The sparks of an intense fire of revenge burned fearfully in her eyes—I recognized the emotion as from the leaves of some forgotten book from the distant past. She went on, in a voice filled with power and tenderness.

"I've come with a purpose. I know you are looking for a story to write, that you are having trouble finding one. I have one in my keeping, a first-class one, which is going to waste for lack of someone to use it. If you agree . . . if you can listen to it without being terrified. . . ."

I had mustered my courage by now. "It's true that I panicked. But isn't that because of the time, the circumstances? But, please, for heaven's sake, tell me who you are. And how you got here at this time of night, through a locked door."

"Who am I?" She burst out laughing. "So you want to know who I am, do you? Whether I'm a human being, or an evil spirit, a ghost or a witch. What superb courage."

She laughed out loud again, sounding like a forest stream that breaks its banks and overflows. Her laughter thudded against the walls of the room. But this time, I did not wince.

"I confess that I am a coward," I said. "But how can I have anything to do with you unless I know who you are? Human beings come to know the very stars in the sky by giving them names and positions of their own."

"Human beings? For heaven's sake, don't count me among them, Sister," she interrupted, looking displeased. "There was a time when I loved to be known as a human being, when I expended my greatest efforts on staying one. But I have learned—and taught others—that I never want to be called a human being again, and particularly not a woman. To be human, how deceitful it is, how cruel, what an experience of agony."

"Maybe you are right," I admitted. "But the pain and agony are gifts that are granted only to human beings. They are links in a divine golden chain."

She shook her head, prevented me from going on: "Stop this foolish raving: 'divine,' 'golden.' What melodious descriptions! A 'golden chain' indeed. Let me ask you, what advantage do golden chains have over iron ones, if they are meant to be fetters? Only this: that iron shows its true colors. And gold? What a glitter. A mere coating. God! What does it prove but the difference between a human being and a devil?"

Her face, which was full of hatred for her fellow beings, seemed transformed into something nonhuman. I could not be certain whether her expression signified sorrow, hatred, pride, or revenge, but I found it a singularly attractive mixture of all these emotions, and my eyes were riveted on her. What deep despair, what grief that life must have experienced in the past!

"So you're waiting to hear my story," she continued, after a short silence. "All right. I've come for that, anyway. It is an old story. It happened more than a hundred years ago and it is a true story, one that shook the world to its foundations when it happened. You had not been born then, neither had your social organizations, with their penchant for debate, nor their leaders. And yet, the turmoil that this story created over a great part of Kerala still continues. Some of the characters who figured in it may still be alive. Have you heard of Thu-Tatri?"

Oh, oh, so this was her. I drew back sharply in fear. This was the woman whose name our mothers had forbidden us even to utter, the very memory of whose name awakened horror. This was—oh, what could I say?

She smiled, with evident delight at my distress. "Yes, yes, you're thinking, which Namboodiri woman has not heard of that unfortunate creature, aren't you? No one says so in so many words. But everyone knows. But, look, child! Do you know for whom, for what, that ill-fated 'thing' sacrificed her life? She too was a pure and untainted young girl once, like all of you. She wove chains of sacred grass. She recited her prayers with a holy thread in her hands. She performed all the ritual fasts. She was as meek as a doll; after the age of ten, she never looked at a man's face, or spoke to him. Grandmothers advised young girls who had started their periods to learn from Tatri's shining example. But you and I know that all this is part of an outward show. By the time we are seventeen or eighteen, we acquire an amazing capacity to keep our feelings under control. As we sit in the veranda by the light of the new moon, chanting our prayers, we hold the sighs that rise in our hearts to ourselves; no one ever hears them. Singing the "Parvathi Swayamvaram" and other auspicious marriage songs, moving our feet in time to their rhythm, we learn to control the trembling in our throats. Yet, do we not listen for the sound of men's footsteps from the living room? Even while struggling with the prickly, exasperating *kuvalam,* our hearts are full of the fragrance of mango blossoms. And we wait. Not just days and months, but years. Till at last one day our mothers come to us with henna and a silver ring. Whether our hands are placed in those of an old man or a young one, a sick man or a libertine, is all a matter of destiny. We can do nothing but endure.

"People told me that I had been singled out for a very special destiny. I was his first wife. And he was not an old man either. He had enough to live on at home. So I started married life with a boundless sense of happiness. He was a passionate man. I nurtured my desires to suit his. I did my utmost to satisfy his preferences in our conjugal life, with the same attention with which I prepared food to please his palate. After all, a husband is considered to be a god in person. It was to give pleasure to this god that I learned a harlot's ways, those talents that were to become so notorious later. It was he who taught them to me. If it had been otherwise, my sister! If I too had become a meek wife, ignored by her husband, like countless women in our society, I wonder whether this cursed happening would have been blown so much out of proportion. I don't know. Maybe the intoxication of physical pleasure crept insidiously into my mind and lingered there as a fragrance. But he was the sole person enclosed within that fragrance, I swear it. That is why I was so upset when we started to drift apart gradually. He began to stay away from home for many nights in succession. Occasionally, it was because he had to perform a religious rite, or attend a temple festival. He would stay in rich, princely houses then. When we met, more and more rarely, I would weep before him, find fault with him. To whom could I unburden my sorrows, except to him?

"He would laugh, indifferent to the pleas of a broken heart. Man is free. He lives for pleasure. Just because he had tied a thali around the neck of a woman—and a woman who is only half Namboodiri at that—he could not waste his youth on her.

"Anger and fury sharpened within me. I wanted to batter myself, I wanted to die. I even cursed myself for having been born. Why had I been born a Namboodiri woman? Couldn't I have been born into some other caste in Kerala, some caste that would have given me the right to answer this arrogant man in his own coin?

"And yet, on every birthday, I bathed and prayed for a long and happy married life. I offered ghee lamps and garlands of *thumba* flowers in the temple. All I wanted now was to see him sometimes so that I could fill my eyes with his presence. Just as when I began to have my periods I had begun to pray for a husband, I longed now for my husband's love.

"Thanks to the generosity of our *karyasthan,* we did not starve.* But emotions and sensations have their own hunger, don't they? Greed. Thirst. Once brought to life, they cannot be quelled. They creep into the bloodstream, into the veins, they melt in them and simmer there. That was what happened to him too. But then. Ha! He was a man, I a woman, a woman born into a cursed society.

"Like all Namboodiri women, I too endured, kept my feelings in check, and went on. It happened without any warning: one evening, he came home with his new wife. They slept in the very room where I had slept with him. I did not mind serving food to that harlot. But though I had read Shilavathi's story a hundred times, making their bed was—** Although I was a Namboodiri woman, I was a human being too. Maybe I accused her of being a prostitute. Maybe I cursed her for being a slut and a harlot. That was the first time I thought of men as devils. The first time my husband became a murderer in my eyes. I could have borne the torture for myself. But when he, my husband, used the same words: 'I brought her home deliberately, knowing she's a harlot. I like harlots. Why don't you become one yourself?'

"Ah, what a cruel blow that was. Even to think of it petrifies me. Imagine a husband telling his chaste, highborn wife, a woman who worships him, 'If you want me to love you, you must become a prostitute.' An irrational, uncontrollable desire for revenge took hold of my mind. But only for an instant. My faith stood in the way. 'No, I can't stay here, even for a single day.'

"After that, I never spoke to him again. I never spoke to anyone. The days went by somehow, empty of events, empty of anyone to love. If only something would move in this hell of darkness! I went back to the house where I was born, my heart full of a limitless grief, a burden of sorrow that it could hardly bear. I thought I would find comfort and relief at home, but I was wrong. In truth, are not all Namboodiri houses a kind of prison? There is little to choose between them. My father was dead, but all my five mothers were still alive. My

---

*The *karyasthan* is a steward who manages the affairs of the estate in the important landowning families.

**Shilavathi is the archetypal figure of a selfless woman whose entire life is given to pleasing her husband.

elder brother was looking for a wife to replace the fourth one, who had just died. Two of my older sisters, both widowed, were staying at home. The third one had gone mad, because her Namboodiri husband had tortured her, and was roaming around somewhere. Two younger sisters had grown up and become a burden on the house, a continual source of worry to their mother. I joined them, going from the frying pan into the fire. Who would not long for whatever small comfort one could grasp amid such grief? At least within the limits that society permitted—I was still young. My body bloomed with good health. I knew I could afford the arrogance of being certain that I was more beautiful than the prostitutes who kept my husband company. And yet, when I combed my hair, placed the bright red *kumkum* between my eyebrows and peeped out through the barred door, all I felt was a desire to see the world, or, at most, an innocent longing that someone should notice how beautiful I was. There were men who met my eyes, returned my smile. After all, people tend to smile if you smile at them. It soon became a habit. Were not those highborn brahmins susceptible precisely because they knew I was a Namboodiri girl? They were aware of the consequences. But so long as nobody knew about them, they indulged in the basest actions.

"Scandalous reports began to spread. And meaningful looks. I heard murmurs. The women's quarters turned into a fifth column. Amma cursed whenever she caught sight of me. 'You sinner, born to ruin the family's honor! Why were you ever born in my womb?'

"My brother's wife said one day, 'Tatri, don't come into the kitchen anymore. I'd rather you didn't touch anything there.'

"I did not understand the nature of the crime for which I was being punished. I had touched no man except my husband. I had not even dared to think of another man that way. If I peeped out of the window, if someone saw me and was attracted to me, how could that be my fault? But the world does not concern itself with such questions. My heart hardened as stones of mockery were hurled at me. My mind whirled with the fear of degradation. Then suddenly, I knew I could take anything that came to me. I had reached a point where I could bear anything. Darkness surrounded me on all sides. My enemies hissed at me from within a smoke-filled darkness like poisonous serpents. They stung me, bit me. To defend myself in this battle unto death, I had to become a poisonous serpent too. The desire for revenge and the hatred that had lain dormant within me blazed high. If I tell you about the decision they forced me to, it will make you draw back in fear. You will tremble, and drive me out of here. Oh, my sister, what I did was as much for your sake as mine. For the sake of all Namboodiri women who endure agonies. So that the world would realize that we too have our pride. I wanted to prove that we have strength and desire and life in us too. I delighted in the sorrow each man had to bear, for not a single tear shed by a Namboodiri woman has value. But, alas, all of you, for whom I did this, despised me. My very name was uttered with disgust, even in my lifetime. I was feared more than a devil. Even in the fashionable world of today, Tatri remains despicable; even you look upon me as a fallen and disgraced woman."

Her voice trembled at this point in her story. Her eyes filled. Weighed down by an unbearable sadness, she put her head down on the table. Silently, without moving, I sat watching that personification of hopelessness. The destiny of a woman like her, placed in such a situation, could take so many directions. If that broken life were to disintegrate completely, if its shattered remnants were to be scattered on the roadside like fragments of broken glass, surely it could not be her fault. Only the base tenets that had made her what she was could be blamed. For a Namboodiri woman who feels the heat of emotion, who feels proud to be alive, there is only one of two ways possible. Either she must go mad, or fall from grace. Both ways are hard.

Maybe she had no tears left to shed. She sat up. A flame that would have burned up even the fires of hell blazed in her eyes.

"No, child! I will not cry anymore. This is my last moment of weakness. I knew I would never be terrified again, not even if the seas swept over me or the skies fell down. Fear ceases to exist when life and death seem no different from each other. I had made my decision. If this was my ultimate destiny, I must transform it into an act of revenge. I must avenge my mothers, my sisters, countless women who had been weak and helpless. I laid my life, my soul, everything I possessed, at this sacrificial altar of revenge and sought the blessing of the gods. Let everyone see—and learn—that not only man, but woman also could bring herself down to the lowest level. My capacity to err or cause to err must become more powerful: if I was to be cast out of society, if I was to be ostracized and excommunicated, I wanted to be sure that I was not innocent. No one was going to punish me for a crime that I had not committed. If I was going to be pushed aside, others who were mean and cruel were going to fall with me. I wanted people to learn a lesson from the event. If justice and fair play really existed, would it not be necessary to excommunicate more Namboodiri men than women?

"From that night onward, a new face was seen at all the temple festivals, the face of a fascinating woman. She was passionate and beautiful. But more than her loveliness, it was a bewitching air of shyness, a gentleness of nature, that attracted men to her. Princes, titled chiefs, noblemen of all ranks crowded around her. I told them all that I was a married woman and not a prostitute. I told them I had a husband, I told them everything, openly, offering them a chance to break free. But the answer that they gave never varied: that bondage to a husband was not stipulated in this land of Parasurama.* All women, except those of one single caste, are free here. They could do as they liked. This was the pattern their comforting excuses followed. Oh, the minds of these men, who pretended to be self-respecting, pure and saintly, even ascetic. If only men who insisted that their wives remain chaste did not deliberately seduce other men's wives.

"Would not a woman who was aware that so many were attracted to her succumb finally, in spite of herself? Particularly one condemned to the women's quarters of a Namboodiri household, whom other women spit on and kicked? It was an age when the greed for flesh knew no bounds. The fame of this new harlot spread far and wide. Those who came to her went away gladdened. Nor did she forget to persuade them to express their satisfaction through gifts to her. And so the reputation of many who swaggered as honorable men of society came into the keeping of this prostitute.

"Only one man was left to come to me. The man I had waited for unceasingly. Surely, he would not fail to come when he heard of this beautiful, strong-willed woman, for he loved a passionate life. It was five years since we had met. Although I recognized him when we met at the trysting place in the temple courtyard, he did not make me out. How could he have recognized me? How could anyone have guessed that this proud and confident woman, this jewel among prostitutes, was that humble Namboodiri wife of long ago?

"That was an unforgettable night. It was the night I had lived for for so long, the night for which I had let myself be degraded. At least I was able to delight him that once. Ever since he had said to me, 'Go and learn to be a prostitute,' his command had lain simmering in my consciousness. If a woman who learns the ways of a prostitute in order to delight her husband can be considered chaste, I was another Shilavathi. I think it was a blissful night for him too. For, a little while before we parted, he said to me, 'I've never been with anyone

---

*Parasurama is a mythological hero who killed his mother at the command of his father.

as intelligent and beautiful as you. I wish I could always stay with you.'

"He had trapped himself. I asked, 'Are you certain that you've never met anyone like me?'

"He lifted his sacred thread, held it high in his hand, and swore, 'By this wealth I possess as a brahmin, this symbol of my caste, I have never seen a woman as passionate and intelligent as you in all my life.'

"A triumphant smile was on my lips. I raised my voice a little and said, 'That's a lie. Remember your wife. Was she not as pleasing as I am?'

"Light was dawning on him. He looked suddenly at my face, screamed and got up. 'Oh God! Is it Tatri! Tatri! Tatri!' I do not know where he went, or when he stopped, when he ran out that day.

"The story is nearly over. You know what happened after that. The affair provoked an ethical debate that rocked Kerala to its very foundations. From great prince to highborn brahmin, men trembled, terrified because they did not know whose names this harlot was going to betray. Some men ran away and escaped. Others performed propitiatory rites, praying that she would forget their names at the time when she was being cross-examined.

"One man's ring, with his name engraved on it. Another's gold waist chain. Yet another's *kashavu angavastram.** The incriminating pieces of evidence were used to prove the guilt of sixty-five men, including scholars well versed in the Vedas. I could have made it possible to excommunicate not just these sixty-five, but sixty thousand men. And not I alone. In those days, any lovely and intelligent woman who practiced this profession could have brought ruin upon entire families of landlords and wealthy aristocrats. And yet, I did not go that far, even though I knew the power of a Namboodiri woman's curse. That historically famous debate had to end there. A longstanding grievance was assuaged. Could it be considered simply an act of revenge performed by a prostitute? Or was it also the expression of the feeling of revenge experienced by all Namboodiri women who are caught in the meshes of evil customs, who are tortured and made to suffer agonies? Tell me, Sister! Tell me! Who is more culpable: the man who seduces a woman in order to satisfy his lust for flesh, or the woman who transgresses the dictates of society in an attempt to oppose him? Whom would you hate more? Whom would you reject? Give me an answer at least now, after so many years have gone by."

---

*A cloth with a border of threads of gold.

I sat amazed, unable to utter a single word while she recounted this extraordinary autobiography. I felt frozen, helpless.

Remarking on my silence, she continued, with an air of profound hopelessness, "So, perhaps I've made a mistake. Why did I come here today? Why did I try to talk to yet another of those Namboodiri women who are without shame or self-respect, another slave among slaves? They will never learn to improve their lot. Never." Her voice trembled with anger and grief.

But I felt no anger toward her. I said to her softly, "My poor sister! I am not trying to find fault with you. On the contrary, I have deep sympathy for you. In truth, you are not an individual anymore; you are society itself. You are timidity and weakness, weeping before strength, helpless womanhood screaming for justice, bloodstained humanity whose desires and talents have been ground into dust.

"How can the expression of that irremediable hopelessness and helplessness be identified with your own? Think of it, there is another side to all this. I have been thinking about it. Fired as you were with the intoxication of revenge, why did you not try to inspire all the other weak and slavish Namboodiri women? Why did you shoulder the burden of revenge all alone? In matters of this kind, Sister, individuals cannot triumph. On the other hand, they can bring disaster upon themselves. Consider, now, what good did it do to society, that hurricane you set in motion? Men began to torture Namboodiri women all the more, using that incident as a weapon. We are close now to bowing our heads once again under the same yoke. Not even the women in the families of the sixty-five who were excommunicated have been released from their agony."

I too was shaken by emotion. I continued, my voice trembling. "So, forgive me, Thu-Tatri sacrificed her very soul, but in the eyes of the world her sacrifice is remembered only as a legal affair involving a prostitute. An affair that certainly created a turmoil, but did not succeed in pointing the way to anything positive. The end cannot justify the means, Sister. Even while I recognize your courage and self-respect, I disagree with you. But Namboodiri society can never forget Tatri. From the heart of a great silence, you managed to throw out an explosive, brightly burning spark. It was a brave warning, a cry of victory. Falling into the minds of the generations to come, the torch it ignited still burns high and threatening. By the fire of its radiance, all the sins of that avenging angel are forgiven."

I held out my hands to that woman's form in affection and sympathy. Its face had paled. Its eyes grew lifeless. "Oh, I am a sinner. A fallen woman. An evil spirit. Even my shadow must never fall over society."

Continuing to talk, her form faded slowly, like the dissolving of a mist from the past. The crowing of a cock woke me from my dream, which of course was of no consequence.

Translated by Gita Krishnankutty.

SHYAMALA DEVI —————————————————

(1910–1943)   *Kannada*

The public career of this short story writer, journalist, activist in the All India Women's Conference, member of the Dharwar Municipal Council, and secretary of a children's association lasted barely a decade.

Shyamala Devi published her first story, "Nannannu Nodalikke Bandaga" (When They Came to See [Whether I Would Make a Good Wife]), 1934, in the journal *Jayakarnataka* (Hail Karnataka), published by her husband, Ramachandra Vinita. Several stories followed and her first collection, *Hu Bisulu* (A Moderate Evening), which contains the story we include here, appeared in 1936. A second collection was in press when she died.

Her short stories, often humorous, depict life around her. Some of them deal with women's issues such as rich old men marrying young girls, as in "Doddamma Nudida Vara" (The Bridegroom Aunt Chose), or the exploitation of daughters by their parents for money, as in the moving story "Karula Kattari" (The Shears of Blood Ties). The main character in "Karula Kattari" is sold into prostitution, and when she finally settles down on her earnings, her family robs her again and she goes mad.

More typical of Shyamala Devi's writing is the rambling humorous narrative, best exemplified by "Muvaru Nagarikaru" (Three Citizens). Three girls are on their way to the municipal office to pay their final respects to a municipal councillor who has died. Many things on the way attract their attention and it is only when they arrive at the office that they realize that the man also had a home and that he had died there! It's too late to go to the house and they start back, worrying now about the questions they will have to face for having stayed away so long.

Many of Shyamala Devi's writings were published in *Jayakarnataka*. In 1941 she became a co-editor and the journal began to pay more attention to women and women's questions. She started a separate section called "Mother and Child," and also published the work of other women writers such as Kodagina Gauramma (1912–1930), Jayalakshmi Devi, Belagere

Janakamma, and Kamala Kumari. The "Mother and Child" section, the editor declared, was designed for discussion of the social and political rights of women and their aspirations to progress. It would introduce women of outstanding achievement, discuss the development of children, and the principles of education. The status of women in the early vedic period was discussed in several issues. The journal also dealt with topics of political significance at a time when India was asserting itself against British rule.

In the preface to the 1945 edition of *Hu Bisulu* her husband and co-worker wrote, "When we had repaid our loans and were about to relax, she died. She was about to begin concentrating on the more permanent aspects of life. We were just thinking of preparing our life on the inside and doing something really worthwhile; before we did so, a call came to her."

◆

NEELEYA SAMSARA
(Neela's Family)

"Do you know why you are back at home, Neeli?"

"No, Father."

"Oh, I see. So you've learned to lie as well, living in a town! You slut!"

Neela's eyes brimmed over with tears.

"Why do you shout like this, Father? First tell me what I've done. Then you can scold me."

"See? That's why I call you a liar. By the way, I heard about the play your school put on. I also heard that you acted very well."

Her father's harsh words hurt Neela. Failing to understand, she rose and went inside. Her father barked without biting.

Leelavathi was the daughter of a landlord in Tegur. Her father lived like a lord, his tenants were the chieftains. His cattle were the army of elephants and horses. The fields, gardens, and the lift well were the arena in which their life struggles were fought.

They were Lingayats by caste. His household was one of the oldest and most respected in the village. The attitudes of the rest of the family were equally traditional and old-fashioned. The world of the women did not extend beyond the home. Household chores were their responsibility, as was looking after the needs of the laborers and extracting work from them. They were expected to live contentedly within the house, where they were pampered, adorned, and secure. They were forbidden even to hear about public meetings, let alone attend school and college. Except on festival days and visits to the temple, they were not allowed to step out of the house. But when the landlord's daughter was born she was named, unconventionally, Leela. For her father, however, she was Neela.

The landlord's sister, Padma, had been married to a successful lawyer. (Even Padma, people felt, was a trifle too modern a name.) Padma and her husband lived quite comfortably in town with their son, Shankar, a young man of twenty. Giving in to his sister's insistence, Gowda, the landlord, had allowed them to bring up Neela. The love and affection showered on her had made life pleasant for fourteen-year-old Neela. She had by then completed three years in a training college and was learning English at home. With Shankar's help, she had also passed a certificate course in English at the Anglo-vernacular school.

Leela's modesty was in tune with her learning. She divided her leisure time between learning to play the harmonium and helping with the household duties. Her aunt would often show her appreciation by pampering her with gifts. She brought hand-spun saris for Leela, as Shankar too liked khadi. The husband and wife fondly hoped that one day Leela would marry Shankar.

Leela's uncle too never returned home empty-handed: flowers, sweets, biscuits, saris, blouses. Each day brought a new present.

Shankar and Leela too loved each other. But the teasing encouragement of the elders only increased their shyness. Mutual conversation seemed impossible.

Both of them had completed their exams and the court had also declared its vacations. So it was decided that all of them would visit Bombay during that month. Their plans were disrupted suddenly, however. An unexpected letter arrived from Leela's father, asking her to return home immediately. At daybreak the next day somebody from the village came to fetch her.

These sudden developments took all of them by surprise. Not wanting to antagonize Gowda, they hesitated even to ask the servant what was afoot. Their excitement evaporated swiftly.

Leela arrived in the village to find her parents silent and uncommunicative. The entire village watched in shocked surprise as the servant carried her belongings into the house. As she approached her mother, she was severely reprimanded, "At least cover your head decently!"

The next day she was told to wear a traditional wide-bordered sari. "I'm here only for a few days. Why should I hurt their feelings," Leela thought as she agreed. The same afternoon she had had that perplexing conversation with her father.

As they sat down for the night meal, the old man spoke in a voice overcome with emotion. "Neela," he said.

Puzzled by the sudden change in his tone, Leela looked at him.

"Neela, you've put our family to shame. It's not your fault, really. I made the mistake of sending you to the town to learn to read and write. But what is this I hear? That you go to movies with them, that you move around with Shankar? Do you want me to lose the village headman's post by your wearing khadi? Your opposing the government will only ruin us. Enough is enough. Stop your schooling at once and stay put at home. Otherwise nobody will agree to marry you. I know what you've been up to at Padma's place. My tenants have told me all about your activities. A landlord from Kyarakoppa is coming to see you soon. If all goes well, the marriage will take place in this month. Yes, and don't forget to take a center parting and plait your hair the day they come. You'd better wear your gold bangles too!"

Leela was ready to dress according to her father's wishes. But the thought of marrying the Kyarakoppa landlord's son upset her deeply.

It was late at night and everybody was asleep. She sat alone, staring without recognition at the group photograph taken at her uncle's home. In her disturbed state of mind she wondered if her marriage to the Kyarakoppa Gowda had already taken place.

Once her aunt had said, "Leelavathi, why don't you get the water ready for your husband's bath? I'll get your meal ready. He's bound to get into a flap over the delay."

From that day had begun Leela's accomplishments in embroidery. She filled in designs on cloth and canvas, and signed her name along with Shankar's. Shyly, she had refused her uncle's offer to get them framed. "There's time enough for everything," he had told himself.

Memories besieged her—memories of Aunt and Uncle, Shankar, blissful memories. They seemed so far away, as though from a previous birth. From today begins a new life, she thought.

Sleep played truant. On an impulse, she sat down and wrote to Shankar, urging him to rescue her. Pleading to all three of them, she begged for a release from these bonds. But how was the letter to reach the postbox?

The very next day brought a letter from her uncle. He asked her to return to the town and mentioned the Bombay trip. But without Leela's knowledge, her father had a reply sent off, saying, "She doesn't want to leave the village for another couple of months."

Upset over the letter, Padma refused to accompany her husband and son to Bombay.

It was decided that Siddalinga Gowda, the son of the Kyarakoppa landlord, would marry Leela. Her cries of protest went unheeded. On the day of the engagement, accompanied by music and fanfare, they were taken in procession to the village temple. Both were dressed in fine clothes and seated on a "swinging cot" placed in the bullock cart.

Halfway through the procession, Leela, who was weeping continuously, felt like throwing up. Unable to get over the biliousness she jumped down from the moving cart. The boor beside her, gloating at the prospect of an "educated wife," anxiously called to the others to stop. As Leela got a grip on herself, the people commented, "She appears to be exhausted." "Maybe the sweets didn't agree with her." She called faintly, "Water!" and collapsed by the mailbox along the road.

After she recovered slightly, they proceeded. The marriage was only two days away. The landlord was reminded of his daughter's angry words: "I will marry only Shankar!" Not wanting to create any complications, he decided against inviting Padma or her relatives.

It was on the afternoon of the wedding day that Padma received both of Leela's letters. One written soon after reaching the village, and the other written on the engagement day. Aghast and desperate at the content of the letters, she had come to a decision. Contacting her husband and son was out of the question. There was no time to lose. Locking the house, she left for the bus stand immediately. Within an hour she was in Tegur.

Padma was confronted with the sight of a sobbing Leela and a dark man beside her going through the wedding rites. Catching her breath, she moaned, "Oh, Leela!"

"Attevvaa . . ." Pathos tinged Leela's cries for her aunt.

The commotion brought Tippa Bhatta from the neighboring house to the scene, who said, "You shouldn't have forced her into marriage, O Gowda. You'll only suffer for it!" In a rage, the landlord hustled everybody out.

Leela's aunt spoke, "What's going on? Is all this finery for a bride or a corpse?"

"A corpse! Here beside her is the husband's body." The bridegroom's tones sounded like the braying of a donkey.

Padma was taken aback. Visibly upset, she saw that it was too late to do anything! Having failed in her efforts to save Leela, she caught the next bus back home.

Leela joined her husband's family the next day. She became a silent but loving presence in the house. Her father-in-law, the landlord of Kyarakoppa, exulted, "Didn't I say she would change after marriage?"

Leela's unfailing service kept her husband content. He never ceased to wonder at her efficiency and generosity.

Her parents too were overjoyed at this transformation. The careful vigil kept on her in the early days of marriage was relaxed. She now had complete freedom.

Meanwhile, Shankar married an educated girl. Leela and her husband, who attended the wedding, stayed on for a couple of months. Later, it became a habit with her to visit Dharwad every month and spend the day with Shankar and his family. His happiness never failed to rouse her spirits. Her husband too learned never to interfere with this pattern. Sometimes, the daily offering to God was overlooked, but never did she falter in this routine of hers.

Translated by Seemanthini Niranjana.

SARASWATI BAI RAJWADE ⎯⎯⎯⎯⎯⎯

(b. 1913)   *Kannada*

Saraswati Bai Rajwade passed her school-leaving examination when she was twenty-five, ten years after her first writings had appeared in print. The family had moved from Maharashtra to a new home in Udipi in Karnataka, where Saraswati Bai still lives. Though her mother tongue was Marathi, this young girl who had had only two years of formal schooling picked up enough Kannada to begin writing in it. The other side of the story is grimmer. Her family was quite poor and Saraswati Bai was married off when she was fifteen to a man of fifty-one. Life in her marital home was very restricted, and things grew worse when she became a widow some years later. But it is probably the intensity of these experiences that gave rise to the clear but angry voice of protest so evident in her earlier writings, where, the critic Vijaya Dabbe writes, "we find strong logic, bold attitudes and glimpses of radicalism."

Her first story, "Nanna Anjana" (My Anjana), appeared in 1929. Since then she has written seventy short stories and several more articles and reviews, as well as poems and plays. Among the better known of her stories are "Badavara Kannira Kate" (The Story of a Poor Man's Tears), "Kulavadhu" (A Bride from a Decent Family), and "Kali." She also translated stories from Marathi, Hindi, and Tamil into Kannada. For some time, she edited a magazine called *Suprabhata* (An Auspicious Morning) and was a regular columnist for *Kathavali* (Series of Stories) and *Nisarga* (Nature).

She wrote on a broad range of themes; there were articles on health, intercaste marriage, and the problems women faced in different walks of life as well as on aesthetics, language, and literature. It is possible that the several pen names she wrote under—Giribale, Vishaka, Vinapani, and so on—were a strategic move to deflect criticism and attack. She is a devotee of the goddess Sharadamba and now lives a life immersed in devotional activities.

The theme of the story translated here is not uncommon in the period, but Saraswati Bai's narrative has a savage intensity quite unusual for the genre. We learn the protagonist's name, Sita, only toward the end of the story. In the epic *Ramayana,* Sita is the wife of the hero, Rama. Kidnapped by the demon Ravana, she is later repudiated by her husband, but her purity is confirmed by the earth, which opens up to receive its offspring. In "Pravaha Patite," the sexual and the spiritual are closely woven, and the woman's outrage at being deceived becomes almost elemental.

◆

Pravaha Patite
(Broken Heart)

The news that Brahmanand the yogi had been murdered spread like a forest fire. People flocked to the ashram. Some of the disciples said, "Surely this augurs some great calamity." Others thought it could be another of the guru's miracles. Everyone ran to the ashram, wanting to know what the truth was! Nobody believed that the yogi could have been murdered.

People crowded around the front gate. The ashram was held in great respect. It was customary, whenever one passed that way, to fold one's umbrella, hold it under the arm, and remove one's shoes. The lower castes didn't even dare enter the ashram. Noisy vehicles were never driven in front of it. It was known to be a holy place. But today a large crowd had gathered there. One could tell from their clothes that they belonged to different castes and religions. Some cars had been driven up onto the veranda of the ashram. People even smoked and chewed pan! Everyone was eager to know whether the yogi had really been murdered and wanted to see the body for themselves. In their anxiety they forgot their natural courtesy and good manners. They trampled on each other's feet and pushed and nudged impatiently.

Suddenly a loud voice called out, "Stand aside, make way." To everybody's surprise, it was a police superintendent, struggling to get through. The crowd fell silent. The superintendent ordered the constables to clear the way. He lifted the sheet that covered the body. It was unbelievable. There were four or five deep gashes in the chest! The right arm had been slit vertically. There was so much blood that the cloth had turned red, and was now dry and stiff. The dead man looked awful! The police officer threw a suspicious gaze around. He wrote something down in his diary and started asking questions.

Then he inspected every nook and corner of the ashram. He found that everything in the treasury, even the safe, was intact. He wondered why the yogi had been murdered. Not for money, it would seem. Suddenly they heard a female voice.

"Arrest her." That was an order given by the superintendent.

Her eyes were bright and she was laughing hysterically. "You don't have to arrest me. I wouldn't have come here if I were afraid of arrest. I'm glad to meet you all!" The strange laughter echoed in the silence.

Everybody looked anxious. They wanted to know what would happen next. The ashram administrator who was watching from a distance suddenly lunged at her and slapped her hard. She turned on him stubbornly and roared like a wounded tigress.

"You, inhuman wretch! I spilled your guru's blood. Now it's time to do *you* in. Come up!" She brought out a bloodstained knife. It had been tucked, along with the end of her sari, into her waist. The police moved in on her.

"So, Sahib. Are you satisfied? I don't want to put you to any trouble. I'm the murderer. I'm Sita. I have killed this yogi, the so-called Holiness, the much-lauded celibate guru. Don't worry. I won't run away. I have no world to escape to. But don't you want to know how the murder took place?"

"Please tell us who you are, madam," the superintendent pleaded. The people around watched in silence.

She said, "You want to know who I am? Come, I will take you to my room. Why do you look so uncertain? I am not mad yet. I promise you, I am not mad. Come with me, it's not far, my room."

She entered an adjacent room. The superintendent followed with two constables. He really would have preferred to arrest her.

"What do you see here?" she asked.

"Nothing," the superintendent said.

"Now?" she asked. Removing a wooden hinge, she turned the key and pushed at the wall. It suddenly gave way. People were convinced that she was a witch. Some even thought that she had supernatural powers.

"This is my place," she said.

Everyone peered in. It was a huge, carefully decorated hall. Nothing like this could be seen anywhere else in the ashram.

"I'm not sure I understand what you are getting at," the superintendent said.

"A little patience, sir. I'm coming to that. Until yesterday I thought there was only one hall like this in the ashram. But now I know that there are many others in this hell called the ashram."

"How did you find out?"

"Find out? Why? What's so wonderful about knowing the truth about my own house? There are many helpless women here and I intend to free them." She laughed wickedly. The superintendent looked around unnerved.

"Not even God will tolerate this, sir! These yogis are just ordinary human beings. They have not renounced the world or accepted *sannyasa*. We say they have to remain celibate. That's too much to expect of a human being with ordinary flesh and blood. Perhaps it's possible in a forest. But even there a beautiful Rambha or an alluring Menaka may tempt them! There may be one Bhishma in a thousand, but this one here was only a phony." She was laughing and crying. Nobody dared interrupt her.

"I've been in this hell for five years now thinking it was heaven! What a cheat he was! A jackal in the guise of a cow! Yes, this was what he deserved. Fools may cry over it. But I—I laugh!"

Then she laughed, and continued. "If he could not control his desire, why shouldn't he die instead of fooling himself and fooling the people? Justice—yes, that's right, I've really helped justice. I was young, I was innocent. Now I know. I was devoted to him, to this cheat. To me, all these days he was a God. Only yesterday I saw his other face.

"Sir, I am happy he's dead. But he was the pulse of my life. I loved him selflessly—he taught me how." Her sorrow-stricken story left people dumb.

She paused for a while, regained her breath, and then continued, "This yogi came to our village five years ago, begging alms like the sannyasis do. As I was washing his 'holy' feet he murmured, 'Have you forgotten?'

"I was startled and looked at him, trembling. His eyes shone with a bright light! He was smiling. I didn't know what he meant. Then he murmured, 'Tonight.'

"Suddenly, I thought, I understand what he has said. I was young. I started dreaming. In a little while, God would be mine. My joy knew no bounds. The day seemed very long. He was waiting at the door when I went to him that night.

" 'Why do you behave like a stranger? Why? Don't you remember our previous births? I have been searching for you all the time. Didn't you recognize me?'

"I was speechless! 'You speak as if you've known me a long time. I can't understand all this.' He took my hand and held it tightly."

She began to cry again. "He told me I had been his wife in our previous birth. He had neglected me for other women. So now he was cursed. He had to be a sannyasi. Because of his mystic power, he said, he knew the truth.

"I was blissfully happy with him. Until now our association was secret. It would have remained a secret if I had not been curious. I have been in this room, from that first day five years ago till now. Today I am responsible for my own widowhood and I feel happy about that."

She laughed again, a loud uncontrolled laughter. The police superintendent listened attentively. She continued, "We'd been together for five years. We were married in the presence of the Almighty. He was still known as a holy man, a celibate. When I worried about our sinful life, he would easily quiet me, talking about higher love. I always thought that it was my great fortune to serve my swami."

She ground her teeth with anger. "Now I know what it all is. Every night I was given a glass of milk to drink, and I drank it. He must have been drugging the milk. As soon as I drank it, I remember, I used to fall asleep. But yesterday, I did not drink it. Swami was in a good mood. We spent some time together. He said, 'Drink the milk and sleep, my golden one.' But I had eaten a heavy dinner. He stretched himself out at my side too. Just as I was about to fall asleep, he offered me the glass of milk again. I couldn't refuse his gift of love. At that moment there was a message for him. A visitor had been waiting for him. So he had to leave the place. I soon fell asleep without having drunk the milk.

"After a while I woke up suddenly. My lord was not near me. He was a very busy person; someone must have come to visit him, I thought. He had gone out. So I came out to wait for him. Suddenly I noticed a light shining through a slit in the wall. I didn't know there was another room like mine. I moved closer to the wall and listened. What a terrible voice it was! Terrible because it was a female. How can I explain to you, sir, what a woman feels when she has been betrayed? You can't imagine what went on in my mind. I went back to my room, picked up a knife, and waited there, by that slit of light. In half an hour, the wall gave way and the yogi came out.

" 'What is all this?' I asked him. The saint just pushed me into the corner and said roughly, 'You have no right to know. No right even to ask me.' 'I am your wife, I have the right,' I said. He kicked out at me. I said, 'You're a true celibate, aren't you? The rules of the ashram don't apply to you, do they?'

" 'Go back to your room,' he said. I fought with him. He kept kicking me.

" 'I am also a human being, am I not?' I cried out. 'There is a limit to anybody's endurance. Is this the reward I get for my love and my devotion?' He was my husband and I couldn't tolerate his being a husband to other women too. I began to investigate.

"I found out there were other women hidden here. Poor victims! All to satisfy this monster's lust! What was till yesterday a heaven for me is now a terrible hell. Should I help some of these women to escape, I wondered? I'm not sure how I came to a decision."

She ran out of the room. The superintendent followed her. He found her near the dead body, moaning. He couldn't ask the police to arrest her. She threw herself on the body and cried out loudly. It was a terrible scene! The yogi's disciples shifted about uncomfortably and said, "She's a madwoman. Take her away from here."

She started. "I am not insane," she said. "It is you, you, who are all mad. I only believed that he was my own. You, all of you, thought he was a holy man. You have all been cheated, haven't you? Sannyasi indeed! He's not even a respectable married man! You mistook this demon, this Ravana, for a saint. You call me mad, do you? It was I who found out the truth. There is another madwoman here. I'll show her to you. But that's not the point. I killed him because he was not loyal to me. Perhaps there are others—how many—hidden away like me. Who will care for me now? My love, my love, are you angry? Are you sulking because I've said all this? Does it worry you to be talked about? Then let me say this: My heart too is broken, splintered to pieces; I have no hope for tomorrow. You cheated me, you did! You are mine. I was your wife in your previous birth and I shall be—"

Before anybody could stop her, she had pushed the knife deep into her own heart. People stood by aghast. Slowly her body fell on the yogi's.

They covered the two bodies. The superintendent turned to the administrator. "So you all helped the yogi to lead his secret life!"

"Sir," he mumbled. "Somebody had to become a sannyasi if the ashram was to continue."

The superintendent discovered eight more women, each with a story almost a copy of Sita's. Each believed that she was the only woman dedicated to the yogi. As the superintendent walked out of the ashram, darkness fell.

Translated by Pushpa Desai.

APPENDIX
GUIDE TO PRONUNCIATION
OF AUTHORS' NAMES AND
TITLES OF WORKS

System of Transliteration

The literary pieces included in this anthology are drawn from ten different Indian languages and English. A system of transliteration that is capable of distinguishing between the many different shades of speech sounds of these languages with appropriate diacritical marks would turn out to be impractical and hard to use by readers who want only to pronounce certain words as correctly as possible. The problem of devising a suitable system is compounded by the fact that there is extensive social and regional variation in pronunciation in any language. Principally, in order to keep the body of the main text "reader-friendly," but also because it is unlikely that a reader will actually be required to pronounce all the Indian-language words accurately, we have not used a systematic transliteration in the main text (see the Preface). As some readers might be interested in learning to pronounce the names of the writer and the title of their work, however, we are providing this guide.

The system of transliteration used here is intended to help the reader articulate the names and titles in a way that is as close to the pronunciation of the native speaker as possible. Separate consonant and vowel charts are provided, with examples. We have used the broad transcription notations of the International Phonetic Alphabet (IPA) with several modifications for this purpose. For instance, among other things, we have opted for /sh/ instead of the IPA form /ʃ/, and /y/ instead of the IPA notation /j/. We have not distinguished among dental, alveolar, and velar nasals and have excluded several other vowel and consonant sounds for which English examples could not be easily found. Where an Indian word and an English word have been given as examples, the Indian word is more accurate and the English one a close approximation. The English words are provided for readers who speak only English, as their pronunciation of the Indian sample words will not give the sound indicated.

VOWELS

The order of the vowels in this chart corresponds to that of most Indian languages.

Symbol	As in word
a	but
ā	bar
æ	bat
i	bit
ī	beat
u	bull
ū	boot
e	bet
ē	bake
o	boredom
ō	bore
ɔ	bought
au	bout
ai	bite
ou	boat
ɔi	boy
ei	bait

CONSONANTS

The order of consonants in this chart corresponds to that of most Indian languages. Some of the examples for aspirates and retroflex sounds are only approximations.

Symbol	As in word
k	**sk**ate
kh	**kh**addar, **K**ate
g	**g**et
gh	**gh**at, log**h**ouse
c	**ch**urch
ch	hit**chh**ike
j	**j**udge
jh	he**dgeh**og
ṭ	**st**ick
ṭh	ligh**th**ouse
ḍ	**dr**um, hun**dr**ed
ḍh	a**dh**ere
ṇ	vi**n**a, butto**n**
t	my**th**ology
th	ple**th**ora
d	kha**d**i, mo**th**er
dh	**dh**oti, with**h**old
n	**n**ap, swi**ng**
p	**sp**in
ph	**ph**agun, **p**in
b	**b**ag
bh	**bh**ang, a**bh**or
m	**m**an
y	**y**es
r	**r**ight
l	**l**ight
v	**v**ery
w	**w**et
s	**s**ee, **s**atem
sh	**sh**ould
h	**h**ouse
ḷ	bott**l**e
z	**z**eal
f	**f**low

The authors are listed alphabetically by first name. The transliterations of the names and titles follow.

Akkamahadevi
akkamahādēvi
[untitled]

Anonymous
anōnimas
a. hindū vidhwānci dukhit stiti: eka vidhawa baine varṇilēli
b. mumbaitil prārthana samāja sambhandhi stīyāncya sabhent: eka baine vāclēla nibhandh

Ashapurna Debi
āshapūrna debi
ja noi tai

Atukuri Molla
ātukūri molla
molla rāmāyana

Auvaiyar
auvaiyār
[untitled]

Bahinabai
bahiṇābāi
ātmanivēdana

Bahinabai Chaudhari
bahiṇābāi chaudhari
a. āṭā maẓa māle jīva
b. man

Bandaru Acchamamba
baṇḍāru acchamāmba
khana

Bhabani
bhabāni
[untitled]

Binodini Dasi
binōdini dashi
ɔmor kɔtha

Chandrabati
chɔndrɔbati
shɔndori mālua

Cornelia Sorabji
kɔnīlia sorābji
inḍia kɔling

Darisi Annapurnamma
darisi annapūrnamma
gnānāmba

Gangasati
gangāsati
[untitled]

Geeta Sane
gīta sānē
hirvaḷi khali

Gul-Badan Begum
gulbadan bēgam
humayun nāma

Hannah Catherine Mullens
hannā kætrin mallins
phūlmɔni o korunār bibɔron

Homvati Devi
hōmvatī dēvi
apnā ghar

Indira Sahasrabuddhe
indirā sahasrabuddhe
baḷutayi dhadhāge

Janabai
jānābāi
[untitled]

Janaki Bai
jānakībāi
[untitled]

Jogeswari
jogēswari

[untitled]

Kakkaipatiniyar Naccellaiyar
kākkaipāṭiniyār naccellaiyār
[untitled]

Kalyanamma
kaḷyāṇamma
sūryāsthamana

Kamla Chaudhry
kamlā chaudhri
kartavya

Kashibai Kanitkar
kāshībāi kaṇiṭkar
pālkīcha gōṇḍa

Kavar Pentu
kāvar peṇṭu
[untitled]

Krupa Sattianandan
krūbāi sattiānandan
sajuna

Kuntala Kumari Sabat
kuntalā kumāri sābat
shefāḷi prati

Lakshmibai Tilak
lakshmībāi tiḷak
smriti citre

Lalithambika Antherjanam
lalitāmbiga antarjanam
pradigāra dēvda

Mahadevi Varma
mahādēvi varma
lachma

Mahlaqa Bai Chanda
mahlakhā bāi canda
[untitled]

Mary John Thottam
mēri jōn tōṭṭam

lōgame yātra

Mettika
mettikā
[untitled]

Mirabai
mīrābāi
[untitled]

Mokshodayani Mukhopadhyay
mokkodāyini mukhopāddhei
bānglār bābu

Muddupalani
muddupaḷani
rādhikā sāntwanam

Muktabai
muktābāi
māng maharācya dukhavishayi

Mutta
muttā
[untitled]

Nanjanagudu Tirumalamba
nanjangūḍu tirumalāmba
nabhā

Nazar Sajjad Hyder
nazar sajjad haidar
pardā

Nirupama Devi
nirupɔma debi
dīdi

Okkur Macattiyar
okkūr mācattiyār
[untitled]

Pandita Ramabai Saraswati
paṇḍita ramābāi saraswati
a. da hai kāsṭ hindū wuman
b. leṭar ṭu mis dorōti bīl, celṭenam

Ramabai Ranade

ramābāi rāṇaḍe
āmcyā āyushyātil kāhi āṭvṇi

Rami
rāmi
[untitled]

Rassundari Devi
rɔshundori debi
āmar jibɔn

Ratanbai
ratanbāi
[untitled]

Rokeya Sakhawat Hossain
rokeya sakhwat hussēn
sultānās drīm

Sanciya Honnamma
sanciya hoṇṇamma
garatiya hāḍu

Saraswati Bai Rajwade
saraswatī bāi rājwaḍe
pravāha patite

Sarat Kumari Chaudhurani
shɔrɔtkumāri chaudhurāni
aḍorar na anaḍorar

Sarojini Naidu
sarōjinī nāiḍu
a. bæŋgl sellarz
b. da ṭempl: a pilgrimej āf lav
c. presiḍeɳshal aḍḍres æt da ahmdābād sṭūdenṭz kānfarens

Savithribai Phule
sāvitrībāi phūle
[untitled]

Shyamala Devi
shyāmalā dēvi
nīleya samsāra

Subhadra Kumari Chauhan
subhadrā kumāri chauhān
ēkādasi

Sudha Chauhan
sudhā chauhān
milā tēj sē tēj

Sughra Humayun Mirza
sughra humāyun mīrza
[untitled]

Sule Sankavva
sūḷe sankavva
[untitled]

Sumangalamata
sumangalamāta
[untitled]

Swarnakumari Devi
swarnakumāri dēvi
kahāke

Tallapragada Viswasundaramma
tallāpragaḍa viswasundaramma
jailu gaḍiyāramu

Tarabai Shinde
tārābāi shinḍe
strī purush tulna

Tarigonda Venkamamba
tarigonḍa venkamāmba
vishnu pārijātamu

Ubbiri
ubbirī
[untitled]

Velli Vitiyar
veḷḷi vītiyār
[untitled]

Venmanipputi
veṇmaṇippūti
[untitled]

Vibhavari Shirurkar
vibhāvari shirūrkar
vīrlele swapna

BIBLIOGRAPHY

Books

Agarwal, Bina, ed. *Structures of Patriarchy: State, Community and Household in Modernising Asia*. New Delhi: Kali for Women, 1988.

Alladi, Uma. *Woman and Her Family: Indian and Afro-American: A Literary Perspective*. New Delhi: Sterling Publishers, 1989.

Altekar, A. S. *Position of Women in Hindu Civilization: From Prehistoric Times to the Present Day*. Delhi: Motilal Banarsidass, 1962.

Amadiume, Ifi. *Male Daughters, Female Husbands: Gender and Sex in African Society*. London: Zed Books, 1985.

Amuta, Chidi. *The Theory of African Literature: Implications for Practical Criticism*. London: Zed Books, 1989.

Asad, Talal. "The Concept of Cultural Translation." In *Writing Culture: The Poetics and Politics of Ethnography*. Edited by James Clifford and George Marcus. Berkeley: University of California Press, 1986.

Athavale, Parvati. *Hindu Widow: An Autobiography*. Translated by Justin E. Abbott. Reprint. New Delhi: Reliance Publishing House, 1986.

Azad, Nandini. *Empowering Women Workers: The W.W.F. Experiment in Indian Cities*. Madras: Working Women's Forum, 1986.

Bala, Usha. *Indian Women Freedom Fighters*. Delhi: Manohar, 1986.

Balasubrahmanyan, Vimal. *Mirror Image: The Media and the Women's Question*. Bombay: Centre for Education and Documentation, 1988.

522

Baldick, Chris. *The Social Mission of English Criticism 1848–1932.* Oxford: Clarendon Press, 1983.

Banerjee, Nirmala. "Working Women in Colonial Bengal: Modernization and Marginalization." In *Recasting Women: Essays in Colonial History.* Edited by Kumkum Sangari and Sudesh Vaid, pp. 269–301. Delhi: Kali for Women, 1989.

Banerjee, Sumanta. "Marginalization of Women's Popular Culture in Nineteenth Century Bengal." In *Recasting Women: Essays in Colonial History.* Edited by Kumkum Sangari and Sudesh Vaid, pp. 127–179. Delhi: Kali for Women, 1989.

Caplan, Pat, ed. *The Cultural Construction of Sexuality.* London: Tavistock Publications, 1987.

Carby, Hazel V. *Reconstructing Womanhood: The Emergence of the Afro-American Woman Novelist.* New York: Oxford University Press, 1987.

Centre for Contemporary Cultural Studies. *The Empire Strikes Back: Race and Racism in 70s Britain.* London: Hutchinson, 1986.

Chakravarti, Uma. *Social Dimensions of Early Buddhism.* Delhi: Oxford University Press, 1987.

Chandra, Bipan, et al. *India's Struggle for Independence, 1857–1947.* Delhi: Viking, 1988.

Chatterjee, Partha. *Nationalist Thought and the Colonial World: A Derivative Discourse?* Delhi: Oxford University Press, 1986.

Chatterjee, Partha. "The Nationalist Resolution of the Women's Question." In *Recasting Women: Essays in Colonial History.* Edited by Kumkum Sangari and Sudesh Vaid, pp. 233–253. New Delhi: Kali for Women, 1989.

Chatterji, Lola, ed. *Women Image Text: Feminist Readings of Literary Texts.* Delhi: Trianka, 1986.

Chattopadhyay, Kamaladevi. *Inner Recesses, Outer Spaces: Memoirs.* New Delhi: Navrang, 1986.

Chattopadhyay, Debiprasad. *Lokayata: A Study in Ancient Indian Materialism.* Delhi: People's Publishing House, 1959.

Chattopadhyay, Kamaladevi. *Indian Women's Battle for Freedom.* Delhi: Abhinav Publications, 1983.

Coburn, Thomas B. *Devi-Mahatmya: The Crystallization of the Goddess Tradition.* Delhi: Motilal Banarsidass, 1984.

Coward, Rosalind. *Patriarchal Precedents: Sexuality and Social Relations.* London: Routledge and Kegan Paul, 1983.

Croll, Elizabeth. *Feminism and Socialism in China.* New York: Schocken Books, 1984.

Croll, Elizabeth. *Chinese Women since Mao.* London: Zed Books, 1986.

De Lauretis, Teresa. *Alice Doesn't: Feminism, Semiotics, Cinema.* Bloomington: Indiana University Press, 1984.

Drew, John. *India and the Romantic Imagination.* Delhi: Oxford University Press, 1987.

Dube, Leela, et al., eds. *Visibility and Power: Essays on Women in Society and Development.* Delhi: Oxford University Press, 1986.

Dutt, Rajani Palme. *India Today.* 1940. Reprint. Calcutta: Manisha, 1947.

Ellmann, Mary. *Thinking about Women.* New York: Harcourt, 1968.

Engineer, Asghar Ali. *Status of Women in Islam.* Delhi: Ajanta Publications, 1987.

Ehrenreich, Barbara, and English, Deirdre. *For Her Own Good: 150 Years of Experts' Advice to Women.* New York: Anchor Books, 1979.

Foucault, Michel. *The Order of Things: An Archaeology of the Human Sciences* [Les Mots et les Choses]. New York: Vintage Books, 1973.

Foucault, Michel, ed. *I, Pierre Reviere Having Slaughtered My Mother, My Sister, and My Brother . . . : A Case of Parricide in the 19th Century.* Translated by Frank Jellinek. Lincoln and London: University of Nebraska Press, 1982.

Ganesh, Kamala. "Gender, Family and Kinship in India: Multidisciplinary Perspectives." In *International Workshop on Women's Studies 26–29 April 1989: Theme Papers,* sponsored by the Indian Council of Social Science Research, Paper VII. Trivandrum: Institute of Management in Government, 1989.

Ghadially, Rehana, ed. *Women in Indian Society: A Reader.* New Delhi: Sage Publications, 1988.

Gilbert, Sandra, and Gubar, Susan. *The Madwoman in the Attic: The Woman Writer and the Nineteenth-Century Literary Imagination.* New Haven: Yale University Press, 1979.

Gilbert, Sandra, and Gubar, Susan. *The Norton Anthology of Literature by Women: The Tradition in English.* New York: W. W. Norton, 1985.

Guha, Ranajit. *An Indian Historiography of India: A Nineteenth Century Agenda and Its Implications.* Calcutta: Centre for Studies in Social Sciences, 1988.

Guha, Ranajit, ed. *Subaltern Studies V: Writings on South Asian History and Society.* Delhi: Oxford University Press, 1987. See especially her essay "Chandra's Death," pp. 135–165.

Hardiman, David. *The Coming of the Devi: Adivasi Assertion in Western India.* Delhi: Oxford University Press, 1987.

Harlow, Barbara. *Resistance Literature.* London and New York: Methuen, 1987.

Hart III, George L. "Ancient Tamil Literature: Its Scholarly Past and Future." In *Essays on South India.* Edited by Burton Stein. New Delhi: Vikas, 1975.

Hobsbawn, Eric, and Ranger, Terence, eds. *The Invention of Tradition.* Cambridge: Cambridge University Press, 1988.

Howe, Florence. *Myths of Coeducation: Selected Essays 1964–1983.* Bloomington: Indiana University Press, 1987.

Hull, Gloria T., et al., eds. *All the Women Are White, All the Blacks Are Men, But Some of Us Are Brave: Black Women's Studies.* New York: Feminist Press, 1982.

Hurston, Zora Neale. *Their Eyes Were Watching God.* Urbana: University of Illinois Press, 1978.

Hutchins, Francis G. *Illusion of Permanence: British Imperialism in India.* Princeton: Princeton University Press, 1967.

Jain, Devaki, and Eck, Diana. *Speaking of Faith: Cross-Cultural Perspectives in Women, Religion and Social Change.* Delhi: Kali for Women, 1986.

Jayawardena, Kumari. *Feminism and Nationalism in the Third World.* London: Zed Books, 1986.

Johnson, Richard, and McLennan, Gregor. *Making Histories: Studies in History-Writing and Politics.* London: Hutchinson, 1982.

Joshi, Rama, and Liddle, Joanna. *Daughters of Independence: Gender, Caste, and Class in India.* Delhi: Kali for Women, 1986.

Kakar, Sudhir. *The Inner World: A Psycho-analytic Study of Childhood and Society in India.* 2nd ed. Delhi: Oxford University Press, 1982.

Kaplan, Cora. *Sea Changes: Culture and Feminism.* London: Verso, 1986.

Karve, Irawati. *Kinship Organisation in India.* Bombay: Asia Publishing House, 1953.

Kaul, Jayalal. *Lal Ded.* Delhi: Sahitya Academy, 1973.

Kaur, Manmohan. *Women in India's Freedom Struggle.* Delhi: Sterling, 1985.

Kopf, David. *The Brahmo Samaj and the Shaping of the Modern Indian Mind.* Princeton: Princeton University Press, 1979.

Kosambi, D. D. *The Culture and Civilization of Ancient India in Historical Outline.* Delhi: Vikas Publishing House, 1987.

Kosambi, D. D. *Myth and Reality: Studies in the Formation of Indian Culture.* London: Sangam Books, 1983.

Krishnamurthy, J., ed. *Women in Colonial India: Essays on Survival, Work and the State.* Delhi: Oxford University Press, 1989.

Kuhn, Annette. *The Power of the Image: Essays on Representation and Sexuality.* London: Routledge and Kegan Paul, 1985.

Lal, Brij V. "Kunti's Cry: Indentured Women on Fiji Plantations." In *Women in Colonial India: Essays on Survival, Work and the State.* Edited by J. Krishnamurthy, pp. 163–179. Delhi: Oxford University Press, 1989.

Loomba, Ania. *Race, Gender, Renaissance Drama.* Manchester: Manchester University Press, 1989.

Madhavananda, Swami, and Majumdar, R. C., eds. *Great Women of India.* Almora: Advaita Ashrama, 1982.

Metcalf, Barbara, ed. *Moral Conduct and Moral Authority in South Asian Islam.* Berkeley: University of California Press, 1984. See especially her "Islamic Reform and Islamic Women: Maulana Thanawi's Jewelry of Paradise," pp. 184–195.

Mies, Maria. *Indian Women and Patriarchy.* Delhi: Concept, 1980.

Ministry of Education and Social Welfare (India). *Towards Equality: Report on the Committee on the Status of Women in India.* New Delhi: Department of Social Welfare, 1974.

Misra, Rekha. *Women in Mughal India.* Delhi: Munshiram Manoharlal, 1967.

Moers, Ellen. *Literary Women: The Great Writers.* New York: Doubleday, 1976.

Mukherjee, Meenakshi. *Realism and Reality: The Novel and Society in India.* Delhi: Oxford University Press, 1985.

Mulhern, Francis. *The Moment of 'Scrutiny.'* London: Verso, 1981.

Murshid, Gulam. *The Reluctant Debutante.* Rajashahi: Rajashahi University Sahitya Samsad, 1983.

Nanda, B. R., ed. *Indian Women: From Purdah to Modernity.* Delhi: Vikas, 1962.

Nandy, Ashis. *Traditions, Tyranny, and Utopias: Essays in the Politics of Awareness.* Delhi: Oxford University Press, 1983.

Nandy, Ashis. *The Intimate Enemy: Loss and Recovery of Self under Colonialism.* Delhi: Oxford University Press, 1988.

Natarajan, S. *Century of Social Reform in India.* Bombay: Asia Publishing House, 1959.

Nehru, Jawaharlal. *The Discovery of India.* London: Meridian Books Limited, 1960.

Newton, Judith L., Ryan, Mary P., and Walkowitz, Judith R., eds. *Sex and Class in Women's History.* London: Routledge and Kegan Paul, 1983.

O'Hanlon, Rosalind. *Caste, Conflict and Ideology: Mahatma Jotirao Phule and Low Caste Protest in Nineteenth-Century Western India.* Cambridge: Cambridge University Press, 1985.

Olsen, Tillie. *Silences.* London: Virago, 1980.

Omvedt, Gail. *Cultural Revolt in Colonial India: The Non-Brahmin Movement in Western India 1873–1930.* Bombay: Scientific Socialist Education Trust, 1976.

Papanek, Hanna, and Minault, Gail, eds. *Separate Worlds: Studies of Purdah in South Asia.* Delhi: Chanakya, 1982.

Pollock, Griselda. *Vision and Difference: Femininity, Feminism and Histories of Art.* London: Routledge, 1988.

Poovey, Mary. *The Proper Lady and the Woman Writer: Ideology as Style in the Works of Mary Wollstonecraft, Mary Shelley and Jane Austen.* Chicago: University of Chicago Press, 1984.

Poovey, Mary. *Uneven Developments: The Ideological Work of Gender in Mid-Victorian England.* Chicago: University of Chicago, 1988.

Qureshi, I. H. *The Muslim Community of the Indo-Pakistan Subcontinent (610–1947): A Brief Historical Analysis.* Hague: Mouton and Co., 1962.

Radha, K., ed. *Feminism and Literature.* Trivandrum: Institute of English, University of Kerala, 1987.

Radway, Janice A. *Reading the Romance: Women, Patriarchy and Popular Literature.* London: Verso, 1987.

Ramakrishna, V. *Social Reform in Andhra (1848–1919).* New Delhi: Vikas, 1983.

Ramanujan, A. K., trans. *The Interior Landscape: Love Poems from a Classical Tamil Anthology.* London: Peter Owen, 1970.

Ramanujan, A. K. *Speaking of Siva.* Harmondsworth: Penguin, 1973.

Rudolf, S., and Rudolf, L. *The Modernity of Tradition.* Chicago: University of Chicago Press, 1967.

Russ, Joanna. *How to Suppress Women's Writing.* London: Women's Press, 1984.

Said, Edward. *Orientalism.* New York: Pantheon, 1978.

Said, Edward W. *After the Last Sky: Palestinian Lives.* London and Boston: Faber and Faber, 1986.

Sangari, Kumkum, and Vaid, Sudesh. *Recasting Women: Essays in Colonial History.* Delhi: Kali for Women, 1989.

Sardar, G. B. *The Saint Poets of Maharashtra.* Translated by Kumud Mehta. Delhi: Orient Longmans, 1969.

Sarkar, Sumit. *Modern India 1885–1947.* Delhi: Macmillan, 1983.

Sarkar, Sumit. *A Critique of Colonial India.* Calcutta: Papyrus, 1985.

Sen, Sunil. *The Working Woman and Popular Movements in Bengal: From the Gandhi Era to the Present Day.* Calcutta: K. P. Bagchi, 1985.

Shah, A. B. ed. *The Letters and Correspondence of Pandita Ramabai.* Bombay: The State Board for Literature and Culture, 1977.

Shiva, Vandana. *Staying Alive: Women, Ecology and Survival in India.* Delhi: Kali for Women, 1988.

Showalter, Elaine. *A Literature of Their Own: British Women Novelists from Brontë to Lessing.* Princeton: Princeton University Press, 1977.

Showalter, Elaine, ed. *The New Feminist Criticism: Essays on Women, Literature, and Theory.* London: Virago Press, 1985. See especially her essay "Toward a Feminist Poetics," pp. 125–143.

Spivak, Gayatri. *In Other Worlds: Essays in Cultural Politics.* London: Methuen, 1987.

Stokes, Eric. *The English Utilitarians and India*. Delhi: Oxford University Press, 1989.

Stree Shakti Sanghatana. *"We were making history . . .": Life and Stories of Women in the Telangana People's Struggle*. Delhi: Kali for Women, 1989.

Tarachand. *The Influence of Islam on Indian Culture*. Allahabad: Indian Press, 1963.

Tattvabhushan, Sitanath. *Social Reform in Bengal: A Side Sketch*. Calcutta: Papyrus, 1982.

Tavernier. *Travels in India*. 1676. Translated by Valentine Ball (1889). Reprint. Oxford: Oxford University Press, 1925.

Thapar, Romila. *Ancient Indian Social History: Some Interpretations*. Delhi: Orient Longmans, 1979.

Vicinus, Martha, ed. *Suffer and Be Still: Women in the Victorian Age*. London: Methuen, 1972.

Walker, Alice, ed. *I Love Myself When I Am Laughing . . . and Then Again When I Am Looking Mean and Impressive: A Zora Neale Hurston Reader*. New York: Feminist Press, 1979.

Articles

Ahmad, Aijaz. " 'Third World Literature' and the Nationalist Ideology." *Journal of Arts and Ideas* 17–18 (1989): 117–135.

Alexander, Meena. "Sarojini Naidu: Romanticism and Resistance." *Economic and Political Weekly* 20,43 (1985): WS 68–71.

Bagchi, A. K. "De-industrialization in India in the Nineteenth Century: Some Theoretical Implications." *Journal of Development Studies* 12 (1975–1976): 135–164.

Bannerji, Himani. "The Mirror of Class: Class Subjectivity and Politics in 19th Century Bengal." *Economic and Political Weekly* 24,19 (1989): 1041–1051.

Bharucha, Rustom. "Haraam Bombay!" *Economic and Political Weekly* 24,23 (1989): 1275–1279.

Chakravarti, Uma, and Roy, Kumkum. "In Search of Our Past: A Review of the Limitations and Possibilities of the Historiography of Women in Early India." *Economic and Political Weekly* 23,18 (1988): WS 2–10.

Chattopadhyay, Ratnabali. "Nationalism and Form in Indian Painting." *Journal of Arts and Ideas* 14–15 (1987): 5–46.

Chhachhi, Amrita. "The State, Religious Fundamentalism, and Women: Trends in South Asia." *Economic and Political Weekly* 24,11 (1989): 567–578.

Choudhurani, Sarala Devi. "A Women's Movement." *Modern Review* October 1911: 344–350.

Clementin-Ojha, Catherine. "Outside the Norms: Women Ascetics in Hindu Society." *Economic and Political Weekly* 23,18 (1988): S 34–36.

Desai, Neera. "Women in the Bhakti Movement." *Samya Shakti* 1,2 (1983): 92–100.

Dube, Leela. "On the Construction of Gender: Hindu Girls in Patrilineal India." *Economic and Political Weekly* 23,18 (1988): WS 11–19.

Forbes, Geraldine H. "In Search of the 'Pure Heathen': Missionary Women in Nineteenth Century India." *Economic and Political Weekly* 20,17 (1985): WS 2–8.

Hansen, Kathryn. "The Virangana in North Indian History: Myth and Popular Culture." *Economic and Political Weekly* 23,18 (1988): WS 25–33.

Indian Literature 29,2 (March–April 1986). Special Issue: "Focus on the Creative World of Our Women Writers."

Jayawardena, Kumari. "So Comrade, What Happened to the Democratic Struggle? Thoughts on Feminism and the Left in South Asia." *Economic and Political Weekly* 23,41 (1988): 2131–2132.

Kapur, Geeta. "Ravi Varma: Representational Dilemmas of a Nineteenth Century Painter." *Journal of Arts and Ideas* 17–18 (1989): 59–80.

Karlekar, Malavika. "Kadambini and the Bhadralok: Early Debates over Women's Education in Bengal." *Economic and Political Weekly* 21,17 (1986): WS 25–31.

Kishwar, Madhu. "Women in Gandhi." *Economic and Political Weekly* 20,40–41 (1985): 1691–1702, 1753–1758.

Kishwar, Madhu. "Arya Samaj and Women's Education: Kanya Mahavidyalaya, Jalandhar." *Economic and Political Weekly* 221,17 (1986): WS 9–24.

Kosambi, Meera. "Women, Emancipation and Equality: Pandita Ramabai's Contribution to Women's Cause." *Economic and Political Weekly* 23,44 (1988): WS 38–49.

Mangala, C. N. "Nanjanagudu Tirumalamba (1887–1982)." *Aniketana* 1,1 (1988): 128–133.

Minault, Gail. "Urdu Women's Magazines in the Twentieth Century." *Manushi* 48 (1988): 2–9.

Mukherjee, Meenakshi. "Reality and Realism: Indian Women as Protagonists in Four Nineteenth Century Novels." *Economic and Political Weekly* 19,2 (1984): 76–85.

Mukta, Parita. "Mirabai in Rajasthan." *Manushi* 50,51,52 (1989): 94–101.

Patel, Sujata. "The Construction and Reconstruction of Women in Gandhi." *Economic and Political Weekly* 23,8 (1988): 377–387.

Reddock, Rhoda. "Freedom Denied: Indian Women and Indentureship in Trinidad and Tobago, 1845–1917." *Economic and Political Weekly* 20,43 (1985): WS 79–87.

Saldanha, Indra Munshi. "Tribal Women in the Warli Revolt, 1945–47: 'Class' and 'Gender' in the Left Perspective." *Economic and Political Weekly* 21,17 (1986): WS 41–52.

Sangari, Kumkum. "Introduction: Representations in History." *Journal of Arts and Ideas* 17–18 (1989): 3–9.

Seminar 165 (May 1973). Special Issue: "The Status of Women."

Seminar 300 (August 1984). Special Issue: "The Sexist Media."

Seminar 318 (February 1986). Special Issue: "Purdah Culture."

Seminar 331 (March 1987). Special Issue: "Femicide."

Seminar 342 (February 1988). Special Issue: "Sati."

Srinivasan, Amrit. "Reform and Revival: The Devadasi and Her Dance." *Economic and Political Weekly* 20,44 (1985): 1869–1876.

Srinivasan, Amrit. "Women and Reform of Indian Tradition: Gandhian Alternative to Liberalism." *Economic and Political Weekly* 22, (1987): 2225–2228.

Thapar, Romila. "Traditions versus Misconception: Interview with Madhu Kishwar and Ruth Vanita." *Manushi* 42–43 (1987): 2–14.

Tharu, Susie. "The Second Stage from the Third World." *Indian Journal of American Studies* 13,2 (1983): 179–184.

Tharu, Susie. "Third World Women's Cinema: Notes on Narrative, Reflections on Opacity." *Economic and Political Weekly* 21,20 (1986): 864–866.

Tharu, Susie. "Thinking the Nation Out: Some Reflections on Nationalism and Theory." *Journal of Arts and Ideas* 17–18 (1989): 81–91.

Viswanathan, Gauri. "The Beginnings of English Literary Study in British India." *Oxford Literary Review* 9 (1987): 2–26.

Viswanathan, Susan. "Marriage, Birth and Death: Property Rights and Domestic Relationships of the Orthodox/Jacobite Syrian Christians of Kerala." *Economic and Political Weekly* 24,24 (1989): 1341–1346.

PERMISSION
ACKNOWLEDGMENTS

We gratefully acknowledge permission to include the following:

AKKAMAHADEVI: [Not one, not two, not three or four] and [Would a circling surface vulture], from *Speaking of Siva,* translated by A. K. Ramanujan (Harmondsworth: Penguin, 1967), © 1973 by A. K. Ramanujan. Reproduced by permission of Penguin Books Ltd.

LALITHAMBIKA ANTHERJANAM: "Praticaradevatha" by permission of N. Mohanan.

AUVAIYAR: "What She Said" and [You cannot compare them with a lute], translated by George L. Hart III, from *Poets of the Tamil Anthologies: Ancient Poems of Love and War* by George L. Hart III, © 1979 Princeton University Press. Reprinted by permission of Princeton University Press.

BAHINABAI CHAUDHARI: "Ata Maza Male Jeeva" and "Mun" by permission of Suchitra Madhusudan Choudhari.

530

SUBHADRA KUMARI CHAUHAN: "Ekadasi" by permission of Sudha Chauhan.

SUDHA CHAUHAN: Excerpt from "Mila Tej Se Tej" by permission of the author.

ASHAPURNA DEBI: "Ja Noy Tai," from *Pratam Pratisruti,* © 1964 by Ashapurna Debi, by permission of the author.

NAZAR SAJJAD HYDER: "Purdah" from *Tahzeeb-e-Niswan,* volume 40, 1937, by permission of Qurratulain Hyder.

KASHIBAI KANITKAR: Excerpt from *Palkicha Gonda* by permission of Dewadatta W. Kanitkar.

OKKUR MACATTIYAR: [Her purpose is frightening, her spirit cruel], translated by George L. Hart III, from *Poets of the Tamil Anthologies: Ancient Poems of Love and War,* by George L. Hart III, © 1979 Princeton University Press. Reprinted by permission of Princeton University Press.

MIRABAI: [The Bhil woman tasted them, plum after plum], translated by J. S. Hawley and M. Jeurgensmeyer, from *Songs of the Saints of India* by John Stratton Hawley and Mark Juergensmeyer, © 1988 by Oxford University Press, Inc. Reprinted by permission of Oxford University Press.

SUGIIRA HUMAYUN MIRZA: [Who will care to visit my grave when I am gone] by permission of Yousuf Ali Mirza.

KAKKAIPATINIYAR NACCELLAIYAR: [His armies love massacre] translated by A. K. Ramanujan, from *Poems of Love and War,* edited by A. K. Ramanujan, © 1984 Columbia University Press, by permission of the publisher.

SAROJINI NAIDU: "Bangle-Sellers" and "The Temple: A Pilgrimage of Love," from *Sceptred Flute: Songs of India* (Allahabad: Kitabistan, 1958), by permission of the publisher.

KAVAR PENTU: [You stand and hold the post of my small house] translated by George L. Hart III from *Poets of the Tamil Anthologies: Ancient Poems of Love and War,* by George L. Hart III, © 1979 Princeton University Press. Reprinted by permission of Princeton University Press.

INDEX

The Feminist Press at The City University of New York offers alternatives in education and in literature. Founded in 1970, this nonprofit, tax-exempt educational and publishing organization works to eliminate sexual stereotypes in books and schools and to provide literature with a broad vision of human potential.

NEW AND FORTHCOMING BOOKS

Allegra Maud Goldman, a novel by Edith Konecky. Introduction by Tillie Olsen. Afterword by Bella Brodzki. $9.95 paper.

Bamboo Shoots after the Rain: Contemporary Stories by Women Writers of Taiwan, edited by Ann C. Carver and Sung-sheng Yvonne Chang. $35.00 cloth, $14.95 paper.

A Brighter Coming Day: A Frances Ellen Watkins Harper Reader, edited by Frances Smith Foster. $35.00 cloth, $14.95 paper.

The End of This Day's Business, a novel by Katharine Burdekin. Afterword by Daphne Patai. $35.00 cloth, $8.95 paper.

How I Wrote Jubilee *and Other Essays on Life and Literature*, by Margaret Walker. Edited by Maryemma Graham. $35.00 cloth, $9.95 paper.

Journey toward Freedom: The Story of Sojourner Truth, a biography by Jacqueline Bernard. Introduction by Nell Irvin Painter. $35.00 cloth, $10.95 paper.

Margret Howth: A Story of Today, a novel by Rebecca Harding Davis. Afterword by Jean Fagan Yellin. $35.00 cloth, $11.95 paper.

Now in November, a novel by Josephine W. Johnson. Afterword by Nancy Hoffman. $29.95 cloth, $9.95 paper.

On Peace and War: A Challenge to Genetic Determinism (Genes and Gender series), edited by Anne E. Hunter. Associate editors, Catherine M. Flamenbaum and Suzanne R. Sunday. $35.00 cloth, $15.95 paper.

Quest, a novel by Helen R. Hull. Afterword by Patricia McClelland Miller. $11.95 paper.

Trifles and *A Jury of Her Peers*, by Susan Glaspell. Afterword by Janet Madden-Simpson. $19.95 cloth, $7.95 paper. *A Feminist Press Sourcebook.*

Truth Tales: Contemporary Stories by Women Writers of India, selected by Kali for Women. Introduction by Meena Alexander. $35.00 cloth, $12.95 paper.

Women's Studies International: Nairobi and Beyond, edited by Aruna Rao. $35.00 cloth, $15.95 paper.

Women Writing in India: 600 B.C. to the Present. 2 vols. Vol. I: 600 B.C. to the Early Twentieth Century. Vol. II: The Twentieth Century. Edited by Susie Tharu and K. Lalita. Each volume: $59.95 cloth, $29.95 paper.

For a free, complete backlist catalog, write to The Feminist Press at The City University of New York, 311 East 94 Street, New York, NY 10128. Send book order to The Talman Company, Inc., 150 Fifth Avenue, New York, NY 10011. Please include $2.00 postage and handling for one book, $.75 for each additional.